PENGUIN BOOKS

WRITING AT THE KITCHEN TABLE

'The story of a singular woman living through extraordinary times'
Arabella Boxer, *The Times Literary Supplement*

'Not only well written, but a refreshingly warts-and-all portrait . . .
She was a woman with a zest for pleasure, who loved beauty . . . If
her work tells us that good food didn't begin in the Fifties, but
stretched its roots into the rich soil of the past, her life is a reminder
that sexual freedom didn't begin in the Sixties. Nobody who loves
her books will be dismayed by this one'
Katharine Whitehorn, *Observer*

'Elizabeth David was a one-off . . . she emerges from this book as
enigmatic, open-hearted but unforgiving'
Richard Whittington, *Spectator*

'Elizabeth David was the most important cookery writer in post-war
Britain . . . the woman who emerges from these pages is a flawed,
sympathetic character . . . Artemis Cooper has uncovered a good
deal of new material about Elizabeth's relationship with Tony David
and has also identified the true love of her life in one of the most
enthralling biographies I have read. Artemis Cooper convinces us
that Elizabeth David's was a heroic life of sorts'
Paul Levy, *Daily Mail*

'It is evident from this biography that she was not by temperament
or desire a teacher, but a revolutionary'
Nicola Shulman, *Sunday Telegraph*

Artemis Cooper's work includes *Cairo in the War 1939–1945* and *Paris after the Liberation* (which she wrote with her husband, Antony Beevor), both of which are available in Penguin. They have two children and live in London.

ARTEMIS COOPER

Writing at the Kitchen Table

* * * * * * * *

THE AUTHORIZED BIOGRAPHY OF

Elizabeth David

PENGUIN BOOKS

PENGUIN BOOKS

Published by the Penguin Group
Penguin Books Ltd, 27 Wrights Lane, London w8 5TZ, England
Penguin Putnam Inc., 375 Hudson Street, New York, New York 10014, USA
Penguin Books Australia Ltd, Ringwood, Victoria, Australia
Penguin Books Canada Ltd, 10 Alcorn Avenue, Toronto, Ontario, Canada M4V 3B2
Penguin Books India (P) Ltd, 11 Community Centre, Panchsheel Park,
New Delhi – 110 017, India
Penguin Books (NZ) Ltd, Cnr Rosedale and Airborne Roads,
Albany, Auckland, New Zealand
Penguin Books (South Africa) (Pty) Ltd, 5 Watkins Street, Denver Ext 4,
Johannesburg 2094, South Africa

Penguin Books Ltd, Registered Offices: Harmondsworth, Middlesex, England

First published by Michael Joseph 1999
Published in Penguin Books 2000

1

Set in Monotype Ehrhardt
Printed in England by Clays Ltd, St Ives plc

Contents

List of Illustrations   vi
Family Tree   viii
Introduction and Acknowledgements   xi

1. The Gwynnes   1
2. The Gwynne Girls Grow Up   10
3. Paris and Munich   28
4. Acting it Out   35
5. Norman Douglas   60
6. The Loss of the *Evelyn Hope*   70
7. Alexandria   84
8. Tony David   98
9. Indian Interlude   117
10. Back in Blighty   124
11. *Mediterranean Food*   139
12. *Italian Food*   161
13. Friends, Editors and Other Enemies   183
14. On the Road in Provincial France   194
15. The Year of Betrayal   208
16. Farewell to P. H.   227
17. The Shop   235
18. Salt and Spice   256
19. Baking Bread   275
20. Omelette and Ice   291
21. Brave New World   316
Epilogue   334

Notes and Sources   337
Selected Bibliography   350
Index   353

List of Illustrations

Section one
1. Stella Gwynne, Elizabeth's mother
2. Rupert Gwynne MP, Elizabeth's father
3. Wootton Manor
4. Portrait of Elizabeth by Ambrose McEvoy
5. Family group at Wootton, 1924
6. Stella and her daughters, late 1920s
7. Elizabeth as an actress
8. Charles Gibson Cowan
9. Peter Laing
10. Norman Douglas
11. Elizabeth, 1944
12. Tony David, 1944
13. Elizabeth at her desk in Cairo, *c.*1943
14. Tony David in Cairo, 1943
15. Cairo friends, 1944
16. Renée Fedden

Section two
17. Elizabeth and George Lassalle, early 1950s
18. Lesley O'Malley at Halsey Street
19. Elizabeth, early 1950s
20. Diana Gwynne's wedding to Christopher Grey, 1941
21. Elizabeth with John Lehmann, early 1950s
22. Elizabeth in her kitchen at Halsey Street, mid 1950s
23. Elizabeth in the kitchen, 1956 or 1957

24. Elizabeth, 1956 or 1957
25. Elizabeth by Anthony Denney, 1964
26. Peter Higgins
27. Elizabeth in the shop, mid 1960s
28. Anthony Denney
29. Elizabeth David Ltd in Bourne Street, Pimlico
30. Elizabeth in France, c.1971
31. Elizabeth's sister Felicité
32. Elizabeth in old age, late 1980s

Photographic Acknowledgements

The author wishes to thank the following for their permission to reproduce the above photographs; those not listed below all come from the Elizabeth David Archives:

Steve Grey: 4

Mrs Aileen Gibson Cowan: 8

Islay Lyons: 10

Hassia, Cairo: 11

Jean Weinberg, Cairo: 12

Jane Blakemore: 15, 18

Doreen Thornton: 19

Mrs Anthony Denney: 25, 27

Georgina Tritton: 26

Piggott: 32

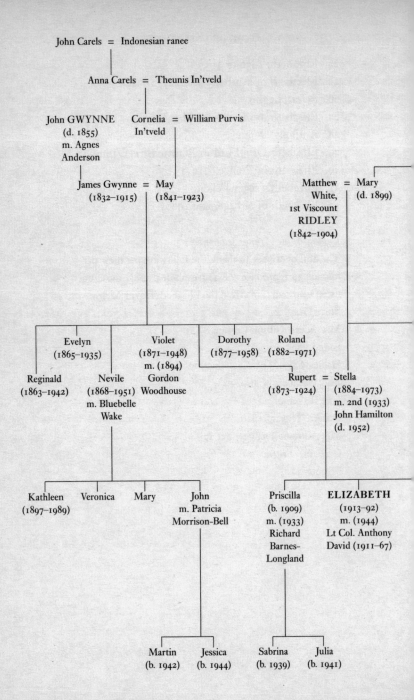

John Carels = Indonesian ranee

Anna Carels = Theunis In'tveld

John GWYNNE
(d. 1855)
m. Agnes
Anderson

Cornelia = William Purvis
In'tveld

James Gwynne = May
(1832–1915)   (1841–1923)

Matthew = Mary
White,   (d. 1899)
1st Viscount
RIDLEY
(1842–1904)

Evelyn
(1865–1935)

Violet
(1871–1948)
m. (1894)
Gordon
Woodhouse

Dorothy
(1877–1958)

Roland
(1882–1971)

Reginald
(1863–1942)

Nevile
(1868–1951)
m. Bluebelle
Wake

Rupert = Stella
(1873–1924)   (1884–1973)
m. 2nd (1933)
John Hamilton
(d. 1952)

Kathleen
(1897–1989)

Veronica

Mary

John
m. Patricia
Morrison-Bell

Priscilla
(b. 1909)
m. (1933)
Richard
Barnes-
Longland

ELIZABETH
(1913–92)
m. (1944)
Lt Col. Anthony
David (1911–67)

Martin
(b. 1942)

Jessica
(b. 1944)

Sabrina
(b. 1939)

Julia
(b. 1941)

FAMILY TREE SHOWING THE GWYNNES, RIDLEYS, MARJORIBANKS, HOGGS AND PALMERS

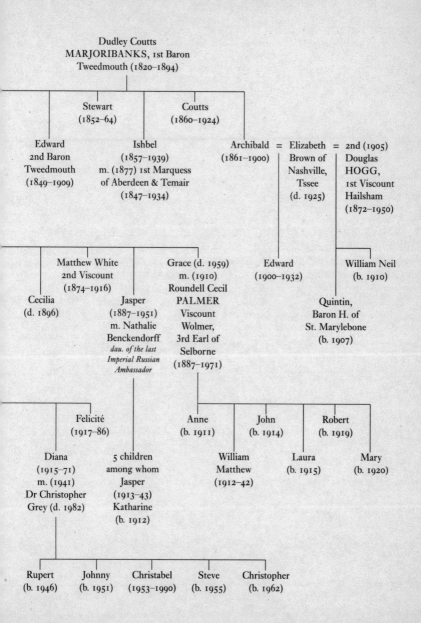

Dudley Coutts
MARJORIBANKS, 1st Baron
Tweedmouth (1820–1894)

Stewart
(1852–64)

Coutts
(1860–1924)

Edward
2nd Baron
Tweedmouth
(1849–1909)

Ishbel
(1857–1939)
m. (1877) 1st Marquess
of Aberdeen & Temair
(1847–1934)

Archibald =
(1861–1900)

Elizabeth = 2nd (1905)
Brown of   Douglas
Nashville,   HOGG,
Tssee   1st Viscount
(d. 1925)   Hailsham
               (1872–1950)

Matthew White
2nd Viscount
(1874–1916)

Grace (d. 1959)
m. (1910)
Roundell Cecil
PALMER
Viscount
Wolmer,
3rd Earl of
Selborne
(1887–1971)

Edward
(1900–1932)

William Neil
(b. 1910)

Cecilia
(d. 1896)

Jasper
(1887–1951)
m. Nathalie
Benckendorff
*dau. of the last
Imperial Russian
Ambassador*

Quintin,
Baron H. of
St. Marylebone
(b. 1907)

Felicité
(1917–86)

Anne
(b. 1911)

John
(b. 1914)

Robert
(b. 1919)

Diana
(1915–71)
m. (1941)
Dr Christopher
Grey (d. 1982)

5 children
among whom
Jasper
(1913–43)
Katharine
(b. 1912)

William
Matthew
(1912–42)

Laura
(b. 1915)

Mary
(b. 1920)

Rupert
(b. 1946)

Johnny
(b. 1951)

Christabel
(1953–1990)

Steve
(b. 1955)

Christopher
(b. 1962)

Introduction and Acknowledgements

On 22 February 1994, two years after Elizabeth David's death, the contents of her two kitchens at 24 Halsey Street, Chelsea, went on sale at Phillips auction rooms in Bayswater. The press had taken up the story as soon as the forthcoming sale was announced, showing photographs of pots and pans, spoons and storage jars, all displayed on her scrubbed-pine kitchen table. Cookery writers and chefs were invited to choose items they coveted or might bid for. From the moment viewing began, a steady stream of people made their way to the showrooms. They were private individuals, not professional dealers, and they spent hours poring over cheese graters and ramekins which could have come from a junk shop.

The day itself took everyone by surprise. The saleroom was packed by nine-thirty in the morning, and the auction, scheduled to take place at midday, was delayed by the crush. 'We brought in every chair we could,' said one of the saleroom staff, 'but the crowd was unbelievable. They were out in the corridor and all the way down the stairs. There must have been three hundred, perhaps four hundred people . . . and there was this sense of excitement, of electricity. I've never seen anything like it.'

When the proceedings finally began, the auctioneer was almost overwhelmed by the sheer volume of bids. People wanted something, anything, even if they didn't know what it was. 'I don't know exactly what I've bought,' said one woman after paying £75 for a lot. 'I just wanted to have some keepsake.' One of Elizabeth's friends recalled how odd it was to see little things that he had given her go for fifty to a hundred pounds. Some people had their eyes on certain pieces: Prue Leith was determined to buy the kitchen table, and a roar of approval went up from the crowd when the table went to her for £1,100. Leith rose to her feet with a whoop of delight, and took a little bow amidst a round of spontaneous applause. 'I'm going to cook on it just like she did, and think of her,' said Prue Leith afterwards. 'She was the most important cookery writer this century. That's why I wanted her table. I can't believe I've got it.' By the end of the afternoon the sale had made £49,000 – more than three times its estimated value. The bidders had not bought pots and wooden spoons, but relics: fragments from someone they had never met, but who had had such an effect on their lives that they wanted to keep a little piece of her for ever.

Elizabeth David's reputation rests primarily on her first five books. *A Book of Mediterranean Food* appeared in 1949 while England was still in the grip of rationing. Her aim was 'to bring a flavour of those blessed lands of sun and sea and olive trees' into English kitchens. At a time when aubergines, lemons and olive oil were almost unobtainable, the book's success amazed both her and her publishers. What Elizabeth had managed to do, in this book and those that followed, was to describe food in such a way as to make people dream of it and want to cook it.

Timing was with her. After the dismal years of war and post-war austerity, the world was opening up. People started travelling as never before, and they were not afraid of garlic and wine sauces as their parents' generation had been. At the same time, new transport systems were established which brought foreign food hitherto unavailable in English shops. Some of Elizabeth David's staunchest supporters declare that it is due to her alone that we can now find Italian olive oil, red peppers and Israeli avocados in every supermarket. This must be an exaggeration, but there is an argument for saying that, in her quiet way, she was the most influential cookery writer of her time. There is scarcely a professional cook of any distinction in these islands who does not acknowledge her as an inspiration. She also taught a whole generation of people how to think about food in ways they never had before, and how to cook the simple, authentic dishes she described. Elizabeth never approached cooking as a chore. It was hard work, certainly, but her writing made cooking a creative act to be enjoyed for its own sake, not something to be got out of the way.

There was also something compelling about her writing. On the surface, it seemed admirably spare, straightforward and to the point. But behind those crisp sentences, one can feel the pressure of her loves and hates, her enthusiasm and her passion. The reader becomes acutely aware of these emotions, although they are never mentioned. This is what makes her prose so powerful, and why she inspired a whole generation not only to take up cooking, but to plunge into it with her own kind of serious enjoyment. 'I think,' she wrote, 'that the ideal cookery writer is one who makes his readers *want* to cook as well as telling them how it is done; he should also leave something, not too much perhaps, but a little, unsaid; people must make their own discoveries, use their own intelligence, otherwise they will be deprived of part of the fun.'

About her private life, Elizabeth left everything unsaid. She hated publicity of any kind, and revealed very few clues about the sort of person she might be. The photographs in the press showed an elegant, rather beautiful woman with clever, cat-like eyes. She wore well-cut, classical clothes, and emphasized her long neck with white shirts open at the throat. Sometimes there was a photograph of her crowded kitchen, with its French armoires and bowls of eggs and lemons on the dressers; but that was as close as the public ever got to her private life. 'Everything I want to say is in my books,' she maintained. She gave out nothing else, and anyone foolish enough to ask an impertinent question would shrivel up in the frozen silence that followed.

*

Fortunately for the biographer, the crockery and kitchen equipment sold at Phillips had not been the only things she left behind. In her house in Halsey Street, books spilled out of every available bookshelf. They had taken over the sitting room to such an extent that the floor was an obstacle course and there was nowhere to sit down. They had advanced up to the first floor in little piles on each stair. Her bedroom contained more bookshelves, also full to bursting; and there was a subsidiary library in her kitchen. She had never been able to acquire them on an expensive scale, but her books made a magnificent collection on the history of cookery and gastronomy in English, French and Italian. First choice went, as she had instructed, to the Warburg Institute. The rest went to the Guildhall Library.

There were also, in every room, innumerable files and cardboard boxes of papers, notebooks, correspondence and catalogues. Elizabeth had appointed her long-time editor and friend Jill Norman to be her literary executor, and before the house in Halsey Street was sold, Jill and her husband Paul Breman moved the archive to their house in Hampstead.

I never met Elizabeth David, although I did talk to her once on the telephone. I was just beginning a book about Cairo during the Second World War when a friend gave me her telephone number. She was a considerable name. I had two of her books and was very keen to meet her, but I had also been told that she could be difficult. While I summoned up the courage to dial, I wrote out what I wanted to say on a piece of paper.

'Hello?' The voice was cold, absent-minded. I threw myself into my introductory patter. By about the third sentence I realized I was getting none of those encouraging little noises that most people make, although I knew she was listening. I rambled on nervously, and finally managed to ask whether I might come and see her. There was a long silence, and then the single word, 'No.' My heart sank. 'But,' she said, 'you can talk to me now if you like.' I was totally unprepared for an interview, and was at that embarrassing stage of very early research when one knows almost nothing. Elizabeth realized this at once, but decided to take pity on me. She told me about her *suffragi* (cook-housekeeper) Suleiman, and the little restaurants on the edge of the Nile where one went to eat freshly grilled pigeon. She also told me a very complicated story which featured a general, several people I had never heard of and the revolving door of the Continental Hotel.

It was not a very satisfactory interview. I tried to find out more, especially about her marriage, which I knew had taken place during the war; but while I talked to a number of people who knew her, they all seemed very vague about her activities. I looked up her own descriptions of Egypt, in *An Omelette and a Glass of Wine*. They were redolent of the time and place, but gave no clues as to what was happening in her life.

Two years later, when my book was nearly finished, I happened to meet Jill Norman and asked if she thought Elizabeth might be willing to talk to me again. Jill thought it unlikely. Elizabeth was not well. A sister to whom she was devoted had recently died, and she herself was in hospital with a broken leg. A few days later Jill rang to say that she had tried to put in a good word for me, but Elizabeth was really not interested. That, I thought, was that. I assumed I would never find out what had happened to her in Cairo.

Ten years later, out of the blue, I received a telephone call from Eleo Gordon of Penguin Books. She wanted to know if I was interested in writing Elizabeth David's authorized biography. My instinct was to say yes at once because I longed to know more about her, but the word 'authorized' made me nervous. What did it mean? If it meant censorship in any form, then my answer would have to be no. However, I was reassured by Jill Norman, and Jenny Dereham of Michael Joseph, who had edited Elizabeth's posthumous book *Harvest of the Cold Months*. Both agreed that what I wrote would be up to me. As far as they were concerned, the word authorized simply meant that I would have full access to Elizabeth David's papers.

Jenny Dereham became my editor when I accepted the commission.

The papers stood in a series of sixty cardboard filing boxes in the studio of Jill's house in Hampstead, taking up two rows of a long set of bookshelves that ran the length of the room. To my immense relief, they had already been meticulously catalogued: an enormous task undertaken by Jill's husband Paul Breman, to whom I am immensely grateful. On that first morning I stood in front of them, awestruck. Here was an impressive collection of papers, but would there be enough material to put together both sides of her life? A swift glance at the contents of each box, neatly labelled on the outside, confirmed that most contained papers to do with her work; but in the course of a morning of mounting excitement, I realized that her private life was here too. There were letters from Sybille Bedford, Mark Boxer, Lawrence Durrell, John Lehmann and Hilary Spurling, not to mention cookery writers such as Jane Grigson and Julia Child. There were albums, photographs, several boxes of family papers and correspondence. Best of all was the discovery that Elizabeth had kept handwritten drafts of almost all the most important letters she sent.

There were also treasures, such as a little blue writing case (smelling faintly of old leather and cumin seeds) that contained bills and snapshots and fabric swatches dating from the 1940s. I found her wartime passport, which charts her passage from France to Italy, the Balkans, Greece and Egypt. Elizabeth's godson, David Watkins, lent me the collection of letters from Norman Douglas that she had given to him. They were kept in a small handbag covered in rust-coloured cloth, and with the letters was an Egyptian leather purse, with another little cache of photographs, papers, letters and old invoices from her days in Egypt.

In the months that followed I began to talk to her friends and family, and piece her life together with the help of the archive. The image that emerged was of an extraordinarily enigmatic woman who was very difficult to pin down. She could be open-hearted but utterly unforgiving. She laughed a lot and was very funny, while taking herself and her work very seriously indeed. Her conversation was challenging, unpredictable and even spiky, yet she was also very shy and reserved. She was utterly without pretension and could sniff out the bogus and pretentious in others with devastating accuracy, but she also played the great lady who expected to be treated as such.

As I immersed myself in her life, the archive that had looked so daunting at first began to seem more manageable. I also began to collect photocopies of long letters she had written to friends and family. And yet, rather like Elizabeth's writing on cookery, what was omitted was as intriguing as what she recorded. In all the thousands of pages of notes, of letters to friends, of drafted articles, there was so little about herself. Sometimes she described what was happening to her, in very funny set pieces: a disastrous trip to Morocco, six weeks of frantic driving all over France for a series of articles in *Vogue*. The only revealing glimpses came indirectly, in letters or articles that seem to have been written in a state of controlled rage.

This was why it was so particularly exciting to read the one long letter in the archive – perhaps the only such letter she ever wrote in her life – which describes the end of an affair with a man she still loved. I had come across it early on, and realized its importance. But since it was part of the second half of her life and I was then concentrating on the first, I did not spend much time on it. When I read it again several months later, I had that eerie sensation of finding the key I had been looking for, while knowing it had been under my nose all along. At that moment, a series of jumbled thoughts that had been clattering around in my head suddenly fell into place. This moment of illumination could never have happened had I not, simultaneously, been talking to and mulling things over with people who had known Elizabeth for years.

The following people have made all the difference in helping me to understand Elizabeth David and her life: Jack Andrews, Sybille

Bedford CBE, April Boyes, Johnny Grey, Rosi Hanson, Veronica Nicholson and Elizabeth Savage. The prolonged conversations I had with them were all crucial to me, because it was only by talking things through with the people who knew her best that I was able to put what I found in the archive into perspective. They have been unfailingly generous with their time and, best of all, they allowed me to feel that I could ring them up whenever I needed help and advice – which I frequently did. I must also at this point mention my husband, Antony Beevor. Quite apart from his constant encouragement and his initial work on the text, he has provided that inestimable asset to any biographer: an outsider's perception.

I was also exceptionally lucky in receiving so much help, and hospitality, from Elizabeth's nephews Rupert, Johnny and Steven Grey. This book is immeasurably richer for the help and support of the Grey brothers and their unfailing honesty in answering my most awkward questions.

I would also like to acknowledge my gratitude to Gerald Asher, Paul Bailey, Ann Balfour-Fraser, Ann Barr, Alan and Olivia Bell, Jane Blakemore, Emma Bolland, Gordon Bowker, Arabella Boxer, Lady Anne Brewis, Nathalie Brooke, Sir Bernard and the late Lady Burrows, Julia Caffyn, James Chandler, Janet Clarke, Patricia Clarke, Derek Cooper, Simon Courtauld, Josette d'Amade, Antony Daniels, Anne Davies, Alan and Jane Davidson, Michael Day, Celia Denney, Jessica Douglas-Home, Barbara Doxat, Roger Eland, George Elliott, the late Roger Ellis, Priscilla Esslin, Frances Fedden, the late Eunice Frost, Christopher Gibbs, Ialeen Gibson-Cowan, Lady May Gore, The Earl of Gowrie, Antonia Graham, Henrietta Green, Professor N. G. L. Hammond CBE, DSO, Anthony Hanson, Sabrina Harcourt-Smith, Frances Harper, John Hatt, Lady Dorothy Heber-Percy, Stephanie Hoppen, Anne Higgins, Derek Hill, Michael Holroyd C.B.E., John and Ellen-Ann Hopkins, Simon Hopkinson, Professor Richard Hosking, Laurette Hugo, Kate Hunloke, Molly Izzard, Rosalind Jenkinson, Hugh and Judy Johnson, John King, Kathleen Laing, Heidi Lascelles, Caroline and the late George Lassalle, Roger

Latham, Richard Leech, Paul Levy, Patrick and Joan Leigh Fermor, Patrick Lewin, Jeremy Lewis, Jenny Lo, Priscilla Longland, Hitch Lyam, Lady Maynard, Jean McAuliffe, Victor Morrison, Patrick O'Connor, Marguerite Patten, OBE, Burnet Pavitt, Neville Phillips, the Countess of Ranfurly, Liz Ray, The Viscount Ridley, Jancis Robinson, Lady Sibell Rowley, John Ruden, John Sandoe, Anne Scott-James, Hilary Spurling, Ann and Franco Taruschio, Doreen Thornton, Peter Trier, Georgina Tritton, Katharine Whitehorn, Audrey Withers, Patrick Woodcock and Michael Zyw.

Lastly I would like to say how hugely indebted I am to Jill Norman. Jill put up with me in her house for what must have seemed far too long, and her help and guidance have been invaluable – as were the powerful espresso coffees and impromptu lunches with which she and Paul Breman kept me going. Jenny has been a wonderfully supportive editor. She has given me every possible encouragement, and has saved me from several mistakes. Any that remain, needless to say, are mine alone.

* * * * * * * *

CHAPTER ONE

The Gwynnes

Elizabeth David's family, the Gwynnes, originally came from Wales. Their fortune was founded in the 1840s by John Gwynne, an engineer who developed the first centrifugal pump for land drainage. With the banker and tea trader Herbert Twining, he also bought up plots of land in London south of the Strand, which became prime sites for development with the completion of the Thames Embankment in 1870.

Like all the best family histories, that of the Gwynnes contains a love match, a secret, a tyrannical patriarch and an intractable will. John Gwynne married Agnes Anderson, who came from a family of well-to-do Scottish professionals. Their first son was James Eglinton Anderson Gwynne, Elizabeth's paternal grandfather, and he is the most important figure in this brief family history. Tall and domineering, with pale eyes, sandy hair and a patrician beard, James inherited his father's engineering firm. He became a good manager and an excellent businessman, but his younger brothers resented the fact that they were given no authority in the family business.

While James's position as head of the family was unquestioned, home life was ruled by their widowed mother Agnes, a strict Presbyterian. On Saturdays she would go round the house putting away every book and paper that was not a sermon, and on Sunday – a day of unmitigated gloom – most of the blinds in the house were kept down.

In 1859, the peace of Mrs Gwynne's family was shattered when

James Gwynne met and fell in love with an eighteen-year-old girl called May Purvis. On one level, the match looked suitable enough: he had met May when visiting his mother's cousins in Edinburgh, and the Purvises were respectable. They were merchants with connections to the Dutch traders of the East Indies. Yet what the Purvises did not like to mention was that May Purvis's Dutch great-grandfather, John Carels, had married a Sumatran 'ranee' (a term that covered every rank from chieftain's daughter to princess), by whom he had had children. The ranee's name has not survived, but she had a considerable effect on the looks of her descendants: for while May was an accomplished young woman with musical talent and a spirited disposition, her Indonesian genes had given her a fragile, exotic beauty that was distinctly un-Scottish.

Right from the start old Mrs Gwynne was suspicious of May Purvis and violently opposed the match. She probably guessed from May's appearance that there was something other than Scottish and Dutch blood in her veins, and she did everything she could to break off the engagement. She nearly succeeded, but James managed to persuade May that their union was only a matter of time if they both stood firm. They were eventually married in 1862. The wedding took place in the house of May's brother in Edinburgh, the Gwynnes and the Andersons being conspicuous by their absence. At the time of her marriage, May's health was not considered good: her doctors feared that she might develop tuberculosis, and one of James's wedding presents to his bride had been a respirator. Yet she proved strong enough to bear nine children, seven of whom survived: Reginald, Evelyn (Eva), Nevile, Violet, Rupert, Dorothy and Roland.

Rupert Gwynne, Elizabeth's father, was born in 1873. He and his brothers and sisters were brought up at Folkington (pronounced Fowington), a large property at the foot of the Sussex Downs near Eastbourne, complete with lodges and a park, a farm, a church and a rectory. The main house was a neo-Jacobean mansion with gabled roofs and tall chimneys, and in James Gwynne's day it made up in comfort what it lacked in architectural distinction. The drawing room was furnished with the most generous sofas and armchairs, every bedroom was well-stocked with books and had a blazing fire in winter, and the greenhouses were filled with heavily scented flowers and Muscat grapes. It was a curious feature of Folkington that, although James Gwynne had been one of the pioneers of electricity supply in London in 1882, his house was lit by oil lamps. There was no plumbing either; though thanks to the teams of servants and fires in every room, a morning bath was hardly a Spartan experience.

The household staff was so huge and well-run that May could claim that she had never been into her own kitchen. She was an affectionate mother, who loved music and riding and entertaining, but her life was lived in the threatening shadow of her husband. As he grew older James became more and more stern and authoritarian, and he could explode into terrifying rages. May, who could not bear rows, became psychologically his prisoner, living in perpetual fear of his temper.

The children grew up in a world of shoots and hunts and point-to-points. Rupert was admired for his reckless courage on a horse, as were Nevile and Dorothy. Violet, on the other hand, developed an exceptional talent for music, which her mother recognized. May saw to it that her daughter had the best teachers, and took her to as many concerts and recitals as she could. Violet was the darling of both her parents, who spoilt her and indulged all her caprices. She and Rupert were curiously alike: both were very dark, with deep-set eyes, and both were endowed with a dazzling and confident charm. May's youngest son Roland was born in 1882, and had the most curious upbringing. His mother doted on him in a way that was almost unhealthy, and insisted that he never leave her side. For once, James gave in to her wishes: the boy was educated entirely at home, first by governesses and then by the rector of Folkington.

Once settled at Folkington, James Gwynne set about turning himself into a country gentleman. It seemed a classic example of British industrial decadence. He allowed the family firm to fall behind, and made no effort to install new equipment or keep up with the rival engineering firm established by his younger brother John. Instead, he turned his attention to land and housing speculation, in London and Sussex. He bought several country estates around Folkington, and members of the local hunt used to say that one could ride all day without ever leaving Squire Gwynne's land.

As James Gwynne's children grew up, their father grew ever more jealous and mistrustful, as if he suspected them all of trying to steal his money and usurp his power. To keep them under his control they were kept on the most miserable allowances, which they overspent at their peril. James's retribution was severe and long-lasting, and he never forgot a grudge. His eldest son Reginald was cut out of his will for reckless extravagance at Eton and Oxford. He fled to Canada, settled there, and eventually prospered, though he and his father were never reconciled. The second son, Nevile, took a degree in engineering at Cambridge and then joined 'the works', as the family firm was known. James treated him in the same way he had treated his younger brothers: Nevile was kept overworked, underpaid and without authority in the firm, despite the fact that James had all but lost interest in it.

Elizabeth's father Rupert was also expected to live on a pittance. Having been to school at Shrewsbury he went to Pembroke College, Cambridge, where he studied history with enough energy to get a degree, but little enthusiasm. Hunting, shooting and social life in general proved far more attractive. One of his closest friends was a shy, good-natured boy called Gordon Woodhouse. Rupert introduced Woodhouse to his musical sister Violet, and they were married in the summer of 1894. Thus began one of the most celebrated and eccentric marriages of Edwardian England, in the course of which Violet acquired three subsidiary 'husbands' without ever losing the devotion of her first.

Having no particular aptitude for engineering, Rupert read for the Bar. He managed to exist on his small allowance thanks to Violet and Gordon, with whom he lived while he was doing his articles in London. At the same time, he spent every day he could at Folkington: not only to keep down his expenses, but also to enjoy the days of hunting, shooting and point-to-point racing at which he proved so skilful.

For those pleasures, there was another, grimmer price to pay, for Rupert had a weak heart. The doctors told him that if he gave up all his active pursuits, he might live as long as most men; but that if he continued with them, he might not survive beyond middle age. Rupert decided that he could not change. He went on riding and racing as hard as ever, and adding to his collection of trophies and silver cups.

Another pleasure in Rupert's life was the exercise of his considerable charm. He talked and laughed easily, danced well, and women blossomed in his company. On one occasion, he exerted a rather stronger spell than he intended. A family friend fell desperately in love with Rupert, going so far as to follow him to his room one night – she might have forced her way in had he not locked the door. She fled the following day accompanied by her mother, leaving Rupert profoundly relieved. He preferred brief, light-hearted affairs with actresses or married women.

Rupert was called to the Bar in 1898, though it did not take him long to realize that he would never rise to the top of his profession. Politics interested him, but he lacked the means to stand for Parliament, and there was not a hope that his father would back such an ambitious venture. Rupert would still have to depend for many years on his small allowance, counting every penny, an austerity only relieved by the rural pleasures provided free at Folkington. Like most young men of his upbringing he loved the country-house world of Edwardian masculinity with its smells of leather, dubbin, Turkish cigarettes and gun oil; the sound of hooves on cobble, as tired hunters were led by stable boys across the yard to their loose boxes to be rubbed down; the reverberation of the dressing gong for dinner, and the prospect of a very hot bath.

Rupert Gwynne was thirty when his father and his older brother Nevile had a quarrel that was to have far-reaching consequences, not least for Rupert himself. Over the years, Nevile had begged his father again and again to invest in new plant and up-to-date technology, essential if the firm were to hold its own in the market; and each time his father had refused. Nevile's final attempt to make his father see reason took place one evening in August 1903. Their discussion started calmly enough, but tempers rose and the quarrel ended in blows and unforgivable words. Nevile was banished from his father's house for ever.

Nevile was stunned by what had happened, but Rupert promised his brother that he would do all he could to heal the breach and reinstate him in their father's affections (and, at least by implication, restore him to his inheritance). Nevile's daughter, Katharine Ayling, had no doubt that Rupert meant what he said at the time. But Rupert, who had seen his two elder brothers banished and treated like outcasts, was now in line to inherit the bulk of his father's fortune – provided he did not repeat their mistakes.

Rupert's position as heir-presumptive grew stronger on 3 May 1905, when he made a most advantageous match. 'A crowd of relatives and guests assembled in St Margaret's Westminster,' wrote one social gazette, 'when Mr Rupert Gwynne . . . was married to the Hon. Stella Ridley, elder surviving daughter of the late Viscount Ridley, sister of the present peer, a granddaughter of Dudley Coutts (first Lord Tweedmouth), and niece of the Countess of Aberdeen . . . Viscount Ridley gave away the bride, a tall, fine-looking girl of twenty-one, with beautiful colouring, who looked extremely well in her long-trained gown of ivory-tinted, rich, soft, corded silk.'

There had been Ridleys in and around the Tyne valley since the twelfth century, although the bulk of the family fortune was founded on coal mining in the early eighteenth century. They had ties by marriage with another well-established local family, the Whites; and when in 1763 Sir Matthew White died unmarried, his baronetcy and the estate of Blagdon were inherited by his Ridley nephews. The arms of the Ridleys were added to those of the Whites over the neoclassical portico of Blagdon Hall, and from then on the eldest son of the family has always been called Matthew White Ridley – right up to the present day. Ridleys had for generations been mayors of Newcastle, and had represented the city in Parliament; but the family's political influence reached a new peak with Stella's father, the fifth baronet. He became Home Secretary under Lord Salisbury in 1895, and was made a viscount in 1900.

Rupert could not have chosen better. He had married a rich woman, whose money would free him from his dependence on his father – and her family's position in the Conservative Party meant that he now had the means and the contacts to enter Parliament. Meanwhile Stella's family and guardians had been allowed to understand that although he had two older brothers, it was Rupert who would inherit Folkington and his father's fortune.

With the help of his wife's connections Rupert now became the Conservative candidate for Eastbourne, which was then held by the Liberals. He fought the 1910 election on the platform of 'Unionism, Empire and Tariff Reform'. He won, and held Eastbourne for the rest of his life. His daughter Elizabeth was very proud of her father. In later life she sought out and collected his election cards and addresses, and kept his photograph in a leather frame beside her bed.

To the surprise of his family, the choleric patriarch James Gwynne began to mellow as his health failed. He became reconciled to his disgraced son Nevile, who was devoted to the old man during his last weeks. Yet when James died in March 1915, Nevile was astounded to discover that neither he, nor his son John (the only grandson James and May Gwynne were to have), were mentioned as beneficiaries in his father's will. It was a disastrous testament: any imagination, caution or foresight James Gwynne might have used when drafting his will was evidently blinded by a desire to control his fortune from beyond the grave.

7

The future Elizabeth David later described her grandfather's will as 'a document which two generations of lawyers and counsel without number have failed to unravel'.[1] The problem was that it set out a rigid line of inheritance. He stipulated that his money must be passed on through the sons he had not disinherited, their grandsons, and their male heirs in the order he set out. Yet all this depended on there being male heirs at crucial points in the line of succession. When these failed to materialize, the family was inevitably thrown into an unseemly squabble over inheritance, which only expensive court cases could decide. For the immediate future, however, all was clear: Rupert and his younger brother Roland were left in possession of the family fortune.

It was the cosseted young Roland, not Rupert, who took over the huge family house at Folkington after their mother's death. Rupert and Stella had already settled into the far more attractive manor house at Wootton, where they set to work on an ambitious programme of extensions. Rupert had never shown much interest in literature and music; but he did have a feel for architecture, and for the work he employed one of the best architects of Edwardian England: Detmar Blow. Blow identified firmly with the principles of the Arts and Crafts movement, and was much used by the Souls, the political and intellectual coterie that clustered around Arthur Balfour (who was prime minister from 1902 to 1905).

To the original building, a compact Jacobean manor dating from the 1670s, Blow added a large staircase and a wing that doubled the size of the house. The lower level of the new wing became the nursery, consisting of a series of rooms opening on to a long corridor. Above it was a library, the largest and most beautiful room in the house. The predominant colours are the rich tones of gold-tooled, leather-bound books, contrasting with the cool grey-painted walls. It is lit by a huge Venetian window overlooking the Sussex Downs, and – unlike many libraries – it gives a feeling of airiness and space.

Detmar Blow also built a gatehouse and two cobbled courtyards connected by a handsome archway. The courtyards were surrounded by a complex of stables, barns and outhouses which, thanks to Blow's sensitivity to texture and his insistence on the very best traditional materials, look as if they had grown out of the centuries.

Stella and Rupert both had a very good eye, and their taste was in harmony with that of their architect. Every object in the house was chosen with care, and was well-made and unpretentious: a taste which profoundly influenced their daughter Elizabeth.

* * * * * * * *

CHAPTER TWO

The Gwynne Girls Grow Up

Initial impressions of Rupert's wife were mixed when she first came and settled in Sussex in 1905. At a time when young women were largely judged by their looks, Stella was considered more handsome than beautiful. Tall and broad-boned, she had a creamy complexion, and her thick chestnut hair was ideally suited to the abundant, swept-up hairstyles of the day. But a heavy jaw and prominent nose gave her face more character than was fashionable. She was proud of being a Ridley, proud of her political connections, and a certain reserve contrasted unfavourably with the warmth and gregariousness of her husband.

As time went on Stella's talents unfolded, and admiration for her grew. She was a keen gardener, became an excellent botanical painter and she developed a real love and knowledge of antiques. Her taste was sure and confident, and she could juxtapose apparently unrelated objects to great effect – a gift that reflected her personality: a close friend and relative described her as 'a high Tory with a strong streak of the rebel'.[1]

Stella was one of a family of four surviving children, with two older brothers, Matthew and Jasper, and a younger sister Grace. She had been born with a powerful and determined character, and when her mother died when Stella was fifteen, she and her sister were put under the care of her aunt Ishbel, Countess of Aberdeen. Lady Aberdeen found her less tractable than her more gentle and obedient sister Grace.

It was said that Stella had come perilously close to a rash marriage before she met Rupert. Some said her first love was her cousin, the Hon. Dudley Gordon, who became Elizabeth's godfather and later 3rd Marquess of Aberdeen. Some even whispered about one of the grooms at Blagdon. There can be no doubt, however, that Stella was very much in love with Rupert when she married him. Their first child, Priscilla, was born in 1909. Their second was Sackville, the only son Stella was ever to bear; but he was still-born.

Her next child, Elizabeth, was born on Boxing Day, 1913. She was christened on 22 January 1914, in the beautiful crypt chapel of the House of Commons, in a family christening robe of fine Irish lace. Her godmothers were May Gwynne and Mrs Detmar Blow, the wife of the architect of Wootton. Her godfathers were Dudley Gordon and the Hon. Alfred Lyttelton.

Diana was born in 1915, and Felicité two years later. As girl followed girl, Stella and Rupert saw their hope of leaving Wootton to a male heir fade away. James Gwynne's will had started to exert its obduracy over them. Stella resented her daughters and grieved for them at the same time. She thought it preposterous that Wootton would pass into the hands of Rupert's sybaritic, childless brother Roland, who already owned Folkington. Rows often developed between husband and wife on the subject. Stella thought they must be able to find some legal loophole – while Rupert told her, with equal force, that there was nothing to be done.

In Parliament, Rupert was noticed more for his performance in debate than for his skills as an orator. Known for being on the extreme right wing of the party, he fought every move towards a relaxation of imperial rule, whether in Ireland, Egypt or India, and he was implacably opposed to women's suffrage. When in London he lived at 47 Catherine Place, which had been given to Stella by her family when she married. It consisted of two Queen Anne houses converted into one, and it boasted a division bell. This useful device rang about eight minutes before a division in the Commons took place, and many private houses around Westminster had them.

The house was also useful for Rupert's occasional illicit afternoons.

The most serious affair of Rupert's life had begun while Stella was pregnant with Elizabeth. A couple called the Cecils came to live in Sussex with their schoolboy son. Vera Cecil was very pretty in a blonde, feminine way; and while she was perhaps not as intelligent as Stella, she made up for it with a lively mind and a warm, light-hearted nature. By 1914 Mrs Cecil and Rupert Gwynne were constantly in each other's company, at hunt balls and race meetings, and they were seen riding together in the early mornings. Mr Cecil did not seem to mind: it was even said that he was rather relieved, since he had a long-standing mistress of his own and it suited him very well that his wife had someone to amuse her.

For Stella, however, the situation was deeply humiliating. At first, Rupert had upheld the conventions of their class: the affair had been conducted discreetly, and he had continued to treat his wife with consideration and respect. However, as time went on his infatuation became more flagrant. Mrs Cecil was often invited over to Wootton, and her son was sent to play with Stella's daughters. Stella did not throw scenes, that was not her style; but one witness to these developments recalled that Stella made no attempt to hide her distaste for Vera Cecil, and that not many women could have supported the freezing looks that Stella gave her rival.

While the pace of life at Wootton remained decorous enough, the children were aware of the tensions: not only between their parents, but with other members of the family. Violet Gordon Woodhouse still adored her brother Rupert, but never got on with Stella: mostly from jealousy, for Violet did not like to see herself displaced in anyone's affections. They saw little of their Uncle Nevile, who never forgave Rupert for failing to intercede with their father. Aunt Dorothy disliked Stella, and some years later she and Rupert fell out once and for all. Roland was disliked and mistrusted by his brothers and sisters, and Dorothy could not forgive him for turning her out of her childhood home. At the heart of all these eruptions was the temper that James Gwynne had passed on to his children, along with his impossible will. 'As children we had had enough of the bitter quarrels,'[2] Elizabeth wrote many years later.

All these tensions and struggles, however, were mere rustles and whispers in the background. In the forefront of everyone's mind was the war.

Rupert attended and spoke at a great many recruiting rallies for the newly formed battalions of the Sussex Regiment, including one at Seaford, where he 'appealed to the employers of labour to make it as easy as possible for their workmen to enlist, by promising that their situations would be kept open for them, and their wives and dependents looked after'.[3] At the same time he never lost sight of his constituency duties, and his assiduous attendance at the meetings of the Eastbourne Rural District Council and the East Sussex District Council was evidently much appreciated.

Stella was to have two more babies before the war was over, but she did not neglect her duty either. She was involved in the League of Mercy and the Eastbourne branch of the Red Cross, for which she organized a matinée in December 1914 at the Devonshire Park Theatre. This consisted of patriotic songs, and tableaux with people representing Glory, Britannia, France, Russia, and Belgium. It was considered a great success, and raised over £121. Stella also chaired the committee of ladies which founded Eastbourne's Union Jack Club, which was a social centre for the wives and children of men on active service. The Club was officially opened in March 1915 by Lady Jellicoe, who was presented with a bouquet by Stella's eldest daughter Priscilla, then aged five. By the following year, Stella was president of the Soldiers and Sailors' Families Association.

Rupert's brother Nevile wanted to join up, but it was decided that his engineering skills were of more use at home making aeroplane engines. Roland joined the Sussex Yeomanry in 1914, though he was not posted to France until September 1916. No one in the family had a high opinion of his courage, whether moral or physical, so it was a great surprise when Roland was awarded the DSO in February

1917 for 'conspicuous gallantry and judgement': he had led a successful daylight raid into enemy trenches. A few months later he returned
to France, and was badly wounded in the knee during the Third
Battle of Ypres. For some time he was in danger of losing his leg.
It healed eventually, but he had a stiff knee and a limp ever afterwards.

Nothing was the same after the First World War, yet while it was
going on the pace of change at Wootton was barely noticeable.
Sometimes, they might just catch the distant thunder of the guns a
little more than a hundred miles away in France. A man was arrested
outside Polegate for shouting abuse at a group of women – it was
said he had been 'shell-shocked'. Hemlines rose dramatically, from
ankle-length in 1914 to mid-calf by 1918. Everyone ate bread made
of Standard flour, and Stella no doubt felt obliged to encourage cook
to experiment with some of the nutritious recipes using maize, lentils
and barley-meal which were supposed to save the country from the
high cost of imported wheat. Yet for the children there were still
eggs and milk, honey and home-made jam. Elizabeth was five when
the war ended, and seems to have had no recollection of it at all.

Stella was not a very demonstrative or affectionate mother. One
cousin described her as 'the most unmaternal woman I have ever
met'.[4] There was in Stella an inner core of rock-solid, egocentric
self-certainty which was rare, at a time when all a woman's cultural
conditioning was focused on devotion to husband and family. Stella
did not care. She had done her duty during the war and in public
she was very much Mrs Gwynne, but after 1918 she led an independent life based on her own interests and pursuits. The result was
that from their earliest years, her daughters were starved of motherly
affection.

Since they received so little love from their mother, the girls
turned to their father instead. The fact that they did not see much
of him made him even more of a godlike figure, and it seemed that
all the warmth and laughter that they enjoyed as children came from
him rather than their mother. He had the gift of making each of

them feel especially loved, though he was not above playing a daughter off against his wife. A cousin noticed it happening with Priscilla in particular; but when she mentioned it years later to Elizabeth, she bristled and said, 'He did that with all of us!'[5]

As soon as they were old enough, the girls were put on horseback. Priscilla, the eldest, took to it easily, as did Diana and Felicité. The only one who never really enjoyed being on a horse was Elizabeth. Since riding was Rupert's passion, he followed this aspect of his daughters' education with some interest. As Elizabeth saw her younger sisters catch up and surpass her own half-hearted efforts on horseback, she felt at a disadvantage in the fierce competition between the sisters for his affection. This was bad enough; but worse was the feeling that she had disappointed her father.

Priscilla, inevitably known as Pris, never allowed her sisters to forget that she was the eldest and exerted her authority whenever possible. Elizabeth, who inherited a great deal of her mother's stubborn integrity, found this profoundly irritating; and her response was to forge a bond of close complicity with her wild, scatty sister Diana. Elizabeth was known as Liza, a diminutive that was linked to the word 'lizard'. Like the animal, Liza seemed to combine both agility and laziness. Until she was two, Diana was known as Bulgie but when Felicité was born, this baby-name devolved on to her. Sadly for Felicité, she enjoyed none of the other indulgent attentions usually lavished on the youngest in a family. Her mother gave her no more love than she gave her other daughters, and Felicité was left with the impression that she was always last, and that however hard she ran she would never catch up.

Although Elizabeth played with the golden retrievers and elk-hounds that lolled about the yard, she developed a particular fondness for cats. She romped and squabbled with her sisters, teased the governess by putting salt in her tea, and made secret houses in the garden; yet very early on Elizabeth began to resist what one of her nieces called 'the wellington-boot side of country life'. At the same time, Wootton and Folkington were the only worlds she knew.

The only escape was reading, which luckily her mother had always encouraged. Elizabeth read everything she could. In later life she recalled 'a childish memory, of primitive coloured pictures and sheets of brightly uniformed soldiers, the Images d'Epinal, which have the same primitive charm as our penny-plain twopence-coloured prints'.[6] Elsewhere she mentions Walter de la Mare's *Come Hither*, an anthology of poetry that made a profound impact on her. The books she returned to again and again were Lewis Carroll's *Alice in Wonderland* and *Through the Looking-Glass*: stories about a curious and intelligent little girl trying to make sense of very peculiar worlds in which she did not belong.

One place where she would have liked to spend more time was the kitchen, which Elizabeth remembered as a centre of bustling activity. Dining room, servants' hall, nursery and schoolroom all had meals of varying quality at different times of day, though it was all cooked on the same coal-burning range. At the same time it was a sociable place, full of laughter and gossip. Throughout the day, 'a massive black iron kettle was kept with water on the simmer for the cups of tea to be administered to any outdoor staff such as the gardener bringing fruit and vegetables, or a stable-boy who might drop in. There would also be a succession of van drivers delivering groceries and household stores . . . the baker and the butcher bringing bread and meat . . . the postman with parcels, a telegraph boy with telegrams from the village post office. All would be offered tea, biscuits, bread and cheese, cake.'[7] The only people who were not welcomed into the warm and busy kitchen were the children.

Instead they had to put up with the horrible food that came out of it, which gave the defiant and provocative Elizabeth something to rebel against at least once a day. Food for the nursery was not made by the cook, but by the kitchen maid, who had much else to do besides. However, she did not have to waste time on making nursery food appetizing. All the emphasis was on nourishment. There was a lot of mutton and beef, and potatoes which had been put through an implement called a ricer, so they appeared in dry, flaky mounds. Like most children Elizabeth hated vegetables, which tended to be boiled yellow marrows and overcooked turnip tops and parsnips. She even hated puddings: 'junket was slippery and slimy, jam roly-poly greasy, something called ground-rice pudding dry and stodgy, tapioca the most revolting of them all . . .'[8] The gastronomic miseries were even worse on fish days. 'The food,' she wrote, 'looked so terrifying even before it was on your plate. Egg sauce didn't do much to compensate for the black skin and monstrous head of a boiled cod; fish pudding, a few spiteful bones inevitably lying in wait in that viscous mass, and whitings biting their own tails, were frightening dishes for children, and often painful too . . .'[9]

All children complain about the food they are given, but when Elizabeth was young there was no avoiding it. Either the child was forced to sit at table until the plate was clean, or, if that became impractical, they would have it served up cold for tea. Elizabeth must have either gone to bed hungry or swallowed the congealed food; but whatever the result, these early battles did more to strengthen her resolve than to break her spirit.

The only pleasant memory was Nannie's illicit cooking over the nursery fire. There was a sort of sticky fudge called 'stuff', scooped up in spoonfuls out of saucers or soap-dishes. In high summer there were gooseberries, red currants and raspberries which Nannie used to throw into a saucepan and heat quickly with sugar: this hot fruit salad embodied, for Elizabeth, the very essence of summer. Best of all, there were mushrooms: real field mushrooms gathered at dawn by Elizabeth and her sisters and carried back to Nannie, who cooked them with fresh thick cream, stolen, Elizabeth surmised, from the kitchen. 'As in most households, Nannie and the cook thoroughly disapproved of each other, and had she known this private cookery was going on upstairs in the nursery, the cook would have made a blistering row. We must have been aware of this, as children always are of tensions between grown-ups, because Nannie's mushrooms had the charm of the forbidden. We must never be caught eating them . . .'[10] It is interesting that her first taste of something really delicious should be associated with naughtiness, complicity, a secret.

The days passed, and a succession of governesses (some more tolerant of being teased than others) came and went. As England returned to the peacetime routine in the early 1920s, the seasons were once more punctuated by hunts and point-to-points, and holidays by the sea with their cousins, the Palmers. Stella's youngest sister Grace had married Roundell Cecil Palmer, Viscount Wolmer (later 3rd Earl of Selborne) in 1910, and had six surviving children; and since she knew her sister Stella was not a motherly woman, Grace would scoop up the four Gwynne girls and, together with her own brood, take them all off to the seaside. One of Grace's daughters, Anne, remembers a sunburnt Liza, aged seven, on holiday with them on Hayling Island. With her shock of dark hair cropped short at the back and with a fringe in front, and a square, determined look about her face, she looked 'just like a little red Indian'.

As they grew older Anne and Elizabeth became closer. They both hated sports, and were not very physically coordinated: Anne remembered one occasion when her father took them all boating in Regent's Park. He took the younger children, while Elizabeth and Anne were given a boat of their own. They got stuck in the middle of the lake because, with one oar each, Anne could not get Elizabeth to row properly; so they went round in circles until rescued by the boatman.

Anne was passionately interested in natural history, and wanted to become, as she put it, 'a female Gilbert White'. When Anne came to stay at Wootton Elizabeth was very happy to go along with this new hobby, looking for plants and examining wild flowers as they walked on the Downs. Their friendship might have blossomed further, but as a pair they were considered a bad influence on each other – a suspicion confirmed after an incident in which the French governess's cardigan was hidden under a pile of weeds. Anne was not invited again.

Whether Elizabeth was bored, frustrated or merely seeking attention, she began to see Wootton as a place to escape from, not to come back to. Several times she ran away from home: 'It was the usual thing,' she once told a friend, 'walking down the drive with your suitcase. You must have done it.' On one occasion, however, the scene was played out with rather more drama than usual. Elizabeth got up at dawn, and whispered goodbye to Diana before setting off once again down the long drive. This time, she seems to have gone further than usual, or her parents had finally had enough. There was all hell to pay when she was finally brought back home. Her father was informed when he came back from London. He stormed into the bathroom where the girls were being bathed. Elizabeth was told that she was a wicked, selfish girl who had put her family to considerable anxiety, and while delivering the lecture he slapped her as she tried to hide behind the towel horse.

When the girls were considered old enough, tea was taken with their mother; and at this point Elizabeth discovered that the food served in the world beyond the nursery was considerably more appetizing. Stella presided over the long tea table, with the silver teapot and the hot-water urn set over a spirit lamp. There was a jug of cream, but that was for guests only. Once her girls were out of the nursery, they were expected to take their tea with lemon. There was always a selection of delicious, elegant food: thin bread and butter, scones, home-made quince or apple jelly, and a sponge cake. For special occasions, there was a cake with orange-flavoured icing. Stella was very fond of chocolate, and sometimes there was chocolate cake too. There was an uproar when one of the golden retrievers found its way into the larder and demolished an entire chocolate cake. 'Who had left the larder door open? Recriminations and arguments raged for days, the younger children fell, as always, under suspicion and the kitchen regions were more strictly than ever out of bounds.'[11]

By 1922, Rupert's health was beginning to cause concern. Although he was an abstemious man who drank little and never smoked, all those years of racing and riding were beginning to take a toll on his weak heart, just as his doctors had warned him. A series of pillboxes and medicine bottles now stood beside his plate at every meal. Yet for Rupert perhaps the greatest worry was that, when he died, everything would go to his younger brother Roland.

The strict provisions of James's will, insisting on the male line of succession, appeared ever more self-defeating. Rupert had only daughters, Roland was what was known as 'a confirmed bachelor' and their sisters were childless. Stella would have a life interest in Wootton, and she was independently rich; but his daughters would inherit nothing of James Gwynne's fortune. Rupert at last took legal advice to try and circumvent his father's will, and a scheme was put forward by which the brothers and sisters who stood in the line of succession would waive their claim in return for a financial settlement. Everyone was agreed, until Rupert quarrelled with his sister Dorothy. In revenge she refused to sign away her birthright, and the plan – which depended on all the siblings acting in unison – fell apart.

In 1923, Rupert was appointed Financial Secretary to the War Office in Stanley Baldwin's government; and to mark the event, the local Conservative Association declared that they would like to give Mr and Mrs Gwynne a handsome present. This consisted of a silver inkwell, an illuminated album containing the signatures of over 9,000 subscribers, and – at Stella's request – a set of portraits of their four daughters. The painter she chose was Ambrose McEvoy, somewhat to the dismay of the Association: McEvoy's painting was energetic and articulate, and he was considered rather too 'modern' for most people's taste.

For some reason Elizabeth was done first, and she remembered being taken to his studio in Grosvenor Road. Elizabeth was then nine years old, and McEvoy was evidently very good with children. 'I was entirely beguiled by your father and his studio,' she wrote to McEvoy's daughter in 1974, 'and it was all the greatest possible excitement for me. It was your father who was responsible I think for giving me what became a very great and permanent interest in painting (although I can't paint at all) . . .'[12] Ambrose McEvoy came down to paint Priscilla, Diana and Felicité in the summer of 1924, and the girls found his company quite delightful. Then Rupert's health took a sudden turn for the worse. McEvoy finished the portraits more hurriedly than he had intended, and returned to London.

Rupert's illness had been brought on by his increased workload. His doctors insisted that he should rest as much as possible, yet he seems to have been particularly restless and anxious that summer, pacing up and down the ballroom when he could not sleep.

He suffered a severe heart attack, after which he needed two nurses around the clock. Once his kidneys failed, it was merely a question of time – although there was little the doctors could do to relieve his agonizing pain. The one person who might have brought him some comfort was Vera Cecil, but she was no longer allowed in the house. Stella argued that it was out of the question for Rupert to see her on the grounds that any emotional excitement was bad for him.

Rupert died on 12 October, aged fifty-two. The local newspaper could be relied on to deliver a respectful eulogy on the occasion, but it also reflected a genuine warmth and sense of loss felt by his constituency. 'It is doubtful if the borough has ever been more moved by the passing of one of its public men,' wrote the *Eastbourne Chronicle*.[13] 'Mr Gwynne occupied a warm place in the hearts of the inhabitants, all the more remarkable in view of his tenacious allegiance to the advanced wing of the Conservative Party.' His coffin of unpolished oak was put on a farm wagon lined with evergreens, and drawn by two horses to St Peter's ad Vincula, Folkington. Stella and Priscilla, attended by Rupert's brothers and sisters and a great crowd of mourners, attended the funeral, but Elizabeth and her younger sisters were not present.

Elizabeth was almost eleven years old. The girls were put under the joint guardianship of their Uncle Top (Aunt Grace's husband Lord Wolmer), and Douglas Hogg, the 1st Viscount Hailsham: a relation of Stella's and a Sussex neighbour. His son Quintin, Elizabeth's cousin, later became Lord Chancellor.

Although Stella had put a great deal of herself into Wootton and its gardens, the animating spirit of the place had been Rupert's. After his death, there were fewer visitors and there was less money. The years that followed were difficult ones for Stella. Roland, who had entertained on a lavish scale since inheriting Folkington, was rapidly dissipating his fortune. He desperately needed money, and by the terms of James Gwynne's will, he had now inherited Wootton. While he could not throw Stella out, he used his position as her effective landlord to make life as difficult as possible.

Stella decided to send her daughters to boarding school. Priscilla, who was still getting over her father's death, was quite unprepared for life at Wycombe Abbey and reacted violently against it. After one term she came home with whooping cough, and then persuaded her mother to let her stay at home to help nurse Felicité, desperately ill with peritonitis. She flatly refused to go back to school after that.

In September 1925, Elizabeth was sent to Godstowe Preparatory School near High Wycombe. According to a fellow-pupil, 'she appeared to be a very solitary being',[14] but she seems to have enjoyed it. In later life she described it as 'a charming, lovely school', and she remembered the history teacher with particular fondness. The records show that she left Godstowe in April 1927, probably due to illness. She was then sent to St Clare's Ladies Private School in Tunbridge Wells. She never had the company of Diana or Felicité at school, since Stella sent her youngest daughters to Moira House in Eastbourne.

Elizabeth herself gave very few details of her schooldays, although she was good at history. In 1929, aged fifteen, she had attended a course of ten lectures on European history in the nineteenth century, culminating in an exam which she passed with distinction. Her cousin Anne remembers Elizabeth mentioning that her interest in the theatre began at school, and that at Godstowe she had had a row with the drama teacher when she was not given a coveted part in the school play. The only thing Elizabeth recorded in later life were her memories of 'limp fried plaice, followed by tinned apricots and custard'.[15]

In Elizabeth's immediate world, the separation from her sisters was the biggest change in her life; but the fact that it had been imposed by her cold and autocratic mother increased her sense of loss from the death of the father she adored. Stella was far from happy herself and was beset with worries; but she took no comfort from her daughters, and gave them none either. Instead, she travelled abroad whenever she could – which was surprisingly often, considering how much she complained of her financial problems. Elizabeth told a friend in later life that 'Mummy always had better things to do than look after us.'[16] She and her sisters began to build up resentment against their mother. In the loveless atmosphere of Wootton and the noisy regimentation of school, Elizabeth soon learned emotional self-reliance.

During the holidays when their mother was abroad, the girls were farmed out to relatives. Sometimes they stayed with their Uncle Jasper Ridley and his wife Nathalie, where they played endless card games. (Nathalie was a Benckendorff, daughter of the last Imperial Russian Ambassador to Britain.) Most often they stayed with their Aunt Grace and her great romp of Palmer children. The four Gwynne girls spent the winters of 1924 and 1925 at Blackmoor, the Palmers' house in Hampshire. They skated on Flash Pond, made a house of snow and – on one occasion – found an old sleigh which had not been used since 1825. In the New Year, Grace's extended family would take the train to Adelboden in the German Alps. If there was not enough snow for skiing they went skating, although Anne, still a keen naturalist, and Elizabeth, who liked winter sports no better than summer ones, often preferred to go walking.

Stella would make periodic visits during the holidays: but it was obvious to the children that she viewed them with a faint distaste, and was relieved when they were all sent off to play. Had she noticed, Stella might have been pleased at how close her daughters were to each other; but at the heart of their complicity was their sense of existing on the margins of their mother's life.

Elizabeth enjoyed being a part of the great clan of cousins, although there was an intense, concentrated streak in her. One holiday, marked by a great many booby traps, ambushes and apple-pie beds, polarized the boys into one camp and the girls in another. It was all quite good-humoured until Liza arrived. She took it all terribly seriously and before long it turned into a veritable battle of the sexes.

Elizabeth was about twelve when she spent one of the happiest holidays of her childhood at Wolcot, on the Norfolk coast, in the summer of 1926. Grace and Stella both took a house there that year, as did their brother Jasper, with his wife and children. Priscilla, by then seventeen, did not consider herself a child any more. She spent most of the holiday sitting on the beach, sewing camisoles. The beaches were quite wild; and while the shells there were not so good as those at Hayling Island, one could find carnelians and amber, supposedly washed up from the shores of the Baltic. There were also shoals of jellyfish. Anne's brother Bob was badly stung, and had to spend the rest of the day in a bath full of bicarbonate of soda.

Anne had been given a small garage in which to do her 'botanizing', with help from Elizabeth and Katharine Ridley (Jasper's daughter). They would go to the beaches, gingerly collecting dead jellyfish in shrimping nets and bringing them back to the garage. Here the girls would press the jellyfish in between sheets of blotting paper, a technique developed by Anne: all the water came out, leaving just the skin. Many years later, Anne wrote to Elizabeth to congratulate her on being awarded the CBE. Elizabeth's reply included the remark that she had never been as happy as that summer, when she and Anne collected jellyfish together.

Life with a happy troop of cousins was very different from life with Aunt Violet, with whom they also stayed during the holidays.

Whereas Grace Wolmer's household was built around the children, Violet Gordon Woodhouse's household revolved exclusively around herself. Elizabeth was fascinated by this 'little creature with her autocratic kingfisher manners and her huge coal-black monkey eyes and her strange dark clothes which never looked sombre but somehow always sparkly and variegated. Her paste-buckled red-heeled Marie Antoinette shoes and the glass bubbles with tiny goldfish imprisoned in them which for years were her favourite earrings helped to make her look like a being from quite another species from our own.'[17]

Mrs Gordon Woodhouse was then in her fifties. She gave up playing professionally in 1927, at the height of her musical talent and her celebrity. She was financially secure, and preferred playing for small audiences of experts rather than for the general public. She was as extravagant as ever, and her every caprice was indulged: not only by her husband Gordon, but also by the other two men of her ménage – the Hon. Bill Barrington, and the Hon. Denis Tollemache. The four of them divided their time between London and Nether Lypiatt Manor in Gloucestershire.

On one occasion, Aunt Violet took Elizabeth and her sisters to see Douglas Fairbanks in the silent version of *The Thief of Baghdad*. 'I remember it still as a magical experience,' wrote Elizabeth, 'with that white horse gliding through the sky. Once was enough for me to remember it for a lifetime, but Aunt V. went to see it day after day, accompanied by Uncle Gordon, Uncle Bill and any other honorary uncles who happened to be around . . .'[18]

Elizabeth admired Violet: here after all was a woman of talent who had been clever enough to live her life exactly as she wished, regardless of the raised eyebrows and the whispers about what went on with all those 'honorary uncles'. She was also very generous, and kept her nieces amused with expensive toys, such as little musical boxes out of which a bird jumps up and sings. Yet with this undoubted generosity, there was a self-centredness of staggering proportions. Felicité stammered as a child, and found it very hard to get out any words at all – particularly when they were expected. One day Aunt Violet gave Felicité a teddy bear. Typically of Aunt Violet, it was a magnificent, fabulously expensive teddy bear, quite the most wonderful thing that anyone had ever given little Felicité. She clutched it, overcome with joy, unable to say a single word. 'Well!' said Aunt Violet. 'She can't even be bothered to say thank you.' With that she snatched the teddy from Felicité's arms, and Felicité never saw it again.

As time passed, however, Elizabeth did find the words, and the courage, to stand up to Aunt Violet. 'The time came when I – I can't speak for my sisters – got bored with Aunt V. saying she was looking after us because we were "Rupert's children", and Rupert . . . had been her favourite brother. One day I said, "Aunt Violet, don't you do anything for us because we're ourselves?" It was horrible of me, but she had asked for it. She was getting at my mother, I think. Children inevitably sense that kind of thing . . ."[19] Elizabeth had been told by a family friend that the feud between Violet and Stella had started during the First World War. Violet came to Eastbourne to give a benefit concert for one of the war charities; but all through her performance, she was driven nearly mad by the steady clicking of Stella's knitting needles. 'I'm afraid it all rings horribly true,' admitted Elizabeth.

Compared to the over-ornamented luxury of Aunt Violet's Nether Lypiatt, Wootton must have seemed a very comfortable and unpretentious place, and Elizabeth could recall some sights and smells of her first home with great affection. Her niece Sabrina, Priscilla's daughter, once gave her some parsley planted in a beautiful old red flowerpot. Elizabeth was delighted, saying that the pot could only have come from one of the old potting sheds at Wootton – which it had. And right at the end of her life, in a list of bequests, she left a picture of white violets to her niece with the words, 'When we were children we used to find white violets on the banks of the ditch or hedgerow along the Wootton back lane, and also somewhere on the way up to the church, also by the back way to Folkington and close to the little lodge.' It seems to have been the countryside rather than the house that she recalled in later life: the bluebell wood at the end of the garden, and the thyme-scented Sussex Downs.

* * * * * * * *

CHAPTER THREE

Paris and Munich

When Elizabeth was about sixteen, Stella made one of her rare and alarmingly sudden appearances at St Clare's boarding school. She was appalled to see her daughter Elizabeth wielding a lacrosse stick. Elizabeth pointed out that, in letter after letter, she had been begging her mother's permission to give up games. But at that moment, the prospect – however unlikely – of her daughter turning into a beefy team-sports girl made Stella decide that Elizabeth had had quite enough of boarding schools.

At that time Elizabeth nurtured an ambition, perhaps encouraged by the art mistress, to become a painter. Since no painting or drawing can be confidently attributed to Elizabeth, it is impossible to say whether or not she had any talent. If she did, it was inherited from her mother, who painted vibrant, precisely detailed flower paintings. Elizabeth scarcely mentions her teenage painting phase, and gives no idea of whether it was an all-absorbing passion or merely a congenial pastime. Yet Stella evidently thought Elizabeth's artistic promise was worth developing, and the natural place to start was Paris.

In Paris Elizabeth attended art lessons, and soon afterwards enrolled at the Sorbonne for a course in French civilization which covered history, literature and architecture. Then she chose to go one step further, and try for a diploma.

On 29 October 1930 Stella wrote, 'I am so glad you have found the Sorbonne what you wanted . . . As Paris suits you it's all to the good, and of course such a diploma would be one of the best things you can get . . . The only thing is be careful of your eyes . . . do see that the light is good as you read and write, as it is only in bad light and bad positions that you get bad eyes.' [1] Sensible advice, but Elizabeth's eyes were naturally weak and she wore spectacles for most of her life (though in youth, she always took them off before being photographed).

Elizabeth, and another girl called Marian Butterworth with whom she kept in touch for much of her life, were two of the three lodgers taken in by a certain Mme Barette. Mme Barette's house had no doubt been recommended to Stella by a friend, who must have told her that Madame was strict, respectable and charged reasonable rates. Stella would not have inquired about the food, beyond establishing that it was ample and wholesome. Yet as it turned out, it was with Mme Barette that Elizabeth was to have her first experience of excellent French cooking.

Mme Barette became 'Mme Robertot' in Elizabeth's later descriptions of her. (She almost always changed the names of people she poked fun at or disliked, while the good cooks she talked about were always accorded their real names.) Mme Barette lived with her grown-up children at 79 rue de la Tour, in the sixteenth arrondissement. Poor Léontine, their cook, worked like a slave for the Barettes, who were exceptionally greedy; but all the shopping was done by Madame. She got up at dawn twice a week to go to Les Halles and returned at about ten, puffing and panting, with four shopping bags bursting with meat and vegetables.

The Barettes did not spend huge amounts of money on food. 'What with the bargains from Les Halles, the wine . . . in casks from Bordeaux, and cream and butter from their Norman property, their food was lovely without being rich or grand . . . So what emerges from those days is not the memory of elaborate sauces or sensational puddings, but rather of beautifully prepared vegetables like *salsifis à la crème*, purées of sorrel and *pommes mousseline*. Many egg dishes, and soups delicately coloured like summer dresses, coral, ivory or pale green . . .' [2]

Yet even the food could not make up for the oppressive atmosphere of the house. The *pensionnaires* ate with the Barettes at lunch, and were closely questioned about the lectures they had attended that morning. They were expected to be present at Madame's gloomy tea parties on Thursdays, attended by half a dozen ladies in black. Then there was the ordeal of the boiled salt cod which appeared every Friday: 'Grey, slimy, in great hideous flakes, it lay plonked on the dish without benefit of sauce or garnish of any kind . . .'[3] The fish was no doubt meant to be a penance, for the Barettes were very devout Catholics.

The atmosphere in the apartment was stifling, as was Madame Barette's preoccupation with food. She took a pride in eating well which had an almost moral dimension, as if her insistence on good food and clever marketing made her a better person. Elizabeth found the way the Barettes' lives revolved around their stomachs positively unappetizing, and she and her co-pensionnaires took every chance they could to escape the rue de la Tour and eat out. They enjoyed patronizing the noisy automatic restaurant in the Boulevard Saint-Michel, where a plate of ham and an orange came out of a slot machine. Madame had declared this place out of bounds, and the girls were interrogated on where they had eaten as soon as they returned home.

To escape Madame, they retired to their rooms to revise for their exams, which provided another excuse for avoiding meals. The result of this enforced studiousness was that Elizabeth gained her diploma. 'I was so very glad to get your news,' wrote her mother, 'and hasten to send my congratulations! Mme B. also wrote, wanting to know by wire, my wishes – it really makes very little difference to me, beyond the fact that I consider you've had enough of Paris, and ought to progress a bit . . .'[4]

A curious portrait of Elizabeth survives from this period, the product of the time one of her friends took her handwriting to be analysed by a graphologist. His report was written in February 1931, when Elizabeth was seventeen. 'She possesses an observant intelligence, served by an excellent memory. She is ambitious, needs to be a star – and is admirably equipped for it. Your young friend never gives herself any trouble unless she thinks it's worth it: she puts herself out only to those who will be useful to her. She is undoubtedly seductive, which many will find very engaging; but she takes a lot and gives little; she does not shine, she absorbs.'[5]

With her course over and her diploma achieved, Elizabeth might have returned to England; but Stella, on consulting her own travel arrangements, decided it was more convenient to keep her daughter in France for a little longer. Elizabeth accordingly went to stay with the Barettes at Biéville, a village near Caen in Normandy. Léontine was having a well-deserved holiday, and the cooking was done by Marie, a local girl only a few years older than Elizabeth. Her cooking was every bit as delicate and delicious as Léontine's; and one day, she came into the dining room with a large tureen of mussels. They were the first shellfish that Elizabeth had ever eaten.

'The appearance, the smell and the taste of those mussels were to me most fascinating and mysterious. The little black-shelled objects didn't seem like fish at all, they had the same kind of magical quality as mushrooms, the real field mushrooms which, as children, we had so often brought home for breakfast after a dawn search in the fields . . . So those Norman mussels, which reminded me, for whatever reason, of our secret childhood feasts, became forever endowed with the mystery of far-off and almost unobtainable things.'[6]

Elizabeth lived in France for no more than eighteen months, and in a few years she had forgotten much of what she had learned at the Sorbonne. She did, however, acquire a taste for good French couture, and the reckless joys of living on credit. By the time she left Paris Elizabeth had an outstanding bill at the dressmaker's for 643 francs. Stella, who was always lecturing her girls on the importance of economy, was furious – but she had to settle the account. It was not the first time, nor the last, that Stella was left to pick up Elizabeth's bills. Elizabeth was of course punished by having her allowance docked until she had paid her mother back, but her response was to run up even more bills. It was one of Elizabeth's ways of getting back at her mother, and a remarkably effective one.

Yet what remained above all was a taste for a kind of food quite unlike anything she had known before. She had taken little notice of it at the time, and had even tried to avoid it rather than eat with the Barettes. 'Ever since, I have been trying to catch up with those lost days when perhaps I should have been more profitably employed watching Léontine in her kitchen . . .'[7]

After the long summer of 1931, Stella sent Elizabeth to study German in Munich in October. She was placed under the wing of the Gräfin Mirbach-Geldern, and took German lessons three times a week. The family had an Austrian cook, who was particularly gifted with cakes and desserts. There was a chocolate and almond confection called *Mohr im Hemd*, tiny apricot and plum dumplings, and a delicious buttery bread which used to appear on Sundays at breakfast. Yet not all their dishes were so appetizing; one of their favourites was 'limp fried eel nauseatingly flavoured with sage'.[8]

In England, Stella was as usual worrying about her finances. In early 1932 she wrote to Elizabeth, 'I can't afford any more Germany after Diana returns in June . . . another year I want to do an *exchange*, possibly if a person came here for the summer holidays . . . Of course it must be understood that there can be no London and no parties . . . It's all I can do to live here [at Wootton] at all, and strict economy must be the order. Foreigners have an idea that English are million-aires. She would see a lot of country life of the best sort here . . .'

Although a German visitor would have to resign themselves to 'no London and no parties', Stella knew that she still had a duty to bring her daughters out into society. Elizabeth's coming-out was scheduled to take place that spring. 'Hope you are returning by April 1st – Countess of Midleton is presenting you, with her grand-daughter, Antonia Meade, some time in May . . .'

Yet if Elizabeth was to make the most of the opportunities that being a debutante provided, she would have to behave properly. 'Will you give me an undertaking, *if* I try and entertain a little for you, will you promise me to be punctual, and down in time to *receive* guests? This is a very important item – Priscilla always arrived after we had sat down to a meal, and gave a very bad impression. I heard a lot of complaints about it and it did her a *lot of harm*. Also she smoked too much. Mothers of Debs don't like it. You were very unpunctual all holidays here – I am not going to think of any entertaining, until I get your promise, as it's a waste of time and money – the whole point is to be asked back . . .'[9]

Coming-out between the wars was a rite of passage on the way to adulthood and independence, and the prospect of some new frocks and evening gowns (even if they were hand-me-downs) was not entirely unappealing. But Elizabeth dreaded the whole business. She also did not want to leave Munich, where she had been blissfully happy. She had developed an intense platonic relationship with an older man who was a friend of the Mirbach-Gelderns. He signed himself 'Lalt', and on the day she left for London he sent her this letter in English:

'Don't forget that sublime walk in Nymphenburg. All I can do today is to send you these few poor roses. Don't bother about them and simply push them into your trunk. I'd prefer that to finding them in the Habsburgstr. when next I go there. Say your English friend sent you them . . .'[10]

His next letter, dated 2 April and written in German, gives a touching picture of the young Elizabeth: 'Just think, the room which you filled with your dear being appears to get bigger and bigger every day. I miss you always more painfully. You were so enchantingly young and open and soft and devoted. In spite of the amusing makeup of your eyebrows, lips and cheeks, you were so natural, genuine, deep and melancholy. You had a certain seriousness which only children have. Your yellow and red flowers have got that from you . . . You and they have nothing of the greenhouse.'[11]

33

Elizabeth was now eighteen. She was very flattered by the attentions of an older man whom she admired, and she must have enjoyed seeing the effect her beauty had on him. Yet it is ironic that what most attracted Lalt to Elizabeth – her youth and innocence – were the very qualities that Elizabeth was keenest to lose.

* * * * * * * *

CHAPTER FOUR

Acting it Out

Shocking news was waiting for Elizabeth on her return to England. Her cousin Edward Marjoribanks, who had been MP for Eastbourne since 1929, had committed suicide. He was only thirty-two, and seemed to have had everything to live for: he had been Captain of School at Eton, President of the Oxford Union, had published three books, and was considered one of the most promising young politicians in the House. He seems to have committed suicide in a moment of extreme nervous exhaustion: he had been overworking himself for some time, and the woman he loved had turned down his proposal of marriage. Stella was distraught: Edward had been her protégé, and had taken the place of the son she had never had.

Nearly forty years later, when her own sister Diana was contemplating suicide, Elizabeth was profoundly sympathetic. 'She knew of course how I felt – and feel – about this question. I thought it all out when my cousin Edward Marjoribanks, for whom I had great respect and whom I greatly loved, blew his brains out. I was seventeen [*sic*] at the time, and have not forgotten.'[1]

A few weeks later, on 11 May 1932, Miss Elizabeth Gwynne was presented at Court by the Countess of Midleton, as arranged by her mother. The dress code was elaborate: those to be presented had to wear a headdress with three small white ostrich feathers to which was attached a short tulle veil, a gown with a court train which trailed some eighteen inches behind the wearer, and long white kid gloves reaching well above the elbow. The debutantes were dressed by three in the afternoon, and had five hours of waiting before being presented to the King and Queen at about eight. Elizabeth endured it all in scowling silence, although Queen Mary thought the evening had gone well. In her diary she wrote that '. . . a good many pretty debutantes came. There were charming toilettes and it was a more interesting Court than usual.'[2] Elizabeth shared her coming-out dance with Karen Harris, who later married Osbert Lancaster.

No doubt coming-out had its pleasures, but by and large Elizabeth despised the gauche young men who could only talk of tennis and horses, the girls who thought only of men and clothes. She had nothing to add to their good-humoured banter, the shrieks and the braying laughs. In Munich, she discovered that she did have the power to charm men; but it was not the sort that could be turned on at will. Trying to make jolly conversation with Elizabeth must have been uphill work for the young men who tried: she hid behind an icy reserve, smoked incessantly and tried to look bored and sophisticated. Besides, the men she was attracted to were not the ones who made an effort. She liked the dangerous ones, the ones mothers disapproved of: but men of that sort were not interested in shy little girls from the Home Counties.

The debutante Elizabeth grew no closer to her mother. She told a friend that Stella's preferred means of communication with her daughters was by letter, which appeared on the breakfast tray brought into their bedrooms by the maid. These letters were basically orders for the day, with instructions of what they had to do and where they would be expected for lunch or dinner. Elizabeth was in London at last: but it was her mother's London, and she was still living on her mother's terms.

Although Elizabeth described painting as her first love, she had reached the conclusion that she was no good at it. She had to find some other way of occupying her time and earning some money. 'After my father's early death,' she wrote in 1985, 'we were very impoverished . . . I knew I would have to earn my own living, although nobody, least of all my mother, provided me with the least idea of how that was to be achieved.'³ Elizabeth did find a way of earning a living, and did support herself for most of her life; but this letter implies that in 1933 her situation was much bleaker than it actually was. Elizabeth was presentable, very attractive and in her early twenties. Both she and her mother expected her to marry sooner or later. Until a man took on the responsibility of supporting her, she had an allowance. That allowance was not enough to survive on; but combined with a small but steady income, it could provide that modicum of good clothes, hats and books that Elizabeth would consider essential to life.

Quite what her job would be was not, at that time, very important. As to how it would be achieved, that was simple: in Stella's class, contacts were all you needed to get your daughter a safe if not particularly well-paid job. Her family were sufficiently rich and well-connected to get her out of any serious financial difficulties. After all, she banked at Coutts – where Uncle Jasper had been a director since 1921.

Thus Elizabeth could please herself in the matter of her occupation, and announced that she wanted to be an actress. Stella was appalled: not because she disapproved of the stage, far from it. But she knew her daughter well enough to know that in a carefree and bohemian world, Elizabeth would become dangerously headstrong. A tremendous tussle ensued between Elizabeth and her mother, in the course of which Elizabeth once again walked out of Wootton with her suitcase, vowing never to return. In the end Elizabeth's determination won. She joined the Oxford Repertory Theatre as assistant stage manager, which included sweeping the stage and making the tea.

For Stella, one redeeming feature of the Oxford Repertory Company was that she was an old friend of the manager, Stanford Holme. No doubt she told him and his wife Thea to keep a stern eye on Elizabeth and not let her get into trouble; but all too soon, the jovial and eccentric Stanford and Elizabeth were finding each other perilously attractive. For him, it was no more than a delicious flirtation; but for the young and passionately intense Elizabeth, it was love.

She was in love not only with Stanford Holme, but with a world in which she felt at ease. Here at last were people who lived entirely as they chose, who accepted her for herself, who didn't care about her family's connections: and to Elizabeth, it came as a tremendous release. Elizabeth was losing her innocence fast, and learning how to deal with the experience she was gaining. In the green room among the girls, she learnt about things her mother would have considered quite unmentionable. She also learnt about hard drinking, at post-performance parties and in long sessions at the pub, and discovered that she had a very strong head.

The actress Joan Hickson, who achieved fame in later life as Agatha Christie's Miss Marple, was also part of the company at the time. She wrote to Elizabeth many years later, saying she had an image of her cooking potatoes in a tin can over the prop-room fire. 'I don't actually remember doing so,' Elizabeth wrote back, 'but if you saw me doing it, I suppose it was for some stage meal. But I'm quite surprised to hear that I actually knew how to open a tin. I know somebody had to show me how to make tea for the cast.'[4] She took small parts occasionally, and these increased, but the training that proved most valuable in the long run was looking for props. She was sent out to find things like an eighteenth-century washstand, a hat-box suitable for putting a head in (as in *Night Must Fall*), plus the odd bed, grandfather clock or sofa. The company could not afford hire charges, so Elizabeth had to wheedle the shopkeepers into lending them – the only incentive she could offer being a credit in the programme. 'Well, one certainly learnt to be resourceful – and undaunted.'[5]

Elizabeth's Uncle Jasper, whose commitments took him to Oxford from time to time, was told to keep an eye on her. Meanwhile her childhood friend, her cousin Anne, was reading zoology at

Somerville. Anne remembers that after rehearsals, she sometimes joined Elizabeth for tea with other members of the cast. The meals were not memorable, but as far as Elizabeth was concerned, two years of 'landladies' food and fish teas at the Cadena Café did their part in sending me to the cooking pots'.[6]

Elizabeth was never afraid of saying or doing what she felt, which did not make her easy to work with – but she was thorough. She was particularly busy in the summer of 1933, since the stage manager was away on holiday for a month, leaving her in charge of *The Faithful Heart*, *The Sign on the Door* and *Almost a Honeymoon*. These were commercial plays, following each other in quick succession and aiming to please the widest possible audience. Stanford Holme kept his company on their toes, and the work was long and demanding.

Meanwhile, Stella's energy was spent on trying to keep Wootton away from her grasping brother-in-law Roland, but he was making her life there such a misery that she began to wonder whether the fight was worth it. It was a fight that she was bound to lose in the end, since although she had an interest in it, Wootton was no longer really her property. In the spring of 1933, Priscilla announced her engagement to a young officer in the Royal Engineers, called Richard Barnes Longland. She was twenty-four, and her life would take her wherever her future husband was posted. Elizabeth had not been back to Wootton for any length of time since she had left to become an actress, and had never shown any particular interest in the place. The two youngest sisters had not yet finished their education, but they were more likely to find employment – and suitors – in London than Sussex.

As for Stella herself, she had been a widow for eight years and was not quite fifty: a handsome woman with a growly aristocratic voice, and magnificent hair always elegantly arranged in a chignon. She wore dark, simple clothes with dramatic jewels. Stella had bought some excellent pieces of Victorian jewellery at a time when it was unfashionable and undervalued.

Stella did not want to waste the rest of her life on a battle for Wootton that she could never win, and her thoughts were turning away from England altogether. She had always gone travelling whenever she could, and had built up networks of friends in Washington, Egypt and Jamaica. It was in Jamaica that she had met Major John Hamilton: sometime ADC to the Governor, and owner of a plantation with a house and overgrown garden to go with it. Soon afterwards Major Hamilton came to England and stayed at Wootton. He seemed pleasant enough, and there was no doubt that Stella was happier than she had been since Rupert's death.

When Stella announced her intention to marry John Hamilton and make her home in Jamaica, her daughters – not unnaturally – took it with all the force of a double betrayal. Uncle Roland would evict them from Wootton, for Stella's life interest in it ceased the moment she remarried. In doing so, she was giving up not only their childhood home but everything that reminded them of their father. As if this were not enough, they were to be left in the care of relations while she swanned off to live with a man she scarcely knew on the other side of the world. Stella had packed up her belongings and left Wootton by the summer of 1933, and as soon as she was gone, Roland installed a tenant.

Stella's sister Grace and her husband Lord Wolmer, on whom much responsibility now fell, might have resented Stella's marriage too; but Grace declared that her elder sister had not been lucky in her first marriage and deserved this second chance to find happiness. In October 1933, Stella Gwynne became Mrs John Hamilton. She waited to see her eldest daughter married, and then sailed with her new husband to Jamaica. Her new house had neither water nor electricity, and the garden was a jungle; but Stella set to work on both with gusto. At the same time, she had not left England completely: she still had three daughters there, and usually returned for several weeks a year.

Priscilla was married from her aunt and uncle's house in Chester Gate in November, and then she too left England: Richard Barnes

Longland had been posted to Malta. Diana, now eighteen, was installed at Marlborough Hill with her Uncle Cony and Aunt Mania – that is, Count Constantine Benckendorff, DSO and his wife Maria Korchinska. (Here was another musical aunt: before escaping from Russia she had taught the harp at the Moscow Conservatoire, and had played at Lenin's funeral in 1924.) Felicité, aged sixteen, spent most of her time in Durham, where she stayed with a family friend and began taking courses in shorthand and typing.

Priscilla was badly missed, particularly by Diana and Felicité. They had lost not only their mother, but their childhood home and the life that went with it. To lose Priscilla as well made them both feel as if they had been cut adrift, though the turmoil was perhaps stronger in Diana, who had always been the most emotional of the four Gwynne sisters. She was also bitterly, hopelessly homesick for Wootton – which was not her home any longer.

In a fit of maternal solicitude, the just-married Stella wrote to Elizabeth from Jamaica: 'I do hope you will *try* at *least* to eat nourishing food even if not appetizing, as only good food will keep you fit and strong for good work – and if you want to get some Bovril and some plain chocolate please do so; that French Marmite, if you can get it is nice, and a change from Bovril, and a cup at night is a help.'[7] Whether her acting improved through drinking these fortifying beverages is doubtful, and when she did get the odd part, the other actors muttered that it was due to her relationship with Stanford Holme more than her talent. Elizabeth's cousin Anne described her acting as 'terrible', adding 'You either have it or you don't.' In any case, Elizabeth was wasting away with the emotional strain of being in love with Holme, who encouraged her one moment and rejected her the next.

Elizabeth's nerves were also being strained by her aunt Grace Wolmer, in whose house in Chester Gate she stayed when she was not in Oxford. Grace felt that Elizabeth's manners were not being improved by the louche company she was keeping. She made her feelings plain at breakfast one morning, and Elizabeth flounced out of the house. Back in Oxford, Holme was at first welcoming and even promised her some parts in his forthcoming productions; but all too soon he had lost interest in her.

In the late spring of 1934 Elizabeth left Oxford, and joined the Open Air Theatre in Regent's Park. This was a new company, founded in 1932 by Sydney Carroll. One of its members was Doreen Brownhill, a young actress who was to become one of Elizabeth's closest friends. Doreen never forgot the company's first sight of Elizabeth, as she stepped into the rehearsal room. 'She was wearing a black sponge-cloth dress with dramatic white organdie collar and cuffs, a black straw hat and gloves. We all stopped and stared at her – she looked stunningly attractive, and completely *wrong*. Everyone else was dressed in slacks and old sweaters.' Elizabeth realized her mistake, and soon she was dressed in slacks and old sweaters too; but she never really joined in the spirit of the company. 'She didn't talk much or give much of herself, just listened,' recalled Doreen. 'To me she seemed terribly grand and sophisticated, because she drank whisky almost non-stop – even first thing in the morning.'[8]

In May 1934, Sydney Carroll put on a production of *As You Like It*. The part of the wrestler, Charles, was taken by a dark, curly-haired actor in his late twenties called Leonard Gibson Cowan. He made the part of Charles so much his own that the name stuck, and that is how most of his friends addressed him. Elizabeth was an extra in this production, as was Doreen. Doreen did not much like Charles Gibson Cowan: she thought he looked dirty and ill-kempt. However, she noticed that many of the women in the company found him very attractive, including Elizabeth.

Leslie French, an actor who worked with Elizabeth in the Regent's Park days, remembers her as 'very serious, very reserved, very eager, and excited really, playing a waiting lady to Olivia; and you never saw a lady waiting so well, or so violently; she had tremendous poise – so much poise I feared she would topple over backwards . . . I remember her in *Twelfth Night* and in *Romeo and Juliet* always as a lady-in-waiting – I suppose she was waiting to be an actress.'[9]

For all the Open Air Theatre productions Elizabeth took part in, she never once had a speaking part. Her busiest season was the summer of 1934, when she was part of a throng of attendants in *As You Like It*, *Twelfth Night*, *The Comedy of Errors*, *A Midsummer Night's Dream*, *Androcles and the Lion*, *Joan* (by Michael Martin Harvey) and *Romeo and Juliet*. The end of the year saw her doing another spell as stage manager, in John Ford's *'Tis Pity She's a Whore* at the Arts Theatre. She enjoyed stage management more than acting, which she knew she was no good at. 'I didn't like it. That's the truth,' she admitted years later. 'I was hopeless. I don't know why I ever thought I wanted to be on the stage . . .'[10]

One summer afternoon she particularly remembered at the Open Air Theatre was when one of the leading ladies treated the whole cast of *A Midsummer Night's Dream* to ice cream ordered from Gunter's. The ices were passed around in huge pots, kept cold in pails of ice.

What an inspired treat. Rich, creamy, pale pink strawberry ice cream and slightly crunchy, grainy, bisque-coloured brown bread ice came out of those pots in a seemingly endless supply of voluptuous scoops . . . The becoming dresses, the magical singing of Leslie French as Puck, the presence on that day of, I think, the legendary stage idol Henry Ainsley, all combined with Gunter's ices to create an absurdly idealistic memory of just one early evening between the matinée and the evening shows in Regent's Park.[11]

After a brief spell with her aunt in Chester Gate, Elizabeth took rooms in a big house in Regent's Park Road, Primrose Hill. She shared them with her old friend Marian Butterworth, with whom she had boarded with the Barettes in Paris. The sitting room was immense, with huge windows; but the kitchen, which was the first Elizabeth had ever had for herself, was really no more than a landing. However, it must have been fairly spacious; for here she installed a gas cooker, a meat-safe with perforated metal sides, and – thanks to a generous twenty-first-birthday cheque from her uncle Jasper – a refrigerator. Refrigerators had only made their appearance in Britain some ten years before, and at that stage they cost almost as much as a car. No wonder Elizabeth's friends thought it a very strange way to spend all that money.

Elizabeth's attitude to money veered from anxiety at how much she was spending, to that youthful disdain for money which often dulls anxiety – at least for a while. She opened an account at Selfridges, and was in the habit of saying 'Oh, just put it on my account' if Charles or Doreen or Marian expressed a desire for something. Elizabeth was also soothed by the knowledge that her mother was a Ridley, and the Ridleys were rich. On the other hand, extravagance was guaranteed to upset her mother. Sometimes Elizabeth didn't care, and on reckless days this might have encouraged her to spend more; but at the same time she did not want to alienate Stella completely. The urge to rebel was very strong; but with it went a healthy sense of self-preservation, and a taste for the good things in life.

The account at Selfridges opened up a new way of spending money. 'I had only to pick up the telephone for roast chickens, smoked salmon, butter, fruit, cheese, cream, eggs, coffee, to be delivered the next day. It wasn't until the monthly accounts seemed to be adding up to much more than I could afford that it began to dawn on me that having a roast chicken always handy in the fridge was a rather extravagant way of entertaining friends, and that anyway bought food . . . was not quite to be compared with the fine cooking I had been exposed to . . .'[12]

It was at Selfridges that she found the answer to the problem of her mounting food bills. When Elizabeth was in the store one day she came across a magnificent display of copies of a thick, enticing book called *Recipes of All Nations*, by a Countess Morphy. She bought it, and read it on the bus all the way home. It made her want to cook; though this impulse had already been activated by another book called *The Gentle Art of Cookery* by Hilda Leyel, a gift from her mother.

Both these books appealed strongly to her imagination, though they were very vague about things like quantities, timing and temperature. This could lead the beginner into serious pitfalls; but far from seeing their lack of technical guidance as a drawback for the beginner, Elizabeth saw it as a positive asset – especially in *The Gentle Art of Cookery*.

'I wonder if I would have ever learned to cook at all if I had been given a routine Mrs Beeton to learn from, instead of the romantic Mrs Leyel with her rather wild, imagination-catching recipes . . .'[13] As it was, Elizabeth felt there was greater merit in trying out Mrs Leyel's '*marrons glacés* in half an hour' than in learning that professional *marrons glacés* involve no less than sixteen separate and distinct processes.

Mrs Leyel spoke of hollowed-out lemons filled with salmon mousse to take on picnics, of pomegranate compotes, of melons steeped in maraschino-flavoured syrup and filled with white grapes, white currants and pistachio nuts. She was particularly fond of fruits, vegetables and salads, which was not surprising since she is principally remembered as the founder of the Society of Herbalists. There was also a chapter on 'Dishes from the Arabian Nights', redolent with honey, rosewater, mint and sweet spices. Here was food for the imagination, though the end result was often far from perfect. 'Had I known,' Elizabeth wrote later, 'how huge was the gap between the urge to cook and the instruction necessary in order to achieve satisfactory results perhaps I wouldn't have embarked on so perilous a course of action. As things were, I blundered on, not much daunted by mistakes.'[14]

An important addition to this fledgling cook's library was Ambrose Heath's *Good Food* which came out in 1932. His jocular style had a broad appeal at the time – 'The jolly lambkin, whose younger brothers leapt so artlessly on to our table in March, now gambols a hint more sedately'[15] – but the chief merit of the book was that it grouped recipes month by month, according to what was in season. It taught her the rudiments of planning a meal around whatever was best and freshest at the time, and what to look out for when she did the marketing.

The most subtle, imaginative and liberating food writer of his day was Marcel Boulestin. One of his most important ideas was that simple dishes like scrambled eggs and anchovy butter, which most people associated with high teas and bed-sits, were 'valuable resources which could be quite differently deployed',[16] as Elizabeth put it. She greatly admired the way he wrote about food, and the fresh, simple elegance of his dishes. But the fact that he was often writing for competent hostesses with cooks to instruct – women, in other words, like her mother – was less appealing, as was his enthusiastic anglophilia. (Boulestin is perhaps the only Frenchman on record who has admitted a liking for mint sauce.) Nevertheless, the profound influence of Boulestin was already permeating Elizabeth's own ideas and experiments.

After a spell in Regent's Park Road, Elizabeth and Marian moved into another flat overlooking the church in Camden Square. In 1934 or so, they were joined by Barbara Hunter, who had been at Godstowe at the same time as Elizabeth. She was having severe family problems at the time, and invited herself to stay in the spare bedroom. Barbara said that while she never remembered Elizabeth cooking a meal, their 'minute kitchen was heavily festooned by Liz with onions, peppers, eggplants and garlic'. (These vegetables, exotic as they were in the mid-thirties, were available in the Greek and Italian shops of Soho and Camden Town.)

One person who was much in evidence at the Camden Square flat was Charles Gibson Cowan, the dark, curly-headed actor whom Elizabeth had met at the Regent's Park Theatre. The double-barrelled name sounds rather middle class: yet in his first autobiographical novel, *Loud Report*, written when he was twenty-four, Gibson Cowan proclaims that his father was the only man he knew who called himself 'lower-class'. Cohen was the family name, but his father changed that to Cowan.

After a stint as a bootmaker, Charles's father had become a

chauffeur; and Charles (or Leonard, as he then was) was the only child of adoring parents. His uncle was a famous freethinker called Chapman Cohen, who encouraged the boy to read widely and question everything. At Leyton County High School for Boys he was the butt of anti-Semitic bullying – but perhaps the bullies also wanted to persecute someone who was clearly more intelligent, imaginative and articulate than they were. He left school at eighteen and, since there was no question of further education, went straight to work. Condemned to what looked like a perpetual grind of nine-to-five among people who saw no further than the next pay packet, he became profoundly depressed. Thanks to his Uncle Chapman, Charles knew there was more to life, though he had no idea how to find it. He gave up his work, stayed in his lodgings as long as he could, and then took to the road with his last half-crown in his pocket.

He spent the next few months scrounging and begging, always on the move, and *Loud Report* is principally an account of this period. While there is no doubt that Charles did live rough for a time, perhaps not all the experiences he recounts are his own: he heard a lot of stories on the road, and he was not a writer to let a good story go just because it hadn't happened to him. Charles later described *Loud Report* as a book of 'boasting confessions'.[17]

Loud Report tells how Charles made his way up from vagabond to fairground barker, and from there to writing his first play. By the time Elizabeth met him he had been making a living from acting, writing and producing since 1926. He knew about the professional theatre, having worked with Basil Dean, Miles Malleson and Robert Atkins; and though he was mainly interested in writing and production, his acting had that 'presence' that Elizabeth always felt she lacked. He was also married, with a young child; but he was already trying to disentangle himself from that commitment when Elizabeth came on the scene.

At that stage, Charles lived with several other people – including his wife – in a large house looking over the river at Wapping. There was a curious moment when Charles talked Elizabeth into delivering his baby daughter Lynn to her mother, who was some distance away by tube. Doreen accompanied Elizabeth, who tried to push the baby on to her but Doreen flatly refused. 'I wasn't going to take it, I didn't know anything about babies. Neither did Elizabeth. Seeing her holding that baby – I suppose it was about six months, perhaps a year old? – was one of the most incongruous sights I have ever seen.'[18] Elizabeth was remarkably free of maternal feelings. She always maintained that she would have made a terrible mother – and if her own mother was anything to go by, she was probably right.

Elizabeth was fascinated by Charles's courage, his sense of adventure, his devil-may-care attitude. She also admired the fact that he was a rebel, which was very much how she saw herself. There was also a gritty sexual attraction about Charles that Elizabeth found irresistible, and she did not seem to mind the fact that she was by no means the only woman in his life. At one point, Charles was having an affair with both her and her flatmate Marian. Marian Butterworth was very different from Elizabeth: she was very kind, and at first glance she seemed shy and rather innocent – yet this mousiness concealed a strong mischievous streak. Marian was, in her way, as naughty and unconventional as Elizabeth, even though she looked as though butter would not melt in her mouth.

As for Elizabeth, Charles was attracted by her elegance, her feline sexiness and her cavalier attitude to money (based on the certain knowledge that Mummy or Uncle Jasper would pick up the bill sooner or later). He was not so impressed by her family, who made no secret of their distaste for him. At one point, Stella summoned Doreen Brownhill to her house and said, 'Can't you get Elizabeth away from that *dreadful* man?' Doreen assured her that it was impossible. To Charles, The Hon. Mrs Gwynne must have looked like a character out of a play by Noël Coward – though it is doubtful that he ever spoke to her. Elizabeth was the kind of over-controlled character who liked to keep her life in rigidly separate compartments, and she was always profoundly uneasy if they overlapped.

What drew Charles and Elizabeth together was that they both

refused to accept the constrictions of their allotted place in the social system, and were reinventing themselves to achieve a new sort of social flexibility. Charles had come a long way from Leyton. Years in the theatrical world had changed his voice, though he never lost the twang of the East End. He was proud of his origins and never denied them. At the same time he evidently felt he could go further with a more resonant name: so he added his mother's maiden name of Gibson to the family one of Cowan.

Elizabeth too was trying to break free from the restrictions of her class. In her case, the problem was how to achieve independence and reject the conventions that irked her, while maintaining the security of an influential family, indulgent bankers and an account at Selfridges.

Elizabeth and Charles also shared a passion for books which are filled with social misfits and mavericks like themselves. It was a time of endless cigarettes, beer and whisky – but as they talked, they became the people they wanted to become. The following morning, when they woke up in grubby sheets with a terrible hangover, things were not so idyllic; but they were both still young and resilient. In 1935, Elizabeth was twenty-two, Charles thirty-one.

Diana was living a much more sheltered life with her Uncle Cony and Aunt Mania, her Benckendorff relations. Diana's gentle, dreamy charm had attracted a string of young men who longed to take her out to tea and the cinema, but Uncle Cony was very strict – at least inside the house. No young man was allowed to sit alone with Diana in the sitting room, for fear the servants might talk. However, she had formed an attachment to a young man called Roger Ellis, who came from a well-to-do family of mine owners in Nottinghamshire. He also knew Elizabeth, whom he remembered as very tall and dark, with a long sinuous neck, but with nothing soft about her sensuality, nor her heavily framed spectacles and her abrasive wit. Diana, in contrast, was a much gentler and less forbidding character.

Roger Ellis had rooms in Gloucester Place, and here he remembered Diana sitting on the floor by the fire while he read poetry to her. She had white skin, a soft voice and dreamy eyes, and none of Elizabeth's challenging sexiness. She was also very absent-minded, and hopelessly unpunctual. Ellis was too much in love to care, but worried about the impression she would make on his parents: they lived in a large house in Nottinghamshire, where everything ran like clockwork.

Diana did not make a very good impression. When the second gong went for dinner – it was a sacred rule of that house that everyone be in the sitting room by the time it was sounded – she was still in the bath. She panicked, rushed back to her room and dressed as fast as she could. The Ellises took a very dim view of her unpunctuality, but worse was to follow. In her hurry, Diana had thrown her sodden sponge on the bed, and by the time she came back to her room it had seeped all the way through to the mattress. 'I hope you never marry that girl,' said Roger's mother when Diana had left.[19]

Roger Ellis did propose to Diana, twice; but she wished he had not, because what she loved was the warmth and comfort of their friendship. She did not see him as a husband because, as he put it, 'she was waiting for someone to sweep her off her feet'. However, when Roger did become engaged, Diana was taken completely off guard: it was, for her, as painful as when Priscilla left for Malta: she had lost her surrogate parent.

Stella had not been settled long in Jamaica before she discovered that John Hamilton was a hopeless alcoholic. Their marriage was over in two years, and Stella moved back to England. She decided to set up an antiques business, and bought the Old School House in Dedham in which to live, do business and house her collection. At the same time, she was much preoccupied by Elizabeth. It was a time when a girl still had to consider her 'reputation'. Elizabeth was ruining her chances of making a good marriage by throwing

herself away on a penniless bohemian, whom Stella suspected of
being after her daughter's money.

Given Elizabeth's conventional upbringing, it is extraordinary
how much independence she had acquired – even before the age of
twenty-one. But Stella had no one to blame but herself for what had
become of Elizabeth. Pris was a steadier character, Diana and Felicité
still young enough to do as they were told. But Stella had abandoned
Elizabeth for Jamaica at the very moment when she most needed
firm guidance – just as she had joined the theatre and was entering
adulthood. The headstrong Elizabeth made sure Stella never
regained control. She was now impervious to any displays of authority
or lectures on morals, because she knew her mother felt guilty.

In an effort to separate Elizabeth from Charles and her dissolute
life, Stella decided that Elizabeth should be encouraged to travel.
Elizabeth was delighted by the idea. Friends of Stella's in Cairo
called the Goodwins invited Elizabeth to come out and stay with
them, and the plan was that after spending several weeks in Egypt
she should go to Malta to visit her sister Priscilla.

In February 1936 Elizabeth acquired a new passport. The photograph shows a young woman with wild black hair, and there is a
hard look about her eyes and her narrow mouth. A few days later,
she equipped herself with a visa for Egypt, but the Egyptian trip
was postponed. It was decided that Elizabeth should go to Malta
anyway, which she did that spring.

Priscilla had been in some ways more of a mother to Elizabeth
than Stella herself, and Stella told Pris that this Maltese holiday was
the ideal moment to bring Elizabeth to her senses. Elizabeth knew
this, and being naturally secretive she didn't talk much about Charles
to Priscilla. Besides, she did not know quite how she felt about him:
with Elizabeth, feelings of love and sexual jealousy went hand in
hand with a kind of irritation that she should be under somebody's
spell.

Richard and Priscilla certainly took a great deal of trouble to
give Elizabeth a lovely time. There were parties and sightseeing

expeditions and picnics, and Elizabeth revelled in the comparative luxury of Priscilla's well-ordered house after her bohemian life in London.

Another bonus of the trip was that, for the first time in her life, Elizabeth had the opportunity to watch an excellent and enthusiastic cook at work. The cook was a Maltese woman called Angela, and Priscilla Longland – herself an excellent cook – allowed Angela a free hand with the meat allowance they were given by the army. Most English women of that time would have insisted that, whatever part of the carcass the meat had come from (and this was often hard to establish) it should be tied up into some sort of joint and served with two veg. Angela, however, was encouraged to make delicious meat stews in the Italian manner, making good use of the rough local wine which cost around ninepence a bottle. Angela could rise to the challenge of the most elaborate dishes; but the most important lesson she taught Elizabeth was that, in the hands of a good and careful cook, even an old bird and a stringy piece of meat can be made edible.

The Maltese trip was a success, but it failed to separate Elizabeth from Charles. As she had suspected, he had not been pining away in her absence – he had never made any secret of the fact that he believed in sexual freedom. So did Elizabeth and, according to her friend Doreen Brownhill, she did not seem to care much about Charles's constant infidelities.

Charles's enthusiasm for the stage was on the wane. He had been working in and around the theatre since the mid-1920s, and realized that he was never going to be a great actor or producer. But he still felt that he might make a good living as a writer, although his life did not inspire him with much to write about. He wanted to travel, and developed a passion for the sea. He bought a small boat, which in July 1936 he had sailed from Wapping to Lowestoft. Charles had plans to sail all the way round the British coast and, eventually, buy a bigger boat and sail the world.

Elizabeth and Charles compiled a book together in the second half of 1936, which they hoped – rather optimistically – would make them some money if they could find a publisher. The title-page reads, '*The King is Dead – Verses on the Passing of Royalty from the earliest printed copies to King George the Fifth, Written by Contemporary hands and collected from various sources. To which is added various notes for the interest of the reader by Gibson Cowan and Elizabeth Gwynne. 1936.*' Not surprisingly, it was never published.

In November, Elizabeth finally set off for Egypt to stay with her mother's friends, Dorothy and Teddy Goodwin. She was accompanied by her cousin Kit (Kathleen) Gwynne, the daughter of her uncle Nevile. Teddy Goodwin worked for Shell Oil. Like most of the bankers, businessmen and cotton brokers of the British community, the Goodwins lived far better in Egypt than they could have done in England. They had a huge house in Cairo, any number of servants and a villa in Alexandria. English social life revolved around racing, polo and cricket matches, all of which took place at the Gezira Club on the southern end of Zamelek Island. On Sundays, everyone assembled at St Mary's in Garden City, for a family service presided over by Bishop Gwynne of Cairo and Khartoum (possibly a distant cousin of Elizabeth's).

Elizabeth loved the expeditions into the desert, the days at the beach and trips to the bazaar; but as she sat around the Gezira Club lido waiting for yet another group of nice young people whom Dorothy Goodwin wanted her to meet, Elizabeth was keenly aware that she was in Egypt on her mother's terms, not her own.

One person who made a big impression on Elizabeth during her time in Egypt was the writer and traveller Robin Fedden, who was then working for the British Council in Greece. Fedden was tall, good-looking, immensely erudite and funny: ideal company for Elizabeth, and they took to each other instantly. Elizabeth could not remember for sure where she first met him, but thought it might have been in the house of Sir Walter Smart. Sir Walter Smart was Oriental Counsellor at the British Embassy in Cairo from 1929 to 1945. His Syro-Lebanese Christian wife Amy was a painter, and their house was filled with books and her brightly coloured paintings. At Walter and Amy Smart's one met not only English people, but Egyptians and Greeks; not only bankers and diplomats, but archaeologists, actors and poets. For Elizabeth, this was a glimpse of a side of Cairene life that she found much more appealing than the Gezira Club.

Before leaving Egypt Elizabeth went on a nine-day trip to the Levant in February 1937, visiting Palestine, Lebanon and Syria. Whether she went with the Goodwins or joined another party is unclear; but it must have felt very different from the comfortable expatriate life she had been enjoying in Cairo. It was closer to the sort of travelling she really wanted to do: rougher, less insulated, more adventurous. Elizabeth sailed from Alexandria in early March, and on her way home she stopped off to spend a month over Easter with Priscilla on Malta. There was a valedictory feeling about this visit, for Richard's posting to Malta was coming to an end.

Elizabeth had been away from home for about five months by the time she returned to England; and although she was now filled with new hopes and determination to get a job, they evaporated quickly. She could not find any work, either acting or stage-managing, and at the same time she was fed up with sharing a flat with Marian. She moved into a small apartment in John Street, Bloomsbury, where Charles too lived on and off. Elizabeth wished she could shake herself free of him. Not knowing quite what to do, she set off for Germany and the Austrian Tyrol, where she spent most of July. At some point that summer she went to stay in the south of France with Doreen, and when Priscilla and her husband came back to Britain on leave, she and her sister took a house in Wales.

Since 1935, Elizabeth and her sisters had got into the habit of spending at least a week together in Wales, usually when Priscilla and Richard were back. They would rent an old farmhouse or cottage, and at a time when their separate lives were inevitably drawing them apart, their holidays in Wales provided a period when they could reaffirm their closeness to each other. Elizabeth came to love the intimate river valleys with their isolated cottages and the wild hills beyond. It was a landscape that never failed to inspire and revive her; and she carried a memory of one particularly magical house, with a brook running through the garden, that she had seen at a place called Machynlleth.

Some of the time that hung heavy on Elizabeth's hands that year was spent on making a present for Marian Butterworth, whose friendship Elizabeth was more inclined to appreciate now they were no longer sharing a flat. She bought a stout exercise book with marbled endpapers, and in this she wrote out a collection of recipes. Among these are Cheese Loafers, Prunes à l'Indienne, Drop Scones, Nègre en Chemise (an attempt to re-create the *Mohr im Hemd* she had tasted in Munich), Hot Beetroot and Roast Rabbit. In a handwritten note attached to the book dated 1979, Elizabeth wrote that the recipes had several sources, among them Countess Morphy, Hilda Leyel and Priscilla's Maltese cook Angela. Some of the dishes sound more appetizing than others. One suggests combining cold chicken with the pulp of a grapefruit, and serving it in the shell; while Bengal Croûtes consist of crushed toasted almonds mixed with Sharwood's Green Label Chutney, spread on home-made cheese biscuits and baked for about ten minutes. Elizabeth took a lot of trouble over the book. The different sections on soup, fish, poultry and so on are marked by a page covered with a sheet of coloured paper, on to which she stuck little Victorian figures, perhaps from a Pollock's cut-out paper theatre.

At the end of that long, listless summer, Elizabeth took on a job as a 'showroom second' for the fashion house of Worth, at 50 Grosvenor Street. Every second was attached to a particular vendeuse, who was usually elderly, unmarried and bent on cultivating her own importance. The seconds were kept very busy dancing attendance on them, and helping clients and models in and out of dresses; but their main function was to order all the materials and accessories with which to make up the outfits which the client had ordered. These young women were theoretically entitled to earn commission, to make up for their miserable salaries (Elizabeth was paid ten shillings a week), but the vendeuses saw to it that they were kept as far as possible from the clients, who included Rose Kennedy and the Queen of Siam. The seconds also had to put up with constant admonitions. 'You are not here to think, but to do as you are told' – 'The seconds don't use the front staircase. Go up the back stairs.'[20]

Their only moments of rest occurred in the airless, windowless staff cloakroom in the basement, where they ate their lunchtime sandwiches. Cockroaches scuttled into cracks in the wall as soon as the light was switched on and, first thing in the morning, the girls often found the insects in their 'house shoes'.

'Still, there were good moments,' wrote Elizabeth many years later to Frances Harper, who had worked at Worth at the same time as Elizabeth. 'I remember the corset-fitter telling me, in a state of deep shock, that she had seen the shameless Lady Whoever stark naked in the fitting room. I never did discover how the lady was supposed to try on her corset without undressing. Then there were those extraordinary model girls. Once, as I was dressing one of them, she suddenly said, "Gwynne, I'd give a *pound* to sleep with Raymond Massey, wouldn't you?"'[21]

The way in which Elizabeth left Worth was perhaps predictable. 'One of the senior vendeuses overheard me telling a customer in the fitting room that the dress she was trying on didn't suit her and I thought it was hideous. There was an almighty rumpus. I'm not sure if they sacked me or if I did a Michael Heseltine, but I was certainly glad to be liberated . . .'[22]

Elizabeth left Worth in the spring of 1938 and spent the summer in the south of France with Doreen Brownhill. Doreen had a friend whose father owned a hotel called Les Roches Fleuris, near Le

Lavandou. As a friend of the family she was given very reasonable rates, which she often shared with friends – in this case, Elizabeth and a girl who was studying at Oxford, called Diana Anderson. They were not expecting to meet anyone else, but it emerged that four Oxford boyfriends of Diana's were staying near by. Their presence enlivened the party considerably. They spent their days in cafés or on the beach, and drank well into the small hours. One might think that this sort of life was only invented in the sixties, but for girls with independent minds and independent allowances, anything was possible in the late thirties – though Elizabeth does seem to have been considerably freer than her friends.

At the end of the holiday, Elizabeth decided to visit Corsica. The other girls very much wanted to join her, but their families would not allow it: the island was considered a dangerous place full of bandits. This did not deter Elizabeth. To the envy and admiration of her friends she set off for Corsica, and settled for a time in the little town of Piana on the west coast.

'I took a room in the house of a very humble family,' she wrote. 'There were a large number of children in their late teens. Their mother was a great big brawny woman with a robust sense of humour. Amid a tremendous clatter we would all sit down to meals at one big table. Madame's cooking was of the same nature as her own: rough, generous, full of character and colour. There were great dishes of ham and tomatoes, eggs and olives, plenty of salads and oil, huge hunks of bread and great bowls of bursting ripe figs. In all the years since then I have never forgotten the very special savour of that food.'[23]

At some point that year, Robin Fedden invited Elizabeth to Chantemesle, some fifty miles north-west of Paris, where his parents lived. On one side of the house was the River Seine, winding between little green islands alive with birds, and on the other, the abrupt ascent of a dry limestone escarpment. Cherry and apricot trees stood about the house. 'It was beautiful there. I have never forgotten it,' she wrote.[24] Perhaps it was then that Robin proposed to her: many years later, she admitted to Robin's daughter Frances that she and her father had been engaged. However, it must be admitted that Robin was very susceptible to women and did have a tendency to propose marriage. It may have been fun for both of them to try on an engagement like a suit of clothes, though it did not fit either of them in 1938.

Elizabeth came back to England and, inevitably, to Charles. They had now been living with each other, on and off, for three years. They were both rather fed up with their aimless lives, disenchanted with the theatre and sick of England. They would probably have drifted apart had they continued as before; but in the winter of 1938 they began to fantasize about buying a boat, and sailing away. It was a mad idea, with little behind it except a strong desire to escape; but it seized their imaginations, and both of them were ready for adventure.

In Charles's case, the urge to travel again may have been rekindled by the publication of *Loud Report*, the autobiographical novel he had written aged twenty-four about his time on the road. Its publication by Michael Joseph in 1938 was partly due to a current interest in accounts of proletarian life and social hardship: Orwell's *The Road to Wigan Pier* had appeared the year before. At any rate, seeing it in print must have given Charles a much-needed boost to morale. Perhaps he could make a living as a writer after all, and a voyage with Elizabeth might give him something to write about.

'We had to live somewhere,' he wrote later, 'and the Mediterranean was cheap. I should continue to write, only slightly more conscientiously. It was true that cruise books of the Mediterranean were ten a penny, and publishers positively curled up at the sound of voyages to the Greek archipelago, but something was certain to turn up to make this different.'[25]

They saved every penny they could, and Elizabeth went to her Uncle Jasper. Sir Jasper usually allowed her to overdraw, though he never failed to remind her gently that she really ought to curb her extravagance. He could not have guessed that, on this particular occasion, the overdraft was 'to enable me to pay for a boat in which to sail for Greece, no less . . .'[26]

* * * * * * * *

CHAPTER FIVE

Norman Douglas

They found the *Evelyn Hope* early in 1939. Although she was basically a two-masted yawl with an engine and was described as a wooden pleasure yacht, Elizabeth thought she looked more like a black fishing boat. She needed a great deal of work, and cost almost twice what they could afford to pay. 'We stood in the mud, heedless of the rain, for the best part of an hour, and agreed it was a ship. We bought it, subject to a survey, and paid a small sum as an earnest of good faith. We went back to London full of enthusiasm for the first time in months.'*

The *Evelyn Hope* contained a cockpit, a saloon, a cabin containing one double and one single bunk and a washbasin, and a galley in the forecastle. The yacht was berthed on the River Hamble, which spills into Southampton Water. Here Charles and Elizabeth fitted her out for the long voyage. Elizabeth's contribution to the boat's library included works by Victorian travellers, seventeenth-century poets and playwrights, several history books, Homer, *Robinson Crusoe* and about a hundred paperback thrillers which she said could be thrown

---

* Charles Gibson Cowan wrote a novel about this voyage which he and Elizabeth made together. It was called *The Voyage of the Evelyn Hope*. Much of this book, written soon after the events it describes, is fairly faithful to what happened. The exception is its dramatic finale, which is purely fictional. Until that episode, the dates tally with those in Elizabeth's passport and other documents, and she herself read most of it in typescript in Alexandria. The only other significant change in the book was to Elizabeth's name. She is called 'Caroline'.

overboard after use. She had also installed cushions and covers and curtains, pots and pans, and tins of provisions. To spread the financial load, Elizabeth and Charles decided to take on a female paying passenger to Marseille. Her identity was never revealed.

As they were making last-minute preparations, Elizabeth was offered a bit part in a short film. She was irritated at the thought of having to postpone the voyage, but by early July she had done the job. Everything was ready. They hoped to be off on the 6th, but a gale sprang up from the south-west. By the 8th, the skies were clearer and the wind was now blowing from the west. 'I went below and started the engine,' wrote Charles. '[Elizabeth] let go forwards. We swung round with the current . . . It was as simple as that; we were under weigh.'[1]

It was warm and the sun was breaking through the clouds as they set out into the Channel, and by lunchtime the following day they had reached Le Havre. They stayed there until the 14th. 'The fête was dampened by a depressing drizzle,' wrote Charles, 'that started in the morning and continued all day . . . The French were either taking the political situation seriously or they were disheartened by the rain, for there was no dancing in the streets.'[2]

They took out the mast at Rouen, and sailed up the Seine in steady rain as far as Paris. After a day of sightseeing they found some friends in the Rotonde, who were much preoccupied with the possibility of war and were discussing it from every angle. Charles and Elizabeth took them for an evening on the river, which must have taken their minds off the Nazi threat for everyone got drunk.

Above Paris they had no charts for the river; but with help from some obliging bargemen, they reached the beginning of the Canal de Bourgogne, which has over two hundred locks. They locked themselves upwards in a leisurely way, shopping in the market of Marigny and drinking the wine of Pouilly, until they reached the two-mile tunnel which passes under the summit of the Côte d'Or. Three days later – the locks now descending – they were in Dijon, 'which possesses what must be the world's best restaurant, and worst museum'.[3] After a sumptuous meal at the Trois Faisans, they continued south: down the river Doubs, down the Saône to Lyon, which seems to have marked a low spot in the trip: 'the paying guest was more conspicuous than usual, Caroline was indisposed and a mechanic was on board most of the time we were there'.[4] They were obliged to take a pilot down the Rhône as far as Arles, sailed through the lagoons of the Camargue and finally dropped anchor in the old port of Marseille in the first days of September.

Elizabeth and the paying guest immediately went off to the Italian market, leaving Charles to enjoy the painted fishing boats, 'which came alongside to sell their loads of black mussels, purple sea urchins, blue crayfish and green and white oysters'.[5] Elizabeth and the paying guest did not come back until after dark, and had great trouble picking their way through the mooring lines back to the *Evelyn Hope*: the war scare had begun in Marseille, and the blackout was already in force. The following day, they found out that Germany had invaded Poland.

The paying guest immediately packed up and went home, but Elizabeth and Charles stayed on in Marseille. Fish, bread and Algerian wine were cheap. Sometimes they ate at a little Italian restaurant, 'where in an open brick oven the chef turned strange vegetable pies with an immense peel'.[6] (These vegetable pies, or pizzas, were not yet the ubiquitous fast food they were to become.) When the air-raid warnings began, they took shelter with the poor people of the Italian quarter in a railway tunnel at the back of the port, its walls dripping with water. 'We were all terribly afraid of gas,' wrote Charles. 'It was a word which crystallized our fear of the unknown chemical warfare we expected to drop from the skies.'[7] But the fear receded, and after a couple of nights in the tunnel, they decided to stay aboard the *Evelyn Hope*.

The boat needed repairs which took almost a week, while Charles and Elizabeth considered their options: whether to move on to a smaller and perhaps safer port, or even to give in and go home. At first, they were ordered to stay where they were; but after a few weeks, under the suspicious eyes of the maritime authorities, they moved to the harbour of Antibes, just south-west of Nice.

Here Elizabeth was delighted to find Mike and Nancy Cumberlege, whom she had met in Malta with Priscilla. Mike's father was an admiral and Mike had been brought up, as his friend Patrick Leigh Fermor put it, 'more or less amphibious. He was bookish, great fun, fantastically good-looking – and he had this small, close-fitting gold earring in one ear which made him look very dashing.'[8] He and Charles spent long sessions on board the *Evelyn Hope* discussing every aspect of seamanship and boats, for Mike at that time had little to do. He was a naval officer on the reserve and hoped to be used in some intelligence capacity, but so far he had not been called up. Unlike Charles, who described himself as a conscientious objector, Mike was very much a patriot and wanted to see action as soon as possible.

Mike and Nancy introduced them to their group of friends, and Charles and Elizabeth found that café life suited them both – even if conversation was dominated by the war and whether Italy would enter it. They also needed to get out. Life on the boat, cooped up in two small cabins within the high walls of the harbour, quickly became claustrophobic. Blackout regulations were strictly enforced, and they had to keep the portholes and skylights covered at night.

Elizabeth's relationship with Charles was based less on true friendship than on an attraction of opposites. The staleness that had begun to creep into their relationship in London became even more marked in Antibes, where there was nothing to do and only an uncertain future ahead. What made it worse was that they were dependent on each other. The boat belonged to Elizabeth more than to Charles, but she needed Charles to sail it if they were ever to leave Antibes.

The situation eased when Charles left in early December with Mike, to fetch a yacht back from Venice to Antibes. Charles, who had never been to Venice before, took the opportunity to do some sightseeing. Meanwhile Elizabeth had stayed with Nan in Antibes, though their friendship was becoming strained by the mood of enervated restlessness that the war had brought about. Elizabeth felt there was nothing to do but drink and write long letters to her sisters. Pris, Diana and Felicité were particularly important to her at this time, especially Pris, who sent her money whenever she could. Stella had more or less washed her hands of Elizabeth. Running off with Charles was bad enough, but the fact that he was a pacifist was intolerable.

Towards the end of 1939 another man came into Elizabeth's life, a man who was to inspire her more than any other. This was the author and traveller Norman Douglas. Norman had been based in the south of France since May 1937, having been forced to leave Florence in a hurry. The cause of his flight was a ten-year-old girl, who had been in the habit of coming to his flat. The very worst interpretation was put on these visits, but for once the old reprobate (whose tastes more often veered towards boys) was probably innocent. The girl's father certainly thought so: it was the puritanical, xenophobic Fascists who chased him out of Italy.[9]

Norman Douglas was then seventy-two, Elizabeth twenty-six, and the difference in their ages was if anything an attraction. They used to meet for drinks in the cafés of the old port, and go on to one of the restaurants where the management took a good-humoured view of the idiosyncrasies of 'Monsieur Doo-glass'. In the restaurant, he would bring a hunk of Parmesan out of his pocket.

'"Ask Pascal to be so good as to grate this at our table. Poor stuff, my dear, that Gruyère they give you in France. Useless for macaroni." And a bunch of basil for the sauce. "Tear the leaves, mind. Don't chop them. Spoils the flavour."'[10]

They also went for what Norman called 'little strolls' in the hills towards Vence – a little stroll, for him, being more like a day's hike for most people. Elizabeth looked forward eagerly to a day in his company, and felt flattered to be chosen as his companion; but she described herself as 'a feeble and unwilling walker', and found it hard work keeping up with him.

In the mid-thirties, she and her friend and fellow-actress Doreen

Brownhill had often walked through the night from Chelsea to Camden Town; while even in later life, she could stay on her feet for hours if she was hunting for books and antiques, or wandering around a market. But the rocky, uneven hills of Vence were another matter, and Norman was a vigorous walker. 'The way he went stumping up and down those steep and stony paths, myself shambling behind, reversed our ages. And well he knew it.'[11] However, at the end of the long haul there was always a café, more often than not what Elizabeth called 'One of those two-chair, one-table, one-woman-and-a-dog establishments.' Norman ordered a litre of wine, but Elizabeth was hungry as well as thirsty.

'Ha! You won't get much out of *her*. Nothing but bread and that beastly ham. Miserable insipid stuff.' From out of his pocket came a hunk of salami and a clasp knife.

'Do you always carry your own provisions in your pocket?'

'Ha! I should say so. I should advise you to adopt the same rule. Otherwise you may have to put up with what you get. No telling what that may be, nowadays.'[12]

In later life she often admitted, quite simply, that she had been in love with Norman Douglas. This was hardly surprising, for one of the strongest loves is that of a disciple for a teacher, and Norman was the best teacher Elizabeth ever had. She admired his rigorous scholarship and broad learning, and everything he said or did struck a chord in her. Much of what he taught her she already knew, on an instinctive level: what Norman did was to express, develop and refine the principles which she wanted to guide her life. Look for what is true and authentic; see things as they are; be constantly vigilant against the pretentious and the sham; above all, please yourself and take the consequences.

He was also, to the core of his being, a Darwinist and an atheist. He did not believe in loving one's neighbour, and loathed any system of thought that advocated either complete equality, or complete submission. Fascism and Communism both wanted to turn people into termites, and were therefore to be abhorred. Democracy was also dangerous because he believed it to be based on a fallacy – to him, people were anything but equal. Norman would not have tolerated Elizabeth's devotion if she had been one of the crowd, but in her he saw someone with the sort of fierce, self-contained individuality that he could admire. She was worth taking trouble over.

Norman was also exceptional – especially among Englishmen – because he talked about food at a time when educated people simply didn't, unless they were self-conscious epicures. He was not an epicure, in that the rarity or delicacy of a dish did not interest him. He talked of food because it mattered, because it was part of civilized life, to be enjoyed as profoundly as every other pleasure and accorded the interest and respect that, in Norman's opinion, too many pretentious people accorded to art. He once shocked the emaciated Nancy Cunard (who never gave a damn what she ate) by saying that 'a good dinner is worth all the Benozzo Gozzolis in the world'.

Norman was no cook himself, though he was acutely aware of the fact that everything worth eating had a family and a history. During the last summer of his life, on Capri in 1951, Elizabeth brought him some figs from the market. He asked her from which stall she had bought them.

'That one down nearest to the steps.'

'Not bad, my dear, not bad. Next time, you could try Graziella. I fancy you'll find her figs are sweeter; just wait a few days, if you can.'

He knew, who better, from which garden those figs came; he was familiar with the history of the trees, he knew their age and in what type of soil they grew . . . I may add that it was not Norman's way to give lectures. These pieces of information emerged gradually, in the course of walks, sessions at the tavern, apropos a chance remark. It was up to you to put two and two together if you were sufficiently interested.[13]

Elizabeth was not only interested: she hung on his every word. Where Mrs Leyel had filled her head with honey and spices, Norman taught her that with a little care and attention, one could eat good food every day. He also taught her how to search out the best, insist on it, and reject all that was bogus and second-rate.

In the course of her career Elizabeth wrote about a great many people including Eliza Acton, William Verral, Mrs Beeton and Marcel Boulestin. In each case she tried to describe their character as well as their work; but she approached them as historical figures. The two essays she wrote on Norman Douglas were completely different in tone, and quite unlike anything else she ever wrote. In those essays, she is not only trying to capture the essence of someone she loved: she is trying to remember, and record, the essence of every conversation she ever had with him.

Charles returned from Venice with Mike Cumberlege in time for a New Year's Eve party. Elizabeth did not turn up till ten that evening: she had been with Norman in Nice. In the days that followed, she showed no particular inclination to be with Charles. Her mornings were spent helping out in a soup kitchen, which had been set up by a wealthy philanthropist in a huge dining room panelled in oak with refectory tables and Jacobean chairs. The evenings she spent with Norman.

Charles liked and admired Norman Douglas. At the same time he resented the way that Elizabeth and the old writer had become friends so swiftly, and how they revelled in each other's company. Between them was a relaxed complicity, an understanding that he had no part of. Elizabeth made no effort to hide her feelings for Norman, and made it clear that he was not welcome to join their excursions. Rather than see them so constantly together, Charles spent more and more time on his own.

'I was too hard up to join in the social life of the Cap. When I could afford it I went alone by bus to Nice, where I spent the day wandering around the Italian quarter . . . and lunching at a restaurant with a small balcony . . . Many afternoons I sat there with the bottle of Armagnac left on the table, finding a companion to talk to, or merely watching the seagulls . . .'[14]

*

He and Elizabeth had now been in the south of France for over six months, and if they did not get out of Antibes that spring the opportunity might vanish altogether. Charles's sudden determination to set sail might also have been prompted by the thought that if he did not make a move soon, Elizabeth might refuse to go with him. He began to get the boat ready for the next leg of their journey, to Corsica.

Whatever she felt about Charles, and her feelings were very ambivalent, Elizabeth found that she was as keen to make a move as he was. Even Norman Douglas's company was not enough to relieve the boredom of life in Antibes. Elizabeth had never liked to mix her friends, and she had not encouraged Charles to develop a friendship with Norman. But she could not keep them completely apart, especially since Charles enjoyed talking to him. Norman urged Charles to travel while there was still time: he said he envied him the prospect of seeing Greece before it became completely spoilt by the twentieth century. Charles pointed out that they did not yet have a permit to leave the harbour.

'Bah! You'll be here for the rest of your life if you wait for permits. What is the use of a permit to a French official? Corsican savages, all of 'em . . . Don't take any notice of 'em. I'd come with you myself if I didn't hate boats. Uncomfortable things, smelly, never get any proper food, nowhere to put your feet.'[15]

Yet if Norman was encouraging Charles to leave Antibes, he rather hoped that Elizabeth might stay. He could see that she was tired of her lover, and that their relationship had been stretched thin by their monotonous and penny-pinching existence. This had not been quite so uncomfortable for Elizabeth as for Charles. Norman would have picked up the bill for most of her outings with him. She still had her allowance and, with the occasional handout from Priscilla, she could just about afford 'the social life of the Cap'.

Shortly before they were due to leave, Norman gave Elizabeth a copy of *Old Calabria*. 'Old-fashioned stuff, my dear,' he said as he presented it. 'Heavy going. I don't know whether you'll be able to get through it.' On the flyleaf he wrote 'Always do as you please, and send everybody to Hell, and take the consequences. Damned good Rule of Life. N.'[16]

Elizabeth understood that the inscription was a message, attempting to jolt her out of her entanglement with Charles. As she recalled the subsequent conversation, Norman said,

'You are leaving with him because you think it is your duty. Duty? Ha! Stay here with me. Let him make do without you.'

'I can't, Norman, I have to go.'

'Have it your way, my dear, have it your way.'[17]

Wise old bird that he was, Norman knew that there is only so much that can be learnt from another person.

* * * * * * * *

CHAPTER SIX

The Loss of the Evelyn Hope

Charles and Elizabeth now realized that while the French authorities would not actually stop them from leaving Antibes in the *Evelyn Hope*, they would never grant them formal permission either. Fuel was already rationed, and what little they possessed had been begged from friends. However, they had managed to obtain visas for Italy and Greece, and decided to take their chances. On the afternoon of 20 May they gave a little cocktail party. 'Even Norman overcame his dislike of boats,' wrote Charles, 'and was on board. It was a brief leave-taking with time but for one drink, slightly sad.'[1] They set out for Corsica that evening, catching the icy mistral which blows from the north.

The exhilaration of the open sea brought back the zest to their relationship. To one of her closest friends, Elizabeth confided that Charles used to tie her up to the mast and whip her – which may have been no more than a joke, but it certainly implies that sex aboard the *Evelyn Hope* was exciting and inventive. They reached Corsica safely and spent some days in and around Bastia, visiting Erbalunga as Norman had suggested. Elizabeth wrote to tell him about it. He answered on 31 May.

> Just got your lovely letter of Sunday [26th May] . . . I suppose you are on the briny once more and can only hope you don't have any trouble with Italian officials, who get more troublesome the further south you go.

Glad you found that restaurant at Bastia; not good, but better than most. And glad you went to Erbalunga, where I had some ultra-pleasant days (*very* rare in Corsica). As to that damned grotto – it is not worth looking at. But I suppose you went there all the same. I was there for the first time with Marion Crawford in 1898. Were you born? I don't think so . . .

My stomach was all right, but I ordered broad beans and bacon the other day and ate about 3 kilos of it, with the result that the business has started all over again, and when I visit the WC (about fifty-four times a day) the explosions are so formidable that – the walls being very thin – Mme Jeanne and her girls rush out of doors, thinking there is an air raid in progress. Heaps of love to Charles. N.

Just before Elizabeth and Charles left Corsica they heard that the Germans had crossed the Meuse. Within three days it had become clear that there was nothing the French army could do to stop a full-scale invasion.

They left Corsica on 28 May, sailing almost due east: past the Italian penal settlement of Pianosa, and past Monte Cristo, then a game preserve for the king of Italy. The weather was turning rough, but they managed to reach the tiny island of Giglio, which lies between Elba and the port of Santo Stefano. Here they were received with the greatest possible courtesy by the *capo doganiere*, and his interpreter, who was the island's schoolmaster. Full of enthusiasm for the new arrivals, the schoolmaster invited them to dinner at his house, promising that all the island would be there to meet them.

As it turned out, they were the only guests. The schoolmaster apologized profusely and was evidently very ill at ease, and the enormous dinner he had laid on was not a success. The following morning, one of the schoolmaster's friends came early, with an urgent warning.

'You must leave early, trouble begins. I cannot tell you more, but war is certain . . . Get your papers as soon as the office opens, but act as though you know nothing. The weather is still bad, but you must go. Everybody here wishes you luck, do you understand? . . . You should be able to reach Messina in five days.'[2]

They collected their papers from the *capo doganiere*, who begged them to come back to the island in happier times, and set off into a gale. It was the first week of June 1940.

The voyage down the west coast of Italy became tiring, for the uncertain and variable winds involved much changing of sail. They bought a lobster from a little fishing boat that drew alongside, near the island of Stromboli, and later they ate it with fresh mayonnaise. As they came closer and closer to Messina without being stopped or questioned, their spirits rose: it was doubtful if the Italians would stop them once they were through the straits and out into the open sea.

The straits came in sight on the evening of 10 June, but their hopes of getting through were dashed. Three Italian destroyers on patrol appeared. One of them approached the *Evelyn Hope*, and they were ordered to proceed to the Sicilian port of Messina. As soon as they had berthed an officer came on board. He was surprised to hear that they did not have a radio, and asked if they had heard the news. They replied that they had not. The officer told them that, as of 5.30 that afternoon, Italy and Great Britain were at war.

The men who came to search the boat were very courteous; but they removed every piece of paper on board – charts, notebooks, address books, photographs. They left an appalling mess, which Charles and Elizabeth had not the heart to clear up. 'Finally we roughly tidied the double bunk, and lay miserably in each other's arms. We tried to imagine what would happen in the morning. At last we slept.'[3]

Now began a period of utter misery for Elizabeth, which in later years she could scarcely bear to recall. The Sicilian authorities, suspicious of a British couple prowling round the straits of Messina just as war was breaking out, decided that they must be spies. Charles and Elizabeth were questioned at the *Questura* (police headquarters) for two hours, and then told to pack. The boat was impounded. Their statements were sent to Rome for verification, and while the Roman authorities decided what was to be done with them, they would be kept as internees in Messina. They were sent to the Pensione Vienna, a squalid little boarding house in the Via Industriale. Their luggage, including a trunk full of books, was delivered the following day.

June in southern Italy was relentlessly hot. Their room was 'fenced off from the kitchen by an unpainted wooden partition about eight feet high, and contained a [single] bed . . . The room opened directly into the main living room, but a certain amount of privacy was afforded by the position of the bed, which allowed the door to only half open.'[4]

From the kitchen ceiling hung a cage with a dead canary in it. When Charles pointed this out, the Austrian landlady merely said, 'Poor thing! He's been dead for fifteen days.'[5] She was a hard, grasping woman with broken teeth. The maid, who worked sixteen hours a day, received only her food in exchange and relied on tips from the guests to feed her illegitimate child. Charles and Elizabeth were kept on a diet of watery soup, a little pasta, dry rye bread and very salty olives – though they later discovered that the *Questura* had asked that they be well-fed, and paid extra so they could have wine with their meals. The small amounts of coffee and sugar that they had brought with them were whisked away and never seen again.

The boarding house consisted of six rooms, which contained various stateless, near-penniless and temporarily homeless people including two Egyptian families, a retired sailor and a pregnant girl who did not dare go back to her parents. Most of them were at liberty to come and go, and some had jobs. For the internees, there was nothing to do but read, and catch fleas on a bar of soap. The fleas were regularly displayed to the landlady, but she was not impressed. The four-year-old daughter of one of their fellow-guests used to stand at the door of their tiny room and stare at them with her mouth open. When Elizabeth and Charles could no longer stand her they would shoo her away, whereupon the child would dissolve into uncontrollable sobs.

Soon both Charles and Elizabeth were suffering badly from the lack of fruit and vegetables. The Austrian landlady made it plain that things might get better if Elizabeth or Charles offered her something to sell, preferably jewellery; but it was obvious that only she would benefit from the deal, so they declined. They had some French francs, but the landlady's husband was unwilling to give Charles more than fifty lire for a one-thousand-franc note. One day Charles took matters into his own hands: he forced his way into the kitchen, and seized two tomatoes and a hard-boiled egg, which he and Elizabeth ate while the landlady screamed at them. They then found out the food belonged to the mother of the four-year-old girl, who had bought them for her child: Charles's moment of defiance turned into one of abject apology. Things only improved when Charles began climbing over the partition that separated their room from the kitchen. He made a key to the pantry door from bent wire. 'We had a meal in our room every morning before [the maid] came down at six o'clock. Even so, by the evening we were usually feeling the want of food.'[6]

By the time they were into the third week of their internment there was still no news from Rome, and their repeated requests to see the American Consul were ignored. Elizabeth decided she could take it no longer. Poor food, claustrophobia and anxiety had already undermined her health, but now her acting talent was employed to make her appear seriously ill.

'Early next morning she awakened the household by a series of piercing shrieks, and as soon as enough witnesses arrived, rushed downstairs in her nightgown. I caught her in my arms at the door and called for help. Signor Pulfer helped me carry her to our room. I wrung my hands in despair . . . Caroline stayed in her bed, staring at any visitor with unseeing eyes, and repeating *The Golden Journey* in a tedious monotone.'[7] Charles told the landlady that he could not be responsible for her actions. She was in such a state that she might run out into the street or even smash up the hotel. Elizabeth's acting on this occasion seems to have been very convincing, for soon after they were told that they were to go to Rome. However, they were not allowed to reclaim any of the papers that had been confiscated, and the boat was to stay in Messina.

They were handed over to two young guards and put on a train, and by nine the following morning they were in Rome. Here they were handed over to another two guards, and told they were going to Venice – after which they would be free to go.

This sounded too good to be true, and it was. In Venice they were taken to the police station and questioned, and to Elizabeth's dismay, Charles was then taken away and locked up in an underground small cell with twenty-four other men while she had to wait in an office. They had had almost nothing to eat for two days. Elizabeth threw a scene in the middle of the afternoon, and was brought a plate of macaroni.

The train for Trieste did not leave until eleven that night, and Charles managed to persuade their Venetian guards that it would be very sad if Elizabeth were to leave their beautiful city without seeing anything of it. After some discussion, the guards agreed. There would be plenty of time to walk them through the Piazza San Marco. Charles had seen it for the first time the previous winter, with Mike Cumberlege, and now he wanted to show it to Elizabeth.

As they walked though the Piazza with their guards, Charles happened to see an acquaintance dining at Florian's, and managed to borrow some money. With it he was able to treat Elizabeth and the guards to dinner in a restaurant where, according to Charles, they drank a straw-covered flask of sweet white Chianti and Elizabeth ate her first *calamaretti*. They took a gondola to the railway station. One of the guards hoped they would come back when the war was over, and gave Charles his address.

Trieste had recently been bombed by the British, which was perhaps why Charles and Elizabeth were both locked up in the cells – but at least they were given a cup of coffee and some bread. The foul smell and scurrying vermin banished any thought of sleep, and Elizabeth was grateful for the company of a couple of prostitutes who were thrown in with her in the course of the night, and kept her supplied with cigarettes.

For the month they had been in custody in Italy they had continually tried to get in touch with a representative of the US Embassy. Finally in Trieste, with the help of the Yugoslav Consul, a meeting was arranged. The American Consul agreed to pay for their tickets as far as Zagreb; and after a few more hours in the cells, they were put on a train to Yugoslavia.

It was 29 June. They had spent nineteen days interned in Italy, and had lost almost everything. Charles was particularly upset about his typewriter, his notebooks and his manuscripts. Elizabeth mourned the loss of her collection of recipes, built up over the years till it was far fatter and more comprehensive than the book she had given her friend Marian as a wedding present. They were both run down and unwell, particularly Elizabeth: but at least they were out of Italy.

They crossed the Yugoslav border and, after several hours, the train stopped at a junction where Charles and Elizabeth were taken to a police station and questioned. The police roared with laughter at their adventures in Italy, and plied them with glass after glass of a fiery liquor made of plums. They were also given some sausage, and a great plate of sauerkraut. But their stomachs were weakened and quite unable to cope with such rough sustenance. They were both violently sick, and were still feeling very ill when they reached Zagreb. They spent three days in rainswept Zagreb, shivering in their thin clothes and drinking black beer, while the British Consul sorted out their visas and train tickets. When all was done they boarded the train, and on 2 July 1940, they reached Athens.

Elizabeth found several letters waiting for her, mostly from her family. There was also one from Norman Douglas.

1. Stella Gwynne, Elizabeth's mother, soon after her marriage in 1905
2. Rupert Gwynne MP, Elizabeth's father, *c.* 1910
3. Wootton Manor, showing the main Jacobean part of the house with later additions by Detmar Blow

4. Elizabeth, aged ten, by Ambrose McEvoy (1878–1927)

5. Family group at Wootton, taken not long before Rupert's
death in 1924: *clockwise starting with Rupert*:
Rupert, Elizabeth, Felicité, Stella, Diana and Priscilla
6. Stella and her daughters, late 1920s:
Felicité, Priscilla, Diana, Stella, Elizabeth

7. Elizabeth as an actress. On the reverse of this publicity photograph
she jotted down her details: '5' 6½"; Dark, fluent French and German.
Leeds, Oxford, Bournemouth, Seafield; Open Air Theatre 2 seasons.'
8. Charles Gibson Cowan. In his book *The Voyage of the Evelyn Hope*,
Caroline (Elizabeth) says: 'Never wear anything but a blue jersey and an old
pair of flannel trousers. Never wash the salt out of your hair ...
Then perhaps I shall stay in love with you.'
9. Peter Laing, in the uniform of the 9th Lancers, *c.* 1942
10. Norman Douglas. 'Always do as you please, and send everybody to Hell,
and take the consequences. Damned good Rule of Life. N.'

11 and 12. Elizabeth and Tony David:

twin portraits taken at the time of their marriage, Cairo, 1944

13. Elizabeth at her desk in the Ministry of Information, Cairo, *c.* 1943.
The silver bracelet she is wearing may be one given to her by
Charles Gibson Cowan
14. Tony David at his desk in Cairo, 1943
15. Cairo group, 1944: Patrick Leigh Fermor, Denise de Menasce,
Patrick O'Malley (who married Lesley Pares) and Major Scott
16. Renée Fedden

3 June 1940. Dearest Liz . . . No particular news here. It is
barely 10 p.m., but this Glacier is already quite deserted, and
the streets are pitch dark . . . I wonder where you are now? I
do hope you passed through the straits of Messina by daylight
and had no trouble with the Italians. They can be very disagree-
able. Won't write any more, as I am being kicked out. All chairs
on the tables. To Hell with them . . . Heaps of love to Charles,
and tell me what the Hotel Mistra is like.

Elizabeth felt homesick and very far from her family, but England
seemed impossibly remote and vulnerable on the other side of
occupied Europe. The Italians and the British had begun fighting
in north Africa and the Mediterranean, Stalin had occupied the Baltic
States and Romania was under German protection by mid-July. The
Germans evidently thought that England could be brought rapidly
to its knees. Elizabeth worried about her sisters, and begged Pris to
send her a telegram to say they were all all right. There seemed little
chance of Elizabeth getting home now, unless she travelled to South
Africa or India first. She did not have the energy, or the money, to
contemplate such a journey.

The terrible precariousness of their situation sank in. She and
Charles were stuck in the honking, crowded, ramshackle squalor
of Athens, struggling with an unfamiliar language and the Greek
alphabet. They had almost no money, no means of having it sent
out from England and Charles had to find a job – though the fact
that he was 'living in open sin' with a woman swiftly got around the
gossiping expatriate cliques in Athens. The British Council were
extremely unhelpful, and no school was prepared to consider him
in the post of teacher. Elizabeth loathed the petty hypocrisy of the
British community in Athens and, sometime later, Norman Douglas
reminded her that it had always been like that.

I am much annoyed to hear about the gossip at Athens, but of
course you don't care a damn. Send them all to hell, and tell
them so. Athens British community has always been known as

the most scandal-mongering brood in Europe. As they are
nearly all sodomites or lesbians you should have no difficulty
in answering back.[8]

But neither Elizabeth nor Charles could afford to antagonize anyone
who might put them in the way of work. When not seeking a job,
Charles joined Elizabeth in wandering around the sights. On a good
day, one of the rich and generous Greeks who kept huge yachts in
the harbour at Piraeus might give them lunch. The evenings were
whiled away at a place called Ekali's, where they drank brandy and
soda into the small hours. In a letter to a friend, Elizabeth said she
could not take much more of this sort of life without going mad.

Charles went from one job refusal to the next. Even freelance
press-work proved a dead end, since there were many well-
established stringers and the Athenian telephones were so tempera-
mental. Eventually, through a Greek friend, he found a job teaching
four pupils English on the island of Syros. He set off in mid-August,
and Elizabeth followed soon after. She had little alternative.

They settled in the village of Vari: a cluster of cottages overlooking
a beach of white sand and a little bay. Their cottage was 'a white
cube of a house, two box-like rooms and a nice large bare kitchen'.[9]
There was no bath and no plumbing, but a well and a fig tree stood
outside the front door, and a few steps further on was the Aegean
sea. The village contained about three dozen houses, two churches,
a shop and a taverna where the men sat outside at wooden tables.
The owner of the taverna was called Josipi, and it was he who
furnished the newcomers with sheets and pillows, cushions and
crockery for their house. His brother-in-law Yannaki was a charming
wheeler-dealer, who assured Charles and Elizabeth that he could
provide them with anything from pins to cars, cigarettes and South
African sherry.

It was not until the asphodels came out that Elizabeth began to
enjoy life on Syros, and put the misery of the past few months

behind her. She learnt how to rely on the ancient, basic foods of the Mediterranean. The only stores she had to bother with were bread, olive oil, olives, salt fish, hard white cheese, dried figs, tomato paste, rice, dried beans, sugar, coffee and wine.

She bought fish from the fisher boys: usually small fry or squid, with the occasional red mullet or langouste. Josipi, who had taken a shine to Elizabeth, often gave her vegetables and fruit from his garden. Eggs were cheap and plentiful, but meat was only available on feast days and consisted of pieces of roughly hewn kid, lamb or pork. Elizabeth described her diet as 'limited, but at least [it] presented none of the meal-planning problems which . . . daily plague the better-off English housewife'.[10] It was also while living in Syros that she discovered rocket, which she used to flavour potato soup instead of parsley.

While Elizabeth and Charles were adapting to this primitive Mediterranean idyll, Spitfires, Hurricanes and Messerschmitts were fighting it out in the skies above the south coast of England. When Goering realized that the battle in the air had been lost, he ordered an all-out bombing campaign on British cities. On 6 September, troops in the south-east of England were told to prepare for invasion. The following day the whole of London's dockland was on fire, and a few days later much of the East End had been reduced to rubble.

On Syros the days passed easily. Three times a week Charles walked the five miles to the village to give English lessons to his four pupils; while Elizabeth swam, read, tried (not very successfully) to learn Greek, kept house, and did her best to provide the English delicacies that Yanniki craved for. It was important to keep Yanniki happy, for he lent Elizabeth his donkey when she needed to go into Ermopoulos, the main town, seven miles away. It was here that she stocked up on beans and oil, cheese and wine, and the boxes of *loukoumia* (Turkish delight) that were a speciality of the island.

What Yanniki really wanted was Heinz tomato soup in tins, and piccalilli pickles. She managed to find four tins of the soup, for which she paid 'a bundle of drachmas that would have kept me in wine and cheese for a month'. The gift was much appreciated: 'in return I was offered baskets of eggs, lemons, oranges, freshly dug vegetables and salads, glass after glass of wine in the tavern'.[11] But Yanniki was still longing to try the celebrated English pickles, and it soon became obvious that he was expecting Elizabeth to make some for him.

And so it came about that Elizabeth found herself on a Greek island, making English pickles. 'Long mornings I spent cutting up cauliflower and onions, carrots and cucumbers. Afternoons, I squatted in my kitchen fanning the charcoal fires into a blaze brisk enough to boil the brew.'[12] She packed them into the only vessels she could get hold of, unglazed earthenware jars holding about three pounds. She didn't like it much, but her Greek friends were delighted. What impressed Elizabeth was that, on the barter system, she might have lived for free had she been prepared to devote her entire life to pickle-making. Elizabeth found that she had made herself a niche in the village community, if not its economy. She was given an emaciated, flea-ridden white kitten, to which she became very attached.

On 28 October the Italians invaded north-west Greece. Josipi was one of many friends who set off to fight that gruelling winter war in the mountains. The Italian advance collapsed a few weeks later, and by 21 November the Greeks were pushing them back into Albania. The mood of the country was triumphant, and in the tavern people hoped Josipi would be home for Christmas.

References to 'Christmas pudding' began to crop up, and Elizabeth realized that this was the next English delicacy she was expected to provide. As one might imagine, she went about it with her usual thoroughness. The beef kidney suet came straight off the carcass and had to be cleaned, skinned, shredded and chopped. Then she had to stone bunch after bunch of raisins 'each one sticky as a piece of warm toffee'. Having made the puddings she then had to think of a way to keep them immersed in boiling water for nine or ten hours. This was quite impossible on the two charcoal fires let into the wall of her primitive kitchen; but she managed to get the villagers to make her a haybox, and when the puddings were finally done, she was pleased with the result.

The optimism that had sprung up with news of the Greek victories in November began to fade as more and more German divisions massed in southern Romania. 'In the church at Christmas,' wrote Charles, 'the peasants prayed before a tinsel crêche in which the infant Jesus was protected by two lead Grenadier Guards. Caroline and I spent the morning in Josipi's garden, where the fallen oranges lay unburied on the ground.'[13] Later that day, they gave a party for the villagers. The famous puddings were consumed, but people were less enthusiastic about them than Elizabeth had hoped. The local raisins, the delicious candied citron made by her neighbours and the Athenian brandy with which the puddings had been liberally doused made them taste disappointingly familiar.

The cottage became increasingly cold and uncomfortable, and fuel was hard to come by. Elizabeth had little to do but write letters. She wrote to Robin Fedden, the writer and traveller whom she had met on her visit to Egypt two years before. He was still working as a lecturer at the University of Cairo, and he urged her to come out to Egypt. 'What I wonder are you planning to do? Do come here! We shall give you what I believe is called "a great reception" – especially me.'[14] Elizabeth did not answer the letter until 16 April 1941, ten days after the simultaneous invasion of Greece and Yugoslavia by the Germans. Charles is not mentioned, as if she had already written him out of her life.

'My dear Robin, I eventually received your letter – in January I think it was – I should have answered it before, but letter-writing seems futile nowadays . . .' She went on to describe her life by the sea with the soothing sound of the waves, and how much she had detested Athens. 'I should like to get to Egypt but I really don't see how it is possible, particularly since the latest development here.

On the other hand don't be surprised if I should suddenly turn up, looking rather wild and probably dressed in rags (that's more or less the state in which I arrived in Athens) after some further ludicrous adventure. In that case I hope I shan't find that you have left Cairo the day before for some un-get-at-able country . . . With much love, Elizabeth.'

On 27 April the Germans marched into Athens, and the following day Syros was bombed. Elizabeth and Charles hastily gathered together as much as they could, and managed to pay their way on to a fishing boat bound for Crete. Elizabeth had to leave her white cat, and grieved for it like a child: its loss seemed to concentrate all the sadness and fear and uncertainty of being a refugee again.

The journey to Crete began on 29 April, and the following day they saw land. They thought it was the island of Sikinos, some eighty kilometres to the south and almost a third of the way to Crete; but unfortunately the pilot had lost his bearings, and the island ahead was actually Mikonos – thirty kilometres due east, in completely the wrong direction. A small mutiny ensued and Charles took the tiller.

They reached Heraklion, the main city of Crete, on 2 May. Here they found Mike Cumberlege, now working with Special Operations Executive (SOE). He was the skipper of a caique, one of those traditional fishing boats that plied their way among the islands of the eastern Mediterranean. This caique was called *Dolphin*. She looked innocent enough, but was armed with four anti-aircraft guns and had a two-pounder gun in the bows. Mike and Nick Hammond, a classical scholar, were reconnoitring possible landing places on the south coast of Crete: both for stores, and for smuggling agents and troops on to the island after the Germans had taken it. This could only be a matter of time.

Charles devoted the last section of *The Voyage of the Evelyn Hope* to a dramatic account of their escape from the island. It tells of how they saw Knossos before the great German parachute invasion began on 20 May, how they were caught on the edge of that terrible battle, how they made their way in an army lorry to Suda Bay on the north coast only to find that the evacuation of civilians was over, how they then had no choice but to turn south and stumble over the mountains – strewn with dead and wounded soldiers – to Sphakia, where at last they were able to scramble aboard one of the last of the Royal Navy warships evacuating the New Zealand, British and Australian troops. This makes out that they escaped on the night of 31 May. The structure of the book needs a dramatic climax, for it is in the course of this final section that Charles and 'Caroline' admit that their relationship is over; although the author implies that their shared experiences of internment, an idyllic Greek island and war have only deepened their friendship. After the book was completed Charles wrote, 'I did not see any shape for *The Voyage of the Evelyn Hope* until Crete suddenly provided me with a climax . . .'[15]

What actually happened was rather more prosaic. They spent a dozen days on Crete, by the end of which the island was undergoing fairly heavy nightly bombing, but they managed to leave on one of the many civilian convoys that were organized at the time. The embarkation permit for 'Mr and Mrs Gibson Cowan' is dated 14 May, and they arrived in Egypt on 16 May 1941. This was four days before the Germans began the massive parachute-born invasion which, after a week of bitter fighting, was to leave them in command of the island.

* * * * * * * *

CHAPTER SEVEN

Alexandria

Elizabeth's first glimpse of Egypt on 16 May 1941 was not encouraging. The great port of Alexandria was filled with warships and other vessels damaged in the evacuation of Crete. The quayside, where the refugees disembarked, was piled high with crates. Milling around them were dusty trucks, gangs of Egyptian dockworkers in their faded blue and white *gallabeias*, and everywhere, soldiers in khaki. The bright red caps of the military policemen blazed out of the mass. The smell of dust and petrol hung heavy, yet from almost anywhere in Alexandria, there was a glimpse of the sea.

From Alexandria Charles and Elizabeth travelled by train to Cairo, which was now the centre of operations for a theatre of war that included the Mediterranean, the Middle East as far as Baghdad, and the north African coast as far as Tunis. The city was ringed with garrisons, and every hospital, street and cinema was filled with Allied troops. The young King Farouk and his government chafed at the way they had been brushed aside to make way for the war, the way the British decreed and commandeered and expected them to fall loyally into line. Entrepreneurial Egyptians, however, welcomed the opportunity. They profited greatly from the situation, as did the naturalized Greeks and Levantines who made up much of the small-business community. Rents soared, new cafés and bars opened, the red-light district flourished, and everyone wanted to help the Allied soldiers spend their pay.

Charles and Elizabeth were lodged at one of the largest refugee hotels – the Luna Park. It boasted a certain amount of plush and gilding on the ground floor, but the rooms above were as small and bare as prison cells. Lawrence Durrell, who had arrived in Egypt from Crete two weeks before with his (first) wife Nancy and their baby daughter Penelope, predictably called it 'Lunatic Park' and spread the rumour that it had been a brothel.

Elizabeth had reached the end of the road with Charles, and yet she lacked the emotional energy to leave him when she felt so vulnerable. For days she was desolate and miserable, yearning for her little white house by the sea, unable to face the task of rebuilding her life in a cacophonous dusty city from which she might be hounded yet again. The authorities, who had a policy of getting civilian women out of the way unless they had secretarial qualifications, tried to put her on a ship to Bombay. This pushed Elizabeth into revolt. She was not afraid of making a scene, and no one in a khaki uniform was going to bully her into going to Bombay. When she started looking for a job and a place to live, she found that the city was filled with refugees like herself, all searching desperately for the same things. Yet Elizabeth did have friends in Cairo: the Goodwins, with whom she had stayed three years before, and Robin Fedden, who gave her the 'great reception' he had promised. Using her few contacts she soon found a job working in the naval cypher office in Alexandria. Her excellent French and good German no doubt proved an advantage.

The early summer of 1941 was a time of great anxiety. Rommel, who had arrived in north Africa in February, had forced the Allies all the way back into Egypt. In Britain, London was undergoing ferocious bombardment – three thousand people had died on the night of 10 May.

Elizabeth's first weeks in Alexandria were spent in a dismal little pension, and her job as a cypher clerk meant long hours and not much pay – but at least it was a job. She bought herself some clothes, having left Greece with little more than what she stood up in, and looked about for somewhere to live. She landed on her feet thanks to Mike Cumberlege, who had repeated his trick of turning up whenever Elizabeth arrived in a new place. 'I had run into him in the street in Alex,' wrote Elizabeth years later to her god-daughter Frances Fedden, 'and he had asked me to keep house for him in an absurdly grandiose apartment he had got hold of – there was even a bar made entirely of mirror glass.'[1]

Cumberlege's flat in the rue des Pharaons had one disadvantage. Its size and scale attracted almost everyone passing through Alex. Elizabeth never knew whether to expect five or twenty-five for dinner, and impromptu parties seemed to take place several times a week. All this did wonders for Elizabeth's social life, although in time it became very expensive – particularly since Mike was often away. He was a vital link, bringing stragglers off Crete under the noses of the Germans, and running in SOE officers and members of Cretan resistance groups.

The first cook Elizabeth and Mike employed was called Anastasia. She cooked very grand dishes like boned stuffed duck in aspic, dressed like a duchess and cheated her employers. She soon found herself in trouble with the military police for handling stolen goods from an Australian supply depot.

Anastasia was replaced by Kyriacou, of whom Elizabeth had far fonder memories. Kyriacou had once been a sponge diver, and suffered from the disease that affects many divers. It took the form of a sudden, agonizing pain in his right arm that forced him to drop anything he was carrying. Even this disability could not account for the amount of teapots he broke – Elizabeth eventually discovered that his way of making tea was to put the teapot directly on the gas burner.

She was working erratic hours based on naval watches, and often did not get back from work till early in the morning. This never prevented Kyriacou from waking her up to show her the contents of his shopping basket. '*Fresco*, Madame, *fresco*,' he would coo to her with pride, dumping his market haul of live fish, crabs and crayfish on to her bed.[2] Elizabeth did not complain about her working hours; but the long periods she had to spend reading put a terrible strain on her eyes. 'I think perhaps it's the long hours working by electric light that make my eyes ache so bad – I have temporarily given up reading outside the office.'[3]

Since both she and Mike Cumberlege were at work all day, Kyriacou took it upon himself to organize much of their social life. He rang up those of their friends he liked best and would invite them to dinner, and not unnaturally, the people he liked were Greek-speaking or involved in the Greek cause. Then came the happy day when he heard that his wife and children had arrived safely in Palestine. Kyriacou invited all their friends and cooked a stupendous dinner to celebrate, the highlight of which was an octopus stew. 'With passionate concentration he prepared it, and I watched him build up in a deep pot a bed of thyme branches on which to lay a huge quantity of onions, tomatoes, garlic, bay leaves and olives, and then the octopus. Gently he poured red wine over his carefully constructed edifice, stirred in the ink from the fish, and left his covered pot to simmer for the rest of the afternoon.'[4] (A version of this recipe appears in Elizabeth's *Book of Mediterranean Food*.)

In July 1941, Elizabeth sent Charles a clipping she had cut out of the Egyptian *Gazette*, which advertised for a diesel engineer and sailors. Charles applied, and on 1 August 1941, he joined the *Samothrace* as bosun. Elizabeth came to say goodbye to him on the 4th, and brought him a present: the much-read copies of *Alice's Adventures in Wonderland* and *Through the Looking-Glass* that she had had as a child. They had accompanied her through all their adventures, and she described them as 'the most precious possessions of my childhood'. The following day, she wrote him a letter:

> We'll both think often of the things we have done together, of
> the canals and the wine and the red rocks of my beloved France,
> of the sea white with nautilus off the coast of Corsica, of dawn
> in the Bay of Naples, of a certain lobster mayonnaise we ate

between one life and another, of mountains of golden oranges in Joseph's garden and those purple islands lying all around us from the top of the hill behind our hovel. Thank you for the lovely experiences you have given me and remember that you made the Isles of Greece more than just a beautiful name for both of us and that these things can be done again.

Charles copied these words into his personal log, with no comment. But when the time came to prepare the dedication for *The Voyage of the Evelyn Hope*, he wrote TO E.G. WITH ALL MY LOVE, followed by the lines just quoted – though he changed the word 'hovel' to 'house'.

Charles had begun the war as a pacifist, but the 'burning convictions' he had held were wearing thin and he wanted to play an active part after all. There was no question of his joining any regular unit of the British Army in Egypt: at thirty-eight he was too old, and too much of a bohemian. One of the reasons he had joined the *Samothrace* was that it was eventually bound for England, where he hoped there might be something for him to do. That wish did not materialize. August 1942 found him in Kenya where he became Port Welfare Officer in Mombasa, and two years later, he was taken on in an official capacity as Chief Advisory and Instructional Pilot, Eastern Mediterranean. He and Elizabeth kept in touch, and Elizabeth's letters to him tell much about her life in Alexandria.

Many people passed through the flat and her life, but the closest friend from this period came through Robin Fedden. He had given Elizabeth a letter of introduction to a girl with whom he was very much in love called Renée Catsaflis. Her mother was Italian, her father an Alexandrian Greek of great charm. She was brought up a Catholic and went to school in France, and from a very early age displayed an iron integrity. In confession one day, the priest asked her to promise not to repeat the sin she had just confessed. Renée said that since she almost certainly would commit that sin again, there was no point promising. The priest warned her that in that case, she could not receive absolution and would therefore be unable to take communion. Renée walked out, and never took communion again.

She had a passion for mountain climbing and walking, which held no charms for Elizabeth; but they were both great readers, and Elizabeth recognized in Renée the same uncompromising honesty and strength of character she had herself. They became very close. On Elizabeth's day off they would make a picnic, and spend the day at the beach.

Renée introduced Elizabeth to Max Bally, a White Russian who had ended up in Egypt after the Revolution. He was an excellent tennis player and something of a playboy. Elizabeth was dazzled – although she took care not to show it, and spared him none of her forceful opinions. 'I do hope,' he wrote after one dinner, 'I will be allowed to reopen our spirited discussions on such grave war problems as the one which produced such eloquence the other evening! And please God, the duck will not have been killed by a landmine this time.'[5]

Elizabeth admitted that 'I was rather taken with Max myself, but he was only interested in Renée.'[6] In fact Renée, at this time, seems to have rather enjoyed the havoc she was causing. In September 1941, Robin Fedden came to Alexandria. 'His arrival was the signal for a series of parties and picnics,' wrote Elizabeth to Charles. 'Robin and Mike started by getting on very well but it didn't last and with Renée doing a butterfly dance between the two of them the situation was rather delicate . . .'[7] It was made worse for Elizabeth by the fact that Robin blamed her for not keeping a closer watch on Renée.

Reassuring news at last arrived from Norman Douglas. He had left Antibes for Portugal, where at her suggestion he had got in touch with her cousin Neil Hogg, who was working for the British Embassy. Neil was a cultivated man who enjoyed Norman's company: they shared a flat in Lisbon, and when Neil was posted back to London at the end of 1941, Norman went with him.

*

The flat on the rue des Pharaons eventually became impossible. So many people were dropping by or using it as a temporary base, and leaving their boxes and tin trunks behind, that it became like a hotel – and a bar, and a restaurant. At the same time, prices were rising every week, and Mike Cumberlege was spending more and more time away on secret operations in the Mediterranean. Towards the end of the year Elizabeth gave it up, and found a tiny flat on her own. When she moved in, the flat was filled with hideous heavy furniture and the walls were covered with dark brown wallpaper. All the furniture, except for bed, bookshelves and a divan, was relegated to the attic, and the whole flat was painted a light cream colour. 'It is thrilling to have my own flat again, and occasionally buy an ashtray or a cushion cover, which to my doting eyes make the place look different.'[8]

She was not lonely, for it was almost impossible to be lonely in Alexandria at that time. 'Hardly a day passes when I don't run into some old friend or relation from England – I am now so used to being clapped on the back and greeted with the words "Hello Liz, I thought you were in an Italian prison camp," that I have ceased to be surprised.'[9] Quite apart from her friends in Alex, there were friends in Cairo and people were constantly shuttling between the two. 'Romney [Summers] is in the Army and has a flat in Cairo . . . The Durrells have a flat also and Larry has a job at the Embassy but is quite unchanged and as amusing as ever . . .' She also enjoyed the company of Professor Robin Furness, who headed the English Department of Cairo University. Elizabeth found him wonderfully restful and refreshing: 'Spending the afternoon with him is like going for a row in a Mediterranean harbour at dawn, after having watched a particularly noisy circus for weeks on end without stopping.'[10]

Elizabeth had always kept in touch with her sisters, and sent home silk stockings, cigarettes and coffee when she could. From Priscilla came parcels of clothes – Elizabeth was particularly grateful for her favourite coat – and bundles of letters. News from home was good.

Priscilla was very happy with her two healthy babies, and Diana had married a young doctor called Christopher Grey on 7 August 1941. 'The wedding was a furore by all accounts,' wrote Elizabeth to Charles. 'Diana wore Mummie's wedding dress and looked gorgeous so Pris says, and Bulgie was bridesmaid, and the family turned up in force and there was a mob of Diana's disappointed boyfriends swooning around the buffet.'[11]

Her great friend Marian Butterworth also married that year, and moved into a house in Lincoln Street, Chelsea. Elizabeth did not much like her husband, whose name was Peter Thomas – which was almost inevitable, because Elizabeth usually disliked the people who married her close friends. 'I do hate all these things going on and me not there to see – and in a way I suppose I have always had the idea that I would like to share a flat or a house again with Marian. It no doubt sounds odd to say such a thing of one's girlfriends but I do feel that there was something between us that was very valuable in my life and hers too I think . . .'[12] But Marian was involved in her domestic life and longing for a baby, and not much good at writing letters. For quiet, intimate friendship with another woman, Elizabeth turned to Renée.

Elizabeth was now a part of that curious middle-class English-speaking society abroad that the war had spawned. She did her bit, worked in canteens set up for servicemen, and for a while she went to dance once a week with the sailors at the Under Twenty Club: 'It makes me feel like a grandmother, but wonderful exercise,' she wrote to Charles.[13] Among the women working as secretaries or cypher clerks for the British authorities, many had, like Elizabeth, fled from occupied Europe, and most were under thirty. So were the young officers in uniform, back for a few brief days of leave. These young men longed for female company: just to walk and talk with a woman was to remember a happier, less violent world, and the women – knowing the men might be dead the following week – were generous with their companionship. They had no children to worry about, no old aunts and neighbours to disapprove of how they spent their time. No wonder that in dimly lit restaurants and nightclubs, and in the rented rooms of once-sumptuous art-deco flats and crumbling *belle époque* palaces, buttons had a way of coming undone.

In that winter of 1941, Elizabeth met an officer in the 9th Lancers called Peter Laing. He had been educated in England, though his family had settled in Canada. When they met, Elizabeth was enjoying her independence too much to want an intense romance, and no doubt Laing felt the same. They had what they liked to think of as an uncomplicated friendship, but soon their feelings for each other began to run deeper than either wanted to admit. They corresponded during the spring and summer of 1942 while he was at the front, and saw each other when he came back on leave to Alexandria. 'I often look forward to getting back to Alex,' he wrote. 'Two hot baths in succession, a complete do at the barber's shop on the first floor of the Cecil, the luxury of the pâté at the Union Bar and many other things beside.'

The war was now entering a critical phase. Rommel had forced the British back into Egypt; but he was on the end of a supply line that went all the way back to Tunisia, and in July 1942 he was stopped at El Alamein. At this point the Germans were caught in a natural bottleneck between the sea to the north and, to the south, the Qattara Depression: an immense dip in the desert floor that was impassable to tanks.

Nevertheless, the unseemly haste with which the British withdrew eastwards in front of the Germans caused considerable unease in Alexandria. Most people did not really start to panic until late June, and the general hysteria came to a head on 1 July, a day which became known as 'The Flap'. Elizabeth came back to her flat to find it being dismantled by her dour Albanian cook, who was convinced that the Germans were already in town. It was a day of mass exodus, of frightened crowds of women and children surging into the railway

ALEXANDRIA

stations, streets blocked with cars piled high with mattresses to protect them from air raids. The British authorities urged calm and restraint, while behind the scenes they were burning their confidential papers as fast as they could.

On 2 July, Elizabeth's office and all its employees – including herself – were transferred to Port Tewfik in the Canal Zone. Out in the desert, Rommel attacked the fortified positions of El Alamein again and again, but he failed to break through. For the rest of July he was on the defensive, while General Auchinleck (who had taken personal command of the battle from the end of June) kept up the pressure with repeated counter-attacks.

Elizabeth, meanwhile, was not well. She had developed an infection in her feet which flared up and died away again, but seemed to get no better. She was still in Port Tewfik, where her office was housed in a troopship, when she received a letter from Peter:

24 July [1942]. My dear Liz – I've gone and got myself in hospital, though with nothing at all serious . . . I contrived to get a pick head driven into my neck, but it has not really impaired my inefficiency in anyway. I got into Alex for one hour on the 29th but you must have left . . . Drop me a line when you have time, Liz, and look after yourself. Love, Peter.

Her reply was robust, to say the least.

PSTOE, Fleet Mail Office, Port Tewfik. I have never heard such a lot of nonsense in all my life – what with pickaxes stuck in your head and bits of shrapnel in your ear you must be in a pretty state . . . I am quite happily settled in a borrowed bungalow on the seashore a few miles out of Suez and living in surprising harmony with three other girls from the office. The whole thing is marred by the fact that we are obliged to keep trailing into the office to work, but otherwise the arrangement is excellent. We sleep outside and listen to the waves, and find heavenly release from the eternal flies and

93

hellish heat of Suez . . . The new Marx Bros. film has by some
sort of miracle arrived here and I'm going to see it tomorrow
and it's the most exciting thing that has happened almost since
I can remember.

In time Peter recovered from his wound and went back to his unit,
but the infection in Elizabeth's feet got steadily worse. She was in
bed for three weeks in Port Tewfik, but that remedy failed and her
walking was now seriously impaired. Nevertheless, she followed her
office on its next move, to Cairo. She took a room in the Continental
Hotel and hoped she would soon be mobile enough to look for a
flat. By now one of her feet was almost right again – but the other
was not improving, and she felt ill and exhausted.

She went to Alexandria on leave, and stayed with her friend
Georges de Menasce. The Menasces were one of the oldest and
wealthiest Jewish families in Alexandria, and Georges was a friend
of Stella's and the Goodwins, who had been Elizabeth's hosts in
Egypt before the war. Georges's passion was music. He was an
excellent pianist, and often gave concerts in his house – although
he always played from behind a screen. In his villa, Elizabeth was
ensconced in luxury; but her bad foot now became so inflamed that
she had to be taken to hospital, where it was operated on. Georges
de Menasce looked after her as though she were one of his family.
He kept Elizabeth in Alexandria for ten weeks, arranged for her to
be treated by his own doctor, and would not allow her to pay the
hospital bill. Elizabeth was grateful: not only for all her friend's
help, but also for giving her the rest she so desperately needed.

She returned to Cairo in the autumn of 1942, where the big event
among her friends was the wedding of Robin Fedden to Renée.
They were married on 3 October, but Elizabeth was still not mobile.
'I am quite unable to walk at all,' she wrote to Norman Douglas on
3 November, 'and I have had to give up my job [with the naval
cypher office].' Yet she could not afford to remain unemployed for
long, and it was Renée – then working with the publicity section

of the British Embassy – who provided the helping hand. 'I needed a job,' wrote Elizabeth, 'and she introduced me to a Canadian called Arnold Smith ... He needed a typist, but my typing was too rudimentary for him so he gave me a job in the newspaper section.'[14]

The newspaper section had started with an Arabic publication called *Akbar el Harb*, 'The Great War', and its purpose was to convince the Arabs that the Allies were going to win it. The office grew as other propaganda newspapers, in Greek, Amharic, Persian and even Serbo-Croat, were set up for distribution throughout the Middle East. Elizabeth had no time to describe what her job entailed in her letters to Charles, but she did say that the work was considerably more interesting and that she was no longer working the inhuman hours that the Navy cypher office had demanded.

That summer, General Bernard Montgomery replaced Auchinleck as commander-in-chief of the 8th Army. Since the winter of 1940, successive commanders had been obliged to spread their forces and equipment over three continents, with supplies and reinforcements constantly lagging behind requirements. By the time Montgomery arrived the war was focused in north Africa, and he could allow himself a period of planning, rearming and re-equipping the 8th Army such as Wavell and Auchinleck had only dreamed of.

On the night of 23 October, a thousand British guns opened fire on the Germans. The battle which was to drive Rommel out of north Africa had begun – but even the bullish Montgomery had never pretended it was going to be easy. Out of a total Allied strength of 220,000, losses numbered about a thousand a day.

One of the casualties was Peter Laing, whose jeep was blown up by a land mine at Mersa Matruh in November. His legs were very badly damaged. He was taken to Cairo and installed in the 63rd General Hospital, where first one leg and then the other had to be amputated. 'I have been a certain amount in the hospitals in Alex seeing friends at various times,' wrote Elizabeth to Charles in early

1943, 'but I haven't come in contact before with the badly wounded and have been completely shattered by the spectacle, and am helpless and hopeless in the face of such loathsome suffering and such fantastic courage.' Over Christmas with Robin and Renée, who had a house out by the pyramids, she visited Peter as often as she could. Elizabeth was in turmoil, for as soon as he was well enough Peter would be moved back to Canada. She knew that she was not the sort of woman who could nurse him through what was obviously going to be a long convalescence, and he did not press her: it was not within the terms of their resolutely 'unemotional' relationship.

They saw each other often in the weeks before he boarded the ship for Canada. He was back in Toronto in mid-April 1943. 'I have been more than a trifle busy,' he wrote on 10 May, 'with scores of relations that seem to infest this town. Most of them I have never seen before and two are clergymen, can you imagine . . . I miss your cooking very much, as everything served out here is very much men's food. You know, big clean vegetables, big clean steaks, big white clean potatoes washed down with a big white clean glass of milk. It lacks the savoury tang of the corrupt Orient . . .' Elizabeth also received a letter from his mother. 'He wrote to me at the time and told me how good you had been, bringing books, cakes and all manner of good things to amuse and divert . . . It was such a comfort to me to learn that he had even one visitor and especially a woman, for I had pictured him lying there with no friends to cheer and encourage him . . . so his news of your visits gladdened my heart greatly.'

Within two years both Peter and Elizabeth would be married to other people, but they kept in touch, and never forgot each other. When Peter came to England with his wife Kathleen McConnell, they sometimes visited Elizabeth in Halsey Street and she never failed to send them her latest book. Many years later, she gave her nephew Rupert Grey an introduction to Peter while he was travelling around Canada. Peter talked a great deal about Elizabeth. 'She gave me back the will to live,' he told Rupert. As for Elizabeth, in later life her regrets were reserved for another man; but in the list of bequests attached to her will she wrote, 'In a box on my dressing table . . . is a pair of heavy gold cuff links with the initials E.G. and P.M.L. These were made in Cairo for a man called Peter Laing who thought he was in love with me, and I with him . . .'

* * * * * * * *

CHAPTER EIGHT

Tony David

In the spring of 1943 the Germans were in full retreat back towards Tunis, and by mid-May the north African campaign was at an end. In Cairo, this meant that the enormous military bureaucracy had to be scaled down and restructured. One of the results was that responsibility for the propaganda office in which Elizabeth worked was removed from the Ministry of State and handed over to the Ministry of Information.

From its headquarters in Cairo, the Ministry of Information had to cover an enormous stretch of territory: from Tunisia to Persia and from Turkey to the Sudan. Officers and agents, experts and diplomats came and went in a constant stream, reporting to the Ministry on changes and conditions in countries all over the Middle East; and from this mass of data the Ministry dispensed information to its masters in Whitehall, to the military and, in varying degrees of fullness and accuracy, to the press.

It was decided that the time had come to start a reference library within the building, and Elizabeth was asked to set it up and run it. She leaped at the chance, and her bosses did not seem to mind that she had not the slightest qualification for the job. They no doubt saw a hard-working, intelligent young woman with an orderly mind and an eye for detail.

The office of the Ministry of Information continued to absorb new responsibilities as the military problems of the Middle East were replaced by political ones. A treasury official called Curteis

Ryan was appointed controller, and he came to Cairo with a small professional team. The office also changed premises: from an Edwardian villa in Garden City, to a soulless modern block facing the Anglican Cathedral. Elizabeth's reference library was housed on the ground floor, and was extremely well-run. A number of books were chosen by the Ministry of Information in London, 'who knew what was good for you'.[1] These included the usual works of reference and informative volumes on Egypt such as Sir Ronald Storrs's *Orientations* and the works of Lord Cromer. Elizabeth could also order books herself. There was a newspaper section too.

Thanks to her job, Elizabeth must have been one of the most well-informed people in Cairo. She had to keep abreast of all developments, both political and military, as reported in every newspaper, journal and magazine the Ministry could get hold of. She then had to index them: so that information on any topic, from production targets to Roosevelt's last speech, could be easily retrieved.

The library was open to anyone who needed information, but it was largely used by press attachés and war correspondents, who at various times included Alan Moorehead of the *Daily Express*; Alexander Clifford of the *Daily Mail*; Freya Stark, who had set up pro-Allied circles among the Arabs all over the Middle East called the Brotherhood of Freedom; Robin Fedden and others from the University of Cairo; and Lawrence Durrell, who ran the Information Office in Alexandria. At coffee time, the library also became a haven where colleagues gathered to laugh at and grumble about the bureaucratic pomposities of Mr Ryan, and Miss Glass, the tight-lipped registrar who sat just inside the entrance.

Roger Eland, who was in charge of *Akbar el Harb* and its satellite publications, remembers Elizabeth as very reserved, with rather severe and conventional clothes. These, combined with her heavy glasses, made her look like a quintessential librarian.

At the same time, there was another side to Elizabeth which those who saw only the librarian would scarcely have recognized. Her friend Christopher Kininmonth saw this naughtier, more rebellious side, and many years later he put a tiny vignette of her into his novel *Frontiers*: 'She laughed with her abrupt and vulgar cackle which contrasted with her speaking voice and her bloodstock kind of beauty. Her laugh brought her off any kind of pedestal one might have set her upon.'[2]

These two very different memories of Elizabeth give an indication of how she could compartmentalize her life; and in Cairo, a hotbed of rumour and gossip, people who were as reserved and secretive as Elizabeth took pains not to make themselves vulnerable. They changed, like chameleons, to blend in with whatever company they found themselves in. Yet whatever facet of herself she was projecting, Elizabeth was still grieving over Peter Laing – although she tried very hard not to think of him at all. All her energies went into her work and her friends, and somehow keeping herself on an even keel.

Cairo was a quieter place than it had been in the past two years, and sadder. So many friends had been wounded, killed or taken prisoner – yet life went on, as did the picnics and parties. Patrick Leigh Fermor remembers Elizabeth at one of them 'looking lovely in a sort of spangly *gallabeia*'. The journalist and seafood-lover George Lassalle, who was then working at GHQ Cairo, also remembered Elizabeth's 'brilliantly ornate ceremonial kaftans'. He never forgot an evening picnic with Elizabeth, Romney Summers and Robin Fedden, sailing lazily up the Nile. 'Romney, Elizabeth and I were reclining on cushions, sipping drinks, and Robin was prancing up and down like an elegant monkey in the rigging . . .'[3]

George Lassalle had ended up studying French at Oxford, after having tried and abandoned both forestry and law. He had been one of the six young patriots who had torn, from the minute book of the Oxford Union, the page which confirmed the motion that 'This House will not fight for King and Country'. He had joined the Sussex Regiment as a private, but was swiftly commissioned. In Cairo, he worked in GHQ for the intelligence service. Elizabeth was instantly attracted: he was light-hearted, charming, and like her he was pining for the life he had once known in the Greek islands. There was a raffish streak in George that Elizabeth found irresistible. He was already on his second marriage; but it did not stop either of them from launching into a companionable affair which, over the years, they were to leave off and pick up again whenever it suited them.

Elizabeth straddled many worlds in Cairo. Through Robin Fedden she had met Lawrence Durrell and Bernard Spencer, the poets who founded *Personal Landscape*, the most impressive poetry journal to come out of the war. They, like her, felt they were living in exile: not from England, but from Greece and the Graeco-Roman and Mediterranean world. Elizabeth was very fond of Durrell, with his verbal fireworks and his rumbustious company. They saw each other fairly often when she went to Alexandria. He had separated from his wife Nancy, but Durrell was not a man to stay single for long. In 1943, a year after he had moved to Alexandria as press attaché, Durrell had met Eve Cohen. She was to become his second wife, and much of her can be recognized in the character of Justine in the *Alexandria Quartet*.

Among Elizabeth's closest friends was the writer and traveller Patrick Kinross, who lived in the shadow of the Ibn Tulun mosque. He shared his flat with two other notable eccentrics: David Balfour, who had been a Greek Orthodox monk (known as Father Dimitri Balfour), and the scholarly diplomat Eddie Gathorne-Hardy. Through them and Robin Fedden, she would have been introduced to the world of British Council personnel and Cairo University lecturers. Unwilling to mix with the hearty polo- and cricket-players of the Gezira Club, the intellectuals and bohemians on the Cairo scene had colonized the Anglo-Egyptian Union. It was a far more democratic place than the Gezira Club, and in the tree-shaded garden they gathered to talk books, poetry and politics.

Among this set was the writer Olivia Manning, author of the Balkan and Levant Trilogies – six novels which, when completed in the 1970s, appeared under the title of *The Fortunes of War*. In these books Manning appears as Harriet Pringle, married to the irrepressible Guy Pringle. This character was closely based on her husband, Reggie Smith: an enthusiastic, bookish man who was intensely gregarious, and very promiscuous. It is possible that he was one of the many men with whom Elizabeth had casual affairs at this time.

Through her mother and the well-connected Goodwins, Elizabeth had friends among the grandest Egyptian families: wealthy British cotton brokers, businessmen and diplomats. Representatives from all these different circles could be seen at the parties given by Amy Smart, wife of the Oriental Counsellor Walter Smart. Amy Smart's parties combined everything that was most glamorous in wartime Cairo: dashing young SOE agents, visiting celebrities like Freya Stark or Cecil Beaton, travellers and intellectuals, as well as the most amusing and sophisticated of what Amy called '*la haute Juiverie, la haute Copterie, et la haute Mussulmanie du Caire*'. There was a cachet in being invited to Amy Smart's parties, and Elizabeth was invited every once in a while. This was an irritation to Olivia Manning, who resented the fact that she was not included on the Smarts' invitation list. She was a touchy, suspicious woman, who might have suspected Elizabeth of being one of her husband's innumerable girlfriends.

The pace of Cairo at that time was frenetic, particularly if one was a young working woman. Elizabeth was expected to be in her office by a quarter to nine, and she worked through till one. There was a long lunch break, with time for a siesta during the hottest part of the day, and people were back in their offices by four. They worked again until seven in the evening. There was just time to dash home for a shower and a change of clothes before going out again. There were not so many tanned young officers as there had been the year before, but there were still plenty of desk-bound ones with war-inflated ranks working in GHQ. A normal evening might well take in a bar, dinner on the rooftop of the Continental Hotel and afterwards a look in at Madame Badia's cabaret or the Auberge des Pyramides. Whisky and Indian gin were still plentiful. French wine had run out, but there was still plenty coming in from Palestine and Algeria.

Elizabeth found herself a tiny ground-floor flat, separated from the Nile by a busy road – part of what is now the Corniche. She always referred to this place as 'the cave', because it was so small and poky. The flat was reached by way of a car park, used by members of SOE and other clandestine organizations, whose nearby offices were known to all Cairene taxi-drivers as 'Secret House'.

Every foreigner with a flat, however humble, had a *suffragi*, an Egyptian or Sudanese servant who ran the household with varying degrees of efficiency. Elizabeth's first Cairene *suffragi* was called Abdul, who contrived to spill soup over her flatmate. After the departure of Abdul (and the flatmate) there was 'Hussein, who threw away the asparagus heads and served the stalks, alleging that that was the way the English liked them (and who was I to contradict him).' Hussein too went on his way. The next *suffragi* was called Suleiman, and Elizabeth soon realized that, as far as *suffragis* were concerned, she had struck gold.

He looked quite different from most people's cooks. His tarboosh was shorter and broader than that worn by other servants, and gave him a unique appearance; tiny eyes, a childlike expression and a rather tremulous smile combined to make him a most engaging figure. We conversed in French; he was very firm about the accounts and forced me to do them every day after lunch ... For £5 a month he cooked, cleaned the flat, did the shopping, took my clothes to the cleaners, dealt with the *dhobi*, took shoes to be mended, brought a clean dress to the office if I had to go straight out to lunch, and in fact did everything for which in England one would employ a cook, a lady's maid, a butler and a housemaid.[4]

Helped by Suleiman, Elizabeth expanded her knowledge of Mediterranean food and entertained as often as she could. '[Elizabeth] was an enthusiastic and very skilful cook,' recalled Jim Richards, who had joined the Ministry of Information in Cairo in the spring of 1943 as Director of Publications. '[She] gave lunch parties every other Sunday after spending much of Saturday scouring the bazaars for the ingredients she wanted. Invitations to these lunch parties were eagerly hoped for.'[5]

The lunches, as Elizabeth was the first to acknowledge, were a joint effort between her and Suleiman, on fairly primitive equipment. They had a portable charcoal grill and two primus stoves, while a square tin box perched on one of the stoves served as an oven. Since there was no ventilation in the kitchen, every time kebabs had to be cooked Suleiman had to run through the sitting room in a cloud of smoke and set the charcoal grill out on the river bank. 'The charcoal, the open air, Suleiman's rather lavish hand with the herbs and seasonings, his devoted watch over the meat all combined to produce a marvellous flavour, even if occasionally the quality of the meat left something to be desired.'[6]

Suleiman also made ice creams, 'with the help of an ancient ice bucket, which made the most fearful clatter as he whirled the handle round. However, everyone was used to it since the old ice pail, like a lot of other equipment, did the rounds in wartime Cairo and everybody was used to talking above it.'[7] As for everyday food, Elizabeth lived on 'highly flavoured, colourful shining vegetable dishes, lentil or fresh tomato soups, delicious spiced pilafs, lamb kebabs grilled over charcoal, salads with cool mint-flavoured yogurt dressings, the Egyptian fellahin dish of black beans with olive oil and lemon and hard-boiled eggs – these things were not only attractive but also cheap'.[8]

Another who remembers her well from those days is Josette d'Amade, a young girl from a middle-class Egyptian-Jewish family who also worked at the Ministry of Information. Josette used to walk home from work with Elizabeth, who often talked of her days in Paris and of the Barettes. Josette was sometimes invited to her lunches, which were very unlike what she was used to at home. 'The other guests were usually men – one was an illegitimate cousin of King Farouk – and most were in uniform. I couldn't join in much of the conversation, which seemed very sophisticated, and I knew it was rude to stare; so I spent most of the time quiet as a mouse, with my eyes lowered . . .'⁹ Josette, who had been brought up in a conventionally bourgeois family, had never met anyone like Elizabeth and found her an inspiration. Josette remembered Elizabeth saying that everyone should cultivate a measure of independence, in however small a way. On the other hand, her liberated attitudes were rather shocking to one who had been so strictly brought up.

Quite fortuitously, Josette had met Charles Gibson Cowan in Alexandria. She was staying with an aunt and uncle, and they had invited the skipper of a yacht in the harbour to dinner. Since he did not know the way, they walked the skipper back to the harbour at the end of the evening. They came on board, where Josette detected a delicious, lingering smell of something like coq au vin, which she immediately associated with Elizabeth. The cook turned out to be Charles. She told Elizabeth about the incident on her return to Cairo, and was amazed to hear that Elizabeth knew him well and that they had been together for the first two years of the war. Josette assumed they had been engaged. 'Good heavens, no!' laughed Elizabeth. 'I would never have *married* him.'¹⁰

Elizabeth and Charles had stayed constantly in touch since she had said goodbye to him in the summer of 1941. He had sent her the early chapters of *The Voyage of the Evelyn Hope* as he had written them, though there were certain passages she would not read. 'After Corsica you remember everything as well as I do,' she told him, 'and I don't want to think about it, talk about it or read about it ever again. From the minute we entered the straits of Messina until about the time the asphodels came out in Syros was just sheer torture.'¹¹

Elizabeth was uneasy and confused about Charles. She wanted to think of him as a friend, but he was also part of an experience she was trying very hard to forget. She wished he would go away, without her having to spell it out – but instead he sent her long, entertaining letters, and presents from his travels around Africa: old coins, a silver bracelet (perhaps the one she is wearing in the photograph of her at her desk in Cairo), books, an African carving – even, on one occasion, two bottles of good French wine. Elizabeth thanked him warmly for these gifts, her gratitude tinged with guilt.

Her real feelings emerged rapidly in August 1943, when Charles announced he was back in Alexandria and would like to come and see her in Cairo. She immediately sent him a telegram[12] begging him to leave her alone, and followed it up with two letters.

Please forgive me for what follows. Really and truly Charles I should prefer not to see you . . . Two years ago I would not have had the courage to so wound somebody, but I have been so inexpressibly hurt and unhappy that I feel I cannot bear any more. I have changed very much and I never want to have anything more to do with my life of before the war. To see you would rake up hellish memories of Athens. Be kind and don't make it happen.

After so many efforts I have met a man with whom I think I could be happy in a very unemotional way. I never want to feel a scrap of emotion for the rest of my life. He has been badly wounded and has gone away.

Her next letter was written along much the same lines, and she added

It's not that I don't feel a great gratitude for the time we spent together, but I rather thought you had understood that it was over really before we ever came to Egypt. I have had two rather painful years since you left, but I think I have found the answer now, and I do absolutely dread any emotion or the reminder of the unspeakable miseries of Italy and Athens and the first weeks in Cairo . . . I will never never return to the kind of existence I led before the war. I am a thousand times happier doing a job I love, living among my friends, than I was bashing around the place never knowing where I should be next week. I have learnt to make up my mind for myself, and not be influenced by emotions.[13]

Charles respected her wishes and, later that month, joined a secret mission organized by the naval section of the American Office of Strategic Services (OSS). This operation took him, mostly by night, to a number of Greek islands – including Syros. 'I passed near enough to Josipi's to see that the lemons were already ripe,' he wrote in his log on 15 September. He also plucked a branch of the dry thorn they had used for kindling, and sent it to Elizabeth when he got back.

This memento, touching as it was, failed to rekindle Elizabeth. She resolutely turned her mind once again to her work, her friends and her lunch parties. Occasionally she went up to Alexandria, staying either with Georges de Menasce or with Eve Cohen and Larry Durrell at the Villa Ambron. They sometimes had Charles to stay too; though Elizabeth made sure they did not coincide.

In February 1944, Elizabeth met an Indian Army officer, Lt Col. Anthony David. Tony David was a small, fastidiously dressed man with kind eyes and a quick, diffident smile. Elizabeth found him attractive and she enjoyed watching the effect she had on him: this young Lieutenant Colonel from the Royal Deccan Horse had obviously never come across anyone like her before.

Tony David was the youngest son of Ivor David, who had been Inspector General of Police in Ceylon. He was born in 1911: ten years after his sister Yvonne, and nine years after his brother Richard. With such an age gap, Tony felt almost like an only child. His father had died in 1913, and his mother Beatrice moved back to Llandaff, where his father's family came from.

He was sent to Bradfield College in Berkshire, where he made friends with a boy called Owen Llewellyn. Owen was a few months older than Tony, who happily tagged along. Owen asked him home for the holidays, and Tony was delighted. For the first time in his life, he found himself in a noisy household full of children and dogs, and – best of all – the Welsh ponies bred by Mrs Griffith Llewellyn, Owen's mother.

This arrangement suited his own mother rather well. A young boy needed the company of other boys and men, and with the Llewellyns Tony would have it – leaving her with more time for her older children, and her own interests. Beatrice David was by all accounts a glamorous, cosmopolitan woman. She had no particular desire to be stuck in Wales with her husband's family, and escaped to Paris or Vienna whenever she could.

With the Llewellyns Tony learned to ride, taking to it naturally, and his happiest childhood holidays were spent with them. But while he was always willing to join in, he did not shine in a crowd. He was always on the edge of the circle.

After Bradfield Tony went to Pembroke College, Cambridge, in 1930. He had already decided on a career in the Army and so did not take an honours degree but an ordinary BA, specializing in history and military subjects. After taking his degree he applied to join the Indian Army, and went out to India in 1934 as an officer cadet attached to the First Battalion The Cameronians (Scottish Rifles). After this spell of service with a British regiment, each young officer spent a probationary period with the Indian regiment of his choice – in his case, the Royal Deccan Horse.

The fact that Tony had gone to Cambridge rather than Sandhurst automatically made him something of an outsider in the tight community of young officers. He soon developed a reputation as a chap more comfortable with women than with men, and his success with the opposite sex did little to endear him to his brother officers. There was also his dark wavy hair, and his name – in other words, the hint of an unspoken suspicion that he might be Jewish. Indian cavalry regiments were not renowned for their liberalism.

'We all tried to be nice to him, but he didn't fit in at all,' said one of his contemporaries. 'He just wasn't one of us.' No doubt Tony felt it too. When he left in 1938, to be ADC to Sir Henry Craik, Governor of the Punjab, his brother officers were relieved. 'We knew he would never come back.'

In 1941, he transferred to the Indian Army Ordnance Corps: which, from a cavalry point of view, was a considerable step down, even if it meant accelerated promotion. He arrived in Egypt in July 1942, at the time of Alamein. A year later, in October, he was posted to GHQ Cairo. Here he met up again with Hermione – by now Lady Ranfurly – and Daphne Llewellyn, his friend Owen's younger sisters. Daphne was then working with SOE. Every morning Tony would pick her up from the Continental Hotel, where she lived, and gave her a lift to work in his car. He treated her with a sort of cosy protectiveness, as though she were a younger sister.

Despite his change of regiment, Tony never lost his passion for horses. He raced and played polo at the Gezira Sporting Club, exercised horses in the desert, and was a regular in a number of Cairene cocktail bars. He was often with a girl, the larger the better. He was particularly smitten by Miranda Lampson, the wild niece of Sir Miles Lampson, the British Ambassador in Cairo.

That this kind, rather uninteresting young man should have fallen head over heels in love with Elizabeth Gwynne is not surprising. He admired her fearlessness, her wit, her sensual beauty, the line of her long neck as she smoked or drank. She gave a sharp edge to life; and in her he saw the colour and the sparkle that he himself lacked. As for Elizabeth, her restless and abrasive character probably found his uncomplicated devotion rather restful. In one of his letters he recalled the first time she had rung him up. When he asked why, she had replied, ' "Just to talk." I think that's the first time I thought you considered me as more than just someone to pass away the time with, and I was so pleased.'[14]

Soon after that, Elizabeth came down with influenza. Tony came round to see her in the little ground-floor flat and asked if he could join her there. 'Thank God you were ill and didn't have the energy to say No,' he wrote later. So Tony moved in. She must have been

quite fond of him because he came with a dog: a large, panting
Alsatian called Bruce.

Her illness proved worse than influenza: it was a form of smallpox
(fortunately too mild to leave scars) which was going around Cairo.
Elizabeth was whisked away to a quarantine hospital in Kantara.
Tony came to fetch her when she was eventually allowed out, and
one of his happiest memories of her was as she ran down the path
towards him.

In the spring of 1944, Elizabeth and Tony became a recognized
couple on the Cairene social scene. Elizabeth's friend and lover,
George Lassalle, sometimes used to borrow his Royal Deccan Horse
mess-dress uniform because he liked it so much. But while George
was swaggering about impressing the girls in Tony's dark green
jacket and gold waistcoat, Tony and Elizabeth led a quieter social
life. It would begin when he came to pick Elizabeth up in the
evenings. 'When I came to fetch you,' he remembered, 'you used
to look up and say in a very quiet voice, "Hello Tony." '[15] From
there they would go for drinks at the Eugène or the Pickwick, where
there was a gramophone, then on for shrimps at Hedjaki's, and
from there to one of the little restaurants by the Nile. Daphne Llewellyn remembers seeing them in a crowd of people. Tony had eyes only
for Elizabeth, but she paid very little attention to him. Back in the
privacy of 'the cave', however, things were different. Tony's letters
imply that their lovemaking was intensely satisfying for them both.

As the weeks wore on, it became increasingly likely that Tony
would have to leave for Italy. They were in bed and asleep when
the summons came, in the early hours of one morning in mid-May.

Elizabeth found herself alone with Bruce the dog, who was not
perhaps the best memento of her lover. She had no alternative but
to take Bruce to the office every day and, if invited out to lunch, she
had to take the dog with her. Tony often found himself having to
soothe Elizabeth's irritation, and excuse Bruce's bad behaviour.
'Sweetheart Bruce has *never* done that previously and I can only
think his tummy must have been upset.'[16] Or, 'I know that hysterical

yap of Bruce's well. It's slightly nerve-racking but shows he is devoted to you . . .'[17]

In Italy, Lt Col. David found that he was either worked to the point of exhaustion or – once the crisis had passed – left with almost nothing to do. Either way he missed Elizabeth cruelly and wrote to her once a day, if not more. One of the most poignant things he wrote to Elizabeth was 'You made me love coming home, a thing I have never done in my life. Everything was such fun. Do you remember cooking supper about two nights before I went, we had fried bananas, eggs, tomatoes, fried bread and bacon. I've seldom enjoyed a supper like it.'[18]

She made life utterly delightful, and he was startled by the intensity of his feelings for her – and his sexual jealousy. Elizabeth had made no secret of her previous affairs and had made no promises to Tony. She was not the sort of girl to sit at home and wait, and there were plenty of men waiting to take her out. Every letter from her, however affectionate, reminded him of these facts.

'I think it nothing short of rude, the three boys renewing their attentions the morning after I left,' he wrote. 'Don't lose your head over Jim Scott-Ellis and if you can hold out for longer than three months this time, for the first time in my life I should mind terribly – Is that an awful thing to say darling?'[19]

Tony became convinced that the only way to hold on to Elizabeth was to marry her. On 21 June, a month after they parted, Tony found out that he would be entitled to return to Cairo on leave in some six weeks' time. He plucked up his courage, and proposed:

'Elizabeth, please marry me darling and if you will, marry me when I come on leave. I want it more than anything else in the world . . . Your letter today was so sweet that I've just said to myself, "I'll try."'

He was in agonies the following day. 'I'm going to spend the most unpleasant fortnight of my life now until I get your letter in answer to mine of yesterday . . . You once said, "It doesn't matter what we do, I'm sure we'll do it well and enjoy it madly." We always did, didn't we and there was never a dull moment, even when you threw the work-basket at me.' (This was what happened on the one occasion Tony asked her to sew on a button.)

Tony's letter threw Elizabeth into turmoil. She knew that she did not really love him, and that he was not her intellectual equal. She did not even like the institution of marriage, which seemed deadening and claustrophobic. Yet she yearned for stability, and was also a pragmatist. It was a fact of her world that until a woman married, she had very little status; and once married, she could command a respect that was seldom granted to a spinster. If she did not accept Tony, who was at least kind and devoted, might she ever be asked again? All the women she felt closest to were married – her sisters Priscilla and Diana, her friends Marian, Doreen and Renée. If she did not join the clan soon, it might be too late. At the end of the year she was going to turn thirty-one. It was a sobering thought.

Her letter back to Tony was anguished, fretful and still undecided. 'Darling I can just imagine the state my letter put you into,' wrote Tony, 'because I do know quite well how madly you've always thought and fought against marriage . . . I know it was an awful thing to . . . spring it on you like that . . . but when I heard I really could come [to Cairo on leave] I just prayed and hoped you wouldn't mind . . . No darling I promise I won't refer to you in your presence as my wife.'[20] In another letter he also promised her that, if they ever went to India together, 'you won't have to flog the natives or watch polo – ever'.[21]

Elizabeth eventually accepted Tony, but everything was to be done in the greatest secrecy, 'with no squawking'. He wrote back at once, assuring her that they would be married in the very greatest seclusion. He begged her to ask Robin Fedden to arrange the calling of the banns: that was what took time, and he wanted that over by the time he came back so that they could be married at once.

In the days that followed, Elizabeth evidently grew more accustomed to the idea, to Tony's intense relief. 'I'm glad that you are happy about marrying me darling, and that you like my name and won't mind being Elizabeth David.'[22]

A few days later, Tony collapsed and was taken to hospital. He had gone to the doctor for sleeping pills, and had mistakenly been given a drug which produced a high fever and dysentery. He was in hospital for a good two weeks, during which time Elizabeth sent him a letter full of misgivings. She pointed out her faults and all her previous affairs, said she did not like the idea of India (apart from the fact that she could wear slacks there more often than in Cairo) and perhaps they should call the whole thing off. Tony lost his temper.

> Now listen, enough of this, whether you get a sensation out of informing me you are going to go to bed with someone or what I don't know, but I was stupid enough to tell you how much I minded once and I can't have these long-drawn dissertations on the reasons for your frailties in the past. I dislike them more than I can say even in the lightest vein, and it's no good saying, 'I thought you would much rather I was frank about it,' because I wouldn't . . . And what's more it is going to be a good idea if we get married. If we can live together in the cave for even the short time we did and not kill each other I think it's a good enough test . . . And you can quite well come to India for a short time and like it. It will be a novelty, and I certainly shouldn't dream of allowing you to wear slacks even if you want to . . . I can't think where you got the idea that the whole of India goes about in them . . .[23]

In Elizabeth's pocket diary for 1944 (a document she used only sporadically) there are no entries at all from 18 August, which was probably the time Tony came back. Perhaps she joined him when he took a few days' leave to visit his mother, who had now settled in Kenya; but they were back in Cairo at the end of August. On the 30th, which was a Wednesday, Elizabeth wrote '*Married*'. The civil service was about as quiet and simple as it could be, since none of Elizabeth or Tony's family were present. It is significant that no photograph of their wedding exists, or has survived.

They spent their honeymoon in Cyprus with relations of Tony's called the Grisewoods, and they were happy – or at least Tony was. After the honeymoon they moved back to Cairo, where Elizabeth resumed her job. In November, Tony was posted back to Italy.

He wrote every day: mostly the stuff of love letters, but one letter gives a vivid picture of their early married life. 'I'm longing to do things with you again,' he wrote on 18 November, 'to dance with you like we did at the Carlton, to go to parties and hear people say how nice you look, to stay at home and mix the drinks while you are giving some unfortunate hell in the kitchen for boiling the artichokes too long. And then to have you erupt from the kitchen and demand your drink as though you hadn't had one for a week, actually . . . having just returned five minutes ago from an hour and a half's solid drinking in our various bars.'

Elizabeth was resigned to domestic life with Tony. After all, many marriages had started with less and fared well, and the advantage of not being wildly in love was that she had fewer expectations. She could never have married Peter, of that she was convinced; and whatever Tony's shortcomings, he loved her wholeheartedly and exclusively. She had never had so much love before, and for the moment, her misgivings melted in its warmth.

Her family wished her well, though her sister Diana recognized that Elizabeth's marriage would never be as fulfilling as her own. 'I'm a little sad for her,' she wrote to her husband Christopher on 2 September. 'It's not a wild love affair on her part – but he sounds very nice, and she wrote to Mummie and said that they would be very happy – he adores her.'

Diana had never met Tony and so was prepared to give him the benefit of the doubt; but Elizabeth's friends in Cairo could not understand why she had married him. Renée Fedden made no secret of the fact that she thought the match a mistake, and Georges de Menasce remarked that Elizabeth marrying Tony was 'like a horse marrying a fish'. Hermione Ranfurly admitted that she knew Tony far better than Elizabeth; but she assumed the only reason for Elizabeth's decision to marry was that 'she needed a good ADC'. Tony was always only too happy to make himself useful, especially as her chauffeur: Elizabeth never did learn to drive.

Elizabeth was too perceptive not to be aware that many of the people she most respected were not impressed by Tony. Perhaps this was why she always seemed rather reluctant to talk about him, and certainly her letter to Peter Laing announcing her marriage was reticent in the extreme. 'Many thanks for your letter telling me of your marriage,' wrote Peter from Montreal on 10 December. 'I hasten to wish you every happiness and I am sure you will be happy too. Your brief note, however, does not disclose in any manner the identity of the fortunate man. In fact, it is written in such a way that all that appears to have occurred is that you have changed your name.'

As for Norman Douglas, the man whom Elizabeth admired most in the world, she could not bring herself to tell him. He found out, of course; but being acutely aware of people's privacy, and perhaps guessing that he would not think much of her choice, he waited for her to mention it first. On 31 July 1945, he wrote, 'Yes! I knew about your marriage ages ago through Neil. But he could not remember your name, and perhaps I haven't got it right either. Anyhow, I hope all goes well?'

Many years later, when Olivia Manning's *Fortunes of War* had been dramatized for television and the books were being read by a new generation, Elizabeth told a friend that she had been 'very much in that world'.[24] There is no character in the novels who is remotely recognizable as Elizabeth, least of all Edwina, a beautiful but empty-headed good-time girl. Yet the point at which Edwina announces that she is going to marry a dull army major called Tony, while still in love with a far more exciting man called Peter, must have given Elizabeth a stab of recognition:

'Good heavens,' said Dobson, 'not Tony Brody!'

'Why not? He's a major and a nice man.'

'I should have thought you could do better than Brody.'

Edwina, sniffing behind her curtain of hair, said dismally: 'There's not much choice these days. The most exciting men have all gone to Tunisia and I don't think they're coming back.'

'Even so. Be sensible and wait . . . You're still as beautiful as a dream and you don't want to marry Brody.'

'Oh, I might as well. If you can't marry the man you want, does it matter who you marry?'[25]

* * * * * * * *

CHAPTER NINE

Indian Interlude

The war was over, but the grief over dead friends and family was still painfully raw. Elizabeth had lost her cousin Jasper Ridley (son of her Uncle Jasper and Aunt Nathalie) in 1943, and Mike Cumberlege had been taken prisoner while trying to plant mines in the Corinth Canal. Elizabeth knew he had been captured; but it was only later that she heard what happened to him. From Greece Cumberlege was eventually taken to Sachsenhausen. There he was interrogated, tortured and kept for many months in solitary confinement. He might have survived; but in 1945, a few days before the arrival of the advancing Allies, he was taken out and shot.

In June 1945, Tony David was posted back to India, as one of the great swarm of staff officers surrounding General Auchinleck in New Delhi. Elizabeth stayed on in Cairo, bound by her job with the Ministry of Information. Towards the end of the year she managed to wangle a trip on Ministry of Information business to Athens. This city, which she had once loathed and where she had been so miserable, now seemed intoxicating and was full of friends. Elizabeth was delighted to be in Greece again, a feeling heightened by the fact that she had already decided she was not going to like India.

She saw in the New Year at the hospitable house at Bulaq Dacrour, where she had spent the miserable Christmas of 1942 with the Feddens while Peter Laing was in hospital. This time, the party consisted of Patrick Leigh Fermor, Patrick Kinross, Eddie Gathorne-

Hardy and Elizabeth. Paddy Leigh Fermor described it as a memorable evening: 'There were a lot of jokes, a lot of loose and reckless talk, and I suppose we all got pretty tight.'

Tony had been allocated a flat in a series of modern blocks on Kingsway in New Delhi. It was bare and cheerless; but Tony had done his best to make it more comfortable before Elizabeth arrived, and while waiting he spent most of his free time at the Gymkhana Club, around which the lives of horse-loving British officers revolved. Among the friends he met at the Gymkhana Club were two people who became so important to Elizabeth that she dedicated two of her future books to them: Veronica Meagher and Peter Higgins.

Peter Higgins was a stockbroker by profession, who was then in the uniform of the King's Royal Rifle Corps. To his regret he did not join his battalion when they went to fight in north Africa in 1941. He was given a staff appointment instead, which took him first to Algeria and then to Italy, before being sent to India, where he became involved in the enormous task of repatriating the British side of the Indian Army before independence (for which he was awarded the OBE in 1945). He appeared in New Delhi some time after Tony: they became friends through a mutual interest in horses and racing. Peter was a man of great charm and entertaining conversation. He was good-looking in a fair, Anglo-Saxon way, though his tendency to put on weight led his less charitable friends to call him Piggins.

Veronica Meagher had come out from England as a junior civil assistant, a post created for young women so that they could take over army desk jobs, thus releasing young officers for more important duties. She, Tony and Peter often found themselves together, and Veronica became more and more intrigued by the idea of Tony's wife. Elizabeth was due to come out and join her husband that winter, and Tony could think of little else. He became increasingly nervous as the time for her arrival drew close.

In January 1946, Elizabeth finally arrived in India. Veronica remembers seeing her for the first time. 'She was wearing a fly-fronted, square-shouldered jacket, and looked terribly chic and sophisticated.'[1] Tony danced attendance on her, eager for her slightest smile; but while she seemed perfectly agreeable to him, she was not demonstrably affectionate. Elizabeth probaby met Tony's friend Peter Higgins at about the same time. It became obvious very soon that Elizabeth did not find India as congenial as Cairo; but with Tony, Veronica and Peter Higgins for company, life was bearable.

Elizabeth was touched by the pains that Tony had taken to make their flat habitable; but she was appalled by the kitchen, a stuffy room which made the one she had had in Cairo look positively well-equipped. One of Elizabeth's favourite writers, Col. Kenney-Herbert, had in the 1870s written in thundering tones about the squalor of the average Indian kitchen: it was usually the dirtiest and foulest room in the compound, with no running water and sited next to the cesspit. Seventy years later, Elizabeth found the state of kitchens was still very primitive – but when she tried to improve matters, even she found that the pace of change could not be forced.

The cook (who more or less came with the flat) was very indignant when he realized that Elizabeth thought of his kitchen as her territory. Memsahibs were there to give orders. They didn't cook, and they certainly weren't supposed to introduce diabolical foreign contraptions (a Primus stove) that might well have burnt the flat down. Two cooks were fired in quick succession, and Elizabeth developed a reputation for upsetting servants.

Veronica was at that time living with the Earl and Countess of Carlisle. Biddy Carlisle was Director of the Women's Auxiliary Corps in India, and cultivated a wide circle of cosmopolitan friends. Through Veronica, the young Davids were invited. Tony, who enjoyed rubbing shoulders with the smart set, was delighted; and one might have expected that Elizabeth would have found Biddy Carlisle's guests more interesting than the usual round of officers and memsahibs. However, Elizabeth refused to be drawn in. She adopted an air of studied nonchalance which infuriated her hostess. 'Where does she come from? What sort of a name is David anyway?' demanded Lady Carlisle. She had no time for young women who did not pull their weight at a dinner table.

Right from the start, Elizabeth loathed British India. She hated the colossal scale of Lutyens's and Baker's ceremonial centre, and the monotony of the residential districts that radiated from it. And in Connaught Circle, the much-vaunted shopping centre that claimed to be the most exciting spot in New Delhi, there was not a single café or bar in which to while away the hours. Part of her frustration with India was that after having held down a responsible job, she had no work and nothing to occupy her time. She did not attempt to get any work, probably because she knew that she could not work with people she found so complacently dull. Even England would look exciting after a few months in New Delhi, surrounded as she was by people whose lives revolved around racing and polo, and who could not see further than the next vice-regal garden party. And however much she hated being a wifely appendage to Tony, she had no excuse for missing the races or polo matches he took part in.

The food too was very frustrating. On the British side, it consisted of boarding-school fare, in which a meal began with a nondescript bowl of Brown Windsor soup, went on to boiled beef and carrots and ended with chocolate shape. Then there were supposedly French dishes spiced with hot green chillies and, 'oddest of all, Edwardian fantasies of the school which liked to present food in any form but its own (mashed potatoes got up to resemble a roast chicken, mushrooms made out of meringue and the like)'.[2] On the Indian side, she was at first rather encouraged: meals were served like Middle Eastern food, with lots of inviting little dishes full of different things; but when she tasted them, Elizabeth found the ubiquitous taste of hot chilli peppers so overwhelming that it killed everything else. However, she did love the pilafs and hot Indian breads.

*

The only thing that made life pleasant was the little clique of herself and Tony, Peter and Veronica, who became her closest friend. Veronica admits that she was nothing like as well-read as Elizabeth, who spent much of her time in India rereading Proust and Henry James. But she was lively and fun, and Elizabeth was grateful for her company. As for Veronica, she found Elizabeth fascinating. One minute she could be so difficult and prickly that everything seemed to rub her up the wrong way; and the next she was being wonderfully funny and light-hearted, and it was with Elizabeth that Veronica most enjoyed 'the giggly side of it all'.

Having nothing better to do, she and Veronica often went to the cinema, or to have their hair done. Veronica remembered that Elizabeth's thick, already greying hair was arranged in short, tight curls which suited her very well. Together they explored the markets of Old Delhi – something Elizabeth also enjoyed doing with her young maid, a beautiful girl scarcely older than a child. At first she was terribly shy, and very reluctant to go to Old Delhi; but Elizabeth befriended and reassured her, and the girl did her best to satisfy Elizabeth's persistent curiosity about everything they saw.

On another occasion Elizabeth, Tony, Veronica and some other friends went for a moonlit picnic in the grounds of the Qtub Minar. They had only just arrived and were pulling the cork out of a bottle of Australian wine when they suddenly found themselves surrounded by a pack of dogs. The dogs did not seem to be interested in the food: 'they simply formed a circle round us at a respectful distance and stared and howled.'[3] They were chased away, but came back in even greater numbers, howling as loudly as ever, and since they made conversation impossible, the party was obliged to pack up and go home. This little glimpse of her Indian life is from *Summer Cooking*, and is one of the very few times when she recalled her time in India in writing.

With the coming of summer, Delhi began to get stiflingly hot. The climate brought Elizabeth a severe attack of sinusitis, and to get away from the cauldron she and Tony went on a trip to Darjeeling.

They took the night train to Calcutta, and then took the astonishing mountain railway to Darjeeling itself. They went to their hotel and, still feeling dazed from the altitude and the ride, repaired to the bar where Tony ordered a couple of martinis. The barman gave the usual virtuoso display with the cocktail shaker, though he confided to Tony that there was no ice: the hotel's refrigerator had broken down. Elizabeth never forgot that warm martini, which they drank while looking on to a landscape of eternal ice: the freezing summits of the Himalayas. Their hotel had other interesting features. Orchids grew out of the mud floor of the bathroom, and just below their bedroom was an open-air cinema where they were showing *Salome* with Yvonne de Carlo – in continuous performances, for most of the night. She and Tony were warned to watch out for cat burglars. These highly skilled thieves, they were told, always tickled the toes of their victims to make sure they were properly asleep before rifling through their possessions. To Veronica, who had just gone to Rome, Elizabeth wrote that all was well, and that so far their toes had not been tickled.

They returned to Delhi on 6 July, but Elizabeth was no better: she was finally taken to hospital on the 12th. The doctors told her she stood no chance of recovery if she spent the rest of the summer in the heat of the plain: she must go home. She hoped to stop off in Cairo on the way back. Eddie Gathorne-Hardy was delighted at the idea, and in a long letter gave her the latest news of the Feddens, and Norman Douglas, whom he had seen in England. 'He had rather been taken under the wing of Viva and Willie King who are old friends of mine. He spoke very affectionately of you. He was just off to Naples. A little gaga he was, and boozing fairly hard, but awfully sweet, amusing and cynical, not to say dirty-minded. I love him.'[4]

Elizabeth left India in early August, and did not stop off in Cairo. Soon after her return, she went to lunch with her Aunt Grace and cousin Anne in London. Anne recalled that Elizabeth was really vehement in describing how much she had loathed India. She and her mother were both left with the impression that something had gone terribly wrong there.

* * * * * * * *

CHAPTER TEN

Back in Blighty

Elizabeth arrived home with even less than when she had set out. Her luggage consisted of a few light clothes, some books and a haphazard collection of recipes. Little remained of the life she had once had: her own possessions, put into storage in 1938, had been destroyed by bombs. She had been away from England for six years, and in that time she, and England, had changed beyond recognition.

In those six years, she had found a mentor in Norman Douglas, spent a winter in Antibes, sailed into the war on the *Evelyn Hope*, been interned, lived in Athens, Syros, Alexandria, Cairo and India. Norman Douglas had laid the foundations of the way she thought not only about food, but about history, the Mediterranean world and the way life should be lived. In Syros she had had to cope with enforced loneliness and idleness; but she had also learnt how to cook the everyday food of the Mediterranean, a process continued in Egypt. She was a long way beyond the 'marrons glacés in half an hour' school of cookery. In Cairo, the experience of setting up and running a reference library had given her a far clearer idea of what she could achieve as a professional working woman, and developed her taste for scholarship as well.

Emotionally too she had grown up, and discovered just how much of herself she could give to a relationship. While she had been prepared to devote herself to Peter Laing in hospital and give him back the will to live, she would not follow him to Canada and share the burden of his disability. She was still brooding and grieving over that decision when Tony appeared. He was perhaps the only man in her life to love her so completely, but she was well aware that while he had married for love, she had made a marriage of convenience.

Seeing her mother and sisters again amply made up for the greyness of London, at least at first. Priscilla had two little girls, Sabrina and Julia, while Diana was expecting her first child. Among all the other family news, Elizabeth also heard the details of the terrible rift that now divided Diana from their Aunt Violet.

Diana had once been Violet's favourite niece, and it was confidently expected that Violet would leave Diana her magnificent collection of jewellery. However, Violet had disapproved strongly of Diana's engagement to Christopher Grey, because she had a pathological hatred of doctors. The final break between aunt and niece had taken place some time after Diana's marriage. Diana had been at lunch with Violet, who had launched into a tirade against the man she held personally responsible for the continuation of the war – Winston Churchill. Diana, whose husband was serving in Burma in the Royal Army Medical Corps, understandably lost her temper. Fierce words were exchanged, after which Diana walked out and never entered her aunt's house again.

Dr Grey had returned home safely, and he and Diana settled into 9 Abingdon Road, Kensington, where he had his practice on the ground floor. The house was set back a little from the road. Two trees had been planted either side of the path, and these had grown towards each other at such an angle that a tall man, like Dr Grey, had to duck under their branches to reach the front door.

Elizabeth moved in with them and, as Diana's first pregnancy wore on, she took over the shopping and cooking. 'One day,' wrote Elizabeth,

I took back to her, among the broken biscuits and the tins of snoek . . . one pound of fresh tomatoes. As I took them out of my basket to show her I saw that tears were tumbling down my sister's beautiful and normally serene face.

'For God's sake, what's the matter?'

'Sorry. It's just that I've been trying to buy fresh tomatoes for five years. And now it's you who've found them first.'[1]

Elizabeth's first flat in London was within walking distance of Diana at 29 Cheniston Gardens, just off Kensington High Street. The kitchen table was also the cover for the bath; but she did have a gas cooker and a small fridge.

She was not without friends, many of them from Cairo: David and Mary Abercrombie, Lesley O'Malley, who had worked with Elizabeth in the Ministry of Information in Cairo, the art historian Cecil Gould, Denis Freeman and Neville Phillips, and Renée and Robin Fedden – he had just started his long career in the National Trust as curator of Polesden Lacey. Elizabeth also ran into Olivia Manning's husband, Reggie Smith, whom she had not seen since Cairo. She was rather startled when he greeted her with the words, 'Elizabeth, how lovely to see you! Let's fuck.'

While descriptions of post-war London are familiar, it always takes an effort of imagination to remember just how bleak it was – particularly to someone who had been living in warm climates without bombs and rationing. For Doris Lessing, fresh from South Africa, London was an assault on the senses. 'It was unpainted, buildings were stained and cracked and dull and grey; it was war-damaged, some areas all ruins, and under them holes full of dirty water, once cellars, and it was subject to sudden dark fogs . . . No cafés. No good restaurants. Clothes were dismal and ugly . . . Everyone was indoors by ten, and the streets empty . . . Any conversation tended to drift towards the war, like an animal licking a sore place.'[2]

As far as rationing was concerned, 1946 had been a very disappointing year. Fears of a world famine meant that bread was rationed for the first time in Britain. Rice was no longer imported, and increases in the allowances of meat, bacon and eggs failed to materialize. Nevertheless, Elizabeth saw rationing as a challenge. 'Everyone else had hoards of things like powdered soups and packets of dehydrated egg to which they were conditioned. I started off untrammelled; an empty cupboard was an advantage. With whatever I could get I cooked like one possessed.'

Elizabeth's satisfaction at her empty cupboard also indicates that while she had to cope with current shortages like everyone else, she had not experienced the solidarity that rationing had given people while the war was being fought. The fact that *everyone* was eating vegetable mince and steamed bread pudding while the lads were at the front had made women feel involved in the war effort. As Marguerite Patten wrote in *The Victory Cookbook*, 'We people at home could not let the forces down, we had to play our part too.'[3] And, as the same author points out, there was much to be celebrated. The population as a whole had a healthier diet than before the war and had become skilful at making the most of what little they had.

Elizabeth, on the other hand, could only compare English food with what she had become accustomed to. 'What I found out when I returned to England . . . was that while my own standard of living in Egypt had perhaps not been very high, my food had always had some sort of life, colour, guts, stimulus; there had always been bite, flavour and inviting smells. These elements were totally absent from English meals.'[4] Entertaining was still possible, with a little imagination. Everyone contributed, and every gift – no matter how odd – was celebrated as a change from the monotony of everyday wartime food: a wild goose, mock liver pâté from Fortnum's, British-Government-bought Algerian wine. 'One of my sisters,' wrote Elizabeth, 'turned up from Vienna with a hare which she claimed had been caught by hand outside the State Opera House.'[5] It was Felicité. She had worked for the Admiralty during the war, which had brought her typing and secretarial skills up to a high level. She had then joined the British administration of occupied Vienna.

'Game was plentiful that year. Even if one didn't actually catch pheasants in Kensington High Street, one could buy them very cheaply in the shops. Wild duck, although distinctly fishy some of them, were not more than a shilling apiece. My landlady, living in the flat below mine, was saintly. Not once did she complain about the cooking smells, the garlic, the onions, those eternal bacon bones simmering in the stock . . ."[6]

No doubt the landlady recognized that whatever was cooking in Elizabeth's pots smelled rather good; but not everyone was convinced by the sort of cooking Elizabeth practised.

'About a year after the end of the war,' she wrote, 'I spent a couple of months in a large, bleak, isolated country house trying to help out a woman friend with the cooking and domestic chores.' This friend of hers, whom Elizabeth calls 'Janet', had two children and no domestic help of any kind; and with grim determination, she cooked what she thought was sensible English food.

What struck Elizabeth was the sheer amount of hard labour that producing such food entailed. Potatoes, sprouts and cabbage all had to be peeled and prepared for the Sunday lunch, and each boiled up separately on top of the stove and cooked till flabby – which was not a very economical use of fuel. Elizabeth suggested that the weekly hunk of ration meat be stewed with the vegetables, which would have meant less work and less fuel. '"The children," said Janet in a chilly voice, "look forward to their Sunday roast. We can't deprive them of it." It wasn't for me to try and deflect Janet from what she conceived to be her duty.'

One day however, 'I got fed up with the loathsome job of making the traditional-style gravy to which Janet had been taught to add the cabbage water as well as some sort of thickening. Deceitfully, I chucked the cabbage water into the garden . . . and added to the meat juices instead a glass of cheap red wine. Janet had no objection to this at first, but suddenly became alarmed at the way the children' (then aged six and four) 'spooned the wine-flavoured sauce into their mouths with such evident relish.' Elizabeth assured her friend that her children would not turn into juvenile alcoholics, since all the alcohol had evaporated in the cooking; but Janet was not convinced. 'Back we had to go to that barbarous gravy routine. And so it went on. Back-breaking cleaning of vegetables, boiling of stodgy puddings, painful waste of fuel. I had always thought it impossible not to enjoy cooking, but now it had indeed become that drudgery of which so many English women complain all their lives.'[7]

Looking back, the woman who refused to let Elizabeth David cook for her attracts the same sort of incredulous pity as the publisher who turned down *Pride and Prejudice* – yet her reaction is understandable. Elizabeth was probably none too tactful in presenting her ideas, and Janet no doubt felt she was being steamrollered into a way of cooking that was, to her, totally alien.

The winter of 1946–7 was the coldest in living memory, and the cold set in in November. Elizabeth, who had spent the last six years in hot climates, had no store of old coats and darned cardigans. 'At this moment somebody put into my head the idea of going to stay, at reduced all-in rates, in a hotel in Ross-on-Wye. You may well ask . . . I didn't. I just went.'[8]

The 'somebody' was George Lassalle, that raffish, funny, fish-loving friend of Elizabeth's who used to borrow Tony's uniform in Cairo. The son of a doctor, George had strayed from his strict Catholic upbringing and, at this stage in his life, was following his inclinations wherever they led him. Unlike many men he was not daunted by Elizabeth.

They had been lovers off and on in Cairo, and now their affair blossomed again with a new intensity. They were both disenchanted with their own marriages, admitted to each other that they had made a mistake. George felt that at one moment 'marriage was in the air'[9] between them, yet Elizabeth would never have taken the idea seriously. She was very fond of George and loved his company, but he lived life for the moment, and did not have the sort of steadiness that Elizabeth looked for in a potential husband. She was also dubious about the combination of her own dark looks and his: 'We might have black babies,' she laughed. (Curiously, Elizabeth's sister Diana worried about having 'black babies' too, and mentioned it more than once to her friend Roger Ellis. Perhaps the Gwynne girls feared that the Indonesian genes of the Purvises might suddenly re-emerge in force.)

Having babies was not, however, something that Elizabeth ever seriously considered. She was remarkably free of all maternal feelings, rather as her mother was; babies stirred nothing in her but a faint distaste. Elizabeth had seen how motherhood, especially on a budget, destroys all independence, and she had no intention of letting it happen to her.

As for George, the idea of marrying Elizabeth was considerably discouraged by the blatantly snobbish attitude of her mother and sisters. One might read their chilliness towards him as dismay: here was another of those ebullient, bohemian, 'not-quite-our-class' buccaneers who, like Charles Gibson Cowan, Elizabeth seemed to find so irresistibly attractive.

They left London with a lot of books and all their warmest clothes and snuggled down in a hotel at Ross-on-Wye. It was one of three hotels belonging to a well-known chain (Trust Houses Ltd), and Elizabeth's room was deliciously warm after London: there was a coal fire in the public sitting room, and a maid to bring hot-water bottles and breakfast in bed.

Ross-on-Wye provided little entertainment, beyond the pubs which were such a feature of the town. She and George went on pub crawls sampling innumerable different varieties of cider, but they also found considerable amusement in Miss Deakin's antique shop. It was piled from floor to ceiling with a jumble of antiques and bric-a-brac, and Miss Deakin had no hesitation in pulling out anything her customers might wish to see from any part of the pile. Elizabeth bought a Leeds dish, the pair to which was (like so much of Miss Deakin's stock) already broken. It was George Lassalle who rescued, and gave to Elizabeth, a white jug with black transfers of John Wesley's head and a building called the Centenary Hall, dated 1839.

As Miss D. took my cheque her elbow jogged the tap of a copper tea-urn perched on top of a model four-masted barque in a heavy box frame. It knocked over a solid silver clock representing General Gordon sitting on a horse, which fell against a scrap screen, a japanned tray and a tortoiseshell and silver-inlaid musical box. The guts of the little musical-box cracked out on to the floor. Miss D. was unshaken. 'Take care how you go out,' she said.[10]

But even the warmth of the hotel and the thrills and spills of Miss Deakin's antique shop could not make up for the misery of the food. 'Conditions *were* awful, shortages *did* make catering a nightmare. And *still* there was no excuse, none, for such unspeakably dismal meals as in that dining room were put in front of me. To my agonized homesickness for the sun and southern food was added an embattled rage that we should be asked – and should accept – the endurance of such cooking.'[11] She thought of going back to London, but by that time the ice and snow had given way to heavy rain and severe flooding. Stuck in Ross-on-Wye, there was nothing to ease the 'embattled rage' but pen and paper.

Elizabeth had been collecting, refining and developing recipes for at least ten years. She lost one collection when she and Charles were forced to abandon the *Evelyn Hope*, and had amassed another during her time in Greece, Egypt and India. Yet all her previous writing had been geared to recipes: what ingredients to use, what one might add, the best way to cook a dish. In Ross-on-Wye, she was not writing lists and instructions; for the first time, she was writing *about food*: a food that was not only unavailable, but that could not even be approached without a completely different set of priorities than those that governed kitchens in wartime England.

She began 'to work out an agonized craving for the sun and a furious revolt against that terrible, cheerless, heartless food by writing down descriptions of Mediterranean and Middle Eastern cooking. Even to write words like apricot, olives and butter, rice and lemons, oil and almonds, produced assuagement. Later I came to realize that in the England of 1947, those were dirty words that I was putting down.'[12]

As soon as travel was possible again Elizabeth escaped the hotel and rejoined George Lassalle, who had moved into a bungalow some friends had lent him near Gloucester. 'I read Julia Strachey's review of Elias Canetti's *Auto da Fé* in *Horizon*, and thought it the most dazzling piece of book-reviewing I had ever seen. By some fantastic chance I found a copy of the book itself in Smiths in the town which was a bus ride away . . .'[13] One evening, however, she and George found a book in the bungalow that was even more riveting.

They had eaten a cassoulet of bacon bones, beans and herbs, accompanied by generous quantities of Algerian wine before finding it, hidden in the shadows of a bookshelf. It was very large, and on the cover was printed CONFIDENTIAL: TO BE KEPT IN THE SAFE. . . It was a pre-1939 Trust House hotel cookery book, catering and food-costing manual.

'I did not steal it,' wrote Elizabeth. 'The temptation to do so was truly appalling: I wish now that I had looked in the neighbourhood for someone with a typewriter to copy out for me some of its most instructive pages. I . . . would have been in possession now of the secrets of Trust House hotel soups; I could have told you how to turn *Potage parmentier* into *Potage cultivateur* with a flick of a ladle . . . How to make lobster patties for twenty-five with one lobster and I forget how many pounds of cod.'[14]

This book of trade secrets also made a profound impression on George, who was struck by two particularly sinister items. 'One was a detailed instruction on how to make imitation French sauces . . . The other was an advisory paragraph on how to meet the need of a sudden influx of casual customers when there was insufficient food in the kitchen to feed them. On no account should such customers be turned away. There followed detailed instructions on how to perform a miracle of the loaves and fishes and turn food already prepared to feed twenty hotel residents into a banquet for forty.'[15] From then on, in their separate lives, George and Elizabeth lived in the hope of tracking down another copy of this book. Both were resourceful bibliophiles, keen trawlers of street markets and second-hand bookshops. They never found one.

Elizabeth's experiences of hotel cookery, combined with the discovery of the caterers' manual, unleashed the source of the creative rage that drove what she wrote. In that miserably cold winter of 1947, she found the heart of her own blazing fire. Of course, she did not always write in the white heat of passion: there is no point wasting emotional energy on custard powder and gravy mix. But whenever she tweaked the noses of pompous restaurateurs, laughed at a factory-made pie or poked fun at the sacred cows of British cookery, she was tapping into the same incandescent exasperation that drove her to put pen to paper in Ross-on-Wye.

Elizabeth felt she owed something to Trust Houses Ltd, because her first book might never have come into being without them. 'I should have dedicated [*Mediterranean Food*] to Trust Houses Ltd. It was ungrateful of me not to have done so. For better or for worse the book brought me a new job and a new life.'[16] In a much later letter to Elizabeth, George wrote, 'Yes, 1947 was a very bad winter indeed but I seem to remember there were compensations for all that snow.'[17]

Tony David came home in the spring of 1947, and her family were profoundly relieved by what they saw. He was well-mannered, eager to please and had a good seat on a horse. The only worry was that he had no job, having left the Indian Army, (his decision to go being more influenced by Elizabeth than by the prospect of Indian independence.)

That summer, Elizabeth and Tony travelled round France with Doreen Brownhill, who had made an unsuccessful marriage during the war and was now separated from her husband. They did not go by barge, as they had once dreamed of doing in Cairo, but in a second-hand Rolls-Royce which they bought for £550. It was a dashing thing to do, and reality caught up all too soon. It ate and drank petrol, the exchange-rate was appalling, the tyres were old, the roads were war-scarred, and they had their first puncture just outside Calais. But despite all obstacles, and the irrevocable puncture of the spare tyre at Lyon, they went as far as the Italian border before heading for home. The way home was even more nerve-racking; but the fact that they got the car home at all was 'a triumph, and like all triumphs it left us in a state of nervous exhaustion'.[18]

That autumn, the Davids were told that the owners of their flat wanted it back. They had by now bought quite a lot of furniture, mostly through Elizabeth's mother Stella. Antique shops were springing up all over the south of England, but Stella Hamilton knew what she was selling.

Rather than rent another flat, Tony and Elizabeth decided to buy: and the house they settled on was No. 24 Halsey Street. Halsey Street is a residential street of white terraced houses, linking Cadogan Street at the south end with Milner Street to the north. That particular area of Chelsea had been one of the first to benefit from the magnificent water closets designed and made by Thomas Crapper, and the lavatory in the basement of the Davids' house boasted an early model from the great man's workshop. The house, though small, was on several floors. The Davids decided to convert it so that the top two floors could be let, to augment their income. They had moved in by early November, and continued to use Stella Hamilton as their main supplier for everything from curtains to sconces, pine tables to soup plates.

Elizabeth had asked for Stella's help in buying the house; but while Stella was willing to underwrite the mortgage, she was also convinced that Elizabeth was financially irresponsible. When Elizabeth was in her twenties, she had indeed been extravagant: not only Stella, but Priscilla had often helped her out, more generously than Elizabeth deserved – although she was always profoundly grateful for their generosity. Elizabeth was by now in her mid-thirties, and had put her reckless youth behind her. Stella, however, still felt it wiser to put the house in Tony's name.

However, the spender in the David ménage was Tony, not Elizabeth. When they went shopping together, he was the one who spent, she the one who held back. The conversion of the house required a certain amount of building work; but that was not the only reason for Tony's spending.

He had gone into partnership with Douglas Grey, the youngest brother of Diana's husband Christopher Grey, who had inherited some money from his mother. Together they bought the lease on No. 12 Herbert Crescent, with the idea of turning it into a relaxed, informal club. Once again, Stella was asked to provide the furniture.

'I have a pine stool which is too low for the bar, but am going to ask my Mr Knott if he can make six bar stools similar – as it is very pretty and will let you know. Should they slant or be quite level and what is the exact height? I suppose you will glamorize the bar – green and gold or somehow embellish it . . .'[19]

This letter shows that Stella, at least, was interested and involved with the project; but Elizabeth was becoming anxious. 'I began to feel uneasy about the amount of money that was being spent on the club scheme. My husband, however, was confident of its ultimate success.'[20] In mid-January 1948, Tony became seriously ill. 'I am more than désolé [sic] to hear about Tony and all,' wrote Stella on the 23rd (of January, presumably). 'Awful strain for you, too, nursing, etc. I am so sorry, and wish I could do something useful. I have found some Jamaican Turtle, but no receipte [sic]. It has to be soaked and boiled . . .' The rest of the three-page letter deals with a Victorian buttoned sofa, a low pine table, a pair of pelmets, a clock, a 'hideous' oak cupboard, and the costs and frustrations of shipping in midwinter. Stella's business was never far from her thoughts.

Quite what Tony was suffering from is difficult to guess, at this distance; but it took him several weeks to recover. In February, he asked for an estimate for work that still had to be done on the club's main room and bar; but it is doubtful that the work was ever done. This was because Tony David and Douglas Grey had gone ahead with their plans without doing much paperwork in advance. They had failed to secure the permission of the local authorities for their scheme, and the club was shut down even before it opened. Elizabeth wrote that 'most of [Tony's] available capital had been spent on it, and little was salvaged'.[21]

Tony managed to find employment for the second half of 1948, managing a firm called Piccadilly Parcels which exploited a clever way of getting around rationing. A great many things, such as orange marmalade and biscuits made with white flour, were available in Britain but only for export. People living abroad wrote to Piccadilly Parcels and ordered export-only goods, for which they paid in foreign currency; the parcels were sent either to them or to their ration-starved relatives in England. For a while the Davids' financial situation improved, while Tony David's nephew Patrick Lewin had the pleasure of receiving real Huntley & Palmer biscuits at Eton – which considerably impressed his schoolfellows and made him very popular.

In the early part of 1949, the sixteen-year-old Patrick Lewin became very ill with bronchitis. His parents lived in Kenya, so Elizabeth and Tony took him away from Eton so as to nurse him back to health in Halsey Street. Patrick felt that they looked after him extremely well, and he never heard a cross word between them. 'Elizabeth and Tony were both good cooks,' said Lewin, 'united in their hatred of the latest gadget on the market – the pressure cooker.'

Veronica Meagher, whom they had last seen in India, got in touch with them, and for a while she lived in the large back room that was then being used as a dining room, and was to become Elizabeth's kitchen. The Davids had hoped that Veronica would take the flat they had made at the top of the house, and at first she had agreed; but friends thought it was a bad idea. The Davids' marriage was under strain. Veronica also felt that while she was very fond of Elizabeth, she was too strong a character to live with.

Instead, the upstairs flat was let to Denis Freeman and Neville

Phillips, whom Elizabeth had met in Cairo. They too were aware of the tension between Elizabeth and Tony, which was not helped by the fact that he was a fish out of water among Elizabeth's friends.

Neville Phillips remembered taking Elizabeth to a matinée performance given by Roland Petit's ballet company, which was then causing a sensation in London. They reached their seats and there, sitting in a box above them, they recognized the great Vaslav Nijinsky. Later that evening, Neville and Elizabeth met up with Denis and Tony for dinner, and Neville mentioned that they had seen Nijinsky. 'Who's he?' asked Tony. Elizabeth explained that he had been a great dancer, star of the Ballets Russes, and celebrated for his breathtaking leaps. 'Oh yes,' said Tony enthusiastically. 'I had a horse just like that in India.'[22] Elizabeth shot Neville a look which implied she had given up on Tony's cultural education.

She was also rapidly losing confidence in her husband, who seemed incapable of finding a 'proper' job. He spent more and more time at home, getting up late and drifting around the house. He was still useful for grinding the coffee, mixing the drinks and driving the car; but it became painfully obvious that Elizabeth's feelings for him had been reduced to irritation and contempt.

Her faith in him was finally shattered in the new year. Tony had always been evasive about their debts; when pressed, he would answer with vague and reassuring noises. But in early 1949, Elizabeth insisted on knowing the details of their financial position: at which point, Tony admitted that nothing whatever had been paid either on the mortgage, or to the builders. He seemed quite relaxed about the situation, and suggested they sell the house. Elizabeth, still in a state of shock, pointed out that this was hardly the best solution since they would be obliged to sell at a very considerable loss. Tony, however, did not see this as a disadvantage, and suggested they go and live abroad. He had no idea of what they might live on. As for the bills, he could not understand why Elizabeth found them such an obstacle: 'He could not understand my attitude. He thought it was very priggish of me to insist that bills and debts must be paid.'[23]

Elizabeth made no secret of her disappointment in Tony. His failure had humiliated her in front of her family, and she was mortified at being so deep in debt.

* * * * * * * *

CHAPTER ELEVEN

Mediterranean Food

The 'agonized craving for the sun' which Elizabeth had begun to work out of herself in Ross-on-Wye had grown into a collection of recipes which she already thought of as *A Book of Mediterranean Food*. They were based on the food she had cooked for the past twelve years, though at this stage she was soliciting contributions from her friends as well. At the same time, prompted by their financial situation, Elizabeth started to write some articles on cookery. If published they might bring in a little money, and it was a good way of turning her back on Tony as she sat at her desk in silent concentration.

It was Veronica Meagher who had, in Elizabeth's words, 'talked, not to say nagged' her into assembling the book; and Veronica now did what she could to find sympathetic readers who might give good advice about publication. One who sprang to mind was John Carter, the European agent for the American firm of Scribner's. His wife Ernestine was then fashion editor at *Harper's*.

'Would you consider showing the MS to [John] Carter?' wrote Veronica. 'A pretty desperate step ... but Mr Carter works for Scribners ... They [he and his wife Ernestine] are also best friends with the Hamish Hamiltons, Messrs Chatto & Windus and the rest ... PS: Alternatively if I could borrow the book I might make Anne abandon Robin Adair.'[1]

Anne was Anne Scott-James, editor of *Harper's Bazaar*, while Robin Adair was the magazine's cookery correspondent. He was a close friend of Marcel Boulestin, but this did not alter the fact that he never filed his copy on time. Veronica knew that Anne, though not particularly interested in cookery herself, might look favourably on any possible replacement. Veronica told Anne that she knew of someone very good, who was just starting; and Anne agreed to look at Mrs David's work.

Elizabeth was very keen for her articles to be accepted, and asked Veronica to help her achieve the right journalistic tone. Veronica did not take her seriously at first; but Elizabeth was so insistent she obliged, and drew the article into line with the bright, cheerful, occasionally girlish 'Harper-ese'. Elizabeth was not impressed. She submitted her work, for better or worse, in its original form.

Anne Scott-James recognized that the articles were written by someone with an independent mind, who had travelled widely: in fact, she liked the way they read more like travel pieces than cookery. From the spring of 1949, Elizabeth's articles appeared regularly in *Harper's Bazaar*.

She was very professional: the copy was always delivered on time, and was never unreasonably overlength. Yet she was not easy to work with. The sub-editors were never allowed to get their hands on Elizabeth's text – if any alterations had to be done, words cut or a line filled in, it was Anne who did it, and then telephoned Elizabeth. 'I would explain what had to be done and there would be a long silence at the other end, before she would say, "I would like it to go in as I have written it." "Yes of course," I would reply, "but the fact remains that either you must cut three words or I must because I cannot make the page any bigger." Difficult as she was, Anne Scott-James could not help admiring her stubbornness. 'Her work was holy and she was the priestess of it . . . She was a perfectionist, and great perfectionists are also great egotists.'[2]

Straightforward as ever, Elizabeth had told the editor of *Harper's* that she was hoping to publish some of her recipes, including those which had made an appearance in the magazine. Anne accepted this with equanimity. 'We were not so worried about copyright as we are now.'

John Carter looked at her manuscript and said that it was no more than a collection of unconnected recipes. It needed more text to bring it together but at this stage Elizabeth had very little confidence in herself as a writer. She did not want to copy Veronica's slick, upbeat journalese, nor the cheerful practicalities of most cookbooks of the time; but she was still unsure of her own voice. She kept her prose as spare as she could, but sometimes it sounded almost terse – on the other hand, she was determined to avoid sentimentality. It was for this reason that she relied heavily on other authors to describe Mediterranean life: Henry James, Marcel Boulestin, Robert Byron, Lawrence Durrell and D. H. Lawrence were among those she pressed into service – and, of course, Norman Douglas. Many of the passages are, not unnaturally, chosen for their seductiveness; but Elizabeth quoted from travel books, not travel brochures, and Mediterranean food was not all olives and sun-warmed figs. Théophile Gautier thought the gaspacho he found in Spain in 1840 was quite revolting, and no one would seriously contemplate starting the day with the gargantuan breakfast Lt-Col. Newnham-Davis recommends in Venice. The descriptions she uses are there primarily to evoke a specific time and place, and to illuminate the Mediterranean approach to food, which was then so alien to the British.

On the other hand, the whole book is infused with that love of the Mediterranean that was so characteristic of the time. She had first found it through the eyes of Norman Douglas, and later, she had made friends with writers who celebrated the Mediterranean for an entire generation: Lawrence Durrell, Patrick Leigh Fermor, Patrick Kinross, Robin Fedden. After the war everyone who had ever been abroad was longing to go again; they were sick of the grey drabness of England and its shattered cities. It was not only warmth and colour they wanted: those little white villages clustering in front of the sea, with olive groves beyond, represented a world that had not yet lost its innocence

The recipes she had put together were made with good but not extravagant ingredients. They had been used year-in, year-out, as the seasons changed, by people who did their own cooking and marketing; and while olive oil and wine and aubergines may have sounded expensive and exotic in the England of 1949, they were not so in the Mediterranean. Elizabeth brought the recipes to life with little details that gave them a history and a personality. The stuffed mussels had been prepared for her on a boat, by a fisherman from Marseille. On late Sunday afternoons in Spanish courtyards, you could see serried ranks of metal paella pans left drying in the sun. (At this stage, she herself had never seen them: she first visited Spain in 1964.) The Greeks sent their lamb to be cooked in the village oven, and it was incomparably more delicious than anything that might emerge from a domestic oven; though in case this pronouncement discouraged her readers, she added that in England one could at least enjoy the dish hot: everything in Greece – even fried fish – was served tepid.

Denis Freeman and Neville Phillips had a friend called Robin Chancellor, who worked for the Museum Press. He had blithely said that he was sure his firm would publish it, but when it was submitted, his superiors turned it down. But he had contacts in other firms as well, and the typescript went the rounds of several publishers. The firm of Herbert Joseph wrote to say that her book was 'a very interesting work but I am sorry to say that we do not feel ourselves able to make an offer . . . Firstly, a part of the contents of your book is already covered by our existing publication *Recipes of All Nations* by Countess Morphy . . . Finally the bookshops are at present flooded with cookery books.'[3] Publisher after publisher turned it down, until the book finally arrived in the office of John Lehmann Ltd.

John Lehmann was best known for being the editor of *New*

Writing, the most influential literary magazine to appear during the war. Its pages featured work by W. H. Auden, Louis Aragon, Stephen Spender, Federico Garcia Lorca, Louis MacNeice, Robert Graves and Laurie Lee, to name but a few; but this gives an idea of how open and attuned Lehmann was to new voices. He had no particular interest in food or cookery, and the 'unprepossessing bundle of grubby typescript', as he called it, was given to Julia Strachey (whose review of *Auto da Fé* had so impressed Elizabeth two years before). She was a niece of Lytton Strachey, and was then working as a reader for Lehmann.

Julia was impressed. Here was a book which was beautifully written, with the quiet authority of someone who knows what they are talking about. The author made no concession to austerity, talked of eggs and cream and butter as if they were freely available, and had the temerity to propose a Turkish Stuffing for a Whole Roast Sheep at a time when meat was still rationed. (Meat did not come off the ration until June 1954.) The book was even extravagant with time: anyone wishing to attempt Senator Couteaux's Lièvre à la Royale must be willing to set aside seven hours for its preparation, and the recipe takes up five pages. Elizabeth did not seriously expect that many of her readers would try stuffing a sheep, or even cooking a hare for seven hours: those recipes are included for sheer pleasure, and for the glimpse they give into a world where it was not considered pretentious, or bad form, to care about food.

Lehmann had never imagined himself publishing a cookbook; but he was delighted by the idea of stuffing a whole roast sheep and trusted Julia's judgement. He wrote to Elizabeth on 27 October 1949.

'Dear Mrs David, I tried to telephone you today, but you were evidently out. Do you think you could ring me here tomorrow (Friday) morning between 11 a.m. and 12.30, so that we can arrange a meeting? I like your book on Mediterranean Food very much, and hope we shall be able to agree about publication.'

*

Elizabeth had no idea what to expect as she walked into the office in Henrietta Street and shook hands with a tall, brisk man with thin hair, and eyes of a startlingly pale blue. Lehmann offered her £100 advance, with half on signature of the contract and half on publication. He said that he wanted to give the book a feeling of cheerfulness and abundance, and suggested that it should be illustrated by John Minton.

John Minton was an immensely talented neo-romantic painter, to whom Lehmann gave a lot of work; but people said there was more to their relationship than that. Minton's charming, gangly figure was often seen at Lehmann's celebrated parties in Egerton Crescent, and he was also a welcome guest at the publisher's cottage near Three Bridges in Sussex. Since both men were homosexual, people naturally assumed they were having an affair. Minton's biographer, Frances Spalding, thinks this is unlikely; but Lehmann was, like many people, fascinated by Minton, in whom he found 'a compelling charm'.[4] Lehmann showed Elizabeth a recent jacket design by his protégé, for a book about Corsica by Alan Ross called *Time was Away*. It showed a man sleeping in a boat under a hot sun in a Mediterranean landscape, and Elizabeth agreed that it was very effective.

All that was lacking was an Introduction, which Elizabeth was to write, and the only problem was the title. For some reason Lehmann did not like *A Book of Mediterranean Food*, and wanted to call it *The Blue Train Cookery Book*. Elizabeth pointed out that the Blue Train, which had epitomized the excitement and romance of foreign travel for the pre-war generation, had never gone as far as Alexandria and Cairo. She felt very strongly that the word Mediterranean was vital, but Lehmann still clung to the Blue Train idea. They both agreed to give the matter some thought.

Elizabeth left John Lehmann's office in a daze of delight and misgivings. Would he really insist on changing the title, and what on earth was supposed to go into the Introduction? She was still puzzling over these things a few days later, when Lehmann rang her up to say that perhaps she was right, and the title could stand. Elizabeth was profoundly relieved, and felt she had won an important victory. She would often say that if Lehmann had had his way, her first book would never have enjoyed the success it did.

That still left the Introduction. Having no idea how to go about it, Elizabeth once again turned to Veronica. Veronica wrote a short piece 'in the buoyant, jokey style I was trained in', but Elizabeth didn't like it. What she wrote instead was short and rather formal. Her aim, she said, was 'to give some idea of the lovely cookery of those regions to people who do not already know them, and to stir the memories of those who have eaten this food on its native shores, and who would like sometimes to bring a flavour of those blessed lands of sun and sea and olive trees into their English kitchens'.[5]

At one point during the preparation of the book, Elizabeth went to visit Lady Sibell Rowley. Before the war, Sibell was one of the three Lygon sisters whose house, Madresfield, had been a constant refuge for the young Evelyn Waugh. In 1939 she had married a fighter plot, Michael Rowley, and they lived in a large house, with its own farm, called Payne's Place near Tewkesbury. Sibell was a countrywoman through and through, who hunted and kept a pack of hounds. Elizabeth had no interest in either, but she was fascinated by the farm on which Sibell did almost everything, from looking after the chickens to killing the pig. She was also a good cook, and a good friend.

'To put up with me for three weeks,' wrote Elizabeth, 'either clamped to the Aga or spreading mountains of papers and books all over the sitting room was really an act of nobility ... You have given me such a gorgeous opportunity to do proper cooking with not only delicious cream and bacon, geese eggs and the rest – I am eternally grateful to you. I am now of course complaining of the difficulties of cooking on a gas stove ...'[6]

Elizabeth had returned to London, and the rapidly cooling ashes of her marriage. As far as she was concerned, it was over – but Tony still loved her, and was deeply hurt when she began a flirtation with one of their friends, Peter Higgins. As a couple, Tony and Elizabeth had kept in touch with Peter, whom they both found entertaining: he could talk horses to Tony, and food to Elizabeth. It was he who introduced her to a book by Lt-Col. Newnham-Davis and Algernon Bastard called *The Gourmet's Guide to Europe*. Peter wrote out for her the colonel's magnificent breakfast in Venice, which she included in *Mediterranean Food*. 'Incidentally,' he added, 'I ate the "steaming risotto with scampi" in June 1946 at the Quadri, but not for breakfast, and very good it was.'[7]

He also very much appreciated the food Elizabeth cooked for him. 'Delicious though the food is in your house always,' he wrote in April, 'that ham which I ate on Thursday night called for appreciation in writing. Don't tell the public how to do it, because it's far too good for them.' This particular letter ends, 'love to you both': Tony was still on the scene, though he had no doubt guessed that something was brewing between Elizabeth and Peter. A friend remembers him at this time as a rather sad, reproachful figure.

In the summer of 1949, Tony was offered a job running a club in Walton-on-Thames. He accepted, and moved down there. When she came to write out the circumstances of their separation some years later, Elizabeth was at pains to make out that this was the moment they moved apart, and that they never again shared a roof. However, the situation seems to have been far less cut and dried, and as far as most of their friends were concerned they were still together – even if they were living apart for the present. When he came up to London Tony stayed at Halsey Street, and they still attended parties and the odd family occasion as a couple.

Elizabeth also emphasized that they were still on cordial, if not intimate terms. They appeared together at the wedding of her cousin Robert Palmer in 1952; and a friend, who happened to be in the sitting room at Halsey Street having coffee, witnessed a moment of affection from Elizabeth as Tony was about to leave. She saw him to the door, put her hand on his arm, and asked him with a smile to stay a little longer; but Tony said he really had to go.

It was during this time of separation from Tony that Elizabeth made herself a new kitchen, in what had been the dining room, which was a few steps down from the tiny hall. With three exterior walls, it had always been the coldest room in the house; but that made it a good larder temperature, and it was rendered slightly warmer by the addition of a wooden parquet floor. Elizabeth relied on an electric heater and the heat generated by cooking to keep the place habitable; but when it became very cold, she lit the gas oven and opened the door.

The kitchen was lit by a window looking out on to the tiny area, where Elizabeth kept a few pots of herbs and, in later years, the overflow from her collection of pots and storage jars. She had no garden, nor did she seem to miss one. For someone who so appreciated the fruits of the soil in their proper seasons, it is curious that she was such an urban animal: in general, Elizabeth preferred markets to gardens.

In front of the window was a chaise longue, where Elizabeth used to rest and read. To the right of the window was the butler's sink, built into a cabinet with a teak draining board. Immediately below was a space for chopping boards and other things that needed to be instantly accessible. To the other side of the draining board stood the New World gas cooker, and above them was a Victorian wrought-iron lamp on a hinged arm. To the other side of the cooker was a white-painted dresser, the shelves of which contained stoneware storage jars and pots overflowing with small implements, with decorative plates propped up behind them. At this stage, the plates were coloured and patterned: Elizabeth's passion for plain white plates did not develop until later. At the end of the room, facing the window, was a heavy French armoire in which she kept glasses, crockery and herbs. (In later years it contained pans and earthenware.)

Elizabeth never liked the idea of having her fridge in the main part of the kitchen. Fridges in those days were a great deal noisier than modern ones, and since her kitchen was both the place where she studied and the room in which she entertained, it is not surprising that she wanted it out of the way. Her fridge was kept cooler and therefore quieter by being on the landing outside: which was easier on the motor and involved less defrosting.

Two more pale wooden dressers occupied the wall facing the cooker, their shelves crammed with madeleine moulds, saucepans, preserved fruits and more plates. On the first dresser stood whatever needed to go in a bowl: eggs, apricots, walnuts, lemons or shallots, depending on the time of year. On the second stood more equipment, plus a collection of liqueur and wine bottles and a large alarm clock. Elizabeth always complained of the clutter in her kitchen, but her curiosity and interest in all culinary objects was insatiable and she was an instinctive collector. As her nephew Johnny remarked, 'She loved the cooking utensils as much as the china and thought them equally worthy of display.'[8] She could never have lived in a minimalist kitchen.

There was nothing that could be described as a work surface, except for the scrubbed pine table that dominated the room. Everything focused on this table, which was lit by a large nineteenth-century oil lamp with a glass shade. This was where Elizabeth read, made notes, and wrote the books and articles that were to make her name over the next decade. Here too she prepared food, checked recipes, measured quantities, checked timings, chopped, diced, whisked and folded.

Then, at lunchtime, all the books and papers were moved down to one end to make room for her friends. It is not unusual for someone to work and entertain in the same room, particularly if space is limited – but the room is usually divided in such a way that work and play take place in different areas. Elizabeth had the use of a sitting room as well as a kitchen. She was also the sort of person who liked to keep her life in separate compartments. Yet the fact remains that she chose to write, cook, entertain her friends, eat, drink, relax and talk, not only in the same room, but at the same table.

As her guests came in, they would be led downstairs and sat at the end nearest the window. Here they would find perhaps a bowl of olives, some radishes, a fresh loaf of bread (she did not yet make her own, since her local baker made what she called 'a passable French loaf') and a slab of butter. There was also, invariably, a bottle of wine.

'When guests were invited to lunch,' wrote Johnny Grey, 'she would only have one dish ready; the ones to follow would be prepared over a lengthy pre-lunch conversation and guests were usually asked to assist . . . If you were lucky and some experiment had taken place the previous day, she would offer it to you in a matter-of-fact way and ask you to try it . . . She never boasted about her cooking skills – her whole attitude to cooking was one of interest, inquiry and very occasionally genuine pleasure when a dish turned out well.'[9] The lunches went on until well into the afternoon, over the kitchen table.

Elizabeth took a great deal of care over her kitchen. Everything was considered to make it comfortable and practical, but it went directly against the mainstream of kitchen design in 1949. Most housewives at that time aspired to spotless acres of laminated surfaces, plastic-covered chairs, linoleum floors and chrome handles to fitted units.

With Tony now drifting into the distance, Elizabeth's emotional life was filled by the elusive, charming Peter Higgins. He used to say that his mother had been a Gibson Girl, 'though not one of the grand ones who dressed up like a cracker',[10] and he claimed to have been born in a hotel in Dorchester. His father Rupert Higgins was a man about town, an Edwardian charmer who enjoyed living close to the rich and grand; and because he was entertaining and amenable, the rich and grand enjoyed his company. Peter was brought up a Catholic and went to the Oratory School near Reading. He did not go to university, the most likely reason being that there was no money to pay for any further education. Instead, he went into the City and became a stockbroker.

He had no particular fondness for his chosen profession; but it provided him with a good living, and enough extra to hunt and ride and go to the races whenever he could get away from London. From his father Peter had inherited a taste for the high life: on the horsy side, he was friends with Harry Stavordale (later 7th Lord Ilchester), and the hunting and racing sets of Dorset and Gloucestershire; while on a more raffish, sophisticated side, he was taken up by Hamish St-Clair Erskine, the son of the 5th Earl of Rosslyn. Erskine, now best-known for being an early love of Nancy Mitford's, used to claim that he had 'discovered' Peter and often referred to him as 'my débutante daughter'.[11] Considering Erskine's homosexual tendencies, and the fact that he and Peter had once shared a house, some people whispered that they were lovers. Peter was in fact firmly heterosexual, and since he was also very attractive to women, he soon had a string of love affairs to prove it.

By the time Peter met Elizabeth in India he already had one marriage behind him, to Kathleen (Kit), daughter of the Canadian lawyer and banker Sir James Dunn. The marriage was over by the end of the war, and she later married Col. Robert Adeane. As for Peter, he seemed quite happy to stick to the principles of his Catholic faith, and said he would not marry again. He settled in Devon, where he became a farmer: an occupation which, he hoped, would enable him to ride more often than if he were still in the City. Yet it soon became obvious that, farmer or not, Peter Higgins could not quite tear himself away from the racing season and the social life of London.

Elizabeth had always liked easy, confident men, the kind who brightened up a room just by walking into it, whom people were always pleased to see. She also noticed that although she herself cared nothing for horses, in later years she had become rather attracted to these hard-riding types: perhaps they reflected something of the intense, childish memories she still cherished of her dead father.

During the early years of their affair, Elizabeth often accompanied

Peter and his friends to the races, to which he was addicted although he never gambled. Elizabeth, on the other hand, hated racing; and her opinion of the racing fraternity was expressed with a distinctly caustic wit over the magnificent picnics she prepared for these occasions. But the highlights of the racing calendar gave her an opportunity to be with Peter, and these were too precious to waste. Peter and Elizabeth sometimes came to spend the weekend with Michael and Sibell Rowley. Sibell remembered them as being very happy. On one occasion, Elizabeth brought Sibell a present of avocados, which (for want of anything better) they ate with Worcestershire sauce.

Priscilla's marriage to Richard Longland was over in 1949, leaving her profoundly depressed. Elizabeth's own marriage was crumbling as well; yet she continually urged her friend Veronica to settle down and choose one of her many suitors. 'It's absurd, of course,' she would say, 'but a woman must marry.' On 21 October 1949, Veronica married Major John Nicholson, who had been courting her for many years and whom she always thought she would settle down with. They went to France for their honeymoon, leaving Elizabeth with the key to their flat; and when they got back, they were very touched to find that Elizabeth and Tony had gone in and made up the bed.

'Then began,' wrote Veronica, 'the era of long luncheons between Elizabeth and me. We would meet at her house or at my flat at about one, and break up just in time to go home for dinner.'[12] Veronica did her best with Elizabeth's recipes when she came to lunch, while Elizabeth's lunches were usually trial runs of the recipes in her next article – though they did not always turn out right. On one occasion clouds of smoke, produced by a batch of choux pastry that Elizabeth had forgotten about, obliged them to abandon the kitchen altogether.

A Book of Mediterranean Food was published in June 1950 and reviewed with great enthusiasm. No one got the point of it better than Elizabeth Nicholas, a travel writer and reviewer, whose piece in the *Sunday Times* gave Elizabeth particular satisfaction. Nicholas called Elizabeth 'a gastronome of rare integrity. She appreciates the present deficiencies of the English larder, but at the same time if she wants to say "take a large piece of rump steak", she says it. She refuses, in fact, to make any ignoble compromises with expediency.'[13] Nicholas also noted with approval that the book contained 'not one reference to Brillat-Savarin'. Even those with reservations about the book could not fail to succumb to its enchantment. John Chandos, in the *Observer*, wrote rather severely that

The book claims that it evokes 'all the colour and sun of the Mediterranean', yet it is precisely those native physical and climactic elements which the recipes require for their proper consummation. Let no one eating in London – with whatever abandon – imagine that he is eating Mediterranean food in the absence of Mediterranean earth and air. With that reservation it may be admitted that Miss [*sic*] Elizabeth David has assembled as potent a bundle of spells as ever made a culinary Witches' Sabbath.[14]

The only real complaint came from the RSPCA, which rightly considered her recipe for Roast Lobster needlessly cruel – it was to be tied to a skewer and roasted alive, basted with champagne, butter, pepper and salt. The recipe came from *Spon's Household Manual*, a book dating from the 1880s. In later editions Elizabeth pointed out that this recipe was not to be taken seriously, but was only given as an example of the 'lavish and somewhat barbaric' recipes of the time.

Elizabeth felt that much of the success of *Mediterranean Food* was due to the authors she was able to quote and John Minton's jacket design. She was not very enthusiastic about his pen and ink illustrations, but the jacket she described as stunning. 'In the shop windows his brilliant blue Mediterranean bay, his tables spread with white cloths and bright fruit, bowls of pasta and rice, a lobster, pitchers and jugs and bottles of wine, could be seen far down the street.'

She was aware that, as a cookbook, it was not unflawed: prevailing conditions dictated that the recipes were more evocative than accurate. And yet for those who knew what they were doing, it was profoundly stimulating.

'I consider it easily the best cookery book that I have read dealing with . . . south European and Arab cookery,' wrote one of her readers. 'Although I really have read an enormous number of books which have purported to touch on this kind of cuisine, they have *all* failed to give me a clear picture of the more exotic recipes. The writers . . . have tasted and seen, but probably not having lived there nor speaking the language, they have failed to understand the fundamentals. You have definitely filled in this gap, and I am very grateful.'[15]

Another grateful recipient was Lawrence Durrell, who wrote to her in June 1950 from Ischia. He was revisiting the Mediterranean for the first time in many months, and he felt back in his natural element at last. Durrell describes his house and his friend Zarian (who appears briefly in the passage Elizabeth had quoted from Durrell's book *Prospero's Cell*), and added, 'All this is to tell you that not only was your book deeply appreciated but we were lucky to be able to take it with us and read it in a proper setting and in good company.'[16]

Elizabeth later described her first book as 'a very primitive effort', but she was fond of it none the less. 'It is a love letter to the Mediterranean.'[17] Although she was 'not the sort to dance a jig',[18] as Veronica put it, Elizabeth was tremendously pleased by the success of *Mediterranean Food*. Of course she saw the limitations of the book; but it showed her that out there were people who were eager and willing to hear what she wanted to say.

Journalistic commissions followed. Lord Kemsley, the owner of the *Sunday Times*, had recently bought up a travel magazine called *Go* in order to satisfy the public's increasing demand for everything foreign. Kemsley put Leonard Russell, the *Sunday Times*'s literary editor, and Elizabeth Nicholas, who had written the most perceptive review of *Mediterranean Food*, in charge of the new venture.

Elizabeth David was one of the first people they contacted; and over the coming months she not only wrote for *Go*, but also contributed a long piece for the *Sunday Times Travel Guide to France* on the area between Marseille and Menton. At the same time, John Lehmann was keen to publish another book by Elizabeth David, and he and Elizabeth agreed that the new book should present the simple, but beautifully prepared dishes of rural France. This was a logical successor to *Mediterranean Food*, for it grew out of the same collection of recipes that Elizabeth had been amassing for years.

The sixty-guinea advance from the *Sunday Times*, plus an advance from John Lehmann, made Elizabeth decide it was time to take a trip to France. In August 1950, two months after the publication of *Mediterranean Food*, she and Tony set off for their last holiday together. They joined another couple in what was supposed to be a comfortable and leisurely trip. The car, however, turned out to be extremely unreliable, and a lot of time was spent walking long distances for help and waiting around for mechanics.

Elizabeth was still writing for *Harper's* on subjects which included pasta, spring vegetables, hors d'oeuvres and alfresco lunches. She even wrote an article in praise of the freshness and convenience of airline food (possibly for *Go*). Two of the pieces she wrote at this time were, however, particularly important. 'Cooking with Wine' (February 1950) began with the words, 'Nobody has ever been able to find out why the English regard a glass of wine added to a soup or stew as a reckless foreign extravagance, and at the same time spend pounds on bottled sauces, gravy powders, soup cubes, ketchups and artificial flavourings.' Many people think of Elizabeth David as a cook for those prepared to take infinite pains. It is worth remembering how liberating and refreshing her work was too, and how she never missed an opportunity to point out when things could be done better, more cheaply and without cluttering up the cupboard.

'Batterie de Cuisine', on the other hand, which appeared in January 1950, shows Elizabeth at her most briskly didactic. Any young bride-to-be must have felt her heart sink as she read that the ideal kitchen should contain at least nine saucepans, four frying pans, earthenware casseroles, egg dishes, soufflé dishes and gratin dishes, plus a large selection of knives, mixing bowls and muslin squares. Too much information was packed into this article, with not enough room to say why all these objects were so vital. However, in its final, more developed form, this piece became one of the most useful and delightful of all her essays.

With one book out, the next commissioned and a fine collection of articles already under her belt, one might assume that Elizabeth had by now mastered the art of typing; yet Elizabeth never got beyond the hunt-and-thump stage. For her, the feel of a pen or pencil in her hand and the paper under it was part of the process of writing and thinking, and, as in her cooking, she did not like to be separated from the creative act by a machine.

For most of her work, the typist was Elizabeth's youngest sister Felicité. Rightly or wrongly, Felicité always saw herself as the runt of the litter. Her low opinion of herself was summed up in the nickname that she had put up with since childhood – Bulgie. It was an affectionate name, and a part of Felicité always answered to it, but another part of her rather wished she could shake it off. She was not quite seven when her father died, and from then until adulthood she lived in an almost exclusively female world. The feeling that she was always trying to catch up with her sisters remained, for she never had enough emotional support from her mother and sisters. As soon as she was old enough, she sought it from her boyfriends instead.

For Felicité, as for many people, the war was one of the happiest and most independent times in her life. She felt at ease in the company of people who had nothing to do with the world she had grown up in, and was more relaxed with her Austrian and Polish friends than she had ever been with the awkward young Englishmen she had come across. But once she was back in England, the past and her family re-exerted its power. She still needed her family's approval, and they teased her about her foreign boyfriends. So she kept them in the background, and once again started to live according to her family's expectations rather than making her own.

She found a job in a bookshop called J. A. Allen. It specializes in horse books, though Felicité ran its small general section on the ground floor. Work in bookshops is not usually very remunerative, and J. A. Allen's was no exception; but Felicité came to a mutually beneficial arrangement with her sister Elizabeth. The top flat had been rented out to Denis Freeman, the actor friend from Cairo, and he had become very short of cash towards the end of his tenancy. Elizabeth asked him to leave; and as soon as he had done so, in 1950, Felicité moved in. Elizabeth kept the rent for the top flat very low, and in return Felicité did Elizabeth's typing.

Elizabeth finished the manuscript of *French Country Cooking* in October 1950, delivering it early in the new year. In her covering letter to John Lehmann, she asked, 'Can I reprint three or four basic recipes from *Mediterranean Food*, or is this cheating?'[19] Lehmann evidently thought it was: 'I can imagine a reviewer making a song and dance about this that would spoil everything.'[20] She had considered another artist to do the illustrations, but Lehmann felt he was 'sophisticated in the wrong way for our public', so once again the drawings were by John Minton. Elizabeth had by now become quite fond of Minton, so she did not complain. The one thing she insisted on was that in this book, there should be drawings of various pots and pans and kitchen implements – not just because they were evocative, but to convey information: the tools that people used to cook with were an integral part of the cooking process. Minton did a number of drawings of these objects, and they have dated better than his impressions of sultry French peasants and the jovial bourgeois family at lunch.

With *French Country Cooking* safely delivered, Elizabeth decided to go and live for a while in France. Not only would she increase her knowledge of the country, but, away from Paris, one could live far more cheaply than one could in England. By renting Halsey Street, she might support herself, and put more distance between herself and Tony – who was by now, in most people's eyes, a sad figure more sinned against than sinning. 'Sympathy with Tony is general,' wrote her mother, 'and I think rightly so . . . People like Tony, and think you are treating him rough, though they don't actually say so.'[21] Elizabeth found a house to rent in the village of Ménerbes in Provence, and let her house. Félicité was still in the upstairs flat, on hand to call in the plumber or the electrician in case of emergencies.

Elizabeth travelled to Provence by train in March 1951, and found Ménerbes magnificently isolated like a stone ship on the top of one of the rocky hills of the Lubéron. The house, belonging to Tony and Thérèse Mayer, was called La Carméjane, after the sixteenth-century Baron de Carméjane who began but never finished it. From the front, La Carméjane presents a massive wall with shuttered windows; but the effect is alleviated by the addition of an ornate little bartizan tacked on to one corner. The main part of the house consisted of three vast rooms, one above the other, which looked on to the hills of the Lubéron. Part of the ground floor room had been partitioned to make a tiny kitchen. There was only a small garden behind the house, but it led to a large terrace looking on to a cherry orchard, with the countryside rolling away beneath it. To one side of the terrace was a little two-bedroom house known as *le cabanon*. All this sounded delightful; but the weather was freezing cold, and everything was in a dreadful state of repair. Elizabeth had to deal with broken windows, a broken lavatory seat, a cantankerous cooker and only a trickle of hot water.

One of the first people to join her there was Romney Summers, the painter whom she had met in Cairo. A friend described Summers as 'Round, kind and the sort of person who did everything no one else wanted to do.'[22] They were soon joined by Hamish Erskine. Hamish went through a period of profound depression for the first few weeks when the weather was so miserable. Elizabeth's friend Doreen arrived at this time too. 'We sat for hour after hour at this huge table, on hard chairs, trying to keep warm and drinking foul wine – I think it was half-French, half-Algerian – out of a huge barrel, while the wind and rain lashed the windows.'[23] The wine was very rough. Elizabeth described it as the sort of wine that should be drunk in tumblers, heavily diluted.

Even on a tight budget (Summers kept detailed accounts of their spending) there was never any lack of what Elizabeth would have regarded as the necessities of life: bread, olives and wine. At first, their staples were chickpeas, lentils, old carrots and tomato paste. Elizabeth did not mind the food so much as the cold, and the constant buffeting of the mistral, the enervating wind that tears its way through the Rhône valley and is at its most violent in the spring.

Eventually the weather cheered up, and so did Hamish. He and Doreen would go for long walks, collecting wild flowers which they pressed. Elizabeth did not join them, since she 'hated walking more than an inch'.[24] Hamish stayed for most of the summer, and when he finally moved on he left his collection of French berets behind. 'You were so very sweet and kind to me,' wrote Hamish to Elizabeth when he finally got around to his thank-you letter in September, 'that except for hangovers and cold my spring and early summer were bliss.'[25]

With the warm weather the wind died, and then came glorious abundance. Eggs were so cheap they were almost given away, and 'we were able to buy a kilo of tomatoes, broad beans, haricots verts, peas, fennel, artichokes or courgettes for a few francs. Asparagus and strawberries were so cheap we could afford them almost every day, and not just for a few days but for weeks on end . . .'[26]

For a real treat she had the truffles of the Vaucluse, which are not considered as fine as those of the Perigord and are therefore cheaper. The centre was Carpentras, where the truffle hunter told her that the best way to enjoy the truffles was to scrub them well and slice them raw into a bowl of eggs, cover the bowl and then leave it to stand for two or three hours before cooking them. Twice a week they went to Avignon to do the shopping, and after the excitement of the market Elizabeth and whoever had come with her would repair, exhausted and laden with shopping, to the Café

Molière, a modest establishment which served a particularly delicious omelette. Parmesan is added to the eggs before cooking, and it is filled with thick cream and gruyère cut into tiny cubes. The secret of this dish is that not more than one tablespoon of each ingredient should be added to three eggs.

The summer brought more friends. Everyone helped with the bills, and many were paying guests. A woman from the village came to cook once or twice a week and clean the house, and Elizabeth did the rest. Some were more appreciative of Elizabeth's cooking than others: Felix Hope-Nicholson, a friend of Hamish Erskine's, was evidently not impressed and claimed to have been poisoned by something he called 'Liza's Balkan stew'. George Lassalle saw Felix a few weeks later in London and wrote, 'Felix H-N you must have bruised a little. He did not give me that instantaneous reaction of praise I expect from people who have lunched and dined with you.'[27]

Stews and casseroles featuring the cheaper cuts of meat seem to have appeared on the menu with considerable regularity, perhaps because they did not require much attention. She was researching at this time – in small hotels, kitchens behind little hardware shops and railway stations – following local recommendations, relying on the bus service to get from place to place. She was also learning the tact, the diplomacy, the patience that is required to persuade the French to give up their recipes. At the same time, she was still producing regular articles for *Harper's*, and in May she sent them a choice of two – one on Catalan cookery, and another on holiday cookery. They decided to go for the Catalan option: as the assistant editor explained, 'The holiday piece we felt entailed rather a lot of effort for women less devoted than yourself, who are generally lazy during their summer holidays.'[28] Elizabeth was also correcting the proofs of *French Country Cooking*, which she dedicated to her mother. 'I shall be greatly honoured should you really dedicate your new masterpiece to me,' wrote Stella. 'I am no cook, in fact, can hardly boil an egg, so it's really too unsuitable . . .'[29] But she was deeply touched.

Elizabeth was so happy in Provence that she even considered buying a house in Ménerbes called the Castellet, which stands beyond the graveyard at the most commanding end of the village and was for many years inhabited by the painter Nicholas de Staël. She never did; but she made a habit of returning to Ménerbes and La Carméjane, and something of those summers is in a soup of courgettes, tomatoes, broad beans and basil which appears, in *Summer Cooking*, as Soupe ménerboise.

It is possible that Peter Higgins came out to join Elizabeth for a week or two that summer, but he would have known the place anyway, since Elizabeth took the house again and again for several seasons. Her happiest memories of Peter were set in the landscape of Provence, which they travelled extensively together, and for many years Elizabeth thought of Ménerbes as a second home. In 1966, when those days were over, a friend sent her a postcard of La Carméjane. 'I arrived home at Halsey Street . . . this evening to find your postcard lying face upwards on the door mat. It gave me a terrible pang.'

* * * * * * * *

CHAPTER TWELVE

Italian Food

Elizabeth left Ménerbes at the end of June 1951, leaving Romney
Summers in charge of La Carméjane, and moved on to Italy with
Hamish Erskine to see Norman Douglas in Capri. She was detained
in Naples by water on her ankle. Resting it helped, but it would
swell up again as soon as she put her foot to the floor.

Since 1947 Norman had been living on the ground floor of the
Villa Tuoro, owned by his friend Kenneth McPherson. But his
health had been deteriorating, and the heat of summer made things
no better. His taste in food was getting very idiosyncratic: he had a
passion for hard-boiled eggs, of which he ate only the whites, and
Elizabeth, hating to see them go to waste, ate the yolks. She left the
island on 25 August, and Norman's parting present to her was a
copy of his autobiographical book *Late Harvest*, in which he wrote,
'For Liz. Farewell to Capri.' From there she made a journey round
the Italian Riviera, to research an article commissioned by *Go*.

Back in England, she went to stay for a few weeks with Doreen
in Cornwall, and then returned to London. Since her own house
was still let, she moved into a flat adjoining that currently inhabited
by George Lassalle and his third wife Judith Richardson (the sister
of Picasso's biographer, the art critic John Richardson.)

French Country Cooking was published in mid-September. It was
not, as she said in her introduction, haute cuisine: it was the everyday
food made by wives and housekeepers for doctors, curés, gendarmes
and post-office officials – the petite bourgeoisie of France, who might

not have had much money, but who loved their food and took it seriously. Elizabeth had learned a great deal since writing her last book; not only about food, but about her readership. She knew that the average post-war English kitchen lacked the necessary equipment to cook the sort of food offered by the recipes, so it opened with a section called 'Batterie de Cuisine'. This was basically the same list that had appeared in *Harper's* the previous year, but now she had larger print and more space at her disposal. Thus the piece became amusing as well as informative, and she was able to develop the reasons why the items she deems essential are so important. In the original article, for example, she only had room to say that earthenware dishes should be in every household. In *French Country Cooking* she can make the point that these dishes are far more than mere containers: they retain heat, add flavour and resonance to the food, and make it more beautiful to look at. In its extended form this piece remains one of the most useful that Elizabeth was ever to write, and holds as good today as it did in 1951. It also contains, in one sentence, a perfect little still life of kitchen gadgetry which sums up the relationship Elizabeth had with the tools of her trade.

As time goes on, you accumulate your own personal gadgets, things which graft themselves on to your life; an ancient thin fork for the testing of meat, a broken knife for scraping mussels, a battered little copper saucepan in which your sauces have always turned out well, an oyster knife which you can no longer afford to use for its intended purpose but which turns out to be just the thing for breaking off hunks of Parmesan cheese, a pre-war sixpenny tin-opener which has outlived all other and superior forms of tin-opening life, an earthenware bean-pot of such charm that nothing cooked in it could possibly go wrong.

This was followed by her (essentially unchanged) piece for *Harper's* on 'Wine in the Kitchen', and another on 'The Menu'. This was a subject she was to develop again in later books, but one part of the message remained unchanged and liberating: there is no commandment which says that meat must be served with two veg and potatoes. One vegetable may be served with advantage as a separate course, dressed with nothing more than butter and parsley; and as for potatoes, they can be omitted altogether. Serving vegetables before the roast was an old French custom, to which Marcel Boulestin had drawn attention in 1937 if not earlier; but the idea still sounded new in 1951.

The book was enthusiastically received, though it did contain one majestic howler. At one point, where Elizabeth had meant to say 'take 2 to 3 eggs', the instruction in print read 'take 23 eggs'. Elizabeth was appalled, but the letter she received from Lehmann's office laid the blame squarely on her. 'The printers could have only taken your mark to mean that the quantity should be 23. I have the proof here and if you care to come and inspect it, please do.'[1]

With another success on her hands, Elizabeth told John Lehmann that her next book would be about Italian food. Very little was known about Italian food in the early 1950s. Elizabeth did not know very much about it either; but her journey through Italy to Capri had given her a glimpse into what was obviously a very rich tradition, in a country that had been unified for less than a hundred years – so the regional differences promised to be every bit as varied as they were in France. Elizabeth had also done enough reading to know that Italian cooking not only had variety, it had history, contained in a bibliography which went back to ancient Rome. Scholars had written endless books on the history and techniques developed by French cuisine; but Italian food had been completely neglected.

John Lehmann was easily persuaded, and not simply because Elizabeth had already produced two excellent and successful books: the time was ripe. In the same way that people were rediscovering the Mediterranean, John Lehmann wrote that one of the most exciting things for his generation, after the war, was the rediscovery of Italy. 'When fascism had at last been brought to its absurd and bloody end, I think that most of us were only too eager to resume a relationship that had brought so much happiness, and had been so fruitful in the past.'[2]

He commissioned Elizabeth to write a book on Italian food, with an advance of £300. It was generous for the times, but Elizabeth was only given £100 of it and had a great deal of travelling to do. She planned to let the house again, and start her sojourn in Italy in the spring of 1952. Elizabeth had promised herself, in what was going to be a period of very hard work, the treat of a visit to Norman Douglas in Capri; but on a dark, rainy day in February, she heard that he was dead. He was old, ill and uncomfortable, and had swallowed two bottles of pills to release himself from the burden of living. Elizabeth missed him painfully. One of his most important messages to her was to say what she thought and damn everybody else; but she had written with him in mind, and without him part of her felt cut adrift.

Elizabeth set off for Italy by train in early March, with an entire trunkful of books. Among the volumes were Osbert Sitwell's *Winters of Content* (1932), Charles Edwards's *Sardinia and the Sardes*, Tobias Smollett's *Travels through France and Italy* (1776) and – of course – Norman Douglas's *Old Calabria*. After a day or two in Paris, she reached Rome on the 9th. It was in the period leading up to Easter (which fell on the 25th that year) and Elizabeth was astounded by the riot of rainbow-coloured sugar work so proudly displayed by the Roman confectioners. In a country in which the food was normally presented with a beautiful simplicity, she mused, it seemed odd that they should dress up their cakes and sweets in such exuberantly bad taste.

Her base in Rome was two rooms in the Palazzo Doria, where loneliness increased her grief over the death of Norman Douglas. But there were friends: Archie Lyall, an enormous gentle elephant of a man who had been in SOE during the war and whom she had known in Cairo, and Arthur and Viola Johnson. Arthur was an international lawyer and art collector who also had a passion for books. His wife Viola was half English, half Italian, and just the sort of woman Elizabeth liked: a generous and highly individual character, whose intelligence was spiked with an irreverent wit. They were also very interested in food, and their knowledge of where to buy the best of everything impressed Elizabeth. 'The Johnsons' Parma ham is better than anything I ever tasted in its way. Sweet, tender, not too fat.' They also had a vineyard outside Rome, at Grottaferrata; and she always associated the taste of its red, heady wine with her months in Rome.

The Johnsons were also regular visitors to Capri, and from Rome the three of them spent Easter at their house there, the Molino a Vento. Elizabeth brought a pot of basil to Norman Douglas's grave, but admitted she never shared his 'melancholy taste for graveyards'. She preferred to remember him in one of his sanctuaries: a little taverna, sheltering in the ruins of the old archbishop's palace now overgrown by a lemon grove. 'Capri wine at the lemon grove . . . white, earthy taste, unmistakably genuine. Country sausage. The scent of lemon skins exquisite. Nobody will get the name of that place out of me.'[3]

At the Café Caprile in Anacapri, Elizabeth found the taste of true southern Italy. The cook was a woman called Mafalda, who gave Elizabeth many of her recipes. Mafalda used to make particularly good bottled pimentos, and Elizabeth badly wanted this recipe; but it was the wrong time of year for bottling them. 'Come back in the summer,' said Mafalda.

Elizabeth took notes all the time, and although only a few of her notebooks survive, they throw interesting lights on the things which struck her, whether meals at specific restaurants or observations people made. The Richietti girls thought that cooking with pork or bacon fat was *vulgare* and heavy; one authority, called Carluccio Civitella, informed her that anything cooked with aubergines was far better with zucchini, and that the celebrated *ragù* (Bolognese sauce) was a *plat de concierge*, stewed until black. She also noticed the way that Roman shopkeepers sold their chickpeas ready soaked.

With little money or experience of Italy, Elizabeth had taken the trouble to get advice from the best possible sources: the High Commissioner for Italian Tourism and the Ente Nazionale Industrie Turistiche. They were very helpful, and smoothed her way into the most celebrated restaurants in Italy. Yet even she was surprised by the extraordinary richness and variety of Italian food, both in its regional specialities and its traditional cookery. She wrote to John Lehmann to tell him, saying she would need more time to research the book. She also complained of the amount she was having to eat, though on this point Lehmann was not very sympathetic: 'You poor suffering martyr to the gastronomical future of the benighted Anglo-Saxons. I have been weeping at the thought of your liver, as I crumble up a little slice of cold luncheon meat.'[4]

Her first series of journeys took her north: first to Siena and Florence, and then to Venice. In Siena she found *panforte* ('like cold plum pudding, with whole almonds and pieces of peel') and little *pecorino* cheeses covered with a red rind. She also noticed that Siena was the only town in Italy where tarragon was much used, and available in all the shops.

Her first call in Florence was to the painter Derek Hill, who occupied the Villino Corbignano in the garden of Bernard Berenson's I Tatti. They ate a memorable meal prepared by his cook, Giulia Piccini: *ravioli verdi*, followed by chicken with anchovy butter, and Mocha pudding, which consisted of a sponge cake soaked in black coffee, smothered in cream and sprinkled with roasted almonds. She later gave Elizabeth some recipes, including one for *riso ricco* which, for all its simplicity, even Elizabeth calls 'a tricky dish'. Derek Hill passed them on, with a note about the wines which had impressed her: 'Osbert Sitwell's white Montegufoni, a light semi-sparkling summer wine, and as red the Contini Bonacossi's Capezzano. The French Consul, who's possibly even greedier than you or I, came to luncheon and said they were the best wines he had drunk here. Rare praise indeed – so after butterpatting myself I had better close as museums always say.'[5]

In the market place in Florence were rolled fillets of pork adorned, 'almost embroidered', with rosemary. Elizabeth thought the Florentines were rather too fond of this herb; but their *finocchina*, a salami flavoured with fennel seeds, was one of her favourites of all Italian salami. She noticed that there were no pizzerias in Florence, and the restaurants seemed more crowded than those in Rome. In the Sabatini restaurant she spent many hours in the kitchens, and found 'the best coffee in Italy so far'.

On her first visit to Venice she was welcomed by Signor Zoppi of the Taverna La Fenice. 'Alfredo Zoppi is a man to clamp to your heart with hoops of steel,' she wrote in her notebook. 'A man who knows his own mind, and furthermore knows the exact anatomy, habits and cooking quality of every beast in the Adriatic sea.' Like Elizabeth he had a particular sensitivity to the appearance of food: in *Italian Food*, a description of his restaurant accompanies one of her favourite desserts: *aranci caramellizzati*.

Elizabeth was keen to do some sightseeing as well. On the way to Verona, she was 'appalled'[6] to find that she was the only person who would get out of the bus to see Palladio's theatre in Vicenza when it was raining; she also thought that the presentation of the Montecchio castle was 'as bogus as Anne Hathaway's cottage'.[7] In Verona she was taken to the Trattoria Molinara, where she ate a very plain risotto, adorned only with a few tiny squares of ham: 'one of the best I have ever had'.[8] It is in Lombardy and Piedmont that the best risottos are made, with the rice of the Piedmont which makes them unique. 'The fact that this rice can be cooked contrary to all the rules, slowly, in a small amount of liquid, and emerge in a perfect state of creaminess with a very slightly resistant core in each grain gives the risotto its particular character.'[9]

She made the journey from Verona to Milan in pouring rain, on a road that passes along the southern shore of Lake Garda. 'Shall never learn to love lake scenery, even in sunshine,' she grumbled, 'and if anyone says Gabriele D'Annunzio again I shall go off my head.'[10]

In Milan she saw mascarpone cheeses wrapped up in white muslin, ate slices of sturgeon in oil, and a particularly good salad of raw artichokes. She also discovered *mostarda di Cremona*: a traditional accompaniment to boiled meat, it consists of figs, apricots, melon, citron, orange peel and pumpkin, in a delicate syrup flavoured with mustard. Now the confection is a shadow of what it was and is sold in small jars; but in Milan, in the early fifties, it was sold in wooden pails. It was also in Milan, on 5 May, that she saw the first of that season's green almonds.

She spent a day in Como, where she ate a risotto made with dried mushrooms, and then moved down to Genoa, 'the noisiest city in the world'. Among its dishes is the *cappon magro*: a combination of vegetables and fish, served on a ship's biscuit rubbed with garlic, and accompanied by a sauce which includes parsley, hard-boiled eggs, garlic and anchovies. Yet the most famous Genoese speciality was, and still is, pesto, which in its place of origin enlivens everything from soup to pasta or red mullet: 'They say the basil in Genoa has quite a different flavour from anywhere else. Also they have it all the year round.'[11] Elizabeth maintained that the Genoese trenette (thin, match-like pasta) with pesto was the best pasta dish in all Italy. She could never resist a fish market, and found the one at Santa Margherita (just to the east of Genoa) particularly beguiling. The shellfish called *moscadini*, brown and pale green, were set out in baskets 'like newly washed pebbles'; and one can imagine her going from one stall to the other, peering closely into everything with a fastidious, inquisitive expression, asking the names of everything. The thin, rose-coloured, slippery little fish for *fritture* were called *signorini*; she also came across a fish called *gallina di mare* – 'sea chicken' – with a huge head and a little body; and tall baskets of *tonnetto*, long fish packed in head first 'like loaves of French bread, shining with phosphorescence'.

From Genoa she went to San Remo, where she was impressed by the wine of Dolcecagna – and amused by 'the candid young man who said he would not invite me to dance, "*parce qu'on fait ça seulement pour des raisons érotiques, n'est ce pas, Madame*"'.[12] She visited Florence again and then Perugia, where the pork was roasted with fennel rather than the ubiquitous Florentine rosemary. She was back in Rome on 15 May, in time to meet Peter Laing, the wounded officer whom she had loved in Egypt. He was on holiday in Italy with his wife Kit.

Elizabeth spent the rest of the month in Rome, and then went back to Venice for ten days. Like many people, she could not have enough of the city. The cooking, with its delicate rice dishes, its fresh anchovies and crabs and scampi, was very much the sort of food she best liked to eat. She also had the company of a delightful friend, Archie Colquhoun, an Italian scholar who was later to translate Giuseppe di Lampedusa's novel *The Leopard*. On 15 June, they decided to visit the Rialto fish market, which has to be seen at dawn. Rather than face the chore of getting up at that hour, Elizabeth and Archie stayed up all night, reaching the market at sunrise. As they wandered around, watching the traders and boatmen hailing each other as they swung the dripping baskets and boxes of fish off the boats and thumping them down on to the stone floor, they came across the Sicilian painter Renato Guttuso who was on his way to the railway station.

Guttuso was considered one of the most important painters working in Italy at the time, and Elizabeth had seen his work at the Venice Biennale. She was overwhelmed by the power of his still-life paintings, in which even artichokes and lemons were embued with a blazing vitality: and there and then, she decided that she wanted Guttuso to illustrate *Italian Food*.

In that particular Venetian dawn everything went Elizabeth's way. Archie Colquhoun was a friend of Guttuso, and they began talking. Colquhoun introduced Elizabeth as a great fan of his work, explained that she was writing a book on Italian food, and – to her astonishment – Guttuso immediately agreed to do the illustrations for it. Whether it was the joy of meeting Guttuso or the magic of the moment, that morning at the Rialto market was to inspire one of the most intensely visual and lyrical descriptions of a market that Elizabeth was ever to write:

The light of a Venetian dawn in early summer – you must be up at about four o'clock in the morning to see the market coming to life – is so limpid and so still that it makes every separate vegetable and fruit and fish luminous with a light of its own, with unnaturally heightened colours and clear stencilled outlines ... In Venice, ordinary sole and ugly great skate are striped with delicate lilac lights, the sardines shine like newly minted silver coins ...[13]

John Lehmann was in Venice too that summer, and Elizabeth had urged him to see the Guttusos: she wanted his opinion, for as her publisher he was the one who would commission and pay for the art work. Lehmann was not impressed. He was put off by the fact that when he was not doing still-life paintings, Guttuso was an ardent Communist, who embraced social realism and all the ideals that went with it.

'If you want your next book to be illustrated in a social-realist manner, with ... a picture of Stalin tasting the macaroni on the frontispiece, then Guttuso is your man. Otherwise heaven forbid. Anyway you might as well ask Picasso to do it.' However, he soon realized that Elizabeth had made up her mind about Guttuso. 'If you are really keen and confident about his capacity, I would not object,' he wrote.[14] But he made it plain that he could not offer much more than £60, and that Elizabeth would have to handle all the negotiations herself.

From Venice she moved on to the airy district of Parma, where she saw the curing of Parmesan cheese or *grana* (the cheese is tested with a skewer, by men who have spent a lifetime learning its secrets) and hams (part of the pigs' diet is the whey from the cheeses).

She returned to Rome to meet up once again with the Johnsons, with whom she took a trip to Sorrento, Salerno and Paestum. Compared to the north of Italy, Elizabeth found the food and wine of the south disappointing; but in the hill town of Ravello, they discovered an unusual red wine called Gran Caruso. The family that made it also owned the local hotel, where the food was as good as their wine.

Elizabeth spent the rest of the summer with the Johnsons in Anacapri. She found plenty of time on her hands, for she was waiting for Mafalda of the Caffè Caprile to announce that the red and orange peppers were finally ripe enough to bottle. For this particular recipe, Elizabeth had to learn the patience of a wildlife photographer waiting to film a particularly elusive specimen.

By the end of August the pimentos, piled in great heaps in the market, looked ready to burst with ripeness; but they were not yet good enough for Mafalda. Elizabeth had to wait nearly a month before the great day came, 'while my host and hostess on the island must have been wondering if I was ever going to leave'.

She was back in Rome by early September, from where she wrote to Renato Guttuso with some trepidation. Guttuso was a serious artist with a world-wide reputation who could command substantial sums of money for his work, and she feared that John Lehmann's £60 might appear insulting.

'I have heard from my publisher John Lehmann. He tells me that unfortunately the most he can offer is £60 (about 100,000 lire) . . . If by any possible chance you would still consent to do the work, I need hardly tell you that I should be overjoyed . . .'[15] To her enormous relief, Guttuso did not go back on his word. 'He said the fee was pretty absurd, but he would do the work all the same.'[16]

Towards the end of September, she took the boat to Sardinia, which was then scarcely visited by tourists. The island was not only wild and beautiful, it had developed a highly individual cookery. Myrtle was much used, for flavouring everything from fish to thrushes to baby pig. The Sardes hunted wild boar and even made hams from it, though by 1950 this was becoming rare; yet perhaps best of all was the multitude of brightly coloured fish so abundantly displayed in the market in Cagliari. She was also struck by the elegance of the Sardinian national dress, on which she took detailed notes: the men wore white linen shirts with black jackets and white breeches, while the women wore finely pleated red or black skirts and medieval-looking headdresses.

Her next destination was Bologna. 'Gastronomically speaking,' she wrote in her notebook, 'Bologna is to Italy rather what Strasbourg is to France.' The food was richer, more heavily laden with cream, truffles, cheese and ham than in most Italian provinces; yet it was also exceptionally good. Like Strasbourg, Bologna's unique culinary tradition was much appreciated all over the country. In almost every Italian town, noted Elizabeth, there was at least one Bolognese restaurant.

In Bologna, the Bolognese restaurant – considered the best in Italy – was the Papagallo, and here Elizabeth tasted *filetti di tacchino in pasta sfoglia*: a turkey breast covered in a sauce of mushrooms, ham and cheese, and served in a puff pastry case. This famous dish was almost too rich and cloying for Elizabeth, and she much preferred the delicacy of their chicken mousse served in broth. Altogether, she felt more at home in the trattoria of Zia Nerina. It was Nerina who gave Elizabeth her recipe for *ragù*: only in Bologna do they add cream to it.

Throughout her Italian journey, Elizabeth had made a point of learning as much as she could about Italian wines. In the early 1950s there were very few of them on the English market, and they were little known because the best ones could not compete in price with their French equivalents. Over the years, more and more Italian wines appeared in England, and more and more people travelled to Italy, so inevitably the chapter on wine is one of those that changed most throughout successive editions of *Italian Food*. Perhaps the wines changed too. In early editions she describes Soave as 'perhaps the most delicious white wine of Italy', whereas in the revised 1987 Penguin edition, she recommends her readers to 'try something other than the Soave, so often flabby and insipid . . .'

She had by now been away for about seven months, and was looking forward to going home; but she felt she could not leave Italy without visiting Turin at the height of the truffle season. She did not regret it. 'Truffles large as tennis balls,' she wrote in her notebook. 'Shops packed with food – game, little birds, cheeses, truffles, huge funghi.' She also visited the Turin market on Saturday, when the piazza was filled with baskets of autumn-coloured mushrooms and truffles, as well as game, sausages and creamy cheeses.

Her engagement book for 1952 charts the journey from town to town. She had contacts in many places, and yet she was touched by the time and trouble people took to show her around their native city, provide guides and introduce her to the *padroni* of the best and most interesting restaurants. The friends she had met in Rome would have passed her on to friends of theirs in other places, but one has the feeling that much of it was a solitary journey. She travelled from one hotel to the next, reading on trains, taking notes in the markets and trattorias and restaurants. She also noted a few of her impressions of Italy. 'They all seem to regard it as the most normal thing in the world that they started the war on one side and finished it on the other . . . they are bitter about Trieste, and clearly see no reason why they should pay for losing the war. Well, why should they?' Yet while Elizabeth developed a tremendous admiration for the abundant creativity and generosity of the Italians, for their rollicking good humour, she could not cope with the noise. Quite apart from the honking horns and roaring traffic, every restaurant was dominated by the sound of cooks pounding veal and turkey breasts; while at night she had to endure the 'excruciating cacophony' of assorted guitarists, violinists and singers.

Italians are not known for their punctuality, so she wasted many hours in waiting for people to turn up, days waiting for the *festa* at which a certain dish was to be made. When the cooks were ready she could not afford to blink or lose the thread for a second, for they talked and cooked with more speed and energy than she felt she could keep up with. Her Italian was, as she described it, 'the wrong side of adequate'.

It was hard work; yet she was utterly absorbed, and exhilarated by a sense of discovery that she had never experienced before. 'As recipe after recipe came out and I realized how much I was learning, and how much these dishes were enlarging my own scope and enjoyment, the fever to communicate them grew every day more urgent.'[17] People at home had told her that she would find Italian cuisine so limited that she would be obliged to invent recipes. Invent! Elizabeth was itching to get home, to tell everyone that Italian cooking consisted of a good deal more than spaghetti, veal and tomato sauce.

She was back in London in late October, and took a room at the Grosvenor Hotel since Halsey Street was still let. From here she got in touch with Peter Higgins, who had given up farming in Devon and had returned to stockbroking, with the Guinness Peat Group in the City. They went out to dinner, stayed out late, and on their return Peter made a fuss because the hotel manager, mindful of his licence, refused to serve them any drinks after hours.

Elizabeth was at the height of her beauty, elated by the success of her trip, and more in love with Peter than ever before. Emotionally, she was about to embark on the happiest years of her life. In her work, she was about to begin a book that (as she already knew) would prove extremely difficult to write, but into which she always felt she had put the very best of herself.

In October 1952, tea came off the ration; and as Christmas approached, Marguerite Patten was able to demonstrate a 'fairly basic Christmas pudding and cake' on BBC television. There were better supplies of fish, vegetables, fruit and poultry, but butter, cooking fat and meat were still firmly controlled by the Ministry of Food. It was not until the following spring that egg distribution was freed of government restrictions.

Ingredients were not the only problem. Generous and obliging as they were, Italian cooks took very little interest in quantities or measurements. Elizabeth had armed herself with a measuring jug, marked out in both imperial and metric measurements, and on occasions 'I stood over the cooks and simply forced them to show me what they meant by a handful.' However, this was not always possible. A handful of flour, a bunch of spinach, a few spoonfuls of sugar, a lot of oil – all too often, these were the instructions she found when the time came to test the recipes.

That too posed a difficulty, for with the house let she did not have a kitchen. She spent the next three months with Doreen and her second husband, Colin Thornton, who had just moved into a house some thirty miles outside London, near Gravesend. Meopham Court was a huge house that had been divided into three. The Thorntons' end was Victorian Gothic and while the rooms were generous enough, the kitchen was minute. In no time at all Elizabeth had taken it over, and there was fresh pasta draped over every chair. The food she cooked was wonderful, but she was so engrossed in her work that she had lost all sense of time. She always offered to make dinner, and when Colin came back from work he was tired and hungry. But Elizabeth had barely begun to cook supper by nine, and often they did not sit down to eat until eleven.

A fast train service to London meant Elizabeth could make the occasional visit to the Italian shops of Soho to buy olive oil, parmesan cheeses and Italian rice. She was also lucky in that there was a farm near by where she could buy cheese and cream, but these were still rationed. So was meat, which came in hunks 'designated as suitable for roasting, frying, grilling, or stewing. To ask your butcher for special cuts (and foreign ones at that) was to ask for a sardonic laugh . . .'[18]

Difficult as it was, the writing of *Italian Food* liberated a lyrical, evocative streak in Elizabeth's writing. In previous books, she had been always inclined to quote from writers she admired, rather than attempt set-piece descriptions herself. In *Italian Food*, she allows herself to be carried away by the extraordinary delicacy of a plain risotto, the market in Venice and the kitchen of Signor Zoppi.

*

In the winter of 1952, when she was still lost in the long and arduous task of writing the book, she received some very bad news. The publishing firm of John Lehmann Ltd was being closed down. Financial control of the company had for many years been in the hands of Purnell, a West Country printing firm. In 1952, Purnell's chairman Wilfred Harvey made it known that he was not satisfied with the profits of John Lehmann Ltd, and planned to wind up the company. With the backing of a young publisher called Robert Maxwell, Lehmann tried to buy the list from Purnell – he was desperate to save it, for the company bore the biggest asset he had in publishing: his own name. But rather than sell John Lehmann Ltd for less than the monstrously large sum he had demanded, Harvey preferred to let the company fold. Journalists, writers and academics sprang to Lehmann's defence with innumerable articles and letters, deploring the fact that such a magnificent and pioneering house should have come to such a miserable end.

John sent Elizabeth a copy of a short statement in which he divorced himself from the company, with a letter dated 2 December: 'I fear the little announcement I enclose will startle and shock you. There is a very nasty story behind it, and I think I should tell it you as soon as possible.'

Elizabeth was deeply shaken by the news; her relationship with Lehmann had been 'friendly, fruitful, civilized';[19] and after hearing the 'nasty story', she was even more alarmed to hear that Purnell wanted to hold on to only two of Lehmann's authors: herself and the American writer Paul Bowles. They were to be handed over to Purnell's satellite company, Macdonald, who published school textbooks and *Jane's Fighting Ships*.

In January 1954, Elizabeth delivered the typescript personally to Wilfred Harvey's son, Captain Eric Harvey, MC, who was the managing director of Macdonald. As she sat in his office in Maddox Street, Elizabeth noticed how Harvey looked at the thick pile of paper on his desk with some distaste. He said it looked very long. It did not conform to the set pattern of cookery books. (The pioneering spirit, that had been such a feature of John Lehmann's company, evidently had no place at Macdonald.) Elizabeth admitted that that was the case, but she had found a great deal of material, and it had anyway been her intention to break new ground. Captain Harvey then looked up the contract in his filing cabinet.

'Good gracious. I see Mr Lehmann contracted to pay you an advance of three hundred pounds. Is that right?'

'Yes.'

'Three hundred pounds. THREE HUNDRED POUNDS? For a *cookery* book? . . . No wonder Mr Lehmann's business wasn't making a profit.' The brave captain sighed a surly sigh. 'Well, all I can say is that I hope we get our money back.'[20]

The delivery of a typescript that represents two or three years of work is always a shaky moment for an author, and to have it received in such a churlishly unsympathetic manner was a shock. 'The surrender into hostile hands of the book with which I had lived for two years and which had caused me much anguish but which I felt did all the same represent some advance over my previous work was traumatic.'[21] Yet that was only the beginning. 'Had I known what I was presently to discover about Macdonald I would certainly have preferred to abandon two years' hard work, return the hundred pounds which was all I had received of that famous advance, and cancel the contract.'[22]

Instead, she began writing pieces for the *Daily Express*, pieces largely written with an eye to value. They had titles like 'Some Leading Questions to Put to Your Butcher This Morning', and 'A Good Dinner Need not be Expensive'. Elizabeth had never had much money, so her concerns in these fields were the same as the editor's and her readership. But Elizabeth could also be rather dogmatic, and the *Daily Express*'s food editor sometimes felt the need to keep her in her place.

In a collective article called 'Is Butter Better?' Elizabeth wrote out why she gave butter an unequivocal 'yes'. However, the cookery editor felt that margarine did have its place for use in cakes, white sauces and strong fish like kippers and bloaters, and ended with 'Perhaps the last word on the question is that the better cook you are the more margarine you can use.'[23]

At the same time, Elizabeth began work on one of her most light-hearted books, *Summer Cooking*. It was a far less demanding project than her previous one, included all the kinds of food that she herself most liked to eat, and she wrote it just as those foods came into season.

By March or April 1954, with the publication of *Italian Food* scheduled for November, Elizabeth had received nothing from Guttuso. He would not answer her letters, while Macdonald were getting restive: time was pressing. Elizabeth turned for help to her friend Derek Hill, who knew Guttuso well. Hill managed to persuade him that Elizabeth needed the illustrations urgently and, in ones and twos, they began to arrive: seven pen and ink drawings, and one magnificent watercolour of artichokes, a bundle of chard and a straw-covered flask. Elizabeth was completely delighted. These intense and vibrant images did not merely illustrate her book: they confirmed everything that she thought and felt about Italy, and that she had tried to convey in *Italian Food*. 'Long before the pictures were out of my hands and delivered into those of the publishers, they had become for me an integral part of my book. Once again, the whole idea made sense.'[24]

Italian Food came out in November 1954, dedicated to Arthur and Viola Johnson, in appreciation for all the help and hospitality they had given her in Italy, and for Viola's work in checking and correcting all the Italian words and phrases. The book received an enthusiastic reception. Freya Stark, writing in the *Observer* on 14 November, observed that in times of 'culinary stress', a good cookery book 'has the same effect on one's morale as the thought of the evening's dinner, gently simmering in an Alpine hotel, has on the tired legs of the returning mountaineer . . . Mrs David may be counted among the benefactors of humanity.'

Her book was also reviewed by Olivia Manning, in her 'London Letter' in the *Jerusalem Post*. She identified *Italian Food* as one of a new breed of cookbooks written for 'the New Poor' – those who would have had cooks and housekeepers before the war, but who now had to do their own shopping and cooking. These books 'do not dictate . . . they inform with all the knowledge and charm their authors can bring to their art'.[25]

The book was undoubtedly a success, but it had very little impact outside the home counties, and none further afield. Even several years after the publication of *Italian Food*, when Ann and Franco Taruschio set up their restaurant at the Walnut Tree Inn near Abergavenny in 1963, their earliest customers had no idea what cannelloni and lasagne were.

However, the first print run of *Italian Food* sold out in three weeks, and Macdonald – despite their direct connection with the printers – reprinted too late, thus missing the Christmas market. In the New Year, Evelyn Waugh wrote in the *Sunday Times* that *Italian Food* was one of the two books he had most enjoyed that year. 'I was, and still am, stunned by the compliment and by Mr Waugh's tolerance at my amateur's efforts at writing,' wrote Elizabeth in her introduction to the Penguin edition. Here was no false modesty. If Elizabeth thought of herself as proficient in anything, it was in food and cookery – she never saw herself as a professional writer, certainly not in the same league as Waugh, and her opinion of her own writing never rose very high. Ten years later she could still write, 'I'm *not* a writer really you know, only a self-made one . . .'[26] Yet whatever she thought of her writing, it was exasperating to have the book out of print when this testimonial was arousing people's interest.

Macdonald held the rights not only to *Italian Food*, but to her two previously published books as well. It seemed to Elizabeth monstrously unjust that they should have such contractual power over work that, if Eric Harvey's reaction to *Italian Food* was anything to go by, they would never have had the imagination to publish themselves. John Lehmann had put Elizabeth in touch with the literary agents Pearn, Pollinger and Higham (later David Higham Associates). She was represented by Paul Scott, later to achieve fame as the author of the *Raj Quartet*. But although he was unable to extricate her first two books and *Italian Food* from their grasp, he did get them to waive their right to a first option on *Summer Cooking*, which in the course of time was published by the Museum Press.

Elizabeth asked her friend Adrian Daintrey to illustrate *Summer Cooking*. Summer had long passed when he took up the commission, and neither he nor Elizabeth liked the idea of setting up fake summer scenes of strawberries and peaches. Instead, Daintrey would come round to Halsey Street, and do sketches of compositions set up mainly by Elizabeth. Daintrey was a curious character, rather threadbare and lugubrious in appearance; yet he had a great many friends and was a fund of stories and gossip, delivered in a very amusing, deadpan manner. His work at Halsey Street was congenial for both of them, and often turned into a long lunch. One of the most evocative of his sketches shows Elizabeth's trusty old gas cooker, on which a stout earthenware pot is cooking something warm and comforting. 'Some people liked Adrian's illustrations,' she wrote, 'others thought them old-fashioned, which they are. I still think they have a good atmosphere, and for those who chose to look there was useful information in them.'[27]

Despite her success, Elizabeth was not yet the household name that she would become. Her first three books had reached an enthusiastic, but still fairly narrow section of the population: mostly those middle-class, educated people who had experienced good food, and were keen – now that they no longer had staff – to train themselves in cooking French and Italian dishes. But she was about to be given an important break, which would open up her work to the paperback market. Penguin Books were interested in publishing an edition of *Mediterranean Food*; and Elizabeth discovered that the person responsible for bringing her book to the attention of Penguin's chairman, Allen Lane, was his only woman director, Eunice Frost.

Eunice Frost had first spotted the book in the Lehmann catalogue, and was intrigued by the new offering – not because it was a cookbook, but because it looked so interesting. 'I am not a cook', she said, 'then no more than now. I read it as an artist, and I felt ravished. It was so visually exciting, so illuminating, with such a sense of purpose and place – it was like finding yourself in an oasis filled with beautiful and delicious things, and it made one realize what one had missed all through the war.'[28]

In the 1988 introduction to *Mediterranean Food* Elizabeth David recorded her debt to Eunice Frost, thanks to whom 'My book had been given a dazzling opportunity.' Elizabeth goes on to say that Miss Frost had supported her book against considerable opposition, though Miss Frost could not recall that *Mediterranean Food* met with many reservations within the firm.

Macdonald passed on the Penguin offer, with a covering letter suggesting that Elizabeth might find it rather 'infra dig' to see her work in paperback. 'Silly asses,' wrote Elizabeth in the margin of the letter. Her reaction was quite the opposite. She wanted her book to reach as many people as possible, and the paperback price of two shillings and sixpence (as opposed to ten and six in hardback) put it within reach of almost everybody.

Macdonald insisted on taking 50 per cent of all the royalties from Penguin. It was quite normal at the time* but Elizabeth thought it scandalous. Her opinion of them sank even lower when, for the second year running, they allowed *Italian Food* to fall out of print just before Christmas.

Most galling of all was Macdonald's reaction to the revisions she

---

* Even now a 50 per cent cut is not unreasonable – though in this country, 60 per cent of paperback royalties is more likely to be the author's cut. The main difference in publishing contracts today is that authors' hardback advances are far higher than they were in the mid-1950s, largely because they take future paperback rights into account.

had made to the Penguin edition of *Mediterranean Food*. These revisions were essential in view of the fact that the book had been written in 1949, and conditions had changed dramatically since then. But Macdonald refused to budge: not only did they forbid Penguin to call their edition 'revised', but they also refused to reset the hardback edition in line with the much-needed changes.

At the most important and productive period in her life, Elizabeth was in the hands of publishers who were, at best, remarkably unsympathetic. This did not, in the long run, damage either her reputation or her books; but in that part of Elizabeth's mind that was always fuming, always enraged, a dangerous resentment was building up.

* * * * * * * *

CHAPTER THIRTEEN

Friends, Editors and
Other Enemies

Whatever he still felt for Elizabeth, Tony David had tired of England. In 1953 he decided he could do better by moving to Spain. With Tony gone, Halsey Street underwent another transformation. The original kitchen, which had been in the basement, was transformed into a tiny bed-sitter into which moved Lesley O'Malley. She made a very dashing entry to Halsey Street, perched on a small sofa which was lashed to the top of a friend's Land Rover.

The arrival of Lesley O'Malley was very welcome. They shared many friends in common, such as the painter Derek Hill, the writer Roald Dahl and his wife Pat, and the rest of the Cairo set; while their own friendship had a delightful complicity that meant they were never bored in each other's company, never wearied of each other's jokes. Lesley was also very close to Felicité; but whereas Felicité and Elizabeth ate together only on birthdays and feast-days, Elizabeth and Lesley ate and drank together several times a week, and often went out to the theatre or the cinema. They had more than friendship in common. Both had been married in Cairo, both were now separated; but while Elizabeth's marriage was over primarily because she had grown bored with Tony, Lesley had had to endure life with a violent and abusive man.

Lesley had found a good job in advertising after the war; but her confidence had been undermined by the dreadful years with her ex-husband, and she was now deeply involved with a married man. She had met Patrick de Morny in Cairo. He had married after

Lesley, and was now as unhappy in his marriage as she had been in hers. But although he was very much in love with Lesley, he felt unable to leave his emotionally fragile wife.

Elizabeth seemed to be drawn to women whose love life had gone wrong, to have a sort of tacit empathy with them. Another of her closest friends was Joyce Murchie, a New Zealand heiress who had come into her fortune at the age of twenty-one and was spending it fast. Small, with ginger hair and freckles, Joyce had married a dentist and tried to become a normal housewife – but the effort was too much for her. She was too much of a hedonist, and was the sort of generous, ebullient person who paid for every round of drinks she and her friends could order. She did not live anywhere in particular, preferring to stay in hotels or the guest bedrooms of her friends. She travelled a good deal, and – when she had run through her fortune – went to live cheaply in a little flat in Asolo. She had been truly in love only once, with a young soldier she had met in Cairo. After the war they had travelled across north Africa; but one day, when her lover was in the car on his own, he drove into a sandstorm and perished.

Lesley and Elizabeth gave a joint cocktail party on one occasion. They had made a magnificent spread of *mezze* (one of Lesley's specialities) and the party went on till four in the morning; but when Elizabeth attempted another cocktail party, it was not a success. She invited far too many people, had no time to heat up the food she had planned under the grill, and one of her dearest neighbours – Walter Baxter, who later became the owner of the Chanterelle restaurant – was insulted by a fellow guest. When it was over, Elizabeth swore that never again would she invite so many people 'who couldn't even get on over drinks'.

Felicité was still living in the top flat, and she and Elizabeth maintained a scrupulous respect for each other's privacy. If Elizabeth was entertaining one of their mutual friends, Felicité came downstairs for a drink but always vanished before dinner. And when Felicité was entertaining, Elizabeth did the same – except that she sometimes brought a terrine or a pâté, and left it as a parting gift with the words 'I thought so-and-so ought to have something decent to eat.'

The underlying reason for this arrangement was that their attitudes to food were so different that they constituted a mutual irritation. In contrast to Elizabeth, Felicité was completely uninterested in food. But sometimes, if Felicité was going to have someone special round for supper, she would ask Elizabeth to cook something for her. Elizabeth always obliged, leaving the dish discreetly in Felicité's tiny kitchen while she was still at work.

One cannot help thinking that Felicité's life might have been more fulfilling if she had left at some point, and branched out on her own. She was very much her own person and knew her own mind, and Elizabeth valued her judgement and her companionship; yet as the years went on, Felicité felt rather oppressed by Elizabeth's fame. She had always wanted to write poetry, but she was much too diffident to show it to Elizabeth, who probably never gave Felicité's writing talents a thought. Felicité was left with the feeling that fate had given all the literary gifts to her elder sister.

At the same time, Felicité had the Gwynne strength of character, and she had that confidence which comes from a certain family pride. She was also a good talker, and a great gossip. She knew everyone in the street, always had time for a chat, and was intensely curious about everything that was going on among the neighbours: 'She was the sort of person who couldn't talk to you for two minutes without trying to ferret something out of you.' She dressed soberly, and bicycled everywhere. Her main extravagance seems to have been her expensive Knightsbridge hairdresser, whom she went to at least once a week – as much for the gossip as for her hair.

Another major element in Elizabeth's life was her sister Diana, who lived in the house with the leaning trees in Abingdon Road. Her first child, Rupert, had been followed by another son, Jonathan (always known as Johnny), in 1951; and two years later she gave birth to her only daughter, Christabel. She was to have two more children: Steven, and Christopher, known as Christo. Diana and her husband were devoted to each other and, although money was always tight, their marriage was happy. Elizabeth used to grumble that Diana's life was one of non-stop drudgery, and that it was Christopher's fault for giving her too many children; but at the same time she was very fond of her attractive brother-in-law, and was one of his patients.

Dr Christopher Grey was doing well. He combined great charm with exceptional skill as a doctor, and he travelled between his patients, and the various academic institutions to which he acted as physician, in the old Rolls-Royce he had bought from Elizabeth and Tony.

It soon became the custom for Elizabeth and Felicité to spend Christmas with Diana and her family. Christopher would come to Halsey Street with the Rolls, and get them – plus all the presents, and baskets of food, wine, preserves and provisions cooked by Elizabeth – into the car. All three sisters were close, and Diana and Felicité were quite capable of standing up to the famous Liza.

Johnny Grey, Diana's second son, was terrified of Elizabeth as a child. But he was also intrigued, and a trip to Aunt Liza's in Halsey Street was always looked forward to. She had an alarmingly brisk manner with children. Yet in her rather aloof and distant way she could respond, because like them she understood the magic of things. He remembers being taken to her house to learn how to cook a chicken, and on another occasion, she noticed that he was fascinated by two or three Japanese paper fans with landscapes printed on them. 'You can have those,' she said – and made a friend for life. Little Johnny was stunned by the generosity of her gift, and lost in admiration that Aunt Liza could give away such precious and beautiful objects.

Her god-daughter Frances Fedden also remembers the nervousness and interest that Elizabeth excited. When she and her sister Kate came to Halsey Street – the Fedden family would always visit Elizabeth on Boxing Day, her birthday – Elizabeth fussed about, trying to keep the children from touching anything. But if either of them expressed an interest in something, she would take the object in caressing hands, talk about it and invite them to hold it. Frances also remembered how good she was at giving just the right present to excite a child's imagination. She did not necessarily wrap it up; but she would stroke and handle the object before bestowing it, giving her gift a significance that no amount of tissue paper and ribbon could have achieved. She remembers in particular a little painted tin box that Elizabeth gave her, cunningly disguised as a pile of books bound with a strap.

Elizabeth's mother Stella had moved from Dedham to a smaller house, in Brighton. She still carried on dealing in furniture and antiques, and used Priscilla's house in Kensington as her London base. Priscilla's younger sisters used to come and visit their mother there; but Pris herself was no longer the centre of their world, as she had been in the thirties and forties. She was wrapped up in her daughters and her own circle of friends, and grew further apart from her sisters – especially Elizabeth, who was rather contemptuous of what she saw as Priscilla's social pretensions.

Within her immediate neighbourhood, Elizabeth had a number of friends: Joyce Murchie, when she was around; Walter Baxter; and Kate O'Malley, who was Lesley's sister-in-law. In 1948 Kate married Paul Willert, who had served with the French Resistance during the war before becoming an oil dealer. Friends from Cairo, such as the Feddens, Burnet Pavitt, Patrick Kinross and Eddie Gathorne-Hardy were still much in evidence, and when George Lassalle married Judith Richardson in 1951, Elizabeth prepared the wedding breakfast. Some friends felt that Elizabeth had been weeping into the salmon she so lovingly cooked, mourning the loss of George; but Elizabeth was probably sadder about losing a friend than a lover. She sometimes resented the women who took away her male friends, and it took time for her to come round to them.

Elizabeth had also kept in touch with one of her mother's most prickly and amusing friends, Arthur Lett Haines. Haines was a painter, now best known for being the partner of the painter and horticulturalist Cedric Morris. Together they had started the East Anglian School of Painting and Drawing, at Benton End, Hadleigh. Their establishment could put up about fifteen students at a time, its most distinguished alumnus being Lucian Freud.

It seems to have been a wonderfully disorganized and stimulating place, not so much a school as a way of life devoted to gardening and painting. Cedric was usually up at dawn to tend his irises, while Lett woke at noon for a cocktail. Lett was an inspired cook, and did the cooking for the whole establishment. He was more interested in food than most, and his strong views usually (though not always) coincided with Elizabeth's.

Elizabeth bought a painting from Cedric Morris called *The Eggs*, which had been painted in 1944. 'Cedric told me he painted the picture during one of the rationing years of the last war and that . . . Arthur Lett Haines repeatedly demanded that the eggs be released because they were actually needed in the kitchen – which was run by Lett, since Cedric never in his whole long life put saucepan to stove . . . I forget just when I bought *The Eggs* from Cedric but I think it was in 1953 because I remember the City bedecked with flags as we drove up to Suffolk in the early morning so it must have been coronation year.'[1] Elizabeth bought the painting for £100, and eventually left it to the Tate Gallery.

Elizabeth never had enough money to collect paintings as well as books; but over the course of her life she bought some beautiful things. She had three pen-and-ink drawings by Henry Moore, and three still lifes by an artist called Eliot Hodgkin, who was a friend of Felicité's. She also had a portrait of herself by John Ward, and a portrait of Norman Douglas by Adrian Daintrey, who illustrated *Summer Cooking*. In her hall hung a set of strange, primitive flower paintings that her mother had found in a junk shop. The painter John Nash, who had taught patients in a mental institution, said they were almost certainly the work of someone very disturbed. 'It's obvious when you look at them,' wrote Elizabeth. 'They are curious and interesting, and very obsessive.'[2] Cedric Morris's *Eggs*, however, remained the most important piece in her collection.

She would sometimes go and spend the weekend with him and Lett Haines at Benton End, and sometimes, when Lett came up to London with one or two of the students, they would all go out together. The painter Antony Daniels remembers one occasion when, after an evening's drinking, they all came back to Halsey Street for supper. While someone opened a bottle, Elizabeth, who had a cigarette in her hand, got a chicken out of the fridge. She dropped it on the floor before it reached the table where – the cigarette now transferred to her lips – she proceeded to hack it up with a cleaver. There were sarcastic comments and much laughter about how uneatable supper was going to be. 'Just you wait,' said Elizabeth. After a little oil, salt and herbs had been thrown on to the chicken pieces, they went under the grill – and emerged, of course, succulent.

The pattern of her life developed its own routine. She woke at four or five in the morning, in her four-poster bed hung with its white crochet-work curtains, and started reading and writing with a thermos of black Nescafé beside her. Work resumed at the kitchen table where she wrote and cooked for most of the morning, and by eleven or twelve, she had done six or seven hours' work and was ready to relax. Elizabeth entertained a great deal at this time, and it was seldom that she had lunch alone: apart from anything else, she was constantly evolving and trying out recipes; and neither she, nor her friends, could bear the idea of those delicious meals going to waste. Often, the food had been cooked – or at least prepared – in advance; although those who did see her in the act of cooking said that she had a marvellous dexterity, an economy of effort. This made everything look easy, though of course such ease can only be achieved with long practice.

She did have a sitting room, and in the fifties and early sixties it had not yet been choked under drifts of books, catalogues and pieces of pottery. But the sitting room was not really where she felt at home, and more often, she took her guests straight down to sit at the kitchen table. The wine was already open – Elizabeth had probably started it while she was cooking – but before handing her guests a glass, Patrick Leigh Fermor remembered how she used to polish it carefully with a clean tea towel. A heap of books and papers had been pushed up at one end to make way for lunch, set with white starched napkins and satisfyingly heavy cutlery. On the table, as always, were a few olives, bread and butter.

Elizabeth was in no hurry. She liked to sit talking, with her back to the stove, and occasionally she would swivel round and adjust a knob or peer into the oven. When the food arrived, it was presented in the earthenware pots it had been cooked in, without fuss or comment, as was the perfect cheese and beautiful fruit that usually followed. If she served a salad, it was dressed at the table and tossed with her hands. This sometimes caused an involuntary gasp from one or two of her guests, but Elizabeth insisted that this was the only way to ensure that every leaf was properly coated with oil.

The conviviality was more important than the food, and Elizabeth liked to sit for hours talking and drinking wine after the meal was over. Yet she was not good at the early stage of a conversation: she seemed preoccupied, not fully engaged, as if her thoughts were still with the work she had been doing that morning. 'She talked obliquely,' said Veronica Nicholson, 'and it was up to you to get the conversational ball rolling; and sure enough it would start to unravel, and soon the whole ball would be coming undone – and late in the afternoon I would go home, thinking what a wonderful talk it had been.'[3]

She went out in the afternoons, or cooked and wrote in the kitchen, and more friends appeared in the evenings (though she did not usually cook more than once a day). She retired to bed, and her books. The light seldom went out until the early hours.

Elizabeth's journalism had appeared mainly in *Harper's Bazaar*. She almost signed a contract with *House and Garden*, owned by Condé Nast, in late 1953; but she was not aware of the intense rivalry between the publications. When it emerged that an agreement with them would prohibit her writing for *Harper's*, owned by the National Magazine Company, she backed down. 'I must say I was absolutely amazed to receive your letter this morning,' wrote *House and Garden*'s editor Anthony Hunt. 'When you left, I believed that we had made an agreement which only needed written confirmation . . . It appears, however, that in the meantime, without letting us know, you reopened negotiations with *Harper's*.' Despite Elizabeth's unprofessional behaviour, Hunt did not close the door in her face: 'I only hope that at some future time we may be able to come to a better arrangement,' he wrote.[4]

Harper's did not object to her writing for newspapers. She had written for the *Daily Express*, which had not made the best of her, and she also worked as cookery reader and editor for the publishing firm of André Deutsch. Then, in 1955, she was taken on by the *Sunday Times*. Leonard Russell had published an extract from *Summer Cooking* in 1955 when the book came out, and Elizabeth wrote for the paper regularly for the next five years.

Elizabeth had great respect for Leonard Russell. He was nominally the literary editor, but he had enormous influence on the whole tone and direction of the paper. He came across as brusque and rather unwelcoming; but this was partly an affectation, and people would find, to their surprise, that he was much more approachable than he appeared at first. Elizabeth described him as the sort of editor who could 'sometimes persuade or cajole me into writing what I had thought I couldn't, although never what *I* knew I wouldn't'.[5] Her pieces for the *Sunday Times* were short, lively and eminently practical: there was one on 'Bedsitter Tips' (eggs can be cooked, covered, on a plate over a steaming saucepan of vegetables) and another on 'Cooking on Your Own'. Elizabeth knew that she was writing for people who did not want to spend a lot of time at the stove, and in her articles she gave them the best she could, without wasting their time or their money. 'The first thing I want to know about a recipe, whatever its cost, is whether it's going to produce real food as opposed to a piece of frippery nonsense.'[6]

However, the nonsense put out by the food industry was always good copy, and Elizabeth could never resist taking a well-aimed shot at food fairs – usually the plumpest of sitting ducks. It is interesting to see what was on offer at the Olympia Food Fair in 1956. Frozen meals had now evolved into the TV dinner with everything all ready on a plastic tray, 'so that the awful fag of transferring the frozen chop and two frozen veg from shopping basket to dish is eliminated'; while the Gas Board was trying to tempt the housewife back to the stove with dishes called Huffkins, Fidget Pies and Bedfordshire Clangers. From Eastern Europe were huge sacks of dried mush-rooms, juicy little plums and a bewildering selection of sausages; from the US, hot-dogs and donuts. Two Spanish senoritas were doing a flamenco in honour of Spanish olive oil, while the English cheeses stood by in 'rugged dignity'.[7]

For the first three or four months, all went smoothly at the *Sunday Times*; until Ernestine Carter was appointed to edit the Women's Pages. Mrs Carter, originally from Savannah, Georgia, was a formid-able woman and had been a curator of the Museum of Modern Art in New York before going into journalism. She was, by all accounts, very effective and good at her job; but her high opinion of her own talents produced a correspondingly low opinion of her contributors. She had no qualms about chopping and changing their copy to suit herself.

Elizabeth always took care to hand her copy in on time, so that she could make any alterations or cuts necessary on the proof that she always insisted on seeing herself. To her editors, she always gave the same reason for this: cookery writing, if it had any claim to honesty, depended on precise instructions, and a line that might seem extraneous to an editor could contain the vital point on which depended the success or failure of a dish; only an experienced cook could recognize what was essential and what could be cut. Most editors were happy to bow to Elizabeth's authority.

Mrs Carter, however, thought she was quite capable of cutting the work of this tiresome woman who took herself so seriously; and as to being a cook, why, Mrs Carter had written a cookbook herself. She describes the book, and her attitude to cooking, in a volume of memoirs entitled *With Tongue in Chic*: 'I had become seethingly resentful of the prepare-lovingly-marinate-for-twenty-four-hours-school of cookery . . . A maximum effect with a minimum of effort was my aim; the recipes were brief and to the point.'[8] (Her book was called *Flash in the Pan*, published in 1953.)

Elizabeth became exasperated by the frequency with which her pieces, already cut to the required length by herself, were being hacked into yet again by Mrs Carter. Every week there was yet another squabble between them, yet another exchange of icy, outraged letters. Elizabeth developed a hatred for Mrs Carter that, to her friends at least, bordered on the obsessive.

* * * * * * * *

CHAPTER FOURTEEN

On the Road
in Provincial France

During the time Elizabeth was locked in battle with Mrs Carter, she also met one of the best editors she was ever to have in her life. In 1956, she was lured away from *Harper's* by Audrey Withers of *Vogue*, an editor of great imagination and energy, who was constantly on the lookout for fresh talent. She not only recognized Elizabeth as a superb writer: she also saw that *Harper's* was not making the best of her. Anne Scott-James, who had been Elizabeth's first editor on *Harper's*, had left the magazine in 1951. Elizabeth stayed on; but by 1956 she had been doing the same sort of piece for years, with very little change in the way of presentation. What Audrey Withers proposed was far more exciting. Elizabeth would be paid more money and have her own page, which would be in the centre rather than the back of the magazine; her work would be illustrated by a full-page photograph, and she would be given star treatment. Elizabeth was delighted by Audrey Withers's proposal, and *Harper's* made very little effort to stop her going.

Vogue announced the forthcoming appearance of 'ELIZABETH DAVID, world-famous cookery expert and author' in their April issue. She would start with a series of monthly articles on 'food in season, and how to make the most delicious use of it'. Since she was now firmly in the Condé Nast stable, Elizabeth also began to contribute regularly to *House and Garden*.

The twelve articles were illustrated with full-page colour photographs by Anthony Denney, another of Audrey Withers's discoveries. She had first seen his photographs in a book, during the war. She was very struck by his work, and keen that he should come into the Condé Nast fold; and with considerable difficulty she tracked him down to India, where he was working for British Intelligence.

After the war, he did come and work for *Vogue* and *House and Garden*; but Denney was much more than a photographer – he was also a very gifted decorator. At the time, it was still uncommon for decorators to juxtapose antiques and objets d'art with the latest Italian and Scandinavian furniture. Denney could do so because he had a profound knowledge of furniture, art, sculpture and design – both ancient and modern – and was a compulsive collector. Over the years, he had developed a sureness of taste and style which was reflected in everything he did.

At first, Elizabeth had been dubious about the idea of food photography. She doubted, too, that she could get herself and a dish of cooked food to the Condé Nast studio without both looking flat and harassed on arrival. It was Denney who suggested he might take the photographs in her house. 'The photographs he took of my food,' wrote Elizabeth many years later, 'were, I think, the first of their kind, in that, as always, I sought to make the subjects of the pictures useful as well as attractive, and atmospheric, but also realistic.'[1] Considering that both she and Denney were perfectionists used to having their own way, these sessions might have become extremely tense. However, in each other they both recognized a true artist, and someone they could learn from. Elizabeth, especially, acknowledged Denney as a formative influence: not only on her taste, but on her powers of observation:

> Anthony showed me what a quantity of small and important details I was missing, and how many inaccuracies and blunders I was allowing to get by. He is the person who sees and notes the difference between the way the French put a knife and fork on the table, and the way the English do it; how the lemons are cut in Spain and how exactly a loaf is cut or broken and

asks why – and detects anything arty quicker than you can say knife. It was the demonstration of this painter's eye, the visual memory he has plus his feeling for authenticity which is a bit like Norman [Douglas]'s that I found such a pleasure, and the stimulus all this produced that made our working relationship so fruitful – it was a slow explosion for me, like a marvellous love affair . . .[2]

It was an immense satisfaction to Audrey Withers to see such a successful collaboration; and with a whole page at her disposal, plus all the run-offs she wanted, Elizabeth could afford to enrich her pieces with many more comments, subtleties and details than those she had written for *Harper's*. At the same time, Miss Withers felt – as good editors do – that she could coax more out of Elizabeth.

During the 'Food at Its Best' series, Audrey and Elizabeth had often talked about her work, over lunch near the *Vogue* offices. Audrey was impressed by the intensely personal way Elizabeth talked of her experiences of eating in specific houses and restaurants in France, and felt that the dishes and foods that Elizabeth wrote about would be even more vivid if accompanied by the stories of how something was displayed in the market, how a certain dish was only made in one place, who had cooked it for her, where she was sitting when she ate it and what wine she drank with it. Hitherto, Elizabeth had reserved her more personal voice for her books rather than her articles.

Audrey Withers's plan to ask Elizabeth for more of herself was bolder than it might appear, because she was so intensely private. She was one of those people whose reserve is like an invisible wall: you know it's there, but you only know you've crossed it when it's too late and offence has been taken. Would she be offended if asked to put more of herself into her pieces? Audrey put her request so tactfully that Elizabeth was not offended; but she pointed out that she only had a certain number of those vivid personal anecdotes and descriptions that Miss Withers required, and new ones could not be conjured up from books and evocative recipes alone. She had to keep her knowledge of France fresh; and while on £20 a month she could afford ingredients, she could not afford trips abroad. Miss Withers agreed, and took the unusual step of allowing Elizabeth the occasional research trip to France, armed with £100 or so of Condé Nast money.

For Elizabeth, this presented a tremendous opportunity. She had already made herself an expert on French food, and had amassed a large collection of French cookery books – as well as an impressive array of traditional French pots, pans and cooking utensils. She had decided that her next book was going to be a definitive work on the everyday cooking of provincial France; but the problem was that this sort of food changed not only from one region to another, but across the seasons as well. There was an enormous amount of research that could only be done on the spot. She would have completed the research by herself, eventually; but the help and encouragement she received from Condé Nast and Audrey Withers now meant that she could go to France more often than before, and be paid for it.

The Condé Nast allowances were not extravagant; but like the clever French housewives she admired, Elizabeth spent the money well. When on the road in France, with whatever friend she had taken along to act as chauffeur, she would usually have a picnic lunch. This gave her the opportunity to see what was in the shops, sample the local cheeses and sausages, and see what vegetables were at their freshest and best in the market. Later on in the day she tried to arrive at her destination in good time for dinner, so as to have time for a chat with the *patron*. She would make friends with Monsieur or Madame, talk to them about what she had seen in the markets and sampled during the day, give them an idea of the sort of things she would like to eat, and listen to their suggestions. The *patrons* were usually flattered to find someone who took such an intelligent interest in the local produce and dishes of the region, and did their best to please her.

'Under such circumstances,' she wrote in *French Provincial Cooking*, 'I have eaten some of the most enjoyable of French country meals; unexacting ones, ordered and served with the minimum of fuss.' And by describing her simple technique for ordering a good dinner, she must have saved many of her readers from ordering an expensive and over-elaborate one.

Elizabeth's diaries are sketchy, and it is difficult to reconstruct the order of her trips to France, who she went with and where she stayed. She often went with Doreen Thornton, who drove her all over France in her Morris Traveller. Elizabeth was good company, and good at map-reading – though because she only looked at the map and not at the signposts, they often got lost in towns. 'Just take the first left and we'll be in the main square,' she would say, unable to appreciate that they were locked into a labyrinthine one-way system. One thing that struck Doreen was how few notes Elizabeth took during these trips. 'We shared a room so often, on so many journeys, but I never saw her writing anything down. She relied on her extraordinary visual memory.'[3]

The presence of Elizabeth's companion – usually Doreen, sometimes Peter – is only referred to in the most indirect way: 'our coffee, when it arrived' – 'I knew where we would go to look for the dish.' What is in these articles, however, is exactly what Audrey wanted. How she chased two hundred miles across France for a dish of pork and prunes, how her memory of the beauty of the Place Stanislas in Nancy is inextricably linked with the little orange and gilt boxes of the Bergamottes de Nancy, how an old lady in a shop in Provence kept everyone waiting while Mademoiselle cut just the right slice of ham for a dish of petits pois.

The series opened with the food of Paris, which was the most personal piece in the series. It is not only a wonderfully funny and penetrating evocation of Mme Barette and her family, their cook Léontine and their lovely food; it also gives the reader a unique insight into how an ordinary (though admittedly very greedy) Parisian family shopped and ate.

In 1956, in Provence, she was appalled to see the damage done by the previous winter. 'The whole landscape was gashed with ugly black wounds. Hundreds of olive trees, withered and blighted by the frosts and the all-blasting mistral winds which followed them, had been cut down or were standing like ancient skeletons . . .'⁴ Only one place had escaped, surrounding a little village in the Ventoux called Beaumes de Venise. On that occasion, she did not taste the golden muscat wine that she later helped to make so famous – for the simple reason that no one in the hotel where she ate lunch thought it worth mentioning.

The following year she made a long research trip that was to prove particularly important, for on it she discovered a lodestar: one of those restaurants which epitomized, to her, everything that was most admirable in the French attitude to food, from its cooking to its presentation. The journey had begun in Alsace, then continued into Lorraine and down through Burgundy, and so to Lyon. Lyon is reputedly the Olympus of French provincial cooking, and here she ate some of the best fish dishes she had ever tasted; but for the most part the food of the Lyonnais, rather like that of Bologna, was rather too rich and heavy for her taste. From Lyon they went south, and then, at Valence, due west into the hills to Lamastre.

The Hotel du Midi already had two Michelin stars and a fine reputation when Elizabeth first visited the establishment in the summer of 1957. At that time there were fifty-nine two-star restaurants in the whole of France, and they were not cheap. They usually boasted about half a dozen *specialités de la maison*, most of which could be sampled at one gargantuan sitting by choosing the *menu gastronomique*. However, it was possible to arrange demi-pension terms. Elizabeth and her companion were so delighted with the hotel and the welcome they received from Mme Barattero that they immediately decided to stay a week – and for her companion, who had driven all the way, it must have been a well-earned rest. The food on offer at demi-pension terms was simple, not extravagant; but the kitchens were run by a master chef, M. Perrier, who put the same care and experience into his vegetable soups as he did into his *pains d'écrevisses sauce cardinal*. Thus they enjoyed, over the course of seven days, some of the simplest and best-prepared food in France – as well as the *pains d'écrevisses*, the *galantine de caneton* and the *poularde en vessie* which were the specialities of the house.

Elizabeth was so impressed by the Hotel du Midi, that every evening's menu was described in her article. This was to make two essential points about French restaurant cooking: first, its variety, and second, how worthwhile it is to eat simple dishes cooked in a first-class manner. When the article was eventually published (in September 1958) it was unique for a *Vogue* cookery article in that it contained not a single recipe.

Yet Elizabeth was not stuck on the perfected principles of French cookery – far from it. The late 1950s were a time when many new food products were coming on to the market, and Elizabeth was naturally bombarded with samples and invitations. She did not always enjoy her experiences. A trip round the Walls sausage factory made a lasting and painful impression. She was, however, willing to try out new things and could make some surprising comments. When sent a sample of Uncle Ben's 'converted' rice, she noted in her diary that it looked rather like Patna rice and she tried it out in a risotto: 'to one (US) cup full of rice, 4 scant cups of liquid, including half a cup of wine. Cooked about twenty minutes. Very good.'[5]

While Elizabeth was working at *Vogue*, her sister Felicité embarked on a new business venture. A young man called John Sandoe, who had worked with her at J. A. Allen, suggested that they go into business together. Felicité had no money of her own to put into it; but she found the premises, in Blacklands Terrace, that the shop still occupies to this day. Felicité was a voracious reader, of everything from novels to histories. She had very strong enthusiasms, which she frequently imposed on her customers. One unwary passer-by, who dropped into the shop for a new book and was unprepared for Felicité's hard-sell techniques, emerged with a full set of the Mapp and Lucia novels by E. F. Benson. Felicité was at John Sandoe's for the rest of her working life, and kept Elizabeth supplied with books and catalogues.

The summer of 1957 marked the high point of Elizabeth's relationship with her publishers, Macdonald. They not only agreed to incorporate her revisions for *Mediterranean Food* and *French Country Cooking* (this last title was also due to be published by Penguin), but they also agreed to lend her two of the Guttuso drawings that had illustrated *Italian Food*.

It was Roald Dahl who suggested to Elizabeth that she should break into the American market, though as he acknowledged, 'everything in this life depends on fucking timing'.[6] He had sent *Italian Food* and a selection of her journalism to his American agents Ann Watkins Inc., and they approached Dahl's publisher Alfred Knopf. Knopf did not offer much because, as they told her frankly, they did not expect to sell many. They did not want the Guttuso illustrations, and they told Elizabeth that the book needed substantial alteration for the American market.

To the astonishment of Alfred Knopf, Elizabeth refused the offer. She heard that Knopf was so furious that her name was never again to be mentioned in his presence – although he was still interested in the book. Elizabeth was only prepared to negotiate on two conditions: they could not publish the book without the Guttuso illustrations, and her book was not to be Americanized. 'I am prepared,' she wrote to her agent Paul Scott, 'to barter financial gain for the minimum of interference with my work. Knopf must surely see that if he wants to preserve the character of the book there is no point in turning it into just another American-Italian cookery book, of which there are already scores.'

Knopf grudgingly agreed, and the work of Americanizing the book without losing its character was given to someone who translated *Fritto misto* as 'Mixed Fry' and *Melanzane e funghetti* as 'Fried Eggplant'. This editor did not last long, and Knopf's next choice of editor was far more suitable. Avis de Voto admired Elizabeth's writing and understood Elizabeth's point of view, but she was equally determined to make the book easier for the American cook. So great were the difficulties of translation that at one point Elizabeth had to send Avis a food parcel, containing things like sultanas, ground rice, haricot beans and a yeast sample. 'None of us have seen anything like it,' she wrote back.[7] After months of work the book came out, and Elizabeth was pleased with the result. Yet it made very little impact in the States, and after all the time and effort put in by herself and Avis de Voto, Elizabeth wondered whether the exercise had been worthwhile.

The articles on French regional cooking were published between May 1957 and April 1958, after which Elizabeth did a series on Italian cooking – this was far less arduous, being based on research already done. It was also very popular, because everything Italian was now fashionable – especially the coffee bar.

The coffee bar is one of the most interesting social phenomena in London in the late fifties, though Elizabeth seldom mentions them. She was never particularly interested in coffee: she had acquired a taste for Nescafé during the war, and never wished for anything better. Another reason was that the coffee bar, and coffee bar culture, was above all a manifestation of youth. One of the most famous coffee bars, The Two I's, had a tiny basement in which people squeezed to hear Adam Faith, Little Richard or Tommy Steele. 'For the first time, the young had somewhere to hang out. The counter was dominated by that hissing, spluttering machine which kept the room (and its windows) reassuringly steamy – and, with the cigarette fug (everybody smoked then) the coffee bar became a teenage sanctuary.'[8] Elizabeth, however, was writing for their mothers. After the series on Italian food Elizabeth went on to 'Cooking Hazards'. This was in direct response to the letters of her readers, who wanted her reassurance on supposedly tricky problems, such as cooking rice and how to roast meat.

Elizabeth's main preoccupation at this time was how to get Tony to agree to a divorce. He had been very much against the idea, but in 1957 he made a blunder which gave Elizabeth the opportunity she needed. While living in Spain, Tony had been cited as co-respondent in a farcical divorce case complete with jealous husband and private detectives. It was gleefully reported in the *Daily Express* by Nancy Spain, one of the most aggressive gossip columnists of her day. Tony was quoted in her article, and made the mistake of referring to Elizabeth as 'my ex-wife'. In July 1958, she filed for divorce, and as far as she was concerned it was not a moment too soon, for Tony was becoming an embarrassment. To avoid the scandal in Spain he had moved to Tangier, where she heard he was running a club-cum-restaurant called the Mille et Une Nuits.

Her main reasons for initiating proceedings were that their marriage had been at an end for the past five years, and that it was based on a misunderstanding: 'He did not realize that my wish was to settle down and lead a reasonably ordered life not more than normally harassed by bills and debts. His broken promises, evasions and deceit in these matters eventually caused me to lose all respect for him.'⁹

Elizabeth had never forgiven Tony for his fecklessness; but perhaps her anger was also partly tinged with guilt – as a wise man once said, it is hard to forgive those one has injured. As for Tony, he was much more forgiving. He never ceased to love her, and followed her career with pride.

Elizabeth spent part of the summer in France with Peter Higgins, and in August she went to stay with Derek Hill at Church House in Letterkenny, Donegal. While Elizabeth was not one for long walks, she loved the wild landscape and the changing light of Donegal. She also loved sitting at the kitchen table, talking to Derek and his cook, Gracie McDermott. Elizabeth said that Gracie was one of the best natural cooks she had ever met. On one occasion when they were talking about salmon, Elizabeth remarked that it was impossible to make a good soup from this fish. Gracie said nothing: but a day or two later, she served up a most delicious, perfectly flavoured salmon soup. From the mid-fifties to the mid-sixties, Elizabeth often spent Christmas with Derek in Donegal. It was a haven of peace and tranquillity, compared to the frenetic, over-commercialized atmosphere of Christmas in London.

She also kept in touch with Doreen and Colin Thornton, with whom she would sometimes spend the weekend. Doreen had been given a copy of Charles Gibson Cowan's book *The Voyage of the Evelyn Hope*, which had been published soon after the war. Doreen had not read it, but on one weekend in 1958 or 1959 when Elizabeth was coming to stay Doreen thought she might be amused to see the book, and put it in her room. It was evidently the first time that Elizabeth had ever seen a finished copy. She had read the early chapters in Alexandria, but she had never read the ending, which is a completely fictionalized account of them escaping from Crete with the German airborne invasion in full swing. Elizabeth was so enraged that she pulled the book to pieces in front of Doreen, hissing, 'Never, *ever*, let me hear that man's name again!'[10]

Elizabeth's journalistic life at this time was sharply divided. She was very happy at *Vogue*, where Audrey Withers had given her work a new dimension. At the *Sunday Times*, on the other hand, her relationship with Ernestine Carter had reached breaking point.

The idea of grouping a series of articles together by theme had been extremely effective and successful, and towards the end of 1958, Audrey Withers and Elizabeth decided that she should do a series on the markets of France; the trip was scheduled for mid-June 1959. A month before that, Elizabeth's battle with Ernestine Carter reached its climax. As she wrote to Jean LeRoy of David Higham Ltd,

two of my recent articles have been hacked about in such a reckless way that I can no longer afford to keep silent. Mrs

Carter's interference is resulting in serious damage to my reputation . . .

Indeed I go further and accuse her either of deliberate sabotage of my work or of selfishness over her own space amounting to egomania. For I cannot believe that anyone in her position is brutishly stupid to the point of not being aware of what she is doing.[11]

With that, she resigned. Harry Hodson, the editor, politely expressed his regret but did not offer to make any changes to existing arrangements. Mrs Carter, for all her abrasiveness, was too valuable to lose.

Glad to be free of the *Sunday Times* but still shaking with rage, Elizabeth set off with Doreen Thornton and Anthony Denney on what proved to be a gruelling trip. The schedule was very tight, and they were badly let down by the weather; but Doreen Thornton had succeeded in getting a very smart car for the journey. In return for an article in the *Standard-Triumph Review*, Doreen was to test-drive the new Triumph Herald Coupé. The trip began badly, with an accident in Kensington High Street. But they had an uneventful crossing to Boulogne on one of the very latest ferries, which boasted *two* car decks.

They arrived in Normandy in a hurricane, hoping to catch the market at Rouen; but despite having gone to enormous lengths to get a list of market days, the information was wrong. However, they were able to see the wholesale butter market at Yvetot, where the butter was sold in huge cones weighing seventy or eighty kilos.

As they went on they discovered that it was the small towns rather than the big ones that were the most photogenic, because many of the large ones had covered markets lit with fluorescent tubes, making photography almost impossible.

Since they had failed to do as much as they had hoped in the first half of their ten-day trip, the second half became manic, with the drivers making dashes of 250 miles in all directions to catch the best markets; but they needed more than just a time and a place, if Elizabeth's written account of the markets was to have any depth; and Audrey Withers wanted her readers informed on a great many details.

Yet as Elizabeth discovered, the French are not inclined to reveal the fruits of their culinary knowledge and experience without 'extensive, cautious and tactful preparation of the ground beforehand. You just cannot blind [*sic*] into a place at eight o'clock, hurl the luggage out of the car, and then expect the cook and the *patron* to jump to attention and produce recipes and local colour before you get up next morning at 4 a.m.'[12]

Some fairly desperate driving enabled them to spend one night with Mme Barattero at Lamastre. 'Although we arrived fairly late she rolled out mink carpets for us in every direction, gave us an absolutely fantastically beautiful dinner, and was in tears at dawn when we went to inspect the market at Valence.'[13]

Dull and stormy weather washed out any hopes of Valence, and there was nothing for it but to head south as fast as possible. The market at Cavaillion was every bit as 'beautiful and abundant' as Elizabeth had remembered it, so there things went smoothly; but the fish markets of the coast presented formidable difficulties since all depended on when the catch came in. At Martigues, there was not a moment to be lost. She and Anthony were sprinting from boat to boat like maniacs looking for the best shots, with their drivers puffing to keep up under the weight of Anthony's equipment, followed by hordes of inquisitive boys and hungry cats. Then they had to try and persuade the anxious fishermen and their wives to stand still for a moment with their loads of fish before they whisked them off to auction.

By the end of this whirlwind tour of French markets, Elizabeth felt that they had got a pretty good cross-section of market life. Wholesale markets, big- and small-town markets, specialized markets like those selling butter in Yvetot, melons at Cavaillion and fish at Martigues. Not only that, but they had managed to find evocative corners of big markets showing such details of French household requirements as the stalls specializing in herbs and salad materials, in vegetables ready tied up for soup, in olives and oil and cheeses.

Anthony went back to Spain after a night at Carré le Rouet ('real postcard Mediterranean'), while Doreen and Elizabeth turned the car north-east. Elizabeth had hoped to move on to Annecy and Chambéry, 'a place where the cooking is famous but which I don't know at all'; but they had to abandon the project: it would have been too expensive a detour, and the bad weather was closing in again.

Doreen's article made the trip sound positively leisurely, compared with Elizabeth's letter to Audrey Withers on which the above description is based. However, there was no doubt that the Triumph made the trip considerably more pleasant than it might have been otherwise. 'My passenger, who had been on many similar journeys with me in other small cars, said that she had never had such a comfortable ride.'[14]

* * * * * * * *

CHAPTER FIFTEEN

The Year of Betrayal

In some ways, *French Provincial Cooking* could be described as a book that only needed assembling. It is prefaced by some of the most evocative articles Elizabeth had written for *Vogue*, and the bulk of the recipes had been in the process of refinement and rewriting for many years. This makes it sound, to use the cookery presenter's cliché, like a 'here's one I made earlier' sort of book. In fact, it was the culmination and synthesis of a decade of work and thought.

During her research trips, the food she sampled was that cooked in good, unpretentious restaurants rather than in private houses; but ultimately, the recipes in *French Provincial Cooking* were presented in such a way that they could be reproduced in Britain, by untrained British cooks in British kitchens. To perfect her recipes, she relied heavily on her collection of French cookery books: not only historical ones of the eighteenth and nineteenth centuries, but also more recent ones with comfortable titles like *Les Secrets de la bonne table* (Benjamin Renaudet), and *L'Art du bien manger* (Edmond Richardin). The recipe for any given dish might vary considerably among the different volumes she consulted and the different restaurants she had eaten it in. Elizabeth's skill was that she knew how to reduce a recipe to its bare essentials, and then reconstruct it – an exercise she recommends to her readers: 'You may well find that the dish is more pleasing in its primitive form, and then you will know that your recipe was too fanciful. If, on the other hand, the dish seems to lack savour, to be a little bleak and insipid, start building it up again. By the end of this process, you will have discovered what is essential to that dish, what are the extras which enhance it, and at what point it is spoilt by over-elaboration.'[1]

Not every reader perhaps feels up to deconstructing their *Râble de lièvre à la crème*, but the point was that Elizabeth had. This is why every recipe is given with such authority: she has tried it and presents it in print at its most authentic, and any departure from the traditional is clearly signposted. In the recipe mentioned above, for example, she calls for two tablespoons of wine vinegar – 'half a claret glass as specified by Tendret being too much for my taste'. This *Râble de lièvre* is a tricky dish, requiring a good deal of blind faith – for much of the cooking the sauce looks as if it is on the brink of separating. But it does sort itself out in the end, and as Elizabeth points out, 'if you don't look at the sauce you won't see any sinister happenings'.

These were the most strenuous years of Elizabeth's life. She was deeply involved in her work, and because she wrote so regularly and so well for a number of different magazines and newspapers, she made herself a fine reputation and acquired the social standing that goes with it. 'I see your name everywhere now!' wrote Lawrence Durrell. 'You have become a sort of Lord Chesterfield of food. How splendid and how deserved.'[2] She had always been independent; but she had developed a taste for scholarship and knowledge that meant that she needed a lot of time to herself. Being no longer married, she had the space she needed; and since she had no one to look after but herself, she could afford the dark tailored suits, white silk shirts and Parisian hats that she loved.

Elizabeth always behaved like a married woman. It was, after all, a part of the job: she had to present herself as, and sound like, a busy woman with people to feed – and it was, for her, the most congenial role. The quality of her hats and shoes, her practicality, and the way she turned the first rather rackety years of her adult life into the authoritative statement 'Mrs David has kept house in France, Italy,

Greece, Egypt', etc., all conveyed the desired impression – and no one had any reason to challenge it.

As a career woman ahead of her time, Elizabeth was to some extent lucky that the professional and personal sides of her life were relatively easy to reconcile. All she wanted from her private life were her family, her friends and Peter – all of whom were easily accommodated around her various commitments. She did not regret being childless and, on one or two occasions, had deliberately chosen to remain so. On the subject of pregnancy she once remarked, 'I always managed to get rid of mine.'

Nothing remotely like marriage existed in her life, least of all with Peter Higgins. Peter loved her wit, her quickness in spotting humbug, the sheer exhilarating fun of being with her – though the speed with which her mood could suddenly change, the way she could take offence over the faintest slight or the most casual remark was rather tiring. As their relationship went on, he also began to resent her jealousy. She wanted to know where he was every minute of the day, and he was irritated by her uncontrollable desire to cross-question him about everyone he saw and everywhere he went.

He probably did not realize the extent to which her emotional well-being depended on him. She still loved and needed him with an intensity that she had never felt for anyone else; but as the 1950s drew on Elizabeth was dismayed to find that Peter's feelings for her were changing. He still enjoyed her company, but he was beginning to get bored, and her reliance on him was beginning to chafe. As he pulled away from her, she became more desperate, and angry. Her jealousy provoked terrible rows between them, which she inevitably regretted. In an undated letter she wrote,

> If I was rude to you as your savage and public rebuke seemed
> to indicate I apologize my love. It must have been due to some
> childish desire to pay you out because you have made me suffer
> so hideously. Whereas my only feelings should be of gratitude
> to you for the years of love and content you gave me. And anyone

who has had the magical good fortune to have experienced happiness such as I had with you in Provence has no right to complain of what happens afterwards.

In the summer of 1958, with *French Provincial Cooking* well under way, Elizabeth's agent Paul Scott had negotiated a contract with the publishers Michael Joseph. Elizabeth knew no one in the firm, and very little about it: but the things she did know were reassuring. Michael Joseph himself, who had died two years before, had built up an excellent reputation as a mainstream publisher who could count C. S. Forester, H. E. Bates and Monica Dickens among his authors. He had also been President of the Siamese Cat Society of the British Empire. This last fact struck a deep chord with Elizabeth, who felt that no firm with such an engaging founder could go far wrong. At that time, she was sharing her house with a black cat called Squeaker. (Elizabeth had adopted Squeaker on impulse, having spent a weekend with Doreen, whose cat had just had a litter of kittens.) Another very good reason for choosing Michael Joseph came from Felicité. As a bookseller of many years' experience, Felicité was of the opinion that Ian Keik – Michael Joseph's London sales representative – was the best in the business.

It was to Anthea Joseph, the editorial director and widow of the publisher, that Elizabeth presented the typescript of *French Provincial Cooking*. She was by all accounts a remarkable woman of great charm, who fought hard for the authors she believed in (she insisted on publishing James Baldwin's *Another Country* against the advice of the firm's lawyers). Yet she and Elizabeth got off on the wrong foot. The typescript was partly to blame: in their earliest stages, Elizabeth's books were a daunting pile of pages, with many handwritten notes, references, corrections and insertions held in place with pins and paper clips. When Elizabeth came in to discuss it, Mrs Joseph looked rather alarmed. 'It isn't quite what we were expecting,' she ventured. 'It seems to be quite different from your other books . . .'[3] She also felt it was in need of serious cutting.

With the high hopes she had built up of the firm, Elizabeth was disappointed, to say the least. It seemed to her that publishers always wanted to see the book she had last published, rather than the one she had just written. Yet in the end she came round to Anthea Joseph, who admitted that she might have been wrong about demanding all those cuts.

Elizabeth got on far better with Peter Hebdon, the firm's managing director. He had always been more involved with the sales and marketing side of the business, but in the early 1960s the division between sales and editing was nothing like as rigid as it is now. Hebdon was a man of unselfconscious integrity, who never hesitated to say what he thought: the sort of person Elizabeth always admired. She saw Hebdon as her best friend and ally within the firm, and felt that the continued success of *French Provincial Cooking* owed much to him. Peter Hebdon promoted it well, was generous with reprints and revisions, and seemed genuinely concerned for the book's welfare. 'Peter cherished his authors,' wrote Elizabeth. 'He was proud of publishing their work. In return his authors, or at least this one, loved and looked up to him.'[4] When the book came out, many people assumed that the dedication *To P.H. with love* referred to Peter Hebdon. Elizabeth made little effort to correct the rumour, which provided an effective smokescreen for the real P.H.'s identity. No one beyond her closest circle of friends knew that P.H. stood for Peter Higgins.

For the illustrations, Elizabeth chose an artist called Juliet Renny. For six months this very shy and retiring artist came to Halsey Street, working more slowly than Elizabeth could have wished; but the fact that she took endless pains to get every rivet, lid and handle exactly right made up for it. 'I was anxious that such details should be put on record,' wrote Elizabeth, 'because some of these regional cooking pots are already becoming very hard to find in France, so that in some sense Juliet Renny's drawings constitute a little historical record in their own right.'[5]

*

The book was published in November 1960, and was received as warmly as her previous books; but hers was not the only cookery book jostling for attention. Two books in particular could be seen as direct competitors: *The Classic French Cuisine* by Joseph Donon, a professional chef's presentation of five hundred recipes from the very summits of haute cuisine; and *The Art of Simple French Cooking* by Alexander Watt, which brought quick bistro cooking into the English kitchen. Books of a kind tend to be reviewed in large batches, the reviewer's job being merely to give a taste of each, but it is interesting to note the little flash of colour and depth coming into the descriptions of *French Provincial Cooking*. Where it was reviewed at greater length, there was a general recognition that the book was beautifully written, profoundly researched, entertaining, informative and more than the sum of its parts: it makes you want to cook. 'If I had my way I would have a copy purchased by public funds and presented to every young wife on her wedding day,' wrote Vivian Rowe in *The Traveller in France*. Even the *Daily Worker*'s reviewer enjoyed it, which should go some way to redressing the absurd contention that Elizabeth David was élitist and only addressed the upwardly aspiring middle classes: 'a textbook not just on French food, but on good cooking and intelligent eating'.[6] She received an enormous number of letters from readers, and the reaction of her friends too was very gratifying. In thanking her cousin Neil Hogg for his letter Elizabeth wrote, 'Of course the book is full of idiosyncrasies and faults of style, and omissions, and repetitions, and it isn't intended to be read right through at one go, although to my dismay that's just what people are doing. They must be getting awful indigestion by about page 150.'[7]

Two other publications from the autumn of 1960 are worth mentioning. One was a pioneer of its kind, and opened up a promising future for a new sort of cookery book. It was called *Cookery in Colour*, edited by Marguerite Patten. The recipes were printed on coloured paper, alternating with double-page spreads of full-colour photographs – which would have been prohibitively expensive to produce in England. Paul Hamlyn could afford to sell it for twenty-five shillings (ten shillings less than *French Provincial Cooking*) because he had invested in a massive print run, and had had the book printed in Czechoslovakia: it sold two million copies.

The past was represented by Ward Lock's centenary edition of Mrs Beeton's famous *Book of Household Management*, now renamed *Cookery and Household Management*. Fifty-five experts were credited for their work on the new edition, and apart from one or two useful chapters, Elizabeth thought the result was a mess: uneven, contradictory and confused. 'We feel that Mrs Beeton promises us the godlike wisdom of a revered professor combined with nanny's protective comfort. We don't get it.'

The article was published in the *Spectator* in October, just as her own book was being launched. 'I know I was asking for trouble writing in those rather thundering tones so soon after the appearance of my own book,' she wrote to Neil Hogg. 'I suppose it would have been more dignified to keep silent on the matter – but . . . I was, and am, really outraged when I think what Ward Lock have perpetrated in Mrs Beeton's name.' She was also rather surprised by the enthusiasm with which the new Mrs Beeton was received: 'it emerges that I seem to be the only person who has said it's pretty mediocre . . . or else I'm utterly wrong'.[8]

The article on Mrs Beeton was one of the first she wrote for the *Spectator*, for which Elizabeth produced some of the best articles she was ever to write. She had first been approached, almost off the cuff, by Katharine Whitehorn, who at that time combined the job of arts editor on the *Spectator* with being fashion editor of the *Observer*. She wrote to Elizabeth on 25 May 1960: 'I do think it would be splendid to have an article on casseroles and other sorts of kitchen equipment; but – this is the first thing that I must admit occurs to me – oughtn't it to be you that writes it and not me? . . . I can think of nothing the *Spectator* would like better than to have you write an article or a series for us. But perhaps, considering our rates, it is an impertinence to suggest it.'

The *Spectator* in those days was owned by Ian Gilmour and edited by Brian Inglis; and although the pay was less than what she was used to, she liked the fact that what the *Spectator* wanted was her writing, her unmistakable voice. What she wrote about was up to her, and no one cared whether she included recipes in her articles or not.

The tone of the magazine was set by what Whitehorn called 'a close-knit gang of disillusioned radicals' which included herself, Cyril Ray, Bernard Levin and Alan Brien. They were all young left-wing liberals, all had jobs on other papers as well; but at the *Spectator*, they felt they were in their element. Work at 99 Gower Street was punctuated by long drinking sessions at the Mortimer Arms, and one afternoon a week was devoted to the *Spectator* lunch. Supplies for this occasion were organized by Cyril Ray, who in the course of his career had been war correspondent for the *Guardian*, Moscow correspondent for the *Sunday Times* and editor of an annual called *The Compleat Imbiber*. He shared a dusty cubby-hole of an office with Katharine Whitehorn, who described his position on the *Spectator* as 'foreign, diplomatic, food, espionage, drink and military correspondent with a spot of labour relations and law reform thrown in'.[9] He was known to many as the Bollinger Bolshevik; and his arrival on lunch days, in a taxi laden with food and unbelievable quantities of wine, rather shocked the younger and more junior members of the *Spectator*'s staff.

It was Cyril who edited Elizabeth's copy; though he often had to bully her for it. She was used to editors who were chiefly interested in recipes or, like Audrey Withers, who had established themes for a series of articles. It was hard to think up ideas when the guidelines were so loose.

She joined the *Spectator* just in time; for she was coming to the conclusion that she no longer wanted to work for *Vogue*. Anthony Denney had left the magazine, and in the second half of 1960, Audrey Withers was succeeded as editor of *Vogue* by Ailsa Garland.

Elizabeth struggled on for a bit, but in October she wrote to the new editor asking to be released from her contract. She felt she was an anachronism in the bright, hard-edged, teasing tones of the new magazine: 'I have a feeling that you may be glad of the opportunity to look for a cookery contributor who takes the whole business a bit more lightly than I do, and I wouldn't blame you.'[10]

Elizabeth also admitted that she was desperately tired. Being as conscientious as she was about her work, it demanded a lot from her both physically and mentally; she had not taken a non-working holiday for years.

Freed from the *Sunday Times* and Condé Nast, her work did ease up a bit: but Elizabeth needed to be busy. She took on a column for the *Sunday Dispatch* in 1960, and another for the *Daily Telegraph* in 1961. It was a particularly interesting time to be writing about food, at a time of such rapid social change. Advances, in everything from technology to ease of transport, were fuelling the huge and fashionable debate about food that raged in every newspaper and magazine.

Elizabeth's line was predictable. She hated the proliferation of supermarkets, the advances in freezing and preserving that were touted at every food fair and the free samples of bottled sauce and packet soup that clogged up her mail and her dustbins. She hated the way fresh vegetables and fruits of the season were being elbowed out by freezer cabinets full of strawberries and 'garden-fresh' peas; yet at the same time, there was much to welcome.

More and more people were going abroad, and they came home wanting to cook some of the dishes they had eaten in France or Italy. This was good for British cooking in general, and the sales of her own books in particular. At Harrods the meat manager, Mr Ducat, was opening a *boucherie* which offered French cuts of meat, and he also began doing Elizabeth's recipe for spiced beef at Christmas. Even if one could not afford to shop at Harrods, one no longer had to go as far as Soho to find good coffee, olive oil and wine vinegar. Elizabeth was delighted when her local Sainsbury's brought out little packets of freshly-grated parmesan, and said so in the *Spectator* – to the rage of one of her correspondents who wrote from Lahore: 'I enjoy your column, although I am occasionally badly shaken when you suggest the purchase and employment of pre-ground Parmesan and such. That kind of thing just *won't do*, and I am sure you know it.'[11]

In wine, too, things were improving. An enterprising wine-merchant called Gerald Asher, one of the founders of Asher, Storey & Co., was exploring French vineyards for unusual, little-known wines that had not been available in England before. 'He used to go looking for . . . wines he had read about, but which no one imported,' said his friend and fellow wine-expert Anthony Hanson. 'Jasnières, to the north of the Loire, the name kept alive by three people growing vines at the back of a vegetable patch, or Jurançon, or Frontignan, or a Costières du Gard . . .'[12] These were just the sort of wines that Elizabeth liked. They were not classed growths or prestige bottles, but they were made by small wine-growers who took trouble, and each wine was an expression of a time and a place.

Despite a rapidly developing food and wine market and a consuming interest in abroad, some English people still insisted on maintaining heavily entrenched positions. At the beginning of 1961, Elizabeth wrote a piece in the *Daily Telegraph* entitled 'Crisp Salads to Cheer Gloomy Days', which provoked a furious response from one reader. Who did that Mrs David think she was? To throw oil and vinegar over pears (the pear Elizabeth had referred to was an avocado) was nothing short of barbarous. She was fed up with hearing about 'those queer messes which foreigners called food', and claimed that a diet of roast beef, Yorkshire and two veg followed by fruit tart with custard was good enough for most people and could not be improved upon.

The insularity of this attitude was eccentric even in 1961 and a host of other readers sprang to Elizabeth's defence; but Elizabeth did not like the way the whole thing had been handled by the

Telegraph. She had been given no warning of the outraged letter, which had been deliberately exaggerated in print by clever editing; and when she was allowed to reply, it was some time later and on the back page.

Elizabeth's articles upset the food industry more often than her readers. In an article she wrote for the *Spectator* called 'Lucky Dip' (29 June 1962), Elizabeth mentioned that she had given the filling for a commercial veal and ham pie to her cat, who had turned it down. A complaint was made to the editor, now Brian Inglis's successor Iain Hamilton. He passed on the indignant letter, with the remark that 'if their pies are anything like their ice cream I'd shoot the lot of them'.[13] Elizabeth had great fun composing her reply to the offended manufacturers.

> The Editor of the *Spectator* tells me that your board takes serious exception to my cat's reported attitude to a . . . pie. Of course, my cat was serious too, but in recording her lack of enthusiasm I did not intend to imply, nor do I think would any intelligent *Spectator* reader infer, that the pie in question would have necessarily been rejected by a human being – or indeed, by all other cats. Standards differ . . .
>
> The Editor also tells me that you have been so kind as to invite me to see over the factory. I have already had this pleasure. I found the experience most instructive and impressions are still vivid in my mind, so I will not put your directors to all the trouble again.[14]

As a cookery writer, Elizabeth was constantly invited to visit commercial premises producing food in one form or another – both in England and on the continent. Like most of her European contemporaries, her work was not much known outside her own country: but people in the food business knew that she wielded enormous influence in Britain. Elizabeth's professional life was punctuated by jaunts organized by cheesemakers, grape growers or houses of commerce. Such trips are not in themselves worth recording; but they often provided

Elizabeth with the raw material for her articles, and it is worth looking at one to see the lengths to which people were prepared to go to impress her.

This particular trip centred on the town of Nantes, where Elizabeth was interested in the sardine canneries. It took place in September 1962, and was organized by the Centre National du Commerce in Paris, treating her as a VIP. In the course of her visit Elizabeth was not only shown over the celebrated canning factory of Philippe Cannaud; she also saw the Biscuiterie Nantaise and several vineyards (Gerald Asher had advised her on which to visit, and given her letters of introduction), and was treated to meals in what were considered the finest restaurants in the area. Elizabeth was touched by the efforts everyone went to on her behalf. She was an appreciative guest, but not an easy one; for once she had become interested in something, she would not let go of it until she had learnt everything she wanted to know. One of her letters was to Mme Audas, who ran the estate of Les Perrières with her husband, producing Muscadet.

'I'm afraid I took up too much of your time, but it was such a beautiful day and everything you showed me was so interesting and such fun, that I quite failed to notice the time. When I realized that you were going to set to work cooking your ducks that evening I was really horrified to think that I had stayed so late . . .'[15]

It was soon after her return that Elizabeth was contacted by a very young, enthusiastic man who, at the age of twenty-four, had just been appointed by André Simon to edit the magazine of the Wine and Food Society. His name was Hugh Johnson. On a copy of the magazine immediately preceding his appointment, Johnson wrote the names of the people he hoped would contribute to 'his' magazine. Top of the list was Elizabeth David. 'I remember saying, "Unless we can get her, there's no point going on." '[16]

Elizabeth always enjoyed the adulation of good-looking young men; but Johnson's enthusiasm, not only for her work but for the whole business of good food and wine, reflected her own inclinations. He wanted to make the magazine more visually exciting, more literary, and hoped eventually to launch it commercially. In all these areas, he eagerly sought her guidance. This was an approach that always brought out the best in Elizabeth, who, whatever her faults, was a great teacher. Before long Johnson was a regular visitor to Halsey Street, sitting at the kitchen table, scribbling notes, while Elizabeth ferreted through her books to find exactly the illustration she was looking for. He also started taking her out to lunch, usually to new restaurants.

Hugh Johnson was editor of *Wine and Food* for two years. During that time, Elizabeth contributed articles which had arisen from research she had followed up for her own interest and enlightenment. Hugh Johnson admitted that he 'never dared to change a comma'.

One of these *Wine and Food* articles was on the eighteenth-century cook, William Verral – her second on the subject, the first having been published the year before in the *Spectator*. This one is particularly interesting, however, since it gives a glimpse of her particular taste for scholarship: a kind of scholarship that looked through the historical text to the people who had written it.

The presence of ingredients which might strike one as outlandish or redundant, recipes which appear preposterously lavish even for large numbers of people are often quite easily explained if one takes the trouble to inquire a little into the personality of the author (it is curious how seldom cookery writers are regarded as people, or even as authors) . . . Was he or she a practising cook, and if so, in what kind of household or catering establishment? Urban or rural? Housekeeper to a great landowning family? A noblewoman more than normally preoccupied with the domestic arts? (You can always tell those. They give a lot of ghoulish recipes for feeding the poor.) Simply a copyist perpetuating a medieval superstition? . . . A physician? (they are the bossiest cookery authors of all.)[17]

Shortly after her trip to Nantes, Gerald Asher invited her to a lunch he was organizing at the premises of Asher Storey. When he had first had the idea of entertaining his friends and clients to regular lunches, Elizabeth had helped him find a cook; and now Asher and the cook went into serious discussions about what to give her. Since she had recently written a piece in the *Spectator* about sardines, they decided to give her a delicacy called Mature Sardines. These were tins which had been ageing for anything from five to twenty years, and according to one aficionado, 'the oldest made foie gras seem maigre. I almost slobber when I recall them'.[18] The tins were duly bought, one for each guest, and the day had arrived before a hideous problem presented itself: how does one serve Mature Sardines? Asher had never eaten them and neither had his cook. In the end, they decided to serve them in their tins, the lid rolled back. With good bread to mop up in every last corner, it was the perfect solution. Elizabeth was very appreciative, and Gerald Asher breathed a sigh of relief.

This lunch with Asher was probably one of the more convivial events in a diary that was filled with appointments: sometimes, even making a date with Higgins was a problem:

> Friday p.m. I never seem to be at home these days. I long to see you, and to cook some civilized food. Next week is hideous. Port on Monday in Belgrave Square, wine on Tuesday at lunchtime at the Aldwych, the French on Wednesday evening, Lyon on Thursday oh God perhaps we could have dinner here on Monday or Tuesday – or lunch on Wednesday. I want so much to see you – I miss you horribly when I don't.
>
> I think it is ten years since I came home from Italy and stayed in that ludicrous Grosvenor Hotel, and you made a scene because they wouldn't give us a drink after hours . . . Darling, for a great deal of perfectly extraordinary happiness in those ten years I have to thank you.[19]

At the end of 1962 Elizabeth turned forty-nine, and was entitled to think that after ten years of extremely hard work she could relax a little and enjoy the fruits of her labours. Yet as it turned out, 1963 was to prove the most turbulent and painful year of her life. It got off to a bad start.

Penguin had decided to drop the John Minton illustration from the cover of their edition of *Mediterranean Food*, and replace it with a food photograph which would bring the book in line with the rest of their cookery list. Elizabeth was appalled by the draft cover she was sent, and wrote a 'cry for help', as she put it, to Eunice Frost, the most senior person she knew in Penguin. 'I don't remember ever writing anything about cooking onions in a Turkish coffee pot with a roll of paper and three slices of slimy tomato; nor about inserting a hard-boiled egg into the belly of a shrivelled aubergine . . . Now what has all that to do with the Mediterranean? Or with cooking?'[20] She had not been that attached to the Minton illustration: what annoyed her was that Penguin had not given her the opportunity to set up the shot herself, and have it taken by Anthony Denney. There was also a principle, which was much on her mind at the time. This was that a book's text could not be divorced from its cover or its index, without substantially changing its impact. 'I am not saying that they are perfect. I am saying that they are all of a piece. John Lehmann made me see the importance of this point . . .'[21]

It was especially true of the illustrations that Renato Guttuso had done for *Italian Food*. To Elizabeth, they were as indispensable to the book as the references to Parmesan cheese – without them, a whole range of colour and taste was lost. They had never belonged to her yet Elizabeth felt intensely proprietorial about the Guttusos: after all it was she who had found him, and she who had conducted the negotiations for his pictures.

Then in March 1963, she was told by the Penguin production department that, in their forthcoming edition of *Italian Food*, they would have to work from the old blocks because Macdonald had mislaid the originals. Elizabeth said that there had been some mistake, and contacted Macdonald herself. It seemed that the Guttusos had been lent to others in the office, or mislaid in the move that the firm had recently made from Maddox Street to Portman Street. No one was really sure.

Elizabeth was very anxious about the illustrations and exasperated

THE YEAR OF BETRAYAL

at Macdonald's incompetence, particularly since they were again
baulking at the idea of a full revision of *Italian Food*. However, she
was reassured that the Guttusos would probably turn up, and three
days later, she set off on a trip to Tangier.

Her hosts (Mr and Mrs Rex Henry) were old friends of Lett
Haines, and they had been looking for someone to teach their
Moroccan-born, Italian-trained cook some of the refinements of
European cuisine. Elizabeth agreed to help, and in exchange they
agreed to pay her air fare and have her to stay as their guest, in a
house which was by all accounts luxuriously comfortable. She needed
a holiday, and thought it might be fun.

It was a nightmare, from start to finish. 'I don't know when I've
ever come across a more odious pair, boring, pretentious, sterile,
utterly without sense of humour, not enough to drink except Moorish
wine at meals and black looks at my cigarettes.'[22] Her host fancied
himself as an epicure, though all he really wanted were basins full
of ice cream and chocolate. Her hostess hated anything with alcohol
in it and fussed over her husband's health. 'There is a fearful lot of
"Chéri, tu n'as pas froid?" and *"Mon amour, tu n'est pas fatiguée?"*
and I fancy they simply hate each other . . .' They had an annoying
habit of saying they did not want any dinner, and then looking
incredulous when there was nothing to eat at dinner time. They also
constantly countermanded each other's orders – and Elizabeth's. All
her frustrations were vented in a long letter to Lesley O'Malley:

> Friday, there was a big lunch for eight which ended, as I
> thought it would, in tears. I prevented them from having *filets
> de sole à la crème* as well as an ice cream, with saddle of lamb
> and three vegetables in between. There were delicious little
> *loups de mer* in the market for grilling. I told the cook to buy
> one per person, and Monsieur sent him back for eight more
> . . . Madame countermanded the second lot, and Monsieur
> insisted. My ice didn't freeze, the lamb was overcooked and
> hacked to pieces. A shambles. Over a dinner of bread and water

there was a fearful post-mortem. I waited until they were both exhausted and then said, now you will listen to me – and delivered my well-known lecture on pretentious food and second-rate grand cooking, and vulgar display and trying to impress people, and giving the cook new dishes to try out for a party, and asking far too much of him and bringing me out here to make a monkey of me, etc., etc., etc. And swept up to bed sobbing . . .[23]

The only person she liked in the household was the cook, who was 'handsome and gay and charming, with beautiful manners . . . and really no end of a dish'. He was also a 'damned good cook, and I hope they lose him. I'm doing my best to undermine his loyalty . . .'

Just when Elizabeth thought she had had enough, Veronica and John Nicholson appeared: they were on holiday, with a car – and for a few glorious days she joined them on a little trip into the desert and the Atlas mountains. With them, Elizabeth was able to vent her frustrations; but at the same time, she seemed to need an emotional whipping boy: Veronica was the butt of all her jokes, and was teased mercilessly from morning till night. John Nicholson had never really liked Elizabeth, and this particular jaunt – during which she was so poisonous to his wife – did nothing to improve his instinctive dislike of her.

Back in Tangier, Elizabeth decided she could take no more. She returned to England at the end of April, feeling ill and run-down. Then Penguin rang with some bad news: Macdonald said the Guttusos were irretrievably lost. When Elizabeth rang Macdonald herself, no one wanted to talk to her; and when she finally buttonholed Walter Parrish, the art director, he told her bluntly that they were 'gone for good'. Elizabeth was still brooding over all the accumulated grievances Macdonald had caused her when she was contacted by a friend of hers and Peter's, who had known them both for years: Lady Sibell Rowley. What she had to say gave Elizabeth a shock from which she claimed she never really recovered.

*

Being the rigidly self-controlled person she was, Elizabeth had learned to live with the sadness of her lopsided relationship with Peter, so passionate on her side, so light-hearted on his; but what she had never imagined was that there could be another woman in his life who might matter more to him than she did. Yet there was, and Peter was in love with her. Her maiden name was Anne Capel, and she was at that time still married to her second husband, Thurston Holland-Martin. Elizabeth had no idea about Anne – although everyone in her circle knew, including Felicité and Veronica Nicholson. Felicité had told Peter that he must tell Elizabeth himself – he was still seeing her once or twice a week; but he always found a good excuse not to.

When Felicité and Veronica realized that Peter would never get around to it, they persuaded Sibell Rowley that only she, as a close friend of both parties, could tell Elizabeth the truth. When she did, Elizabeth turned on her in a fury. She became extremely unpleasant, more or less accusing Sibell of inventing the story out of jealousy; but when Sibell had gone the truth sank in. Felicité came downstairs, in an attempt to calm and comfort her sister – but Elizabeth was beside herself with grief and rage, flinging herself about and hurling things across the room.

Soon after, Elizabeth collapsed. She was found one morning by Lesley O'Malley, who was horrified to see Elizabeth trying, but unable, to talk. She was taken by ambulance to the National Hospital for Nervous Diseases in Queen Square and treated for a cerebral haemorrhage. Often triggered by stress, a cerebral haemorrhage is something like a stroke, and this is how Elizabeth's friends referred to it: they said it was astonishing that she should sustain such a thing, at her comparatively young age. Yet Elizabeth had been working too hard for years, and took very little exercise. Doreen Thornton, who used to come to Halsey Street at this time to help Elizabeth with typing and filing, also noticed that she was taking sleeping pills and drinking a great deal of brandy.

On 4 May, Elizabeth received a telegram from Peter: 'HOPE YOU ARE COMFORTABLE WILL COME AND SEE YOU SAT.' When he came, she thrust a letter into his hand and turned away.

* * * * * * * *

CHAPTER SIXTEEN

Farewell to P. H.

Elizabeth remained in hospital for a few weeks. Her speech returned. The doctors advised complete rest, but Elizabeth was back at work even before she left hospital, finishing an article she had begun for the *Spectator* called 'Points de Venise'. Her description of the fish market was, if anything, even more intensely visual than that which she had written in *Italian Food* all those years ago. 'In the dawn light of the Rialto markets . . . a sole isn't made of old white cricket flannels but of pale lilac silk, and . . . if you are looking you may see a pyramid of apricots radiating rose and gilt reflections from a catch of red mullet . . .'[1] This piece elicited a particularly warm fan letter, from the journalist and novelist Sybille Bedford.

> Dear Mrs David,
>
> Your article in June 14th *Spectator* has given me such intense pleasure that I feel I ought to write to thank you. I read 'Points de Venise' about six times, and aloud to friends, it is so beautifully written.

On first reading it, she had been on the point of leaving Asolo; but on the strength of Elizabeth's article:

> I drove off to Venice, walked the streets till after midnight, slept at the Albergo Fave (ten steps from the Rialto and built inside a live printing press and very cheap), and up again – alarm clock – at 4.40 a.m. for the Adriatic dawn. There's the power of the pen for you.[2]

This generous letter could not have arrived at a better time. It not only gave her a much-needed boost to the morale, but from her reply there's a sense that Elizabeth felt she had found a true friend.

Dear Mrs Bedford,

You wrote me such a beautiful letter about my Venice article. I have written you at least three replies. None of them has reached the letter box (one actually got lost on the way to the typist – it was too lengthy to send to you in longhand. At least you were spared that one) . . . I think I may have told you on a previous occasion how great is my admiration and love for your own beautiful books. Two copies of *The Legacy* are always near me – one in my bedroom, one near my work table. The passage about Melanie and the *loup de mer* I know by heart like I know Durrell's piece about black olives from *Prospero's Cell* – all the same I still want to get the sensation of actually reading them on the printed page . . .

Incidentally, about that Venice article, I have been told since (*a*) that Alfredo Zoppi of the Fenice has died . . . (*b*) that Proust did go to Venice (*c*) that there is no early morning market near the Rialto. What has happened? . . . I wrote part of the Venice article in hospital, with the doctors telling me that I had better not – perhaps they were right . . . I only hope I didn't make you get up for nothing.[3]

21 Sept., Les Bastides
Dear Mrs David,

Such a very delightful letter. I am overcome. To be told that one's books are actually *used* . . . that seems to me the only real reward of writing. But then I don't write with ease. Do you? You read as if you did, but I know that is no indication. To me, it is all anguish and stone-heaving work . . .

As to the rest, Mrs Bedford was reassuring: Proust had dithered so much about whether to go to Venice that no one knows for sure whether he did or not; and when she reached the Rialto at dawn, there was the fish market, just as Elizabeth had described it.

They had already met, at publishing parties and the like; but after their exchange of letters, Elizabeth invited Sybille to dinner. Sybille passed through the narrow hall, made so much narrower by the piles of books on either side – 'you could only just pass through'.[4] Elizabeth gave her a white Beaujolais, which Sybille had never tried before; and the meal consisted of *mezzes*, a few grains of perfectly cooked rice, a salad, and a bottle of red wine – 'good, but not great'.[5] They were neither of them at ease in a crowd; both preferred books, wine, simple dinners and intimate conversation that went on till 'birdsong', as they called the early hours of the morning. Sybille would drag herself away and then, as was her habit, walk around the quiet streets for a while before returning to her London base, which was a small flat in Chesham Place. They were both nocturnal: walking back through Halsey Street, Sybille often noticed that Elizabeth's bedroom light was still on, at two or three in the morning.

Sybille knew a great deal about food, and even more about wine: she could appreciate fine vintages in a way that Elizabeth always claimed she never could. Whenever Elizabeth was given a really fine bottle of wine she would give it to Sybille: 'It was true generosity, because she knew I would take it away and drink it by myself.'[6] Sybille's idea of a perfect evening was to drink a great wine, with just the right piece of music to go with it. That was another taste that Elizabeth did not share. She was untouched by music in any form – whereas Sybille positively needed it.

Over the next decade, Sybille and Elizabeth had endless lunches and dinners together, usually in restaurants. 'I was an innocent in those days, I thought we were equals,' said Sybille. However, she did not fail to notice Elizabeth's somewhat prima-donna-ish style in restaurants, and she soon found out that their friendship was on Elizabeth's terms, not hers. The invisible wall she had erected around herself could not be crossed with impunity. One evening Sybille happened to mention, because she was so full of it, that she was in love –

'and I knew it was the wrong thing to say the moment I had said it'.[7] Elizabeth froze and glanced away. The conversation moved on.

Another friend Elizabeth made at this time was the American cookery writer Julia Child. With her co-authors Simone Beck and Louisette Bertholle, she had written a classic of American cookery writing *Mastering the Art of French Cookery*, the English edition of which had just been published by Cassell. Elizabeth had given it a very favourable review, and Mrs Child was deeply grateful.

> We are simply overwhelmed with your review of our book. It's the first time we've had a serious comment from a pro, and you have brought out the gist of what we tried to do in writing it. That we have succeeded, in your eyes, to make cooking a bit easier and more understandable is of the deepest satisfaction ... The important thing is that you quietly and firmly get back your health ... Thank heaven you can be quiet and work on the *Spectator* articles, and have nothing else pushing at you.[8]

As soon as she was well enough, Elizabeth went to France and from then on down to Italy, to stay with Viola Johnson. She and Viola visited the truffle town of Alba near Turin, which led to another of her best-known *Spectator* pieces, 'Trufflesville Regis'.[9]

Another particularly effective piece she wrote for the *Spectator* at this time was called 'Golden Delicious' celebrating a wine called Beaumes de Venise. Elizabeth was introduced to this golden muscat dessert wine by Gerald Asher, who had begun importing it and gave her a bottle shortly before Christmas. Elizabeth was entranced; and the aura of mystery which seemed to hang about the wine added another dimension to its haunting, flowery taste. Elizabeth told her readers that 'Nobody, it seems, quite knows when the muscat grapes of Beaumes de Venise were first planted nor how the sweet wine from the vineyards of this tiny area protected by a fold in the hills from the savage north winds acquired its reputation. Certainly that reputation has always been a local one only.'[10]

All that was about to change. In the mid-sixties there were only two growers of Beaumes de Venise, producing about 200 hectolitres a year. But thanks to Elizabeth's enthusiasm the wine caught on to such an extent that, thirty years later, Gerald Asher wrote '200 hectolitres would now scarcely keep the market going for half a week'.[11] During her weeks in hospital and the brief convalescence she allowed herself, Elizabeth had found herself doing a lot of re-reading: of writers who had been formative influences, and also of earlier English cookery writers. The previous year, she had written about Eliza Acton and William Verral. In the later half of 1963, the *Spectator* published pieces by Elizabeth David on Hilda Leyel, Florence White and Countess Morphy; on Mrs Beeton; and (an honorary Englishman) Marcel Boulestin. As far as any casual reader of her work could see, all was well.

Elizabeth had not given herself the time to recover fully from her stroke. She did not want anyone outside her immediate circle to know how ill she had been, particularly among those who commissioned her work; and besides, she hated the idea that her friends might be discussing her health behind her back. The result was that that winter, she succumbed to a bout of severe depression. It was not just that she still felt physically and emotionally drained; the cerebral haemorrhage had also impaired her sense of taste and, unlike her speech, it was not coming back. Friends noticed that she was doing much less cooking than she used to, and when she did, she often asked them to taste whether the food was properly salted. Friends might arrive at Halsey Street to find four or five little white dishes, each containing a differently salted sample of whatever she was cooking. The guest had to try each one and say which was the best. At the same time, she could not bear the smell of fried onions, which seemed ten times more pungent and pervasive than it had been before.

Elizabeth had always had a strong head for alcohol, and had been drinking a good deal of spirits before her stroke. The doctors had warned her off the hard stuff, and she seldom drank spirits again; but she still drank a great deal of wine to dull the pain of what seemed like an emotionally empty life. A friend recalled that she was profoundly unhappy at this time; and when she came round of an evening, she used to drink till she became 'quite sodden. Not violent, not unpleasant, just sodden.' She stopped writing for the *Spectator*, though this was mostly because she could not think up enough subjects to be able to fill a page twice a month; and while Cyril Ray and Katharine Whitehorn were full of ideas, none of them seemed to appeal to her.

Instead she brooded over the Guttusos, fretting and fuming over their loss in a way that was clearly obsessive for she had never owned them: they had been paid for by her publisher. She hired a solicitor, Michael Rubinstein, to prepare a case against Macdonald. Rubinstein told her that she stood very little chance of proving that she would lose either royalties, or the prospect of a future edition of *Italian Food*, due to the loss of the illustrations. But when she set out the list of incompetence, obstructions and aggravations she had had to endure from Macdonald since she had had the misfortune to fall into their hands, Rubinstein thought that they might be persuaded to release the rights they held over her first three books. This case took up an enormous amount of her time and energy, and she talked about it to anyone who would listen. It was a way of channelling the anger that burned inside her, the real cause of which could never be mentioned: the loss of Peter Higgins.

Peter's new love, Anne Holland-Martin, was young, rich and much more in tune with Peter's hunting and racing set than Elizabeth could ever be. Their affair had been going on for about a year, during which time they shared the top flat of a house in Chapel Street. At some point soon after they started living together, perhaps in the autumn of 1963, Peter had had a serious riding accident in Rotten Row which had badly damaged his pelvis. He was in hospital for months in traction, during which time Elizabeth had come to see him. Anne and Peter planned to be married as soon as her divorce came through. But Peter did not want Elizabeth to think that he had merely discarded her, no longer cared for her; and in the spring of 1964, a year after her haemorrhage, he rang her up. They agreed to meet for lunch on 6 May. Elizabeth wrote 'Beau Higgins lunch' in her diary, and drew a little heart beside his name.

If she had any hopes, they were soon dashed. Peter told her that their affair was over, but he was still very fond of her and wanted to stay friends. He assumed she had another lover by now, but Elizabeth told him there was no one else – no one who mattered. Painful as it was, all this was bearable; but when he began to apologize and make excuses for not telling her sooner about Anne, Elizabeth lost all patience. She felt bitterly disappointed and humiliated, and as always, these feelings turned to anger. Over the next few days she wrote Peter a letter, which she worked over and over. Even in its fullest form it is not complete, and some paragraphs stand by themselves without being incorporated into the main text. It seems less of a letter than an attempt to make sense of her emotional turmoil.

20 May 1964

I think it must be just exactly a year ago to the day that I started writing you the letter which, as things turned out, I shoved into your hands the night you came round to see me after I had had that brain haemorrhage. If you ever read the letter you will have thought it was the product of an already disordered brain boiling up for an explosion. Certainly I was already ill and in a state of shock following the disastrous trip to Morocco and the revelation by my publishers of the loss of the Guttusos. But as far as you were concerned my head was perfectly clear. There were things which had never been said, and could be said only when I knew for certain and sure that a long period of emotional misery was forever over.

The little tiny malign blow which wrecked my sense of taste has also put an end (some might think high time too) to any interest I might still have had in sex. After you got bored with me I didn't think much of the whole idea anyway. But now it wouldn't be any use even if I did. I am half-numbed physically,

233

and can't feel anything. Relinquishing something I cannot have is therefore of no account, since I do not want or need it. I am lucky. Most people have to learn this the hard way. You, with all your endearing lack of the possessive instinct, have never wanted to renounce entirely any woman you have ever fancied.

Your emotional confidence suited me, (all other serious attachments I ever had came to grief because I could not stand being suffocated with love) and your gaiety was, and still is, adorable. For a long time, during all those years of excruciating pain after you got bored of me and I wasn't bored with you I fought to get rid of you. Once or twice I nearly succeeded but in the end you always defeated me and betrayed me into making a spectacle of myself. Of course you made me work too. The book I dedicated to you was the product of those hateful years.

I dedicated my book to you because it was you who provided the conflict and the stress which, for such as I, alone make writing possible. For that matter, for better or worse, it was you who were responsible for all my books, right from the beginning. It was childish, but I had to show you, while you were busy down in Devon pretending to be a farm labourer, that I could do something with my time . . . It is not, you know, my illness which has stopped me writing. It is the ending of a necessity, and of a prolonged torment . . .

This letter is unique in that it makes a connection between Elizabeth's work and her private life. It is hard to believe that Peter was 'responsible' for all her books. He might have inspired and encouraged the writing of them; but to make him 'responsible' for them was a way of telling Peter what she felt at the time – that he had ruined her life, and that she would probably never write another book again.

* * * * * * * *

CHAPTER SEVENTEEN

The Shop

Anthony Denney came to the rescue. He was one of the few people who could not only stand up to Elizabeth, but bully her as well. Her doctors had told her she needed a rest and a complete change of scene, and he was going to see that she got it. He persuaded her to come to stay with him in Spain, on a little estate he had in the almond- and lemon-growing country near Valencia. It was called La Alfarella.

Elizabeth had never been to Spain before; but as soon as she felt the sun and the pull of the Mediterranean again, she began to feel better. The isolated, whitewashed farmhouse built around a stone courtyard had been a ruin when Denney bought it in the late fifties. Now it had water and electricity, but the cooking arrangements were still rudimentary. The food was usually prepared in earthenware dishes, heated directly over the Butagaz or on the hearth. It was served on the veranda whenever possible, and eaten overlooking a magnificent view of the mountains.

The pieces that Elizabeth wrote from La Alfarella have an extra-ordinary freshness, as if she is seeing a new-born world for the first time: discovering that, after all the pain and illness of the past year, she can write again – even eat onions again.

'The enormous ridged tomatoes were cored with a little sharp knife, cut round roughly into sections, thrown into a shallow bowl, mixed with thickly sliced raw onions, mild and very sweet. Salt, a sprinkling of olive oil and wine vinegar were the only seasonings

... It has no regional or picturesque name. It is just *ensalada*.'[1] Among the lemon and almond trees of La Alfarella, and in that very simple dish, 'so rich in flavour, so sweet, so cool, fresh', Elizabeth found that life was still worth living.

A muddle over dates with the travel agent meant that Elizabeth was forced to stay in Spain a few days longer than she intended, and had to miss a signing session that she had committed herself to in the book department of Harrods. She was very unhappy at having to drop this professional commitment, and as soon as she was back in England she went to apologize. The management were very understanding, and from the sales staff she learnt that the paperback of *French Provincial Cooking* had been one of the top six best-sellers for the last three weeks – 'after the latest James Bond and before the Kama Sutra, which gives one a certain amount of pleasure'.[2]

In her letter of thanks to Anthony, she described her three weeks in Spain as 'a door to new and marvellous things ... which only you could have shown me, and I feel my life is quite changed, and none too soon, either. Except for the small inevitable leftovers of that annoying illness of last year, the ones which will always remain, all the rest is forgotten, as if it had never been. A lot more unhappinesses and anxieties [are] gone too. In their place a tremendous whirl and surge of new vistas and a different outlook on everything.'[3]

She visited Anthony again in October of 1964; and the feeling of renewal that La Alfarella bestowed shines through one of the most beautiful of her *Spectator* articles, 'Para Navidad'. The title refers to the way everyone in that part of Spain was making delicious things and storing them up for Christmas: the piece is imbued with the excitement of something to work towards and look forward to.

La Alfarella was the perfect rest cure, and in Denney's stimulating company she found the strength to face the future. No one since Norman Douglas had taught her so much or been on her wavelength to such an extraordinary degree. They shared not only a highly developed artistic taste, but also the same mischievous sense of humour, the same sharp nose for humbug. Denney had once had a school report which described him as 'naughty and defiant', and part of him still was. As with Douglas, sex did not come into it. Denney had three children from a previous marriage but that had long been over, and the only other guest at La Alfarella was his Australian partner Alex Collins, who ran the financial side of Denney's decorating business. They were just the people with whom to discuss the project that she had been thinking about for some time: a shop for cooks.

In the late 1950s, most people in England bought their cookware, dishes and utensils from hardware shops, where they were displayed alongside dusters and shoe polish, fly swatters and clothes-pegs. What there was was serviceable, and some of it was excellent: Union-Brand enamelware, Kenrick cast-ironware, fine stainless steel knives from Sheffield, beechwood rolling pins and spatulas, Pearson's stoneware, and bakery tools from Errington's of Portsmouth.

For the sort of cooking Elizabeth wrote about, however, the local hardware shop was not so well stocked. Earthenware was scarcely used for cooking any more, having been replaced by paler, less porous dishes from the big china manufactories since the mid-eighteenth century. Sheffield knives were good and easy to look after; but they were no substitute for the carbon-steel knives used in France, thin as paper and sharp as razors. The other problem was that even in the better-stocked shops, very few of the sales assistants knew anything about what they were selling.

There was only one shop in England where real French utensils could be bought, things like mandolines, carbon-steel knives and snail tongs: Madame Cadec's in Soho. Madame Cadec, a sprightly figure with dark hair and almond-shaped glasses, had run the shop single-handed for the past fifteen years since her husband's death. She had become an institution, and a password: those who mentioned her name in a knowledgeable way were assumed to be serious cooks. Her shop was small and dark, filled to bursting with equipment which was piled, higgledy-piggledy, from floor to ceiling.

Elizabeth wanted a shop where the staff would know about what was on sale, and where all the beautiful cooking tools that she herself would use could be found. Unlike Mme Cadec's, which looked like an old tool shop cum ironmonger's, she wanted hers to look stunning. Only one man could design such a place, and that was Anthony Denney. Denney agreed in principle, which must have been a relief to Elizabeth. She trusted his eye completely, and she would have felt far less confident about the project had he not been a part of it. She went back to London full of hope for the future, and feeling stronger than she had for many months.

The idea for a shop was not hers alone. In the late 1950s she had made a new friend called Peter Trier. He owned a company which made copper pans and also re-tinned them, and in 1960 he began importing Le Creuset's enamelled cast-iron ware. Elizabeth had long been complaining of the paucity of good cooking utensils in England, and kept urging Peter to make more things himself. Over long sessions at Halsey Street, they talked about what might be done to rectify this hole in the market. Others became involved. Peter Trier brought in his wife Jenny, and Elizabeth pressed Renée Fedden into joining them; at the time Renée was deeply troubled and unhappy, and Elizabeth felt she needed something to occupy her time and fill a part of her life. On several occasions, this small group had got together to think about whether they could raise the money to get the idea off the ground.

One of the factors that inspired them to go ahead was the appearance in May 1964 of a new shop, on the corner of the Fulham Road and Sloane Avenue, owned by an enterprising young designer called Terence Conran. It was called Habitat, and among many other things it sold bright textiles, china, glass and furniture for urban nomads. Conran had found inspiration for his ideas across the world, from Scandinavia to Japan; but he was always particularly fascinated by the solid, unpretentious work of French ironmongers. Their knives, their beautiful black pots and pans, ladles and tongs were on display alongside carafes, pepper mills and butchers' aprons, and Japanese-inspired paper lampshades. The shop was a sensation: Habitat not only offered a world that everyone under thirty wanted to be a part of – it was on sale at an affordable price. In later years, Elizabeth was rather scathing of 'Tattycat' as she used to call it; but there was no denying that it filled a gap. To a reader she wrote, 'They have the French [Le Creuset] vitreous-enamelled cast-iron cooking pots and quite a lot of good sensible things.'[4] Another factor that encouraged Elizabeth and her friends to clinch their decision was the announcement that Madame Cadec was about to retire. Elizabeth got in touch with her, offering to buy her leftover stock.

Towards the end of 1964, Elizabeth was persuaded to join the team of writers that was being gathered together for a new magazine called *Nova* – probably because they had promised that Anthony Denney would illustrate her pieces. Every magazine claims to be new, but *Nova*'s claim was justified. There was an immediacy in the way big black headings jumped out at the reader, the way a single photograph of a bowl of lemons filled an entire page right to the edges. It was not only more topical than most women's magazines: it also had a mind of its own. Magazines had discussed divorce before, but *Nova* was among the first to question the usual conclusion that it was the woman's duty to stick by a marriage come what may. Elizabeth contributed eight articles for *Nova*, from February to November 1965; and her appearance in the newest and most radical women's magazine gave her just the right 'profile' when the time came to launch the shop.

Another factor keeping Elizabeth firmly in the public consciousness was that all her books save *Summer Cooking* were now published by Penguin. Elizabeth had never ceased to bless Eunice Frost for bringing *Mediterranean Food* to the attention of Allen Lane, and putting her books within reach of a far wider readership. However, given the public interest in cooking, Penguin's cookery list was relatively small and in the mid-sixties the management felt the time had come to build it up. They had only one woman editor at the time, Jill Norman, so she was automatically given the cookery list –

though she was also handling contemporary poetry, the Penguin Classics and foreign literature.

Soon after taking over as cookery editor, Jill had to prepare Penguin's first edition of *Summer Cooking*, which Elizabeth had revised and enlarged. She used to go round to Halsey Street, and together they worked at the kitchen table. Elizabeth got on very well with Jill: she was not only sympathetic (all Elizabeth's best editors had a good desk-side manner), she paid rigorous attention to detail, and had a determination to get things right.

In the early spring of 1965, shop premises were found at 46 Bourne Street, just behind Sloane Square. Jenny Trier, who had inherited some money, bought the lease. They planned to open in the autumn, but before then the stock had to be ordered and the shop set up, and Elizabeth was still writing her articles. There were times when the immensity of what she had undertaken and the stress of ever getting it all ready in time got the better of her.

'Sorry about the outburst yesterday,' she wrote to Denney. 'I'm harassed and tired beyond endurance, and feel trapped like an escaping prisoner, back to bashing out another of those god-awful articles just when I thought I was free ... [The shop] *has* to go right. I've involved three people in it, and you're involved too, I can't help it.'[5]

At this point two more people joined the venture: Bryan Llewellyn, who had experience in marketing and was then the Controller of Regional Marketing for Thomson Newspapers, and his wife Pam Pugh. Bryan Llewellyn had been approached by the Triers, who felt that the venture needed someone who had experience of marketing. He and Pam Pugh formed two of the five partners in the shop, the others being Jenny Trier (not Peter), Renée Fedden and Elizabeth.

Madame Cadec had told Elizabeth that she would be delighted to sell what was left of her stock – though perhaps the partners expected rather more than there was. Elizabeth wrote that she, Bryan and Pam 'spent an exhausting but entertaining afternoon with Mme Cadec in her warehouse, going through crates of rusty knives and ancient ironware, which I suppose we have to buy from her in return for information and her blessing plus a few bottles of her tarragon vinegar'.[6] Throughout 1965, Peter and Elizabeth made a number of trips to France in his van. They would park it in the courtyard of one of Peter's friends, who was a sculptor, and then do the rounds of all the old wholesale firms dotted about in the Parisian suburbs. Elizabeth had been collecting the names of good firms for many years, long before she started thinking of a shop. Once inside a warehouse she would not rest until she had explored every corner of the premises, and once she found something right her excitement was palpable. During these trips, they ate in a wide variety of restaurants – some not bad, some very rough indeed; but Elizabeth never seemed to mind, and Peter found himself learning a lot in her company. 'She was so funny, so cynical – her language was pretty rich too . . . and no one could bullshit her when it came to food. She was a great debunker.'[7] At the same time, the shop was being made ready. Elizabeth told Anthony that Bryan Llewellyn had bought a letter box and got the glass-cutters in to make an aperture in the plate-glass window, but 'they said it was much too dangerous to tamper with it. It's armour-plate glass. The wall took nearly a week to knock down. The place must have been built as a gangster's refuge.'

Elizabeth's excitement and enthusiasm, so long dormant, bubbled into a sort of skittish quality that was quite uncharacteristic. Her letter to Denney hopes that he is already planning the next shop, which will have '(*a*) a place for a letter box and (*b*) a staircase so we don't have to put a net at the bottom to catch the customers as they fall down . . .'[8]

She also has plans for books, lavishly illustrated by Anthony. 'I'm fed up with working for nothing. It's very nice having a lot of compliments and grateful readers and knowing that one has done some not bad work which everyone has tried to copy . . . and

E. David Ltd is going to make money too. You'll see. You've only known me as a writer, so it seems wrong to you that I should try and be anything else."[9]

There was no doubt in anyone's mind, least of all Elizabeth's, what the shop would be called. By now even people who did not cook had heard of Elizabeth David, and those who had never read a word she had written had probably absorbed the idea that her name was synonymous with good food and a certain integrity. As for her loyal and ever-growing band of followers, they would travel from all over England to visit what they saw as her shop. To her partners, the words ELIZABETH DAVID LTD that hung over the shop in massive, hand-forged, gold-painted iron letters were a lucky amulet. They were essential to publicize and launch their venture, and they would remain a symbol of the quality of the shop. To Elizabeth, however, the name meant far more. Only she knew how much work it had taken to make that name what it was, and in the window of the shop it was a promise to her customers. They would know that everything on display was there because she had chosen it, and it carried the stamp of her approval. At the same time, there was a risk in giving one's name to a business venture, as her first publisher, John Lehmann, had discovered to his cost.

Renée and Jenny were rather worried by the fact that although Anthony Denney had agreed to design the shop, he produced no plans or sketches at all. Elizabeth told them to have faith: she had complete confidence in him, and she was right – for when all was ready, the shop looked spectacular. Immediately behind the great wall of armour-plated glass was a massive wooden table, on which Anthony Denney erected dizzying, acrobatic pyramids of wire whisks, brioche tins, sugar casters, soufflé dishes, wire egg baskets and ramekins. These displays were lit from above, and stood out dramatically. Inside, a series of plain white shelves stood against the pale grey-blue walls, each supported by a deep iron frieze (designed by Denney) which hid the lighting of the shelf below. On these stood piles of the largest and heaviest items of stock: casseroles, bean-pots, storage jars, cheese stands and fish platters. On the black-and-white tiled floor were more piles of bowls and casseroles, and a round marble table at the back of the shop provided further room for displays. On the back wall, painted a deep blue, a white arrow invited the customer into the basement, which was reached by a narrow flight of stairs. Here the only decoration was bare brick and whitewash, with wooden warehouse shelves supported on perforated steel units; but the piles of fish kettles and sugar boilers, the drifts of omelette pans and terrines, and the warm russet colours of earthenware cocottes and gratin dishes, the bags of *gros sel* and the baskets of wooden and horn spoons gave the place all the exoticism of a Middle Eastern bazaar. Under the stairs was a little office.

The shop opened on 1 November 1965, on which occasion Elizabeth received good-luck telegrams from several of Britain's most cele- brated gastronomes: Philip Harben, Len Deighton, Fanny and John- nie Cradock, Robert Carrier and Robin McDouall. Terence Conran sent a huge bouquet of flowers, and she also received telegrams from Peter Higgins, and Tony David, who had now settled in St-Juan-les-Pins. Elizabeth had granted the *Sunday Times* an exclu- sive interview to be published the day before, on Sunday 31 October; but word got out before the paper went to press, and so many papers took up the story that by nine o'clock on Monday morning there was a queue outside the door. The day passed in a flurry of tissue paper and the ringing of the till, and at the end of the afternoon it appeared as if they had made over a million pounds – but this was primarily due to Renée's daughter Frances, who had obviously not quite mastered the cash register.

For the past fifteen years, Elizabeth had spent her working days by herself. The writer's life is one of solitary concentration, immense effort in an empty room. Now she was with other people, and rather enjoying it. She was, after all, the star of the show; and she was also a natural teacher, to pupils of any level. Jill Norman, who had known

Elizabeth only as a very reserved and retiring person, was astonished at the transformation that came over Elizabeth in the first few years of the shop. 'Suddenly she was available to everyone. She tried to establish exactly what people wanted, what they needed; she'd give them advice on presents, on cooking – and she loved it. There was an enthusiasm, a desire to share all her knowledge and experience, and the reclusiveness was just . . . *gone*.'[10] One observer remembered Elizabeth taking endless pains to find just the right sort of pan for an American lady with three children, who needed a skillet large enough to fry three pancakes at the same time. Sometimes, no trouble was too much. On one occasion, someone came in looking for a specific implement in just the right size, and was very crestfallen when told it was not in stock: 'But if you come back tomorrow,' said Elizabeth, 'I *think* I've got one at home . . .'

There were some things she refused to sell, such as wall-mounted knife sharpeners and – one of her pet hates – garlic crushers: 'Squeezing the juice out of garlic doesn't reduce its potency, it concentrates and increases it. I have often wondered how it is that people who have once used one of these diabolical instruments don't notice this and throw the thing into the dustbin.'[11] Elizabeth urged people to use the flat blade of a knife and a scrap of salt instead, but not all customers were happy to accept this particular tablet from the mountain. One was heard to say, 'And who are *you* to tell me I can't buy a garlic crusher?' To which Elizabeth tartly replied that the lady was at liberty to buy one wherever she pleased, but not in *her* shop.

When not upstairs with her customers, Elizabeth spent most of the day in the basement in her little office. Much of her time was spent working on mail-order catalogues, to which she devoted the same fanatical attention to detail as she did to her books. She also, in the early days, checked orders and dealt with suppliers. While working, she smoked untipped Gauloises by the packet; but while she never minded working with the bustle of the shop going on around her, she could not bear the noise of the air-conditioning and always switched it off as soon as she came in. Sooner or later, someone unable to breathe through the cigarette smoke any longer surreptitiously turned it on, and it would clatter away until Elizabeth turned it off again.

Elizabeth shared her office with a huge collection of reference books on food and cookery. These were tools she could not have lived without, and they were also used to answer the customers' questions. Customers were encouraged to use the shop as what one would now call a help-line, whenever their soufflé fell or their sauce curdled, and they availed themselves freely of this extremely useful service. Behind the desk were Elizabeth's treasures: pots and pans and tins, specimens of white china rimmed with shades of blue, different bowls and moulds all crowded together on a series of deep shelves. These were her personal things, not for sale; but each was a benchmark of its kind, and Elizabeth used them for reference and comparison with the orders.

To Drusilla Beyfus, who interviewed her for the *Telegraph* Magazine, she confided that 'this life is a million million times easier than writing a book';[12] but it was not plain sailing either. Many years later, she told Jane Grigson that dealing with suppliers was exhausting. 'Visits entailed endless argufying. And in spite of it all the sizes ordered were seldom sent, lids rarely tallied with the pots (but of course duty still had to be paid, no matter how long you had to sit on both waiting for them all to be matched up before you could sell them . . .)'[13]

Elizabeth was also responsible for generating certain discrete little crazes. Once it was coeur-à-la-crème dishes, and once – having got in a consignment of vinegar jars – Elizabeth started a vinegar 'mother'. This slightly opaque, gelatinous mass is required for the proper fermentation of good vinegar. A piece of it can be removed and, like a yeast, it can be used to form a new vinegar mother. People were constantly coming in to ask for a bit, till there was such a demand (it was like having the relic of a culinary saint) that Elizabeth wished she had never introduced it.

One thing she never regretted introducing was the olive oil of Poggio Lamentano. She had always loved real, unfiltered olive oil; but she did not know about this particular one until, one day in the late 1960s, she received a parcel. It was very badly wrapped, very greasy, and inside were the smashed remains of a bottle of olive oil. She wrote back to inform the senders, and they sent her another bottle – this time more carefully packaged. It was dark, murky green, intensely aromatic, and the best she had ever tasted. The people who made it were Lesley and Aleksander Zyw, and their son Michael. Aleksander was a Polish artist, Lesley came from Edinburgh. They had known nothing about olive oil when they bought the property with its eight hundred abandoned olive trees in 1961. Elizabeth described the oil as 'one of the supreme pleasures of my life', and the shop soon stocked it in five-litre cans, driven back from Tuscany in the Zyws' Land Rover. Michael Zyw was particularly grateful that she allowed them to use her name for publicity, and on the bottle labels: 'Not many people understood about good olive oil and having E.D.'s seal of approval convinced them to try it out,' wrote Michael Zyw. 'She most definitely did make a practical contribution both to the sale of our olive oil, and our perseverance in producing and marketing it.'[14]

The shop also generated a certain amount of publicity, which Elizabeth tried to keep strictly on her own terms. Whenever anyone wanted to interview her, the first reaction was, 'Why should anyone want to know about me?' In 1966, when the *Sunday Times* said they would like to do a profile of her, Elizabeth agreed only on condition that Sybille Bedford do the interview and that no personal questions should be asked. The interview was conducted over a series of dinners; and to reassure Elizabeth, Sybille showed her the finished piece. On handing in the copy to the features editor, however, Sybille was appalled to hear her say, 'Well, now that Elizabeth's checked it, let's put in some personal bits.'[15] Sybille indignantly refused to add a word.

Sybille told Elizabeth what had happened, but was unprepared for the force of her reaction. Not only was she outraged that the editor could have dared to suggest such a thing: she never forgot it, and never forgave the editor concerned. Fifteen years later, at a party to celebrate Sybille's OBE, the editor came to say hello to Elizabeth, who was enthroned in a chair with many people dancing attendance about her. Elizabeth cut her dead.

The shop became the focus of Elizabeth's life and she more or less settled into it. It was her club. In Bourne Street family and friends knew they could always find her, and here country readers breathless to meet the great Mrs David were granted an audience. An order was made for a case of wine per week, from Asher Storey: six bottles of Soave, and six of an inexpensive red wine Elizabeth called 'Flaming Carthage'. She often brought lunch for the staff: delicious terrines and egg dishes, olives and radishes, that were beautifully laid out on a little marble table downstairs.

Over the years, there was quite a turnover of staff in Elizabeth David Ltd. Some were very young, like Renée's daughter Frances Fedden and Celia Royde-Smith, who had been introduced to Elizabeth by her godmother, the cookery writer Margaret Costa. It was a first job too for Antonia Graham, who went on to found her own shop, Graham & Greene, some years later. Some were old friends of Elizabeth's – like Joyce Murchie, who came in once or twice to help out.

Rosalind Jenkinson, a bohemian and strikingly beautiful ex-model who became manageress of the shop in 1970, felt that it had a particularly intimate and relaxed atmosphere. It was generated by a collection of people who had nothing in common except that Elizabeth had seen, in each of them, something that she herself responded to. There was April Boyes, who became Elizabeth's most trusted right hand and who eventually undertook the cataloguing of Elizabeth's library; Rosi Hanson, who had learnt to cook in France and only read Elizabeth's books after returning to England with her husband Anthony, who was writing a book about wine. There was also

Ellen-Ann Ragsdale from Little Rock, Arkansas, and Elizabeth Savage, who succeeded to April's role when April decided to devote more time to her husband and daughter. Each felt particularly grateful to Elizabeth: to work with her was an education in itself. But to some she had also given new confidence, and a new lease of life.

When Anthony Denney and Celia Royde-Smith announced their engagement in 1969, almost everyone in the shop was taken by surprise – except Elizabeth. She had engineered their coming together from the first. Frances Fedden remembered seeing her mother Renée and Elizabeth together one evening with their backs to the fire, giggling delightedly, while Elizabeth tacitly congratulated herself on this fine bit of matchmaking. 'Some marriages are made in Heaven,' said Celia; 'ours was made in Halsey Street.'[16]

She was a thoughtful friend. Birthdays were marked by the little presents she was so good at giving, or a dedicated recipe. Yet she expected a lot from her staff, and anyone who slipped from her exacting standards was immediately corrected. April remembered that while everyone was expected to know what things were for and encouraged to ask if they did not, their ignorance was not always met with understanding. 'Sometimes she would be happy to tell you but at other times she would say rather severely, "Haven't you read my books?" We were all expected to be familiar with the sacred texts.'[17]

On window nights, everyone was expected to work late. Elizabeth would bring a picnic supper, and several bottles of Flaming Carthage helped to make it a convivial evening – but it was hard work. The girls went up and down the stairs with armloads of things for Anthony Denney, who constructed new ziggurats and miniature Chrysler Buildings with madeleine tins and asparagus kettles on the display table. When Anthony moved to Spain, the window was entrusted to a young artist; but it was Elizabeth who decided the theme, what would be displayed, and until she was satisfied the work went on – sometimes until nine or ten at night.

The mood among the staff was very cheerful, although there was a general feeling that it was more fun to be downstairs in the basement where Elizabeth held court. Most customers went downstairs too, for that was where the less bulky items of stock were. Someone was always supposed to be on duty upstairs, where there was a till, but the rule was not always obeyed. The result of this negligence was that on one occasion, not just the money in it but the upstairs cash register was stolen – and it was some time before the loss was noticed. The loss of the money was not as bad as the loss of the till, which was a brand-new one purchased to cope with the decimal coinage introduced in 1971. 'Now that's what I call cash and carry,' remarked Ellen-Ann in her Southern drawl.

Behind the scenes, however, cracks were opening up between the directors. The Triers, Bryan Llewellyn and Pam Pugh felt that the business should lead the enterprise: new suppliers should be found, new stock lines considered; Elizabeth should be compiling kitchen starter-packs, presentations for brides, arrangements for wedding lists. Elizabeth was impatient of such things, seeing it as her role to concentrate on publicity and aesthetics. Items ordered by another partner, or even items she had chosen herself but changed her mind about when they arrived, would be pronounced '*Hideous!*' and banished from sight. The fact that money had been paid for them and that they were there to be sold seemed no longer relevant. Renée was caught between the two. Helped by a friend called Rosemary Peto, she had put about £5,000 into the shop – more than twice Elizabeth's financial stake; but out of loyalty, she usually backed Elizabeth.

The shop failed to make as much money as they had hoped in the first year, and in 1966 they branched into mail-order and wholesale. Elizabeth was in charge of compiling the catalogues, and with her scholarly mind and eye for detail, they were very good. The company took a lease on a warehouse under the railway arches at Vauxhall (which Elizabeth used as a dump for the 'hideous' things that she could no longer bear to see in the shop). The office here was big enough to house Renée, Pam – who worked on the orders and accounts – and Mrs Goldsworthy, the book-keeper. Mrs Goldsworthy was in close contact with the spirit world, and kept a crystal ball and tarot cards in a drawer beside the petty cash.

In Bourne Street, at least outwardly, things went smoothly enough. Princess Margaret paid it a visit, and everyone was rather shocked that she walked around smoking a cigarette through a long holder – though there were usually at least two or three overflowing ashtrays downstairs in Elizabeth's office. The *gros sel* was joined by herbs, grainy French mustard and green peppercorns – though this only provoked more questions from the customers on how to use them. Since this was not a question that could be answered in one go, in 1967 Elizabeth wrote what was to be the first of a series of little booklets – *Dried Herbs, Aromatics and Condiments*. This was followed in 1968 by *English Potted Meats and Fish Pastes*, and in 1969 she brought out *Syllabubs and Fruit Fools* and *The Baking of an English Loaf*. The little books were not only for immediate sale: they were stepping stones towards a future series of books. Since she had so little time for cooking and writing, she saw the booklets as a way of getting the ideas and main headings together one by one.

Apart from these little books and the odd article, Elizabeth was working too hard in the shop to write; but the resonance of her name, and the impact of her work had never been stronger. Her books to date had made food as much a subject for discussion as the latest novel, foreign travel or French cinema, and there were more cookery books on the market than ever before. She had proved that people liked their cookbooks well-seasoned with history and travel writing, and that they were not afraid of sound scholarship either. Three writers emerged at this time whose work was influenced by Elizabeth and who benefited from the fact that she had blazed the trail.

In 1966 Elizabeth had been sent the typescript of a book called

Charcuterie and French Pork Cookery, by Jane Grigson. She was impressed. Here was someone who researched her work with as much thoroughness as she would have done herself, while at the same time writing with an enthusiasm that brought the subject to life with a wealth of historical detail and anecdotes. A year later, the *Observer* contacted Elizabeth and asked her to write a food column. Being too busy with the shop, Elizabeth declined – but suggested they ask Jane Grigson, who wrote for the *Observer* from then on until her death in 1990.

Jane Grigson was profoundly grateful to Elizabeth, and they became close friends. They were very different in character: Jane was much more open and accommodating than Elizabeth, who expected everyone to come up to the standards she set for herself. Yet they shared a boundless curiosity about everything to do with food, corresponded on subjects such as medieval English bread laws and eighteenth-century French ice creams, talked on the telephone every Sunday, and often had lunch or dinner together when Jane came up to London. Jane once said that she had only met two people in the world with perfect taste – her husband, the poet and critic Geoffrey Grigson, and Elizabeth David.

Another writer to emerge was Claudia Roden, who came from a close-knit Jewish family in Cairo. In 1956 her family, like many others, was banished from Nasser's new Egypt. As they spread all over Europe and the Americas the traditional food they had eaten in Egypt, which had always been important, began to take on a far greater significance. People preserved their cultural identity by giving feasts to entertain visiting cousins, by talking about what they had lost, by recalling the food from the past and preserving the stories and recipes that went with it. There is a parallel in the way that Claudia Roden and Elizabeth were impelled to write about food: both wrote from a place of exile, in an attempt to re-create the tastes they had known. Roden also acknowledges her debt to one specific sentence in Elizabeth's *Mediterranean Food*, which describes her few Middle Eastern recipes as 'the tip of the iceberg' and urges someone to explore further. 'Why not me?' thought Roden; and the stories and recipes she had been collecting for many years took form as *A Book of Middle Eastern Food*.

Elizabeth was not as impressed by Roden's work as she had been by Grigson's. She felt that, like her own first book, the recipes were inconsistent, and the whole not sufficiently scholarly. She was much happier to encourage Alan Davidson, a career diplomat who had produced what he called a 'primitive booklet' called *Seafish of Tunisia*. He had been attached to the British Embassy in Tunis at the time, and his booklet had been cyclostyled in the office of the information officer, Roger Eland – who had known Elizabeth in Cairo. Eland sent a copy of the booklet to Elizabeth, who was very appreciative. She had long been puzzling over the difficulties of correctly identifying Mediterranean fish, each of which might be known by a handful of different names in different countries; and in April 1963, in the pages of the *Spectator*, she had saluted Davidson's little book for tackling the problem head on. This had created a considerable demand: on 10 June 1963 she wrote to inform him, 'A lot of maddened *Spectator* readers and friends are still shrieking for your book.'

Elizabeth felt he could find a publisher; but Davidson was still a diplomat, and it was not until 1969 that he approached Elizabeth again. If he had his book – now much enlarged and called *Seafish of Tunisia and the Central Mediterranean* – privately reprinted, would she be willing to sell it in the shop? Elizabeth wrote back at once, with a decisiveness that Davidson found very encouraging. On no account was he to contemplate a reprint. His work must be presented as a proper book. He should immediately approach Jill Norman at Penguin and mention her name. Davidson followed her orders: the consequence was that Penguin did publish his *Mediterranean Seafood*, and it has been in print ever since. Soon after, he gave up diplomacy to become a full-time writer and editor.

Elizabeth never failed to notice food writers whose work she found good, and she was generous in her praise – even of one, like Jane

Grigson, who might have been seen as a direct competitor. Unfortunately, she was less quick to see how her attitude in the shop was beginning to arouse resentment. Minor differences between the partners were turning into fault-lines and getting deeper. Elizabeth, who was on a retainer of £1,000 a year as 'consultant' for the firm, felt that she should be paid more for her work on the catalogues. The other directors, already irritated by her high-handedness, pointed out that they too were working long hours with little to show for it, but this was something that Elizabeth seemed unwilling to acknowledge. In 1969 she nearly walked out of the shop because she felt Pam Pugh hated her. This was an exaggeration: what Pam objected to was the way that Elizabeth, thwarted of any rise in salary, tried to make up for it with perks and privileges that Pam did not think were valid. She also disliked Elizabeth's cavalier attitude to bills: some were incomplete, some badly calculated, and she had a tendency to give away small items of stock (admittedly these were usually slightly imperfect 'seconds') to people she liked. In the end it was Pamela who resigned.

Elizabeth and Renée made several buying trips to France during these years. Renée would plan the journey and do all the driving, while Elizabeth saved her energies for the suppliers and the warehouses. It was probably on one of these trips with Renée that Elizabeth had her last meeting with her ex-husband, Tony David. He had left Tangier after the zone lost its international status in the late 1950s, and moved to Ibiza. Here he ran a guest house with his French girlfriend Lélie, and when Tony's divorce came through in 1960 they married and moved to France. Eventually they settled in St-Juan-les-Pins where – quite fortuitously – they had a shop selling kitchen equipment. Quite what Elizabeth and Tony made of each other on the occasion of their meeting is not known, but Elizabeth was glad that she had made her peace with him because Tony died in 1967, at the age of fifty-six. One of Elizabeth's friends remembered the tears coming into her eyes, as she said that Tony David was dead. She mourned the only man who had ever loved her unconditionally, and whom she had been incapable of loving back.

Elizabeth needed Renée very much at this time, for she was becoming increasingly disenchanted with her other partners. Everyone who knew Renée Fedden agrees that she was very supportive when her friends were in trouble, and no doubt she listened to Elizabeth with a great deal of sympathy – particularly about Pamela, with whom Renée had her own differences.

Yet the shop was not Renée's only concern. Robin had left her for another woman, and Renée had found solace with an old friend – the painter Rosemary Peto, with whom she was to spend the rest of her life. Rosie Peto told Elizabeth that she had never loved anyone as much as she loved Renée, who inspired her paintings – although Renée was not very complimentary about them. She often told people that Rosie's paintings were no good, which obviously hurt the artist. When people urged her to be kinder Renée would say 'I can't help it, it's true.' Despite this forthright honesty, Rosie felt intensely protective towards her. For Renée's sake Rosie invested in the shop, although she soon began to resent the way the business seemed to devour all of Renée's time and energy. Rosie wrote impulsive letters to Elizabeth on the subject, complaining that Renée was being exploited by Elizabeth and the other partners.

It has been suggested that Elizabeth herself was lesbian, and that she and Renée were lovers. It has even been rumoured that Elizabeth felt betrayed when Rosie and Renée began living together, though this is highly unlikely. The loves of Elizabeth's life were all men. As for Renée, Elizabeth wrote that Rosie was 'in love with Renée, and I am not, and never have been – we were friends'.[18]

On one of their buying trips, Elizabeth and Renée visited the medieval town of Conques in south-western France, and stood in silence in front of the golden, jewelled figure of Sainte Foi – Holy Faith – whose hands are ever open and forgiving. Both Elizabeth and Renée were pagan, if not atheist; but they were both going through a period of change and upheaval, and they found themselves strangely moved by this tenth-century figure and its ancient benediction.

* * * * * * * *

CHAPTER EIGHTEEN

Salt and Spice

Elizabeth's failure to notice the storm gathering at the shop came partly from a growing tragedy within her own family. Her favourite sister, Diana, was being inexorably destroyed. For some months, she had been suffering from tinnitus, ringing in the ears. Many people have to endure this condition in varying degrees; but Diana's case was particularly severe, and the fact that nothing – even electric shock therapy – could be done to alleviate the incessant torture had brought on a profound depression.

Her condition cannot have been helped by the fact that still having three teenage children and one under ten to look after, Diana was often tired and run-down. Dr Christopher Grey made a good living, but with seven to support, money had always been tight. When Diana came into a little inheritance she bought a small cottage in Hampshire, where they spent their holidays; but there was no let-up in the work Diana had to do, to keep her household washed and fed.

Elizabeth and her brother-in-law Christopher agreed that a rest and a change of scene would do Diana a great deal of good; so Elizabeth decided to take Diana and her husband on holiday to Venice, a place that Diana had always wanted to visit. It was the first foreign holiday the couple had had without their children. The tickets were arranged through Christopher's brother Douglas (once Tony David's partner in the ill-fated club in Herbert Crescent), who was then deputy traffic and sales director of BEA. Douglas did a lot to smooth their way. They were met at the airport, and taken by water-taxi to the Hotel Monaco, a few steps from St Mark's Square and next door to the best restaurant in Venice, Harry's Bar.

It was early May 1969, and Venice was every bit as magical as Diana had hoped it would be. Elizabeth took them to see the Byzantine cathedral on the island of Torcello, and they had lunch a short walk away at Cipriani's Locanda. They had ordered and settled down to the jug of wine when Elizabeth noticed an elegant couple near by, in raptures over their risotto. 'They in turn noticed my curiosity. With beautiful Italian manners they passed some across to me, explaining that it was a risotto unique to Venice and unique to this particular season. It was made with a green vegetable called *bruscandoli* . . .'[1] Elizabeth thought it so good that she called the waiter and changed her order. The manager told her that *bruscandoli* was a sort of wild asparagus, which can only be found in the flat marshy country of the Veneto during the first ten days of May.

They ate it the following day on the island of Burano, and returned to Torcello again to eat it once more; it was the last of the season. Elizabeth was told that if she hurried, she might still find some in the Rialto market. She was up at dawn the following day, and found one old lady with a few bunches for sale. She took the *bruscandoli* back to the hotel and put it in a glass of water, planning to draw it later; but when she returned to her room, the over-zealous chamber-maid had thrown it away – and the following day at the Rialto, the old lady was no longer there. This was just the sort of mysterious encounter with something delicious that Elizabeth relished, and back in England she was even more intrigued when she could find no reference to *bruscandoli* in all her books. It took her months to unearth a reference, which described them as wild hop-shoots.

Diana had been enchanted with the vegetable market, and especially the astonishing variety of salad greens that could be bought there. She came back to England with a passion for rocket, several limp samples and packets of seeds, and planted her garden in Hampshire with every variety of salad she could find. Yet while Diana and Christopher had returned feeling a great deal better for their holiday, the effects were only temporary. The tinnitus, which had never completely gone away, came back with a vengeance.

Elizabeth returned to the bustle of the shop; but she had felt for some time that she ought to be writing another book, and a lunch with Jill Norman sparked off a new trail of ideas. They were in an Indian restaurant, somewhere near the Post Office Tower; perhaps chosen because Elizabeth had recently been reading around the subject of Anglo–Indian food.

She had no particular interest in learning more about the food she herself had eaten in India: that was a part of her life she had no wish to relive. But she was very intrigued by the use of spices, and one of her favourite cookery writers was Colonel Kenney-Herbert, who in the great days of the Raj had thundered against the filth of Indian kitchens and the memsahib's reliance on tins and bottled sauces. At the same time she was contemplating, without much enthusiasm, the prospect of writing a book about Christmas food. The family festival of Christmas held no particular attraction for Elizabeth. As a child she must have suffered from the fact that her birthday on Boxing Day was invariably an anticlimax, and resented those relatives who gave her one present for both occasions. (It must have been just as bad for Priscilla, who was born on 27 December.) Yet the food associated with Christmas did hark back to an earlier tradition of cooking in Britain, when spices were used far more liberally than they are now.

As Elizabeth and Jill talked and talked over lunch that afternoon, they became fascinated by the English taste for hot spicy food. The conversation grew into a discussion of English food in general, and Elizabeth talked of other books that could be developed from the little booklets she had written: on spices and condiments, the baking of an English loaf, potted meats and syllabubs. Jill felt that they should become a series, which Elizabeth decided to call 'English Cooking Ancient and Modern'.

The following year, 1970, Elizabeth published the first book she had written for a decade. It was called *Spices, Salt and Aromatics in the English Kitchen*, and it heralded a new departure in her work. One glance at it shows that it is not a recipe book. Elizabeth had had enough of that particularly laborious and painstaking process, and most of the recipes she includes in this book are either her own tried and trusted ones, or quoted straight out of old cookery books, some dating back to the seventeenth century.

The point of this remarkably elegant book is not just how to use salt (to which she devotes five pages) and spices. It also explores the particularly English attitude to them. Contrary to many claims that the English like their food plain, the history of the subject tends to prove the opposite. The English went to great lengths and prodigious expense to acquire spices. They used them in their food not just as status symbols, nor to disguise the taste of bad meat – but because they liked the taste of spicy food. This taste was rediscovered by the soldiers and civil servants of British India who came back with their kedgerees and curries and was subsequently developed and refined by the Indian immigrations of the 1960s. She also points out that the English fondness for spices is enhanced by their appeal to our sense of romance and our longing for the exotic, so powerfully evoked by writers like Mrs Leyel.

This theme weaves through a book that is as full of stories and quotations as Elizabeth's previous works, but there is also a new note of rather intimate, relaxed reflection – perhaps the result of there being more text and fewer recipes. She recalls making pickles and Christmas pudding in Greece, and the curries and Edwardian nursery food of New Delhi. The book does, however, still bear traces of the Christmas book that was still in the back of her mind: in it are recipes for spiced beef, plum pudding and mincemeat.

There were one or two enthusiastic reviews, but because *Spices, Salt and Aromatics* was not what people had come to expect from Elizabeth David it was not given the rapturous welcome accorded to her earlier books. In the public mind, Elizabeth was firmly associated with France, Italy and the Mediterranean. The switch to

English food was seen as rather abrupt; but in the shape of Elizabeth's life and work it was a development that had been coming for some time.

Arabella Boxer, a writer who has been particularly interested in the subject of English food, began writing when Elizabeth was at the height of her fame. She has always acknowledged Elizabeth's achievement; but in the introduction to her book on English food, published in 1991, she expresses reservations about the nature of her influence. By introducing cheerless post-war England to the delights of olive oil, parmesan and garlic, Elizabeth diverted our attention from the 'brief flowering' of English food that had taken place between the wars.

In the 1920s and 30s, the pomposity and heaviness of Edwardian repasts had given way to informal meals, of three courses rather than eight. Egg and vegetable dishes were given greater prominence, simple grills and roasts were followed by fruit fools, summer puddings or Bakewell tarts, while cold meats and salads became more interesting. This type of cooking had absorbed a lot of French and American ideas; but it was still based on traditional, home-produced ingredients. It had begun in the sophisticated houses of London and the home counties, and might have spread its beneficial influence throughout society had it not been cut short by the Second World War.

When the war and its aftermath of austerity was over, Arabella Boxer feels that we should have picked up this promising thread where it left off; but thanks to Elizabeth David, whose vision of the Mediterranean was so intoxicating, we threw ourselves happily into coq au vin and daubes, vitello tonnato and ossi bucchi. 'All this is intrinsically good,' argues Boxer, '. . . but it does seem slightly ridiculous that pesto should have become a national dish.'[2] She goes on to say that 'Our two greatest food writers, Elizabeth David and Jane Grigson . . . both wrote one or two books about English food in the end, but it came low on their list of priorities.'[3] Elizabeth is unquestionably responsible for inspiring the English to cook Mediterranean, French and Italian food with unaccustomed gusto. But to say that English food was low on her list of priorities is not entirely fair.

Right from the start, her recipes were geared to what could be done by English people in their own kitchens. Throughout her journalism, even at times when French and Italian food was uppermost in her mind and those of her editors, she was informing people about what locally grown food was in season. In this context, she rarely lost an opportunity to give her readers some simple, perfectly English ways of making chutneys and jams, and what to do with spring lamb, or a glut of apples, or herrings and mackerel. At the same time, she was pouring scorn on the 'worked-over, worried, teased-up food' purveyed by English magazines, while the English catering trade received the regular tongue-lashings it deserved. Time and time again she remarked that English cookery, like our language, is one that is remarkably open to new influences – we have been using currants and spices, rice and potatoes for so long they hardly seem foreign at all. Her point, in presenting authentic French or Italian recipes to the public, was not that our cooking should become French or Italian: it is that we should learn from their techniques and absorb their ideas, and use them to develop and enliven our own home cooking.

Elizabeth could perhaps be accused of not acknowledging the renaissance in English food that took place between the wars – although she had been inspired by Hilda Leyel, Countess Morphy and, of course, Boulestin.

From the 1960s on, she wrote more and more about English cookery, and several *Spectator* pieces were devoted to those who had written best about English food: William Verral, Eliza Acton, Mrs Beeton, Dorothy Hartley and Lady Llanover. Several more pieces were devoted to specifically English food: pears and quinces, spiced beef, Cumberland sauce. Had she written the series of books to be called 'English Cooking Ancient and Modern', they would have more than balanced – in numbers and weight – those she had written in the first half of her career. And yet, inevitably, they would have sounded different. Elizabeth never found a lyrical voice to describe England, or even Wales, in the way that she had described France and Italy: perhaps, as an Englishwoman, she was too close. When there is a glimmer of it, she seems to be evoking an England that is so far away that it no longer seems real.

Yet it was not the state of English cookery that was preoccupying Elizabeth, nor even the shop; it was her sister Diana. By the beginning of 1971, Diana's suffering had become terrible. The incessant ringing in her ears was making her life unbearable, and affected her balance: Rosalind Jenkinson remembered that when Diana came to the shop, she had to be helped down the narrow stairs. She was profoundly depressed, and now openly talking of suicide. Her eldest son Rupert, who was then in his mid-twenties, was spending a year in Nepal; he was called home and for a while she seemed more cheerful. But although Diana was comforted by the presence of her children, the peace and quiet she so desperately needed was not enhanced by having five young people and their friends around the house.

Dr Christopher Grey's anguish and anxiety about his wife's suffering was made worse for him by the fact that he, a doctor, could do so little to help; yet he was by temperament an optimist, and hoped that the crisis she was undergoing would ease in its own time. Elizabeth was more pessimistic, feeling that there was only one way out of Diana's agony. She began to neglect the shop, spending more and more time with her sister. She tried to persuade her to eat, but Diana could manage no more than chicken broth and Dr Grey was too distraught to want anything else either. When Elizabeth was not with her, Diana telephoned her perpetually. Elizabeth had become her lifeline.

On one occasion, Diana rang Elizabeth and said she had to get out of the house. She and Christopher came round to Halsey Street, and together they all went to a local restaurant. Elizabeth and

Christopher talked about their forthcoming trip to Venice: Diana had so loved it the first time that they hoped the city would work its magic on her again. Flights and hotels had already been booked. But at dinner that night Diana kept saying 'I'll never make it Liza, I'll never see Venice again.'[4]

A few days later she went down to her cottage at South Harting in Sussex, for quiet was what she needed above all. Elizabeth spent hours on the telephone, while Diana, half-crazed by the terrible noises in her head, talked and talked of suicide. She asked Elizabeth if she thought it was wrong; Elizabeth assured her that it was not wrong, just very sad. Diana was more concerned for Christopher and his old age than for her children, who were almost grown up and had their lives ahead of them. She made Elizabeth promise to look after Christopher, and would not take no for an answer when Elizabeth tried to remonstrate. Elizabeth promised, and Diana thanked her. It was the last time they spoke.

The next day, 31 March 1971, Christopher called to see Elizabeth at the shop. He told her that Diana was in a pretty bad way and he was taking no chances: he had removed all dangerous pills, and was commuting from his London practice to Hampshire every day. But Diana had made up her mind, and had already arranged how to end her life. Christopher telephoned Elizabeth again that evening, soon after she had got home from the shop. Diana had been found dead in her bedroom, a suicide note beside her. She was buried at South Harting.

Christopher was heartbroken at his wife's death, and exhausted by the emotional strain that had preceded it. Fortunately he had his children to think of, his demanding work to get on with and sympathetic friends. Within a few years he was married again, and he and his children began to spend their Christmases in the Isle of Wight, where his new wife had a house.

For Elizabeth, Diana's death was harder to come to terms with. Although their lives were so different, for many years there was a sort of complicity between Elizabeth and Diana, an understanding which Priscilla and Felicité did not share. Elizabeth also felt protective and indulgent towards Diana, whose scattiness seemed more of a lovable characteristic than a fault. The main recipe in her little booklet called *The Baking of an English Loaf* begins with the useful reminder, 'Take off your rings and leave them in a safe place.' The recipe had been written for Diana, 'whose tendency to mislay her engagement ring while cooking has caused many a household drama'. With Diana's death, Elizabeth had also lost a focus of family life, particularly when the Greys began spending their Christmases on the Isle of Wight. When friends invited her out for lunch on Boxing Day, her birthday, they noticed that she would not be drawn on what she had done the day before.

Elizabeth had stayed at Wootton for Easter after the funeral, and on 18 April she and Renée left on their regular spring buying trip to France. 'I hope Renée's old Fiat proved reliable,' wrote Peter Higgins in a brief note on her return; but it was Renée herself who, with Elizabeth in such a fragile state, proved the most reliable and sympathetic friend she could have wished for. The thank-you letter she wrote when they came back, on 3 May, is a good indication not only of Elizabeth's state of mind, but of how much she leant on Renée and appreciated her.

My darling Renée,

You will never know how much you have helped me. As you know, I didn't believe that I could manage the trip at all, and certainly with anyone but you there could have been no question of my going away. As things turned out I think you were right, and anyway the job had to be done. You have done all the work, all the planning and coping, and at the same time you have comforted me and kept me going, and provided many moments when grief was forgotten and we could both give our minds to the work we were supposed to be doing – and like every one of our journeys together this one produced what will prove to be happy memories of waterfalls and lakes and flowers and trees, nice hotels, delicious wine, even sometimes a good meal.

You must be very tired. As I well know from my sessions with poor Diana during the last weeks of her life, sustaining somebody who is in misery is totally exhausting. Your patience and understanding are not gifts for which one can exactly say thank you I suppose – I can say thank you, my love, for using them so wonderfully. Dearest Renée, I do love you very much.

Elizabeth

Elizabeth and Renée had known each other for nearly forty years, and seen each other through periods of misery and desolation. At that moment, Elizabeth must have felt as close to Renée as they had ever been. But from then on, events in the shop were to drive them not only apart, but beyond the point of forgiveness.

Another source of comfort was Ellen-Ann Ragsdale, who had joined the staff of the shop in 1971. Warm and emotional, Ellen-Ann had none of the reserve that so characterized Elizabeth and Renée; but Elizabeth took to her instantly ('I think she was amused by the fact that I had never heard of her').[5] Yet what had really brought them together was that Ellen-Ann, like Elizabeth, had recently suffered the loss of someone very close. Soon she and Elizabeth were having lunch together – 'our requiem lunches, I used to call them. Elizabeth needed someone to mourn with, to get weepie with – and I had nothing else to do. Our friendship was based on shared regret and loss, encouraged by wine and long lunches.'[6]

That summer, Elizabeth's niece Sabrina (Priscilla's elder daughter) married an officer in the Life Guards called Charles Harcourt-Smith; and many of the wedding presents, both from Elizabeth and other friends and relations, came from the shop. For Priscilla, the wedding was a moment of joy after Diana's death and at an extremely difficult and anxious time as the inheritor-in-waiting of her Uncle Roland

Gwynne's estate. In the troubled years that followed, Wootton and its future were much on Elizabeth's mind.

The estate was nothing like what it had been in her father's day. Roland Gwynne had lived in considerable style, way beyond his income. For many years before the war, when he was Mayor of Eastbourne, he had been blackmailed by his sinister butler, who knew the secret of his homosexuality. His fortunes might have recovered, had he married the very rich lady who loved him; but she grew tired of being kept at arm's length, and left him to his own devices.

The bulk of the land had been let, sold or mortgaged to finance the luxury in which he liked to receive his friends; and over the years the houses at Wootton and Folkington became seriously dilapidated. One of his nieces described walking 'down passages and through unused rooms where the walls were covered in damp and mildew and the fittings were mouldering away'.[7] The years of good living eventually caught up with Roland. He was taken off to a nursing home in Eastbourne from which he never returned, and gave his power of attorney to his lawyer.

In the late 1960s, the lawyer died suddenly leaving Priscilla – as Roland's heir – in an impossible situation. For months there was no one to administer the estate and all money was frozen, so Priscilla could not carry out the repairs that Wootton so desperately needed. The only way to raise the necessary cash was to sell Folkington Manor. 'It just didn't seem possible,' wrote the same niece. 'To us in our youth Folkington had always stood for solid strength and security.'[8]

Priscilla had moved into Wootton to look after the estate some time before Roland's death in November 1971. Soon after, Stella was moved into Wootton as well. She was miserable at losing her garden and her independence, but Priscilla insisted because she was getting so old and frail. With both Stella and Priscilla now firmly in control of Wootton, it seemed as if the long line of male heirs set down by James Gwynne had finally been sidelined.

Priscilla, who felt that Wootton was hers by right of primogeniture, certainly thought so. Elizabeth supported her firmly: 'Pris has worked so hard to restore the wreckage left by Roland,' she wrote.[9] Elizabeth had not taken any part in the revitalizing of Wootton, but she admired the energy and determination with which Priscilla set about it. Indeed Priscilla had made a real commitment to Wootton, and had sunk all her own capital into it. But if Priscilla were going to leave the house to her eldest daughter Sabrina, she would have to dissolve the complex entail set up by James Gwynne in his will. Elizabeth was thought to be the only heir intervening between Priscilla and Sabrina, and she happily signed away her right to inherit a house for which she had little attachment, in return for a lump sum from the estate.

Diana too was sent a legal document to sign, for reasons that were not entirely clear. So Christopher suggested that it might be wise to ask his brother Martin, a lawyer, to go over the papers. The result was that Martin Grey discovered that Diana's claim was every bit as strong as Elizabeth's because, in inheritance law, a person's existence is calculated from the moment of conception rather than birth. If Diana spent the normal nine months in the womb, she would have been legally 'alive' at the time of her grandfather's death – and of the four sisters, she had produced the only sons. As Martin Grey confirmed, that not only gave Diana's eldest son Rupert a strong claim to the estate but, even more inconveniently, all of Diana's sons had a potential claim if Rupert died before they did.

This revelation was completely unexpected, and plunged Diana into a difficult dilemma. She was not a grasping woman, and hated the idea of sparking off another family feud. On the other hand, she did not see why Rupert's claim should not be recognized, in the same way that Elizabeth's had. What she did insist on was that if Rupert's claim was admitted by the Wootton estate, it was to be considered a one-off settlement and he would divide the money equally between all his siblings. Diana made this clear to Rupert before she died.

However, it must also be remembered that as this problem was developing, Diana had been reduced to a very fragile emotional state by tinnitus. The idea of a family confrontation was more than she could bear, and to Elizabeth and Priscilla she stressed that she wanted no part of Wootton for herself. Elizabeth records that at the time the whole thing blew up, Diana wrote to Priscilla 'renouncing totally and unequivocally any interest in the inheritance. Of course she hadn't any right to do so, any more than I have until I receive permission from the Courts – but she didn't know that – neither did I.'[10] Yet her attitude was nowhere near so clear-cut. She never expressly forbade Rupert to proceed with the claim, and her son Johnny remembers his mother telling him that Rupert, acting for his siblings, should be compensated.

After Diana's death in 1971 Rupert pressed his claim, encouraged by his uncle and his father. The matter was settled by the Wootton estate, and the money divided equally between all the Grey children.

Elizabeth was so angry that she did not speak to Rupert for ten years. She continually maintained that Diana had never recognized Rupert's claim to Wootton, and refused to listen when Johnny and Christopher both tried to explain that Diana's feelings had been much more equivocal than Elizabeth was prepared to admit. Rupert was particularly hurt by her attitude, since his claim to Wootton had been settled in the same way as her own.

Elizabeth's attention had returned to the shop after Diana's death; but tensions between the partners and the staff had not eased, and after six years in business the shop was still failing to make a significant return.

In 1970, a man called John Smith had been brought in as general manager of Elizabeth David Ltd, in an attempt to make the shop more streamlined and, it was hoped, profitable. He knew nothing about cookery but he did know about retailing, and he stormed into the intimate atmosphere of Bourne Street like a bull in a china shop. He had a broad grin and flirted with the girls; the first thing he did

17. Elizabeth and George Lassalle on the steps of Halsey Street,
early 1950s

18. Lesley O'Malley in the basement flat at Halsey Street, early 1950s

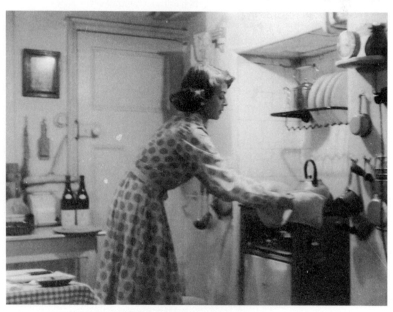

19. Elizabeth, taken by Doreen Thornton, early 1950s.
This was one of her favourite photographs
20. Elizabeth's sister Diana's wedding to Christopher Grey, 1941
21. Elizabeth with her publisher John Lehmann, early 1950s

22. Elizabeth in her kitchen in Halsey Street, mid 1950s
23. Elizabeth, mid 1950s: 'She laughed with an abrupt and vulgar cackle
which contrasted with her speaking voice and her bloodstock kind of beauty.'
Christopher Kininmonth, *Frontiers* (1971)
24. Elizabeth, 1956 or 1957. She noted on the reverse:
'Had forgotten I once had a white streak in my hair. Oh dear, that raggedy
finger bandage would never get past today's salmonella vigilantes.'

25. Elizabeth by Anthony Denney, 1964

26. Peter Higgins

27. Elizabeth in the shop, mid 1960s
28. Anthony Denney arranging the stock, mid 1960s
29. Elizabeth David Ltd, 46 Bourne Street, Pimlico

30. Elizabeth, taken by Renée Fedden on one of their last buying
trips to France, c. 1971
31. Elizabeth's sister Felicité, early 1980s

32. Elizabeth in old age, late 1980s

was organize a stocktake. For Elizabeth, the arrival of John Smith was not merely an intrusion, it was an invasion. To her dismay he ordered the removal of some of the most beautiful things in the shop, because they had never sold; while many of the 'hideous' things that had languished for years at Vauxhall were given another chance, dusted off and put back on display.

John Smith's feeling was that since the wholesale end was the most profitable side of the business, this was where efforts should be concentrated. He also felt that the range of stock was too narrow, and should be developed to give it a broader appeal. The more business-minded of the partners agreed that this was the right direction. Elizabeth, however, fought it with every ounce of her determination. Over the next two years there was a series of quarrels, misunderstandings, threats, accusations and blunders; but they all stemmed from this fundamental disagreement in policy.

She felt that in their new emphasis on wholesale trade, the partners were deliberately neglecting the shop. In her eyes, it began to look tacky and rundown. It is hard to imagine just how passionately Elizabeth identified herself with her shop. It had been created with her taste and expertise, represented years of work and was the tangible expression of her own vision. The signs of neglect that Elizabeth saw everywhere were all the more distressing because they represented a refusal to acknowledge what she had brought to the business: not just the shop itself, but the publicity her name had generated and the loyalty her name inspired.

Renée too was finding life in the shop increasingly distressing, and in March 1972 she resigned as a working director – even though she was still a shareholder in the business, and continued to sit on the board. Elizabeth was very sorry to see her go, and sent her a little present 'with my love, and to say goodbye because what else can I say? Except that perhaps one day Sainte Foi will be good, and restore something of what has been destroyed.'[11]

A brief respite from the storm that was gathering over the shop took place in May, when Elizabeth took a trip to Denmark. The

British Food Export Council were taking part in a British trade drive (which included everything from heavy industry to food). Among the many attractions were a double-decker bus, policemen from Liverpool, a nursery garden expert, and Elizabeth David, 'culinary expert and writer, who is well-known throughout Denmark'. The Danes gave her a very enthusiastic reception and, considering how naturally wary of publicity Elizabeth was, she was very amenable. The press took photographs of the '*engelsk gastronomik skribent*' with eminent Danes and wrote respectful articles, while Elizabeth did a number of signing sessions and interviews. She also spent time each day at the English stand of the food exhibition.

The crisis in the shop reached its climax in the first week of July 1972. There was a meeting of the partners, after which Elizabeth stormed out in tears. 'I am still in a state of shock,' Elizabeth wrote to Renée on 5 July, 'over the events which took place at Bourne Street immediately succeeding our last company meeting, and at the part which you played in those events. I think that you allowed yourself to be used to create a situation which could only result in my instant departure from the shop.'

Elizabeth chose to see a situation in which Renée had 'allowed herself to be used' by the other partners; but it is far more likely that Renée was trying to tell Elizabeth, in the quietest and most tactful way, that she was going align herself with their more businesslike methods.

In fact, Elizabeth had already reached the conclusion that things had become so tense and uncomfortable that she would have to leave sooner or later. She had told April Boyes, saying that her partners were becoming increasingly difficult and that anyway it was time she got back to her writing. She then asked April whether she would come and work for her at Halsey Street, to make a proper catalogue of her collection of cookery books. 'But what about the shop?' asked April. 'Oh, they'll get on well enough without me,' she said – a casual line which scarcely reflected her sense of betrayal.[12]

All these anxieties and upheavals were compounded by Elizabeth's increasing bad health. The chronic fatigue that was a natural sequel to Diana's death did not lift. The trip to Denmark had tired her more than she cared to admit, and her legs – which had never been good – were swollen and often ulcerous. One specialist she consulted asked, 'Why do you look so much older than you are?' She knew exactly who to blame, in her letter to Renée after the partners' meeting. 'The company could certainly answer that one – it is not only personal grief which has got me into the state in which I now find myself.'[13]

Over the next few weeks Elizabeth sat and lay around the house 'like a zombie'[14] and hardly knew what to do with herself. She could scarcely imagine an existence without the shop. She saw some people from the London Museum, who were looking for objects to show in an exhibition about London in the 1930s. Elizabeth had had the idea of starting a museum of kitchen artefacts herself, and sometimes thought about it in a desultory way. When she and Renée met for lunch, her mood was profoundly bleak. Later on that summer Renée sent her a postcard from Conques of Sainte Foi, with the message 'I came to ask if she could help us – love Renée.'[15] But Sainte Foi was invoked more from sentiment than from faith in a cure for their growing separation.

April Boyes came round to the house five mornings a week, and began work on the catalogue. The bookshelves in the sitting room had long ago been filled, both vertically and horizontally. Piles and drifts of books and magazines had gradually occupied the chairs and sofas, while stalagmites of books were steadily rising on the floor. Outside in the hall, Sybille Bedford described how one had to make one's way through 'a positive trench made of books – one's shoulders touched them either side, and one had the feeling they might fall in on one at any moment'. More books were set in piles on the stairs, and in the kitchen there was a further small library. April kept asking for instructions: she did have some experience of cataloguing, but Elizabeth had been so dogmatic about how things were done in the shop that she did not want to get off on the wrong foot. Elizabeth, however, was only sporadically interested. Much of April's time was spent driving her about, to see exhibitions and go shopping, and keeping her company over long lunches.

The death of Diana and the increasing tensions at the shop had left Elizabeth with some very raw wounds. In December 1972 she had found solace at La Alfarella, where Celia Denney had just received the news that her beloved grandmother had died. 'Elizabeth and I wept companionably, a glass of local plonk to hand, a cat on each lap.'[16]

In February 1973, April drove Elizabeth and her mother to Heathrow. Stella was going on what was to be her last visit to Jamaica, and a wheelchair had been ordered to meet her at the airport. Once Stella was safely enthroned in the wheelchair, April was surprised to see how Elizabeth fussed and fretted around her mother. Stella, however, was very much enjoying all the attention and remarked, 'My dear, do you know what I feel like? I feel like the Queen of Sheba!'[17] This broke the ice for a moment and they laughed; but Elizabeth was still very much on edge.

Once they had seen Stella safely on to the plane and had got back to the car, Elizabeth dissolved into tears. 'How could I have let her go on her own? I should be going with her! How on earth is she going to manage the other end?'[18] Her mother's frailty had touched a nerve of remorse and regret that was not usually so exposed in Elizabeth.

Stella came back safely from Jamaica; but her strength was failing, and she died at Wootton on 8 June 1973. Elizabeth, who had still not got over Diana's death, was in mourning once again. The funeral took place on 13 June, and coincided with an extraordinary general meeting of the partners. Elizabeth always laid great emphasis on the date, as an example of how callous her partners were to expect her attendance.

A week or so after the funeral, Elizabeth and Doreen Thornton drove through France and Spain, and were with the Denneys at La Alfarella a week later. The main excitement was a trip that took in

SALT AND SPICE

Albacete and Teruel, staying overnight at the Venta de Contreras. Elizabeth, determined to put the shop out of her mind, enjoyed it all – and was particularly touched by the hospitality they received at the Venta de Contreras. They dined on *gazpacho manchego*, and the following morning, they were sent on their way with little posies of mint and carnation.

At the same time, she was still absorbing the loss of her mother. At one point she confided to Celia Denney that she had recently given Stella a little hand-wound musical box, which had got mislaid; and that in the last days of her life, her mother became almost obsessed in her determination to find it again. It was only a small detail, but to Elizabeth it seemed to have significance. Once home, she had to go to Wootton to help Priscilla and Felicité sort out Stella's things. 'It will be painful, and going to Wootton is always a terrible penance to me. I fear the inevitable squabbles.'[19]

The meeting of 13 June, which took place while Elizabeth was at her mother's funeral, formally agreed to pursue the shift the business had already made: towards wholesaleing and mail order, away from the shop. They also agreed to expand the range of their stock. On that last point, Elizabeth had been willing to compromise (in so far as she could, which was not very far). But the deliberate neglect of the shop in the interests of the wholesale and mail-order end was more than she could stand. Elizabeth said that it had declined from being 'a well-stocked, elegant, efficient and profitable unit to a rather tatty corner hardware shop. That situation is intolerable, as it affects my name and reputation, earned and built up over many years.'[20]

Yet what Elizabeth could never get over was that Renée had, on this occasion, openly aligned herself with the rest of the partners. In a way, Renée had no choice. She felt responsible not only for her own stake in the business, but that put in by her friend Rosie Peto. Renée had been persuaded that the only way to make good and build on the efforts of the past seven years was to endorse the tough decision – and she knew, as they all did, that this would probably precipitate Elizabeth's resignation.

Elizabeth did indeed resign: from the board and as a consultant, and she announced her intention of selling her shares as soon as possible and publicly severing all connection with the shop. The worst of it was that when she walked out, she had to leave her name above the door.

Had Elizabeth put herself in Renée's shoes she might have seen where Renée's interests and loyalties lay. But Elizabeth was not always very good at that. Some of her most recent behaviour – in which she had accused Renée of stealing – was so exaggerated that it is possible that her mind was affected, perhaps by some drug she had been prescribed for her legs or her blood pressure. At all events Renée's defection came as a complete shock, and it amounted to high treason. That night she sat at the kitchen table sobbing and shouting, 'How *could* they! How *could* they!' as she slammed her fists down on the table.[21] It was as if a great poisonous wound, opened first by the loss of the Guttusos and the defection of Peter Higgins, had opened up again with a vengeance.

A year or so later, Renée's friend Rosemary Peto tried to force them to make up. In an undated letter to Elizabeth she wrote, 'I can't bear it that you and Renée should be separated . . . it seems so silly – but I believe strongly that [John Smith] was the only practical money-maker of you amateur hopeless lovely idealists . . .' Elizabeth wrote back as she did to everyone who tried to make her see reason about Renée: '. . . friendship betrayed is friendship slaughtered'. Rosie persisted. 'I long to bang your heads violently together and say "You bloody silly bitches, you love each other, you are amused by each other . . . how can you allow the nonsenses of business to stand in the way of your friendship?"' Elizabeth remained adamant. Peter Higgins was forgiven, but Renée would never be.

* * * * * * * *

CHAPTER NINETEEN

Baking Bread

While Elizabeth had no time for the Englishwoman's passion for cakes and biscuits, she had always been drawn to bread. One of the works that had sparked her interest was the little book called *Home Baked* by George and Cecilia Scurfield, which Leonard Russell had coaxed her into reviewing in 1956. The magical effect of yeast on flour and water, the sensual pleasure of kneading a substance as soft and springy as flesh, the smell as it baked ('even bad bread smells good in the oven'), all gave her a profound satisfaction; and a table without fresh bread, and a pat of butter, was not a table at which she would choose to eat. Bread is timeless; and made with the right ingredients, it never let her down – unlike friends, lovers, editors, business partners. As the authors of *Home Baked* had pointed out, 'the great thing about baking with yeast is the difficulty of failure'.

Back in England, she immersed herself in work. *English Bread and Yeast Cookery* is the first book on which she tried to concentrate almost full-time, precisely what she wanted to do – but it was not easy. She could not summon up the energy she had once possessed, and as her research went deeper and deeper into the subject she wondered whether she would ever emerge to complete the book. Yet the hours in libraries, the fascination of what she was learning, the endless experimentations were soured by one constant nagging thought. Her name was still above the shop in Bourne Street, and there seemed to be no way of getting it back.

Some of her friends feel that she went into the whole business with too much enthusiasm, and too little professional advice; and that had she consulted a lawyer at the time, he might have warned her of the dangers inherent in putting one's name to a company. No doubt that is true, but even if Elizabeth had thought of what had happened to John Lehmann, it is unlikely that she or her partners would have considered a different name. The shop had to be called Elizabeth David: that was what gave it its unique selling point, and an edge over the competitors that sprang up in its wake.

Her first move was to put an announcement in *The Times*, which said that 'Mrs Elizabeth David wishes it to be known that she has no personal connection with the shop trading under her name.' And yet, while supposedly trying to rebuild her life as a writer, she could not take her eyes off what was going on in Bourne Street. She continued to press her claim that she was entitled to more pay because of the work she had done on the catalogues. The partners refused, but issued new catalogues largely based on her work. They then started redistributing recipe leaflets of Elizabeth's without asking her permission; on another occasion, she wrote a stiff letter about the exorbitant prices the shop was charging for the postage and packing of her books sold through the catalogue. There was a nasty moment in the summer of 1974 when it looked as if an Australian entrepreneur might start up a line of 'Elizabeth David' cookshops in Australia, and she was advised that neither she nor her erstwhile partners in Elizabeth David Ltd could do anything about it – but this particular threat never materialized. For the next ten years Elizabeth badgered the company at regular intervals to change its name, which the company had once allowed itself to say it might 'reconsider'. Eventually it did, but not to Elizabeth's satisfaction.* In the meantime, she had to content

---

* In 1986, after incorporating with Peter Trier's company Clarbat Ltd, the company did change its name to The Kitchenware Merchants Ltd. Bryan Llewellyn suggested that he might be willing to surrender the name 'Elizabeth David Ltd', which was still being used for one of the subsidiaries, in return for her shares. Elizabeth flatly refused: she wanted her name back as a matter of principle, and

herself with rapping the knuckles of any hapless journalist who made the mistake of mentioning 'Elizabeth David's shop'.

Elizabeth's rage, whether it was in its creative manifestation that made her write or the destructive one that made her bitter, was never contained: it managed to spill out in a modified form into whatever else she was doing, and the anger provoked by her dealings with the shop inevitably spilled into the bread book. A draft of her announcement to the press, in which she severed all connection between herself and Elizabeth David Ltd, was written on the back of a draft of the opening page of the chapter entitled 'The Bread Factories', one of her most trenchant chapters.

In it Elizabeth admits that English bread, and particularly London bread, had been bad for at least two hundred years. She quotes Tobias Smollett, who in *Humphrey Clinker* (1771) wrote that 'the bread in London is a deleterious paste, mixed up with chalk, alum and bone ashes; insipid to the taste and injurious to the constitution'. The people of London were well aware of this adulteration, 'but they prefer it to wholesome bread because it is whiter than the meal of corn'. This ancient tradition of over-processing bread had been taken ever further after the war. In an earlier chapter entitled 'Milling', Elizabeth takes the reader through the series of government orders concerning bread. Since the war these have permitted the great bakery conglomerates to make vast profits on a flour that is so refined that – by law – it has to be 'enriched' with all the nutrients that were taken out of it in the processing. The *coup de grâce* for English bread came with the invention of the so-called Chorleywood process in the 1960s. Instead of leaving the dough to stand for up to two hours to mature, it is agitated violently in high-speed mixers

---

had no intention of paying for it in any way. To Elizabeth's fury, a new shop was opened in Covent Garden in 1986. The Kitchenware Merchants then put out a press release saying that the founding shareholders 'remain in control of the new business: Mr Peter Trier, Mr Arthur Lewis, Mrs Elizabeth David CBE, Miss Pamela Pugh and Mr Bryan Llewellyn'. The Bourne Street shop was closed down in 1989, though the one in Covent Garden is still trading.

for a few minutes, thus making an enormous saving on time and human resources. 'Of any advantage to the bread itself,' remarks Elizabeth bleakly, 'nobody has anything much to say.'[1]

She meant the book to sound as plainly factual as a serious work of history; but her indignation at the all-conquering steamed loaf, her impatience with the government that could not control it and the public who are prepared to accept it, are palpable nonetheless.

Elizabeth went into every detail of bread manufacture: from its earliest beginnings, the ovens it was cooked in, the tools that people used, how the baking of bread – and the brewing of beer, which also depended on yeast – were a focus of people's lives. She knew well enough that the past was not romantic. That while the bread they ate might have been better than it is now, people's lives were hard and the baker's was no easier. While he might be envied for being the only man in the village who could keep warm, his job was more like that of a stoker on a steamship – as hot, as dirty and often as dangerous. At the same time, there was something very comforting about the past. It posed no threat, and made no demands.

Historical research also brought her closer to Felicité, who put her bibliographical experience to use with considerable enthusiasm. She combed the most recondite catalogues for books and references, sought out obscure works from the London Library, and had an instinct for nosing out what Elizabeth would find most useful and interesting. When the bread book was published, she gave Elizabeth a tiny gold pill-box in the shape of a loaf.

Those who had accompanied Elizabeth on her research trips also deserved a present; for once Elizabeth was on the scent of something, she did not let go. Elizabeth Savage, who had worked in the Bourne Street shop, drove Elizabeth around Normandy in 1974. Towards the end of the trip, Elizabeth was bitterly disappointed to find that the bakery to which they had driven from Rouen to inspect was closed. To make matters worse, it was effectively their last day in France. Nothing daunted, Elizabeth found out where the baker lived and persuaded him to show them round his bakery. He showed them everything he could, but the whole visit was very frustrating because none of the ovens was working and no bread was being made. However, they did find another good bakery that was open: 'This is a point for English visitors to look out for,' wrote Elizabeth in the bread book. 'Don't assume, if you . . . find the nearest bakery closed, that all bakers all over France are closed that day.'[2] Elizabeth bought a sample of all the loaves they had, and back at the hotel, they were all laid out on the bed and photographed.

It was the first trip that Liz had taken with Elizabeth, and she found herself rather tense, wanting to please and get everything right. It was a feeling Elizabeth often inspired in people: the feeling that sloppiness of any kind would not be tolerated. But on that trip, Elizabeth was a wonderful companion, full of information and interested in everything – although her curiosity to try out different establishments once meant that, in the square of a large market town, they sat down in a different restaurant for each course of their lunch.

April Boyes was another companion on Elizabeth's research trips, which were never undertaken without a good picnic lunch – fresh bread, pâté, perhaps that vegetable gratin that was such a feature of Provençal picnics, the tian. The Guildhall Library was a particularly convenient spot, because near by was a pond with an overhanging bush. A bottle of white wine was attached with a piece of string (Elizabeth never packed a picnic without including a corkscrew, a stout knife and some string) to the bush and lowered into the water, while they did a morning's work; and by lunchtime it was deliciously cold. They did this on several occasions, and their bottle was never spotted or stolen.

Once installed in a library, April Boyes was astonished at the way Elizabeth could become so utterly absorbed in her work that it became the only imperative. The lengths to which she was prepared to go to get what she wanted were demonstrated when Elizabeth and April took a trip to Leicester in March 1975, where Elizabeth wanted to see the two reconstructed querns (for grinding grain) in a certain museum.

Once inside a city, Elizabeth was such an unreliable map-reader that April had to drive and navigate on that rainy day. Finally they found the museum, and Elizabeth was delighted with the querns – particularly since grain was provided, and visitors were encouraged to try them out. Seeking for more information she asked to see the director, and was told he was not in that day. She and April then did a little tour of the museum, which was deserted. Elizabeth found a door and opened it: inside some students were larking about, but seeing Elizabeth and April they quickly got back to their work. 'Where is the director's office?' asked Elizabeth in a voice of quiet authority. One of the students led the way. The door was not locked, and Elizabeth marched in with April behind her. The student looked a bit uncertain, but was dismissed with an imperious wave from Elizabeth.

Once inside, she started opening drawers and filing cabinets and generally peering around. Then she installed herself at the director's desk, moved his papers out of the way, and settled down to work. April was kept busy bringing her photographs and folders, and the piles of paper mounted on the director's table; but April noticed that one pile was being carefully put aside, consisting largely of photographs and press cuttings. April began to feel that Elizabeth's intentions towards this pile were not strictly honourable, and that she might be planning to 'borrow' them without the director's permission.

Elizabeth could work with such concentration, such total absorption in her notes that she did not notice when April surreptitiously removed the pile. First she simply moved it to another part of the desk; and then, since she was still bringing Elizabeth more documents, she removed it altogether and returned the items to their proper places.

After about an hour or so, Elizabeth decided it was time to leave. It was still raining. She got up from the desk, looked around and gave an involuntary gasp. 'Where is that pile I had here?' – 'What pile?' asked April innocently. 'You know very well what pile. Where is it?' April said everything had been put away; but that since she had made a note of everything in the pile, it would be easy to request the information and have it sent or copied. This made no difference to Elizabeth, who was shaking with fury. 'Do you realize what you have done? You have set my book back by six months.' 'But –' '*Six months.*' Elizabeth did not say a word all the way back to London; and when April let her out at Halsey Street, she got out of the car, let herself into the house and slammed the door without looking round.[3] Elizabeth came round in the end, for April's help is gratefully acknowledged in *English Bread and Yeast Cookery*.

Jill Norman had been deeply involved in the book from the start because, as she explained, 'Elizabeth needed a sounding board.' Her first books had been largely based on information already acquired, and the big Italian and French books had demanded a great deal of travelling and practical kitchen work. This was the first time Elizabeth had ever worked on a book that demanded so much scholarly research. She had never gone into a subject in such depth and detail, and she wanted to make sure that she stayed on course. As time went on and Jill's interest deepened, she gave Jill recipes to try out with the words, 'Have a look at these.' She also showed Jill each chapter in draft as she wrote it.

As the writing progressed, they made several research trips in Jill's car: to look at mills, buy flour and search out small firms who made baking equipment. On one occasion they visited Jordan's flour mill in Bedfordshire, which was then quite a small concern. Elizabeth questioned their guide with extraordinary thoroughness and concentration: as if she was trying to understand the nature of flour itself, how it behaved. She did not take many notes at the time; but once they were back in the car she would talk over what they had seen and found out.

The first of what became several journeys to Wales was to visit Jean Bolland, who had bought a cottage called Ty Isaf near Llandeilo.

It had belonged to the same family for generations, and when Jean bought it, it had no electricity or running water; but it did have a brick bread oven, which had been in continuous use since it was built. Elizabeth had first got to know Jean when she worked in the shop, which she did two days a week, commuting from Kent. She was a hearty, jolly woman, who hid a certain melancholy under her determination to live life to the full. To some she might have sounded brusque, but Elizabeth appreciated her straightforwardness, her company and the fact that she still used her brick oven for baking. Baking with Jean gave Elizabeth great pleasure, and allowed her to try her hand at the techniques she was writing about.

Had Elizabeth travelled only for reasons of work, she might not have spent so much time in Wales. She wrote that in Norfolk, Suffolk and Cambridgeshire, 'traditions of cooking and baking seem to have remained intact long after they had been destroyed in areas subjected to the upheavals of the early nineteenth century'.[4] But at the time she was working on bread, Wales was very much on her mind. It was where her father's family had originally come from, and as she grew older, she began to feel the invisible ties of her unknown ancestors more deeply. She tried to find out more about them, and trace the Welsh side of the family tree: but as Elizabeth herself admitted, 'whether [we are] descended from the Gwynnes of Taliaris or Glanbran, or from one of the numerous families of that name who once flourished in mid-Wales, nobody seems to have established'.[5]

While Elizabeth had always loved the Sussex countryside around Wootton, she had never really felt a part of its life: neither when her mother was mistress of the house, nor when Priscilla took over. Too much had gone on there for Elizabeth ever to make her peace with the place, but Wales was different. She had always been refreshed by its unspoilt beauty, and it held memories of the holidays that she and her sisters had spent there before the war. Even in the 1970s, there were still vestiges of the old way of life. The work she was doing – and baking bread in Jean Bolland's oven – brought her in touch with them.

Quite apart from these satisfactions, it was also the site of one of her favourite restaurants in the British Isles: the Walnut Tree Inn at Llandewi Skirrid. Ann and Franco Taruschio had bought the Walnut Tree in 1963. Over the years they had developed a network of local suppliers, which meant that only the freshest and best of what was in season went into Franco's cooking. What Elizabeth loved, as much as the food, was the Taruschios' hospitality in what is still essentially a pub. Elizabeth sat in the bar, at a corner table in the window, and would ask Franco to prepare something for her that was not on the menu. He always obliged: serving it in tiny portions, and arranging little samples of this or that dish which had taken her fancy or aroused her curiosity. She even enjoyed his salad: 'I ate every scrap of it,' she wrote after one salad at the Walnut Tree, 'and I think perhaps yours is the only restaurant in these islands where I would even order a salad, let alone be able to eat it.'[6]

Such were the pleasures offered by Wales that Elizabeth thought she would like to buy a little house there. The estate agents were given very strict instructions. Anything they wanted to show her must be very quiet, but within walking distance of a few homely shops. The house should also combine the utmost tranquillity, while also being within half an hour of a main-line station with frequent and direct trains to London. But while she dreamed of Wales and always yearned to go back, she would never have abandoned London altogether. She could never have lived so far from a fishmonger such as Burkett's and Mr Ducat at Harrods, let alone her family and friends.

Elizabeth was now in her early sixties. Her thick grey hair, which had been worn short for much of the previous decade, was now in a chignon at the back of her neck. Her style of dress had scarcely changed. When going out she still favoured cream silk shirts and dark jackets, but the shirts were now worn with scarves or bows at the neck, and whenever possible she wore well-tailored trousers in preference to skirts. She had never had good legs; but her hands were beautiful, and her eyes – of a colour once described as 'prunes-in-brandy' – still held their challenging glint.

In 1975, her engagement book shows that she often saw Peter Higgins. Although he had lived in Spain for many years, he still came over to England fairly regularly; and he was in London, off and on, throughout that summer. 'Higgins will be interrupting us,' Elizabeth might say to Jill as they sat working at the kitchen table in Halsey Street. He was always beautifully dressed, having come straight from some meeting in the city. Elizabeth communicated with him very discreetly, leaving messages at White's Club. Peter Higgins's messages were even more discreet: they took the form of postcards, informing Elizabeth of the dates when he would be passing through London.

It was not until the following April that Elizabeth could write 'finished last chapter of bread book'. It was a considerable relief – not only to her but to Jill. To celebrate the event, Elizabeth asked Jill to dinner: this in itself was a rarity, for she seldom entertained in the evenings any more. She cooked a dish of ham in brioche for the occasion. They talked of future books in the 'English Food Ancient and Modern' series; Elizabeth felt that she might tackle meat next.

In June 1976 the proofs of the bread book were ready. Elizabeth rented a large cottage in Portmeirion, where she and Jill went to go over them. They took it in turns to cook, bought wine from the hotel, talked a great deal and read in the evenings. Elizabeth was in an excellent mood, and was more interested in the picnics and expeditions they organized than in the task on hand. *English Bread* was an enormous book; but they had brought all the various drafts of the manuscript to check against the proofs, and Elizabeth could still rely on her extraordinary memory.

In the autumn, George Elliott drove her down to visit the Denneys, who were becoming disenchanted with the countryside around Valencia. It was still beautiful, but tourism was on the increase; and for those who had known it before the rise of 'the Benidorm factor', it was not the same. Anthony and Celia had decided to move out, and had found an old castle in Badajoz that looked promising. It was called Salvatierra, and was going to require a great deal of work. For Elizabeth, however, a period of work was over. She had finished the bread book at last, and she was much gratified that her contribution to Britain's cultural life was publicly recognized with the OBE. She had received the award on 17 February 1976 from the Queen, who asked her what she did. 'Write cookery books, Ma'am,' said Elizabeth. 'How useful,' remarked Her Majesty.[7]

In 1977, Elizabeth increased her efforts to find a house in Wales, but finding the right one was evidently going to take time. Her first trip that spring produced no likely candidates, and she was back in London in early summer. Soon after she wrote a message and a poem to John Lehmann, her first publisher, who was celebrating his seventieth birthday. She says the poem is 'unoriginal and unworthy of you, but you will know it comes from the heart of a most affectionate and loyal friend, one also much in your debt. I could say so much more – but this is a greeting, not a testimonial, so I'll leave it at that.'[8]

The poem was called 'Scrambled Eggs Variation 77'. It is perhaps longer than it should have been, and not all of it is quoted here; but is almost certainly the only recipe Elizabeth was to write in free verse.

You must first find fresh eggs laid by hens running about
In the open air and pecking on corn and other wholesome things
Not reared in a cage and crammed with pellets and fish meal
This is the most difficult part
Then you take two or three of those eggs
And a not very large lump of butter,
About half as large as one of the eggs
And a frying pan or sauté pan, seven or eight inches in diameter
You need also a fork. Salt only comes later, although that is
*   against all the rules*

You put the pan over low heat and melt the butter
You break the eggs straight into the pan
You beat them and fold them with the fork
For just about twenty-five seconds until they are in soft and creamy
    flakes
Now you pour them out into a little dish
I forgot to say that this should be warmed –

                                but not too much –

Or the eggs will go on cooking and they will be spoiled.
Now you sit down and eat them, with the crunchy salt you have
    put ready on the table
And pepper from a mill . . .
With a slice or two of brown bread and some good butter
You now have a feast fit for a poet.

Her next visit to Wales took place in August, where she stayed with Jean Bolland and made bread again. On 7 August her diary records that she made 'two beautiful loaves with white Mill flour'. Two days later she saw three houses, and on the 11th she records that during a picnic on the banks of the Edw they sighted a kingfisher. The next two days were spent at Ty Isaf, and more bread was baked. It seemed an idyllic holiday, even if she had not found a house; and she returned to London in good spirits to pack up the kitchen, before having it rewired and repainted.

Elizabeth had enlisted the help of her nephew Johnny Grey to put up shelves in her refurbished kitchen. He was then twenty-four, had studied architecture and was already planning to specialize in kitchen design. That autumn, he joined her house-hunting efforts in Wales. He had a car, was a willing driver and his architectural training would be put to good use on those houses where the main question was, 'Is it fixable?'

They saw a beautiful vicarage at Abergwesyn, and on the 23 September, visited what looked like a very promising cottage at Newbridge-on-Wye. The following day, with a case of red wine in the back of the car, they were on the road from Portmeirion to Builth Wells, where they had to see another cottage. Johnny was not driving fast, because Aunt Liza didn't like it; but he did notice that the roads were slippery. He urged her to put on a seat belt. There was a snort of derision: like many of her generation, Elizabeth did not believe in seat belts. Prompted by a sort of misplaced gallantry Johnny decided not to wear his either. Shortly afterwards, while taking a corner, Johnny lost control of the car. It swerved across the road and smashed into a telegraph pole. He sustained no more than a broken arm, but Elizabeth had been thrown forward and her mouth had hit the dashboard. In the silence that followed the crash, Johnny saw that she was very badly injured. There was also a sickly, vinegary smell from the bottles of wine that had smashed in the back of the car. It was about ten years before Johnny could bring himself to drink red wine again.

Elizabeth received emergency treatment locally, and on 26 September she was transferred to the Princess Grace Hospital in London. The first thing she did was to send Johnny a case of wine (white this time), and urge him not to feel guilty for what had happened. The police too had said that the accident was not his fault, but Johnny could not help blaming himself.

'I have a fractured right wrist and left elbow,' she wrote to Peter Higgins on 7 October,

> also smashed knee cap, and teeth all over the place. Johnny also has a broken arm, a bill from the PO for damaging their property and terrible misery about the damage to me. Poor boy, it was in no way his fault, just rotten luck. I fell in love with the doctor who set my arm at the local hospital but I was whisked away by ambulance to London to have my knee and elbow operated on and to get Mr Moreton [her dentist] to work on my teeth. Am lolling in great comfort in a hospital a few yards from Devonshire Place so I don't have to get out of bed

to go to Mr M., that's lucky because I can't anyway, just like you when you fell off your horse. Going down to the operating theatre is like a ride through the souk. There's a beautiful Arabian prince next door and two security guards outside. I have a lovely view of the Post Office Tower, at night it's all coloured lights, very pretty. There should be a muezzin calling to prayer on the top.

I expect I shall be here several more weeks, isn't it lucky my book was finished before I had the accident. So annoying, I just had my kitchen rewired, lovely new lights and beautiful clean paint, I was enjoying it, and Wales was lovely too. I'll be quite all right, but it's a slow business. I just long to see you my love. E.

From this letter it is obvious that Elizabeth was completely reconciled with Peter and still, from the way she is trying to sound cheerful and amusing, eager to please him. But although various friends had tried to reunite her with Renée from time to time, here she remained implacable. When Robin Fedden died that year, Elizabeth did write to Renée. But her letter of condolence, however well-meant, sounded hard and cold.

George Lassalle came to see her in hospital. He had just married his fourth wife, the publisher and novelist Caroline de Crespigny, and they were about to move to Cyprus. The weather was very cold, and George appeared wearing an overcoat with a Persian lamb collar. 'So, Vronsky, you've come,' said Elizabeth.[9]

She did not think much of the food she was given. One friend was with her when the nurse came in with her lunch, and on top of the aluminium plate cover was a piece of pitta bread. Handing it to the nurse she said, 'Please take this away and find a patient who needs a poultice. It's not good for much else.' When asked if she needed anything she said, 'Stamps, just stamps, I can never have enough of them.'[10]

*

English Bread and Yeast Cookery came out in November, while Elizabeth was still in hospital. The fact that the reviews all hailed it as a great and important work of scholarship must have done much to raise her morale. 'I doubt if anyone who reads this book,' wrote Hilary Spurling in the *Observer*, 'will ever feel quite comfortable with a supermarket loaf, whether white or wheatmeal.'[11]

Another generous review came from Paul Levy in *Books and Bookmen*. The piece begins with a paeon of praise for her work, and says that her OBE was 'a rather mingy honour for someone who has made a social and cultural revolution. Who else in recent time can be said to have changed the *habits* of so large a section of the population of an entire country? Surely she should be Damed as soon as possible.'[12]

Levy went on to point out that Elizabeth was not a crank. What she detested was the factory loaf, and what she provided was the instruction and the information required by those who were not prepared to tolerate it any longer. Elizabeth wrote Levy a note to thank him, saying he had understood exactly what she was trying to say.

Elizabeth's book was a very important milestone in the campaign for better bread, which so far had been fought on two fronts that were sometimes inimical to each other. On the one hand were the health-food lobbyists, who argued that the only wholesome flour was one made of 100 per cent stoneground wheat. On the other were the people who simply wanted bread that tastes good, as it does in other countries. Elizabeth took a sensible middle course between these two positions. She did understand the health benefits of wholewheat bread, but she did not disapprove of white flour – provided that it had not been refined and bleached of all its goodness and taste. At the same time, she had gone into the subject in such depth that every twist and turn in the story of bread legislation and the rise of the factory-made loaf was made alarmingly clear. In fact, the big concerns were already aware of this change in the air, and were beginning to turn it to their advantage. A whole new range of steamed, sliced brown loaves had appeared, promising health and nutrition, while Tesco opened their first in-store bakery in Newport in 1970. It did not take them long to notice that the smell of 'fresh' bread made their customers feel good, and thus encouraged them to spend more time in the store – and more money.

Elizabeth was still in hospital when Peter came over in December. She had needed a series of operations to mend her arm, elbow, knee and teeth. He had lunch with her on several occasions, and no doubt did much to raise her spirits; but her friends felt that Elizabeth never really made a complete recovery. The accident had taken something out of her, and she would never have the same strength and energy again. There was no more talk of buying a house in Wales.

* * * * * * * *

CHAPTER TWENTY

Omelette and Ice

On 13 April 1978 Elizabeth was made Author of the Year in the Glenfiddich Awards, given annually for excellence in writing, publishing and broadcasting on food and drink. She received the prize for *English Bread and Yeast Cookery*, and in her speech of thanks, Elizabeth alluded to the recent collapse of Spillers, one of the big three milling companies in England: 'I received a card from a friend,' she announced, 'which simply said: *One down – two to go*.'[1] In the following year, the University of Essex decided to award Elizabeth an honorary doctorate. Elizabeth was particularly proud of this acknowledgement of her scholarship, and was accompanied to the ceremony by John and Veronica Nicholson. In her long black gown and mortarboard, Veronica thought Elizabeth looked rather small; but she was in great spirits, and tipped Veronica a big wink as she went up to the rostrum. In her speech, she laid particular emphasis on her debt to Veronica, who had 'nagged and bullied' her into journalism all those years ago.

English Bread and Yeast Cookery was an important part of a general drive for better bread which did then gather speed. In 1979 the *Sunday Times* launched a Campaign for Real Bread, headed by Caroline Conran and the health correspondent Oliver Gillie. Considering that its aims were to improve the variety of shop bread and make wholemeal bread available everywhere, the campaign could claim a measure of success. As the 1980s wore on, other campaigns

– for organic fruit and vegetables, and better conditions for animals, all gathered momentum. Elizabeth, almost at the end of her working life acknowledged as the best food writer of her generation, might have lent the weight of her name to those campaigns. She chose not to. Campaigning, even in print, is a very public endeavour, and Elizabeth was turning inwards.

She had become absorbed in history and research. Through Felicité, she came across two herb farmers – Guy Cooper and Gordon Taylor – who had just become co-directors of the Herb Society. She wrote occasional articles for *The Herbal Review*; but what particularly interested her was the seventeenth-century still-room book of Lady Granville, which belonged to the Society's library. It contained one of the earliest English references to ice cream, and led to further research which took her into Bishop Ken's Library under the eaves of Longleat.

She first visited Longleat in June 1979, with Alan Davidson. The archivist had gone to great trouble to find samples of the handwriting and signature of Grace Granville. However, Lord Christopher Thynne (son of the Marquess of Bath) was keen that she should also see the *Pynson Boke of Cokery*, which – dated 1500 – is the only surviving copy of the first cookery book ever published in England. Elizabeth went back to Longleat again a few years later, to discuss a possible reprinting of the book with Lord Christopher. Nothing came of it, for Elizabeth felt that she could only participate if the reprinting were done to the most exacting academic standards, while the Thynnes were evidently thinking of a publication with more general appeal.

At about this time Elizabeth met an antiquarian book dealer called Stephanie Hoppen, who had a strong interest in books on food and wine. Elizabeth was particularly drawn to books compiled by the *maestri di casa* of the sixteenth and seventeenth centuries, who managed the kitchens of the most powerful families in Italy. These books were much more practical than their French equivalents, more descriptive of the food itself and the techniques of cooking. Elizabeth

also took an intense interest in Stephanie's work of compiling catalogues and bibliographies, and questioned her every reference and
assumption: 'She was always telling me to go back to the source:
whenever you're in doubt, go back to the source. She made me do
everything that much better than I would have done without her.'
Elizabeth bought several books from Stephanie, some of which cost
well over a thousand pounds: 'She loved books with such a passion.'[2]

She also became fascinated by a small, stout, handwritten book
dated 1604, which the biographer Hilary Spurling had been cooking
from for the last ten years. Elizabeth said, most emphatically, that
it ought to be published: 'she wasn't a person you said "no" to
twice', said Hilary Spurling.[3] Elizabeth was a great help in the
preparation and presentation of *Elinor Fettiplace's Receipt Book*:
when sent the notes that were to accompany the text, the five pages
of corrections and suggestions Elizabeth sent back reveal the range
of her knowledge, and the accuracy she insisted on.

Professional chef is a designation which didn't become usage until the mid
nineteenth century. Chef is an anachronism. Master cook would be the
correct designation of Robert May . . . *The Prince de Condé's chef*. Not only
an anachronism, but an error of fact. Vatel . . . was never Condé's head
cook. He was his maître d'hôtel, which in the case of a great establishment
like Chantilly, meant that he was in overall charge of organizing the supplies
. . . *Artificial colourings*. In the light – if one can call it that – of present-day
usage of the term, saffron and the rest are surely natural colourings?
Perhaps you could say additional colouring?[4]

In March 1979, Elizabeth emerged from her studies to join John
and Ellen-Ann Hopkins for a holiday in Tangier, where the Hopkinses then lived. Several years had passed since Elizabeth and Ellen-
Ann had mourned together over their 'requiem lunches', but they
had always kept in touch. Since 1977, when Ellen-Ann Ragsdale
had married the writer and novelist John Hopkins, she had often
asked Elizabeth to come and see them.

They spent a few days in southern Spain before sailing to Morocco, eating in all sorts of little restaurants and *ventas* – the smaller and more rustic the better. As usual, people were flattered by Elizabeth's boundless curiosity, and she was an appreciative guest. The only time she misbehaved was in the Marbella Club, where she ordered a consommé. It was the sort of place that pretended to a knowledge of French cuisine so Elizabeth had no qualms about sending it back with the words, 'This is horrible.' The chef took it back and the dish was presented for the second time: 'This is even worse!'[5]

As soon as she arrived in Tangier she was happy. She wrote in the morning as usual, then dressed and went exploring – usually with Ellen-Ann. She became obsessed by a green leafy vegetable she saw in the Socco Grande, the great market of Tangier. In Morocco it is called *b'khola* and John Hopkins always thought it was a kind of kale. No, said Elizabeth, it was more like a sort of Swiss chard, but not one she had ever come across before. The result was that John and Ellen-Ann were put to work trying to find out what it was, and Elizabeth would not let the subject go – she worried at it, like a terrier with a bone.

She was also fascinated by John's collection of the conical cooking pots called *tagines*, which he had built up over seventeen years in Morocco. Some had been bought in extremely remote places, in the mountains or the desert, and many were adorned with beautiful designs. When the Hopkinses moved back to London a year later, several of the tagines arrived broken and had to be thrown out. When Elizabeth heard of this she was very upset. She thought they could have been repaired, and all were worthy of being in a museum. John was quite taken aback to see how distressed she was.

The Hopkinses introduced her to the writer Paul Bowles, with whom she had one thing in common – they had been the only authors on John Lehmann's list to be retained by Macdonald, when his publishing company was forced to fold in 1954. They got on famously; and Paul Bowles's Moroccan helpmate Abdelouahid took her on a memorable day out.

Elizabeth had said she wanted to see how Moroccan bread was

made, from beginning to end. 'Abdelouahid obligingly drove her out to the countryside where Moroccan women in their colourful costumes harvest wheat with sickles. Then to the threshing floor where animals go round and round. Then to the huge watermill where the huge stone pulverizes the grain. Abdelouahid then took Elizabeth to his home so that she could watch his mother prepare the loaf. Then to the local oven where it is baked. A perfectionist and notoriously difficult to please, Elizabeth returned thoroughly satisfied.'[6]

She had not been back in London for more than a month when Elizabeth received one of the saddest letters she was ever to read in her life. Her old friend Viola Johnson, to whom she had dedicated *Italian Food*, had committed suicide in Greece. The letter she sent to Elizabeth was not so much a suicide note as a grateful farewell. 'Alas, you and I will never again sit together at a table with a bottle or two, for I have reached the end of the road . . . Goodbye, dear Liz. Thank you for your friendship, and the many good times and good laughs we have shared.'[7]

The year 1979 saw the creation of a new cookery journal called *Petits Propos Culinaires*. It was founded by Alan and Jane Davidson, who had for some time been thinking of launching such a publication. They had discussed the idea with Elizabeth, who expressed enthusiasm – the magazine would be the perfect showcase for certain pieces of research she herself had done. But the spark that got the magazine started came over lunch one day with Richard Olney.

Richard Olney was born American, but realized early on that his only natural home was France. He rapidly became an authority on French food and wine. He was also as close to being a French chef as is possible without the formal training. 'Elizabeth teased me mercilessly,' he wrote after her death, 'claiming that my cuisine and my taste in wines were much too grand for the "likes" of her.'[8]

Richard Olney had recently been appointed chief consultant for an ambitious series of cookery books planned by Time-Life Books, called *The Good Cook*. Since its American editors wanted it to be as authoritative as possible, they laid down a great many rules – one of which was that no recipe could be included that had not already been published. At lunch one day with the Davidsons, Olney was venting his rage over this particular rule, which forbade him to include one or two perfectly straightforward dishes for which no satisfactory recipe existed. The answer was, of course, to publish them himself – in *Petits Propos Culinaires*. The first issue contained an article by Elizabeth called 'Hunt the Ice Cream', and two by Olney – posing as Nathan d'Aulnay for an aubergine gratin, and Tante Ursule, for crayfish à la bordelaise. Elizabeth was to contribute several articles for *PPC*, as it came to be called, and took her position as honorary president very seriously – she had no hesitation in telling those concerned when she felt it was getting too rarefied and scholarly. 'For every ten postcards or telephone calls to us expressing pleasure or congratulation . . . there would be one telling us that we had gone off the rails.'[9]

Olney admired Elizabeth, and when she came to visit him at the Time-Life flat he used while living in London, he gave her only the simplest food: elvers in oil, scrambled eggs with truffles; but she happily joined him in the 'Montrachets, Chambertins, Lafites and Yquems that I sometimes imposed on her'.[10] On one occasion, however, Elizabeth joined him in a meal that was far from simple.

Olney's fiftieth birthday fell on 12 April 1978, when he happened to be in England staying with Lesley Marple, ex-wife of the film director John Huston. A brilliant young Californian chef called Jeremiah Tower did the cooking, Sybille Bedford chose the wines, and the guests were Richard Olney and Elizabeth. The menu was carefully noted by Sybille Bedford, along with the wines that went with it.

First they had prosciutto, with bread made by Elizabeth: with this went a bottle of Roederer Crystal Vintage Champagne 1969. Then, after a *fumet de poisson* (with a Sauvignon de St-Bris '76) they went on to the entrée, roast saddle of lamb with a sauté of spring vegetables: tiny onions, turnips and broad beans, and a chiffonade of lettuce and sorrel. This was accompanied by Château Pape-Clément '66. With the fresh goat cheese and a Saint-Nectaire they drank another bottle of Pape-Clément, this time a '61. Then came a Blanc Manger, accompanied by a Château Climens 1961.

The occasion provides another example of Elizabeth's talent for giving presents. Her gift to Olney was 'a large, heavy, oval porcelain platter – antique restaurant service – with a faded burnt-orange rim, a thread of the same colour just inside the rim. I love it. When not in use, it is always on view.'[11]

That summer, Felicité fell gravely ill. She was taken to St George's Hospital. The main cause was heart trouble; but when Elizabeth came to talk to Felicité's doctors, it emerged that they were concerned by the fact that she was alarmingly undernourished.

Felicité's habitual lack of interest in food was quite genuine, not just a way of underlining her independence from her famous sister. People who took her out to lunch or dinner noticed that she ordered the plainest and dullest things on the menu, and the pleasure she took in going out was entirely in the talk. According to John Sandoe, in whose bookshop she worked for so many years, Felicité felt the need to keep her weight down. She ate the yogurt she made herself, or bed-sit stand-bys like eggs and baked beans, or the sort of self-consciously spartan health food that Elizabeth would have had no time for – but whatever she ate, it was in tiny quantities, and as she grew older she started skipping meals altogether.

Over the years, Elizabeth had had little occasion to think about what Felicité ate. She did not notice her tiny appetite on family occasions, because her own appetite was small too. Both sisters scrupulously respected each other's privacy: neither of them encroached on the other's territory without a telephone call beforehand. But on hearing that Felicité was suffering from malnutrition, Elizabeth was profoundly shocked. Quite apart from her concern for Felicité's health, the idea that someone might find out that

Elizabeth David's sister, who lived in her house, was half-starved, was too terrible to contemplate.

She immediately concurred with the doctors' recommendation that Felicité be given rich, tempting food, in very small quantities. Elizabeth had not cooked regularly for many years, except for the fresh loaves that she loved; but now she started cooking again for Felicité. Starting with soups and broths, which were all that her sister could manage at the beginning, she moved on to tiny pâtés, rich jellies, little egg dishes, delicious morsels of fish or chicken in cream – all served in the doll's house proportions that Elizabeth herself liked. John Sandoe often drove her to the hospital, with the dishes in a basket. Felicité was very touched by her efforts, but very weak and could scarcely manage more than a mouthful.

Her stay in hospital was succeeded by a long period of convalescence in a nursing home; and although she did get her strength back, she was never quite the same again. She went back to work in the shop, but only three mornings a week to open the mail and answer the telephone. On the one hand, she could not get used to having her role in the shop so reduced; and on the other, she had become so forgetful and absent-minded that she had become more of a hindrance than a help. John Sandoe finally had to ask her to leave. Elizabeth and the rest of her family never forgave him.

The tiny basement flat in Halsey Street was empty much of the time, though it was still nominally occupied by Lesley O'Malley. Several years before, Lesley had been persuaded by her old friend Roald Dahl to buy three little cottages, side by side, in the quiet street of a village called Great Missenden in Buckinghamshire. Dahl and his wife, who lived nearby, had helped her with the purchase. Two were rented, and Lesley used the third at weekends.

When Lesley was sacked from her job in advertising at the end of the 1970s, she decided to go freelance. She spent more and more time at Great Missenden, where she now occupied two of the cottages, converted into one by her architect niece, Jane Blakemore.

Elizabeth immediately noticed that Lesley was not using her bed-sit as much as before, and let it be known that she would like the space back. This was not done as tactfully as it might have been: Lesley was deeply offended, and moved out at once. They did make it up a few years later; but for the time being a distinct coldness existed between them.

Some years before Elizabeth had given her nephew Johnny Grey his very first commission, for a new sink cabinet. He built it in the street, and installed it himself. Then, in 1983, she asked him to design a new kitchen in the basement flat. Johnny describes Elizabeth as a surprisingly easy client: she had her own very definite ideas, but was not particularly demanding because her kitchen require-ments were very simple. There was no microwave, no dishwasher, no kitchen gobbler – although her cleaning lady, Jean McAuliffe, did persuade her to install a washing machine, the first there had ever been in Halsey Street.

Over the course of her life in Halsey Street Elizabeth had had a succession of cleaning ladies, most of whom left after a few months, but Jean was different. She was very retiring and sweet-natured, and Elizabeth found her easy to get on with because she never disturbed her books and papers. Her relationship with the builder was far more difficult. On the one hand, she did not like the idea of him being there at all, he was invading her space; while on the other, Elizabeth felt he had left the job before it was finished. She described him as 'a proper tease. I have to *beg* him every day to come back, and put up a plate rack or fix handles on the cupboard doors – as elusive as Higgins.'[12]

However, she was very pleased with the results. The new kitchen had more space, and more natural light than the old one. It also had a 'soft' area which was carpeted; and around the table in this space went an upholstered banquette. The cupboard and sink cabinet were made of London plane and English ash, which glowed against the pale, blue-grey paint with which she painted not only this room, but almost every other room in the house. An enormous daybed was another feature, although it would not go downstairs. Jack Andrews had to spend a morning taking out the area window so as to get it in that way. Johnny suggested that the new one should be the 'winter kitchen', while the old one remained as the 'summer kitchen'. Elizabeth liked the idea of a seasonal migration, between one kitchen and the other – but it did not turn out that way.

The door of the old kitchen was shut, as if she had shut off a part of her past. It was not locked, merely abandoned, left to its own devices, rather like the sitting room. At one point the sitting room had had a proper turnout, and a new sofa was bought. 'For a while, it was actually usable; but since she never used it, the books and papers started to pile up and soon it was unusable again.'[13] Elizabeth had four rooms at her disposal, but retreated into two of them: her new kitchen and the bedroom.

Elizabeth felt very close to Johnny, and certainly he inherited her tastes for cooking and design more than his brothers and sister. The building of the new kitchen had been a satisfying time for them both, sharing long lunches and suppers at the kitchen table. He tried to persuade her to move: the Halsey Street house was very dark, and he knew that she sometimes found it depressing: 'She, of all people, shouldn't have to live in the dark! I thought she would be much happier in a big first-floor flat with huge windows, like the ones in Cadogan Square, where she could enjoy the sun streaming in all day.'[14]

She never moved, but Johnny seemed to move out of her life. He contracted glandular fever, after which he could no longer take the late-night drinking sessions. They began to see each other less frequently, and Elizabeth began to feel slightly neglected.

In fact, she was far from neglected. Rosi Hanson took her on picnic jaunts outside London, as did Liz Savage, Jill Norman and Jack Andrews. With April Boyes she went to any number of exhibitions. Elizabeth was fascinating company in an art gallery: she looked at pictures as keys to the past, filled with the sort of information that did not appear in books. She still kept in touch with old friends like

Doreen Thornton and Sybille Bedford; though since Sybille now only liked going out for dinner while Elizabeth wanted to go out for lunch, they saw each other less frequently than before. She had not seen as much of Hugh and Judy Johnson as she used to, for they had moved to the country and had young children; but she retained a very wide circle of friends. She was particularly good at long-distance friendships, because she remembered what amused or interested the people she liked. Out of the blue would come a newspaper cutting, or an extract from a book catalogue, or an advertisement from a magazine, accompanied by a postcard from Elizabeth saying, 'I thought you might be interested.'

Similarly, her correspondents knew what would interest her. 'I currently find myself with considerably raised blood pressure,' wrote Anthony Denney from Spain, 'having just finished reading M. F. K. Fisher's *Two Towns in Provence*. . . In the Aix section she describes proudly how she was able several times to resist being told and shown the preparation of *calissons d'Aix*: her own version of the recipe then follows.'[15] For Elizabeth, who never turned down an opportunity to see how a local speciality was made, this just about summed up the difference between herself and Mrs Fisher.

One person who was very interested to meet her was the cricket commentator John Arlott, who also ran the *Guardian*'s Wine Club. They had met at some formal occasion but he wanted to know her better, and Rosi and Anthony Hanson arranged a dinner for them to meet. They were astounded by the way that Arlott was not only curious about her early life, but quite openly so. He asked her questions about her childhood, her youth, and her husband that they would never have dared ask her – and even stranger was the fact that she did not seem offended. In fact she seemed to be rather enjoying it. At one point she mentioned some uncomfortable moment in her youth and Arlott exclaimed, 'If only *I'd* been there, you wouldn't have had to go through all that!' Elizabeth was flattered and amused; but she replied, 'I think not, John. You see, I was a bolter.'

In her thank-you letter to Rosi she wrote,

I wasn't able sufficiently to deflect John from his apparent purpose of conducting a 'Face to Face' interview across the dining table, in front of an unpaid, unwilling and captive audience. It must have been boring for you two . . . On the whole I can't help thinking that it was just as well our paths didn't cross when he was a lusty – or did he say lustful – Hampshire policeman. When I said I was a Bolter he didn't get the allusion. I was thinking of Nancy Mitford's Bolter, Fanny's mother in *Love in a Cold Climate*, who was always running away from husbands and other gentlemen. John would have been very disillusioned, very quickly I fear . . .[16]

Many friends came into Elizabeth's orbit thanks to Félicité, who met them in John Sandoe's bookshop. One was Michael Day, a cheese connoisseur and wholesaler – later founder of the Huge Cheese Company – who used to swap cheese for proof copies of books at Sandoe's. When he first came to see Félicité at Halsey Street and came upstairs, she jokingly told him that the bottom half of the house was occupied by 'my terrifying sister'; but when Michael himself came to meet Elizabeth, she was not a bit frightening and they began to see each other. Michael was young and very good-looking, and Elizabeth enjoyed going out to lunch with him. She also enjoyed long evenings with him in Halsey Street, where he kept her entertained with stories of his different girlfriends.

One friend whom she met through Jane Grigson was the broadcaster and novelist Paul Bailey. In the early 1980s he was involved in a series for Radio Three called 'Third Ear', which consisted of interviews with writers: not because they had a book to plug, but simply because they were worth talking to. He had already interviewed Jane Grigson, and after the companionable lunch with Jane at which he had met Elizabeth, he tried to persuade her to be interviewed as well. Paul Bailey understood that she was very shy, and tried to make the interview he proposed sound as undemanding as possible. She would not have to say anything personal, she would be talking exclusively as a writer, and it could all be done at Halsey Street with the minimum of fuss. Elizabeth dithered and dithered – and finally said she simply couldn't, she was too terrified. Paul accepted this, with regret but with grace: he did not try and change her mind. Elizabeth was grateful for his understanding, and their friendship developed.

Two years later, in the autumn of 1982, Elizabeth was invited to take part in an edition of *The Food Programme*, presented by that veteran food campaigner and connoisseur of single malts, Derek Cooper. The programme was going to be devoted to bread, and Elizabeth was suspicious from the start. 'Who else is going to be interviewed?' she wrote on the letter of invitation. 'Don't ask me to taste any bread.' On balance, she decided to say no: she was not a natural performer. However, the producer approached Jill Norman, and she persuaded Elizabeth to change her mind. After all, Derek Cooper's programme had an excellent track record, and was widely respected.

The programme was recorded on 22 October, and got off to a bad start. Derek Cooper launched into a fulsome introduction in praise of her work, and described Elizabeth as the woman who had done more to change British attitudes to food than anyone else this century. He then turned to her and asked, 'Is that true?' There was an agonizing silence as Elizabeth sighed inaudibly, tilted her head and looked around the studio. She finally replied, 'You tell me.'

The interview never really recovered, but Derek Cooper plugged on manfully. Elizabeth answered his questions in a way that started clipped and brusque, and then died away with a hesitant 'don't you think?' She was obviously not enjoying it, and every attempt to ignite a spark in her fizzled out. When discussing the time it took to bake bread Cooper asked, 'What about women who work all day?' – 'That's their problem.' – 'What do you do when you are served terrible bread at dinner?' – 'I don't go to dinners like that.' At one point, thinking that Elizabeth had taken against him, he asked his colleague Christopher Driver to take over, hoping that perhaps he might do better. Elizabeth did not appreciate the change and was, if anything, even frostier and more monosyllabic. In despair, Cooper thought the only thing to do would be to tie up the interview as if it had ended, and keep the tape running. This was done, but Elizabeth never really loosened up. By the time she left they had hundreds of feet of tape, and by dint of a great deal of skilful splicing, the producer Joy Hatwood managed to put together something like an interview.[17] At one point, they did give Elizabeth some rice bread to try, and she made a stab at being more forthcoming. 'This is rather *damp*. . . not at all like mine . . . it's interesting . . . someone's trying, anyway . . .'[18]

The programme had been a great deal of hard work, and Derek Cooper felt it had been a disaster: 'She just couldn't play the game, and she knew it. I blame myself, I should have respected her initial refusal.' At the same time he was glad that she had been recorded because her voice is now in the BBC Archive; and the fact that people had actually heard it was so exciting that they did not notice the shortcomings of the interview. Derek Cooper recalled one listener who said what a joy it was to hear Elizabeth David, but then added 'what a pity Cooper didn't give her the chance to say more'.

Elizabeth now had two books in mind: one called *Ice and Ices*, for which the research seemed (like the bread book) to be expanding exponentially, and the other was a volume of her journalism. It was an idea suggested by Jill Norman as a way of getting her back into making books as opposed to researching. Elizabeth was enthusiastic, and for the moment, this book was known as 'Early Works'.

As far as Elizabeth was concerned, Jill was now irreplaceable: they worked together so well that she never wanted to have another editor. When Jill left Penguin in 1979 to set up on her own, Elizabeth followed her. By 1983, however, Jill had discovered that going solo had its disadvantages. She had to spend too much time on the administration of the business, and not enough on books. For these reasons she decided to maintain her independence and her list, while sheltering under the umbrella of a larger publisher who would provide services like warehousing, sales teams and distribution. In January 1984 Jill moved her list to Robert Hale Ltd.

Part of the deal was that Robert Hale acquired certain rights over Jill's list, though the sum paid by him did not reflect its value: it was a kind of insurance measure, repayable by Jill if she left the company within eighteen months. It was understood, at least by Jill, that she should retain her own imprint. Since Elizabeth was one of her most important and best-selling authors, Jill was keen to present a new book by her in the first list she produced that autumn.

This was to be 'Early Works', the collection of Elizabeth's journalism. She and Jill went through the dusty files that sat on the bottom shelf of the bookcase in the hall, where Elizabeth kept all her articles. When Elizabeth went to Uzès in February, Jill was left with the keys of Halsey Street to get on with the selection. Soon after Elizabeth came back she developed a painful skin complaint on her legs and feet. This became so bad that she had to be prescribed painkillers, and could not go out for days on end. Jill came round very often, bringing a picnic lunch, and worked at weekends too.

The pieces they gathered together included the best of the work she had done for *Vogue* and the *Spectator*; and it was Elizabeth's idea to include extracts from the little books that she had written for the shop. The pieces were, with very few exceptions, left as they stood – Elizabeth preferred to write introductory notes where necessary, rather than change them. But the book still took six months of hard work. Elizabeth decided to call it *An Omelette and a Glass of Wine*.

By mid-July, the book was in page proof. Jill and Elizabeth corrected it together, but the contract for it had not yet been signed. Elizabeth had let the matter slide because she was not entirely happy with it: under the new terms, the publisher was Robert Hale Ltd, and not Jill Norman. But John Hale (son of Robert) was pressing Jill for the contract, and Jill was reassuring. Elizabeth signed.

On Friday 13 July, Jill delivered the corrected page proofs and the contract for *An Omelette and a Glass of Wine* to John Hale. She then set about clearing her desk, since she was going on holiday the next day. At the end of the afternoon, John Hale came in and gave her a letter. It told her that she had been dismissed. 'I was so astounded I couldn't take it in; I think I just carried on with what I was doing.'[19]

It was not until she returned from holiday that reality sank in. Jill was barred from entering the building – even to retrieve her own filing cabinets. These contained the contracts, correspondence and work-in-progress of her authors, and all the papers relating to her backlist. She was told that all her papers were now the property of Robert Hale Ltd, including her name, which she was no longer allowed to use as a publishing imprint. Among the assets seized were a great many draft chapters of *Ice and Ices*, and the hardback rights of the 'Elizabeth David Classics': a collective title that, iron-ically, covered the books that Elizabeth had extricated from Mac-donald with so much difficulty.

Elizabeth was appalled by what had happened. She felt that Jill had been sacked so that Hale could get his hands on her list, and that she herself had been tricked into giving him two books that she had always wanted Jill to handle. They saw a great deal of each other over the next few weeks: not only for mutual support, but to think about what could be done. The only hope was to go to law but it is a fact of life that large companies can afford lawyers, while individuals very often cannot.

Elizabeth was particularly concerned about the draft chapters of her ice book. On several occasions she demanded their return; and when finally they were returned to her, in mid-September, it was obvious that the papers had been photocopied: they were out of order, and all the paper clips had been removed.

Thus Elizabeth had publishers very much on her mind when, on 30 September, she attended Ellen-Ann Hopkins's fortieth birthday party at the Quat' Saisons restaurant in Oxford (this was before Raymond Blanc had moved into his Manoir). She found herself at a table with three people: the writer and publisher Jeremy Lewis, the American publisher Jerry Epstein and Clare Astor. These three had, by surreptitiously changing the place cards, contrived to sit next to each other; but they did not know her.

Jeremy Lewis described the occasion in his memoir *Kindred Spirits*. As yet unidentified, Elizabeth appeared as

a white-haired woman in her sixties, whose elegance and rather washed-out beauty was sadly upset by an unhappy expression and the abstracted air of someone who would obviously prefer to be somewhere else . . . Clare – eager to make her feel at home, and worried in case she was baffled by the menu – began, in the kindest of ways, to translate the various items on offer and explain, very slowly, what they tasted like. Far from showing gratitude for a helping hand, our dinner companion looked unhappier than ever; and when – unwisely, perhaps – I revealed that I was in publishing, she embarked on a tirade against the iniquities of publishers, and how shockingly she had been treated by a particular firm.[20]

Lewis had charitably put Elizabeth in her sixties; she was in fact seventy, and the situation she found herself in was a terrible replay of what had happened with *Italian Food* thirty years before. Through no fault of her own, she had fallen into the hands of a remarkably unsympathetic publisher. In the revised page proofs of *Omelette*, Jill's name was removed from the title and credits pages. This revised proof was hurried through and circulated to the press before being sent to Elizabeth. She immediately hired a lawyer, and Robert Hale Ltd were obliged to put back the original dust jacket and alter the tampered proofs. Hale then had the nerve to deduct £400 for 'excess proof corrections' from her first royalty cheque.

An Omelette and a Glass of Wine delighted Elizabeth's legion of fans. In the *TLS* Jane Grigson praised it for including all the dishes most closely associated with her (spiced beef, salted Welsh duck, syllabub), as well as all her pet hates (fake mayonnaise, Bird's custard, the rise and flop of the quiche). She also pointed out that 'Mrs David has been more to us, I think, than Mrs Beeton was to aspiring Victorians.'[21]

She did not mean so much to the novelist Angela Carter, who as a food critic was a notoriously loose cannon. She distrusted any woman whose books sent other women 'back to the stove' and loathed anything that smacked of Upper Class Writing. 'An enthusiasm for the table, the grape and the stove itself is characteristic of the deviant subsection of the British bourgeoisie that has always gone in for the arts with the diligent enthusiasm of (as they would put it) "the amateur in the true sense of the word". This class is more than adequately represented by Mrs Elizabeth David.'[22] Yet even Carter could tell the difference between the oh-so-civilized Mrs David and the pretentious, slurping foodie culture which seemed to have infiltrated everything. 'Piggery triumphant,' fumed Carter, 'has invaded even the pages of the *Guardian*.'[23]

The economic boom of the eighties had ushered in the age of the yuppies: the young upwardly-mobile professionals, who had money to burn on designer clothes and designer food. Their attitude to life was summed up by the character of Gordon Gecko in the film *Wall Street*, who proudly pronounced that 'Greed is good.' Triumphant piggery was in the air. It was also on the minds of both the above-mentioned reviewers, because *An Omelette and a Glass of Wine* had appeared at the same time as a book that was being celebrated, disputed and deplored in equal measure: *The Official Foodie Handbook*, by Ann Barr and Paul Levy.

The *Handbook*'s time had come, as its authors were well aware: 'Foodism is glamorous, Foodism is fun. "I am a Foodie" is as proud a boast as the old Roman citizen's "Civis Romanus sum" . . . What they both mean is "I am a winner". Eating is a vocation worth devoting your life to.'[24] It aimed to inform as well as amuse, and much of it is based on considerable research. But it was seen as a successor to the Sloane Ranger books, and it was taken as a bluffer's guide to the latest social craze.

From the days when Elizabeth had started writing, when food was not a topic of conversation, fashion had gone to the opposite extreme. Now it was not only acceptable to talk about food, one could show off one's knowledge. It was permissible to ask the waiter whether the salmon was farmed or wild, to ask which side of Lucca the olive oil came from, and to thrill with excitement on being told that the baby broad beans had just come into season. Yet there was something fake, pretentious about it all: in the word of the moment, 'pseud'. The real food and wine experts hated the word, for it lumped them together with pretentious cookery writers, duff wine buffs and the prancing TV chefs.

Elizabeth had always disliked Paul Levy, a dislike which he traces back to his early days on the *Observer*. When he became the food correspondent in 1980, he was hailed as an innovator and heaped with prizes because his pages talked about food in an intelligent way without getting clogged up with recipes. 'I didn't know about the articles she had written twenty years before in the *Spectator*, but when *Omelette and a Glass of Wine* came out I realized that on several occasions I had written about precisely the same things – Madame Barattero, truffles . . . I can imagine what she thought: plagiarism. It's not uncommon – I sometimes feel I've been ripped off, too.'[25]

Elizabeth never found out that Paul Levy had initiated the campaign to award her the Fellowship of the Royal Society of Literature, to which she had been elected in 1982. Michael Holroyd, who was on the council, was her official champion and the council had voted for her unanimously. Among all her honours it was the one that gave her the most satisfaction and pleasure; but knowing that she owed it to Levy would have taken a lot of gilt off the gingerbread.

She did like Ann Barr, who had once been her sub-editor when she worked for Hugh Johnson on *Queen*. When she heard that Barr and Levy were going to collaborate on the *Foodie* book she warned Barr against him and said 'Miss Barr, you'll never pull it off.'[26] They did pull it off: the book did not have quite the impact of the Sloane Ranger books, but it became a best-seller nonetheless.

The success of a book that, to Elizabeth, represented the worst aspects of the eighties food culture was galling enough; but that she was included in the 'Foodies Who's Who' was unforgivable. Derek Cooper's name was not included because he had told Levy that if his name appeared in the book he would sue. Elizabeth wished she had done the same – but it was too late now. *The Official Foodie Handbook* came out when she was still boiling with anger and indignation over what she had been subjected to with Robert Hale; and in a pattern that was now becoming familiar, her hatred boiled over and fixed on another object. Paul Levy became her *bête noire*, and in order to account for the fact that her friend Ann Barr was co-author, she persuaded herself that Levy had somehow conned Barr into doing the book with him.

Her only revenge was to review the book. The cartoonist Mark Boxer, who was then editor-in-chief of the *Tatler*, persuaded Elizabeth to write it for him. It appeared in February 1985, entitled 'Scoff Gaffe'.

She began with what they had written about her. There was no Ministry of Information in occupied Greece during the war; it was in Cairo that she had been librarian, not Alexandria; and she had never, at any time, been married to a Lieutenant Colonel in the Bengal Lancers. The real criticism, however, was deeper. 'To be sure they are skilful enough in the arts of toadying to their public and providing it with a little giggle at itself, but the meaning of satire in the true sense eludes them. Their truly awful brand of teasy jocularity isn't any kind of substitute.'

Mark Boxer was delighted with this corruscating review, and asked Elizabeth to write for the *Tatler* on a regular basis. She was very fond of Boxer, who knew how to handle her and never messed about with her copy; but there was another reason for taking up journalism again. She had spent a lot of money in legal fees.

Jill's dismissal from Robert Hale Ltd. the year before had shocked the publishing world. Jane Grigson and Kit van Tulleken, an editor at Time-Life, launched a campaign to gather funds for Jill's legal costs, to which a great many authors and almost all the publishers in London contributed. The case went to independent arbitration in April 1985. Jill's plea of unfair dismissal by Robert Hale Ltd was upheld, and Hale was not allowed to hold on to her name as an imprint; but all Jill's backlist was deemed the property of Robert Hale Ltd. Only two books were returned to Jill: one of them was *An Omelette and a Glass of Wine*.

With the help of her solicitor Clifford Harris and the firm of Payne Hicks Beach, Elizabeth had managed to wrest the ice book and the 'Elizabeth David Classics' from Robert Hale; but Hale had not let them go without huge compensation payments for loss of expected revenue. This was in part borne by the publisher Dorling Kindersley, for whom Jill was now working.

Paul Levy, well aware of Elizabeth's dislike of him, never wavered from his profound admiration of her. He was not the only person who felt she deserved to be made a Dame: so did the writer and editor Drusilla Beyfus and, surprisingly enough (in December 1978), the *Guardian*. In their different ways, they all tried to do something about it. The result was that in the 1986 New Year's Honours, Elizabeth was made a Companion of the British Empire. Peter Higgins wrote, 'A rather belated communication to congratulate you on HM The Queen's birthday present. It is agreeable to know that someone sees that merit is recognized.'[27] Elizabeth was then plunged into the problem of what to wear. Her legs were now so bad that she never wore skirts any more, but at the same time it would never do to wear trousers to Buckingham Palace. She compromised with a long skirt, and set off for the palace on 7 March with Jill Norman and Kit van Tulleken. Once there, she found that she was the only woman not wearing a hat. Elizabeth received the CBE from the Prince of Wales, who mentioned in passing that 'My wife loves Italian food.'[28]

A few days later, Felicité was taken to the Cromwell Hospital. Once again, the trouble was her heart, but there was little that could be done and she was sent home a few days later. On 20 March she had a stroke: 'I found her sitting on her bed,' wrote Elizabeth to Celia Denney, '. . . fully dressed and obviously expecting to go out, but unable to speak . . . She was making frantic efforts to make herself understood. It was terribly distressing.'[29]

For four days she fought to make a recovery, and her speech did begin to come back. But 'on the morning of the 24th when I took her papers up there was no sound of early morning news on her radio. She was lying dead, half in and half out of bed.'[30]

One of the first people Elizabeth rang was Stephanie Hoppen, who had by that time become a close friend. Stephanie recalled that Elizabeth was 'like a child, she was so devastated'.[31] She was also in urgent need of emotional support. 'I don't yet know what I will do in this house without her . . . although we lived such different lives we were each dependent on the other for many things. She was really a very remarkable person . . . She was sixty-eight and she didn't really have a lot of luck in her life. But she was happy during the shop years, and must have encouraged scores and scores of people to read . . . Gerald always says, "Felicité educated me."'[32]

Stephanie accompanied Elizabeth to the funeral at Folkington. 'I sat beside her in the pew because she insisted, though it was reserved for family . . . Elizabeth could not bring herself to go to the burial itself, but afterwards we went back to Wootton for the reception. I knew almost nobody there, but Elizabeth clung to my arm . . . It was strange because I had always seen her as such a confident person, but she would not let me go out of her sight for a second. It was as if she dreaded being left alone with her family.'[33]

Felicité was buried in the same ground as her parents and her infant brother. Rupert Grey noticed a handsome old man milling among the guests, who stood out because of his tan. Rupert did not recognize him; but during the service the stranger, who was standing behind him, whispered, 'I made love with Felicité on the Downs in the summer of 1942.' 'Who are you?' asked Rupert. The man replied, 'Peter the Pole.' Rupert wanted to talk to him again, but by the time the service had ended, Peter the Pole had vanished.[34] But it was good to know that he had not forgotten her, and had come to her funeral.

Felicité's death sank Elizabeth into a profound, silent grief. When she did talk, she seemed almost unable to believe that her sister was dead. She had never understood how much she relied on Felicité; not just as a friend and sister, but as someone who kept her in touch with the outside world and as a friendly presence in the house. It felt oppressively big, and Elizabeth had never felt so desolate.

As the weeks went by, the grief turned into a depression and Elizabeth began to suffer from chest pains. She was frightened that she might be developing lung cancer. X-rays established that she had nothing to fear on that account, but the doctors suspected that she might be suffering from tuberculosis – of which her brother-in-law Christopher Grey had died in 1982. She was admitted into hospital, and Stephanie, who accompanied her, was asked to sign in as Elizabeth's next of kin. Stephanie was reluctant but Elizabeth urged her to get on with it, implying that it really didn't matter who signed.

Elizabeth was put under very heavy sedation, and was receiving drugs for TB which, apparently, put a very heavy strain on the liver. At the same time, the hospital was also allowing her wine. The combination of alcohol and these powerful drugs began to undermine not only her health, but her mind.

Stephanie Hoppen was on holiday when her ex-husband, Richard Leech, telephoned her to say that he was seriously worried about Elizabeth, who seemed desperately ill. Stephanie flew back at once, though by the time she reached London she fully expected to discover that Richard had been exaggerating and that Elizabeth was not as ill as he had made out. However, as soon as she saw Elizabeth she realized that things were even worse. 'She was wandering, completely and utterly out of it – she didn't recognize me.'[35] Stephanie immediately sought out the matron and Elizabeth's doctor, who were obviously very worried about her but seemed to have no idea what was wrong – perhaps cancer, perhaps a brain tumour? They did not know. One of the consultants who was looking after her definitely felt that alcohol was the main culprit, and he had already said that he would no longer treat her if she went on drinking. The fact that Elizabeth had had a succession of doctors over the past few years complicated matters, for no one was really certain of her medical history. Their only solution was to give her more and more drugs.

It was obvious to Stephanie that whatever was wrong with Elizabeth, she was getting no better where she was. She therefore arranged for her to be transferred to King Edward VII Hospital for Officers (Sister Agnes). There was a good deal of resistance from the first hospital, but Stephanie used her authority as 'next of kin'.

Elizabeth arrived at Sister Agnes's on 8 September. All the medication she had been on was stopped, and she was not allowed any wine. Almost immediately she began to recover, but the lack of wine made her very angry. She said King Edward's was as strict as a boarding school, and she was furious with Stephanie for transferring her – 'It was the only time she ever shouted at me.'[36] Many of Elizabeth's friends and family, however, felt that Stephanie had saved Elizabeth's life by moving her when she did.

As the days passed and Elizabeth came out of the fog of drugs, her anger turned from Stephanie and King Edward's to the hospital she had been in previously. She was distressed, frightened and furiously angry at the way she had been treated. The loss of memory upset her most, and the idea that things had been done to her without her consent. Elizabeth came out of hospital on 26 September, having been in for almost three months. She needed a long rest, preferably in the sun.

As soon as she could be moved, Gerald Asher arranged for her to go and stay with him. He lived in a warm, sunny place where Elizabeth always felt happy and well: California.

* * * * * * * *

CHAPTER TWENTY-ONE

Brave New World

Elizabeth had already been to stay with Gerald Asher in San Francisco on a number of occasions. After Asher Storey & Co. stopped trading in the summer of 1970, Gerald moved to New York and then, in 1974, to San Francisco where he settled with his two sons. He continued working in the wine business, and wrote regularly for *Gourmet Magazine*.

He had first persuaded Elizabeth to come and visit him in the spring of 1981, which was quite a feat in itself, for Elizabeth did not like the idea of America. Only two years before, when her nephew Johnny had told her excitedly that he was going to the United States, Elizabeth's reaction was 'Why on earth do you want to go there? What a waste of time.'[1] Gerald Asher had evidently been very persuasive, for Elizabeth did start contemplating the idea, but she was nervous of undertaking such a long journey alone. Hugh Johnson had encouraged her. But what finally made up her mind to take up the invitation was that her Californian friend Chuck Williams was in London at the time, and she could travel to San Francisco with him. Chuck Williams was the director of one of the largest cooking equipment stores in California. Over the years, Elizabeth had often helped him with names of suppliers, and she occasionally wrote little pieces for the magazine which accompanied his catalogue.

At that stage Elizabeth could still get about, and on that first visit Gerald Asher showed her as much of California as he could. They drove north to see the redwoods, south to Big Sur and into the

Napa valley to visit the vineyards. Elizabeth was enchanted by San Francisco: a place where fresh fruit and vegetables were not only abundant, but as beautifully presented as in France or Italy. As for the restaurants, fresh bread, good salad, real espresso coffee and cheerful service were taken for granted from the cheapest to the most expensive. The San Franciscans enjoy food and take it seriously: 'The latest restaurant,' observed Asher, 'is of more interest in San Francisco than the latest movie.'

Perhaps the biggest surprise of all was that Elizabeth, whose books had never really taken off in the States, was something of a celebrity. Her photograph, blown up to poster size, hung in the back of Chuck Williams's shop. Alice Waters, whose restaurant Chez Panisse was considered the purest expression of West Coast or Californian cuisine, always maintained that Elizabeth David was the greatest influence on her cooking. Not only that, she and her partners had come together over her books and she attributed a large part of the restaurant's success to the fact that they had held firmly to her principles. Chuck Williams, Alice Waters and Gerald Asher had spread the word and works of Elizabeth David, and in California they fell on remarkably fertile soil.

When Asher decided to take Elizabeth to Yosemite National Park, he did not worry about the lack of good restaurants on the way. They would just have to eat in a hamburger bar: 'It would have done her good, and amused her.'[2] Alice Waters had another idea. To thank Elizabeth for everything she meant to her, Alice prepared a picnic: the ultimate, fantasy picnic. The food included roast quails, herb salad, plus three different bottles of Zinfandel wine, each decanted and re-stoppered. She hunted down beautiful old linen, found just the right glasses, packed everything lovingly into huge baskets. Perhaps the most generous part of this gift was that Alice herself left Gerald and Elizabeth to enjoy it alone, which they did: on a perfect afternoon in May, by the side of the San Pedro Lake.

They spent the night in a hotel in the Yosemite mountains, and woke the next morning to six inches of snow. Then they drove back to San Francisco through the relics of California's history. Many of the old ghost towns are now firmly on the tourist track; but in Mendocino they found a shop crammed with old records of the 1930s, and in Murphys, another Gold Rush town, they discovered an ice-cream parlour which had, behind the store, the remains of a nineteenth-century above-ground ice-house. At that time, ice, cut from the Alpine Lake and stored in blocks weighing 50–100lb, was bought by householders in 25lb blocks which cost 3 cents a pound in June which rose to 12 cents in August.

It was on another trip to San Francisco that Elizabeth, following her nose, arrived at a modest eatery which served tea and grilled sandwiches. There was no proper kitchen: the food was cooked over mesquite wood, on a grill on wheels that stood out in the alley. Elizabeth could not stay to lunch; but she talked to the owner-cook, Billy West, and noted the name of his little enterprise: the Zuni Café.

Elizabeth went to the Zuni Café as often as she could, taking Gerald and other friends of his. Before long, thanks to her enthusiastic endorsement, everyone on the food scene was talking about the Zuni Café. The place took on bigger premises, installed ventilators and wood-burning stoves, and went from strength to strength; but no matter how crowded and fashionable it became, there was always a place for Elizabeth when she came to San Francisco.

Elizabeth returned year after year, between 1981 and 1990. Sometimes in the spring, sometimes in the fall, she would come and stay for one month or even two, depending on Gerald's work schedule. She loved the markets, and the second-hand bookshops. Asher remembers how out of a whole bank of books she could pick out just the one that was of interest, and talk about it as she caressed and turned it over in her hands. There was a Lebanese shop which she loved, because it contained things she had not seen since she was in Cairo: the leathery sheets of dried apricot that is softened to make a drink called *amar-el-din*, and little implements for gouging out courgettes before stuffing them.

When Elizabeth came to California in the autumn after Felicité's death, she was still very weak from her long stay in hospital. She spent a month in bed before she was strong enough to get up and about, but after that her spirits soared. She enjoyed the occasional visit to her favourite restaurants, the afternoon drives, the not-too-strenuous outings Gerald arranged to entertain her. An exhibition of jewellery by Lalique she found particularly fascinating. Some of the pieces were so large and elaborate that it was hard to work out how they would have been worn at all. She went back to see it several times.

The only worry was just how much of her time in hospital was a complete blank. She was appalled to find out that she had no recollection whatever of certain friends having come to see her, and feared that the medication she had been given had wiped out great chunks of her memory.

Gerald Asher's apartment was on the sixteenth floor of a building set high on a hill. It looked out over the Bay and the Golden Gate Bridge, and the views from the dining room were particularly fine; but Elizabeth always preferred to eat in the kitchen. Almost everything in the kitchen had been bought at her shop, and reflected her taste. They would talk at the kitchen table as she stroked his cats, while he cooked a fritatta or a risotto. Gerald knew how to awaken her appetite, merely by putting a fresh loaf, a few olives and a thick slab of butter on the table.

On one of her visits, Gerald hoped to arrange a meeting with the celebrated writer M. F. K. Fisher. Gerald wanted to meet her, and Mrs Fisher was keen to meet Mrs David. But when Gerald proposed it to Elizabeth, she was far from enthusiastic. 'Gerald,' she said, 'what on earth would we two old women have to talk about?'[3] Elizabeth did not want to see many people, preferring to be left in peace; so Gerald accepted few invitations, and chose the guests he invited to dinner with special care. 'She always wanted to know about who was coming, and why they were being asked. It was difficult for me because there were many here who wanted to meet her, and I must have given the impression that I wanted her all to myself.'⁴ So the evenings passed quietly, often with a rented movie. Sometimes a recent one, such as *Amadeus* and *The Last Emperor*, or one of the old Garbo films she was so fond of. *Citizen Kane* was another favourite, which Gerald thought they must have watched at least half a dozen times.

Within hours of her arrival, the bed looked exactly like her own in Halsey Street. On a tray were her pens and scissors, plus the little wooden-handled Opinel knife that she never travelled without. The rest of the bed soon vanished under piles of books, newspapers and magazines, marked with little yellow stickers, with her annotations and exclamations carefully written out in green ink. Beside the bed was a thermos of black coffee and a cup, at which she sipped occasionally. More black coffee arrived early in the morning, with toast and tropical fruits. The room she was given was ample and comfortable. It looked east; and on clear days, sunlight streamed in all morning.

To return to the cold, dank air of London in November 1986 was particularly depressing, even though she felt better and stronger in herself. Jean and Liz Savage saw to it that she came back to a warm house with fresh sheets and flowers. Yet Halsey Street, silted up with books, cardboard boxes full of files and papers, smelling faintly of electric fires (she had never installed central heating) must have seemed particularly cramped and dingy after California. It also brought back just how painfully she missed Felicité: at that time, Elizabeth could barely hear her sister's name without weeping.

A few days later, she saw her nephew and godson Steven Grey, who was over from Australia. Steve had never had much in common with his Aunt Liza, and was seventeen before he discovered that she was his godmother. But rather to his surprise, she was beginning to warm to him. He was a happy-go-lucky character, with that raffish, irreverent charm she had found so attractive in her youth. He seemed to enjoy a long evening spent chatting over the wine as much as she did, and he made her laugh with his wild Australian stories. When he had given up hope of any food, she leaned over her chair and peered into the oven. Out came a few little potatoes cooked in a *diable*, and a piece of salmon baked in tinfoil.

Her nephew Johnny, with his love of cooking and kitchens, had always seemed to be her natural heir; but Johnny was rather out of favour. In 1984, while Elizabeth and Jill were locked in battle with Robert Hale Ltd, he had married. Johnny and his wife Rebecca moved out of London and soon after, they had their first child. On top of all this Johnny was trying to get his business established, and looking after his sister Christabel who was a diagnosed schizophrenic. Emotionally, he could not cope with Elizabeth as well.

Johnny arranged to have lunch with her in London. She was obviously in a bad mood, and feeling resentful of what she saw as his neglect. A different character might have expressed these feelings with more sadness than anger, and so given Johnny the chance to talk about the changes and upheavals in his own life. But that was not Elizabeth's way: if she felt wronged, she had to draw first blood. Before they had even sat down at the table she announced, 'I'm leaving all my money to Steve.' To which Johnny indignantly replied that what she did with her money was her own business, and no concern of his. They made it up, and became close once more in the final years of her life; but Elizabeth's testamentary plans were never referred to again.[5]

About a year after Felicité's death, Elizabeth fell down the stairs of Halsey Street. Once again she was back in hospital. The bone was just beginning to mend when, in May, she slipped on the bathroom floor again and fractured another bone. Fortunately the Lister was a friendly hospital and Elizabeth rather enjoyed being looked after, and occupied her time on an illustrated edition of *Italian Food*. She managed to buy or borrow a small fridge. This was kept well-stocked with half-bottles of white wine ordered from Anthony Hanson's firm of Haynes, Hanson & Clark, and the foie gras and smoked salmon brought by the steady procession of friends and well-wishers. Antonio Carluccio used to bring her delicious baskets of food from his restaurant.

She emerged from hospital and resumed her normal life; but she stopped all but the simplest top-of-the-stove cooking, because she did not trust her brittle bones to support her any longer. She lived on Roka cheese biscuits, omelettes, Parma ham and the occasional delivery of oysters or smoked salmon. Otherwise, there were restaurants: the Kundan in Horseferry Road, the Phoenicia in Abingdon Road and the Hilaire in the Brompton Road. She visited this last restaurant with Richard Olney, when Simon Hopkinson was the chef. He was very pleased to be to told that she was there, and asked whether she would be willing to try some of his shrimp consommé. 'Here we go again,' grumbled Elizabeth, who did not like the ritual of the chef's specials being trotted out for her to taste; but on this particular occasion, the shrimp consommé was so good that she asked for another bowl. When Simon Hopkinson moved to Bibendum in 1987, that soon became a favourite too. There was a dish of aubergines he made, a variation of the Turkish *Imam Bayeldi*, which she ordered time after time. Soon Hopkinson was taking her out to dinner; the evening always started with a bottle of wine in the kitchen at Halsey Street.

Elizabeth's work on ice and ices had been in progress since she had finished *English Bread and Yeast Cookery*, and was still not finished. She took great pleasure in describing the elaborate feasts of the Medici and the Sun King, the sherbets of Persia, and the painstaking work of the Italian and French confectioners in creating everything from iced drinks to iced creams and sorbets. By careful research into contemporary recipes, she also conjures up an idea of what the earliest ices would have tasted like. Like her Gwynne forebears, she was fascinated by technology: of ice gathering, ice houses, iceboxes, ice pails, and the leaden moulds and *bomba*s into which the iced confections were pressed. Perhaps the greatest attraction of the work lay in the way that so many legends and conflicting accounts had grown up around the development of ices; these she was determined to unravel so as to reveal, with incontrovertible scholarship, the facts. It is not an unhappy book. Rich in anecdote and curious detail, it even includes little stories from her own past: the ices from Gunter's on a summer afternoon at the Open Air Theatre, and the barman in Darjeeling shaking ice-less martinis for her and Tony as they gazed out towards the Himalayas. Yet this is a book she wrote for herself. She set out into this frozen, sunlit landscape for her own reasons, without particularly caring whether readers would follow her or not.

Because Elizabeth herself had been so reticent, the crystallizing of her image into an icon went a few steps further. In January 1987, Radio 4 broadcast an appreciation of her work by Melissa Bakewell called *A Matter of Taste*, with contributions from, among others, Jane Grigson, Prue Leith, Michel Roux and (the late) John Lehmann. One person described it as 'a premature obituary'.[6] All the distinguished food writers and cooks interviewed had placed her work on such an Olympian level that the impression was hard to avoid. Two years later, a similar piece was put together for *Woman's Hour*. Even Elizabeth could not object to this sort of attention; but she was annoyed, almost frightened, when untrue stories about her came into circulation. She knew that these stories were like ticks: once established in print they were difficult to dislodge, and tended to grow bigger.

Some years before, Jilly Cooper had put together an anthology of women's writings and sayings with the gruesome title of *Violets and Vinegar*. Introducing a piece by Elizabeth, Jilly Cooper wrote:

'During her first flush of popularity, when the whole of the middle classes were trying out her recipes for daubes and coq au vin, a friend went to interview her and was invited to stay for dinner. He was totally enchanted by her lack of pretension. She matched him drink for drink for several hours, then, muttering that she'd better do something about dinner, went off and threw two partridges into the oven, and returned to match him for several hours more until the partridges were burnt to a cinder!'[7]

In a letter to Hugh and Judy Johnson Elizabeth explained that she had been obliged to share her meal with the journalist in question, because he simply would not leave. 'When I wrote to Jilly Cooper that her story was a complete fabrication, that the occasion had been lunch and not dinner, that there aren't too many partridges around in mid-August [when the interview took place] and I was wondering whether to reach for Lord Goodman or Sir David Napley, she replied saying she thought it was *such* a lovely story, she admired me *so* much, and the story showed how human I was, just like other people. You can't win . . .'[8]

In December 1988 Elizabeth received a letter from Nick Lander, who had been part-owner of a restaurant called L'Escargot. He was married to the writer and broadcaster Jancis Robinson, and they were putting together a series of food programmes for Channel 4 television. Nick Lander said that he would like to make a programme about her. It would be an attempt to put Elizabeth and her writing into a historical context; to look at the British diet before her books were published, and again after their impact.

Both Nick and Jancis were warned that Elizabeth was notoriously difficult to interview, and that she would probably refuse outright; but there was nothing to be lost by asking, and they were blessed with beginners' optimism. Although Jancis Robinson was an experienced presenter, this was the first time that she and her husband had produced a television programme.

To their astonishment, Elizabeth did not turn down the idea. She had her misgivings, and wondered why anyone should be interested in seeing her on television; but she liked the thought of a programme that would reaffirm her own work, at a time when the fashion in food was all nouvelle cuisine on octagonal plates. Jancis Robinson's approach to food and wine was exactly in line with Elizabeth's, and Jancis feels that she had an added advantage in being a wine writer. 'If I had been a food writer,' she explained, 'I expect I would have put my foot in it before now . . . but she was more lenient with wine writers, because she didn't know so much about the subject.'[9] The programme would be firmly restricted to her writing, and it would all take place at her favourite restaurant – the Walnut Tree at Llandewi Skirrid.

Over the first half of 1989, Elizabeth saw a lot of the Landers. They had friends in common such as the Hansons, Gerald Asher and Hugh and Judy Johnson; and she felt happy and stimulated in their company. They talked of the programme, and she particularly looked forward to seeing Ann and Franco again at the Walnut Tree Inn. A date for filming was set for 17 July. About a week before, Elizabeth got cold feet. She never threatened to pull out, but she was obviously considering ways of escape. For Nick and Jancis, who had made a considerable commitment to the programme, it was a very nasty moment; but they succeeded in reassuring her.

'Remember that no "performance" is expected of you,' wrote Jancis on 12 July. 'There are no time constraints. We can nip, tuck and destroy the tape at any point. The aim is to take you to see some old friends in a jolly nice place. You and I will talk over a glass of wine as we would do anyway and hope that some snippets of our conversation will make interesting television.'

Early on the morning of 17 July, Jill Norman accompanied Elizabeth in a hired car on the three-hour journey to Wales. The cameras started rolling the minute Elizabeth arrived at the kitchen door of the Walnut Tree, leaning heavily on Jancis, who was already there to meet her. Elizabeth was given a chance to rest, as the make-up artists powdered her nose and did her hair. The first part of the interview was the 'set-up lunch', in which Jancis and Elizabeth talked over a glass of wine and a dish of stuffed zucchini flowers. Elizabeth was disappointed that they were not allowed to sit at the table by the bar which she habitually occupied. For technical reasons they had to be in the dining room, at a table with a brown cloth. Elizabeth made it clear that she did not like tablecloths unless they were white, and she particularly hated brown ones; but the director was adamant. Not only that, he had put the camera on tracks so it could zoom in and out of her plate or her face, which made her profoundly uneasy. 'You could see the stress building up in her face as the filming progressed,' said Ann Taruschio.

When the filmed lunch was over they went out into the garden, for a real lunch with Ann and Franco. Elizabeth and Jancis, now released from the formality of interview on camera, enjoyed this a great deal more: it was a beautiful day, and by the end of the meal they were thoroughly relaxed. Then they returned indoors to another setting, and the camera was set up again to take the final part of the interview. Elizabeth was doing her best to 'perform' in so far as she was able, but by now she was tiring. The long silences were evident, and she obviously resented some questions more than others. At one point, Jancis admired the fact that Elizabeth had written her first four books in five years, and asked how she had done it. Elizabeth fidgeted impatiently, gazed over her shoulder, and when she leaned forward there was a dangerous glint in her eyes. 'Why does anyone write books?' 'For money?' ventured Jancis. Elizabeth looked at her as a teacher might look at an inattentive schoolgirl who had finally got the right answer.

The film, entitled *A Matter of Taste*, was due to be broadcast on Elizabeth's birthday: Boxing Day 1989. As the time drew nearer, Jancis wrote a piece in *The Listener* to publicize it. To Jancis, this was a straightforward publicity exercise, designed to arouse interest in the programme. To Elizabeth, it was a violation – made worse by the fact that other papers had picked up the story. She wrote an outraged letter to Jancis that went through several drafts, saying that when she had agreed to do the programme, 'I did not bargain for also being the subject of vulgar and insensitive journalism nor for finding myself bounced around every magazine and newspaper in the country. I suppose I have only myself to blame for breaking my rule of not giving interviews . . . I should have known all this could only end in tears.'[10]

One might imagine that Elizabeth resented being cast as an elusive wild animal while Jancis played David Attenborough, but it is not that to which she was objecting. Elizabeth's tone is that of a well-brought up gentlewoman who only expects to read her name in the papers in the hatched, matched and dispatched columns of *The Times* and the *Daily Telegraph*. She expected to be treated as such, even though she had been a journalist and a writer all her life.

She wrote an article about her day's filming at the Walnut Tree, but never watched the programme.[10a] When Jean McAuliffe said, 'I saw you on the telly last night, Mrs David,' Elizabeth made no answer. Many of her friends were saddened. The television camera in close-up exaggerated her age and emphasized the slightly slumped muscles to one side of her face, which had never fully recovered from the cerebral haemorrhage she had suffered twenty-five years before. This had the effect of slurring her words, and some people even reached the conclusion that she was drunk. This was not the case. According to Jancis Robinson, she consumed no more than she would normally have done at lunch with friends.

A letter from Jane Grigson must have offered much more comfort. 'Of course I wanted to appear in the Jancis Robinson programme,' she wrote.

> You know well how I have always admired you, been in awe of you, and been well aware of how much I owe you in a personal way. I was not happy about the programme. It did not emphasize your intellectual standing as a scholar, or your wonderful eye for a painting. You belong to that notable group of people that I got to know when I first met Geoffrey in the fifties, people of first-class minds who tried to share their knowledge with the rest of the population. It was an extraordinary time, all those TV programmes and good books about archaeology and painting. Geoffrey always said it took a first-class mind to popularize a subject . . . You opened a new world to us, not just the world of the Mediterranean, but a mental world as well as a sensual one.[11]

The letter must have been all the more moving to Elizabeth, who suffered the deaths of so many friends and relatives during this time, because Jane herself was dying of cancer. 'I'm going to try the Bristol Cancer Clinic for a week in March. It's a blend of raw carrots, meditation, counselling and visualization. At times I can see it will be difficult keeping a straight face, but people who've been say it's well worth going . . . Just as long as they don't expect me to go to that place in Mexico where you have to give yourself *coffee enemas* every four hours. That would be no laughing matter.'[12]

In late 1989, shortly before *A Matter of Taste* was broadcast, Elizabeth received a letter from George Lassalle in Cyprus. They had always been in touch, and he was often grateful for her advice on his cookbooks.* He now wrote to explore the possibility of writing her biography. 'Dear Liz, please don't immediately fall down and break a leg with shock, but there it is. I can do it well, I want to do it and it would give me a marvellous year's work.'[13] The answer came back swiftly: 'Dear George, I can't stop you writing a biography of me – I'm sure you have ample material – but please don't expect me to cooperate.'[14]

The spectre of a biography was bad enough; but the idea that posterity had a right to her papers was intolerable. One of her American friends had written to urge her to leave her archive to some academic institution, implying that failure to do so would be an act of irresponsibility. This had infuriated Elizabeth to such an extent that she had begun throwing out her papers there and then. April Boyes had arrived to find her outside, in her dressing-gown, stuffing file after file into her dustbins. April persuaded her to come indoors and calm down over a cup of coffee. The mood passed, and Elizabeth took no further steps to destroy her archive.

At the same time, as she grew older, she sensed that a biography

---

* On one occasion he wrote to thank her 'for saving me from the exploding pizza and the seed cake gaffe' (letter of 5.11.75), but his proof-reading skills had been of use to Elizabeth in the past. In her first book she described an Arab soup called *melokhia*. She also gave its name in Latin and Greek, but owing to an unfortunate misspelling, the Greek word read 'masturbation'. Luckily, George caught this slip before the book went into print.

would eventually be written. Through Paul Bailey Elizabeth had met Jeremy Round, a young writer who had joined the *Independent* as its food correspondent in 1986. His pieces had turned Elizabeth into a regular reader of this recently launched newspaper, for Round's blows against the adulterated, the overpriced, the over-packaged and the over-hyped were always well aimed and extremely funny. Paul and Jeremy had taken Elizabeth out to lunch one day when the subject of biography came up, and Elizabeth turned to Jeremy and said, 'If anyone writes my biography, I hope it's you.'[15] Elizabeth became very fond of Jeremy. Perhaps the little yellow stickers that occasionally appear in her archive, with comments that could only be of interest to a biographer, were addressed to him. But Jeremy Round died in 1989, aged thirty-two, before the idea was ever seriously mooted.

In the spring of 1990 she went to San Francisco again. She always dreaded coming back, and this time she returned to find that Jane Grigson was dead. It was a bitter blow, closely followed by another. Her niece Christabel Grey, then in her thirties, had committed suicide by jumping off the cliffs at Beachy Head.

Christabel's tragedy was all the more poignant because she had been a particularly gifted and beautiful child. The onset of schizophrenia had happened at the time of her mother's death, eighteen years before. Since then her mental condition had deteriorated steadily, but the note Christabel left before she killed herself shows that when she took the decision to end her life her mind was clear. Christabel had been Elizabeth's godchild, the sole daughter of her favourite sister. In fits and starts Elizabeth had tried to help her, encouraging her interests and giving her little secretarial jobs from time to time; but as her nephew Johnny remarked, 'Liza couldn't cope with mental illness. Some people can, but she simply couldn't.'

At the end of the month there came another blow: Anthony Denney died at Salvatierra, on 30 April 1990. Celia rang to tell her, and Elizabeth wrote to her soon afterwards. 'Ever since your sad telephone call – somehow I knew what you were going to say – you have seldom been out of my thoughts . . . at Salvatierra Anthony will always be with you. For that matter he will forever be sitting beside you in the car, jeep whatever – saying there's a right turn now or that's a no-entry street – You made such a happy life for Anthony. Truly, I wonder if he had ever been really happy, before he met you.'[16]

Of the four Gwynne sisters, only Elizabeth and Priscilla remained alive. They had been close in their youth, and Priscilla had had a part in Elizabeth's culinary education; she was also a skilled and enthusiastic cook in her own right. But although they exchanged bottles of olive oil at Christmas, they had drifted apart with the years; and Michael Day, who knew them both, thought it sad that they should only see each other at funerals. He arranged a dinner for Elizabeth and Priscilla at the Colony Club, hoping it would revive a certain sisterly warmth; but it did not quite work out like that. Priscilla was in a cheerful and sparkly mood, but she devoted all her attention to Michael. Elizabeth was rather disgruntled by the way Priscilla was hogging the limelight; but she liked the food, and complimented John King, who came out of the kitchen to meet her.

This was not out of politeness. Elizabeth had always set herself the highest standards; and while she was generous in her praise to any friend who cooked for her, professional chefs were expected to get things right. On one occasion, Jancis Robinson remembered taking Elizabeth to a smart new restaurant where she ate a dish of 'wild' mushrooms. Elizabeth might have kept her opinions to herself, had not the chef emerged to be introduced; but instead of the praise he was expecting, Elizabeth tore a strip off him – beginning with the fact that the mushrooms he had served her were certainly not wild.

The deaths of others could not help but remind Elizabeth of her own frailty. 'Right leg won't work,' Elizabeth wrote in her diary on

8 September; and a few days later, just as she was about to get into a taxi with Jill Norman outside Sally Clarke's restaurant in Church Street Kensington, she tripped and fell. She was helped up, and the taxi took her straight to the Lister. The break was bad and her leg took a long time to heal, and once again, she was prescribed a drug that caused her considerable alarm. To a friend she wrote, 'It was lucky for me that you came in on Friday. If you hadn't heard me – and I hadn't heard myself jabbering like an ape . . . I'd have been in a box by now . . . I'm pretty certain the new heart medication was the cause.'[17] She was home before Christmas, but from now on she could not move without a stick.

A little fridge was installed in her bathroom, so that she should not have to go all the way down to the kitchen; and although she still went out from time to time, she was more or less bed-bound by the time Jenny Lo moved in to the top flat in the summer of 1991. Jenny Lo was Chinese, as discreet and reserved a character as Elizabeth herself. She was going through a painful divorce at the time, and Elizabeth was very sympathetic.

Jenny used to bring Elizabeth her post and the papers before she went out to work. Sometimes they would fall into conversation. Elizabeth talked about how she had started cooking, her nephews, her days at Ménerbes and the Greek islands. Olivia Manning's Balkan and Levant Trilogies, collectively called *Fortunes of War*, had been dramatized for television. It was while they were talking about it that Elizabeth mentioned that 'something of me is in those books', and recalled her Cairo life with Tony. They also talked about food writers. She rated Jane Grigson very highly indeed, and approved of Delia Smith: no great stylist, but someone whose understanding of cooking was based on solid principles and experience.

Jean McAuliffe came to clean every morning, accompanied by her little daughter Carly. When Jean had first taken on the job in the early 1980s, she had explained that she could not come without the child, who was then only two years old. Elizabeth had been very uneasy about Carly at first, fearing that she would upset things or pull them about. But Carly never did cause any trouble, and as she grew older Elizabeth became very fond of her. Sometimes Elizabeth would ask Carly to take something downstairs or pass her a hairbrush, and for these little services, at the end of the week, Elizabeth would solemnly tip the child a pound.

Elizabeth was fastidious about her clothes and her immediate surroundings, and visitors to the house remember the faint smell of Penhaligon's Bluebell scent that hung in the air. Jean concentrated on the bedroom, kitchen and bathroom, for the boxes of files, the books and magazines, and the piles of paper had taken over to such an extent that cleaning the rest of the house was almost impossible; Elizabeth did not seem to mind. (There were corners of Halsey Street that had remained untouched for years: when the house was cleared it was found that pigeons were nesting in the cistern of the downstairs lavatory, which had been out of use since Elizabeth filled it with all the pots and pans she had brought back from Egypt.) So when the washing and cleaning and ironing was done, Jean also spent time keeping Mrs David company. They talked about the great 'ifs' in history, particularly those of the Tudor and Stuart periods. They were both great fans of Pepys, and told each other a lot of cat stories too.

In mid-May 1992, Elizabeth suffered a stroke. Jean came in to find her on the floor, and managed to get her up into a chair. Elizabeth was conscious but her speech was impaired, and she had lost the use of one arm. From then on she had nurses round the clock, and a stream of family and friends came to see her. To several of them she said, 'I'm going to beat this thing'; but Liz Savage remembers one of the doctors saying to a nurse, 'We are not here to cure her, just to make her comfortable.'

Gerald Asher came over from Paris as soon as he could. He described her last evening, with himself and Liz Savage, as 'much like any other, except that she couldn't move very much'.[18] Liz remembers Gerald sitting on Elizabeth's bed, making her laugh, trying to persuade her to eat. Propped up on the pillows, Elizabeth announced that she needed 'a bottle of good Chablis', and Gerald brought up some caviar which she told him he would find in the fridge. She was surprised that he did not pick up an allusion to Sir Philip Sidney. She told him to look it up, since she might have misquoted Sir Philip's famous last line: as he lay dying on the battlefield, Sir Philip gave the water he was offered to a wounded foot soldier with the words 'Thy necessity is yet greater than mine.'

'I pulled the *Chambers Biographical* off the shelf. "It doesn't help much," I told her. "There's nothing here about a glass of water." We were both still wondering about Sir Philip Sidney's glass of water when I kissed her before leaving.'[19] Gerald and Liz left before twelve: the night nurse was there, but Liz still regrets that she did not stay the night as she sometimes did. Liz was woken by the telephone at two o'clock, on the morning of Friday 22 May. Elizabeth David was dead.

The funeral took place at St Peter's ad Vincula, Folkington, on 28 May. It was a cloudy day, but the bluebells were out, glimmering through the woods. The little church was filled to bursting, the floral tributes were stupendous. And among the wreaths and baskets of lilies and blue iris, and the violets she loved, someone had left a loaf of bread, and a bunch of herbs tied up in brown paper.

* * * * * * * *

Epilogue

In her lifetime, Elizabeth was often tagged 'the doyenne' or 'grande dame' of cookery writers – to her intense irritation. 'I would thank you *not* to use that phrase,' she said with some asperity to an American journalist who had come to interview her. 'I know it means something different in America, but in England it suggests some ghastly old dragon who's stamping about with an ebony stick.'[1]

Poor Elizabeth. As soon as she was dead, such phrases larded almost every tribute and obituary that appeared in the British press. For *The Times* she was 'the doyenne of cookery writers', for the *Daily Telegraph* she was 'the grande dame of the kitchen'. The *Observer* hailed her as a 'household goddess', while the *Yorkshire Post* called her 'a latter-day Mrs Beeton'. She was the saviour of English cooking, and her pen inspired a thousand cooks. 'It is no exaggeration to say that for middle-class British people of the second half of the century she did more to change their way of life than any poet, novelist or dramatist of our time,' wrote Richard Boston in the *Guardian*.

All agreed that Elizabeth David had changed British cooking for ever, although it is hard for anyone not familiar with pre-war English attitudes to food to understand just what an impact she had made. In France and Italy it is taken for granted that food is one of the greatest pleasures in life, that one should take time and trouble to find the best ingredients one can afford, that shoddy compromises with margarine and stock cubes are unnecessary. In the England of the 1950s and 60s, this message – as championed by Elizabeth – had had all the power of startling novelty.

Her influence crossed the Atlantic. Every American cookery writer was familiar with her work; the *New York Times* wrote that 'Dozens of young chefs who have brought glory to American cooking over the last two decades are indebted to Mrs David. Alice Waters, often described as the mother of contemporary American cooking, considers Mrs David her greatest inspiration.'[2]

Ironically, the biggest side effect of the revolution started by Elizabeth David came with the proliferation of cookery programmes on television. The food writer Nigel Slater wondered whether a young, unknown cookery writer with original ideas would even get into print in today's market. 'Some of our greatest cookery classics sell just a few hundred copies a year . . . whereas a troop of all-singing, all-dancing clowns with a daytime cookery television slot may sell a quarter of a million.'[3]

Elizabeth's last book, *The Harvest of the Cold Months*, never aspired to become a best-seller, if only because the subject of ice and ices was too specialized for her regular readership. Elizabeth nevertheless wanted to see it in print. In the last years of her life, she realized she would never finish the manuscript herself and asked Jill Norman to take on the task. 'The trouble was that the book had grown without a structure,' said Jill. 'There was no logical flow. It was a collection of essays really, and images of ice and snow in different cultures at different times.' The book was published in 1994, two years after Elizabeth's death.

Elizabeth's memorial service took place at St Martin-in-the-Fields, on 10 September 1992. It was a sunny day, and the church was filled with the scent of white flowers, arranged in great pyramids by Stephanie Hoppen. There had not been more than a brief announcement in the press, but the church was packed with chefs and restaurateurs, food critics, cookery writers and wine writers – not to mention a great throng of family and friends. Leslie French, who had played with her at the Open Air Theatre, remembered her poise. In a letter read out by Sally Clarke, Alice Waters spoke of the gratitude she felt to Elizabeth and recalled the fantasy picnic she had made for her in California. Hugh Johnson observed that she 'combined the writing of an angel with a certain celestial invisibility, made your heart beat faster, turned you (or at least me) into an adoring fan with a sentence, and into a disciple with a paragraph'. Gerald Asher remembered her sitting in his kitchen in San Francisco, looking intently at a slab of butter on a white dish. 'How beautiful,' she had said.

Everyone that day had their own memory of Elizabeth and what she had meant to them; but the best expression of it came from Sally Clarke, who with Simon Hopkinson and Martin Lam, gave a celebratory picnic in her memory for friends and family after the service. In a perfect world it should have taken place on a sunny hillside, with a river near by in which to cool the wine. But although the Nash Room of the Institute of Contemporary Arts in the Mall can hardly be described as a pastoral setting, it looked beautiful nonetheless. The fireplace had been decorated with great garlands of hops and brambles and rowan berries, and on the long tables stood flower pots, some containing artichokes, some filled with fresh herbs. In between were little white bowls of olives, radishes, butter, and loaves of cornmeal and rosemary bread. At each place was a menu, rolled up with a sprig of rosemary held together with twine: rosemary for remembrance.

The rest of the meal was set out on round tables spread with blue-and-white gingham picnic cloths: *bocconcini* with basil leaves, marinated lentil and goat-cheese salad, tarts of spinach and gruyère, baby beetroots and chives, Piedmontese peppers, spiced aubergine salad, grilled tuna with red onion and beans, and a *salade de museau*. With it the guests drank a Macon Prissé 1991 and a Morgon Château Gaillard 1991. The sun streamed in through the tall windows. It was a profoundly happy and convivial meal. Everyone there understood that the best way to remember Elizabeth, then as now, was at a table with wine and talk and friends.

* * * * * * * *

Notes and Sources

EDP: Elizabeth David Papers; AC: Artemis Cooper.
Unless otherwise stated, all quotations from ED's published works
are taken from the Penguin edition current in 1999.

CHAPTER ONE: *The Gwynnes*
Main source: 'My Father's
Family', an unpublished memoir
by Katharine Ayling (daughter of
Nevile Gwynne) 1980. Also
'Wootton Manor', *Country Life*,
7 April 1955.

1. ED to Mr Shah of Nabarro &
   Co, 4.8.74.

CHAPTER TWO: *The Gwynne
Girls Grow Up*
1. Obituary of Stella Gwynne by
   Lord Archie Gordon, *The
   Times* 18.6.73.
2. EDP: draft letter to Pelham
   Maitland, undated, spring
   1974.
3. *Eastbourne Chronicle*, 12.9.14.
4. Lady Anne Brewis in
   conversation with A.C.
5. ibid.
6. *French Provincial Cooking*, p. 32.

7. *Kitchens and Their Cooks*,
   Smallbone, summer 1989.
8. ibid.
9. *French Provincial Cooking*,
   p. 279.
10. 'A la marinière', *An Omelette
    and a Glass of Wine*, p. 86.
11. *Kitchens and Their Cooks*,
    Smallbone, summer 1989.
12. EDP: draft of a letter to Mrs
    Bazell, McEvoy's daughter,
    undated; written after a visit to
    an exhibition of McEvoy's
    work at the Morley Gallery,
    Feb./Apr. 1974.
13. *Eastbourne Chronicle*, 18.10.24.
14. Barbara Doxat, letter to AC,
    25.8.97.
15. *French Provincial Cooking*,
    p. 279.
16. Jill Norman in conversation
    with AC.
17. EDP: undated draft of 'Point
    de Venise', *c.* 1963.

18. 'Remembering Aunt V': piece written by ED for Jessica Douglas-Home, biographer of Violet Gordon Woodhouse.
19. ibid.

CHAPTER THREE: *Paris and Munich*
1. EDP: undated letter from Stella Gwynne.
2. *French Provincial Cooking*, p. 24.
3. ibid. p. 23
4. EDP: undated letter from Stella Gwynne.
5. EDP: analysis by A. Dreyfus Hirtz, Paris, 24.2.31.
6. *An Omelette and a Glass of Wine*, p. 86.
7. *French Provincial Cooking*, p. 24.
8. 'Better Ways of Eating Fish', *Harper's Bazaar*, August 1955.
9. Undated letter from Stella.
10. Letter, in German and English, from 'Lalt' to EG.
11. ibid.

CHAPTER FOUR: *Acting it Out*
1. EDP: draft of a letter to Pelham Maitland, undated, spring 1974.
2. Queen Mary's diary, 11 May 1932; quoted by gracious permission of HM The Queen.
3. EDP: undated letter to the journalist Suzy Benghiat, 1985.
4. EDP: undated draft of a letter to Joan Hickson, *c.* April 1989.
5. ibid.
6. EDP: draft of undated letter to Mrs M. P. Silverman.
7. EDP: undated letter from Stella Hamilton, autumn 1933.
8. Doreen Thornton in conversation with AC.
9. Leslie French, speech at ED's memorial service, St Martin-in-the-Fields 10.9.92.
10. ED interviewed by Nancy Mills, *Daily News* (U.S.), 18.6.80.
11. *Harvest of the Cold Months*, p. 351.
12. 'Survival', *Spectator*, 28.6.63.
13. ibid.
14. ibid.
15. Ambrose Heath, *Good Food*, Faber & Faber 1932, p. 75.
16. 'Having Crossed the Channel', *Wine and Food*, spring 1965.
17. Letter to AC from Aileen Gibson Cowan, 27.10.98.

18. Doreen Thornton in conversation with AC.
19. Roger Ellis in conversation with AC.
20. Letter from Frances Harper to AC, 10.5.98.
21. Letter from ED to Frances Harper, 24.1.86.
22. ibid.
23. *French Provincial Cooking*, p. 234.
24. EDP: draft of a letter to Frances Fedden, early 1992.
25. [Charles] Gibson Cowan, *The Voyage of the Evelyn Hope*, Cresset Press 1946, p. 11.
26. EDP: ED's memoir of Sir Jasper Ridley.

CHAPTER FIVE: *Norman Douglas*
1. *The Voyage of the Evelyn Hope*, pp. 11–38.
2. ibid.
3. ibid.
4. ibid.
5. ibid.
6. ibid.
7. ibid.
8. Patrick Leigh Fermor in conversation with AC.
9. Mark Holloway, *Norman Douglas*, Secker & Warburg, 1976, pp. 424–9.
10. 'Have It Your Way', *An Omelette and a Glass of Wine*, p. 122.
11. ibid.
12. ibid.
13. op. cit., p. 123.
14. *The Voyage of the Evelyn Hope*, p. 59.
15. op. cit., p. 57.
16. 'Have It Your Way', *An Omelette and a Glass of Wine*, p. 120.
17. ibid.

CHAPTER SIX: *The Loss of the Evelyn Hope*
1. *The Voyage of the Evelyn Hope*, pp. 61–106.
2. ibid.
3. ibid.
4. ibid.
5. ibid.
6. ibid.
7. ibid.
8. Norman Douglas to EG, 23.9.40.
9. 'Pudding and Pickles', *Spectator*, 24.11.61.
10. ibid.
11. ibid.
12. ibid.
13. *The Voyage of the Evelyn Hope*, p. 158.
14. Robin Fedden to EG, 28.11.40.

15. Charles Gibson Cowan, personal log, 16.11.43.

CHAPTER SEVEN: *Alexandria*

1. EDP: draft of a letter to Frances Fedden, early 1992.
2. EDP: draft of 'Two Cooks', *Wine and Food*, 1951.
3. Elizabeth to Charles Gibson Cowan, 16.10.41.
4. EDP: draft of 'Two Cooks', *Wine and Food*, 1951.
5 Undated letter from Max Bally to EG.
6. EDP: draft of a letter to Frances Fedden, early 1992.
7. Elizabeth to Charles Gibson Cowan, 8.10.41.
8. Elizabeth to Charles Gibson Cowan, 9.12.41.
9. ibid.
10. ibid.
11. ibid.
12. ibid.
13. Elizabeth to Charles Gibson Cowan, 18.3.42.
14. EDP: draft of a letter to Frances Fedden, early 1992.

CHAPTER EIGHT: *Tony David*

1. Roger Eland in conversation with AC.
2. Christopher Kininmonth, *Frontiers*, Davis Poynter, 1971, p. 9.
3. George Lassalle, *The Fish in my Life*, Macmillan, 1989, pp. 27, 28.
4. EDP: unpublished article in MS (Anastasia, Suleiman).
5. J. M. Richards, *Memoirs of an Unjust Fella*, Weidenfeld & Nicolson, 1980, p. 180.
6. EDP: unpublished article in MS (Anastasia, Suleiman).
7. ibid.
8. 'Fast and Fresh', *An Omelette and a Glass of Wine*, p. 22.
9. Josette d'Amade in conversation with AC.
10. ibid.
11. Elizabeth to Charles Gibson Cowan, June 1942.
12. Telegram dated 12.8.43.
13. Two undated letters from Elizabeth to Charles Gibson Cowan, August 1943.
14. EDP: Tony David to EG, 15.6.44.
15. ibid.
16. EDP: letter from Tony David, 28.5.44.

17. EDP: letter from Tony David, undated.
18. EDP: letter from Tony David, 29.5.44.
19. EDP: letter from Tony David, 25.5.44.
20. EDP: letter from Tony David, 8.7.44.
21. EDP: letter from Tony David, 20.7.44.
22. EDP: letter from Tony David, 24.7.44.
23. EDP: letter from Tony David, 8.8.44.
24. Jenny Lo in conversation with AC.
25. Olivia Manning, *The Levant Trilogy*, originally published by Weidenfeld & Nicolson, Penguin Books, 1982, pp. 457–8.

CHAPTER NINE: *Indian Interlude*
1. Veronica Nicholson in conversation with AC.
2. *Spices, Salt and Aromatics in the English Kitchen*, p. 161.
3. *Summer Cooking*, pp. 214–15.
4. EDP: undated letter from Eddie Gathorne-Hardy.

CHAPTER TEN: *Back in Blighty*
1. 'Look to Your Tables', *Spectator*, 2.3.62.

2. Doris Lessing, 'The Roads of London', *Granta: Ambition*, summer 1997, pp. 54–5.
3. Marguerite Patten O.B.E., *The Victory Cookbook*, Hamlyn 1995, p. 10.
4. 'Fast and Fresh', *An Omelette and a Glass of Wine*, p. 24.
5. 'John Wesley's Eye', *An Omelette and a Glass of Wine*, p. 19.
6. ibid.
7. EDP: untitled, perhaps unpublished piece.
8. 'John Wesley's Eye', *An Omelette and a Glass of Wine*, p. 19–20.
9. Letter from Caroline Lassalle to AC, 22.9.96.
10. 'John Wesley's Eye', *An Omelette and a Glass of Wine*, p. 20.
11. EDP: early draft of piece entitled 'How it All Began', *Spectator*, 1.2.64 (re-named 'John Wesley's Eye' by ED, and reprinted in *An Omelette and a Glass of Wine*).
12. 'John Wesley's Eye', *An Omelette and a Glass of Wine*, p. 21.
13. EDP: early draft of 'How it All Began'.
14. ibid.

15. George Lassalle, *The Adventurous Fish Cook*, Macmillan 1976 p. 52.
16. EDP: early draft of 'How it All Began'.
17. EDP: letter from George Lassalle, undated; first part of letter lost.
18. EDP: unpublished piece (cars/holidays) undated.
19. EDP: Stella Hamilton to Tony, undated, mid-November 1947.
20. EDP: draft of petition for divorce, July 1958.
21. ibid.
22. Neville Phillips, in conversation with AC.
23. EDP: petition for divorce, July 1958.

CHAPTER ELEVEN: *Mediterranean Food*

1. EDP: undated letter from Veronica Meagher, 1949.
2. Anne Scott-James in conversation with AC.
3. EDP: letter from Herbert Joseph, 2.2.49.
4. Frances Spalding, *Dance Till the Stars Come Down: a Biography of John Minton*, Hodder & Stoughton, 1991, p. 106.

5. Introduction to *A Book of Mediterranean Food*.
6. Letter from ED to Lady Sibell Rowley, undated.
7. EDP: Peter Higgins to ED, 17.1.49.
8. Johnny Grey in conversation with AC.
9. Johnny Grey, *The Art of Kitchen Design*, Cassell, 1994, pp. 53–4.
10. Veronica Nicholson in conversation with AC.
11. Lady Sibell Rowley in conversation with AC.
12. Veronica Nicholson in conversation with AC.
13. Elizabeth Nicholas, *Sunday Times*, 4.6.50.
14. John Chandos, *Observer*, 18.6.50.
15. EDP: O.W. Darch to ED, 23.6.50.
16. EDP: letter from Lawrence Durrell, June 1950.
17. EDP: draft of a letter to Patricia Siddall of Penguin Books, February 1963.
18. Veronica Nicholson in conversation with AC.
19. EDP: undated letter to John Lehmann.
20. EDP: letter from John Lehmann, 2.10.50.

21. EDP: letter from Stella Hamilton, 9.8.51.
22. Doreen Thornton in conversation with AC.
23. ibid.
24. ibid.
25. EDP: letter from Hamish Erskine, September 1951.
26. 'The Cooking of Provence', *Harper's Bazaar*, June 1955.
27. EDP: letter from George Lassalle, 4.7.51.
28. EDP: letter from Jane Stockwood to ED, 5.6.51.
29. EDP: letter from Stella Hamilton 27.7.51.

CHAPTER TWELVE: *Italian Food*

1. EDP: letter from J. C. Hall, 19.10.51.
2. John Lehmann, *The Ample Proposition*, Eyre & Spottiswoode, 1966, p. 151.
3. EDP: Italian notebooks, 1952.
4. EDP: letter from John Lehmann, 22.5.52.
5. EDP: undated letter from Derek Hill.
6. EDP: Italian notebooks, 1952.
7. ibid.
8. ibid.
9. *Italian Food*, p. 123.
10. EDP: Italian notebooks, 1952.
11. ibid.
12. ibid.
13. *Italian Food*, p. 169.
14. EDP: letter from John Lehmann, 24.6.52.
15. EDP: draft of an undated letter to Renato Guttuso.
16. EDP: draft to Michael Rubinstein of her dealings with Macdonald.
17. *Italian Food*, Introduction to the first Penguin edition.
18. ibid.
19. EDP: draft of 'Grabbies', which appeared as 'How Publishers Like to Have Their Cake and Eat It', *Tatler*, October 1985.
20. ibid.
21. ibid.
22. ibid.
23. 'Is Butter Better?', *Daily Express*, 21.6.54.
24. Introduction to the first Penguin edition.
25. Olivia Manning, *Jerusalem Post*, 12.11.54.
26. EDP: draft of a letter to Anthony Denney, spring 1965.
27. EDP: letter from ED to Lynette Hunter, 27.2.89.
28. Eunice Frost in conversation with AC.

CHAPTER THIRTEEN: *Friends, Editors and Other Enemies*

1. EDP: draft of a letter to Nicholas Serota, 19.11.91.
2. EDP: list of bequests attached to ED's will.
3. Veronica Nicholson in conversation with AC.
4. EDP: letter from Anthony Hunt, *House and Garden*, 27.11.53.
5. Introduction to *An Omelette and a Glass of Wine*, pp. 16–17.
6. *Sunday Times*, 9.11.58.
7. *Sunday Times*, 2.9.56.
8. Ernestine Carter, *With Tongue in Chic*, Michael Joseph, 1974, pp. 85–6.

7. EDP: letter from Avis de Voto, 8.2.58.
8. Simon Hopkinson and Lindsey Bareham, *The Prawn Cocktail Years*, Macmillan, 1997, p. 137.
9. EDP: deposition for divorce, 14.7.58.
10. Doreen Thornton in conversation with AC.
11. EDP: draft of letter to Jean LeRoy of the *Sunday Times*, May 1959.
12. EDP: letter to Audrey Withers, 6.7.59.
13. ibid.
14. Doreen Thornton, *Standard-Triumph Review*, No. 10, 1959.

CHAPTER FOURTEEN: *On the Road in Provincial France*

1. EDP: piece on cookery book illustration.
2. EDP: undated letter (*c.* late sixties) to Sybille Bedford.
3. Doreen Thornton in conversation with AC.
4. 'Golden Delicious', *An Omelette and a Glass of Wine*, p. 83.
5. EDP: pocket diary, 3.1.58.
6. EDP: undated letter from Roald Dahl.

CHAPTER FIFTEEN: *The Year of Betrayal*

1. 'French Cooking in England', in *French Provincial Cooking*, p. 17.
2. EDP: letter from Lawrence Durrell, autumn 1956.
3. EDP: draft of 'Grabbies', which appeared as 'How Publishers Like to Have Their Cake and Eat It' in *Tatler*, October 1985.
4. EDP: short piece on connections with Michael Joseph.

5. EDP: draft of an introduction to *French Provincial Cooking*.
6. *Daily Worker*, 8.12.60.
7. EDP: letter to Neil Hogg, 29.11.69.
8. ibid.
9. Katharine Whitehorn, 'The Compleat Imbiber: A Profile of Cyril Ray', *Wine* Magazine, Christmas 1973.
10. EDP: letter to Ailsa Garland, on resignation from *Vogue*, October 1960.
11. EDP: Daniel S. Watson, Lahore, 8.11.61.
12. Anthony Hanson, 'Personal Memories of Elizabeth David', speech given at the PEN Club, June 1998.
13. EDP: Iain Hamilton to ED, 2.7.62.
14. EDP: draft of a letter to the management of Walls.
15. EDP: letter to Mme Noëlla Audas, 6.10.62.
16. Hugh Johnson in conversation with AC.
17. EDP: draft of an article for *Wine and Food* on William Verral.
18. EDP: letter from Leslie Nye, undated, *c.* October 1962.
19. EDP: draft of a letter to Peter Higgins, undated.

20. EDP: draft of a letter to Eunice Frost of Penguin Books, February 1963.
21. ibid.
22. EDP: letter to Lesley O'Malley from Tangier, 24.3.63.
23. ibid.

CHAPTER SIXTEEN: *Farewell to P.H.*
1. 'Points de Venise', *Spectator*, 14.6.63.
2. EDP: letter from Sybille Bedford, 9.7.63.
3. EDP: draft of a letter to Sybille Bedford, 8.9.63.
4. Sybille Bedford in conversation with AC.
5. ibid.
6. ibid.
7. ibid.
8. EDP: letter from Julia Child, undated, 1963.
9. *Spectator*, 18.10.63; reprinted in *An Omelette and a Glass of Wine*, p. 280.
10. 'Golden Delicious', *Spectator*, 10.1.64; reprinted in *An Omelette and a Glass of Wine*, p. 83.
11. Annotation by Gerald Asher to Anthony Hanson's 'Personal Memories of Elizabeth David',

speech given at the PEN
Club, June 1998.

CHAPTER SEVENTEEN: *The Shop*

1. 'Para Navidad', *Nova*, July
   1965; reprinted in *An
   Omelette and a Glass of Wine*,
   p. 94.
2. Letter to Anthony Denney,
   13.7.64.
3. ibid.
4. EDP: letter to Mrs A.
   Mather, 26 March 1965.
5. EDP: draft letter to Anthony
   Denney, spring 1965.
6. EDP: drafts of letters to
   Anthony Denney, 1965.
7. Peter Trier in conversation
   with AC.
8. EDP: drafts of letters to
   Anthony Denney, 1965.
9. ibid.
10. Jill Norman in conversation
    with AC.
11. 'Garlic-presses are Utterly
    Useless', *Tatler*, February
    1986.
12. Drusilla Beyfus, *Telegraph
    Magazine*, November 1965
13. EDP: draft letter to Jane
    Grigson, March 1988.
14. Michael Zyw, letter to AC,
    5.6.98.
15. Sybille Bedford in
    conversation with AC.
16. Letter from Celia Denney to
    AC, 3.5.99.
17. April Boyes in conversation
    with AC.
18. EDP: draft of a letter to an
    unnamed correspondent.

CHAPTER EIGHTEEN: *Salt and
Spice*

1. 'Bruscandoli', in *An Omelette
   and a Glass of Wine*, p. 107.
2. Introduction to *English Food:
   A Rediscovery of British Food
   from before the War*, by
   Arabella Boxer, Hodder &
   Stoughton, 1991, p. 1.
3. op.cit., p. 13.
4. EDP: draft of a letter to
   Pelham Maitland, *c.* 1974.
5. Ellen-Ann Hopkins in
   conversation with AC.
6. ibid.
7. Katharine Ayling, 'My
   Father's Family', unpublished
   memoir, 1980, p. 287.
8. ibid., p. 291.
9. EDP: draft of a letter to
   Christopher Grey, *c.* March
   1974.
10. ibid.
11. EDP: letter to Renée, 29.5.72.

12. April Boyes in conversation with AC.
13. EDP: to Renée, 5.7.72.
14. EDP: to Renée, 27.7.72.
15. EDP: postcard from Renée Fedden, 2.9.72.
16. Letter from Celia Denney to AC, 14.1.99.
17. April Boyes in conversation with AC.
18. ibid.
19. Letter to Anthony and Celia Denney, 14.6.73.
20. EDP: letter to Mr Crowe, June 1973.
21. George Elliott in conversation with AC.

CHAPTER NINETEEN: *Baking Bread*
1. *English Bread and Yeast Cookery*, p. 195.
2. ibid., p. 364.
3. April Boyes in conversation with AC.
4. *English Bread and Yeast Cookery*, p. 172.
5. EDP: draft letter to Lynn Hughes, 14.7.87.
6. EDP: draft of a letter to Franco Taruschio, 29.11.80.
7. Jill Norman in conversation with AC.

8. EDP: draft of a letter and poem to John Lehmann, *c.* May 1977.
9. Letter from George Lassalle to AC, 28.7.96.
10. Jack Andrews in conversation with AC.
11. Hilary Spurling, *Observer*, 18.12.77.
12. Paul Levy, *Books and Bookmen*, Jan. 1978.

CHAPTER TWENTY: *Omelette and Ice*
1. *Daily Telegraph*, Peterborough column, 14.4.78.
2. Stephanie Hoppen in conversation with AC.
3. Hilary Spurling in conversation with AC.
4. EDP: notes on typescript of *Elinor Fettiplace's Receipt Book*, edited by Hilary Spurling (Salamander Press and Penguin Books, 1986).
5. Ellen-Ann Hopkins in conversation with AC.
6. John Hopkins, *The Tangier Diaries 1962–1979*, Arcadia Books, 1997, p. 239.
7. EDP: letter from Viola Johnson, 2.4.79.

8. Jill Norman, ed., *South Wind through the Kitchen*, Michael Joseph, 1997, p. 1.
9. *Petits Propos Culinaires*, 41, p. 8. Tribute to ED.
10. Jill Norman, ed., *South Wind through the Kitchen*, p. 1.
11. Letter from Richard Olney to AC, 6.5.99.
12. EDP: draft of a letter to Sybille Bedford, undated.
13. Jill Norman in conversation with AC.
14. Johnny Grey in conversation with AC.
15. EDP: letter from Anthony Denney, 18.4.86.
16. Letter to Rosi Hanson, 15.7.82.
17. Derek Cooper in conversation with AC.
18. Recording of *The Food Programme*, with ED, 22.10.82.
19. Jill Norman in conversation with AC.
20. Jeremy Lewis, *Kindred Spirits: Adrift in Literary London*, HarperCollins, 1995, pp. 233–4.
21. Jane Grigson, *Times Literary Supplement*, 21.12.84
22. Angela Carter, 'An Omelette and a Glass of Wine and Other Dishes', *London Review of Books*, vol. 7, no. 1.
23. ibid.
24. Ann Barr and Paul Levy, *The Foodie Handbook*, Ebury Press, 1984, p. 7.
25. Paul Levy in conversation with AC.
26. Ann Barr in conversation with AC.
27. EDP: letter from Peter Higgins, 22.2.86.
28. Jill Norman in conversation with AC.
29. Letter from ED to Celia Denney, 4.4.86.
30. ibid.
31. Stephanie Hoppen in conversation with AC.
32. Letter from ED to Celia Denney 4.4.86.
33. Stephanie Hoppen in conversation with AC.
34. Rupert Grey in conversation with AC.
35. Stephanie Hoppen in conversation with AC.
36. ibid.

CHAPTER TWENTY-ONE: *Brave New World*

1. Johnny Grey in conversation with AC.

2. Gerald Asher in conversation with AC.
3. ibid.
4. ibid.
5. Johnny Grey in conversation with AC.
6. EDP: Nick Lander, letter to ED, 29.12.88.
7. *Violets and Vinegar, an Anthology of Women's Writings*, ed. Jilly Cooper and Tom Hartman, George Allen & Unwin, 1980, p. 103.
8. Letter to Hugh and Judy Johnson, 28.2.85.
9. Jancis Robinson in conversation with AC.
10. Draft of an undated letter to Jancis Robinson.
10a. *Sunday Telegraph Review*, 24.12.89.
11. EDP: letter from Jane Grigson, 16.1.90.
12. ibid.
13. EDP: letter from George Lassalle, 15.12.89.
14. EDP: draft of a letter to George Lassalle, 24.12.89.
15. Paul Bailey in conversation with AC.
16. EDP: draft of letter to Celia Denney.
17. EDP: letter to Ellen-Ann Hopkins, November 1990.
18. Gerald Asher, Obituary of ED, *Independent*, 25.5.92.
19. ibid.

Epilogue
1. Nancy Mills, *Daily News*, 18.6.80.
2. *New York Times*, 10.6.92.
3. Nigel Slater, *Waterstone's Magazine*, Winter/Spring 1997.

Selected Bibliography

Ayling, Katharine, 'My Father's Family', unpublished memoir, 1980

Boulestin, Marcel, *Having Crossed the Channel*, Heinemann, 1934

Boxer, Arabella, *Arabella Boxer's Book of English Food*, John Curtis
at Hodder & Stoughton, 1991

Burnett, John, *Plenty and Want: A Social History of Diet in England
from 1815 to the Present Day*, Routledge, 3rd edn, 1989

Barr, Ann and Levy, Paul, *The Foodie Handbook*, Ebury Press, 1984

Chaney, Lisa, *Elizabeth David: A Biography*, Macmillan, 1998

Cooper, Artemis, *Cairo in the War 1939–1945*, Hamish Hamilton,
1989

Cowan, [Charles] Gibson, *Loud Report*, Michael Joseph, 1938; *The
Voyage of the Evelyn Hope*, Cresset Press, 1946

David, Elizabeth

    A Book of Mediterranean Food: first published John Lehmann,
        1950; revised editions 1955, 1958, 1965, 1988; new introduction
        1991

    French Country Cooking: first published John Lehmann, 1951;
        revised editions 1958, 1966

    Italian Food: first published Macdonald & Co., 1954; revised
        editions 1963, 1969, 1977, 1987

    Summer Cooking: first published Museum Press, 1955; revised
        edition 1965

    French Provincial Cooking: first published Michael Joseph, 1960;
        revised editions 1965, 1967, 1970

Spices, Salt and Aromatics in the English Kitchen: first published
Penguin Books, 1970; revised editions 1973, 1975

English Bread and Yeast Cookery: first published Allen Lane, 1977

An Omelette and a Glass of Wine: first published Jill Norman at
Robert Hale Ltd, 1984

Harvest of the Cold Months: first published Michael Joseph, 1994

Douglas-Home, Jessica, *Violet: The Life and Loves of Violet Gordon
Woodhouse*, Harvill Press, 1996

Grey, Johnny, *The Art of Kitchen Design*, Cassell, 1994

Grigson, Jane, *Good Things*, Michael Joseph, 1971; *English Food*,
Macmillan, 1974

Hardyment, Christina, *A Slice of Life: The British Way of Eating
since 1945*, BBC Books, 1995

Hartley, Dorothy: *Food in England*, Macdonald, 1954

Holloway, Mark, *Norman Douglas*, Secker & Warburg, 1976

Lasalle, George, *The Fish in My Life*, Macmillan, 1989

Leyel, Mrs F. C, and Hartley, Olga, *The Gentle Art of Cookery*,
Chatto & Windus, 1925

Norman, Jill, *South Wind through the Kitchen: The Best of Elizabeth
David*, Michael Joseph, 1997

Patten, Marguerite, *The Victory Cookbook*, Paul Hamlyn, in association with the Imperial War Museum, 1995

Spurling, Hilary, *Elinor Fettiplace's Receipt Book*, The Salamander
Press, in association with Penguin Books, 1986

Index

ED stands for Elizabeth David

Abdelouahid 294–5
Aberdeen and Temair, Countess of 10
Adair, Robin 139–40
Alexandria
  ED in during war 84–5, 90, 91–4
Anastasia (Alexandrian cook) 86
Anderson, Diana 57
Andrews, Jack 300
Angela (Maltese cook) 52, 55
Arlott, John 301–2
Art of Simple French Cooking, The
  (Watt) 213
Asher, Gerald 336
  and ED's last evening 332–3
  in San Francisco 315, 316, 319–20
  and sardines 220–1
  and wine 217, 230, 231
Astor, Mrs David (Clare) 307
Auchinleck, Gen. Sir Claude 93, 95, 117
Ayling, Katharine (née Gwynne) 6, 53

Bailey, Paul 302–3, 329
Bakewell, Melissa 323
Baking of an English Loaf, The
  (booklet) 250, 264
Balfour, David 101
Bally, Max 89
Barattero, Mme 199, 309
Barette, Mme 29–30, 198
Barr, Ann 309–10
Barrington, Bill 25

Bastard, Algernon 146
Baxter, Walter 184, 187
Beaumes de Venise 230–1
Bedford, Sybille 227–9, 246–7, 271,
  296, 301
Beeton, Mrs 214, 231
Benckendorff, Count Constantine 41, 49
Beyfus, Drusilla 245, 311
Blakemore, Jane 298
Blow, Detmar 8–9
Bolland, Jean 281–2, 286
Bologna 172
Book of Mediterranean Food, A 87,
  139–45, 151–4, 239
  agreement to publish by John
    Lehmann 143–4
  appreciation of and success xiv, 153
  illustrations 144, 152
  initial rejections from publishers 142
  Penguin edition 180–1, 181–2, 222
  publication and reviews 151–2
  use of other authors in 141
Boston, Richard 334
Boulestin, Marcel 46, 140, 163, 231, 261
Bowles, Paul 176, 294
Boxer, Arabella 260–2
Boxer, Mark 310–11
Boyes, April 247, 248, 270, 271–2,
  279–81, 300, 328
bread book *see English Bread and Yeast
  Cookery*

Brien, Alan 215
British Food Export Council 270
Brownhill, Doreen *see* Thornton,
    Doreen
Butterworth, Marian *see* Thomas

Cadec, Madame 237–8, 239, 240–41
Carels, John 2
Carlisle, Earl and Countess of 119–20
Carluccio, Antonio 322
Carroll, Sydney 42
Carter, Angela 308
Carter, Ernestine 139, 192–3, 204–5
Carter, John 139, 141
Catsaflis, Renée *see* Fedden, Renée
Cecil, Vera 12, 21
Chancellor, Robin 142
Chandos, John 152
Charcuterie and French Pork Cookery
    (Grigson) 251
Child, Julia 230
Clarke, Sally 336
Classic French Cuisine, The (Donon) 213
Clifford, Alexander 99
Cohen, Chapman 47
Collins, Alex 237
Colquhoun, Archie 169
Conran, Caroline 291
Conran, Terence 238, 243
Cookery in Colour (Patten) 213–14
Cookery and Household Management
    (Beeton) 214
Cooper, Derek 303–4, 310
Cooper, Jilly 323–4
Cooper, Guy 292
Costa, Margaret 247
Crespigny, Caroline de 288
Cumberlege, Mike 63, 82, 86, 89, 90,
    117
Cumberlege, Nancy 63–4
Cunard, Nancy 66

Dahl, Roald 201, 298
Daily Express 177–8, 191
Daily Telegraph 216, 217–18

Daintrey, Adrian 180, 188
d'Amade, Josette 104–5
Daniels, Anthony 189
David, Anthony (Tony) (ED's
    husband) 156–7
  army career 108–9
  background 107–8
  death 253–4
  ED's feelings for 112, 114, 125,
    137–8
  filing for divorce by ED 146, 203
  involvement in setting up club
    135–6
  leaves Indian army 133
  love for ED 109–10, 114, 125,
    145–6, 203
  marriage and honeymoon 111–14
  moves to Spain 183
  posted back to India 117, 118
  strains in marriage 136–7
David, Beatrice 107–8
David, Elizabeth (née Gwynne)
  Food and Cooking 127–9, 159
    attitude towards 149
    auction of kitchen contents xiii–xv
    in Cairo 103–4
    dealing with rationing 126–7
    first cookery books 44–6
    first introduction to French
      cooking and seafood 29, 31
    influence of Boulestin 46
    influence of Norman Douglas 66–7
    kitchens and utensils 147–8, 149,
      162, 299–300
    learning to cook 38, 43–5, 79
    loss of sense of taste 231
    love of olive oil 246
    making pickles in Syros 80
    in Morocco 223–4
    photographs of food 195
    shop venture *see* Elizabeth David
      Ltd
    taste in wine 172, 217, 229, 247,
      296, 333
    testing of recipes 151, 175, 189

David, Elizabeth – *cont.*

Early Years

birth and christening 11

childhood and upbringing 12, 14, 15–16, 18–19

debutante and presentation at court 32–3, 35–6

and father's death 21, 23

holidays 23–5

lack of affection shown by mother 14, 15, 23, 24

love of reading 16

memories of Wootton 26–7

in Munich 32, 33, 36

nursery food 16–18

in Paris and attending the Sorbonne 29–31

platonic relationship with older man 33–4

portrait by McEvoy 20–1

relationship with Aunt Violet 25, 26

relationship with cousin Anne 18, 24

relationship with father 7, 14–15

relationship with sisters 15

running away 18–19

schooling 22–3, 28

tea with mother 19

Personal Life

ancestry and family background 1–9

appearance and dress style xv, 51, 283–4

attachment to Wales and visits to 54–5, 282–3, 285, 286

attitude towards children 48, 130, 186–7, 210

attitude towards money 31, 44, 59, 134

attributes 29–30

awarded CBE and OBE 24, 285, 289, 311–12

awarded honorary doctorate from University of Essex 291

book collection and love of books xvi, 271–2, 293

car accident and injuries sustained 287–8, 290

and cats 15, 211

cerebral haemorrhage 225–6, 231, 327

characteristics xvii–xx, 30–1, 99–100, 109

circle of friends 184, 187–8, 300–3

daily routine 189

and death of ex-husband 253–4

death and funeral 333

and death of mother 273

and death of sister Diana 263–4

and death of sister Felicité 312, 313, 320

deterioration of marriage and divorce 136–7, 145–6, 151, 203

diet in later years 322

and drinking 225, 231–2, 314

early married life 114–15

entertaining 189–90

flats in London 43–4, 46, 54

fragility in later years 321, 330–1

and Halsey Street 134, 136–7, 183

handwriting analysis 30–1

interest in history 292

interviews of 245, 246, 303–4

job as 'showroom second' for Worth 55–6

London life after return from India 125–6

marriage and honeymoon 113–14

memorial service 335–6

obituaries 334

and painting 28, 36

painting collection 188–9

in Ross-on-Wye 130–1

and Rupert Grey's claim to Wootton 268

stroke 332–3

television programme on 324–7

theatre career 37–9, 41, 42–3

David, Elizabeth – *cont.*
  on Tory Island 203–4
  Relationships and Friendships
    Anthony Denney 235, 236–7
    Charles Gibson Cowan *see* Gibson
      Cowan
    Diana (sister) 262–3
    Doreen Thornton 42, 64–5, 175,
      204, 225, 301
    Edward Marjoribanks, 35
    Felicité (sister) 184–5
    George Lassalle 100–1, 110,
      129–30
    husband *see* David, Anthony
    mother 36, 37, 51, 272
    Norman Douglas *see* Douglas,
      Norman
    Peter Higgins *see* Higgins, Peter
    Peter Laing 92, 93–4, 96–7, 100,
      124, 169
    Priscilla (sister) 64, 187
    Renée Fedden *see* Fedden, Renée
    Stanford Holme 38, 41, 42
    Sybille Bedford 227–9, 301
  Second World War
    in Alexandria 84–5, 86, 87, 90,
      91–3, 94
    in Athens 77–8
    in Cairo 94–5, 100, 101–3
    escape from Crete 82–3
    in France 62–3, 68, 70
    internment in Italy 72–6
    leaving of Corsica for Giglio 71–2
    leaving of France for Corsica
      68–9, 70–1
    leaving of Syros for Crete due to
      bombing 82
    running of reference library in
      Cairo 98–9, 124
    in Syros 78–81, 124
  Travels
    buying trips in France for shop
      241, 253, 254–5, 264
    Capri 161, 163, 165
    Corsica 57

    Denmark 269–70
    Egypt 53–4
    France 56–7, 154
    French travels in *Evelyn Hope*
      60–3
    India 118–23
    Italy 164–72, 172–4
    Malta 51–2, 54
    Ménerbes (France) 156–60
    research trips to France 197–200,
      205–7, 278–9
    San Francisco 316–20, 329
    Sardinia 171–2
    Spain 235–7, 272
    Tangier 293–5
    Venice 167, 169–70, 256–7
  Writing Career 155
    attributes xv
    'Author of the Year' in
      Glenfiddich Awards 291
    awarded Fellowship of the Royal
      Society of Literature 309
    begins to write in Ross on Wye
      131–2, 133
    booklets written for shop 250
    contribution to *Sunday Times
      Travel Guide to France* 153–4
    and *Daily Express* 177–8, 191
    and *Daily Telegraph* 216, 217–18
    and editors 140, 192–3
    and English food 261–2
    enhancement of reputation 209
    and *Go* 153
    and *Harper's Bazaar* 139–40, 154,
      155, 159, 190–1, 194
    and *House and Garden* 190–1, 194
    influence and impact of xv,
      334–5
    influence on other writers 250–2
    little books 250
    and Macdonald publishers *see*
      Macdonald
    and *Nova* 239
    opinion of own 179
    and *Petits Propos Culinaires* 296

David, Elizabeth – *cont.*
    reviews of books 151–2, 178–9,
      213, 289
    and Robert Hale publishers
      305–6, 307, 311
    and *Spectator* 214–15, 218, 220,
      221, 227, 230, 232, 236, 261
    and *Sunday Dispatch* 216
    and *Sunday Times* 191–3, 204–5
    and *Tatler* 310–11
    upsetting of food industry 218
    visit to sardine cannery in Nantes
      219
    and *Vogue* 194–7, 198, 200, 202,
      215–16
    Wine and Food articles 220
    see also individual books
David, Ivor 107
Davidson, Alan 252, 295
Davidson, Jane 295
Day, Michael 302, 330
Denmark ED's trip to 269–70
Denney, Anthony 194–5, 195–6, 205,
    206, 215, 284–5, 301
    background 195
    death 329–30
    and design of shop 238, 241, 242
    engagement to Celia 248
    relationship with ED 235, 236–7
Denney, Celia (née Royde-Smith) 247,
    248, 272, 329
Douglas, Norman 89, 122, 141, 165
    in Capri 161
    death 164
    and ED's marriage 115
    and food 66
    forced to leave Italy 64
    influence of on ED 66–7, 124
    letters to ED 70–1, 76–8
    relationship with ED 64–5, 68–9,
      164
Dried Herbs, Aromatics and Condiments
    (booklet) 250
Ducat, Mr 216
Durrell, Eve (née Cohen) 101, 107

Durrell, Lawrence 85, 99, 101, 153,
    209

Eland, Roger 99, 252
'Elizabeth David Classics' 306, 311
Elizabeth David Ltd. 240–50, 275–6
    attempts by ED to change its name
      after her departure 275–6
    buying trips in France 241, 253,
      254–5, 264
    design 242–3
    ED working in 243–5, 247, 248
    mail-order and wholesale 249–50
    naming of 242
    opening 243
    plans for 237–9
    premises and stock 240–1
    resignation and severance of all
      connections with by ED 274,
      276
    staff 247–8
    tensions and growing crisis between
      ED and partners 249, 253,
      68–9, 270, 272, 273
Ellis, Roger 49–50, 130
English Bread and Yeast Cookery 275,
    277–8, 284
    ED receives award for 291
    importance of in campaign for better
      bread 289–90, 291–2
    publication and reviews 289
    research for 279–82
English Potted Meats and Fish Pastes
    (booklet) 250
Epstein, Jerry 307
Erskine, Hamish St-Clair 150, 157, 158
Evelyn Hope, The Voyage of the, 60–63,
    72–3

Fedden, Frances 58, 86, 186–7, 247,
    248
Fedden, Renée (née Catsaflis) 91, 94–5
    background 88–9
    buying trips to France with ED
      254–5, 264

Fedden, Renée – *cont.*
  on ED's marriage 114
  falling out with ED over shop 271,
    272, 273, 274, 288
  friendship with ED 88, 89, 91,
    264–5
  marriage 94
  resignation from shop 269
  and Rosie Peto 254
  and shop 238, 249, 253, 270
Fedden, Robin 81, 85, 88, 89, 101, 126,
    254
  death 288
  marriage 94
  relationship with ED 53–4, 57–8
Fisher, M.F.K. 301, 319
Florence 166–7
Folkington Manor 2–3, 8, 266
Food Programme 303
Fortunes of War (Manning) 102,
    115–16, 331
France
  ED's buying trips 253, 254–5, 264
  ED's research trips 197–200, 205–7,
    278–9
  visits to by ED 56–7, 154, 156–60
Freeman, Denis 126, 136–7, 142, 156
French Country Cooking 156, 159,
    161–3
French, Leslie 42, 335
French Provincial Cooking 198, 208–9,
    211–13
  dedication 212
  illustrations for 212
  publication by Michael Joseph 211–
    13
  reception 213
  research trips for 197–9
Frost, Eunice 181, 222, 239
Furness, Professor Robin 90

Garland, Ailsa 215
Gathorne-Hardy, Eddie 101, 117, 122
Gautier, Théophile 141
Gentle Art of Cookery, The (Leyel) 44, 45

Gibson Cowan, Leonard (Charles)
  in Athens 77–8
  background 46–7
  ending of relationship with ED 83,
    85
  French travels in *Evelyn Hope* 60–3,
    67–8
  internment in Italy 73–5
  joins *Samothrace* as bosun 87–8
  Loud Report 46, 47, 58
  relationship with ED 47–9, 54, 58,
    63, 67, 70, 105–7
  teaching job in Syros 78, 79
  theatre career 42, 47, 52
  and *The Voyage of the Evelyn Hope*
    60, 82–3, 88, 105, 204
  ED's reactions to 105, 204
Gillie, Oliver 291
Gilmour, Ian 215
Glenfiddich Awards 291
Go 153
Goldsworthy, Mrs 250
Good Food (Heath) 45–6
Goodwin, Dorothy and Teddy 51, 53,
    85
Gordon, Dudley 11
Gould, Cecil 126
Grace, Aunt *see* Palmer, Grace
Graham, Antonia 247
Granville, Lady (Grace) 292
Grey, Christabel 321, 329
Grey, Diana (née Gwynne) 129–30
  birth 11
  character 49
  early years and schooling 15, 22
  and ED's marriage 114
  holiday in Venice with ED 256–7
  living with Benckendorffs 41, 49
  marriage 91, 125, 186
  relationship with ED 262–3
  relationship with Roger Ellis 49–50
  rift with Aunt Violet 125
  suffering from tinnitus 256, 258, 262
  suicide 35, 263
  and Wootton 267–8

Grey, Douglas 135, 256
Grey, Dr Christopher 91, 125, 186,
    256, 262, 263, 267, 313
Grey, Johnny 148, 149, 186, 286–7,
    299, 300, 321, 329
Grey, Martin 267
Grey, Rupert 96–7, 262, 267, 268
Grey, Steven 320–1
Grigson, Geoffrey 251
Grigson, Jane 251, 252–3, 260, 302,
    307–8, 311, 323, 327–8, 329
Guttuso, Renato 169, 170, 171, 178,
    222
Gwynne, Agnes (née Anderson) (great
    grandmother to ED) 1, 2
Gwynne, Diana (sister) see Grey,
    Diana
Gwynne, Dorothy (aunt) 2, 3, 12, 20
Gwynne, Evelyn 2
Gwynne, Felicité (sister)
    attitude towards food 185
    birth 11
    bookselling career 156, 200–1, 211
    character 155, 185
    death and burial 312–13
    during Second World War 127, 155
    early years and schooling 15, 22, 25–
        6, 41
    and ED's bread book 278
    ill-health 297
    relationship with ED 184–5
    stroke and death 312
    suffering from malnutrition 297–8
    typing of ED's articles 155, 156
Gwynne, James (grandfather) 1–2,
    3–4, 6, 7, 11, 12, 20
    will 7–8, 11, 20, 22, 267
Gwynne, John (great grandfather) 1
Gwynne, Kathleen (cousin) see Ayling
Gwynne, May (née Purvis)
    (grandmother) 2, 3, 11
Gwynne, Nevile (uncle) 2, 3, 4, 6, 7,
    12, 13
Gwynne, Priscilla (sister) see Longland,
    Priscilla

Gwynne, Reginald (uncle) 2, 4
Gwynne, Roland (uncle) 2, 3, 12, 20
    awarded DSO during First World
        War 13–14
    dissipating of inheritance 22
    and Folkington 8, 11, 266
    in nursing home 266
    relationship with Stella 39
    upbringing 3
    and Wootton 40
Gwynne, Rupert (father) 2, 3, 4–6
    affair with Vera Cecil 11–12, 21
    death and funeral 21
    early years 2–3
    education and career 4–5
    and father's will 20
    marriage 6, 7
    political career 7, 11, 13, 20
    weak heart 5, 19–20
    and Wootton 8
Gwynne, Stella (née Ridley) (mother)
        135, 266
    and antiques 50, 134, 135, 187
    appearance and dress style 10, 39
    attitude towards Charles Cowan 48,
        51
    death 272
    and death of Edward Marjoribanks
        35
    end of marriage to Hamilton and
        move back to England 50
    feud with Violet Gordon
        Woodhouse 12, 26
    finances 32
    first husband's affair 12
    first husband's death and after 22
    first marriage 6, 11
    and First World War 13
    and James Gwynne's will 11
    lack of affection shown towards
        daughters 14, 15, 23, 24
    and painting 28
    personality and talents 10, 14
    relations with Rupert's family 12
    relationship with ED 36, 37, 51, 272

Gwynne, Stella – *cont.*
  relationship with Roland 39
  second marriage to John Hamilton
      and move to Jamaica 40
  Wootton 22, 39
Gwynne, Violet *see* Woodhouse, Violet
      Gordon

Habitat 238–9
Haines, Arthur Lett 187–8, 189, 223
Hale, John 305, 306
Hamilton, Iain 218
Hamilton, Major John 40, 50
Hamlyn, Paul 214
Hammond, Nicholas 82
Hanson, Anthony 217, 325
Hanson, Rosi 247, 300, 325
Harcourt-Smith, Charles 265
Harcourt-Smith, Sabrina (née
      Longland) 26, 265–6, 267
Harper, Frances 56
Harper's Bazaar
  ED's articles 139–40, 154, 159,
      190–1, 194
Harris, Clifford 311
Harris, Katherine 36
Harrods 216, 236
Harvest of the Cold Months, The 304,
      306, 322–3, 335
Harvey, Captain Eric 176, 177
Harvey, Wilfred 176
Heath, Ambrose 45–6
Hebdon, Peter 212
Herbert Joseph 142
Henry, Mr and Mrs Rex 223–4
Herbal Review, The 292
Hickson, Joan 38
Higgins, Kathleen (née Dunn) 150
Higgins, Peter 119, 146
  affair and relationship with ED 149,
      150–1, 160, 174, 203, 210–11,
      212
  and Anne Holland-Martin 225,
      232
  background 118, 149–50

  ED keeps in touch with 284
  ending of affair with ED 232–3
Higgins, Rupert 149
Hill, Derek 166, 178, 203
Hodgkin, Eliot 188
Hodson, Harry 205
Hogg, Douglas (1st Viscount
      Hailsham) 21–2
Hogg, Neil 89, 213
Hogg, Quintin 22
Holland-Martin, Anne (née Fane) 225,
      232
Holme, Stanford 37–8, 39, 41, 42
Holme, Thea 37
Holroyd, Michael 309
Home Baked (Scurfield) 275
Hope-Nicholson, Felix 159
Hopkins, Ellen-Ann (née Ragsdale)
      248, 265, 293, 294, 306–7
Hopkins, John 293, 294
Hopkinson, Simon 322
Hoppen, Stephanie 292–3, 312,
      313–14
Hotel du Midi 199–200
House and Garden 190–1, 194
Hunt, Anthony 191
Hunter, Barbara (later Doxat) 46

India
  ED in 118–23
Inglis, Brian 215, 218
Italian Food 167, 175
  and American market 201–2
  commissioning of 164
  illustrations 169–70, 178, 222–3
  Penguin editions 172, 179, 222
  publication and reception of 178–9
  reaction to by Macdonald publishers
      176–7
  success 179
  wine chapters 172
Italy
  ED in 164–72, 172–4
  food in 163
  wine 172

'Janet' 128–9
Jasper, Uncle see Ridley, Jasper
Jenkinson, Rosalind 247, 262
Johnson, Arthur 164, 165, 178
Johnson, Hugh 219–20, 301, 336
Johnson, Judy 301
Johnson , Viola 164–5, 178, 230, 295
Joseph, Anthea 211, 212
Joseph, Michael 211
Josipi 78, 79, 80

Keik, Ian 211
Kemsley, 1st Viscount 153
Kenney-Herbert, Colonel 119, 258
King, John 330
Kininmonth, Christopher 100
Kinross, Patrick 101, 117
Knopf, Alfred 201
Korchinska, Maria 41
Kyriacou (Greek cook) 86, 87

Laing, Peter 92, 93–4, 95–6, 96–7,
    100, 115, 124, 169
'Lalt' 33–4
Lampson, Miranda 109
Lander, Nick 324, 325
Lane, Allen 181
Lassalle, George 132, 328
  affair with ED 100–1, 110, 129–30
  marriages 187, 288
Leech, Richard 313
Lehmann, John 154, 156, 180, 222, 242
  closure of company 176
  ED's poem for 285–6
  and Italian Food 163, 170
  and Mediterranean Food 142–3,
    143–4, 144–5
Leigh Fermor, Patrick 100, 118, 190
Leith, Prue xiv, 323
Léontine (Parisian cook) 29, 32
Lessing, Doris 126
Levin, Bernard 215
Levy, Paul 289, 309, 310, 311
Lewin, Patrick 136
Lewis, Jeremy 307

Leyel, Hilda 44, 45, 55, 231, 259, 261
Llewellyn, Bryan 240, 241, 249
Llewellyn, Daphne 109, 110
Llewellyn, Hermione see Ranfurly
Llewellyn, Owen 107–8
Lo, Jenny 331
Longland, Priscilla (née Gwynne) 90–1
  birth 11
  daughters 125
  early years and schooling 13, 15, 22,
    24
  ED's visits to Malta to see 51–2, 54
  end of marriage 151
  engagement and marriage 39, 40–1
  and marriage of daughter Sabrina
    265
  relationship with ED 64, 187, 330
  and Wootton 266–7
Longland, Richard Barnes 39, 40–1,
    51, 151
Longleat 292
Loud Report (Gibson Cowan) 46, 47, 58
Lyall, Archie 164
Lyon 199
Lyttelton, Alfred 11

McAuliffe, Carly 331–2
McAuliffe, Jean 299, 331–2
McConnell, Kathleen 96
McDermott, Gracie 203–4
Macdonald (publishers) 201, 224
  and Italian Food 176–7, 179–80, 181
  losing of Guttuso illustrations 222,
    224, 232
  and Mediterranean Food 181–2
McEvoy, Ambrose 20–1
McPherson, Kenneth 161
Mafalda (cook, Capri) 165
Manning, Olivia 101–2, 115, 179, 331
Margaret, Princess 250
Marjoribanks, Edward 35
Marple, Lesley 296
Mary, H.M. Queen 36
Mastering the Art of French Cookery
    (child) 230

Matter of Taste, A (Radio 4 broadcast) 323, 328

Mayer, Tony and Thérèse 157

Meade, Antonia 32

Meagher, Veronica *see* Nicholson, Veronica

Mediterranean Food see Book of Mediterranean Food, A

Menasce, Georges de 94, 114

Middle Eastern Food, A Book of (Roden) 251–2

Midleton, Countess of 32, 35

Milan 167–8

Minton, John 144, 152, 156, 222

Montgomery, General Bernard 95

Moorehead, Alan 99

Morny, Patrick de 183–4

Morphy, Countess 44, 55, 231, 261

Morris, Cedric 188, 189

Murchie, Joyce 184, 187, 247

Museum Press 142, 180

Nash, John 188

Nerina, Zia 172

New Writing 142–3

Newnham-Davis, Lt Col. 141, 146

Nicholas, Elizabeth 151–2, 153

Nicholson, Major John 151, 224

Nicholson, Veronica (nee Meagher) 190, 291 and ED's writing 139–40, 145 in India 118–19, 121 marriage 151 relationship with ED 136, 224

Nijinsky, Vaslav 137

Norman, Jill xvi, xvii, 243–4, 258, 284, 300, 304–5
and Robert Hale 306, 311
editing of ED's books 239–40, 281, 304

Nova 239

Observer 251

Official Foodie Handbook, The (Levy and Barr) 308, 310

olive oil 246

Olney, Richard 295–6, 297

Olympia Food Fair (1956) 192

O'Malley, Kate 187

O'Malley, Lesley (née Pares) 126, 183–4, 225, 298–9

Omelette and a Glass of Wine, An xvi, 304, 305–6, 307–8, 309, 311

Open Air Theatre (Regent's Park) 42

Oxford Repertory Theatre 37–9

Palmer, Anne (ED's cousin) 18, 23, 38–9, 41, 122–3

Palmer, Grace (née Ridley), Viscountess Wolmer, Countess of Selborne (aunt to ED) 10, 18, 23, 40, 41–2

Palmer, Roundell Cecil (Viscount Wolmer), 3rd Earl of Selborne (uncle to ED) 18, 21

Parma 170

Parrish, Walter 224

Patten, Marguerite 127, 174, 213

Penguin 180–1, 222, 239

Perrier, M, chef at Hôtel du Midi 199–200

'Peter the Pole' 313

Petits Propos Culinaires 295–6

Peto, Rosie 249, 254, 273, 274

Phillips, Neville 126, 136–7, 142

Piccini, Giulia 166

Pugh, Pam 240, 249, 253, 254

Purnell 176

Ragsdale, Ellen-Ann *see* Hopkins, Ellen-Ann

Ranfurly, Hermione, Countess of (née Llewellyn) 109, 114–15

Ray, Cyril 215, 232

Renny, Juliet 212

Recipes of All Nations (Morphy) 44

Richards, Jim 104

Richardson, Judith 161, 187

Ridley, Katharine 24

Ridley, Grace *see* Palmer, Grace

Ridley, Jasper (son of uncle Jasper) 117

Ridley, Sir Jasper (uncle to ED) 23, 37, 38, 58–9
Ridley, Nathalie 23
Ridley, Stella *see* Gwynne, Stella
Ridley, 1st Viscount 6
Robert Hale Ltd (publishers) 305–7, 311
  dismissal of Jill Norman from 306
Robinson, Jancis 324
Roden, Claudia 251–2
Round, Jeremy 329
Rowe, Vivian 213
Rowley, Lady Sibell (née Lygon) 145, 151, 224, 225
Rowley, Michael 145, 151
Royal Society of Literature 309
Royd-Smith, Celia *see* Denney, Celia
Rubinstein, Michael 232
Russell, Leonard 153, 191

San Francisco 316–20
San Remo 168
Sandoe, John 200, 297, 298
Sardinia 171–2
Savage, Elizabeth 248, 278–9, 300
Scott, Paul 180, 201, 211
Scott-Ellis, Jim 111
Scott-James, Anne 139, 140–1, 194
'Scrambled Eggs Variation 77' 285–6
Scurfield, George and Cecilia 275
Seafish of Tunisia (Davidson) 252
Selborne, 3rd Earl and Countess of, *see* Palmer
Slater, Nigel 335
Smart, Lady (Amy) 54, 102
Smart, Sir Walter 54, 102
Smith, Arnold 95
Smith, Delia 331
Smith, John 268–9
Smith, Reggie 102, 126
Smollett, Tobias 277
Spectator
  ED stops writing for 232
  ED's articles for 214–15, 218, 220, 221, 227, 230, 232, 236, 261

Spencer, Bernard 101
Spices, Salt and Aromatics in the English Kitchen 259–60
Spurling, Hilary 289, 293
Stark, Freya 99, 178–9
Strachey, Julia 132, 143
Suleiman xvii, 103–4
Summer Cooking 121, 160, 178, 180, 240
Summers, Romney 90, 157, 158
Sunday Dispatch 216
Sunday Times
  Campaign for Real Bread 291
  ED's articles for 191–2
  interview with ED 246–7
  relationship between ED and Ernestine Carter 192–3, 204–5
  resignation of ED 205
  series on French markets 204, 206
Sunday Times Travel Guide to France 153–4
Syllabubs and Fruit Fools (booklet) 250
Syros
  bombing of by Germans 82
  ED's life in during war 78–81, 124

Taruschio, Ann and Franco 179, 283, 326
Tatler 310–11
Taylor, Gordon 292
Telegraph magazine 245
Thomas, Marian 29, 43, 46, 48, 55, 91
Thomas, Peter 91
Thornton, Colin 175, 204
Thornton, Doreen (née Brownhill) 48, 56–7, 157, 272
  accompanies ED on French trips 133, 198, 205, 207
  first impression of ED 42
  friendship with ED 42, 64–5, 175, 204, 225, 301
Thynne, Lord Christopher 292
Tollemache, Denis 25
Tory Island 203, 204
Tower, Jeremiah 296

Trier, Jenny 238, 240, 249
Trier, Peter 238, 241, 249
Trust House Hotel's catering manual
    132–3
Tulleken, Kit van 311
Turin 173
Twining, Herbert 1

University of Essex 291

Venice
    ED's visits to 167, 169–70, 256–7
Verona 167
Verral, William 231
vinegar 'mother' 245
Vogue
    ED's articles 194–5, 198, 200, 202,
        215–16
    'Food at Its Best' series 196, 198
Voto, Avis de 202
Voyage of the Evelyn Hope, The
        (Cowan) 61, 82–3, 88, 105, 204

Walnut Tree Inn 179, 283, 325
Waters, Alice 317, 335, 336
Watt, Alexander 213

Waugh, Evelyn 145, 179
West, Billy 318
White, Sir Matthew 6–7
Whitehorn, Katharine 214, 215, 232
Willert, Paul 187
Williams, Chuck 316, 317
Wine and Food 219–20
Wine and Food Society 219
Withers, Audrey 194–5, 196, 197, 204,
    215
Woodhouse, Gordon 4
Woodhouse, Violet Gordon (née
        Gwynne) 2, 3, 4, 5, 24–5
    character 25–6
    feud with Stella 12, 26
    men friends 4, 25
    musical talent 3
    rift with Diana 125
Wootton house 8–9, 266

Yannaki 78, 79, 80

Zoppi, Signor 167
Zuni Café 318
Zwy, Lesley 246
Zwy, Michael 246

Dignity in Healthcare

A practical approach for nurses and midwives

Edited by

MILIKA RUTH MATITI

PhD MSc BCur (I et A) MCM RGN

Lecturer

University of Nottingham, School of Nursing,
Midwifery and Physiotherapy (Boston Centre), UK

and

LESLEY BAILLIE

PhD MSc BA(Hons) RNT RGN

Reader in Healthcare

Faculty of Health and Social Sciences, University of Bedfordshire, UK

Foreword by

PAULA McGEE

RN RNT PhD MA BA Cert Ed

Professor of Nursing

Birmingham City University, City South Campus, Birmingham, UK

Radcliffe Publishing

London • New York

Radcliffe Publishing Ltd
St Marks House
Shepherdess Walk
London
N1 7BQ
United Kingdom

www.radcliffepublishing.com

Electronic catalogue and worldwide online ordering facility.

British Library Cataloguing in Publication Data

A catalogue record for this book is available from the British Library.

ISBN-13: 978 184619 390 3

The paper used for the text pages of this book is FSC® certified. FSC (The Forest Stewardship Council®) is an international network to promote responsible management of the world's forests.

Typeset by Phoenix Photosetting, Chatham, Kent, UK
Printed and bound by TJI Digital, Padstow, Cornwall, UK

Contents

Dedication   vii

Tribute to Paul Wainwright   viii

Foreword   ix

Preface   xii

About the editors   xviii

Contributors   xix

Acknowledgements   xxiv

Abbreviations   xxv

Section 1   Dignity in healthcare: setting the scene   1

1   The importance of dignity in healthcare   3
         Milika Ruth Matiti

2   The concept of dignity   9
         Milika Ruth Matiti and Lesley Baillie

3   Professional and ethical expectations for dignity in care   24
         Paul Wainwright

4   Dignity as a policy issue in healthcare   37
         Alistair Hewison

5   Care environments that support dignity in care   52
         Ann Gallagher

6   Staff behaviour and attitudes that promote dignity in care   62
         Lesley Baillie

Section 2   Dignity in different healthcare settings   79

7   Dignity for children   81
         Paula Reed

8   Dignity in maternity care   95
       Barbara Burden

9   Dignity and older people   109
       Wilfred McSherry and Helen Coleman

10 Dignity at the end of life   126
       Davina Porock

11 Community care and dignity   142
       Candice Pellett

12 Dignity in acute and critical care   156
       Lesley Baillie

13 Dignity in mental health: listening to the flying saint   171
       Gemma Stacey and Theodore Stickley

14 Dignity and people with learning disabilities   186
       Bob Hallawell

Section 3   Developing dignity in healthcare   199

15 Education to promote dignity in healthcare   201
       Liz Cotrel-Gibbons and Milika Ruth Matiti

16 Enabling dignity in care through practice development   220
       Kate Sanders and Jonathan Webster

17 Dignity in care: the way forward   239
       Lesley Baillie and Milika Ruth Matiti

Index   255

Dedication

This book is dedicated to pre-registration healthcare students and all health-care workers who are committed to promoting dignity in healthcare but have been frustrated due to the lack of a comprehensive text book on the subject that they can use. We also hope that it will be an inspiration to those in training or healthcare workers who have not yet realised the importance of dignity in healthcare.

Tribute to Paul Wainwright

Paul died suddenly on 16 June 2010 as this book was going to press. His very significant contribution to nursing philosophy, ethics and medical humanities was acknowledged in the many tributes from colleagues around the world. Paul will be greatly missed for his generosity of spirit, intellectual rigour and commitment to the value of nurses and nursing. He had the ability to make complex ideas accessible and applicable to everyday practice. Paul was an exemplary teacher, researcher and academic and contributed to the flourishing of many colleagues, practitioners and students. He demonstrated dignity in his everyday and professional lives, offering wise counsel when invited to and giving freely of his time. His contribution to dignity scholarship and research has been substantial, and the field has suffered a tragic loss.

Foreword

Dignity is one of a cluster of interrelated concepts that are difficult to unravel: respect, status, privacy, self-esteem, shame. These concepts form part of the taken-for-granted element of our daily lives. We do not often talk about them overtly, and consequently do not find them easy to explain. When pressed, we tend to draw on negative rather than positive factors. We all know, or think we know, what it means to lose one's dignity by, for instance, being made to look foolish or belittled. Inherent in these feelings is the notion that we have, somehow, been reduced or exposed in ways that affect our self-worth. We are diminished as human beings both in our own eyes and in the estimation of others. Dignity is, therefore, a matter of concern to everyone. It is a global concern in healthcare and fundamental for every patient or client. Quality care requires a commitment to dignity, irrespective of the setting in which that care is delivered.

Certain situations are particularly likely to produce feelings of an assault on our dignity. Our sense of ourselves, the images we project to others, and how we expect them to treat us are easily undermined by sickness and disease. Our bodies or minds no longer behave as we wish and, consequently, we find ourselves depending on others. It is in the shift to dependence that our dignity is first compromised. Pain, illness and suffering threaten our security and lead inexorably to the unmaking of our world (Scarry, 1985).

The behaviour of those to whom we turn for help can make matters worse. Nurses, midwives and other healthcare workers, whose roles bring them into intimate contact with others, can easily undermine their patients' self-worth. Usually this is through sheer thoughtlessness, such as neglecting to make sure that curtains are drawn right around a bed or that someone is not exposed while being transported to the bathroom. At other times it may be due to the pressures placed on practitioners that cause them to appear brusque in their dealings with patients and families. There is no intention in such events to undermine patients' dignity. Nurses and midwives simply overlook the details, turning what should be a caring encounter into an uncaring one.

If these were the only examples, there would perhaps be less need for this book, but, unfortunately, numerous reports have highlighted shortcomings on a much larger scale. Individuals make mistakes and benefit from reminders but where leaders cease to pay attention to direct patient care, systemic failures occur throughout an organisation. Such failure was markedly evident in the inquiry into events at mid-Staffordshire hospitals, where patients were left in soiled sheets, unable to care for themselves. Relatives had to:

> spend extended periods attending to their relatives' hygiene needs. This included having to get the patient to and from the bathroom, washing, and attending to other personal care needs. Little assistance was offered . . . and there was a fear that if families did not attend to such care the staff would not do so (Francis, 2010, p.11).

Patients did not receive sufficient food or drink. Wards were not cleaned properly. There was evidence that patients were treated with 'rudeness or hostility' (Francis, 2010, p.13). The inquiry's report makes disturbing reading. Clearly, something was seriously wrong but it would be incorrect to think that the mid-Staffordshire hospitals are the only example of such failings. As this book makes clear, numerous other reports have demonstrated similar shortcomings over and over again, since Barbara Robb first reported the warehousing of elderly people in the 1960s (Robb, 1967). Time and again promises are made that nothing like this will ever happen again. Time and again promises are broken because human nature does not change; people will not change without conscious effort.

This book is a welcome attempt to address the crux of the matter. Ultimately, the art of helping others lies in the way in which that help is given. This calls for the development of a heightened sense of self-awareness, a process described as *emotional labour* (Smith, 1992). As the term suggests, this is not easy. Working on the self requires honesty and effort in examining our own practice, the humdrum, day-to-day procedures that we scarcely think about but that can so profoundly affect the well-being of others. Urinary catheterisation, administering medication, bed bathing, and forceps delivery may be among the things we do every day, but to our patients they are unusual, often unwelcome, experiences. The attitude and communication skills of the individual practitioner can do much to ensure that these and other similar experiences are not made worse; indeed, I would hope that they are actually improved by careful attention to the patients' dignity (Campinha-Bacote, 2002).

While there have been previous attempts to address dignity, for example through the Dignity in Care campaigns run by the Department of Health and the Royal College of Nursing, there is no other text devoted solely to the subject. This book will, I am certain, make a major contribution to the initial preparation of nurses and midwives. It explores dignity in care from a multidimensional perspective. It will promote an understanding of the nature of dignity in healthcare and how dignity can be promoted in practice. I hope that, in years to come, readers of this book will follow the examples of professional leadership demonstrated here by the two authors in compiling this book, and always seek to make the maintenance of patient dignity one of their foremost priorities.

REFERENCES

Campinha-Bacote J (2002) Cultural competence in psychiatric nursing: have you 'asked' the right questions? *Journal of the American Psychiatric Nurses Association* 8:183–7.

Francis R (2010) *Independent Inquiry into Care Provided by Mid-Staffordshire NHS Foundation Trust January 2005–March 2009*, Volume I. Chaired by Robert Francis QC. London: The Stationery Office.

Robb B (1967) *Sans Everything: a case to answer.* London: Nelson.

Scarry E (1988) *The Body in Pain. The Making and Unmaking of the World.* Oxford Paperbacks.

Smith P (1992) *The Emotional Labour of Nursing.* London: Macmillan.

Paula McGee
RN RNT PhD MA BA Cert Ed
Professor of Nursing, Birmingham City University
November 2010

Preface

To our knowledge, no book exists that exhaustively focuses specifically on the subject of dignity in healthcare. This book therefore has two major aims: to explore the importance of dignity for patients and clients in different healthcare settings and to stimulate healthcare workers to understand ways of promoting dignity for patients and clients. This book suggests that healthcare workers should translate dignity into straightforward practical terms and apply these in day-to-day practice. While the book is primarily aimed at nursing and midwifery students, it is also relevant interprofessionally and applicable to those who work in healthcare in general. Thus, where possible, the book explores the concept of dignity in care from multiprofessional perspectives. At the time of writing, the contributors were all based in the UK but they draw on research conducted in a wide range of countries, highlighting the relevance of this topic across the world. Most of the book's content is applicable worldwide although the legislation, health policy and profession-specific content discussed are largely UK derived.

THE CONTRIBUTORS AND THE STRUCTURE AND CONTENT OF THE BOOK

The book's editors and other contributors come from different areas of healthcare, reflecting the importance of dignity in every healthcare specialty. All contributors are committed to the promotion of patient and client dignity and they offer their experiences in research, teaching and clinical practice. Together, they comprehensively address dignity with practical application, drawing on their experiences and knowledge. The contributors recognise that the concept of dignity is relevant to healthcare workers at international level and although they use UK-based scenarios to exemplify their ideas, they hope that readers from other countries will find their discussions applicable to their own settings.

The book has 17 chapters divided into three sections.

Section 1 – Dignity in healthcare: setting the scene

This section explores the meaning of dignity and the context in which dignity is understood and applied in healthcare practice. It would be difficult for healthcare workers to promote patient or client dignity if they did not understand and reflect on the concept of dignity. Promoting dignity is influenced by a number of factors; therefore, it is also essential for healthcare workers to understand how factors such as expectations of professionals, health policy, the care environment and staff behaviours and attitudes affect dignity. This section comprises six chapters. In Chapter 1, Milika Ruth Matiti discusses the importance of dignity in healthcare, reviewing research from patients' and healthcare professionals' perspectives as well as professional guidelines. In Chapter 2, Milika Ruth Matiti and Lesley Baillie explore the concept of dignity and what promoting patient or client dignity entails; they draw on a wide range of literature, including their own research, to explore the concept's varying aspects, perspectives and applications to healthcare. The chapter uses scenarios and reflective exercises to enable readers to relate the content and application of the concept of dignity to their own experiences and healthcare practice. In Chapter 3, Paul Wainwright explores the concept of dignity from the perspective of professional practice and from the expectations of the general public and service users. He explores the popular understanding of the concept of dignity as revealed by the media and everyday usage. He relates this account to the purpose and practice of nursing and examines the implications in terms of the expectations of both professionals and service users.

In Chapter 4, Alistair Hewison commences by explaining how policies are developed, and follows with an examination of England's Dignity in Care campaign, launched by the Department of Health. The chapter explores how 'dignity' has become an important consideration for all who work in UK healthcare. The chapter identifies the dilemmas that occur where policy and practice intersect, and different strands of policy are in conflict. In Chapter 5, Ann Gallagher examines the relationship between care environments and dignity. The chapter discusses the meaning and contribution of the care environment to dignity in care. Two aspects of the care environment are discussed: the physical care environment and other aspects of the organisation, which include the culture and leadership. Some of the concerns relating to undignifying care environments are examined, and examples of good practice discussed. It is concluded that reflection on, and improvements to, the care environment makes a significant contribution to patients, relatives and staff feeling valued and respected.

In Chapter 6, Lesley Baillie explores staff behaviour and attitudes affecting dignity in care, with a particular focus on healthcare workers' communication with patients, their provision of privacy for patients and delivery of fundamental care. With illustrative examples, the chapter reviews research findings of how staff behaviour affects patients' dignity, demonstrating how this behaviour can support dignified care in situations where dignity is under threat. The chapter considers how staff behaviour and attitudes may be influenced by the culture within which they work and how staff can respond when colleagues compromise the dignity of patients and clients.

Section 2 – Dignity in different healthcare settings

This section discusses dignity for people at different stages of their lifespan and when undergoing healthcare in various settings, thus acknowledging that dignity is important to all patients and clients. Readers will be able to select those chapters that are most relevant to their area of healthcare practice, while also developing a broader understanding of dignity across the healthcare spectrum. Each chapter explains the particular factors that influence dignity in this area of practice and illuminates how dignity can be promoted for specific patients and clients.

There are eight chapters in this section. In Chapter 7, Paula Reed explores the meaning of dignity for children, drawing on her ethnographic research undertaken with children and their families in hospital. She points out that dignity for children is often overlooked and that, indeed, sometimes it is considered of lesser value or relevance than the dignity of adults. The chapter explores some of the issues that are pertinent to the dignity of children, illuminating the vulnerability of children, with particular reference to power, control and decision making. The chapter explores the relationship between family-centred care and the dignity of children and examines how the care environment affects dignity, including aspects such as privacy and staff–patient relationships.

In Chapter 8, Barbara Burden focuses on how women's dignity can be affected during pregnancy and childbirth; in particular, she explores the relationship between dignity and privacy. The chapter draws on work undertaken during Barbara's doctoral research in maternity care environments, which used observation and interviews with mothers. She illuminates the strategies that mothers use to deal with affronts to their dignity and what healthcare professionals can do to support them.

In Chapter 9, Wilfred McSherry and Helen Coleman explore dignity with reference to older people and why they are vulnerable to a loss of dignity. The chapter discusses what is important for older people's dignity. This is illustrated with examples of where dignified care for older people might not have been achieved in various settings. The discussion draws on research findings and reports. Practical ways of promoting dignity for older people are provided in the chapter.

In Chapter 10, Davina Porock considers the meaning of dignity at the end of life and the context of death and dying, with particular reference to the UK and current trends of where people die. The purpose of this chapter is to explore why dignity is so important at the end of life and how health professionals can facilitate respect for dignity with the dying person and their family. The chapter is divided into two main sections: the meaning of dignity at the end of life and facilitating dignified dying. The main focus is on dying and death in older age groups because that is predominantly when death occurs in our society. The chapter explores preferences for end-of-life care and examines how healthcare workers can facilitate dignified dying through their interventions, as patients, residents and clients approach the end of life.

In Chapter 11, Candice Pellet examines dignity in care for patients in community settings, taking the UK context as an example. The importance of promoting the dignity of clients and patients in settings such as the patients' own homes, care homes, clinics and general practitioner surgeries is discussed. Challenges faced by health professionals in maintaining dignity within the community are analysed. Community nurses often work with patients and their families over a long period of time, so it is imperative to build trusting relationships in order to promote independence, choice and empowerment on their healthcare journey. The chapter includes case studies relating to community patients with chronic wounds, those undergoing palliative care and those who have long-term conditions.

In Chapter 12, Lesley Baillie explores the vulnerability of patients undergoing acute and critical care, highlighting the patients' anxiety, lack of control and dependency that may result from their acute health problems. She considers the activities and processes that are experienced in acute and critical care and how these can undermine patients' dignity, due to their invasive nature. The chapter considers the challenges and barriers to dignity in acute and critical care, such as rapid patient throughput, workload pressures and technology. She specifically addresses how dignity can be promoted in accident and emergency departments, intensive therapy units, and during peri-operative care.

In Chapter 13, Gemma Stacey and Theodore Stickley focus on dignity in mental health practice, starting with a brief history of mental healthcare. The notion of 'recovery in mental health' is discussed with the promotion of patient dignity in mind. Dignity and self-esteem are recognised as essential to recovery in mental health, although it is conceded that the views of those who use mental health services and routinely feel stripped of dignity are often ignored. The chapter explores the key areas identified within recent policy and research, which require substantial attention if practitioners are to maintain the dignity of people who use mental health services. The impact of practitioners' attitudes towards people who use mental health services in healthcare settings is critically considered, challenging stigma and discrimination.

In Chapter 14, Bob Hallawell examines dignity for people with learning disabilities, focusing on specific aspects of dignity related to the concept of learning disability and the particular context of the promotion of dignity within services designed to meet the needs of people with learning disabilities. The historical and social influences that have created devalued identities for people with learning disabilities and a consequent lack of dignity in their lives are discussed. The author also explores how social policy may both hinder and promote dignity in the lives of people with learning disabilities and he considers contemporary thinking about the promotion of dignity within health and social care settings for people with learning disabilities. The chapter suggests ways that individuals and services may promote dignity through their thinking and actions.

Section 3 – Developing dignity in healthcare

Section 3 is about developing dignity in practice and looking at ways of taking dignity forward. The section has three chapters. The first two chapters focus on the strategies required to assist healthcare professionals to promote dignity in care, through education and practice development, and the final chapter identifies key messages and considers future developments needed, including future research.

In Chapter 15, Liz Cotrel-Gibbons and Milika Ruth Matiti focus on the approaches to education that can be employed to promote dignity in care. The chapter is aimed at both students and educators, with particular reference to pre-registration nurse education, but the content can be applied to other students receiving their initial education in healthcare. In the first section of the chapter the rationale for 'values education' in nursing and the position of dignity within 'values education' are presented, and challenges to dignity education are identified. The educational theories of deep learning, andragogy, constructivism and transformative learning, and their relevance for dignity education, are discussed. It is believed that these theories provide a solid theoretical foundation for the section on the implementation of educational strategies. An example of a programme for dignity education is outlined, accompanied by specific examples of how to implement this programme.

In Chapter 16, Kate Sanders and Jonathan Webster focus on practice development in relation to patient or client dignity. The authors believe that defining dignity is complex and that, similarly, helping practitioners to develop practice in the context of complex work-based cultures and ever-changing services can be challenging. The chapter considers how practice development can enable practitioners to improve dignity in care through creative, transformational ways of learning supported by skilled facilitation. The chapter first provides a history of practice development, to set it into the context of the UK healthcare modernisation agenda. Practice development is then defined and the key characteristics identified. Two pictures from practice are used to illuminate how practice development can facilitate the development of people, practice and workplace. This chapter also acknowledges some of the challenges within complex healthcare contexts and identifies core components that will help sustain and enable ongoing practice development.

In the final chapter, Chapter 17, Lesley Baillie and Milika Ruth Matiti identify key messages from the book, and highlight challenges in promoting dignity in care and areas for development from management and educational perspectives. The chapter reviews research studies focused on dignity, identifying gaps and limitations, and suggests further research needed to underpin dignity in care. The emphasis in this final chapter is on the way forward for promoting dignity in care.

Case studies and reflective exercises

Throughout the book, there are case studies, practice scenarios and reflective exercises that enable readers to explore patient and client dignity from different perspectives. These take into account everyday encounters and challenges faced by healthcare workers. This interactive approach has been adopted to help readers to reflect on practice and consider promoting patient and client dignity in concrete and practical terms, rather than addressing the notion of dignity at purely abstract level. This will allow qualified healthcare professionals and students to explore the dimensions of dignity, enhance their self-awareness and identify practical ways of promoting dignity to apply in their own healthcare practice.

About the editors

Dr Milika Ruth Matiti is a lecturer in the Division of Nursing (Boston Centre) in the University of Nottingham, School of Nursing, Midwifery and Physiotherapy. In 2002 she obtained a PhD with a thesis entitled: *Patient Dignity in Nursing – a phenomenological study*. She has achieved a great deal since completing her PhD but her greatest interest has been in dignity education for pre- and post-registration healthcare students and clinical staff. In 2004–2007, Milika developed and carried out a dignity education programme at a local NHS trust for clinical staff. In 2006 she was part of the Nursing and Midwifery Council working group developing the Essential Skills Clusters (ESCs) for Communication, Care and Compassion. In 2008 she was part of a team developing the Royal College of Nursing Dignity E-learning resource. She has presented and published nationally and internationally about dignity in care.

Dr Lesley Baillie is Reader in Healthcare at the University of Bedfordshire. Lesley's PhD thesis (completed 2007) was *A Case Study of Patient Dignity in an Acute Hospital Setting*. From 2007 to 2009, Lesley was a consultant to the Royal College of Nursing's 'Dignity at the heart of everything we do' campaign, which included an online nursing workforce survey, development of a practice support pack on dignity, and an evaluation of the campaign. In 2010, Lesley was part of a team evaluating the UK's Design Council's 'Design for Dignity' project, which focused on enhancing the care environment through design innovation. Lesley has published and presented widely on patient dignity and is very interested in dignity in different care settings and the education of healthcare students about dignity in care.

Contributors

Barbara Burden RN RM ADM PGCEA MSc Social Research PhD
Barbara Burden is Head of Community Services and Lead Midwife for Education at the University of Bedfordshire. She has a background in midwifery and women's health. She has undertaken research into midwifery supervision and management, provision of maternity care at NHS Direct, and privacy within maternity care settings. She has published a number of chapters in *Mayes Midwifery*, a textbook for midwives, on child protection, preconception care and birth injuries. She has also published on bereavement and the midwife. Barbara is a member of the Royal College of Midwives Research Advisory Group and has worked for them as a research consultant.

Helen Coleman RN Dip Health Management
Helen Coleman is Head of Nursing Practice at Shrewsbury and Telford Hospital NHS Trust. Helen has been a registered nurse since 1979. She has held a variety of senior clinical, management and professional leadership roles. Her field of clinical expertise is in critical care, where the dignity of this vulnerable group of patients is paramount. As Head of Nursing, Helen is committed to improving the patient experience and is currently on the National Patient Experience programme run by the Institute for Innovation and Development. Her project is 'Dignity in Care: making it happen' where her aim is to embed the Dignity in Care challenge into the culture and everyday working methods of her organisation.

Liz Cotrel-Gibbons MMed Sci Clinical Nursing BA(Hons) PGCEA RGN Cert Health Ed
Liz Cotrel-Gibbons is a lecturer based in the Boston Centre of the University of Nottingham, School of Nursing, Midwifery and Physiotherapy. With Milika Ruth Matiti, she was a co-founder of a patient dignity education programme in the United Lincolnshire Trust from 2004 to 2007, which aimed to raise awareness and encourage active involvement of clinical staff in promoting patient dignity. She is involved in facilitating the integration of teaching of dignity in the curriculum for the pre-registration programme.

Ann Gallagher SRN RMN BA(Hons) MA PGCEA PhD
Ann Gallagher is Reader in Nursing Ethics and Director of the International Centre for Nursing Ethics in the Faculty of Health and Medical Sciences, University of Surrey. She was a consultant to the Royal College of Nursing Dignity Campaign ('Dignity: at the heart of everything we do'), and worked with Dr Baillie on the campaign evaluation. Ann's research areas include dignity in care, information giving in mental health, and healthcare ethics. She is editor of the journal *Nursing Ethics.*

Bob Hallawell PhD MBA BA Cert ED RNLD RMN
Bob is currently the Academic Lead for Learning Disabilities in the School of Nursing, Midwifery and Physiotherapy at the University of Nottingham. He began his career in learning disability nursing in 1977 and held a variety of positions within health services around England. He has worked in nurse education since 1987. He has been a member of the Royal College of Nursing learning disability advisory group and an external examiner to a number of UK universities. Bob was formerly Secretary of the Association of Practitioners in Learning Disability (APLD) and is a trustee for a learning disability charity. He is currently a reviewer for the *British Journal of Nursing* and an editorial advisory board member for *Learning Disability Practice.* He has published and spoken at conferences on a variety of topics, including quality in health services, user involvement, curriculum challenges and e-learning.

Alistair Hewison PhD MA BSc RN
Alistair Hewison is a senior lecturer in the School of Health and Population Sciences at the University of Birmingham. His professional background is in nursing, with experience as a staff nurse, charge nurse and nurse manager in the NHS in Birmingham, Oxford and Warwickshire. Having undertaken a number of roles in higher education, including Head of Nursing and Head of School, his current research and teaching activities are centred on the management and organisation of care. His main focus at the moment is a five-year project examining service redesign in three acute NHS trusts. He has written widely on healthcare management and policy issues in papers published in scholarly journals and chapters in edited collections. He recently completed a Nursing Policy Fellowship in the United States and is editor of the *Journal of Nursing Management.*

Wilfred McSherry PhD MPhil BSc(Hons) PGCE(FE) PGCRM RGN NT ILTM
Wilfred was appointed Professor in Dignity of Care for Older People in August 2008. This is a joint appointment between the Faculty of Health, Staffordshire University, and The Shrewsbury and Telford Hospital NHS Trust. He is currently working on a number of projects promoting the dignity of care within

the acute healthcare sector. Wilfred has published books and articles addressing different aspects of nursing care, and has an international reputation for his work on the spiritual dimension. Prior to being appointed to his current role, Wilfred was a Senior Lecturer in Nursing at the University of Hull, where he was also instrumental in creating with colleagues the Centre for Spirituality Studies, of which he was director.

Candice Pellett BSc(Hons) DipHE DN RNA IndNP CPT Queen's Nurse
Candice Pellett is a Case Manager District Nurse at Lincolnshire Community Health Services. In 1999 she obtained a double-award BSc in Community Health Nursing and Specialist Nurse Practitioner (District Nursing). In 2007 she was awarded the Queen's Nurse title, which is recognition of excellence in practice, and innovation and improvement in patient care. Candice works in clinical practice and is also currently seconded to the Department of Health as Clinical Lead for Nursing on the Transforming Community Services Programme. Candice cares for people with long-term conditions and delivers palliative and end-of-life care in the community setting. She is passionate about patient dignity in the community, particularly when caring for people at the end of their lives. She has presented nationally for the Department of Health and has published on end-of-life care.

Davina Porock RN PhD
Davina Porock is Professor and Associate Dean for Research and Scholarship at the State University of New York at Buffalo, where she moved in 2010. She has worked in nursing practice and research in Australia, where she received all her formal nursing education, in the UK, and in the USA, and holds adjunct professorships at Edith Cowan University, Perth, Western Australia and at the University of Missouri, USA. Her focus for research and scholarship is with older people with life-threatening or life-limiting conditions. Specifically, her interest is in understanding the transition from recovery-focused care to palliative care and ultimately comfort care at the end of life. Davina continues to collaborate with colleagues at the University of Nottingham where she holds a special professorship and actively participates in a number of nationally funded studies. Davina has published widely on hospice and end-of-life care.

Paula Reed PhD SCPHN (SN) PgDip(Couns) BSc(Hons) RGN
Dr Paula Reed completed her PhD, entitled *The Meaning of Dignity for the Child in Hospital*, in 2007 at the University of Surrey. Paula applied an ethnographic approach to the research based in a hospital ward. Paula remains passionate about the development of a greater awareness and understanding of dignity, especially in relation to children. She has published in peer-reviewed journals and presented her work at national and international conferences.

Paula works for Surrey Community Health, but has followed an unconventional career path. She commenced her working life as a dancer but has worked as a nurse, in acute, community and public health, a lecturer, counsellor and researcher. She is committed to the promotion of health and well-being in children and is currently pursuing play therapy as a way of hearing and understanding the worlds of children in research and therapy.

Kate Sanders MSc BSc(Hons) RHV RGN
Kate Sanders joined the Foundation of Nursing Studies (FoNS) as a Practice Development Facilitator nearly 10 years ago. Prior to this, she worked in a variety of acute and community settings where she became increasingly interested and active in practice development. At FoNS, Kate leads a number of practice development programmes, and has editorial responsibility for the Developing Practice Improving Care Dissemination Series and FoNS website. Kate has actively represented FoNS on a range of national and international events and initiatives. She also works as an external facilitator to support nurses, midwives and health visitors across healthcare practice to develop their knowledge and skills in facilitating and evaluating sustainable improvement and change. She has a keen interest in the characteristics that enable effective development in practice, and in particular the impact of workplace culture.

Gemma Stacey MN RN(Mental Health) PGCHE
Gemma Stacey is a Lecturer in Mental Health and Social Care in the School of Nursing, Midwifery and Physiotherapy at the University of Nottingham. Gemma's research, teaching and clinical practice focus on approaches and interventions that support recovery-orientated mental healthcare. She has published research on the values of mental health nurses and has developed educational approaches that aim to address the factors that challenge the realisation of recovery focus values in practice. These innovative educational approaches have been integrated into interprofessional pre-registration curricula internationally.

Theodore Stickley PhD MA Dip Couns Dip N PGCHE RMN
Theodore Stickley has trained in both counselling and mental health nursing and has worked and taught in both disciplines. He is now Associate Professor of Mental Health in the School of Nursing, Midwifery and Physiotherapy at the University of Nottingham. Theo is a keen gardener, motor cyclist and artist.

Paul Wainwright SRN DipN DANS MSc RNT PhD FEANS
Paul was Professor of Nursing and Associate Dean (Research) in the Faculty of Health and Social Care Sciences, Kingston University and St Georges University of London. He was previously Reader in the Centre for Philosophy and Health

Care at Swansea University. He published books, book chapters and articles on many aspects of philosophy, professional ethics and medical humanities, as well as completing a range of empirical studies. He was a member of two clinical ethics committees and chaired the Faculty Research Ethics Committee and the Royal College of Nursing Ethics Forum Committee. He was also a Fellow of the European Academy of Nursing Science.

Jonathan Webster PhD BA(Hons) MSc DPS(N) RGN
Jonathan is Assistant Director for Quality and Clinical Performance, Bexley Care NHS Trust and Honorary Senior Research Fellow at Christ Church Canterbury University. Jonathan qualified as a Registered General Nurse in 1990 and has worked in both secondary and primary care in the UK and Australia. Up until October 2009 he was a Consultant Nurse, Older People, initially in West Sussex before joining University College London Hospitals in 2005. In this role, he worked with teams and individuals who focused on improving quality of care for older people and their supporters through practice development. During his time there, Jonathan completed his PhD research, which focused upon evaluating a programme of emancipatory practice development centred upon developing person-centred assessment with older people. In his current post he provides the organisational lead for clinical quality within a commissioning primary care trust, along with the clinical lead for nursing. Key to this role is the need to work with stakeholders, ensuring that commissioned services have 'quality' at their core. Jonathan's professional interests lie in developing person-centred ways of working that enable both individuals and teams to work in partnership with service users and their supporters, through practice development and action research.

Acknowledgements

Our idea for this book came about as we identified the need for a comprehensive and practical book about dignity in healthcare. We very much appreciate the positive responses from all the chapter contributors, the high quality of their writing and the wealth of information they have provided for readers. We are sure that all this will make this book informative, enjoyable and stimulating. We also thank all those who have encouraged and supported us, including our families and colleagues, and Radcliffe Publishing for taking our book idea forward to publication.

Abbreviations

A&E	accident and emergency (department)
AMHP	approved mental health practitioner
ANA	American Nurses Association
APLD	Association of Practitioners in Learning Disability
DH	Department of Health
DN	district nurse
FoNS	Foundation of Nursing Studies
GMC	General Medical Council
GP	general practitioner
HAS	Health Advisory Service
HASCAS	Health and Social Care Advisory Service
HCC	Healthcare Commission
ICN	International Council of Nursing
ITU	intensive therapy unit
NDU	nursing development unit
LINk	local involvement network
MP	member of parliament
NHS	National Health Service
NMC	Nursing and Midwifery Council
NPSA	National Patient Safety Agency
NSF	National Service Framework
PDU	practice development unit
RCN	Royal College of Nursing
SCIE	Social Care Institute for Excellence
SCMH	Sainsbury Centre for Mental Health
SWOB	strengths, weaknesses, opportunities, barriers
UK	United Kingdom
UN	United Nations
US/USA	United States of America

SECTION 1
Dignity in healthcare: setting the scene

CHAPTER 1

The importance of dignity in healthcare

Milika Ruth Matiti

INTRODUCTION

The concept of dignity is not new. Many scholars have written on the subject and there seems to be a global consensus that dignity is an important concept to every individual in every society. Dignity is imbedded in Article 1 of the United Nations General Assembly Declaration of 1948, reiterated in 1996 by the United Nations International Bill of Rights, which states that all human beings are born free and equal in dignity and rights (United Nations, 1996). Dignity is reflected in Article 3 of the United Kingdom's (UK) Human Rights Act (1998), which states that 'no one shall be subjected to torture or inhuman or degrading treatment or punishment'; this article applies across society, including healthcare. The 1994 Amsterdam Declaration on the promotion of patients' rights recognises dignity as one of the main rights for patients (World Health Organization [WHO], 1994), regardless of nationality, race, tribe, creed, colour, age, sex, politics, social and educational status, cultural background or the nature of their health problems.

This first chapter highlights the importance of patient and client dignity in healthcare settings, drawing on patients' and healthcare professionals' viewpoints.

DIGNITY IN HEALTHCARE: PATIENTS' AND HEALTHCARE PROFESSIONALS' VIEWS

Worldwide empirical evidence confirms that, for a positive healthcare experience, patients and clients need to feel that their dignity is upheld and that healthcare professionals (most studies are from nurses' perspectives) also view dignity as important for patients and as a valuable part of their professional practice. Confirming the universality of dignity, these studies have been conducted in a range of specialties and some of these are presented next.

Patients in varied hospital settings have identified that dignity is important to them: in maternity care (Lai and Levy, 2002), medical and surgical wards (Matiti, 2002) and for older people in hospital (Jacelon, 2003). Joffe *et al* (2003) surveyed 27 414 patients following their discharge from acute care in the United States of America (USA) to identify how involvement in decisions, confidence and trust in care providers, and treatment with respect and dignity, influenced patients' evaluations of their hospital care. They found that perceptions of respectful, dignified treatment correlated most closely with high satisfaction with the hospital stay, thus indicating that patients who perceive that they are treated with dignity are happier with their overall hospital experience. In the USA, a survey by Beach *et al* (2005) of 6722 adults found that involving patients in decisions and treating them with dignity and respect were associated with positive outcomes. Recently, in Norway, a qualitative study using semi-structured interviews with 12 older people who had had strokes found that being treated with dignity and respect was a core factor contributing to the patients' satisfaction with their rehabilitation (Mangset *et al*, 2008). This main factor was further subdivided into: being treated with humanity, being acknowledged as individuals, having their autonomy respected, having confidence and trust in professionals and dialogue and exchange of information.

In terminal care, a number of research studies have identified dignity as one of the most important issues, from patients', relatives' and/or staff perspectives (Payne *et al*, 1996; Keegan *et al*, 2001; Miettinen *et al*, 2001; Vohra *et al*, 2004; Volker *et al*, 2004; Touhy *et al*, 2005; Aspinal *et al*, 2006). Chochinov *et al*'s (2002a) study of dignity with terminally ill patients indicated that patients viewed loss of dignity very negatively. In a further study, the same authors (Chochinov *et al*, 2002b) indicated a link between loss of dignity and various negative effects, such as psychological and symptom distress, heightened dependency needs and loss of will to live. In critical care settings, nurses stated that facilitating dying with dignity is important in end-of-life care (Kirchhoff *et al*, 2000; Beckstrand *et al*, 2006).

In several other studies, the importance of being treated with dignity has also emerged. Holland *et al* (1997) interviewed 21 patients about their recollections of their stay in the intensive therapy unit (ITU). Participants stated that it was easier to cope with the stress of ITU if nurses treated them with respect and dignity. In a further ITU-based study, Engström and Söderberg (2004) studied the experiences of seven ITU patients' partners, who all stressed that it was important that staff showed respect for the patient's dignity. Clegg (2003) explored perceptions of culturally sensitive care with older South Asian patients who were being cared for in two community hospitals. 'Demonstrating respect' emerged as a core category, with 'Retaining dignity' being a subcategory. The results indicated that promoting dignity was necessary for cultural sensitivity and involved preserving humanity and self-respect in the hospital setting.

Worldwide, healthcare professions have agreed that promoting patient or client dignity is a core element of their practice and this is also evidenced by empirical studies. Kelly's (1991) study aimed to examine what English nursing undergraduates internalised as professional values. The 12 students interviewed perceived two concepts as central to their professional values: 'Respect for patients' and 'Caring about little things'; these both link with patient dignity. Fagermoen (1997) surveyed Norwegian nurses (*n* = 731) with varying experience about their underlying values and found that human dignity was the core value, with all other values either arising from it or being aimed at preserving it. In Yonge and Molzahn's (2002) study, 18 registered nurses from varied settings in Canada gave examples of going to great lengths to preserve patients' dignity in situations in which they were vulnerable, demonstrating the importance these nurses placed on dignity. In Australia, Johnstone *et al* (2004) surveyed 398 nurses regarding ethical concerns encountered in practice. Protecting patients' rights and human dignity was a frequently cited ethical concern, which could indicate high staff awareness of dignity as an ethical issue. Perry (2005) conducted an internet-based study, accessing a self-selected, international sample of nurses (*n* = approximately 200) who were asked to share a story related to career satisfaction. Nurses who were satisfied with their careers believed that they provided quality care; defending patients' dignity was one of the four core values that emerged.

From a professional perspective, international bodies of different professional groups acknowledge that patient and client dignity is important and they have adopted the notion of dignity in their professional charters and policies; here are some examples. The European Region of the World Confederation for Physical Therapy (2003) urges physiotherapists to promote patient dignity at all times in their practice. In terms of midwifery, one of the perinatal principles of the WHO is that care should respect the privacy, dignity and confidentiality of women (Chalmers *et al*, 2001). The International Council of Nurses' Code of Ethics for Nurses (2006) affirms that inherent in nursing is respect for human rights, including cultural rights, the right to die and to choice, and the right to dignity and to be treated with respect. In the UK, under the duties of a doctor registered with the General Medical Council (GMC), doctors are expected to treat patients as individuals and respect their dignity (GMC, 2006). The General Pharmaceutical Council (2010) expects pharmacists to respect the dignity of clients and patients. The Occupational Therapy Association of South Africa (2005) asserts the expectation that occupational therapists should promote patient dignity. These global examples signify that different professions recognise the importance of patient or client dignity.

From these discussions, then, there is a widely shared view among patients and healthcare professionals that dignity is important in healthcare practice. However, while legislation and different professions urge healthcare workers to respect the dignity of patients and clients, the practicalities of promoting dignity for individuals in different situations and diverse settings have not been clearly articulated. There is evidence from different healthcare settings and drawing on patients' and healthcare workers' perspectives that the notion of dignity is neither clearly understood nor appropriately or consistently applied in practice (Porkony, 1989; Street, 2001; Matiti, 2002; Enes, 2003; Jacelon, 2003; Reed *et al*, 2003; Matthews and Callister, 2004; Calnan and Tadd, 2005; Baillie, 2007).

Dignity in care is influenced by multiple and interconnecting influences and, furthermore, the concept is abstract and difficult to define and is consequently not adequately understood, contributing to a lack of clarity about what kind of caring activities preserve dignity in practice (Anderberg *et al*, 2007). Therefore, there is a need to help healthcare workers in practice to identify practical ways of promoting patient and client dignity.

CONCLUSION

This introductory chapter has emphasised the importance of dignity from patients' and professionals' perspectives. The book contributors address the central issues in the current debate on the concept of dignity in healthcare. We hope that the work of the authors in this book will inspire you and help you to further develop your practice as a healthcare worker or student, to better promote the dignity of patients and clients in healthcare practice. We hope this book will be useful to everyone who reads it in their day-to-day practice. At the end of each chapter, authors have provided an extensive reference list which will be very useful for readers to further explore the dignity field.

ACKNOWLEDGEMENTS

I would like to thank Dr Henry Matiti and Professor Jack Mapanje for their valuable comments while writing this chapter.

REFERENCES

Anderberg P, Lepp M, Berglund A, Segesten K (2007) Preserving dignity in caring for older adults: a concept analysis. *Journal of Advanced Nursing* 59(6): 635–43.

Aspinal F, Hughes R, Dunckley M, Addington-Hall J (2006) What is important to measure in the last months and weeks of life? A modified nominal group study. *International Journal of Nursing Studies* 43(4): 393–403.

Baillie L (2007) *A Case Study of Patient Dignity in an Acute Hospital Setting.* Unpublished thesis. London South Bank University.

Beach M, Sugarman J, Johnson RL *et al* (2005) Do patients treated with dignity report higher satisfaction, adherence, and receipt of preventive care? *Annals of Family Medicine* 3(4): 331–8.

Beckstrand RL, Callister LC, Kirchhoff KT (2006) Providing a 'good death': critical care nurses' suggestions for improving end-of-life care. *American Journal of Critical Care* **15**(1): 38–46.

Calnan M, Tadd W (2005) Dignity and older Europeans: methodology. *Quality in Ageing: Policy, Practice and Research* **6**(1): 10–16.

Chalmers B, Mangiaterra V, Porter R (2001) *WHO Principles of Perinatal Care: the essential antenatal, perinatal and postpartum care course.* http://onlinelibrary.wiley.com/doi/10.1046/j.1523-536x.2001.00202.x/pdf (accessed 26 October 2010).

Chochinov HM, Hack T, McClement S, Kristjanson L, Harlos M (2002a) Dignity in the terminally ill: a developing empirical model. *Social Science and Medicine* **54**(3): 433–43.

Chochinov HM, Hack T, Hassard T *et al* (2002b) Dignity in the terminally ill: a cross sectional, cohort study. *Lancet* **360**(9350): 2026–30.

Clegg A (2003) Older South Asian patient and carer perceptions of culturally sensitive care in a community hospital setting. *Journal of Clinical Nursing* **2**(2): 283–90.

Enes SPD (2003) An exploration of dignity in palliative care. *Palliative Medicine* **17**(3): 263–9.

Engström Ä, Söderberg S (2004) The experiences of partners of critically ill persons in an intensive care unit. *Intensive and Critical Care Nursing* **20**(5): 448–58.

European Region of the World Confederation for Physical Therapy (2003) *European Physiotherapy Benchmark Statement.* Barcelona: European Region of the World Confederation for Physical Therapy. www.fysiot.ee/dok/01.pdf (accessed 8 October 2010).

Fagermoen MS (1997) Professional identity: values embedded in meaningful nursing practice. *Journal of Advanced Nursing* **25**(3): 434–41.

General Medical Council (2006) *Good Medical Practice: duties of a doctor.* London: General Medical Council. www.gmc-uk.org/guidance/good_medical_practice/duties_of_a_doctor.asp (accessed 8 October 2010).

General Pharmaceutical Council (2010) *Standards of Conduct, Ethics and Performance.* London: General Pharmaceutical Council. www.pharmacyregulation.org/pdfs/other/gphcstandardsofconductethicsandperflo.pdf (accessed 26 October 2010).

Holland C, Cason CL, Prater LR (1997) Patients' recollections of critical care. *Dimensions of Critical Care Nursing* **16**(3): 132–41.

Human Rights Act (1998) C.42. London: Her Majesty's Stationery Office.

International Council of Nurses (2006) *International Council of Nurses Code of Ethics for Nurses.* Geneva: International Council of Nurses.

Jacelon CS (2003) The dignity of elders in an acute care hospital. *Qualitative Health Research* **13**(4): 543–56.

Joffe S, Manocchia M, Weeks JC, Cleary PD (2003) What do patients value in their hospital care? An empirical perspective on autonomy centred bioethics. *Journal of Medical Ethics* **29**(2): 103–8.

Johnstone MJ, Da Costa C, Turale S (2004) Registered and enrolled nurses/experiences of ethical issues in nursing practice. *Australian Journal of Advanced Nursing* **22**(1): 24–30.

Keegan O, McGee H, Hogan M *et al* (2001) Relatives' views of healthcare in last year of life. *International Journal of Palliative Nursing* **7**(9): 44–56.

Kelly B (1991) The professional values of English nursing graduates. *Journal of Advanced Nursing* **16**(7): 867–72.

Kirchhoff KT, Spuhler V, Walker L *et al* (2000) Intensive care nurses' experiences with end-of-life care. *American Journal of Critical Care* **9**(1): 36–42.

Lai CY, Levy V (2002) Hong Kong Chinese women's experiences of vaginal examinations in labour. *Midwifery* **18**(4): 296–303.

Mangset M, Dahl TE, Forde R, Wyller, TB (2008) 'We're just sick people, nothing else': factors contributing to elderly stroke patients' satisfaction with rehabilitation. *Clinical Rehabilitation* **22**: 825–35.

Matiti MR (2002) *Patient Dignity in Nursing: phenomenological study*. Unpublished thesis. University of Huddersfield, School of Education and Professional Development.

Matthews R, Callister LC (2004) Childbearing women's perceptions of nursing care that promotes dignity. *Journal of Obstetric, Gynecologic and Neonatal Nursing* **33**(4): 498–507.

Miettinen T, Alaviuhkola H, Pietila A (2001) The contribution of 'good' palliative care to quality of life in dying patients: family members' perceptions. *Journal of Family Nursing* **7**(3): 261–80.

Occupational Therapy Association of South Africa (2005) *Occupational Therapy Code of Ethics.* Hatfield: Otasa.

Payne SA, Langley-Evans A, Hillier R (1996) Perceptions of a 'good' death: a comparative study of the views of hospice staff and patients. *Palliative Medicine* **10**(4): 307–12.

Perry B (2005) Core nursing values brought to life through stories. *Nursing Standard* **20**(7): 41–8.

Pokorny ME (1989) *The Effects of Nursing Care on Human Dignity in Critically ill Adults*. Dissertation. University of Virginia.

Reed P, Smith P, Fletcher M, Bradding A (2003) Promoting the dignity of the child in hospital. *Nursing Ethics* **10**(1): 67–76.

Street A (2001) Construction of dignity in end-of-life. *Journal of Palliative Care* **17**(2): 93–101.

Touhy TA, Brown C, Smith CJ (2005) Spiritual caring: end of life in a nursing home. *Journal of Gerontological Nursing* **31**(9): 21–35.

United Nations (1996) *The International Bill of Human Rights*. Fact Sheet No 2. Geneva: United Nations.

Vohra JU, Brazil K, Hanna S, Abelson J (2004) Family perceptions of end-of-life care in long-term facilities. *Journal of Palliative Care* **20**(4): 297–302.

Volker DL, Kahn D, Penticuff JH (2004) Patient control and end-of-life care. Part 11: The patient perspective. *Oncology Nurse Forum* **31**(5): 954–60.

World Health Organization (1994) *Declaration on the Promotion of Patient's Rights in Europe – Amsterdam*. Copenhagen: WHO Regional Office for Europe.

Yonge O, Molzahn A (2002) Exceptional non-traditional caring practices of nurses. *Scandinavian Journal of Caring Sciences* **16**(4): 399–405.

CHAPTER 2

The concept of dignity

Milika Ruth Matiti and Lesley Baillie

INTRODUCTION

To be able to promote dignity in healthcare, we need to understand the meaning of dignity. However, while dignity is frequently referred to in the media and health policy, it is by no means a universally understood concept. The French philosopher Gabriel Marcel believed that the 'mysterious principle at the heart of human dignity' cannot be preserved unless its 'sacred quality' is made precise (Marcel, 1963, p.128). Shotton and Seedhouse (1998) suggested that dignity is a vague and poorly defined concept, warning that unless dignity's meaning is clear, it can disappear beneath more tangible and measurable priorities. The Social Care Institute for Excellence (SCIE; 2006) pointed out that although defining dignity may be difficult, 'people know when they have not been treated with dignity and respect'.

In this chapter we will therefore explore the concept of dignity, drawing on a range of perspectives. We start with reflective exercises to enable you to explore your own understanding of dignity and develop a personal definition of dignity. The chapter continues by reviewing definitions of dignity from the healthcare literature, drawing on concept analyses and research with patients and healthcare workers. We will use scenarios to help you to understand how the concept of dignity is perceived by patients or clients. The chapter also aims to explore factors that influence how people perceive their own dignity.

LEARNING OUTCOMES

By the end of the chapter you will be able to:
➤ recognise your own understanding and perceptions of dignity
➤ discuss how dignity has been defined in the healthcare literature and the core elements of dignity
➤ understand how dignity is maintained and promoted through other related concepts.

REFLECTIONS ON YOUR OWN UNDERSTANDING OF DIGNITY

We suggest that you start by reflecting on your own understanding of dignity by carrying out Reflective activity 2.1. The activity guides you to reflect on what 'dignity' means to you and then to ask a friend to do likewise. You will then have insights into your own understanding of dignity and how understandings of dignity might differ between two individuals.

Reflective activity 2.1 The meaning of dignity

1. Write down some notes on what dignity means to you.
2. Now, read through what you have written and list words that describe dignity for you.
3. Reflect on each of the words in your list:
   a What exactly does each word mean?
   b Did you find it easy or difficult to define what dignity means?
4. How would you need to behave in order to promote dignity as you have described it?
5. How should other people promote the kind of dignity you have in mind? Look again at each word you have listed and state exactly how you would like others to promote it.
6. *Where* did you learn the behaviour that relates to your definition of dignity?
7. *How* did you learn the behaviour that relates to your definition of dignity?

When you are satisfied that you have fully explored your understanding of dignity, ask a friend to do the same exercises (1–7) and compare your notes.

8. How do your views on the meaning of dignity compare with your friend's?
9. Were there any differences or similarities between you and your friend's views about the behaviour that promotes dignity?
10. Were there any differences or similarities in how and where you and your friend learnt the behaviour relating to dignity?
11. If there are differences in your views, discuss the reasons why with your friend.
12. In your own words, write a summary of what you have learnt from this exercise.

The next sections of this chapter explore published definitions of dignity.

DEFINITIONS OF DIGNITY

There are definitions of dignity in dictionaries, while other definitions have developed from philosophical exploration and concept analyses and through research.

Dictionary definitions of dignity

Collins English Dictionary (2003) states that the word dignity comes from two Latin words: *'dignus'*, meaning worth, and *'dignitas,'* meaning merit. Most definitions of dignity have assumed the relevance of these two roots, as you will see if you look up 'dignity' in a dictionary or thesaurus. Now carry out Reflective activity 2.2.

Reflective activity 2.2 Dictionary and thesaurus definitions of dignity

Look up 'dignity' in a dictionary (hard copy and/or an online dictionary) and a thesaurus and consider:

➤ how do the definitions and words in the dictionary or thesaurus relate to the Latin meanings of 'worth' and 'merit'?
➤ how helpful are the definitions in clarifying what the concept of dignity means?
➤ how applicable are these definitions in relation to dignity in healthcare?

You will probably have found that most words in definitions of dignity in dictionaries, and the words listed in the thesaurus, are abstract and need defining themselves. Some definitions include internal qualities like having pride in oneself, self-respect and self-esteem. Others relate to how one is viewed in society, including notions of nobility and being in an esteemed position. This exercise illustrates that dignity can be defined and interpreted in different ways; some of these may be more applicable to healthcare than others. We will next examine the meaning of dignity proposed in philosophical and theoretical explorations.

Theories of dignity

The German philosopher Immanuel Kant's views on dignity have been widely referred to in discussions of the meaning of dignity. He defined dignity as an intrinsic, unconditional and incomparable worth or worthiness that should not be compared with things that have economic value because, unlike market value, a person's value does not depend upon usefulness and cannot be replaced (Kant, 1948). Kant argued that dignity should be accorded on the basis of ability to reason and that as humans are able to reason, they possess dignity (Kant, 1909). He related rationality with autonomy: 'Autonomy then is the basis of the dignity of human and of every rational nature' (Kant, 1909, p.54). However, Beauchamp (2001) asserted that Kant's (1909) philosophy failed to acknowledge the dignity of those who lack the capacity for autonomy, which is particularly relevant in healthcare. A number of definitions have been influenced by Kant's ideas about dignity however.

Nordenfelt (2003) developed a theoretical framework for dignity from reviewing the literature. His work was related to dignity in older people and is further discussed in Chapter 9. He proposed four categories of dignity:

➤ *Menschenwürde* (a German word) refers to the dignity that each individual has by virtue of being human; everyone has this human value to the same degree regardless of sex, age, race or religion

➤ *dignity as merit* includes rank in society, earned or inherited; this also entails a set of rights and honours installed in this position – for example, a king, queen, chiefs, lawyers – and therefore this varies from one person to the other. This definition closely relates to some of the dictionary definitions found in Reflective activity 2.2

➤ *dignity of moral stature* includes respect of oneself as a moral human being and respect from others related to performances and attitudes, and may vary in relation to one's own acts

➤ *dignity of personal identity* focuses on human beings' self-respect, including notions of integrity and autonomy, and may be violated when a person is prevented from doing what they want to do or are entitled to do, or by physical assault and humiliation.

In a later paper, Nordenfelt and Edgar (2005) emphasised that while *Menschenwürde* (human dignity) cannot be diminished or lost while a person is alive, the presence and degree of the other three types of dignity varies in each individual. They acknowledged that dignity of identity is most relevant in the context of illness, as disability restricts autonomy and threatens personal identity. Baillie (2009) argued that the categories 'dignity as merit' and 'dignity as moral stature' have questionable relevance to healthcare because all patients should be treated with respect for dignity, regardless of perceived merit or moral status. Wainwright and Gallagher have also critiqued Nordenfelt's analysis (*see* Chapter 3 of this book).

Jacobson's (2007) analysis identified two distinct meanings of dignity: human dignity (a value that belongs to every human being because they are human) and social dignity. Jacobson (2007) explained that social dignity is experienced through interaction and, while human dignity cannot be removed, social dignity can be 'lost or gained, threatened, violated, or promoted' (p.295). She elaborated that social dignity always arises in a social context and comprises two linked elements: 'dignity-of-self' (includes self-confidence and self-respect), which is created through interaction, and 'dignity-in-relation', which concerns the conveyance of worth to others and is situated in time and place. Jacobson (2007) also asserted that traditional definitions of dignity relating to status and merit (as in Nordenfelt's model) are included in social dignity; thus, this broad category of social dignity encompasses various interpretations. Jacobson (2007) suggested that being clear about whether human or social dignity is being discussed may help to reduce some of the vagueness associated with dignity. She also asserted that the concept of human dignity can be used to argue for the right to health.

Concept analyses of dignity

Concept analyses of dignity have mostly comprised theoretical analysis and literature reviews (Johnson, 1998; Fenton and Mitchell, 2002; Griffin-Heslin, 2005; Coventry, 2006), but a few included views from convenience samples of students (Mairis, 1994; Jacobs, 2000) or friends, colleagues and family (Haddock, 1996; Marley, 2005). One United States (US)-based concept analysis of dignity in older people appropriately included focus groups with older people (Jacelon *et al*, 2004). Some concept analyses drew on popular literature, visual art and poetry, recognising that the word 'dignity' is used in a broad context. The concept analyses highlight that dignity is complex and multidimensional. Mairis's (1994) concept analysis identified critical attributes of dignity as being the maintenance of self-respect, self-esteem and appreciation of individual standards. Her definition referred to individuals being able to apply control or choice over their own behaviour and surroundings and how others treat them. The definition also included being able to understand information and make decisions and feeling comfortable with oneself, both physically and from a psychosocial perspective.

Haddock (1996) concluded that the dignified self comprises self-respect; self-confidence; self-control; control of environment; pride of self; being trustworthy, happy with self, humorous, autonomous, independent, private; positive self; striving to keep boundary, integrity and identity of self when under attack. Her operational definition of dignity included feeling, and being treated as being, important and valuable when in situations that are considered threatening. The definition also highlighted the link between one's own dignity and the ability to promote the dignity of others; this is an important consideration for healthcare professionals working with patients (*see* Chapter 3).

Fenton and Mitchell's (2002) concept analysis of dignity in older people included, like Mairis's concept analysis, control, choice and decision making. However, they also included being valued as an individual and feeling comfortable (physically, emotionally and spiritually). Jacelon *et al*'s (2004) concept analysis also focused on older people. Their definition included dignity as part of being human, dignity as an attribute of self, and related concepts and 'behavioural dignity' with attributes including self-worth, self-respect and pride. Marley's (2005) concept analysis of dignity led him to emphasise dignity as being two-way: 'a quality that existed both in and for people; that it is both a possession and a gift' (p.84).

In the next section we focus on healthcare research which gained understanding of dignity from patients' and healthcare professionals' perspectives.

Research findings about the meaning of dignity

Researchers have often focused on experiences of dignity rather than the meaning of dignity; here we review studies that have specifically explored what dignity means. Nearly all studies were qualitative, involving in-depth interviews with patients, healthcare professionals (mostly nurses) and occasionally relatives; a few used observation too. Understanding the meaning of dignity in healthcare is clearly of universal concern as researchers have explored the meaning of dignity in the US (Porkony, 1989; Jacelon, 2003), the UK (Seedhouse and Gallagher, 2002; Matiti, 2002; Enes 2003; Reed *et al*, 2003; Baillie, 2009), Sweden (Randers and Mattiasson, 2004), Canada (Chochinov *et al*, 2002) and Europe – the 'Dignity and Older Europeans' project (Ariño-Blasco *et al*, 2005; Bayer *et al*, 2005; Stratton and Tadd, 2005). Most studies were conducted with adult hospital patients but Enes' study was hospice based, Chochinov *et al*'s (2002) research was in a palliative care unit, and Reed *et al*'s (2003) study was with children (*see* Chapter 8). The 'Dignity in Older Europeans' project, based on Nordenfelt's (2003) theoretical framework, included members of the public as well as healthcare professionals. Both chapter authors have conducted their own doctoral research into the meaning of dignity and we present some of these findings here.

Using a phenomenological approach, Matiti (2002) conducted interviews with patients and nurses about dignity in hospital wards in England. Patients described their concept of dignity as: privacy, confidentiality, need for information, choice, involvement in care, independence, forms of address, decency, control, respect and nurse–patient communication. Patients also described dignity as something everyone has, that it is about self-worth and personal standards, how they present themselves and are perceived by others. Privacy was highly rated by all participants as a main attribute of dignity. Matiti (2002) found that patients went through a process of adjustment in hospital, which she referred to as 'perceptual adjustment level' and thus she developed the following definition:

> Patient dignity is the fulfilment of patients' expectations in terms of values within each patient's perceptual adjustment level, taking into account the hospital environment (Matiti, 2002, p.105).

The definition indicates the individuality of dignity to patients, implying that the meaning of dignity varies according to what the patient expects, how they have adjusted to being in hospital, and the impact of the hospital setting on them.

Baillie (2007) conducted a multi-method qualitative case study on a hospital ward in England using participant observation, interviews with nurses and patients and documentary analysis. The central component of dignity in hospital emerged as being how patients feel, which was linked with their physical presentation and behaviour towards and from others. Feelings associated with dignity related to feeling comfortable (for example, safe, happy, relaxed), in control (for example, confident, able to cope) and valued (for example, of consequence, cared about). About half the patients and most staff associated dignity with appearance: patients being dressed appropriately and not having their bodies exposed. Many participants associated dignity with behaviour towards and from others, as this influenced how comfortable patients felt and whether they felt valued. Most patients and staff referred to behaviour, with 'respect' being the most commonly used term. Some felt that dignity entailed reciprocity: mutually respectful behaviour. Some staff and patients identified privacy as a behaviour associated with the meaning of dignity. Baillie's definition of dignity, developed from the patients' expressed meanings of dignity, is:

> Patient dignity is feeling valued and comfortable psychologically with one's physical presentation and behaviour, level of control over the situation, and the behaviour of other people in the environment (Baillie, 2007, p.247).

There are similarities between the findings of our doctoral research and with the concept analyses and other research studies, as we will discuss next.

The meaning of dignity: a summary from the literature

For our review we summarise the key themes as:

➤ *dignity is inherent in human beings* (Matiti, 2002; Nordenfelt, 2003; Jacelon, 2003; Reed *et al*, 2003; Jacelon *et al*, 2004; Griffin-Heslin, 2005; Marley, 2005; Jacobson, 2007)

➤ *dignity is dynamic*: patients adjust their perceptions of dignity during hospitalisation (Matiti, 2002; Jacelon, 2003) and as illness progresses (Enes, 2003)

➤ *dignity is an internal quality*: an aspect of self (Haddock, 1996), self-dignity (Jacelon, 2003), dignity-of-self (Jacobson, 2007), an attribute of the self (Jacelon *et al*, 2004), a possession (Marley, 2005), and closely linked to each patient's individuality, their feelings and uniqueness as an individual (Mairis, 1994; Fenton and Mitchell, 2002; Marley, 2005)

➤ *dignity relates to feelings*: self-esteem (Matiti, 2002; Chochinov *et al*, 2002; Enes, 2003), self-worth (Matiti, 2002; Enes, 2003), pride (Seedhouse and Gallagher, 2002; Chochinov *et al*, 2002; Matiti, 2002), confidence (Seedhouse and Gallagher, 2002; Baillie, 2007), self-respect (Seedhouse and Gallagher, 2002; Chochinov *et al*, 2002; Matiti, 2002; Baillie, 2007), feeling important and valuable (Baillie, 2007), being happy with self (Baillie, 2007), well-being (Chochinov *et al*, 2002; Baillie, 2007), hope (Chochinov *et al*, 2002) and feeling comfortable (Fenton and Mitchell, 2002; Baillie, 2007)

➤ *dignity relates to behaviour*: behavioural dignity (Jacelon *et al*, 2004), dignity-in-relation (Jacobson, 2007), a gift (Marley, 2005). Examples are: behaving according to one's personal standards (Matiti, 2002; Jacelon, 2003; Baillie, 2007), courteousness (Matiti, 2002; Baillie, 2007), conveying respect (Seedhouse and Gallagher, 2002; Matiti, 2002; Enes, 2003; Jacelon, 2003), reciprocal respect (Jacelon *et al*, 2004; Baillie, 2007) and treating people as individuals (Enes, 2003; Baillie, 2007), as competent adults (Seedhouse and Gallagher, 2002) and as important and valuable (Haddock, 1996; Baillie, 2007)

➤ *dignity and relationships*: interpersonal dignity (Jacelon, 2003) and relationships involving reciprocal behaviour (Enes, 2003; Jacelon, 2003; Reed *et al*, 2003; Baillie, 2007)

➤ *control as a component of dignity* (Matiti, 2002; Jacelon, 2003; Reed *et al*, 2003; Baillie, 2007). Related concepts are: autonomy (Chochinov *et al*, 2002; Randers and Mattiasson, 2004) and independence (Pokorny, 1989; Seedhouse and Gallagher, 2002; Chochinov *et al*, 2002; Matiti, 2002; Enes, 2003; Baillie, 2007)

➤ *presentation of self in public*: physical appearance (Seedhouse and Gallagher, 2002; Chochinov *et al*, 2002; Matiti, 2002; Enes, 2003; Baillie, 2007) and modesty (Matiti, 2002; Baillie, 2007)

➤ *privacy* (Porkony, 1989; Seedhouse and Gallagher, 2002; Chochinov *et al*, 2002; Matiti, 2002; Enes, 2003; Reed *et al*, 2003; Jacelon, 2003; Randers and Mattiasson, 2004; Baillie, 2007). Other examples are: being private and able to keep one's boundaries (Haddock, 1996), protecting privacy to convey respect (Jacobs, 2000; Jacelon, 2003; Griffin-Heslin, 2005), being in control of one's own privacy (Marley, 2005).

Following this review, now carry out Reflective activity 2.3.

ATTRIBUTES OF DIGNITY

The previous section indicated that other concepts have been used to describe the concept of dignity and that despite studies being carried out in a wide range of countries, there are some similar ideas about dignity. Chinn and Jacobs (1983) state that if a concept is difficult to define, its meaning can be inferred from other theoretical concepts, which they call 'attributes'. These are concepts that appear repeatedly in the literature to describe a concept. It may therefore

Reflective activity 2.3 Comparing definitions of dignity

Look back at the definitions and meanings of dignity included in this section and list all the common words that are used. Now compare these to the words you used in the definition you developed in Reflective activity 2.1.

➤ Do any of these definitions match with your definitions?
➤ Do the definitions from the literature make the concept of dignity clearer to you?
➤ Has the literature review led to any different perspectives of dignity for you?
➤ What conclusions can you draw?

be easier to describe or define the notion of dignity by using attributes but these attributes are also abstract and need defining further. Attributes associated with dignity include respect, privacy, autonomy and worth but what do they mean exactly? Think critically and look at the list of attributes that you compiled in Reflective activity 2.1 to describe the concept of dignity. Now consider: is it more practical to explain what dignity means by using its attributes?

Owing to the abstract nature of the concept of dignity, you will find that sometimes attributes of dignity (for example, privacy, respect, worth) are used interchangeably with dignity or attached to dignity (see examples in Box 2.1). This interchangeable use of the concept of dignity with its attributes further blurs the meaning of dignity and can cause confusion. In Chapter 3, Paul Wainwright explores this issue further, drawing on a range of literature and media reports.

BOX 2.1 *Examples of how dignity is used interchangeably or linked with its attributes*

1. The rights designated as human are justifiable by reference to the principle that all humans are beings with intrinsic worth and dignity (Blackstone, 1970, pp.34–5)
2. *Privacy and Dignity – A Report by the Chief Nursing Officer into Mixed Sex Accommodation in Hospitals* (Department of Health, 2007)
3. Privacy and dignity of cancer patients: a qualitative study of patients' privacy in UK National Health Service patient care settings (Woogara, 2005)
4. Care of the body: maintaining dignity and respect (Bernick *et al*, 2002)

At this juncture, you are probably realising that it is through its attributes that dignity is maintained and so it is important to discuss what influences perceptions of these attributes in relation to one's dignity. A person's background, their age, previous experience and social standing in the community might influence their perception of dignity. The situation in which a person finds himself or herself also influences the way they perceive the maintenance of their dignity. Another factor is hospitalisation, as the type of illness and treatment also influences a person's perception of their dignity. Now consider the scenario and questions in Reflective activity 2.4 , which will help you to explore how a patient might perceive their dignity and what might influence their perception.

Reflective activity 2.4 Perceptions of dignity

Mrs Smith, an 80-year-old widow who had worked as a nurse and rose through the ranks to retire as a matron, has been admitted, with a bladder tumour, onto a ward she had worked on 40 years before. She is having difficulties controlling her bladder and cannot go to the toilet unassisted as she has arthritis, which limits her mobility. She is told that she needs a urinary catheter. A young nurse goes over to her and calls her by her first name. You overhear her talking to the patient in the next bed: 'Things have changed these days, during my time patients were addressed properly using their surnames. I personally do not feel respected being addressed by my first name; at least I should be asked if I mind. This is how I have been brought up'.

➤ First, identify some attributes through which Mrs Smith's dignity might be promoted.
➤ Can you identify what would influence her perception regarding the maintenance of her dignity while in hospital?

The factors influencing dignity will be discussed further in the next section.

FACTORS INFLUENCING PERCEPTIONS OF THE ATTRIBUTES OF DIGNITY

Each community or family has its own perception and sets its own standards regarding attributes of dignity, such as respect, privacy and forms of address. Take, for example, the attribute 'respect'. Most families teach their children the expected mode of behaviour that constitutes respect; that is, how to respect oneself and others. Other factors that influence a child's perception and understanding of respect include institutions such as schools. As we grow up, the environment in which we live, including the people we work, live and socialise with, continues to influence our understanding of the concept of respect. Healthcare professionals' understanding of dignity is influenced by their education and experience of working with patients in healthcare settings.

Regarding the attribute of privacy or 'being decent': children are taught dress codes, which in some cultures require covering almost the whole body. As they grow up, children learn these shared standards of beliefs and values which are internalised and become part of a person's self-concept. Self-concept comprises three components: self-image, ideal-self and self-esteem (Gross, 2005). Self-image refers to the way in which each individual describes themselves. Ideal-self refers to what kind of a person each individual would like to be and might include appearance and personality. Self-esteem refers to the extent to which one likes, accepts or approves of oneself and how worthwhile one is (Oliver, 1993). Self-esteem can be influenced by how other people view us. Within healthcare settings, how patients feel they are viewed by staff caring for them, or how staff feel they are viewed by colleagues and patients, can affect self-esteem. If a person's own standards are met, they develop a sense of pride, have high self-esteem and feel worthy.

Various other factors are involved in the process of socialisation, which can affect a person's perception and promotion of dignity. Culture is dynamic as the values of community change over time. The scenario of Mrs Smith (Reflective activity 2.4) demonstrates the change in perceptions of 'respect' relating to form of address. Help the Aged (2007) highlighted that many older people find themselves routinely addressed by their first names or endearments in hospital, which they perceive as disrespectful. Acceptable dress codes have also changed in UK society. For example, young people may feel comfortable wearing clothing that exposes their underwear, which would previously have been perceived in our society as undignified.

Previous experiences might also influence one's perception of respect and therefore how a person feels that their dignity has been promoted. For example, abuse in childhood or experience of torture at an early age may affect a person's self-belief or self-concept and the perception of how their dignity is promoted in future. Social standing in the community might influence how one sees oneself; for example, a vicar might expect to be addressed as 'Reverend' instead of by their first name or surname. The situation in which a person finds themselves also influences the way they perceive the maintenance or promotion of dignity (Seedhouse, 2000). For example, you might want to be addressed in a different way in different social settings. The healthcare setting, healthcare procedures and the various interactions with healthcare workers affect how attributes of dignity are maintained. Although dignity is important to people across the age range, perceptions of the attributes of dignity may differ between children and adults (*see* Chapter 8).

The '3Ps' model (Royal College of Nursing, 2008) is useful for considering influences on dignity. These relate to: people (patients, relatives and staff), place (care environment, including organisational culture) and process (care activities). Now consider the scenario and questions in Reflective activity 2.5, which relate to a young woman's experience of healthcare in a community setting. The scenario is a real experience, used with permission and pseudonyms. You will notice that although Bethany was having a procedure performed that was exposing and invasive (process), it was not the actual procedure that affected her dignity so much as the care environment (place) and the staff behaviour (people).

Reflective activity 2.5 A community healthcare experience

Bethany is 25 years old and had her first baby (Amy) four months ago. She is on maternity leave from her job for the local council where she works directly with the public. Her employers emphasise 'excellent customer care' and Bethany won her department's customer care award last year. Bethany's appearance is important to her and she is always smart. She was asked to attend her local doctor's surgery for a cervical smear. Only morning appointments can be made for these and she had no one with whom she could leave Amy. She hoped that Amy would sleep in her buggy during the appointment. She wasn't worried about having the smear as she rationalised that it was important to have it done.

Bethany pushed the buggy into the surgery. The receptionist, who was a lot older than Bethany, shouted at her across the waiting room that buggies must be left outside due to 'health and safety'. Bethany found it embarrassing to be shouted at across a crowded waiting room as though she 'was a child' but she did as she was told and then carried Amy into the waiting room. The nurse called her in and Bethany said that she might cancel her appointment as she had had to leave the buggy outside. The nurse was unsympathetic repeating that it was 'health and safety' and she said that Bethany could hold Amy on her chest.

Bethany found it distressing having to hold Amy on her chest during the smear. Amy was now crying and she vomited over Bethany's face and hair. The nurse offered no assistance. Bethany left the surgery feeling very upset about how she had been treated and aware that she now smelt strongly of 'baby sick'. She considered making a complaint but instead she changed the family's registration to a different surgery.

➤ What attributes of dignity might have been important to Bethany?
➤ What influenced these attributes during her visit to the surgery? Consider the 3Ps: people, place and process.

SUMMARY: THE MEANING OF DIGNITY

This section's discussion has illuminated that patients and clients come from varied backgrounds with different values and expectations regarding the maintenance of their dignity. For example, Mrs Smith expected to be addressed by her title and Bethany expected to be spoken to politely and with concern, as she does when working with the public. Healthcare workers have their own values influenced by their upbringing, age and experiences too. Perceptions of dignity may vary according to the situation we find ourselves in. All these factors influence the maintenance and promotion of patients' or clients' dignity. Key points are that:

➤ everyone has a unique and dynamic concept of dignity
➤ although there is no universal definition of dignity, there are commonly identified attributes of dignity through which it is maintained and promoted
➤ each individual perceives these attributes differently, depending on how they perceive the influencing factors
➤ perceptions of dignity are influenced by experiences in healthcare; the care environment, procedures and healthcare workers' behaviour can all affect perceptions of dignity.

CONCLUSION

This chapter has explored the concept of dignity, firstly by guiding you to reflect on your own perceptions of dignity and then through reviewing theoretical perspectives and research findings. We have suggested that dignity can be defined using its attributes so that we can use a practical approach in the care of clients and patients. We have also introduced the 3Ps of people, place and process, which all influence dignity; these are addressed in detail in this book's other chapters. The chapter has set the scene for the exploration of practical issues concerning the concept of dignity and promotion of patient or client dignity in healthcare. In Chapter 3, the concept of dignity is explored from philosophical and professional perspectives, drawing on media portrayals and a range of literature, thus further expanding your understanding of dignity as a concept.

REFERENCES

Ariño-Blasco S, Tadd W, Boix-Ferrer JA (2005) Dignity and older people: the voice of professionals. *Quality in Ageing* 6(1): 30–5.
Baillie L (2007) *A Case Study of Patient Dignity in an Acute Hospital Setting.* Unpublished thesis. London South Bank University.
Baillie L (2009) Patient dignity in an acute hospital setting: a case study. *International Journal of Nursing Studies* **46**: 22–36.

Bayer T, Tadd W, Krajcik S (2005) Dignity: the voice of older people. *Quality in Ageing* **6**(1): 22–7.

Beauchamp TL (2001) *Philosophical Ethics: an introduction to moral philosophy.* Boston: McGraw-Hill.

Bernick L, Nisan C, Higgins M (2002) Care of the body: maintaining dignity and respect. *Perspectives* **29**(4): 17–21.

Blackstone WT (1970) Human rights and human dignity. In: Gotesky R, Laszlo, E (eds) *Human Dignity – This Century and the Next.* New York: Gordon and Breach, pp.3–36.

Chinn PL, Jacobs MK (1983) *Theory and Nursing – A Systematic Approach.* St Louis: CV Mosby.

Chochinov HM, Hack T, McClement S, Kristjanson L, Harlos M (2002) Dignity in the terminally ill: a developing empirical model. *Social Science and Medicine* **54**(3): 433–43.

Collins English Dictionary (2003) *Collins English Dictionary – Complete and Unabridged.* Glasgow: Collins.

Coventry M (2006) Care with dignity: a concept analysis. *Journal of Gerontological Nursing* **32**(5): 42–8.

Department of Health (2007) *Privacy and Dignity – A report by the Chief Nursing Officer into Mixed Sex Accommodation in Hospitals.* London: Department of Health.

Enes SPD (2003) An exploration of dignity in palliative care. *Palliative Medicine* **17**(3): 263–9.

Fenton E, Mitchell T (2002) Growing old with dignity: a concept analysis. *Nursing Older People* **14**(4): 19–21.

Griffin-Heslin VL (2005) An analysis of the concept dignity. *Accident and Emergency Nursing* **13**(4): 251–7.

Gross R (2005) *The Science of Mind and Behaviour.* London: Hodder Arnold.

Haddock J (1996) Towards further clarification of the concept of dignity. *Journal of Advanced Nursing* **24**(5): 924–31.

Help the Aged (2007) *The Challenge of Dignity in Care: upholding the rights of the individual.* London: Help the Aged.

Jacelon CS (2003) The dignity of elders in an acute care hospital. *Qualitative Health Research* **13**(4): 543–56.

Jacelon CS, Connelly TW, Brown R, Proulx K, Vo T (2004) A concept analysis of dignity in older adults. *Journal of Advanced Nursing* **48**(1): 76–83.

Jacobs BB (2000) Respect for human dignity in nursing: philosophical and practical perspectives. *Canadian Journal of Nursing Research* **32**(2): 15–33.

Jacobson N (2007) Dignity and health: a review. *Social Science and Medicine* **64**(2): 292–302.

Johnson PRS (1998) An analysis of 'dignity'. *Theoretical Medicine and Bioethics* **19**: 337–52.

Kant I (1909) *Kant's Critique of Practical Reason and Other Works on the Theory of Ethics* (6e). London: Longmans.

Kant I (1948) *Groundwork of Metaphysic of Morals* (Translated by Paton HJ). New York: Harper and Row Publishers.

Mairis ED (1994) Concept clarification in professional practice. *Journal of Advanced Nursing* **19**(5): 947–53.

Marcel G (1963) *The Existential Background of Human Dignity.* Cambridge, MA: Harvard University Press.

Marley J (2005) A concept analysis of dignity. In: Cutcliffe JR, McKenna, HP (eds) *The Essential Concepts of Nursing*. Edinburgh: Elsevier, Churchill Livingstone, pp.77–91.

Matiti MR (2002) *Patient Dignity in Nursing: a phenomenological study*. Unpublished thesis. University of Huddersfield School of Education and Professional Development.

Nordenfelt L (2003) Dignity of the elderly: an introduction. *Medicine, Health Care and Philosophy* **6**(2): 99–101.

Nordenfelt L, Edgar A (2005) The four notions of dignity. *Quality in Ageing: Policy, Practice and Research* **6**(1): 17–21.

Oliver RW (1993) *Psychology and Healthcare*. London: Baillière Tindall.

Porkony ME (1989) *The Effects of Nursing Care on Human Dignity in Critically Ill Adults*. Dissertation. University of Virginia.

Randers I, Mattiasson A (2004) Autonomy and integrity: upholding older adult patients' dignity. *Journal of Advanced Nursing* **45**(1): 63–71.

Reed P, Smith P, Fletcher M, Bradding A (2003) Promoting the dignity of the child in hospital. *Nursing Ethics* **10**(1): 67–76.

Royal College of Nursing (2008) *Defending Dignity: challenges and opportunities for nurses*. London: Royal College of Nursing.

Seedhouse D (2000) *Practical Nursing Philosophy. The universal ethical code*. Chichester: Wiley.

Seedhouse D, Gallagher A (2002) Undignifying institutions. *Journal of Medical Ethics* **28**: 368–72.

Shotton L, Seedhouse D (1998) Practical dignity in caring. *Nursing Ethics* **5**(3): 246–55.

Social Care Institute for Excellence (2006) *Practice Guide 15. Dignity in Care*. www.scie.org.uk/publications/guides/guide15/index.asp (accessed 8 October 2010).

Stratton D, Tadd W (2005) Dignity and older people: the voice of society. *Quality in Ageing: Policy, Practice and Research* **6**(1): 37–45.

Woogara J (2005) Privacy and dignity of cancer patients: a qualitative study of patients' privacy in UK National Health Service patient care settings. *Journal of Cancer Education* **20**(2): 119–23.

CHAPTER 3

Professional and ethical expectations for dignity in care

Paul Wainwright

INTRODUCTION

Steven Pinker has said that 'The problem is that "dignity" is a squishy, subjective notion, hardly up to the heavyweight moral demands assigned to it' (Pinker, 2008), while Bostrom has argued that the notion of dignity has uncovered a 'winning formula' encompassing 'a general feel-good quality, and a profound vagueness', which enables all to assert their commitment to it but without 'endorsing any particular course of action' (Bostrom, 2008, p.174). Of these attributes, it is perhaps the 'squishyness' or 'profound vagueness' that has created the biggest problem for healthcare professionals, politicians and the media. It suits many to assert their allegiance with the idea of dignity but few have managed to clear away the vagueness.

In this chapter I explore the concept of dignity from the perspective of professional practice and from the expectations of the general public and service users. In doing so, I explore popular understanding of the concept as revealed by the media and everyday use in common language. I then relate this account to the purpose and practice of nursing and explore the implications of our account in terms of our expectations of professionals and the expectations that service users may reasonably have.

LEARNING OUTCOMES

By the end of the chapter you will be able to:
> discuss the common language use of the concept of dignity
> explore the relationship between common usage and more theoretical accounts
> explain two applications of dignity: to the character of the practitioner and to the treatment of others
> debate the meaning and relevance of respect
> discuss the relationship between dignity and the purpose of nursing as a practice.

DIGNITY IN COMMON LANGUAGE

In common parlance we talk of people having dignity, behaving in a dignified way or upholding the dignity of their office. We may feel we have been placed (or placed ourselves) in an undignified position, like Mr Pooter who 'left the room in silent dignity but caught my foot in the mat' (Grossmith and Grossmith, 1998, p.77) or that we have been treated in an undignified way. We may be accused of being 'on our dignity'. We may treat others with dignity. And we may dignify others by the way in which we treat them. We say things like 'I won't dignify that remark by replying to it . . .', meaning that to respond would give the offending utterance an importance it did not deserve.

Dignity is a favourite word for journalists. Recent examples from London-based newspapers include many comments about the behaviour of people caught up in the recent earthquake in Haiti, of which Reed Lindsay's is typical: '. . . but then I would witness an act of unsolicited kindness or solidarity or perseverance or dignity, and I would be reminded of the spirit and strength of the Haitian people' (Lindsay, 2010). The novelist Hilary Mantel talks of the perils of writing personal memoirs and the difficulty of emerging 'with a scrap of dignity' (Mantel, 2010), while in a more frivolous tone *The Guardian's* Pass Notes column says, of a minor celebrity, that 'she's appearing on Celebrity Big Brother without completely surrendering her dignity' (*The Guardian*, 2010). And on the more serious side of performance, Eric Siblin, discussing the cellist Pabo Casals, quotes the newspaper *Diario de Barcelona* as praising Casals' performance for 'its diction and dignity' (Siblin, 2010).

An editorial in the *Independent on Sunday* gives several examples of people who, the writer claims, personify dignity. They describe Henry Allingham, a First World War veteran who had died recently, saying that there was 'something about the reticence of Mr Allingham that gave him dignity'. They refer also to the broadcaster, the late Walter Kronkite, whose announcement of the death of President John F Kennedy was 'notable for its restraint and dignity' and to Nelson Mandela, 'another man whose dignity has inspired millions' and whose 'public bearing and lack of bitterness were exemplary', arguing that South Africa 'would be in a much worse position today were it not for his moral stature, and the world would be a less hopeful place'. The editorial concludes with the suggestion that what these men have in common is modesty, and their greatness 'moves and inspires us all the more for their restraint and absence of self-advertisement . . . we believe that quiet dignity still commands respect' (*Independent on Sunday*, 2009). Finally, President Obama, in his Nobel Peace Prize acceptance speech, referred to the 'quiet dignity of reformers like Aung Sang Suu Kyi' (Obama, 2009).

The concept of dignity is used in connection with many things. The preceding examples emphasise the dignified behaviour of the individual but in recent times dignity has been particularly applied to the way we treat other people.

Even in death, dignity is important. A British Coroner states that 'Every case is important to somebody, therefore it's important to me . . . each, I would hope, is treated with sincerity and the dignity it deserves' (McGregor, 2010). Media coverage of disasters has resulted in the publication of photographs of the dead and dying, and this presents challenges for photographers and cameramen, with agencies claiming, for example, that they 'do not use pictures that lack dignity' (Gormley, 2010). But it is in the context of healthcare and, in particular, the care of older people that dignity in the treatment of others has received particular attention in recent years. A typical example is that from Wynne (2010), who offers a graphic account of patients who were unable to get out of bed being instructed by nurses to soil themselves instead of being offered bedpans. Wynne suggests that this was 'an obvious assault on dignity and respect'. We thus have two accounts of dignity. On the one hand it is used to refer to the character of the person, the man with quiet dignity, while on the other it is used to refer to the way others are treated, in ways that protect or threaten dignity. This distinction roughly equates to the distinction made by Beyleveld and Brownsword (2001), between dignity as constraint and dignity as empowerment.

A vivid account of dignity in professional roles comes from the novel by Kazuo Ishiguro, *The Remains of the Day*. Ishiguro has his character Mr Stevens, the butler at Darlington Hall, discuss at some length the nature of dignity in the context of 'great butlers'. The (fictional) Hayes Society, a kind of professional body for butlers, describing the necessary characteristics of applicants for positions in great households, asserts that 'the most crucial criterion is that the applicant be possessed of a dignity in keeping with his position' (Ishiguro, 2005, p.33). Ishiguro has Stevens agree, saying that what distinguishes great butlers from those who are just very competent is 'most closely captured by this word "dignity"'. Stevens describes arguments he had with his friend and fellow butler Mr Graham, who felt that this dignity was akin to a woman's beauty 'and it was thus pointless to attempt to analyse it'. Stevens observes that this would mean that 'this "dignity" was something one possessed or did not by a fluke of nature', just as it would be impossible for an ugly woman to try to 'make herself beautiful'. Stevens believed that dignity, at least in the context of butlering, was 'something one can meaningfully strive for throughout one's career' and he described other butlers who he was sure had 'acquired it over many years of self training and the careful absorbing of experience'. Stevens recounts several anecdotes about butlers who demonstrated great dignity, the point being that in each case the butler had behaved impeccably, successfully managing the situation in spite of the great difficulty with which he was confronted.

Stevens' character is deeply flawed, and one would not want to suggest that professional nurses (or any other professionals) should live their lives in the rather extreme way depicted in the novel. However, Ishiguro's account offers several useful pointers as to the nature of professional dignity.

Dignity thus seems to be attached to persons, their positions and their actions. We may feel that we, or others, possess dignity and we may judge that we or others have acted with dignity. We may describe something or someone as possessing dignity or as being dignified and we may describe an action that bestows dignity on something or someone as dignifying. Dignity appears to be inextricably bound up with our identity and the roles we play. However, from Ishiguro's account and the others quoted above, the character of the person is central. The ability 'not to abandon the professional being he inhabits' must be a quality of the person, not a quality of a professional role, even though the role calls for certain qualities, including dignity, in those who would occupy it. Extending this to ordinary life, away from professional practice, one might say of people like Henry Allingham and Aung Sang Suu Kyi that they had or have the ability not to abandon the person they are, the being they inhabit; 'quiet dignity' means having the strength not to be shaken by the unexpected, the difficult or the distressing. Primo Levi, writing about his experiences in the Nazi concentration camps, notes that it takes a brave man to go to his own death with dignity (Levi, 1991); retaining one's dignity in such appalling circumstances does seem the ultimate in courage and moral strength. This focus on the character of the individual and the challenge of remaining dignified in difficult circumstances is one aspect of Beyleveld and Brownsword's (2001) concept of dignity as constraint. Retaining our dignity in the face of difficulties places constraints on our behaviour, requiring that we do not abandon ourselves, do not give in to fear or anger, and so maintain our quiet dignity.

PROFESSIONAL EXPECTATIONS

Professional expectations of dignity appear to be a central concern for nurses throughout the world. The International Council of Nursing (ICN) Code of Ethics states:

> Inherent in nursing is respect for human rights, including cultural rights, the right to life and choice, to dignity and to be treated with respect. Nursing care is respectful of and unrestricted by considerations of age, colour, creed, culture, disability or illness, gender, sexual orientation, nationality, politics, race or social status (ICN, 2006, p.1; Copyright ©2006 by ICN – International Council of Nurses, 3 place Jean-Marteau, 1201 Geneva, Switzerland).

Later in the document the ICN Code also says: 'The nurse, in providing care, ensures that use of technology and scientific advances are compatible with the safety, dignity and rights of people' (p.3). Other codes, such as the Nursing and

Midwifery Council (NMC) in the UK and the American Nurses Association (ANA) in the USA also include strong statements concerning dignity. The ANA Code, for example, says in Provision 1 that nurses should practise 'with compassion and respect for the inherent dignity, worth and uniqueness of every individual . . .' (ANA, 2001), while the NMC Code states: 'You must treat people as individuals and respect their dignity' (NMC, 2008).

These accounts of dignity and others that appear in national and international codes and charters represent Beyleveld and Brownsword's concept of dignity as empowerment. There is a real danger, however, that such approaches may devalue dignity and render it of little use. The tendency to refer to any and every discomfort or mishap as 'undignified' is not helpful. It is never acceptable for nurses to be rude to patients and still less so for them to neglect people or give poor care. But where we used to talk plainly of poor-quality care, of neglect, of poor management, now everything from thoughtless but minor errors to major failures of care are labelled a matter of dignity. It is not clear what is gained by doing this.

PHILOSOPHICAL BASIS FOR DIGNITY

The philosophical grounds for treating people with dignity are contested but several criteria have been offered and these are critiqued elsewhere (for example, Gallagher and Seedhouse, 2002; Gallagher, 2004, 2007; Gallagher *et al*, 2008; Wainwright and Gallagher, 2008). In brief, a plausible summary would be to follow Nordenfelt (2004) and argue that human beings are of intrinsic worth, what Nordenfelt refers to as *Menschenwürde*, that they may also command respect in the light of their moral conduct and their achievements in life, and finally that a distinctive individual identity is both a source of self-respect and sets up some aspects of the grounds on which we should respect others. I take issue with some of the detail of Nordenfelt's analysis (see for example Wainwright and Gallagher, 2008) but I will simply assert here that both *Menschenwürde* and dignity of identity are helpful concepts for nurses, establishing as they do that we should treat all human beings with respect, regardless of any qualitative account of their lives or health status, and that we should demonstrate contextually appropriate respect for individuals, acknowledging individual preferences and offering individualised care.

DIGNITY AS THE BASIS FOR NURSING

At this point I will take a short digression to consider the goals and purpose of nursing. This seems appropriate as, I will argue, our understanding of nursing is very much about the intention that defines the action. The idea of nursing is a common one in everyday speech and is not confined to the professional usage.

'Nurse' and 'nursing' crop up regularly in literature, with, for example, 34 inclusions in the *Oxford Dictionary of Quotations* (Oxford University Press, 1975). Milton's *Comus* speaks of 'Wisdom's . . . best nurse Contemplation', Campbell says 'and if you nurse a flame . . .', and Goldsmith speaks of 'The land of scholars, and the nurse of arms'. Burke, in his *Reflections on the Revolution in France*, says '. . . the nurse of manly sentiment is gone' and Blake in his *Proverbs from Hell* advises us to 'Sooner murder an infant in its cradle than nurse unacted desires'. Field tells us that 'Public schools are the nurseries of all vice and immorality' and Burns speaks of 'our sulky sullen dame . . . nursing her wrath to keep it warm'. There are many examples that refer to the other notions of nursing, as in Shakespeare's baby, mewling and puking at the nurse's breast, and teachers who continue what the nurse began, but this particular selection has been chosen because they better capture the idea of the purpose of nursing, as opposed to the tasks with which it is associated.

From the examples above and from general usage of the words 'nurse' and 'nursing', a shared meaning emerges, which has to do not with specific actions or tasks but with the intention behind those actions or tasks. To say that contemplation is the best nurse of wisdom is to say that contemplation is the best way to develop the quality of wisdom, to nurture and sustain it. To speak of nursing a flame suggests something fragile, which might be extinguished, but which one might want to protect and to keep alight, sheltering it and keeping it burning. Blake's reference to 'unacted desires' also suggests carrying something and not letting it die or be extinguished, while Burns's sullen dame nursing her wrath reminds us that anger, if it is allowed to, may fade away, while an anger that is fed and nurtured, in other words nursed, will continue to burn.

One can imagine other ways in which one might use 'to nurse' as a verb. For example, we might nurse a business through hard times or perhaps, in schoolboy fiction, imagine our hero nursing his crippled aircraft back to base. A child might nurse her doll, or a kitten or other pet. In forestry it is the practice to plant what is called a nurse crop of fast-growing trees to protect and encourage growth in slower-growing species, and young bees, before they go out foraging, spend some time as nurse bees, feeding the developing larvae of the next generation. The shared intention behind all of these applications of the verb 'to nurse' is thus to indicate some means of preserving, nourishing, sustaining, carrying forward, developing, supporting, holding or protecting something, and this something might be a thing, a plant, a creature, an idea, an emotion or an enterprise.

To identify something – call it for the moment a project – as deserving of being nursed and requiring to be nursed implies some recognition of the worth or value of the project and also of its vulnerability, while to undertake to nurse it requires the motivation that comes from a sense of caring about the success of the project because it is recognised as being of worth. Something that is of no consequence will not call forth the motivation required for it to be nurtured and protected, and a worthy project that is flourishing will not require nursing, although it may still require some care, maintenance and protection. So nursing, I would argue, requires the conjunction of three circumstances. It requires that there be some project of a certain worth (or dignity), that this project is vulnerable or at risk of failing to flourish in some way, and that there is someone prepared to engage with the project so as to try to ensure its survival or flourishing.

Nursing as a healthcare profession illustrates this framework quite well. The project that is the focus of the professional nurse, or indeed the lay carer or the individual sufferer himself or herself (we do, after all, frequently nurse ourselves) is the person who is recognised as having some health need or vulnerability. The particular vulnerability will be health related – the presence of some disease process, some pathology, mental distress or something of the sort. The motivation or intention, the desire to nurture and protect the individual sufferer and protect their dignity, comes from two main sources. The first is society, through the mechanism of the state. Countries like the UK that have state-provided healthcare and support a nursing profession do so out of a collective belief that individuals who need healthcare should be provided with it. The provision of healthcare for all, free at the point of need, is not entirely altruistic – it is to the wider benefit of society that the population is healthy – but clearly rests in part on a belief in the individual worth or dignity of the people who make up that society.

The second factor in the provision of nursing is the character of those who nurse – the individuals who care. It is unfashionable to talk about nursing as a vocation in the religious sense, but there can be no doubt, from the pronouncements of professional regulatory bodies such as the NMC in the UK, that there are clear requirements for nurses to be of a certain character. To become a nurse is to become a certain kind of person, with certain values, attitudes and beliefs.

To nurse in the full sense, to pursue the purpose of nursing as understood from the common language examples above, requires not just the willingness but the desire on the part of the practitioner to engage with people, with a view to nurturing them and pursuing their flourishing and promoting their dignity. Why should both society and individual practitioners desire this? For society and for individual practitioners to invest so much in nursing requires the recognition of something in those who need nursing to call forth the caring response. This, I would argue, is the recognition of the intrinsic worth of human beings, which we might otherwise call human dignity.

WORTH, DIGNITY AND RESPECT

If we equate dignity with worth, then to say that something or someone has dignity is to say they have worth. And to acknowledge worth is to acknowledge that we should treat the worthy object with appropriate respect. The important questions then are: on what grounds do we decide whether a thing has worth or dignity, and, in the event that we decide that it does, how then we should respond. From a nursing perspective, the discussion has mostly focused on the dignity of the individual person and, not surprisingly, the person of the patient. The majority of references to dignity in the healthcare literature and the popular press relate to the way in which patients (in particular vulnerable older people, the dying and the dead) are treated by nurses and by the health-care system in general, and whether and to what extent they are treated with respect.

What amounts to contextually appropriate respectful conduct towards others is, of course, also contentious. Gallagher offers a more detailed discussion of this that draws from the work of Joseph Raz (Raz, 2001; Gallagher, 2007). For Raz, the most basic level of respect involves 'appropriate psychological acknowledgement of value, that is, regarding objects in ways consistent with their value' (Raz, 2001, p.161). Raz argues that there is 'a general reason that if we think of an object which is of value, we should think of it in ways consistent with its value' (p.161). Thus, from a nursing perspective, if we accept the basic premise that all human beings are of fundamental worth, then we should think of them in ways consistent with that worth. Similarly, if we think that a person's individual identity, their preferences and so on, are of value, we should also think of those in ways that are consistent with that value.

Raz suggests a second level of respect, arguing that there is also 'a general reason to preserve what is of value', the strength of that reason varying with the value of the object. As Raz says (p.162), 'we have reason not to destroy, and furthermore, to preserve what is of value'. Thus, Raz's argument supports our earlier analysis of the ordinary language view of nursing: we take steps to nurture, preserve and protect those things that we find to be of value, and we take those appropriately in the context of their value and their need for preservation. We informally nurse our projects and we formally create professional nursing and provide nursing services to people with health needs. There are, as Raz acknowledges, some 'difficult questions regarding the nature and limits of these reasons' but we will not attempt to resolve these here.

Merely preserving things of value represents a rather neutral or static approach, suggesting a curator's concern for a collection rather than the more active and progressive nature of nursing, which we might expect to be concerned with the move from vulnerability to well-being. This brings us to the third stage of Raz's analysis, the need for engagement. Engagement requires, according to Raz, attention and discrimination, and would include, for example, 'spending time with friends in ways appropriate to our relationship with them' (p.163). Contrasting this third stage with the previous two, Raz argues that thinking of valuable objects in appropriate ways and preserving them is only a preliminary, while 'value is realised when it is engaged with'. For nursing to achieve its purpose, whether informally when we nurse our favoured projects or more formally when we deliver professional nursing, if we are to realise the worth of our projects or our patients, there is the requirement for engagement, for caring about as well as caring for the object of our nursing.

THE DIGNITY OF A PRACTICE

As we noted above, the main focus in the healthcare literature is on the dignity of people in their experience as patients. However, I want to introduce a further dimension to the debate, which is to consider the value, or worth, or dignity of a practice, specifically the practice of nursing, and of the dignity of the nurse.

To take the idea of the dignity of a practice first, it may seem odd to apply the concept to a socially constructed notion such as that of a practice. For Kolnai, the characteristics of those things that possess dignity include:

> First – the qualities of composure, calmness, restraint, reserve, and emotions or passions subdued and securely controlled without being negated or dissolved . . . Secondly – the qualities of distinctness, delimitation, and distance; of something that conveys the idea of being intangible, invulnerable, inaccessible to destructive or corruptive or subversive interference . . . Thirdly, in consonance therewith, Dignity also tends to connote the features of self-contained serenity, of a certain inward and toned-down but yet translucent and perceptible power of self-assertion . . . With its firm stance and solid immovability, the dignified quietly defies the world (Kolnai, 1976, pp.253–4, reproduced with permission from Cambridge University Press).

As characteristics of a person, we can probably relate to these and recognise them in individuals for whom we have great respect and who we see as being of particular moral worth, very much in line with the examples given at the beginning of this chapter. But can we apply such a description to an inanimate object? Kolnai suggests that:

> The predicates . . . [of dignity] are chiefly applicable to so-called 'human beings', i.e. persons, but . . . not exclusively so: much dignity in this sense seems to me proper to the Cat, and not a little, with however different connotation, to the Bull or the Elephant . . . is not the austere mountainous plateau of Old Castile a dignified landscape . . . ? And, though man-made, cannot works of art (especially of the 'classic' though not exactly 'classicist' type) have a dignity of their own? (Kolnai, 1976, p.254, reproduced with permission from Cambridge University Press).

While it seems reasonable to view animals and inanimate objects as having intrinsic value or worth, they would lack any capacity for morality. While we acknowledge the notion of the fundamental worth of human beings, the dignity of *Menschenwürde*, any notion of the dignity of people beyond this basic intrinsic worth seems typically to be based on the notion of morality. Thus 'the qualities of composure, calmness, restraint, reserve, and emotions or passions subdued and securely controlled without being negated or dissolved' in a person would reflect their moral character, and while 'the austere mountainous plateau of Old Castile' may invoke feelings of calmness in the observer, this must be a projection, rather than any intrinsic quality in the landscape. Calmness is a human quality and judgement.

But a practice is rather different. It is not a kind of mammal, nor is it an inanimate object, nor even a landscape, although it may have some of the characteristics of at least two of these. It is, first and foremost, a human activity and, fundamentally, a moral activity (*see*, for example, MacIntyre, 1985). Practices result in the realisation of goods, and they demand the pursuit of standards of excellence that are themselves definitive of the practice. A practice has a goal or purpose, which is, by definition, a moral purpose, and in this way practices differ from animals and inanimate objects. It is perhaps not stretching the point too far to suggest that the collective intention of its practitioners, together with the other moral characteristics, gives a practice the kind of intrinsic value or worth that we might well call dignity.

One test of this proposition is to consider the kind of response that practices demand from us. When we reflect on the nursing profession, the medical profession, the clergy or the judiciary (or at least on some notion of them as ideal types), or even Mr Stevens's notion of the 'great butlers', we must surely accord them respect. As Kolnai says of the way we should respond to those things that have dignity, our response:

> must bear a close resemblance to our devoted and admiring appreciation of beauty (its 'high' forms at any rate) on the one hand, to our reverent approval of moral goodness (and admiration, say, for heroic virtue) on the other. Dignity commands empathic respect, a reverential mode of response, an 'upward-looking' type of the *pro* attitude: a 'bowing' gesture if I may so call it (Kolnai, 1976, p.252).

Leaving aside modern cynicism, an idealised or aspirational view of a practice as a moral enterprise or a social good would surely qualify for such a response.

It is perhaps rather easier to understand the dignity of nursing and of the nurse as embodied in the practice of the individual. Nordenfelt includes as one of his types of dignity the idea of dignity of merit, which he says accrues from the attainment of some position of status or significance, either by birth or through one's own success. If we accept the brief sketch offered above of the nature of practices, then achieving admission to a professional practice through one's study, success in examinations and acceptance by one's peers, surely represents the type of situation that Nordenfelt would have in mind. But going beyond the mere elevation to the status of registered nurse, which is on the face of it perhaps the kind of position that Raz would suggest we label simply 'social status' rather than as having dignity, the good nurse, the expert practitioner, might well be expected to display the qualities that Kolnai (1976) describes, 'qualities of composure, calmness, restraint, reserve, and emotions or passions subdued and securely controlled without being negated or dissolved'. Like Mr Stevens's great butlers, the good nurse has the '. . . ability not to abandon the professional being [s]he inhabits'. Good nurses are perhaps good 'by virtue of their ability to inhabit their professional role and inhabit it to the utmost; they will not be shaken out by external events, however surprising, alarming or vexing'.

CONCLUSION

Dignity, despite the reservations of some authors, does appear to have some value as a concept for nursing and, indeed, for other healthcare professionals. It does not have a great deal of specificity or precision as an idea but its vagueness or even 'squishyness' is perhaps part of its value. I would argue that dignity is, at least in some respects, regarded as a virtue, but as with all the virtues it therefore requires the application of prudence or wisdom. Our position can thus be summarised as follows:

➤ dignity is best regarded as essentially a moral quality or virtue
➤ it relates to the intrinsic worth of an object, rather than its exchange value
➤ because of its essentially moral nature, it is best applied to humanity and human activity. Other animals and inanimate objects may possess some similar qualities but these are best regarded in the Aristotelian sense, as characteristic, but not fully characteristic, of dignity
➤ human beings have intrinsic worth, and thus dignity, but beyond this minimal qualification it is the quality of human behaviour and the intention underlying that behaviour that determines its dignity
➤ objects that are of value demand respect, and those that have dignity are of moral worth and demand a particularly moral respect
➤ following Raz (2001), we understand three levels of response to objects of worth: acknowledgement; preservation; engagement
➤ the precise nature of our response must be to the particularity of the situation and thus unpredictable in the detail, but predictable in general principle. In this I follow Kolnai (1976), suggesting a style of response that should be similar to our appreciation of beauty and to our approval

of moral goodness and admiration for virtue on the other. As Kolnai says, 'Dignity commands empathic respect, a reverential mode of response, an "upward-looking" type of the pro attitude: a "bowing" gesture. . .'

I argue that there are three classes or categories of objects, in the context of nursing and healthcare, to which dignity is relevant:

> the first of these is the patient (client or service user, and all those associated with the patient, including carers, family members and so on). All such people demand our acknowledgement, preservation and engagement, in recognition of their intrinsic worth as human beings and of their individual identity

> second, the individual nurse, as a human being, is entitled to respect in terms of basic humanity, individual identity and in recognition of his or her expertise and professional standing. The professional nurse must also behave with dignity, exhibiting the qualities that characterise the good nurse and the good professional life

> thirdly, the practice of nursing has moral worth and demands respect. As a moral endeavour, nursing demands acknowledgement, preservation and engagement, but only in so far as this is justified by the preservation of its purpose and the recognition of its excellence.

Put even more simply, I would argue that the concept of dignity can be reduced to the recognition of moral worth and the appropriately respectful response to that worth, in all areas of human life. In the context of professional nursing, this entitles the patient to expect respectful treatment and behaviour from nurses and places the responsibility on the nurse to embody the notion of respect. This suggests that wisdom, respectfulness and dignity itself are core virtues for nursing as a practice.

REFERENCES

American Nurses Association (2001) *Code of Ethics for Nurses*. Silver Spring: American Nurses Association.

Beyleveld D, Brownsword R (2001) *Human Dignity in Bioethics and Biolaw*. Oxford: Oxford University Press.

Bostrom N (2008) Dignity and enhancement. In: *Human Dignity and Bioethics: essays commissioned by the president's council on bioethics*. Washington, DC: The President's Council on Bioethics, pp.173–207.

Gallagher A (2004) Dignity and respect for dignity – two key health professional values: implications for nursing practice. *Nursing Ethics* **11**(6): 587–99.

Gallagher A (2007) The respectful nurse. *Nursing Ethics* **14**(3): 360–71.

Gallagher A, Seedhouse D (2002) Dignity in care: the views of patients and relatives. *Nursing Times* **98**(43): 38–40.

Gallagher A, Li S, Lee D, Wainwright P, Jones IR (2008) Dignity in the care of older people – a review of the theoretical and empirical literature. *BMC Nursing* 7(11). www.biomedcentral.com/1472-6955/7/11 (accessed 8 October 2010).

Gormley B (2010) I wasn't very charitable. *The Guardian*, 23 January.

Grossmith G, Grossmith W (1998) *Diary of a Nobody*. Oxford: Oxford Paperbacks.

Independent on Sunday (2010) Editorial. *Independent on Sunday*, 19 July.

International Council for Nurses (2006) *Code of Ethics for Nurses*. Geneva: International Council for Nurses.

Ishiguro K (2005) *The Remains of the Day*. London: Faber.

Kolnai A (1976) Dignity. *Philosophy* **51**: 251–71.

Levi P (1991) *If This is a Man*. London: Abacus.

Lindsay R (2010) Spirit and strength will pull Haiti's people through. *The Observer*, 24 January.

MacIntye A (1985) *After Virtue: a study in moral theory*. London: Duckworth.

Mantel H (2010) A memoir of my former self. *The Guardian*, 23 January.

McGregor J (2010) On coroners' courts. *The Guardian*, 23 January.

Nordenfelt L (2004) The varieties of dignity. *Health Care Analysis* **12**(2): 69–98.

Nursing and Midwifery Council (2008) *The Code: standards of conduct, performance and ethics for nurses and midwives*. London: Nursing and Midwifery Council.

Obama B (2009) *A Just and Lasting Peace*. http://nobelprize.org/nobel_prizes/peace/laureates/2009/obama-lecture_en.html (accessed 8 October 2010).

Oxford University Press (1975) *Oxford Dictionary of Quotations*. Oxford: Oxford University Press.

Pinker S (2008) The stupidity of dignity: conservative bioethics' latest, most dangerous ploy. *The New Republic*, 28 May. http://pinker.wjh.harvard.edu/articles/media/The Stupidity of Dignity.htm (accessed 8 October 2010).

Raz J (2001) *Value, Respect and Attachment*. Cambridge: Cambridge University Press.

Siblin E (2010) How Bach's cello suites changed Eric Siblin's life. *The Guardian*, 16 January.

The Guardian (2010) Pass notes. *The Guardian*, 18 January.

Wainwright P, Gallagher A (2008) On different types of dignity in nursing care: a critique of Nordenfelt. *Nursing Philosophy* **9**: 46–54.

Wynne A (2010) Shortcuts to bad health care. *The Guardian*, 13 January.

CHAPTER 4

Dignity as a policy issue in healthcare

Alistair Hewison

INTRODUCTION

There has been a lot of talk about dignity recently – politicians, charities, even celebrities are talking about it (Cann and Lishman, 2009). Indeed, since 2006 there has been a growing interest in, and concern about, dignity, or rather the lack of it, in care services in the United Kingdom (UK). This has arisen in part from a series of exposés such as the undercover filming for the BBC Panorama programme, which revealed hospital patients being left in pain without medication, nurses failing to respond to people who desperately needed to use the toilet, patients who were unable to eat going hungry, and some patients dying alone and unnoticed (Whyte, 2008). Similarly when summarising a recent report from the Patients Association (Patients Association, 2009), Boseley (2009) concluded that 'vulnerable and elderly' NHS patients were receiving poor-quality care and being denied their basic dignity in hospitals across the UK. This recognition of failure, in maintaining the dignity of clients, has resulted in it being given prominence in recent health policy focused on quality. The *Next Stage Review* (Department of Health [DH], 2008), or the Darzi review as it is generally referred to, named after its author, states:

> Quality of care includes quality of *caring*. This means how personal care is –
> the compassion, dignity and respect with which patients are treated. It can only
> be improved by analysing and understanding patient satisfaction with their own
> experiences [emphasis in the original] (DH, 2008, p.47).

The purpose of this chapter is to examine how patient dignity became a pressing policy issue in the UK, and what the response to this has been. In order to do this, it is necessary to discuss briefly some key aspects of the policy process to demonstrate how dignity came to be placed on the policy agenda. Next the policy action taken to address the 'dignity problem' will be examined, and finally consideration will be given to whether or not progress has been made.

This is not as straightforward a task as might first appear, because not only is the policy process complex, but there is no agreement on the precise definition of dignity in policy terms. However, this serves to underline the importance of exploring this area of policy. The UK health and social care sector is subject to constant scrutiny, review and policy direction. Without an understanding of this context, practitioners may experience difficulty in maintaining clients' dignity, as they will not be aware of how it is expressed in policy terms, what is expected of them as individual clinicians, or the challenges it presents.

LEARNING OUTCOMES

By the end of the chapter you will be able to:

➤ summarise the policy process in healthcare
➤ examine the role of the government, pressure groups and the media in the UK dignity campaign
➤ discuss policy implementation and how this relates to practitioners and clients in the National Health Service (NHS)
➤ identify the organisational and structural challenges affecting the implementation of the dignity policy
➤ review progress to date and consider the implications for future practice.

THE POLICY PROCESS IN HEALTHCARE

Two definitions usefully summarise the policy process and signal the particular aspects of it that need to be explored in more detail if its effects on health services and patient care are to be understood. For example:

> Health policy refers to the laws and directions from governments that seek to affect and to regulate or to supply state-run health care services. In industrial countries health policy is a major area of political interest and public debate (Cox, 2010, p.294; reproduced with permission from Polity Press).

While this characterisation of policy provides a helpful starting point, it does not fully convey its inherent complexity and tangled nature. This is more evident below:

> Policy making is complex; it is a political activity which crosses national borders. Policies can be made by individuals and organisations, as well as by governments and other agencies, and they can be made at a local level, as well as at regional, national and international levels. Policies at local and national levels often emerge from other policies that have been determined at a global level; however, local policy and practice can also influence global policy making (Earle, 2007, p.5; reproduced with permission from Sage Publications).

In view of this, rather than seek an all-encompassing definition, a way of trying to make sense of policy is to approach it as a process made up of a series of stages (*see* Box 4.1).

BOX 4.1 *The stagist model of policy (adapted from Dorey, 2005)*

Agenda setting
↓
Recognition of the problem/issue
↓
Consideration of the options for action
↓
Agreement/decision on the most suitable option
↓
Introduction of the policy (may involve legislation)
↓
Implementation

The manifesto of a political party or the underlying ideology of a particular government sets the overall direction for the way it addresses policy issues. For example, the commitment to lower taxation and less public ownership of services such as health and education would result in a distinct policy programme, whereas a party or government with a belief in collective responsibility and the provision of a wide range of public services provided by the state would produce a contrasting set of policies. This overall orientation then influences what are deemed to be 'problems' in need of action. Consequently, unemployment can be a problem, in that it is something that needs to be dealt with. Or it can be perceived as an inevitable consequence of the way the economy works and therefore not requiring attention or specific intervention on the part of government. Once a problem is identified, the options for how best to address it are evaluated, in order to inform a decision about selecting the most effective way of solving it. Finally the policy is put into practice.

Although 'stagist' accounts such as this present an impression of order and logic, this is not accurate by any means. The agenda-setting stage, for example, is not conducted in isolation; it is influenced to a large extent by public opinion and the media (see below). Policy is not always developed in a planned and ordered way; it is often reactive and incremental (Lindblom, 1959, 1979). The use of evidence has been identified as central to the policy process in terms of its design, or 'consideration of options for action'; essentially 'what counts is what works' (Cabinet Office, 1999). However, even when it is agreed that evidence should underpin policy, the availability of different forms of evidence serves to make the process more challenging (Gauld, 2001). In addition, evidence does not provide answers to difficult questions about 'what should be done'; these remain moral and ethical judgements (Greenhalgh and Russell, 2009). Implementation is not a simple act of taking a policy and introducing it, because sometimes the policy is ignored, or more often it is changed by those putting it into practice (Hannigan and Burnard, 2000; Schofield, 2004).

Even this brief review of the stagist model indicates that it is by no means a complete and inclusive account of the policy process. This being the case, why include it here? It is beyond the scope of this chapter to conduct a detailed examination of policy, yet a framework is needed to shape the discussion that follows. So although the stagist model can be called into question for oversimplifying things, it does provide a useful conceptual description of the complex policy process, which breaks it up into manageable parts (Thurber, 2003). With this in mind, the subsequent sections will focus on particular stages of the process as a way of illustrating how dignity became a prominent issue in UK healthcare that demanded action.

GETTING DIGNITY ON THE POLICY AGENDA

If an issue is to appear on the policy agenda, Ham (2004) suggests it must:
➤ attract attention
➤ claim legitimacy
➤ invoke action (Solesbury, 1976; Ham, 2004).

The agenda has been defined as the list of subjects or problems to which government officials, and people outside government closely associated with those officials, are paying some serious attention at any given time (Kingdon, 2003). The 26 departments of the UK government each have more specialised agendas and the key concerns in health are different from those in the Ministry of Justice, for example. Kingdon (2003) offers the useful analogy of a 'policy window' to describe how problems, solutions and decisions come together to generate action. A policy window opens when three streams – problems, proposals and politics – come together. The way these elements came together to raise the profile of dignity in healthcare indicates how an issue that might have been assumed to be a 'given', in the sense that maintaining patients' dignity was a normal and expected part of care, was highlighted as a problem, placed prominently on the policy agenda, and invoked action. The work of Ham (2004) and Kingdon (2003) will be used to inform the explanation of how dignity became a policy issue in healthcare.

Attract attention

In 2006, the Health Care Commission (2006) reported that it found that some older people experienced poor standards of care on general hospital wards, including poorly managed discharges from hospitals, being repeatedly moved from one ward to another for non-clinical reasons, being cared for in mixed-sex bays or wards and having their meals taken away before they could eat them. It recommended that all users of health and social care services should be treated with dignity and respect. This report, along with a series of damning articles in the popular press, such as one in the *Daily Mail* newspaper which estimated that the number of elderly patients starving in NHS wards doubled to 30 000 between 2005 and 2007 (Martin, 2008), all served to ensure that dignity 'attracted attention'.

Claim legitimacy

This issue clearly claimed legitimacy, as it was of interest and concern to politicians and the public. This is reflected in the impetus given to the DH's dignity campaign by a range of bodies and organisations once it was launched. However, in the first instance legitimacy was conferred on this area of policy making through the initiative launched by the Secretary of State for Care Services at the time, Ivan Lewis.

In presenting this policy development, Ivan Lewis acknowledged that health and social care services had made significant progress in reducing waiting times and improving access to services; however, the emphasis on throughput and targets had compromised the quality of patients' experience. The Dignity in Care campaign was aimed at redressing that balance and putting dignity at the heart of care (DH 2006a). Thus, political legitimacy ensured that the need to provide dignity in care would invoke action.

Invoke action

The main way in which action was invoked was through the dignity campaign.

THE DIGNITY IN CARE CAMPAIGN

Formally launched on 14 November 2006, the Dignity in Care campaign (DH, 2006a) was intended to stimulate a national debate around dignity in care, end tolerance of services that did not respect the dignity of those using them and raise the profile of respecting people's dignity. It involved:

➤ the allocation of £67 million to local authorities to enable them to improve the physical environment of care for older people; to help older people living in care homes to do so with dignity; and to enable care homes to be more responsive to the needs of older residents

➤ the issuing of the dignity challenge, a ten-point plan that sets out the national expectations of what constitutes a service that respects dignity (*see* Box 4.2) and the plan to establish a network of local champions of dignity, described as an army of volunteers who would work to raise the profile of dignity in care locally

➤ the issuing of the *Dignity in Care Practice Guide* intended to help frontline staff, practitioners, managers, commissioners, older people and their carers to take up the dignity challenge.

There was also a commitment to review policy in the following areas:

➤ safeguarding vulnerable adults
➤ complaints reforms
➤ training and registration of the workforce
➤ improving the care environment (DH, 2006a).

BOX 4.2 *The dignity challenge (DH, 2006b, 2009a)*

High-quality care services that respect people's dignity should:
1. have a zero tolerance of all forms of abuse
2. support people with the same respect you would want for yourself or a member of your family
3. treat each person as an individual by offering a personalised service
4. enable people to maintain the maximum possible level of independence, choice and control
5. listen and support people to express their needs and wants
6. respect people's right to privacy
7. ensure people feel able to complain without fear of retribution
8. engage with family members and carers as care partners
9. assist people to maintain confidence and a positive self-esteem
10. act to alleviate people's loneliness and isolation.

(Department of Health, 2006b, Crown copyright; reproduced with permission from the Controller of HMSO and the Queen's Printer for Scotland)

It was made clear at the launch that the campaign was not intended to be a 'one-off' event. It was a major priority for the DH and would involve a sustained series of actions, events and policy development (DH, 2006a). This endorsement of the importance of this issue at government level served to cement its legitimacy, and the subsequent programme of events associated with it helped to ensure that sustained action would follow and keep dignity on the policy agenda. For example, two days later (16 November) the Secretary of State wrote to the chairs and chief executives of all the strategic health authorities in England, chairs and chief executives of primary care trusts, chairs of NHS acute trusts and directors of adult social services, amongst others, to explain the campaign and issue the dignity challenge (*see* Box 4.2). He concluded by stating: 'I hope I can count on your support and that together we can create a care system where there is zero tolerance of abuse and disrespect of older people' (DH, 2006b, p.2).

The second major event of the dignity campaign was on 23 January 2007 in Birmingham. The Secretary of State made a speech about dignity, with particular emphasis on the importance of nutrition. During the event he also called on those in attendance to become 'dignity champions', who would challenge bad practice and encourage colleagues and others to look at how dignity can be improved in their locality (DH, 2007a). A dignity champion is someone who believes passionately that being treated with dignity is a basic human right and that care services must be compassionate and person centred, as well as efficient, and are willing to try to help achieve this (DH, 2009a). Examples of such activities include:

➤ challenging disrespectful behaviour
➤ acting as a positive role model by treating other people with respect, particularly those who are less able to stand up for themselves
➤ discussing how to improve the way that services are organised and delivered, in order to maintain dignity
➤ influencing and informing colleagues
➤ listening to and understanding the views and experiences of citizens (DH, 2009b).

Champions are committed to taking action, however small, to create a care system that has compassion and respect for its clients. Each champion's role varies depending on their knowledge, influence and the type of work they do. They include health and social care managers and frontline staff. They also include doctors, dieticians, porters, care workers in care homes, Members of Parliament (MPs), councillors, members of local action groups and local involvement networks (LINks), people from voluntary and advocacy organisations, people who use care services and their relatives and carers as well as members of the public (DH, 2009b).

The campaign is supported by the Royal College of Nursing (RCN), the British Geriatrics Society and Help the Aged, and was boosted by the recruitment of veteran broadcaster Sir Michael Parkinson as its Dignity Ambassador in July 2008. He reported how his mother was starved of care and compassion in a range of establishments leading up to her death, and how this fostered his desire to change the attitude of the NHS and British society to old people (Parkinson, 2008a). He expressed his pride in becoming the ambassador for the campaign that aims to put dignity and respect back at the heart of care by giving a voice to those who need care and encouraging them to stand up and tackle services that do not respect dignity (Parkinson, 2008b). The support of the organisations listed above, and media coverage of further high-profile events such as the National Dignity Tour (BBC, 2008; *Health Service Journal*, 2008) are examples of how the issue continued to be highlighted and helped to ensure that it remained on the policy agenda.

IMPLEMENTING POLICY

As a result of the DH's Dignity in Care campaign, there is no shortage of guidance indicating what practitioners, and indeed all those working in health and social care, need to do to maintain the dignity of clients. For example, guides have been produced by a number of organisations, including Age Concern (2008), the Royal College of Nursing (2008a,b), the Nursing and Midwifery Council (NMC, 2009), and the Social Care Institute for Excellence (SCIE, 2009). This illustrates how charitable bodies, professional regulatory bodies and professional organisations all seek to shape the formation and implementation of policy. They provide detailed instruction and 'best practice' examples to demonstrate how dignity can be delivered. The advice provided is founded on particular definitions of dignity, which are examined in detail in Chapter 2; however, in policy terms, consideration needs to be given to what happens next. Policy can be regarded as both a statement of intent by those seeking to change or control behaviour, and a negotiated output emerging from the implementation process (Barrett, 2004). In practice, this means that putting policy into action often takes place through informal networks and contacts between people rather than through the mechanisms of formal institutions (Newman, 2002). The individual actions of those working in care environments are key to determining whether clients are looked after in a way that promotes and maintains their dignity. However, as in other areas of policy, the success or failure of implementation is affected by a range of factors including the organisational context, leadership, and resources.

CHALLENGES IN IMPLEMENTING DIGNITY POLICY

Two challenges practitioners face in implementing policy related to dignity will be examined briefly to illustrate how policy is of direct relevance to those delivering care. These are the environment of care and working practices.

The environment of care

One of the factors that presents a particular challenge in relation to dignity is the nature of the care environment. The importance of accommodation in the maintenance of patient dignity is examined in Chapter 5; consequently, the focus here is on how action to improve the care environment is being driven by the DH, and in particular the measures being put in place to address the issue of mixed-sex accommodation. This is necessary because in a study involving 2000 interviews with members of the general public, two-thirds of the respondents reported that mixed-sex accommodation was unacceptable because it led to a lack of privacy (DH, 2007b).

Recent policy guidance has made it clear that men and women should not have to share sleeping accommodation or toilet facilities, and from 2010 to

2011 hospitals that fail to achieve this will face serious financial consequences, unless there is an overriding clinical justification (DH, 2010). To help ensure that this target is achieved, an allocation of £100 million has been made to strategic health authorities in England in the form of a privacy and dignity fund which must be used to make the changes in buildings and processes necessary to comply with this requirement (DH, 2009c). Delivery against the privacy and dignity fund plans is being monitored fortnightly, and payment will be with-held if satisfactory progress is not being made (DH, 2009d). This will be man-aged using 'rigorous and transparent performance measures' from April 2010, to ensure same-sex accommodation is provided for every NHS patient (DH, 2009e). This combination of incentives and penalties is intended to ensure that the sensitive issue of mixed-sex accommodation is addressed and so taken off the policy agenda. However, this can be regarded as 'work in progress' and in the meantime nurses may have to care for people in wards or departments that make it difficult to maintain patients' dignity. Yet the potentially adverse effects of unsuitable surroundings can be offset to a large extent by the actions of those delivering care. The most important consideration for people concern-ing their privacy and dignity is the attitudes of staff. The seemingly small acts, such as ensuring curtains are completely drawn and toilet doors are closed, have a real impact on the extent to which people feel they have been treated with dignity and respect (DH, 2007b). Chapter 6 considers in detail how staff behaviour can promote dignity.

The NMC (2009) guide states that part of the nurse's responsibility is ensur-ing that older people are cared for in single-sex accommodation whenever possible (p.12), although it is conceded that 'you may have to work in an envi-ronment which is not conducive to delivering care which meets the specific needs of older people' (p.32). In addition, a list of practical actions has been developed by the Chief Nurse to guide nurses in maintaining dignity (Box 4.3).

Now carry out Reflective activity 4.1.

Reflective activity 4.1

As an implementer of policy how can you ensure you comply with the Chief Nurse's list of practical actions (*see* Box 4.3)?

Working practices

The way that care work is carried out is another element of implementation that needs to be considered if the policy commitment to ensure that clients are treated with dignity is to be met. Few conditions are more important than continence with regard to privacy and dignity (Wagg *et al*, 2006), and so data extracts from a recent research report examining privacy and dignity in this

BOX 4.3 *The Chief Nurse's advice on dignity (DH, 2007c)*

Practical actions at individual level
➤ Give as much control as possible to patients, for example:
  – do not enter closed curtains unannounced
  – ask patients how they wish to be addressed
  – try to offer a choice of single-sex room or bay if available
➤ Challenge poor practice
➤ Consider becoming a dignity champion
➤ Apologise for every episode of mixing
➤ Give extra personal nursing support to patients in mixed bays, for example:
  – use a separate quiet room for personal conversations
  – avoid giving personal care (for example, toileting) in the bay where possible
  – allocate extra nursing time to confused patients who may act inappropriately.

area will be used to illustrate how conflicting working practices need to be balanced by practitioners to maintain clients' dignity. A total of ten individual semi-structured interviews were conducted as part of a broader observational study, seven with nursing home residents and three with hospital patients aged 68–89 years (Billings *et al*, 2009). It is not possible to examine the findings in detail here; however, two brief accounts from the participants are presented as a means of illustrating how different demands in relation to working practices need to be managed by those providing care.

I mean some people have to be hoisted to the toilet, well I'd hate that. That's what happened when I went into [. . .] hospital for the two weeks, they hoisted me everywhere and boy did I get sick and tired of that. . . . They took all your dignity away. Well as they say you've got no dignity left, I said "No, all the dignity's gone, stand up, pull your pants down, pull them up when you get up" (NH3:4:v3:p.19).

No. There wouldn't be a choice. The reason is that the hoist is in constant use with other patients and trying to get hold of it is very difficult and I think if you wanted the bed pan, invariably that means that you need to go so they're quite quick with it and they don't hang about, they might take 5 minutes or maybe 10 but there is not a choice, you only get the hoist if you have already got it and you make the opportunity of it. It's not a toilet requisite if you like, it's not, "we'll hoist him out and he can go to the toilet", that doesn't happen (H2:15:V1:p.19).

There is a requirement that all healthcare workers discharge their duty to use machinery and equipment, such as handling aids, where it has been provided for the employee in accordance with the training and/or instruction provided (Health and Safety Executive, 1992). However, in the incidents recorded above, the use of the hoist was implicated in reducing clients' dignity, either because they thought its use undignified or its limited availability presented a risk in relation to safe transfer to the toilet. There is no simple answer here, as both sets of requirements must be met. Safety and dignity need to be maintained. If the potential for a clash between the two competing local policies of maintaining client safety and dignity is to be reduced, then care staff need to deploy a range of skills and knowledge. The RCN (2008b) guide for unit managers, ward managers and team leaders is intended to provide practical support for those wanting to promote and maintain dignity in the workplace. Key to this is 'influence' and 'understanding your organisation' (RCN, 2008a,b). In essence, this requires that practitioners learn more about how their organisations work and seek to influence those around them to focus on dignity as a priority in care. In the situation outlined above, it would involve working closely with clients to build agreement about how best to balance these care priorities in an acceptable manner. In the context of policy implementation, this further emphasises the observation others have made that those delivering services can have a significant effect on how policy is put into practice (Barrett, 2004; Schofield, 2004). Getting results from a policy depends to some degree on the manner in which professionals interpret the policy and incorporate it into their day-to day work (Barton, 2008), which serves to underline how the different elements of the policy process need to fit together if change is to occur. In the case of dignity, a high-profile media campaign has ensured it is prominent on the policy agenda; support and direction from senior politicians and a range of other organisations have combined to ensure that it claims legitimacy, and those same organisations along with health workers are in the process of invoking action.

PROGRESS

Examination of selected issues in the context of the policy process sheds light on the nature of the challenges involved in ensuring that dignity for clients is managed effectively in a large and complex care service. In this final section, the way these challenges have been addressed will be discussed to evaluate progress. The DH's Dignity in Care campaign has been supported by an investment of £2.5 million and has involved 11 events including conferences, four ministerial 'web-chats', award ceremonies and stakeholder lunches, attended by the Dignity Ambassador. Many resources have also been produced to promote and support the dignity champions (DH, 2009d). In October 2008 it was announced that the 3000th person had volunteered to become a dignity champion (Health4Media, 2008), and by 11 November 2009 the number had risen to 10 000 (DH, 2009f). The success of the campaign has raised the profile of dignity as an issue, and this has been reflected in the emergence of reports charting how initiatives to address dignity issues have improved care.

For example, as part of an initiative conducted between 2007 and 2008 in a district general hospital in Surrey, a series of awareness-raising workshops were undertaken, a bay area in a ward was designated solely for the care of female trauma patients with dementia, and a working group was convened to develop practice further, in order to enhance the privacy and dignity of patients with dementia (Haak, 2009). Elsewhere, staff and patient involvement in the creative arts has been used as a way of exploring and improving shared under-standings of dignity (Webster *et al*, 2009 – *see* Chapter 16, 'Enabling dignity in care through practice development'). Finally, Maxwell and Sigsworth (2009) explain how a judgement of non-compliance against the Care Quality Com-mission's standard on privacy and dignity (20b) stimulated a £10m trust-wide capital redevelopment programme to ensure that the physical environment was changed to improve privacy and dignity in the trust. The project also resulted in a complete culture change, with the maintenance of privacy and dignity being regarded in the same terms as other performance targets.

These examples demonstrate how policy action at a national, organisational and departmental level is needed if it is to be successfully introduced. The challenge for the future will be to ensure it remains on the agenda and does not get sidelined by other pressing issues.

CONCLUSION

Without an understanding of how policy works and an awareness of the influence it has on practice, it is difficult for healthcare workers to bring about change in their organisations. Despite all the high-level activity noted earlier, what dignity means in practical terms can be lost (Cann and Lishman, 2009). Ultimately it is the actions of health and social care staff working with clients that will determine whether or not people are cared for in a dignified manner. If the risk of it becoming a 'buzzword' (Cann and Lishman, 2009) is to be averted, then a continuing and concerted effort is required at every level of policy making to ensure that dignity is kept on the 'agenda'. As Cann (2008) concludes: 'Dignity must not become the victim of political slogans – a concept that everyone agrees is important but no one quite knows how to deliver' (p.2).

REFERENCES

Age Concern (2008) *Quality not Inequality: Age Concern's vision for the future of quality social care.* London: Age Concern.

Barrett SM (2004) Implementation studies: time for a revival? Personal reflections on 20 years of implementation studies. *Public Administration* **82**(2): 249–62.

Barton A (2008) New Labour's management, audit and 'what works' approach to controlling 'untrustworthy' professions. *Public Policy and Administration* **23**(3): 263–77.

BBC News (2008) *Parkinson in Dignity Campaign.* http://news.bbc.co.uk/1/hi/health/7410034.stm (accessed 8 October 2010).

Billings J, Alaszewski H, Wagg A (2009) *Privacy and Dignity in Continence Care Project – attributes of dignified bladder and bowel care in hospital and care homes* (Phase 1 Report). Canterbury: Centre for Health Service Studies, University of Kent/Royal College of Physicians/British Geriatric Society. www.rcplondon.ac.uk/clinical-standards/ceeu/Current-work/Documents/Privacy-and-Dignity-in-Continence-Care-Phase-1-Report-Nov-2009.pdf (accessed 8 October 2010).

Boseley S (2009) Patients 'demeaned' by poor-quality nursing care. *The Guardian* 27 August. www.guardian.co.uk/society/2009/aug/27/patients-association-poor-quality-care (accessed 8 October 2010).

Cabinet Office (1999) *Professional Policy Making for the Twenty-First Century.* London: Cabinet Office.

Cann P (2008) Why does dignity matter? In: *On Our Own Terms: the challenge of assessing dignity in care.* London: The Picker Institute/Help the Aged, p.2.

Cann P, Lishman G (2009) Liberty, equality – and dignity. *Health Service Journal* **119**(6148): 14.

Cox D (2010) Health policy. In: Denny E, Earle S (eds) *Sociology for Nurses* (2e). Cambridge: Polity Press, pp.293–310.

Department of Health (2006a) *£67Million Pledged to Improve Care Homes for Older People.* London: Department of Health. www.mmnetwork.nhs.uk/med-man-new-details.php?newsid=1200 (accessed 8 October 2010).

Department of Health (2006b) *Dignity in Care.* Gateway Reference 7388. London: Department of Health.

Department of Health (2007a) *Speech by Ivan Lewis MP, Parliamentary Under Secretary of State for Care Services, 23 January 2007: Dignity in Care regional event, Birmingham.* London: Department of Health. www.dh.gov.uk/en/News/Speeches/DH_064793 (accessed 8 October 2010).

Department of Health (2007b) *Public Perceptions of Privacy and Dignity – Research Study conducted for the Department of Health.* London: Department of Health.

Department of Health (2007c) *Privacy and Dignity – A Report by the Chief Nursing Officer into Mixed Sex Accommodation in Hospitals.* London: Department of Health.

Department of Health (2008) *High Quality Care for All: NHS next stage review final report.* London: Department of Health.

Department of Health (2009a) *The Dignity Challenge.* London: Department of Health. www.dh.gov.uk/prod_consum_dh/groups/dh_digitalassets/documents/digitalasset/dh_085105.pdf (accessed 8 October 2010).

Department of Health (2009b) *Dignity in Care. Becoming a champion.* London: Department of Health. www.dignityincare.org.uk/_library/Dignity_in_Care_A5_final.pdf (accessed 8 October 2010).

Department of Health (2009c) *The Story so Far. Delivering same-sex accommodation: a progress report.* London: Department of Health.

Department of Health (2009d) *Chief Nurse's Letter: eliminating mixed sex accommodation.* London: Department of Health.

Department of Health (2009e) *Input Assessment – Dignity in Care Campaign.* London: Department of Health.

Department of Health (2009f) *Sir Michael Parkinson's Dignity Champions Reach 10 000.* London: Department of Health. http://webarchive.nationalarchives.gov.uk/+/www.dh.gov.uk/en/MediaCentre/Pressreleasesarchive/DH_108178

Department of Health (2010) *Majority of NHS Trusts Declare Same-Sex Accommodation.* www.wired-gov.net/wg/wg-news-1.nsf/0/73BD8A0278835DE6802576F70038C97E?OpenDocument

Dorey P (2005) *Policy Making in Britain: an introduction.* London: Sage Publications.

Earle S (2007) Promoting public health in a global context. In: Lloyd CE, Hansley S, Douglas J, Earle S, Spurr S (eds) *Policy and Practice in Promoting Public Health.* London: Sage Publications/Open University, pp.1–32.

Gauld R (2001) Contextual pressures on health – implications for policy making and service provision. *Policy Studies* 22(3/4): 167–79.

Greenhalgh T, Russell J (2009) Evidence-based policymaking: a critique. *Perspectives in Biology and Medicine* 52(2): 304–18.

Haak N (2009) Maintaining privacy and dignity of patients admitted to a District General NHS Trust. In: Shaw T, Sanders K (eds) *Foundation of Nursing Studies Dissemination Series* 5(2): 1–4.

Ham C (2004) *Health Policy in Britain* (5e). Basingstoke: Palgrave Macmillan.

Hannigan B, Burnard P (2000) Nursing, politics and policy: a response to Clifford. *Nurse Education Today* 20(7): 519–23.

Health4Media (2008) *Minister of State for Care Services Announces 3000 Dignity Champions.*

Health and Safety Executive (1992) *The Manual Handling Operations Regulations 1992 (as amended) (MHOR).* London: Health and Safety Executive.

Healthcare Commission (2006) *Living Well in Later Life: a review of progress against the National Service Framework for Older People.* London: Commission for Healthcare Audit and Inspection.

Health Service Journal (2008) Ivan Lewis Begins National Dignity Tour. www.hsj.co.uk/ivan-lewis-begins-national-dignity-tour/1374632.article (accessed 8 October 2010).

Kingdon JW (2003) *Agendas, Alternatives and Public Policies* (2e). New York: Longman.

Lindblom CE (1959) The science of 'muddling through'. *Public Administration Review* 19: 78–88.

Lindblom CE (1979) Still muddling, not yet through. *Public Administration Review* 39: 517–25.

Martin D (2008) Number of elderly patients starving in NHS wards doubles to 30 000 in two years. *Daily Mail,* 30 July. www.dailymail.co.uk/health/article-1039562/Number-elderly-patients-starving-NHS-wards-doubles-30–000-years.html#ixzz0We1pbpLJ (accessed 8 October 2010).

Maxwell S, Sigsworth J (2009) Eliminating mixed sex accommodation in hospital to improve patient experience. *Nursing Times* 105(44): 12–14. www.nursingtimes.net/nursing-practice-clinical-research/acute-care/eliminating-mixed-sex-accommodation-in-hospital-to-improve-patient-experience/5008248.article (accessed 8 October 2010).

Newman J (2002) Putting the 'policy' back into social policy. *Social Policy and Society* 1(4): 347–54.

Nursing and Midwifery Council (2009) *Guidance for the Care of Older People*. London: Nursing and Midwifery Council.

Parkinson M (2008a) Parky's quest for the elderly. *The Sun*, 22 May. www.thesun.co.uk/sol/homepage/showbiz/tv/article1194437.ece (accessed 7 November 2008).

Parkinson M (2008b) Michael Parkinson on dignity. *Telegraph*, 20 May. www.telegraph.co.uk/news/uknews/1997085/Michael-Parkinson-on-Dignity.html (accessed 18 December 2008).

Patients Association (2009) *Patients . . . Not Numbers, People . . . Not Statistics*. London: Patients Association.

Royal College of Nursing (2008a) *Defending Dignity – Challenges and Opportunities for Nursing*. London: Royal College of Nursing.

Royal College of Nursing (2008b) *Small Changes Make a Big Difference: how you can influence to deliver dignified care*. London: Royal College of Nursing.

Schofield J (2004) A model of learned implementation. *Public Administration* 82(2): 283–308.

Social Care Institute for Excellence (2009) *SCIE Guide 15: Dignity in Care*. London: Social Care Institute for Excellence. www.scie.org.uk/publications/guides/guide15/index.asp (accessed 8 October 2010).

Solesbury W (1976) The environmental agenda. *Public Administration* 54(Winter): 379–97.

Thurber JA (2003) Foreword. In: Kingdon JW. *Agendas, Alternatives and Public Policies* (2e). New York: Longman.

Wagg A, Peel P, Lowe D, Potter J (2006) *National Audit of Continence Care for Older People*. London: Clinical Effectiveness Unit/Royal College of Physicians. www.rcplondon.ac.uk/clinical-standards/ceeu/Current-work/Documents/GenericHospital2006.pdf (accessed 8 October 2010).

Webster J, Coats E, Noble G (2009) Enabling privacy and dignity in care: using creative arts to develop practice with older people. In: Sanders K, Shaw T (eds) *Foundation of Nursing Studies Dissemination Series* 5(3): 1–4.

Whyte A (2008) What is going on? *Nursing Standard* 13(22): 18–22.

CHAPTER 5

Care environments that support dignity in care

Ann Gallagher

INTRODUCTION

Care activities are conducted in many different environments, for example, in hospitals, residential homes, patients' own homes, in ambulances and in prisons. Within these environments there is the potential to both develop and diminish dignity. This chapter discusses the meaning and contribution of the care environment to dignity in care. Two aspects of the care environment will be the focus of discussion: the physical care environment and other aspects of the organisation. Some of the concerns relating to undignifying care environments will be examined and examples of good practice discussed. It is concluded that reflection on, and improvements to, the care environment make a significant contribution to patients, relatives and staff feeling valued and respected.

LEARNING OUTCOMES

By the end of this chapter you will be able to:
➤ define the care environment
➤ identify factors that promote dignity in the care environment
➤ identify factors that diminish dignity in the care environment, learning from examples of care environment failings
➤ critically reflect on dignifying and undignifying aspects of one's own care environment
➤ work with colleagues to develop strategies supporting dignity in the care environment.

CARE ENVIRONMENTS

An understanding of the nature and scope of the 'care environment' is a necessary precursor to a discussion of factors that support or diminish dignity. We can think of the environment in narrower and broader terms. As I write, I might think of my immediate environment – the computer, table and sunlight streaming through the window. Or I might think of the wider environment – other buildings in my area, trees, the local town, country and the global context I live within. My environmental concerns may therefore be local and parochial and global. Care environments can also be thought of in more and less limited terms. A healthcare professional may think of the care environment as the immediate area within which he or she delivers care, that is, the bedspace, the outpatients' clinical room or the bathroom. However, for patients, relatives and staff, it is likely that the impact of a care environment will be experienced in relation to the people they encounter, the reception area, cafeterias, and corridors to areas where they receive treatment and care or within which they work.

The scientist Albert Einstein is quoted as saying 'The environment is everything that isn't me' (*see* http://quotationsbook.com/quote/27957). This helpfully reminds us that the environment includes all aspects of our surroundings and includes both people and places. We are, of course, part of the environment of others. The 'care environment' can be defined, therefore, as all aspects of people's surroundings wherein care is received or delivered.

It becomes clear that there are, therefore, many opportunities and challenges regarding the promotion of dignity in the care environment. The reception area and receptionist, for example, have the potential to make patients and families feel welcomed and respected or a nuisance and an inconvenience. Hospital corridors and waiting areas have the potential to make patients and staff feel that they are worthwhile and deserving of cleanliness and comfortable surroundings or, alternatively, disrespected.

Recent reports from United Kingdom (UK) inspection and investigative bodies support the view that there is room for improvement in relation to dignity in care environments. The 13th and final report from the Mental Health Act Commission (2009), for example, detailed environmental conditions reported by commissioners and patients within mental healthcare environments:

> There is use of strong bedding and blankets on the unit, but the blanket had not been washed regularly and there was no bedding between the patient and the plastic mattress. The patient was also not given a pillow to use and had to use her slippers as a make-shift pillow (Mental Health Act Commission, 2009, p.12; reproduced with permission from the Stationery Office).

There were also examples of undignifying care environment conditions in the Patients Association (2009) report *Patients . . . Not Numbers, People . . .Not Statistics*. Ron Kirk's account of his father's experience is as follows:

> Toilets were not cleaned properly with faeces clearly left from several previous uses. My sister often had to clean them herself before she'd let my father use them. My father's swallowing wasn't safe because of his stroke but drinks of

> orange juice and water were supplied when the counter instruction over the bed was nil by mouth. We saw dirty and bloodstained food trays. We saw soiled and dirty linen left on floors and mixed with fresh supplies. Personal items for his own comfort frequently went missing (Patients Association, 2009, p.10; reproduced with permission from the Patients Association).

Other relatives reported broken equipment, dirty and uncaring hospital environments, lack of responses to patient needs and requests and moving patients to other wards without consultation. *The Final Report of The Independent Inquiry Into Care Provided by Mid Staffordshire NHS Foundation Trust* (Francis, 2010) was introduced by inquiry chairman, Robert Francis QC, as follows:

> I heard so many stories of shocking care . . . The Inquiry found that a chronic shortage of staff, particularly nursing staff, was largely responsible for the substandard care. Morale at the Trust was low, and while many staff did their best in difficult circumstances, others showed a disturbing lack of compassion towards their patients. Staff who spoke out felt ignored and there is strong evidence that many were deterred from doing so through fear and bullying (Francis, 2010, Crown copyright; reproduced with permission from the Controller of HMSO and the Queen's Printer for Scotland).

One example of the 'shocking care' described by Francis is from the wife of a 67-year-old patient. She recalled that call bells were rarely answered and in any case were frequently placed out of reach of patients. She documented that her husband:

> . . . soiled his bed time and time again because no-one had answered the call-buttons. On numerous occasions when I arrived on the ward, he was lying in faeces and several times he had been lying in it so long that it dried and caked onto him. Time and again I had to fetch the necessary equipment from the sluice and attend to him myself because there was no staff in evidence on the ward (Francis, 2010, p.392, Crown copyright; reproduced with permission from the Controller of HMSO and the Queen's Printer for Scotland).

These examples are indeed shocking and may be taken to support a view that the UK healthcare system diminishes rather than enhances patient and staff dignity. It is essential to try to understand why these bad experiences come about and why care environments become uncaring and undignifying. There are indications and suggestions within the reports above as to why these situations arise. The Francis (2010) report, for example, identifies low staffing levels, low morale and staff fears of speaking out about poor practice. He also pointed to the impact of a trust making financial cuts when staffing levels were already inadequate. What is evident from this and other reports regarding dignity fail-ings in care environments is that it is rarely the case that the failing is due to an individual but rather a mix of *micro-level*, *meso-level* and *macro-level* factors.

The Royal College of Nursing report (RCN, 2008) outlines what is meant by each of these levels. The *micro-level* relates to the role of individual respon-sibility and accountability. Individual healthcare workers should take advan-tage of opportunities to learn about dignity in care, to be aware of the impact of role modelling and to develop strategies with patients and colleagues that develop dignity in care environments. The RCN survey revealed that almost 80% of nurses left practice feeling that they were unable to deliver dignifying care. It is suggested that this inability is due to organisational (*meso-level*) con-straints such as the lack of human and material resources such as equipment and laundry. The *macro-level* factors are attributed to the role of government policy in targets that may diminish dignity in care environments. The lack of progress with single-sex care environments and waiting-time targets would be two examples (RCN, 2008; *see* Chapter 4 for an analysis of health policy relat-ing to single-sex accommodation). The point that staff need to keep the focus on patients was also emphasised by Robert Francis QC (2010):

> People must always come before numbers. Individual patients and their families are what really matters. Statistics, benchmarks and action plans are tools not ends in themselves. They should not come before patients and their experiences. This is what must be remembered by all those who design and implement policy for the NHS (Francis, 2010, p.1, Crown copyright; reproduced with permission from the Controller of HMSO and the Queen's Printer for Scotland).

Thus far it may seem that there is little to celebrate regarding dignity in care environments. There is much scope for improvement but there is also much good practice. A recent RCN evaluation of the impact of a dignity in care cam-paign (Baillie and Gallagher, 2008) provided many examples of nurse-led ini-tiatives supporting dignity in very diverse care environments.

The 2008 RCN report *Defending Dignity – Challenges and Opportunities for Nursing* distinguishes between two aspects of the care environment – the physi-cal environment and other aspects of the employing organisation. The physical environment has three themes:

1. aspects of the environment maintaining informational and physical pri-vacy (for example, curtains, screens and private spaces for consultation)
2. aesthetic aspects of the physical environment (for example, colour, space, furnishings, décor and music)
3. the provision of single-sex accommodation.

Other aspects of the employing organisation include:

> ➤ staff attitudes, awareness and knowledge

➤ leadership and role modelling
➤ teamwork
➤ resources (human and material)
➤ organisational culture and philosophy.

Focusing on composite vignettes drawn from previous research and practice experience, the next section explores aspects of the physical environment.

DIGNITY AND THE PHYSICAL ENVIRONMENT

The physical environment has the potential to enhance or diminish the dignity of patients and staff. In the previous section, there was consideration of examples of undignifying aspects of the care environment. The examples here (Box 5.1 and Box 5.2) suggest how opportunities to promote dignity in care environments might be maximised.

BOX 5.1 *Vignette 1*

Martha lives alone and finds that she has become increasingly forgetful. She is embarrassed about this and her family are concerned. Her general practitioner has suggested to Martha and her family that she should consider an assessment at the local memory clinic as this may be a form of dementia. Martha is not keen to follow this advice, saying she prefers to retain her independence. After a fall when she is out shopping, she is taken to the accident and emergency (A&E) department at the local hospital. She is not badly hurt but is fearful and appears confused. One of the A&E team (Jean) has expertise in dementia and takes Martha from the curtained A&E area to a quiet room. The room is clean and comfortable and there is a clearly marked toilet nearby. Jean makes Martha a cup of tea and asks her who she would like to be contacted. She contacts Martha's daughter with her consent. Jean spends time with Martha and her daughter talking through support options such as community services and local day centres. Martha admits to feeling lonely and fearful at times and says she would welcome the opportunity to meet other people and to have support to remain at home.

These two vignettes suggest some of the aspects of the physical environment that are likely to develop dignity. In relation to Martha's experience, it seems that Jean was sensitive to her needs and vulnerability. Given her embarrassment regarding her memory lapses and confusion, it seems likely that conducting an interview behind a curtain would not be ideal. She may have had

---

BOX 5.2 *Vignette 2*

Roshan manages a busy acute mental health unit. He was aware that space is limited on the unit and that staff did not have a coffee room or area to store their belongings. One of the rooms had been used as a store-room for another ward. Roshan negotiated an alternative space on an adjoining ward and arranged for the store-room to be converted to a staff room. He presented a case for resources to the unit manager and argued that this initiative supports dignity at work. The manager was sympathetic and allocated a modest budget for the work. Roshan involved staff in selecting the colour scheme and furniture. He also ensured that there is space on the corridor notice-board for the 'staff member of the month' notice.

---

physical privacy (if, that is, the curtains closed properly and people did not intrude) but would not have had informational or auditory privacy as conversations can be overheard. A quiet room is likely to have been more peaceful and private. It is also significant that Jean was able to take time to talk with Martha and her daughter and to offer information about a range of appropriate services. The A&E department at Southampton University Hospitals NHS Trust has such an initiative (Nuffield Council on Bioethics, 2009, p.53). Members of a team, based in the A&E department, provide specialist assistance to people with dementia. It should not be assumed, of course, that Martha has dementia as there may be other explanations for her memory deficits and confusion. However, it is important that she is taken seriously and offered an assessment and appropriate interventions that are respectful of her dignity. The fact that the private room is comfortable and clean is also significant in terms of a dignifying environment.

The second vignette (Box 5.2) relates to dignity at work and suggests how a creative manager might advocate for staff, contributing to their feeling valued by the organisation they work for. Having a notice-board with staff awards is part of the physical environment and also relates to other aspects of organisations.

DIGNITY AND OTHER ASPECTS OF THE ORGANISATION

The RCN report (2008) identified other aspects of the care environment with the potential to enhance or diminish dignity. These include leadership and role modelling, team working, resources and organisational philosophy and culture. Good leadership and 'forward thinking management' were identified as contributory factors to dignifying care (RCN, 2008, p.24). Leaders and managers need, therefore, to act as dignity-promoting role models, being seen, as it were, to 'walk the talk'. Examples of good practice include matrons who accompany ward staff to walk around their ward on a 'stop-and-look' programme. This initiative allows staff to scrutinise their practice area from the perspectives of patients and family members (RCN, 2008; Gallagher *et al*, 2009).

It is suggested that ethical leadership, supporting dignity and other values, may be promoted in at least three ways (Gallagher and Tschudin, 2009). First, having a critical and multidisciplinary approach to professional practice involves learning from the social sciences and public reports detailing and explaining good and poor practice. The Bristol Inquiry, for example, highlighted flawed behaviour, lack of insight, inadequate leadership and 'a club culture' as contributing to unethical practice (Kennedy, 2001). Observing the dignity-promoting practice of others involves reflection on, and learning from, the behaviour and approach of others. Inviting feedback on one's own practice and providing constructive feedback to colleagues are also helpful strategies to promote dignity-promoting leadership. This requires a team ethos and organisational culture that is supportive, open and trusting. The third approach is to provide opportunities for practitioners to develop particular dispositions or virtues such as care, respectfulness, integrity and professional wisdom (Banks and Gallagher, 2009).

A culture of openness where constructive feedback is invited and welcomed is a component of a dignifying organisation echoed in the RCN report. One respondent stated that:

> We work as a supportive team, where mistakes are not judged but used as opportunities to learn. We try to be open about our failures and seek help from each other constantly. We encourage our patients to do the same. If our patients can see where things can improve, we want to know (Staff Nurse, NHS Trust, Acute Hospital) (RCN, 2008, p.25; reproduced with permission from the Royal College of Nursing).

The philosophy of care and website of a healthcare organisation also have the potential to support dignity in care, making explicit the values and priorities of that organisation.

The vignette in Box 5.3 suggests how these aspects of the care environment might support dignity in care.

Features of this vignette illustrate many examples of good practice regarding dignity in care environments. The RCN (2008) report, for example, emphasised the importance of leadership and of leaders role modelling dignifying care. Blake ward appears to be an area where the dignity of both patients and staff is taken seriously. Views may differ regarding the recognition of staff who demonstrate an exceptional ability to deliver dignifying care. Staff recognition awards

Box 5.3 *Vignette 3*

The members of staff on Blake ward are proud of the standards of care
they deliver. They describe themselves as a supportive multicultural
team with strong leadership. The 'team', they say, includes everyone,
from the ward clerk and housekeeper to nurses, doctors and porters.
The ward manager works alongside new members of staff, students and
healthcare assistants, demonstrating, by her example, how to enhance
dignity in care. Although the ward does not have single rooms, staff
members insist on single-sex sleeping and bathroom areas. A peg and
privacy sign is attached to curtains to prevent colleagues inadvertently
barging in when an intimate care procedure is under way. The team use
the Essence of Care as dignity benchmarks and also meet regularly for
dignity training and discussion. Staff, patients and relatives are invited
to nominate a staff member for the monthly 'dignity in care' awards.
Staff members are encouraged to disclose 'near misses' and to report any
aspect of the care environment that appears to compromise dignity in
care. All staff members are encouraged to make suggestions as to how to
enhance dignity.

was one initiative reported in the RCN dignity evaluation (Baillie and Gallagher, 2008). There is evidence that staff may fear the consequences of reporting
near misses, errors or poor practice. This suggests that there needs to be a culture where such reporting is commended rather than criticised, and viewed as
a learning opportunity rather than as disloyalty. In conducting the RCN dignity
evaluation (Baillie and Gallagher, 2008), the author was made aware of many
dignity initiatives that resulted from staff members being encouraged to make
suggestions as to how to enhance dignity. Examples included an initiative to
make the dining room in a nursing home 'more like a restaurant', with napkins and matching tablecloths and with disposable 'bibs' replaced with linen
clothes protectors. Other examples included improvements in privacy, with
occupied/unoccupied signs on bathroom doors, pegs to hold curtains together
and curtains inside toilet doors to prevent exposure.

PRACTICAL APPLICATION

In Chapter 2, you were introduced to the idea that dignity in care is promoted
or diminished by people, place and processes. This chapter has focused on *place*
in terms of the physical care environment and other aspects of the organisation. The discussion has focused on care in inpatient environments. Health-

care professionals do, of course, deliver care in very different environments including patients' homes, ambulances and prisons. Much of the discussion is transferable to other care environments; however, there will be additional challenges and opportunities. It is, therefore, important that readers reflect on and think creatively about dignity in relation to their own particular environment, taking all who spend time in that environment into account. The focus has been on patients and staff members; however, the dignity of students and visitors should also be considered. In Section 2 of this book, there are chapters considering specific care environments and how they interact with dignity in care.

To apply learning from this chapter to one's own practice it may be helpful to work through Reflective activity 5.1.

Reflective activity 5.1

➤ What does the care environment I work within consist of? Is there, for example, a reception or waiting area, sitting room, staff room, patients' own home?
➤ What aspects of the care environment could be improved regarding dignity in care?
➤ How might these areas be improved, for example, cleanliness, comfort, choice, taking more time?
➤ Who do I need to influence to bring about the necessary change?
➤ If I confront obstacles to the necessary practice change, who might I recruit as allies, for example, other health professionals, managers, patient and carer groups?
➤ How can I evaluate the effectiveness of the change, for example, patient and staff satisfaction?

CONCLUSION

This chapter has explored the relationship between the care environment and dignity. Readers have had the opportunity to reflect on the meaning of the care environment. Examples from reports detailing failings in organisations resulting in patient and staff dignity being compromised were discussed and the importance of appreciating the interrelationship amongst micro-level, meso-level and macro-level factors. Factors that promote and diminish dignity in care environments have been discussed and vignettes providing illustrations have been included. It is hoped that the discussion and reflective questions enable readers to perceive and respond effectively and creatively to dignity deficits in the care environment.

REFERENCES

Baillie L, Gallagher A (2008) *Evaluation of the Royal College of Nursing's 'Dignity at the Heart of Everything We Do' Campaign – The Little Things Make a Difference.* Unpublished report for the RCN.

Banks S, Gallagher, A (2009) *Ethics in Professional Life: virtues for health and social care.* Basingstoke: Palgrave Macmillan.

Francis R (2010) *Final Report of The Independent Inquiry Into Care Provided By Mid Staffordshire NHS Foundation Trust.* http://midstaffsinquiry.com/pressrelease.html (accessed 8 October 2010).

Gallagher A, Tschudin V (2009) Educating for ethical leadership. *Nurse Education Today* **30**(3): 224–7.

Gallagher A, Wainwright P, Baillie L, Ford P (2009) The RCN Dignity Survey: implications for leaders. *Nursing Management* **16**(4): 12–16.

Kennedy I (2001) *The Report of the Public Inquiry into Children's Heart Surgery at the Bristol Royal Infirmary 1984–1995.* CM5207(I). London: The Stationery Office. www.bristol-inquiry.org.uk/final_report/the_report.pdf (accessed 8 October 2010).

Mental Health Act Commission (2009) *Coercion and Consent: monitoring the Mental Health Act 2007–2009 Thirteenth Biennial Report.* London: The Stationery Office.

Nuffield Council on Bioethics (2009) *Dementia: ethical issues.* London: Nuffield Council on Bioethics.

Patients Association (2009) *Patients . . . Not Numbers, People . . . Not Statistics.* London: The Patients Association.

Royal College of Nursing (2008) *Defending Dignity – Challenges and Opportunities for Nursing.* London: RCN.

CHAPTER 6

Staff behaviour and attitudes that promote dignity in care

Lesley Baillie

INTRODUCTION

Staff behaviour and attitudes have a major influence on whether patients experience dignity in care; indeed, Widäng and Fridlund (2003) argued that promoting dignity is *dependent* on how patients are treated by their caregivers. In my doctoral research (Baillie, 2007), a patient who had had major surgery described a nurse who cared for him and maintained his dignity as being:

> . . . sensitive, explains what she's going to do before she does it, she's cheerful, she has a sense of humour, she appears interested in me as an individual, she has a caring approach, appears to enjoy her work – doesn't appear as though it's a chore (Baillie, 2007, p.206).

Clearly the nurse's attitude underpinned her behaviour and approach to care. Other studies have also highlighted the impact of staff attitude on dignity-promoting behaviour. Nåden and Eriksson (2004) found that nurses who promoted dignity had a strong moral attitude underpinned by values such as respect, honesty and responsibility; such nurses had a 'genuine interest and desire to help patients' (p.90). In a study by Bayer *et al* (2005), older people considered that attitudes of caregivers were central to dignified care, as they can portray that the person is valued. In the Royal College of Nursing (RCN, 2008) survey, nurse respondents considered that attitudes of staff themselves particularly influenced the delivery of dignified care. Humanistic caring approaches have been found to promote dignity: treating patients as human beings (Enes, 2003) and holistically (Widäng and Fridlund, 2003) and conveying a caring attitude (McClement *et al*, 2004). Walsh and Kowanko (2002) identified that patients wanted to be acknowledged as a 'living, thinking and experiencing human being not just an object' (p.149).

This chapter explores how staff behaviour and attitudes affect patients' dignity, with a particular focus on communication, privacy and quality fundamental care. The chapter also considers how organisational culture affects individual staff behaviour and how staff should respond when colleagues compromise dignity through their behaviour. The chapter draws on international research findings illuminating the impact of staff behaviour on patients' dignity. Throughout this chapter, for simplicity, the term 'patient' is used, although it is acknowledged that in some care settings the term 'client', 'resident', 'service user' or another term may be more appropriate.

LEARNING OUTCOMES

By the end of the chapter you will be able to:
➤ explain the types of staff behaviour that can diminish patients' dignity
➤ discuss how staff behaviour can promote dignity for patients
➤ analyse how organisational culture can affect individual staff behaviour
➤ consider responses to colleagues' behaviour that compromises patients' dignity.

BEHAVIOUR THAT DIMINISHES THE DIGNITY OF PATIENTS AND CLIENTS

Unfortunately, many reports that refer to loss of dignity suggest that staff behaviour plays a major role. As Chapter 5 explained, the physical care environment and resources also affect dignity but healthcare professionals must acknowledge that their own behaviour and that of their colleagues is highly influential.

Staff behaviour that diminishes dignity is essentially that which is uncaring, as uncaring behaviour from others affects how people feel and whether they feel valued as human beings. Arman and Rehnsfeldt's (2007) study led them to conclude that an uncaring approach was demonstrated when patients were not viewed as 'whole human beings' and caregivers did not recognise their 'existential suffering' (p.373).

Halldorsdottir (1991) highlighted the vulnerability of patients who experienced uncaring. She found that dependent people who felt uncared for felt a sense of loss and dehumanisation, feeling that they had no value as a person: 'an object': 'I was ... a piece of dust on the floor'. In the United Kingdom (UK) in 2009, the Patients Association published *Patients . . . Not Numbers, People . . . Not Statistics*, which provided detailed and shocking accounts of patients' experiences of poor hospital care. The report showed many deficits of management, systems and the care environment, including poor staffing levels, but these reports also referred to individual staff behaviour and attitudes that diminished patients' dignity, including poor communication, and failure to provide pain relief and personal care.

Staff behaviour and attitudes diminish the dignity of patients when they breach privacy, display poor communication and attitudes and deliver inadequate fundamental care. These behaviours clearly contravene professional codes of conduct, legislation and health policies yet continue to be reported.

The UK's Healthcare Commission (2007, p.14) reported on the dignity of older people in hospital and listed 11 categories of commonly received complaints about dignity compromises. Notably, most categories arose from staff behaviour (inappropriate form of address, being spoken about as though the person is not there, not being properly informed, not seeking consent or having wishes considered, being exposed, being left in soiled clothes, lack of help with eating and drinking, being left in pain, abuse and violence). Only a few categories resulted from deficits in the care environment (mixed-sex accommodation, lack of sleep due to noise at night, lack of cleanliness, lack of protection for people's own property, for example, hearing aids). Reflective activity 6.1 relates to the Healthcare Commission's findings.

Reflective activity 6.1 Compromises of dignity

Re-read the previous paragraph: consider the Healthcare Commission's examples of compromises of dignity and reflect on practice in your setting:

➤ have you or your colleagues ever behaved in any of these ways?
➤ if you have observed any of these compromises, what did you do in response?

This chapter later discusses how staff can respond when colleagues compromise patients' dignity.

PROVIDING PRIVACY

Many studies in diverse settings have highlighted that staff behaviour that ensures privacy for patients helps to promote dignity (McClement et al, 2004; Matthews and Callister, 2004; Baillie, 2009a).This section considers privacy of personal space, privacy of patients' bodies and confidentiality.

Privacy of personal space

Some studies found that in hospital, patients' personal territory, their bedspace and locker, was not respected by staff (Matiti, 2002; Woogara, 2004). Patients may feel that their personal space has been breached when staff move patients' belongings around in their bedside lockers or other furniture without discussion, or when staff enter closed curtains or doors without asking. Box 6.1 summarises actions to maintain privacy of personal space in different care settings.

BOX 6.1 *How staff can maintain privacy of personal space*

People's own homes

➤ Book appointments in advance (conveys respect and provides people with some control over their own environment).

➤ Knock on the door and introduce yourself, show an identity badge and check the identity of the person answering the door. Explain the purpose of the visit and ask for permission to enter.

➤ Only enter areas of the property necessary for carrying out the care activity, always checking with patients first.

➤ Approach any concerns about their home (for example, safety issues such as lack of heating, trip hazards) constructively and tactfully. Do not make judgemental comments about people's homes.

➤ If using a key to enter a person's home, knock before entering, then call out a greeting and state who you are.

➤ Assess whether to pull curtains, depending on the reason for the visit, the room's position and the potential for people to see in from the street.

➤ Be aware of other people's presence; check discreetly whether the patient wants their relative, friend or neighbour present for support, or whether they would prefer to be alone with you.

Single rooms in care settings

➤ Tell colleagues that you are going to be in a person's room carrying out a procedure, so they will be less likely to enter the room.

➤ Place an 'Engaged' sign on the door as a deterrent to other staff to enter during care delivery or examinations.

➤ Knock before entering and ask whether you can come in. Close the door and cover any window on the door (with the shutters or curtain, as provided) when you are going to carry out care, examine the patient, etc.

➤ Ask first before opening cupboards/drawers to take out items and replace items after use.

➤ Before leaving the room, move any furniture (for example, bed table) back into the position the patient would like and ensure that the person has their call bell.

➤ If possible, negotiate whether the person would like the door left open or shut. N.B. Clinical needs may influence this, for example, infection control, patient safety.

Multi-patient areas (for example, hospital bay)

➤ For personal care, intimate procedures, examinations or private discussions: whenever clinically possible, assist patients out to the toilet, bathroom, treatment or private discussion room, where you can close the door and put on an 'Engaged' sign.

➤ In toilets or bathrooms there may be a 'dignity' curtain inside the door to give added privacy.

➤ Whenever possible, leave patients to use the toilet or shower or bath alone. First assess risk, as some patients will be unsafe to leave alone or might require assistance. Ensure that patients left alone have a call bell.

➤ For patients who are too unwell to leave the bedside or are confined to bed due to their medical condition, explain that their curtains can be pulled whenever needed for privacy.

➤ Apply a clip or a 'do not disturb' notice to the pulled curtain to deter intrusion. Ensure all staff are aware that closed curtains should not be entered by staff without warning.

➤ When pulling curtains, take care that the edges are pulled closely together; report ill-fitting curtains and ask that they are replaced.

➤ If you need to enter the curtains before the patient calls you, ask first if you can enter.

➤ As you enter curtains take care that you do not make a gap so that others can see in.

➤ Show respect for people's belongings and furniture; ask permission before removing items from a locker and before moving furniture.

➤ Ensure that you replace the items where the person would like them and ensure that the person has their call bell.

Privacy of patients' bodies

People undergoing healthcare are at risk of bodily exposure as they often need to undress for procedures or examinations and need help with personal care. Patients may feel that their bodily privacy is violated if they are unnecessarily exposed. Unfortunately, many studies have reported that staff exposed people's bodies and were inattentive to their privacy (Turnock and Kelleher, 2001; Matiti, 2002; Woolhead et al, 2005) and that staff intruded behind curtains during intimate procedures involving bodily exposure (Lai and Levy, 2002; Ariño-Blasco et al, 2005; Baillie, 2009a). Box 6.2 provides an example of a patient's experience of a breach of privacy in a hospital ward. The patient had a blocked catheter and was having a bladder washout performed when another ward staff member entered the curtains without warning, to talk to the nurse. The patient could not clearly see who had entered the curtains and was acutely aware of his bodily exposure. Not only was his privacy breached but the two staff members talked over him and ignored him. The nurse carrying out the procedure, rather than asking the person to leave and covering the patient, instead engaged in conversation.

BOX 6.2 *A breach of privacy during a bladder washout (Baillie, 2007, p.160)*

'A nurse comes in, draws the curtains round so I'm there, I'm on my back, my frock's [nightshirt's] up round my waist . . . my legs are apart – they've got a bowl in me – and she's syringing me . . . she [another staff member] puts her head through the curtain. Chats to this nurse who's treating me. And I thought – what are you doing – as far as I know, you're not a nurse – you've not come in here for my benefit . . . I felt a bit annoyed. And a bit embarrassed. At the thought that someone who was not medical staff as far as I know . . . I don't know what they were talking about. But it was nothing to do with me. So I got a bit narked. And felt a bit embarrassed. And a certain loss of dignity because I was not in a very dignified position.

Other examples of breach of privacy include bedside curtains that are not fully closed during personal care, removal of clothing without discussion or consent, or providing clothing that does not cover patients' bodies adequately, for example hospital gowns (Baillie, 2009a).

Sometimes, tradition leads to unnecessary bodily exposure, for example patients being expected to undress into nightclothes or hospital gowns long before it is necessary, and for staff convenience, rather than patients' well-being. As well as causing bodily exposure, this practice diminishes dignity by reducing individuality. It also creates a power imbalance between staff who are dressed in uniforms or day clothes, and patients who are dressed in nightwear. Edvardsson's (2008) study highlighted that a person's own clothes were linked with a person's identity; wearing hospital clothing was depersonalising and carried a social stigma. Wilson (2006), in a small project based on a ward for older people, successfully implemented a system to enable patients, where possible, to wear their own day clothes.

Box 6.3 lists ways to minimise indignity resulting from bodily exposure.

BOX 6.3 *Minimising indignity caused by bodily exposure*

➤ Whenever possible, assist patients to dress in their own clothes; if they have to wear nightclothes, provide dressing gowns.
➤ In hospitals there are rarely facilities for washing clothes, so do explain this to relatives. Many relatives will agree to bring in nightwear (including a dressing gown and slippers) and day clothes. Ensure that soiled clothing is bagged separately from clean clothing

so it can be taken home for washing, which will help to ensure a constant supply of clean clothing.

➤ When hospital gowns must be used for operations or examinations, ensure that they are fastened properly. There are newer styles available that are less exposing.

➤ Never expect a patient to walk around in a gown without a dressing gown. If there are no dressing gowns available, provide another hospital gown to wear like a dressing gown.

➤ Ensure that patients sitting out in a chair or wheelchair in nightwear or a gown are covered up adequately; for example, use a blanket to cover their legs.

➤ When patients need to undress for procedures or examinations, if they can undress unassisted, leave them to do so unobserved and provide a gown and blanket to cover themselves after undressing.

➤ When you need to expose an area of the patient's body for a procedure or examination, always ask permission first. If possible, ask the patient to move clothing themselves, and only move clothing the minimum amount necessary, ensuring that the rest of the patient's body is covered, by bed linen or clothing. Replace clothing as soon as possible.

➤ Chaperoning (used for protection of both staff and the patient) increases the 'audience', potentially causing further embarrassment for patients. Chaperones should always introduce themselves and give their name and job role. Whenever possible, a chaperone should stand or sit where the patient can see them, and they should talk to the person and avoid looking at their exposed body areas. It is unacceptable for non-healthcare staff (for example, a receptionist) to act as a chaperone.

➤ Some patients will not wish to expose their bodies to staff of the opposite sex, and certain religions may stipulate this requirement. In these situations behave sensitively and ensure that their wishes are respected.

Maintaining confidentiality

Maintaining privacy of information (confidentiality) is another staff behaviour that can promote dignity (Matiti, 2002; Calnan *et al*, 2005). Lack of confidentiality occurs when personal information, for example, about incontinence, medical diagnosis or home circumstances, is overheard or displayed in public areas. Patients are usually well aware that information about them must be shared between healthcare workers to ensure their safety, continuity of care and appropriate referrals. However, information should not be shared unnecessarily between healthcare workers, it should not be shared with patients' families or friends without their permission (except in extreme situations such as an unconscious patient), and patient information must not be shared with other patients, visitors or the media. Most health and social care organisations have confidentiality policies that provide specific guidance about information giving. When families and friends request information about patients, staff should first ask the patient what information they would like to be shared with the enquirer and, if possible, enable them to talk to their relative or friend themselves. In patients' own homes, staff should consider the confidentiality of patients' notes that are left in the home. When information is passed between team members (for example, during a ward round or ward handover), staff should prevent other patients and visitors overhearing. In outpatient areas or waiting rooms, staff should not ask personal questions or carry out procedures, like weighing, in front of other patients.

In curtained areas in hospital, curtains provide a visual barrier but auditory privacy can still be breached. Therefore, taking patients to toilets, bathrooms or a private discussion room is always preferable. When carrying out exposing or intimate procedures at the bedside, staff should communicate discreetly, by keeping voices low and using non-verbal communication. This is particularly important when dealing with personal care, for example incontinence or during an intimate procedure (for example, catheterisation) or examination (for example, vaginal or rectal examination). In a research interview, a patient expressed her embarrassment to me that her consultant spoke so loudly on the ward round that other patients could hear about her urological surgery:

> I just thought, you know "Don't speak too loud" – I'm not exactly proud of what's going on (Baillie, 2007, p.135).

Staff should ensure that patients with hearing impairments have working hearing aids in place and that they can see staff who are talking to them. Potentially embarrassing smells should be dealt with sensitively, by not referring to them verbally or non-verbally and using strategies such as window-opening or sprays quietly and discreetly.

Apart from lack of attention to privacy of the body, there are other forms of behaviour towards people's bodies that can threaten dignity. These include treating people's bodies like objects (Walsh and Kowanko, 2002) and not treating a person's body with respect after death (Söderberg et al, 1997).

COMMUNICATION AND ATTITUDES

While privacy is crucial, underlying staff attitudes and values are key to staff behaviour that promotes dignity. Indeed, Applegate and Morse (1994) asserted that privacy-promoting actions such as pulling curtains are of little value if not accompanied by respect for personhood. Similarly, Walsh and Kowanko (2002) concluded that while privacy was important, it was not enough to promote dignity; patients also needed to feel like unique human beings. Women in Widäng *et al*'s (2007) study felt that they were respected when treated as a person, not an object. Staff are more likely to see, and therefore treat, patients as unique human beings if they get to know them; this can be achieved even in acute and short-stay settings through conversation during assessment and essential treatment and care. In care homes for people with dementia, constructing a biography of residents can help caregivers to understand them (Newson, 2008), which should help staff to approach them as individual human beings.

Staff can promote patients' dignity if their interactions help patients to feel comfortable, in control and valued; *see* Box 6.4.

BOX 6.4 *Interactions that help patients to feel comfortable, in control and valued (adapted from Baillie, 2007; RCN, 2008)*

Interactions that help people to feel comfortable
➤ Sensitivity
➤ Empathy
➤ Developing relationships
➤ Conversation
➤ Professionalism
➤ Family involvement (if desired by the patient)
➤ Friendliness and reassurance.
➤ Humour (if used sensitively and appropriately)

Communication that helps people to feel in control
➤ Explanations and information giving
➤ Informed consent
➤ Offering choices and negotiating
➤ Enabling independence

Communication that helps people to feel valued
➤ Listening
➤ Giving time
➤ Showing concern for patients as individuals
➤ Being kind, considerate and helpful
➤ Courtesy: addressing people by their preferred name, introducing self, being polite and respectful, including respect for culture and religious beliefs

---

Now carry out Reflective activity 6.2.

> **Reflective activity 6.2** Communication to promote dignity
>
> Think back to a recent situation with a patient. You could have been carrying out care or a treatment, investigation or examination. Reflect on the communication that you used during this situation and try to identify specific examples of your verbal and non-verbal communication that might have:
>
> ➤ helped the patient to feel comfortable
> ➤ helped the patient to feel in control
> ➤ helped the patient to feel valued.

Staff interactions that threaten dignity

Jacobson (2009) focused specifically on behaviours that violated patients' dignity and listed them as rudeness, indifference, condescension (for example, talking down to), dismissal (when practitioners discount patients' concerns, needs, feelings, etc.), disregard (for example, ignoring), dependence (owing to the patient's condition but exacerbated by practitioners' attitudes), intrusion (breaching privacy), objectification (treated as a 'thing' not a person), restriction (of movement, access to belongings), labelling (for example, 'difficult'), contempt (treated without value), discrimination, revulsion, deprivation (for example, preventing access to necessities), assault and abjection (being forced to compromise one's beliefs). Matiti (2002) identified that nurses did not recognise the need for respect to be integral to all procedures, only associating it with personal care. Woogara (2004) reported a general lack of courtesy towards patients, for example, doctors rarely introduced themselves and patients were frequently interrupted by staff while they were eating.

Patients' dignity can be threatened when staff adopt an authoritarian attitude, for example, 'telling' rather than 'asking' patients (Baillie, 2009a). Help the Aged (2007) asserted that talking to older people as though they are children is fairly common, and that endearments like 'sweetheart' or 'darling' may be used rather than an older person's preferred name. Other studies have reported that patients may not be asked how they would like to be called, and first or second names are assumed (Matiti, 2002; Woogara, 2004; Woolhead *et al*, 2005). An interview extract in Goodrich and Cornwell's report (2008) related that during a seven-week stay following a fall, the ambulance crew were the only members of staff who introduced themselves and asked the interviewee's mother how she would like to be addressed. Throughout her hospital stay, staff addressed her mother by her first name, which she had never previously been called by – she had always been called by her middle name. Matiti and Sharman (1999) found that while most patients on a surgical ward preferred first-name terms, some preferred surnames. It is therefore best to ask patients how they wish to be addressed.

More extreme staff behaviour that threatens dignity is inhumane treatment and care (Nordenfelt, 2003). There are reports of staff shouting at patients (Patients' Association, 2009), which could constitute emotional/psychological abuse (World Health Organization, 2002). Abusive behaviour is clearly unacceptable and breaks professional codes of ethics.

QUALITY FUNDAMENTAL CARE

Providing quality fundamental care implies respect and that the person is of value. Examples that have been associated with dignity include ensuring good standards of hygiene and dress (Health Advisory Service [HAS], 2000; Bayer *et al*, 2005), assisting with elimination needs (Calnan *et al*, 2005) and promoting nutrition (Help the Aged, 2007). Textbooks such as Baillie (2009b) detail a caring approach to delivering fundamental care, and UK health policies such as the Essence of Care (NHS Modernisation Agency, 2003) and Fundamentals of Care (Welsh Assembly Government, 2003) set benchmarks for quality fundamental care. Box 6.5 includes two examples of how patients' dignity can be promoted during care activities. Both examples include careful planning, preparing appropriate equipment, thoughtfulness, patient involvement, attention to privacy, and effective communication.

BOX 6.5 *Maintaining dignity during care activities*

Assisting with eating (p.34)
Modified diets are served onto everyday plates; use of the correctly sized spoon or fork; where there is dribbling, the use of a tissue to clean excess; the involvement of the individual in the activity (even in a small way); privacy is offered; verbal interactions with the individual are adult and not infantilising; checking to see that the individual is comfortable with the way that I am 'assisting' them; the individual is offered the opportunity to wash their hands before and after the meal (even if they will play no part in the activity); care is taken to spill no food, but if clothes are soiled, assistance is given to change them (Ward Manager, Acute Hospital).

Bedbath (p.37)
Patient involved in discussion regarding care for the day and is in agreement. Ensure that I have all equipment I require. Ensure I have an assistant to facilitate safe moving and handling. Inform colleagues that I will be undertaking bedbath. Ensure curtains closed. Encourage patient to do as much as they can for themselves during the procedure.

Ensure that only the area being washed is uncovered, that patient is covered and warm throughout procedure. Ensure that patient is involved in conversation. Do not speak about 'what did you do last night' over patient. Offer patient toilet if required. Ensure teeth and mouth clean. Offer drink. Tidy up. Leave patient comfortable with buzzer, drink and ensure that patient has everything they need before leaving them (Practice Development Nurse, Acute Hospital).

(RCN, 2008; used with kind permission from the Royal College of Nursing)

Now carry out Reflective activity 6.3.

Reflective activity 6.3

Consider a care activity or procedure that you regularly carry out in practice. Reflect on how you can carry this out in a way that promotes dignity. Consider careful planning, preparing appropriate equipment, thoughtfulness, patient involvement, attention to privacy, and effective communication.

Inadequate fundamental care

There are many reports of dignity being diminished by staff delivering poor fundamental care; for example, respondents in the Department of Health's (2006) 'Dignity in Care' survey identified lack of assistance with eating, hygiene and elimination. A review of complaints to the Healthcare Commission (2008) included many relating to poor nutrition and hygiene, including patients being left in soiled bedding. Woolhead *et al* (2005) identified a lack of attention to older people's appearance as threatening their dignity. Age Concern's (2006) *Hungry to Be Heard: the scandal of malnourished older people in hospital* described many instances of older people being left hungry in hospital. The Patients' Association (2009) report includes deficits in all aspects of fundamental care, leaving relatives as well as patients devastated. Patients experiencing inadequate fundamental care will feel uncomfortable, uncared for and unvalued as well as experiencing incontinence, hunger, thirst, pain and poor hygiene. All staff should ensure that fundamental care is maintained to a high standard, with privacy and communication that promote dignity.

HOW ORGANISATIONAL CULTURE AFFECTS INDIVIDUAL STAFF BEHAVIOUR

As Chapter 5 explored, organisational culture is influential and includes the social norms of staff and the policies, systems and accepted practices within care settings. Hospital culture can have a positive or a negative effect on how staff behave (Baillie, 2009a). In Walsh and Kowanko's (2002) study, a dehumanising hospital culture was found to diminish the dignity of patients. Conversely, the HAS (2000) study indicated that some wards had a culture of respect for patients and sensitivity to privacy; dignity was highly dependent on the ward manager's leadership.

Staff should reflect on how their own attitudes and behaviour affect patients' dignity but also how these are influenced by institutional culture and their colleagues' behaviour. Each individual staff member should consider how they would respond if colleagues diminish the dignity of patients. In the RCN (2008) nursing workforce survey, respondents reported that other staff, of all disciplines, often breached privacy by entering curtains or rooms without warning. Reflective activity 6.4 explores these issues.

Reflective activity 6.4

➤ How does your organisation's culture influence your attitude and behaviour with patients?
➤ Do you feel that your organisation's culture influences the attitude and behaviour of your colleagues?
➤ How might your own attitude and behaviour towards patients affect those of your colleagues?
➤ What would you do if you observed colleagues displaying attitudes or behaviour that could diminish patients' dignity?

In many cases where abusive behaviour has been uncovered, it has been because of the actions of individual staff members (often junior) speaking out. In the UK, following the 1998 Public Interest Disclosure Act, employees speaking out about malpractice are protected by law, and employers are expected to have whistle-blowing policies (Department of Health, 2003). However, Firth-Cozens et al's survey (2003) identified many barriers to reporting bad practice and that only 56% of nurses reported concerns about practice. They also found that nurses' experiences of reporting bad practice were often negative, highlighting a need for support. Ray (2006) argued that when organisations do not support people who whistle-blow, there is 'a failure of organisational ethics' (p.438). The Healthcare Commission (2008) reported that while 78% of staff said that they would report concerns about negligence or staff wrongdoing, 36% did not know about confidential reporting systems. Organisations must ensure that they have sound systems in place to support staff who report bad practice, and that staff know how to access these.

Box 6.6 makes practical suggestions as to how you could deal with behaviour of colleagues who diminish dignity.

BOX 6.6 *Dealing with colleagues who diminish patients' dignity*

Immediate action

Aim to restore dignity by demonstrating compassion and meeting immediate dignity needs. Some examples:

➤ if a colleague exposes a patient unnecessarily, depending on the situation, cover the patient up, offer a dressing gown or help the patient to dress, pull the curtains fully closed
➤ if a colleague fails to introduce themselves, introduce them to the patient
➤ if a colleague talks over a patient, instead involve the patient in the conversation
➤ offer explanations and information (when they are not offered) and ensure patients' consent and involvement in decisions, where absent
➤ apologise to patients for your colleagues' behaviour, where appropriate.

Speaking to your colleague

➤ Raise the issue in privacy by taking them to a quiet room to discuss.
➤ Focus on their behaviour, not them personally.
➤ Encourage them to reflect on how their behaviour might make the patient feel.
➤ Aim to be constructive: suggest how they can adjust their behaviour to promote rather than diminish dignity.
➤ Where applicable, reinforce any positive behaviour that they showed.

Reporting

➤ If a colleague's behaviour consistently lacks attention to dignity, or an isolated incident was particularly serious, talk to their manager or use your organisation's whistle-blowing policy to report the behaviour.
➤ Document the details of the incident(s), writing clearly exactly what happened and the people involved.

CONCLUSION

Dignity in healthcare is 'everybody's business'; all staff who work with patients, regardless of their qualification and role, have a crucial influence on whether patients' dignity is promoted. Even if the environment is far from ideal, the individual interactions between staff and patients and their families can have a major impact on whether they feel cared for and valued as human beings. Privacy, communication and quality fundamental care are key aspects of staff behaviour that promote dignity in care. Staff should be aware of how organisational culture affects their own behaviour towards patients. They should also be prepared to deal with diminished dignity arising from the behaviour of colleagues, using whistle-blowing policies as necessary.

REFERENCES

Age Concern (2006) *Hungry to Be Heard: the scandal of malnourished older people in hospital.* London: Age Concern.

Applegate M, Morse J (1994) Personal privacy and interaction patterns in a nursing home. *Journal of Ageing Studies* **8**(4): 413–34.

Ariño-Blasco S, Tadd W, Boix-Ferrer JA (2005) Dignity and older people: the voice of professionals. *Quality in Ageing* **6**(1): 30–35.

Arman M, Rehnsfeldt A (2007) The 'little extra' that alleviates suffering. *Nursing Ethics* **14**: 372–86.

Baillie L (2007) *A Case Study of Patient Dignity in an Acute Hospital Setting.* Unpublished thesis. London South Bank University.

Baillie L (2009a) Patient dignity in an acute hospital setting: a case study. *International Journal of Nursing Studies* **46**: 22–36.

Baillie L (2009b) *Developing Practical Adult Nursing Skills* (3e). London: Hodder Arnold.

Bayer T, Tadd W, Krajcik S (2005) Dignity: the voice of older people. *Quality in Ageing* **6**(1): 22–7.

Calnan M, Woolhead G, Dieppe P (2005)Views on dignity in providing health care for older people. *Nursing Times* **101**(33): 38–41.

Department of Health (2003) *Whistle-blowing in the NHS Policy Pack.* London: Department of Health.

Department of Health (2006) *Dignity in Care Public Survey October 2006 – Report of the Survey.* Gateway reference 7213. London: Department of Health. www.dh.gov.uk/prod_consum_dh/groups/dh_digitalassets/@dh/@en/documents/digitalasset/dh_4139558.pdf (accessed 11 October 2010).

Edvardsson D (2008) Balancing between being a person and being a patient – a qualitative study of wearing patient clothing. *International Journal of Nursing Studies* **46**(10): 4–11.

Enes SPD (2003) An exploration of dignity in palliative care. *Palliative Medicine* **17**(3): 263–9.

Firth-Cozens J, Firth RA, Booth S (2003) Attitudes to and experiences of reporting poor care. *Clinical Governance* **8**(4): 331–6.

Goodrich J, Cornwell J (2008) *Seeing the Person in the Patient.* London: King's Fund.

Halldorsdottir S (1991) Five basic modes of being with another. In: Gaut DA, Leininger MM (eds) *Caring: the compassionate healer.* New York: National League for Nursing Press, pp.37–49.

Health Advisory Service (2000) *'Not Because They are Old': an independent inquiry into the care of older people on acute wards in general hospitals.* London: Health Advisory Service.

Healthcare Commission (2007) *Caring for Dignity: a national report on dignity in care for older people while in hospital.* London: Commission for Healthcare Audit and Inspection.

Healthcare Commission (2008) *Learning from Investigations.* London: Healthcare Commission.

Help the Aged (2007) *The Challenge of Dignity in Care: upholding the rights of the individual.* London: Help the Aged.

Jacobson N (2009) Dignity violation in healthcare. *Qualitative Health Research* **19**(11): 1536–47.

Lai CY, Levy V (2002) Hong Kong Chinese women's experiences of vaginal examinations in labour. *Midwifery* **18**(4): 296–303.

Matiti MR (2002) *Patient Dignity in Nursing: a phenomenological study.* Unpublished thesis. University of Huddersfield School of Education and Professional Development.

Matiti M, Sharman J (1999) Dignity: a study of pre-operative patients. *Nursing Standard* **14**(13–15): 32–35.

Matthews R, Callister LC (2004) Childbearing women's perceptions of nursing care that promotes dignity. *Journal of Obstetrics, Gynaecologic and Neonatal Nursing* **33**(4): 498–507.

McClement SE, Chochinov HM, Hack T *et al* (2004) Dignity-conserving care: application of research findings to practice. *International Journal of Palliative Care* **10**(4): 173–9.

Nåden D, Eriksson K (2004) Understanding the importance of values and moral attitudes in nursing care in preserving human dignity. *Nursing Science Quarterly* **17**(1): 86–91.

Newson P (2008) Dignified care for staff and residents. *Nursing and Residential Care* **10**(1): 608–13.

NHS Modernisation Agency (2003) *Essence of Care: patient-focused benchmarks for clinical governance.* London: NHS Modernisation Agency.

Nordenfelt L (2003) Dignity of the elderly: an introduction. *Medicine, Health Care and Philosophy* **6**(2): 99–101.

Patients Association (2009) *Patients . . . Not Numbers, People . . . Not Statistics.* London: Patients Association.

Ray SL (2006) Whistleblowing and organisational ethics. *Nursing Ethics* **13**: 438–45.

Royal College of Nursing (2008) *Defending Dignity: challenges and opportunities for nurses.* London: Royal College of Nursing.

Söderberg A, Gilje F, Norberg A (1997) Dignity in situations of ethical difficulty in intensive care. *Intensive and Critical Care Nursing* **13**(3): 135–44.

Turnock C, Kelleher M (2001) Maintaining patient dignity in intensive care settings. *Intensive and Critical Care Nursing* **17**(3): 144–54.

Walsh K, Kowanko I (2002) Nurses' and patients' perceptions of dignity. *International Journal of Nursing Practice* **8**(3): 143–51.

Welsh Assembly Government (2003) *Fundamentals of Care: guidance for health and social care staff.* Cardiff: Welsh Assembly.

Widäng I, Fridlund B (2003) Self-respect, dignity and confidence: conceptions of integrity among male patients. *Journal of Advanced Nursing* **42**(1): 47–56.

Widäng I, Fridlund B, Martenssen J (2007) Women patients' conceptions of integrity within health care: a phenomenographic study. *Journal of Advanced Nursing* **61**(5): 540–8.

Wilson D (2006) Giving patients a choice of what to wear in hospital. *Nursing Times* **102**(20): 29–31.

Woogara J (2004) *Patient Privacy: an ethnographic study of privacy in NHS patient settings.* Unpublished PhD thesis. University of Surrey.

Woolhead G, Calnan M, Dieppe P, Tadd W (2005) Dignity in older age: what do older people in the United Kingdom think? *Age and Ageing* **33**(2): 165–70.

World Health Organization (2002) *The Toronto Declaration on the Global Prevention of Elder Abuse.* Geneva: World Health Organization.

SECTION 2
Dignity in different healthcare settings

CHAPTER 7

Dignity for children

Paula Reed

INTRODUCTION

In this chapter I discuss dignity in relation to children. For the purposes of this chapter, the term 'children' is used to cover all children and young people from the age of 0 to 16 years. 'Dignity' is a term that is not always associated with children, especially young children and babies. As those who work with children and young people will recognise, there is huge variation of developmental stage including awareness, dependency, abilities and understanding within these ages. In order to address this spectrum I have used three case studies to illustrate some of the issues that are pertinent to this diverse client group: two from the acute hospital setting and one in the community. Dignity campaigns (Department of Health [DH], 2006; Royal College of Nursing, [RCN] 2008) have raised the profile of dignity in care in the United Kingdom (UK) (*see* Chapter 4: 'Dignity as a policy issue in healthcare'), but dignity remains a concept associated with older people rather than a term linked with children. In this chapter, I explore the meaning of dignity for children and demonstrate how dignity-promoting practice is as important for children and their families as for any other group.

I commence by reviewing what is currently understood by dignity and children. I have made particular reference to work undertaken around promoting the rights of the child and their participation in both society and their own healthcare. I will then explore the social construction of children and their position in society, and look at areas in which dignity can be promoted or diminished for children in practice and consider the environment, the processes and the people involved in the care of the child (Gallagher *et al*, 2009). Gallagher *et al* (2009) distil the themes that underpin dignity into: places, people, processes. Important too are the values at the level of society, the institution, for example the hospital, and the individual people involved.

To be able to protect and promote the dignity of children and young people in a range of settings, we need to understand what dignity means when it is linked with young people. It is easy to make assumptions about dignity for children based on what is understood about adult dignity, but is dignity for children the same or different from that of adults? There has been a groundswell of interest in promoting the dignity of older people, particularly in hospital, but there has been limited research on dignity and children. However, recent research has been undertaken to challenge adult-centric assumptions and demonstrated some of the particular aspects of care that affect children's and young people's sense of dignity. Examples in this chapter have been informed by an ethnographic approach to understanding the meanings of dignity for children, their parents and the staff looking after them on a children's ward (Reed *et al*, 2003; Reed, 2007). Ethnography is a useful methodology to tap into the direct experience of participants. In this example, the study involved a nine-month period of fieldwork on a children's ward in a district general hospital. The research took a broad approach to understanding dignity for children, focusing not only on, for example, the need for privacy, but exploring the entirety of the experience of children in hospital or other care settings and linking it back to the impact on the child and their feelings and sense of dignity. The research identified themes central to the promotion of dignity for children. This chapter's case study examples are drawn from my research; all names have been changed to protect confidentiality.

I conclude the chapter with an exploration of the practical application of dignity-promoting practice in child healthcare settings. I have included some questions to encourage reflection on practice and stimulate further discussion. In my final summary, I will draw together the key points covered in this chapter.

LEARNING OUTCOMES

By the end of the chapter you will be able to:

➤ understand some of the issues pertinent to the protection and promotion of dignity for children
➤ identify some of the threats to dignity for babies, children and adolescents
➤ challenge your own beliefs/practices with regard to children and young people.

DIGNITY AND THE CHILD

The inherent dignity of the child is emphasised by the United Nations (UN) Convention of the Rights of the Child (1989). Children should be treated with humanity and respect for the inherent dignity of the human person and in a manner which takes into account the needs of persons of his or her age (Article 37). The rights of disabled children are described in Article 23, which demands that they be able to enjoy a full and decent life, their dignity is ensured, and self-reliance and active participation in the community are promoted. The convention also recognises that by reason of physical and mental immaturity, children need special safeguards and care, with their best interests being the primary consideration. I will discuss some of the challenges to these ideals in caring for children when they are in hospital or cared for in the community and how dignity-promoting care can be delivered in practice.

POWER AND THE CHILD

An acknowledgment of the vulnerability of a child is also the recognition of an imbalance of power between the child and adults. These power relations are built upon the view that childhood is a discrete category of human life (Lloyd-Smith and Tarr, 2000). Balen *et al* (2006) suggest that children are constructed as 'human becomings' rather than human beings in their own right, and that their present is sublimated with their future in mind. There have been recent UK government initiatives to improve outcomes for all children and raise the profile of the well-being of children, for example *Every Child Matters* (Department for Education and Skills, 2004), as well as multi-agency initiatives to increase the participation of children in society and ensuring that children and young people have a strong voice in the development, delivery and evaluation of services that affect their lives (Participation Works Partnership, 2010). Nevertheless, at a societal level, the voices of children remain quiet. Adults assume a considerable degree of power over children and what happens to them. Rather than placing importance on the here and now experiences of children, it has been argued that children are judged, nurtured and protected with the future adult in mind (Christensen, 1998). The child and their childhood matter less.

Powerlessness may be compounded by ill health and admission to hospital. Research with adults indicates that a feeling of powerlessness and loss of control has a negative impact on one's sense of dignity (RCN, 2008). Within a hospital setting, the lives of the children, and to a lesser extent their families, are subjugated to the routines of the hospital. Dignity has been linked with the feeling of being in control and being able to make decisions for ourselves and yet these are feelings that many children and young people lack, especially when they are unwell or hospitalised.

There are individual and socially constructed reasons why children and young people are vulnerable to having their dignity unacknowledged or overlooked. Children are used to adults having control over them; young children are small and can be carried or moved at the whim of the health worker. Young children may not be able to talk or articulate their views and staff may be tempted not to communicate directly to them. Attempts by babies to communicate, such as crying, may not always be listened to by busy staff and staff may communicate with parents but this is not always adequate.

FAMILY-CENTRED CARE

Baillie *et al* (2009) identify the culture of the organisation as influential in promoting the dignity of patients. Central to the care of children and young people is the ideology of family-centred care. This has grown up in recognition of the importance of parental presence and involvement in the way children are cared for when they are ill. The National Service Framework for Children (DH, 2003, 2004) upholds the ideal of care being integrated and coordinated around the particular needs of the child as well as the needs of the family. This trend is based upon the premise of the beneficial influence of the family in the care of children (Corlett and Twycross, 2006).

The ethos of family-centred care has been promoted on children's wards and situates the child within his/her family. Care is planned by health staff around the whole family rather than just the individual child, with the aim of minimising emotional trauma and assisting recovery. Family-centred care has intuitive appeal to health carers and yet there is a lack of evidence to demonstrate that family-centred care improves the child's experience (Shields *et al*, 2007; Carter, 2008). Family-centred care assumes a cohesive family unit. However, at times of stress such as when a child becomes ill, even the closest families can become discordant. Adolescents may naturally be in conflict with parents, and agreeing an approach to care can become very difficult. Coyne (2006) showed that parents were not always able to take part in family-centred care due to other commitments and some resented doing what they considered to be the work of the nurses.

Where family-centred care works, it can promote communication between the parents, child and staff. Parents can advocate for their child and ensure that their needs are met. They can help their child understand about their illness and what is happening as well as providing safe and familiar support. However, the voice of the child and their opinion, especially if it conflicts with the staff, can be lost (Reed, 2007).

Researchers investigating the experiences of children in hospital have drawn attention to the way the desire to protect children, or a paternalistic attitude by healthcare workers, can have the effect of limiting a child's opportunity to express their opinions. Carter (2002), in her discussion of chronic pain, argues that the professional can base their interpretation of a child's pain on clinical experience alone rather than an appreciation of the lived experience of the child. It can be difficult for children to communicate effectively; they may have limited verbal skills due to their condition or their stage of development. There may be opportunities now for children to play in hospital and express themselves in this way, but neither doctors nor nurses are regularly involved in these activities and they are not able to capitalise on these episodes to understand the children more holistically.

Staff and parents may work together in the 'best interests' of the child. Respecting the dignity and experience of a child is fundamental to determining best interest. Promoting the dignity of a child may, in some circumstances, mean challenging the basis on which decisions are made or treatments initiated. Procedures may be undertaken despite the protestations of a child, with the intention of doing what was best, either for the child now or for their future well-being. Carnevale (1997) uses the uncomfortable term 'aggressive care' following his ethnographic research in a paediatric intensive care unit. Children may need to be 'held down' or restrained for procedures. However, where staff are busy and under pressure themselves, clinical expediency can determine their actions. For example, it can be tempting to take blood from a baby before he/she has finished their feed or while they are still asleep. It is important to question for whose best interests we work: the child, the member of staff, or the parent? Sometimes, for the well-being of all the patients on a ward, procedures have to be undertaken at a particular time in order that the staff member can attend to others on the ward. There is always the tension of the needs of another taking priority at ward level; this can threaten an individual's dignity.

Dealing with patients and their parents who challenge the way we work can be difficult. Promoting the dignity of such children and parents can be testing. Equally, parents and their children may be overly compliant and there is evidence to suggest that children and their families do not challenge decisions and practice because they want to keep on the right side of staff. As one mother of a 17-month-old boy explained:

> We are scared of upsetting them, you know. A lot of the time we let things ride because we thought maybe there's a bigger battle round the corner (Reed, 2007, p.288).

In either situation, the best interests of the child may not be achieved.

THE ENVIRONMENT

The importance of the environment in safeguarding the dignity of an individual is widely recognised in the discourse (Coyne, 2006; Baillie *et al*, 2009). Children and young people are cared for in a variety of settings, from acute hospitals, to hospices, in their own homes and in schools. Every setting raises its own particular challenges to the promotion and protection of the dignity of an individual child. The environment is key to putting children at their ease:

> An appropriate, well cared for environment engenders feelings of worth especially among children, young people, their parents and possibly staff (Baillie *et al*, 2009, p.28).

The layout of the ward is important. Many wards now have a play area/room, but if a child has to walk a long way or past the nurse's station then they may be discouraged to go.

In hospital the ward, its layout, the lack of privacy, the bright lights, food and routines are strange to a child and their parents. Those who stay in hospital for up to 48 hours can suspend their normal way of living as if they were just visiting. However, those who must stay in for a prolonged period or who have to return frequently have to live in hospital and adapt their way of living accordingly. Meal times, bed times and the timings of procedures are all taken out of their hands. This can deny them their sense of control and independence; in turn this can undermine their self-esteem and sense of dignity.

Children and young people appreciate comfort and seek out comfort on the ward. Where children are placed in mixed open bays, they have little opportunity to personalise their space around them. In side rooms one can observe the way children and their families will fill the space with their personal effects. Self-expression and identity can be threatened in hospital and yet it is an intrinsic part of both dignity and the young person's personal growth. Lewis *et al* (2009) describe the benefits of using the hospital bedside space to give visual cues to nurses, thereby enabling them to know their patients more intimately and in a way that is more meaningful.

Normality is something that we all crave; particularly in times of stress and distress, we yearn for the familiar and that which is safe. Hospitals and other healthcare settings can be very alien places to children, young people and their parents, in terms of both the physical environment and the sights, sounds and smells they encounter. It can be this very strangeness that threatens the individual's sense of control, ease, self-expression and determination. By acknowledging some of this strangeness and thinking of ways to overcome it, we can go a long way in putting patients and their families at ease, and arguably promote their sense of dignity.

Dignity can be more difficult to maintain where the ward caters for a variety of ages. Older children can find it insulting being put in a bed next to a young child. They can find adhering to early lights out and early rising an additional strain and a disregard for their needs as adolescents. Equally, in wards that have a range of conditions, staff may have more empathy for those children and families who are 'truly' sick with long-term and serious illnesses, and lack compassion for those recovering from routine yet nevertheless painful and upsetting procedures. Equally, parents of children with chronic illness may regard the families of children with minor ailments with disdain and be aware of uninvited interest of other families on the ward.

PRIVACY

There is a considerable body of research to support the idea that the maintenance of privacy is fundamental to the promotion of dignity (Walsh and Kowanko, 2002; Webster and Bryan, 2009). Research indicates that children are perceived by staff and parents to have an increasing sense of bodily privacy, from very little in babies, to an acute sense of bodily privacy in adolescence (Reed, 2007). This growing awareness is thought to be modelled by parents and promoted by staff.

There are some important areas when the privacy of individual children and young people can be undermined. Staff, seeking to promote privacy, adopt stylised behaviours, such as pulling curtains, that demonstrate that dignity is being addressed. However, children do not necessarily recognise these behaviours as such. They may feel more secure with the curtains not closed or they may be particularly sensitive to the crack in the curtain left open, or the reality that sounds and conversations are not kept confidential by curtains alone.

Staff manage the bodies of children throughout their hospital stay, covering exposed bodies, observing, measuring and breaching body boundaries with the insertion of drips and drains. In hospital, the bodies of children are no longer private but become the objects of interest, discussion and examination, with their appearance being the source of speculation and conjecture as to what may be wrong with them. The children and their bodies can become defined by the clinical gaze and medical measurements. Foucault (1973) documents the transformations in medical practice that took place towards the end of the 18th century. He describes the way the body became the new 'anatomical atlas' to be interpreted through the 'clinical gaze'. The role of the patient diminished as the body became the object of study (Williams and Bendelow, 1998). Children who have many or prolonged periods of time in hospital can experience a considerable amount of handling by relative strangers. Staff and even parents can become desensitised to drips and drains and handle them without regard to the sensitivities of the patient. Yet children and young people may be acutely aware of their physical appearance and stigma.

Dignity for children is complex, as the discussion has so far identified. The case study in Box 7.1 raises a few points for discussion; for example, what features of this scenario are pertinent in considering the dignity of the young person involved?

Sometimes, when providing intimate care or undertaking intimate procedures, staff may seem not to react to a potentially embarrassing task. Staff may use behaviours or words to minimise the size, significance or severity of an event. These 'minifisms', suggests Lawler (1991), protect the member of staff and the patient from having to acknowledge and deal with embarrassment. However, Carl (in Box 7.1) found the episode where the female nurse took a swab degrading. Children's developing sexuality is often avoided, yet is an important part of their developing sense of self.

Children develop and redevelop their sense of identity as they grow up. Fundamental to establishing self-identity are the choices we make over the way we present ourselves. Choices for children over presentation of self are very limited

---

BOX 7.1 *Case study A*

Carl was a 14-year-old boy with cystic fibrosis. He had been admitted many times, and on this occasion with an acute infection requiring intravenous antibiotics. He expressed his feelings of humiliation when a nurse, just a few years older than he, took a swab from his groin.

Carl felt ridiculous in a hospital gown and was reprimanded when he wore just boxer shorts on the ward, as they were judged unsuitable. He pulled out a nasogastric tube as he found it stigmatising and sensed that people stared at it.

Carl missed his friends from home. He also commented on how he would make friends with children and young people on the ward and then they would 'disappear' and he would not know how they were unless they were readmitted. He felt that staff did not respect his need for friendships. He resented having to, yet had to put up with their noise early in the morning. Carl longed for normality and felt that the world was passing by, leaving him behind.

Carl's mother had a difficult role to play. She wanted to be there to advocate for her son and yet she was aware that at 14 he did not want to have her around all the time. She felt some of the staff did not like her and thought she interfered. She was not medically trained, yet over the years she had acquired a detailed understanding of cystic fibrosis and thought she had the right and ability to question the staff about the treatments and their care of her son.

---

on a children's ward. Children can be humiliated by being forced to wear clothes that are not their own. Hospital gowns can be particularly disliked by boys who see them as dresses and, rather than devices to protect their dignity, perceive them to be embarrassing. Moreover, children and young people, such as Carl, may be taken from the relative privacy of the ward through more public areas of the hospital dressed in hospital wear with an assortment of drips and drains.

Adolescence is a time of great changes in a young person, both physical and emotional. It is a time characterised by emerging independence and dis-attachment from the primary caregivers (usually parents). Yet in hospital this natural progression is compromised as parents are frequently resident, spending a great deal of time with their adolescent child, and important friendships and the establishment of peer groups are undermined.

Despite acknowledgement of the dignity of all persons, even the very young (UN, 1989), in practice it can be a difficult notion to appreciate with very young children. Babies are unable to communicate their needs verbally. They are small and unable to move themselves around and their daily needs have to be met through another. This makes them vulnerable to being overlooked in terms of dignity. Reed (2007, p.256) cites the acknowledgment of this vulnerability from a staff nurse:

> They are only babies, so people think it doesn't matter

and later:

> People think "Oh it's a baby we can just go ahead and do it".

The case study in Box 7.2 illustrates privacy issues related to a young child in hospital.

BOX 7.2 *Case study B*

Jaynie was a 21-month-old girl. She had been readmitted with pneumonia for the sixth time and was waiting in the eight-bedded assessment bay to be seen by the registrar. Since birth she had been subjected to a raft of tests, but still a definitive diagnosis had not been made. Privacy was difficult to maintain in this area as it was next to the entrance and held children of all ages and their families prior to admission or discharge home. Jaynie's mother found the attentions of other families painful, and repeatedly telling and retelling her story to different health professionals in such an environment was distressing. Jaynie's routines were disrupted and she had undergone several painful procedures, including a lumbar puncture, during previous admissions.

Autonomy is recognised as important in the preservation of dignity. Indeed, it has been argued that autonomy is a more tangible and useful concept to measure and therefore achieve than the more nebulous notion of dignity (Macklin, 2003). The idea of autonomy for babies and very young children at first seems impossible and inappropriate (Pullman, 1999). Yet autonomy for children the age of Jaynie (*see* Box 7.2) has been described by a mother (Reed, 2007) as the freedom to listen and respond to bodily needs such as sleep and hunger when they need to.

Children and their families are particularly aware of the eyes and ears of the other families on the ward. They are constantly scrutinised not only by staff but by other patients and their families. Darbyshire (1994) described this phenomenon as 'parenting in public'. Parents of disabled children have described their loss of normal parenting and described the transformation of parenting from private to being conducted under the gaze of healthcare workers (Kirk *et al*, 2005). Thus, parents can be upset by the others looking on and even by doctors, where they perceive their interest to be disingenuous, for example, curious about the medical condition rather than the child's well-being.

STAFF–PATIENT RELATIONSHIPS

Research demonstrates that children and their parents appreciate the relationship they develop with the staff (Reed, 2007). However, the position of the trained children's nurse is ever further from the child and their intimate care, leaving limited opportunities for staff on a ward environment to establish relationships. A sense that they were treated with dignity and a feeling that their dignity remained intact were reported to be integral to the relationships between children and their parents and the staff. The style of communication is fundamental to the promotion and protection of an individual (Wainwright, 1994).

Children and their parents want to feel that they matter. They want to be listened to and have their opinions respected. Parents do not want their child objectified but acknowledged as an individual. They want staff to demonstrate interest in their child as people and as individuals, and appreciate it when staff make an effort to get to know them. Children want to be spoken to and not over (Reed, 2007).

Several papers identify communication along with environment as key to the promotion of dignity (RCN, 2008). I have already described some of the issues to be aware of in family-centred care, but there are also other aspects of interaction that are important to consider. One needs to be aware that even if you have seen a child coming in for a routine tonsillectomy or appendectomy, it is the first time for the child, and for many the first time in the strange hospital environment with strange nurses and doctors. Another issue is attention to pace and timing. Sometimes, information is badly received because the timing was wrong and the healthcare professional was communicating within their own timeframe, unaware of the needs of the patient. For example, soon after Jaynie (Box 7.2) was born, a junior doctor came to check her over before discharge, but suggested that she was seen by the registrar first. The registrar had come swiftly over, stating 'I understand that you are worried about Down's', to which Jaynie's parents had replied 'No but we are now'.

Research (Reed, 2007) indicates that some children are likely to receive more attention from staff than others. Teenage girls, for example, are able to establish a rapport readily with the nurses, the majority of whom are female and often not much older. For teenage boys, this relationship can be more awkward, as in Carl's experience. In a general children's ward, children with learning difficulties or mental illness may be avoided by staff and communication may be limited, with parents/carers expected to undertake most of the caring role (Brown and Guvenir, 2008). Stockwell (1972) first identified characteristics of patients who were not popular. Those that received more attention were those with whom staff could develop reciprocity in their relationship.

Children and young people, especially those with chronic health needs, grow up whist undergoing treatment and care. The DH (2003) identified that the changing needs of children were not always considered. Box 7.3 presents an extract from an interview at home with Luke (aged 6 years) and his mother, reminiscing about the tough times they spent together in hospital when Luke was being treated for cancer and had a Hickman line ('Wiggly').

BOX 7.3 *Interview extract (Reed, 2007, p.301)*

Luke (aged 6 years) at home with mum 24 months post treatment.

Mum: 'She used to give him something to drink, didn't she, and then we take out some ketchup'.

Luke: 'It was blood, Mum!'

Mum: 'Oh I am sorry, was it, Luke? We called it ketchup at the time'.

Box 7.3 demonstrates how those in a caring role need to be alert to the developing and maturing child. Ways of communicating and explaining treatments effectively need to be modified as children grow up.

Reflective activity 7.1 presents a list of reflective questions to help you to explore dignity for children and their parents in your care environment.

Reflective activity 7.1

➤ Try entering the ward or the environment in which you work and imagine yourself as a child coming to this place for the first time. What does it smell like, what does it look like, what are the people around you doing, are there other children, how do they seem? What can you hear? How does this make you feel? You can test out your hunches with the children themselves, or their parents.

Consider

➤ How do I feel about this patient (and their parents)? How does this influence my response to them, and in particular my attention to protecting and promoting their dignity?

➤ Are there patients/families that I avoid? Why is this? How does this influence their stay in hospital?

➤ Are there patients I enjoy being with/looking after? How does this affect their dignity?

➤ What activities do I do to promote dignity? Are they working? Do they work in every case?

CONCLUSION

In this chapter I have explored the importance of dignity for children and young people in healthcare. To assume that dignity is of lesser importance for children and young people arguably denies their very humanness and is a reflection of their position in society. At a practical level, there are some particular issues pertaining to children and young people to consider when promoting dignity in healthcare.

I have not provided a 'dignity checklist', but rather drawn attention to some points to consider for best practice when caring for children and young people. I have discussed the impact of the environment in promoting dignity for children, with particular reference to the hospital ward. Particular to the care of children in hospital is the presence of family and family-centred care, which creates its own challenges to maintaining dignity. Linked to the environment is the individual's need for privacy and their parents'/carers' need for privacy and refuge from the scrutiny of fellow patients and staff. Patient confidentiality is fundamental to a relationship between patient and staff, but this can be difficult to maintain on an 'open' ward with the privacy of family life made public. Nursing and medical staff can become desensitised to bodily exposures, and without careful attentiveness can inadvertently cause a patient humiliation and distress. Loss of autonomy and independence has been noted as fundamental to feelings of a loss of dignity in older people; children, by contrast, may be prevented from developing this independence and have their presentation of themselves severely restricted. It should be borne in mind that there is a power differential between the child and an adult, which is compounded by their role of patient. This, combined with barriers to communication, means that questions of best interest must be carefully negotiated.

Paramount to the promotion of dignity is the interaction between the child and the healthcare worker. To engage fully with a child, one must engage with that child's subjective experience. This requires challenging traditional accepted ways of doing things by taking the perspective of the child. Listening to children and communicating using child-friendly methods such as play improve this understanding. Being reflective and aware of one's own attitudes and resultant behaviours can assist human encounters and communication, no matter what the age.

REFERENCES

Baillie L, Ford P, Gallagher A, Wainwright P (2009) Dignified care for children and young people: nurses' perspectives. *Paediatric Nursing* **21**(2): 24–8.

Balen R, Blyth E, Calabretto H *et al* (2006) Involving children in health and social research: 'human becomings' or 'active agents'. *Childhood* **13**(1): 29–48.

Brown F, Guvenir J (2008) The experiences of children with learning disabilities, their carers and staff during hospital admission. *British Journal of Learning Disabilities* **37**: 110–15.

Carnevale F (1997) The experiences of critically ill children: narratives in the making. *Intensive and Critical Care Nursing* **13**: 49–52.

Carter B (2002) Chronic pain in childhood and the medical encounter: professional ventriloquism and hidden voices. *Qualitative Health Research* **12**: 28–41.

Carter B (2008) Commentary on Shields L, Pratt J, Davis L, Hunter J. Family-centred care: a review of qualitative studies. *Journal of Clinical Nursing* **5**: 1317–1323.

Christensen P (1998) Difference and similarity: how children's competencies are constituted in illness and its treatment. In: Hutchby I, Moran-Ellis J (eds) *Children and Social Competence: arenas of action*. London: Falmer, pp.187–201.

Corlett J, Twycross A (2006) Negotiation of care by children's nurses: lessons from research. *Paediatric Nursing* **18**(8): 34–7.

Coyne I (2006) Children's experiences of hospitalisation. *Journal of Child Health Care* **10**(4): 326–36.

Darbyshire P (1994) *Living with a Sick Child in Hospital: the experiences of parents and nurses*. London: Chapman and Hall.

Department for Education and Skills (2004) *Every Child Matters: change for children*. Nottingham: DfES Publications.

Department of Health (2003) *Getting the Right Start: National Service Framework for Children*. London: Department of Health.

Department of Health (2004) *Children and Young People Who are Ill: National Service Framework for Children, Young People and Maternity Services: standard 6, part II*. London: Department of Health.

Department of Health (2006) *Dignity in Care*. Gateway Reference 7388. London: Department of Health.

Foucault M (1973) *The Birth of the Clinic: an archaeology of medical perception*. Translated from the French by AM Sheridan. London: Tavistock.

Gallagher A, Wainwright P, Baillie L, Ford P (2009) The RCN Dignity Survey: implications for leaders. *Nursing Management* **16**(4): 12–16.

Kirk S, Glendinning C, Callery P (2005) Parent or nurse? The experience of being the parent of a technology dependent child. *Journal of Advanced Nursing* **51**(5): 456–64.

Lawler J (1991) *Behind the Screens: nursing, somology and the problem of the body*. Melbourne, Edinburgh: Churchill Livingstone.

Lewis P, Kerridge I, Jorden CFC (2009) Creating space: hospital bedside displays as facilitators of communication between children and nurses. *Journal of Child Health Care* **13**: 93.

Lloyd-Smith M, Tarr J (2000) Researching children's perspectives: a sociological dimension. In: Lewis A, Lindsay G (eds) *Researching Children's Perspectives*. Buckingham/Philadelphia: Open University Press, pp.59–70.

Macklin R (2003) Dignity is a useless concept. *BMJ* **327**: 1419–20.

Participation Works Partnership (2010) *About us*. www.participationworks.org.uk/about-us (accessed 25 October 2010).

Pullman D (1999) The ethics of autonomy and dignity in long term care. *Canadian Journal of Aging* **18**(1): 26–46.

Reed P (2007) *Dignity and the Child in Hospital*. Unpublished PhD thesis. University of Surrey.

Reed P, Smith P, Fletcher M, Bradding A (2003) Promoting the dignity of the child in hospital. *Nursing Ethics* **10**(1): 67–76.

Royal College of Nursing (2008) *Defending Dignity: opportunities and challenges for nursing.* London: Royal College of Nursing.

Shields L, Pratt J, Davis L, Hunter J (2007) Family-centred care for children in hospital. *Cochrane Database of Systematic Reviews* **1**: CD004811.

Stockwell F (2002) The unpopular patient. In: Rafferty AM, Traynor M (eds) *Exemplary Research for Nursing and Midwifery.* London: Routledge, pp.23–42.

United Nations (1989) *Convention on the Rights of the Child.* www.unicef.org/crc/ (accessed 11 October 2010).

Wainwright P (1994) The observation of intimate aspects of care. In: Hunt G (ed) *Ethical Issues in Nursing.* London and New York: Routledge, pp.38–54.

Walsh K, Kowanko I (2002) Nurses' and patients' perceptions of dignity. *International Journal of Nursing Practice* **8**: 143–51.

Webster C, Bryan K (2009) Older people's views of dignity and how it can be promoted in a hospital environment. *Journal of Clinical Nursing* **18**(12): 1784–92.

Williams S, Bendelow G (1998) *The Lived Body: sociological themes, embodied issues.* London and New York: Routledge.

CHAPTER 8

Dignity in maternity care

Barbara Burden

INTRODUCTION

Ask any midwife about dignity within maternity care and they are likely to tell you the age-old adage that mothers leave it 'at the door to the maternity unit and collect it on the way out'. Over the years that I have practised as a midwife I have found this portrayal of dignity intriguing and somewhat difficult to qualify. The notion of dignity being removed from a person poses a number of questions; for example, what is it about being pregnant that requires mothers to lose or relinquish their dignity? Is this a midwife's perception of what happens to mothers or do mothers acknowledge it as occurring? Can a woman have a baby with dignity? And at what stage in her pregnancy does a mother feel that she has parted with her dignity and, if so, does she get it back and how? These questions became one element within a grounded theory research study on privacy in maternity care environments (Burden, 2007), which explored the perception of privacy and its inherent relationship with dignity, the results of which provide the foundation for this chapter. The case studies and quotations used throughout the chapter are from the research study; all names used are pseudonyms.

LEARNING OUTCOMES

By the end of this chapter you will have:
- ➤ explored the concept of dignity in relation to privacy in maternity care environments
- ➤ considered the strategies mothers use in maternity settings to enable them to maintain dignity in childbirth
- ➤ reviewed how the concepts explored in this chapter relate to your own area of practice.

PRIVACY AND DIGNITY DURING PREGNANCY AND CHILDBIRTH

Privacy and dignity are concepts which, while generically defined, are interpreted by us as individuals. We each have identified boundaries of privacy which, while predominantly unique, have commonalities such as shame, embarrassment and need for respect and solitude (Halmos, 1953; Schneider, 1977; Bloustein, 2003). As individuals we usually have reasonable control over our privacy (Bloustein, 2003) but this can change with the circumstances in which we find ourselves. In the case of pregnant women, these boundaries are influenced by contact with health professionals, the need for health surveillance and the environment of care (Burden, 2007). The outcome is a process of adaptation where mothers attempt to maintain their privacy and dignity by putting in place strategies that enable them to deal with the intimacy involved with the process of childbirth, and then revisit their privacy and dignity after the birth has occurred. These strategies focus upon losing one's inhibitions, solitude and withdrawal, self-introversion, dealing with the indignity of ward-based procedures and losing face in a public environment. The chapter explores all these areas in detail.

The idea of creating new life and delivering a baby into the world is an exciting experience for most mothers; it does result, though, in women being subjected to a range of intimate examinations or processes that, if undertaken at other times, may be perceived as intrusive. During the process of pregnancy, birth and the early postnatal period, mothers find themselves subjected to varying degrees of physical assessments, from abdominal examinations and vaginal examinations to fetal blood sampling or induction of labour. It is the repetitive nature of early examinations that mothers describe as desensitising them to subsequent and more invasive examinations later in their pregnancy and that ultimately concludes with a loss of their inhibitions.

LOSING ONE'S INHIBITIONS

Inhibition can be described as the defence mechanisms or barriers we put in place to protect us from the embarrassment of our actions, or the actions of others, and which in turn impose restraints on our behaviour. For example, some women feel comfortable sunbathing topless on the beach whereas others would not consider exposing themselves so openly in a public place. It is the level of inhibition that we have for a given activity that predicts our level of embarrassment. Therefore, if a mother is happy to expose her breasts in public, the notion of breastfeeding in a public place may not be such an issue for her. Where our level of inhibition is consciously reduced this is mirrored by a subsequent decrease in our levels of embarrassment and shame. This is shown where mothers, as they become accustomed to physical examinations such as abdominal and vaginal examinations, put in place strategies based upon their previous experiences, to manage lowering both their inhibitions and their embarrassment during such interactions.

Women know their boundaries of privacy and dignity in any given situation and are usually able to ensure that their privacy needs are met. As with the development of any experience, privacy status is governed by previous actions and experiences (Goffman, 1963, 1967; Rosen, 2001). It is therefore inevitable that expectant mothers commence their pregnancy with their own unique require- ments for privacy and dignity, based on prior experience. Within my study there were mothers who, for example, had never had a cervical smear or a vaginal examination before becoming pregnant, in some cases actively postponing examinations because of the embarrassment and indignity they perceived would result. This meant that some mothers embarked upon pregnancy either with no preconception of what would happen to them during the birth or with a some- what idealistic view that they would remain in control of their bodily privacy and their dignity during pregnancy. For some mothers this came with a naivety relating to the type and number of examinations they would be subjected to and a view that they could refuse, or keep examinations to a minimum.

Upon entering pregnancy mothers in my study described themselves as 'pri- vate in mind and body' and 'shy'. Most mothers had an idealistic view that they would not be admitted to hospital until they were in labour, at which time they would have their own room and their own midwife who would be provid- ing all their care, and would labour with their clothes on. For example, it was only with hindsight that the following two mothers were able to consider how private their bodies were prior to pregnancy and how their privacy and dignity boundaries changed throughout their experience.

> Before I had the baby, I didn't realise it but I was quite a private person . . . Look- ing back I think, knowing now how private I was, how did I get through that whole experience?

> You go into it [pregnancy] thinking I don't want to show myself at all and I don't really want too many people in the room. I am quite shy and what have you.

Mothers perceive routine examinations to be embedded in the process of preg- nancy, as an acknowledgement of both their pregnancy and the need to deter- mine the viability of their baby. They are viewed as something over which they have little control if they want a successful outcome to their pregnancy.

The process of being 'prodded' and examined during pregnancy was deemed by mothers to intensify as pregnancy progressed, with mothers becom- ing complicit first in abdominal examinations and then with more physical and invasive procedures. Once mothers considered an examination as routine or necessary to ensure the health and well-being of their baby, they legitimised their compliance with it.

> I think I got so used to being prodded, you just get used to it . . . it is one of those things that you have to accept when you have your checks on a regular basis. You just have to get used to it.

The repetitive nature of examinations meant mothers relinquished control of access to their bodies during procedures, accepting this as the monitoring procedure associated with pregnancy, stating that it no longer 'bothered me' or that they 'didn't care'.

It is the sense of control over personal circumstances and interactions that is central to maintaining a sense of ownership over one's body (McHale and Gallagher, 2003) that is necessary for privacy maintenance. Where mothers retain a sense of ownership of, and control over, their body, they are able to deal with repetitive examinations and bodily exposure while perceiving their dignity to be intact. A decrease in the level of inhibition, linked to an increase in embarrassment of the examination, enabled mothers to temporarily transfer ownership of their privacy to the midwife in order to maintain their dignity. Midwives were then able to legitimately perform tasks on mothers' bodies without mothers challenging the need for explanations. The following mother explained:

> I don't think that it is explained enough what they are doing and why they are doing it and why it is necessary. It was just a case of right here we go, and you just lay back without any sense of explanation really.

Mothers described how a lack of explanations prior to what were considered routine procedures resulted in depersonalisation, a decline in interactions with professionals and a perceived reduction in staff's need to show them respect. Mothers in return felt unable to ask questions because of their lack of understanding of what was happening and their embarrassment caused by the processes involved. This is particularly relevant for healthcare practitioners, as guidance on informed consent prior to all procedures is explicit within professional guidance documentation (Berg *et al*, 2001; Aveyard, 2002; Royal College of Nursing, 2005). Where explanations were not given, mothers felt midwives were disrespectful and breached their privacy and dignity. This lack of respect resulted in mothers constructing strategies for dealing with invasive procedures by psychologically withdrawing from the situation in order to preserve their dignity.

Now consider Reflective activity 8.1.

Reflective activity 8.1

Consider your own area of practice and how invasive or embarrassing procedures are explained to patients:

➤ do patients ask questions about procedures that could be perceived as embarrassing?
➤ how are these procedures explained?

SOLITUDE AND WITHDRAWAL: A DIGNITY PROTECTION

Withdrawal from social interaction is portrayed within classic privacy literature as synonymous with social isolation, or being separated from a group
and free from observation (Westin, 1970; Simmel, 1971). The need for withdrawal or solitude is portrayed as necessary to our everyday lives and necessary to enhance our freedom to define ourselves (Fried, 1970; Rossler, 2005).
It is required to enable us to 'break from role-playing and the opportunity
for "making fools of ourselves"'' (Rossler, 2005, p.149) and needed for 'deso-
cialisation' from others (Halmos, 1953). During pregnancy and childbirth,
withdrawal is identified by two concepts. Firstly, women may withdraw from
social interaction, as an attempt to psychologically escape from overcrowded
rooms, being viewed while breastfeeding, or reducing interactions with people
with whom mothers are not acquainted. In these instances mothers perceived
themselves as having little control over their privacy maintenance, with a subsequent result of a loss of privacy and dignity that was outside their control.
Secondly, mothers use withdrawal positively as a method of dealing with pain
during labour or examinations, which I have labelled self-introversion, that is,
withdrawing psychologically into their bodies with the aim of concentrating
on pain management. This withdrawal or self-introversion is a subconscious
adaptation process adopted by mothers as a means of securing personal privacy and a sense of control over their dignity and personal respect. Now consider Reflective activity 8.2.

Reflective activity 8.2

Most hospital wards consist of multi-occupancy rooms. Think what it must
be like to be in one of these rooms:

➤ what would you like and dislike about sharing a room with other
   people?
➤ how would you feel if invasive procedures took place in this
   environment?

Self-introversion

Self-introversion is a coping mechanism adopted by mothers while concentrating on managing the physical side of labour. It enables mothers to ignore social
events, social interactions and the discourse surrounding them. For most individuals, isolation, under normal circumstances, is a function associated with
defining and redefining ourselves. Its function is to enhance personal autonomy, aid emotional release and promote self-evaluation while limiting and
protecting interactions and communication with others, all of which are per-

ceived as necessary for daily living (Westin, 1970; Rossler, 2005). The process of daily living requires us to 'act a part' within society or, as Goffman (1959) states, the 'belief in the part one is playing'. By utilising self-introversion, mothers are able to suspend the role they usually play as partner, wife or mother and concentrate on the process of childbirth. This allows them to act differently from the norm during labour, without any associated embarrassment. For example, mothers in labour may remove all clothing without being inhibited by their nakedness, and upon reflection they promote this as a normal action.

By psychologically separating the body from the pain, such as that caused by labour or invasive physical examinations, the experience becomes something that happens physically *to your body* and not personally *to you*. Bodily detachment or disassociation from the body enables mothers to disassociate themselves from procedures, what Rachels (1975) describes as 'property rights', as a coping mechanism and to reduce any later embarrassment. By temporarily disassociating from the body, mothers subconsciously enable others to claim ownership of it, with subsequent right of possession and legitimate access. While Rachels perceived this disownership of the body as detrimental and disempowering within nursing, within midwifery, ownership is temporarily transferred by the mother voluntarily to the midwife. As temporary ownership is re-established to the midwife, she becomes the new *'owner'*, with right of access to the mother's body, enabling her to act on her behalf and address her privacy needs without consent, what Lawler (1991) calls 'an environment of permission'. As witnessed during participant observation, mothers handed over control of addressing privacy requirements to the midwife, so that when people knocked on doors or accessed rooms mothers no longer needed to pull down their clothing, cover themselves, or even acknowledge that person, leaving these superficial tasks to their midwife. This reallocation of basic privacy management was not verbally acknowledged between mothers and midwife, but undertaken through a subconscious awareness of each other, focused upon the individual needs of the mother.

It is important to note that self-introversion only takes place in the presence of a distraction, such as pain. Where a mother finds herself in a situation where pain is removed, such as when an epidural is used or where she has an operative delivery under spinal anaesthesia, then the need for introversion is decreased. In instances such as these, mothers' senses increase as they listen to and observe what is happening around them.

Now read through Box 8.1 and consider how Jessica might have felt in this situation.

When visiting Jessica in the postnatal period, we discussed her birthing experience, and in particular her experience at and following the birth. She described her sense of shame and embarrassment at being exposed like a 'slab of meat' for all to see, and of her 'horror' of events. She clearly remembered

> **BOX 8.1** *Jessica's story*
>
> During a participant observation I shadowed an experienced midwife
> in the operating theatre when a mother arrived for an emergency birth.
> The birth progressed quickly under spinal anaesthesia and the baby
> was born in good condition. At the end of the operation the mother
> was observed lying naked on the table with her gown around her neck.
> Her body was completely exposed and no-one took the time to cover
> her. In the room was her partner, the anaesthetist, an operating theatre
> technician, a midwife, a student midwife and a healthcare assistant.
> It wasn't until the senior midwife returned that the mother was
> covered and her sanitary towels reapplied and someone spoke to her.
> Throughout the observation the door to the operating theatre was open
> and visitors could be seen walking along the adjoining corridor.

people talking in the theatre and walking by in the corridor. For example, she
told me all about the social life of two members of staff as they described what
they would be doing at the weekend. Jessica also described two activities experienced just before and just after the birth. She outlined how before the birth,
once her pain was removed through spinal anaesthesia, she became more
aware of those around her. She described how she listened to every word, fearing for the safety of her baby, watching everything that everyone was doing. She
feared that there was a problem with her baby and ended up lying completely
still and non-participative in order not to distract the professionals from their
work, for fear of hindering their attempts to deliver her child. Once the birth
was completed, this heightened awareness of senses remained, but at this stage
she knew that her baby was safe and removed to the care of her partner. She
then focused on what was occurring around her. She found herself looking at
her naked body lying on the operating table. No-one appeared to be concerned
for her dignity or respected the need for her body to be covered. Staff started
to tidy up and move items around the room; the operating theatre doors were
opened, exposing her to visitors walking along the corridor. She felt very alone
and disrespected and at this stage she cried:

> . . . the whole time I was like "Oh my god" what have they seen? That was quite
> important to me but of course at the time you don't care too much but you still
> do, it is still your dignity.

Staff deal with mothers in the operating theatre as if they are unconscious
patients, forgetting that the majority have spinal anaesthesia and are awake

throughout the process. By ignoring their privacy needs and showing a lack of respect for mothers' bodily needs, mothers perceive themselves as no more than slabs of meat on the table. In contrast, midwives within the privacy study stated that one of their key roles was to protect the privacy and dignity of mothers by acting as advocate for them in situations where they perceived the mothers to be compromised. This appeared to be the case in situations where mothers laboured in individual rooms, under the auspices of a single midwife, but was not the case where the pregnancy became compromised.

In situations of compromise mothers perceived themselves to be watched by others, and ignored during conversations between practitioners. This resulted in mothers perceiving care as something that is 'done to them' rather than a mutual participation between parties. Subsequently, mothers experience a loss of ownership of their body which increased their sense of vulnerability and exposed them to increased physical contact by healthcare professionals, all of which were compounded by the attitudes of hospital staff, which mothers perceived to be patronising and authoritarian. In a study by Applegate and Morse (1994), where care home residents were viewed as objects, privacy needs were violated and patients became invisible or dehumanised, with privacy considered unnecessary or unimportant. Being treated as an object is not always initiated or perpetuated by staff. Within my study, mothers also adopted the role of inanimate object in order not to influence the work of doctors and midwives, when the safety of their baby was perceived to be compromised. Adopting this role was sensed as positive by mothers – as something they had to do short-term, was requirement specific, and necessary to achieve their primary goal of a healthy baby and safe return home.

In contrast, mothers admitted into single rooms on delivery suites, when in established labour, are more likely to achieve physical control of their privacy through isolation from the rest of society, by staking a claim on their room and having their birthing partner present. If mothers felt safe and secure in their environment, and with their midwife, they expressed some control over associated events. This sense of control over their labour ensured that as pain levels increased they were able to achieve privacy and maintain a sense of dignity by managing their pain through self-introversion. Where mothers felt in control of their labour pain they were able to concentrate on their body and their breathing, resulting in them becoming desensitised to surrounding events, for example:

> . . . you are in a bubble. You are in your own world and as far as I was concerned it was just me and my husband.

> Partner: I think during the delivery Rose wouldn't have noticed if there had been a coach full of Japanese tourists come through quite frankly [laughter].
> Rose: No, I can't remember half the things that I went through.

Goffman (1961, p.61) describes this type of situational withdrawal as 'regression' or 'plateaux of disinvolvement', where the person withdraws their attention from everything apart from what is happening in their immediate vicinity, and views these events in a different way than other people present do. This withdrawal enables mothers to remain in a 'birthing reality', which is then exited at the point of the birth. This enables mothers to disassociate themselves from the pain and in some cases the indignity of childbirth, in order for them to progress into their new role as a mother.

THE INDIGNITY OF WARD-BASED TREATMENT

In a number of cases, mothers are admitted to hospital in early labour. These mothers do not remain on the delivery suite but are transferred to the antenatal ward until labour is established. During this admission mothers are cared for within 4–6-bedded rooms, having all of their treatments and examinations undertaken within this public environment. Treatments and examinations undertaken include insertion of vaginal pessaries, vaginal examinations and daily examinations of abdomen and vaginal loss. While these treatments are not usually problematic if undertaken in the right environment, they become problematic when completed in the public environment of the ward. It is human nature that visitors and other mothers like to eavesdrop on conversations in the wards, as we all like a good gossip and the drama of unusual events. In the ward environment, mothers envisage eavesdroppers visualising invasive procedures taking place behind the curtains and confirmed that they too listened to conversations between mother and midwife. The following mothers described their experiences:

> This person just arrived and said "right I am going to put this pessary in" and nobody told you how awful this was going to be, on the ward there was just like a thin curtain around you and like other women on the ward as well and it was horrible.

> I think it depends where you are because I was in the ward with six other women that was fine when they were coming round giving you treatments but they were quite painful and some of them were due in visiting times when men were there and all you have got is a very thin curtain and some treatments that are quite intimate. You know, they are being described to you exactly what is going to happen and what you are going to feel and then they are pushing and shoving and what have you, and you are reacting to this, or are going to and on the other side of the very thin curtain you know, is a lady with her family and her husband and what have you. I found that most embarrassing.

Induction of labour and the insertion of vaginal pessaries caused most concern for mothers in relation to embarrassment caused by a loss of privacy and dignity during examinations. They were concerned that they might scream and embarrass themselves and others. There was a perception that staff perceived the curtains to provide enough privacy for them and, although this may be the case with protection from visual privacy, this was counterproductive when midwives described in detail the process of examinations. One mother stated: 'you are private but you are not, you can hear everything'.

The outcomes of procedures in the ward were embarrassment, a loss of dignity for mothers and a sense of loss of control over personal details and intimate aspects of care. The embarrassment caused to mothers was enhanced by the silent acknowledgement of the experience by others present in the room. As the curtains were drawn back each person in the room had some idea of what had occurred, yet there was no acknowledgement of such and so mothers remained embarrassed. One mother, when discussing the implications of her care in the ward, said 'I hate to think about it'. In response to discussions on improving privacy in the ward mothers in the study suggested the use of a 'treatment room' where they could go for treatment, 'just you and the midwife', without the fear of being overlooked or overheard by others.

Now carry out Reflective activity 8.3.

Reflective activity 8.3

How do you think privacy and dignity could be achieved in a ward environment? Consider both the environment and staff behaviour in your response.

LOSS OF FACE: BEING OVERHEARD WHILE IN LABOUR

Mothers who find themselves on an antenatal ward when in early labour describe themselves as 'performing' in front of others. Their need to act instinctively in labour is hindered by the number of people in the environment and mothers' feelings of being in a public setting. They describe themselves as wanting to be able to be themselves and act as they wanted by 'screaming out' or 'moaning', but felt restricted in the presence of others. This is because mothers are acutely aware of the impact their actions have on other occupants and describe themselves as not wanting to lose face in front of others. This loss of face is described as not being able to cope with pain or of making a fool of yourself, which is in turn perceived by them to reflect their failure as a mother. Where mothers deemed themselves unable to cope with examinations or being overheard by others, this resulted in a sense of shame and loss of face (Goffman, 1959, 1963; Rykwert, 2001). These feelings were compounded by the perception that midwives 'aren't bothered' about the mothers' privacy and have no respect for them or their pain or discomfort. One mother stated:

> It [privacy] is of absolutely no importance to the staff there at all. Because you are on the production line, in fairness to them, they are racing around like people possessed, there is hardly any staff and there are far too many people and they have to try and get on with the job in hand and unfortunately as quickly as possible.

The mothers' perception of being on a 'production line' does nothing to enhance self-worth or empowerment, and results in feelings of stupidity, uselessness, vulnerability and disempowerment. As staff were perceived as too busy, privacy became compromised and care became something that was 'done to you' without regard to privacy needs, and completed in a busy and overcrowded environment. Once mothers' private 'face' became public, personal information about them moved into the public sphere, to include the way they behaved and their personal and intimate details, all of which were perceived as an invasion of personal privacy and a loss of personal dignity.

The notion of labouring in front of other people makes mothers feel they are on display and having their ability to cope examined by others. Prospective mothers described how during labour they were going to remain mobile, dressed and maintain a sense of dignity throughout. In reality they found themselves in a public environment, on display and in fear of impending events due to the observation of others. The onset of labour is associated with onset of pain, however minor. Often, as seen during participant observation, mothers laboured in wards behind closed curtains resulting in other mothers overhearing them during labour without witnessing the event. This can be linked to the experience of visiting the dentist, where the dental drill is heard and the level of perceived pain we are going to experience enhanced, even before we have entered the surgery. Overhearing another mother's pain was deemed to be an extensive privacy breach at what mothers perceived to be a private time.

> There were people in the early stages of labour in beds around this ward with only a curtain around them, who were clearly in pain, there were people moaning and so on and I thought "I can't face this" . . . I thought that there was no privacy for me.

> There were all these women, I think it was busy downstairs [on the delivery suite] and they would be walking up and down, moaning in pain and waiting to go down and we would have paid the midwives not to hear that.

Mothers perceived that the idea that you are being watched or overheard when in labour, reflected on their ability to remain unseen or unheard at this very private time. They did not want to feel compromised by the views or attitudes of others and did not want to feel that they were making a fool of themselves in public.

Mothers' perceptions were that once pain commenced they should be transferred to a single room on the delivery suite. In retrospect mothers felt they were kept on wards far too long and in so doing were deprived of the privacy of a single room. Mothers determined that if labour progressed to the point where they were in pain, then they should be 'allowed to go on to the delivery suite' and that decision should be theirs and not the practitioner's, the rationale being:

> when your labour does start, you need to be taken somewhere even if it is not delivery suite because they can't take you [on delivery suite] but a side room, where you are not worried about screaming in front of a lot of people.

Overhearing mothers in pain was not the only perceived breach of privacy and dignity. As the ward environments are spatially challenged, the possibility of other people overhearing conversations involving personal aspects of your life or pregnancy is significantly increased; this was the case with Lindsey (see Box 8.2).

BOX 8.2 *Lindsey's story*

Lindsey had been admitted to the accident and emergency department following the onset of acute abdominal pain. She subsequently delivered a healthy baby boy. Lindsey had a concealed pregnancy, stating that she was not aware that she was pregnant. After the birth she was admitted to a six-bedded postnatal ward. The midwife ensured Lindsey was placed in bed and then brought a portable telephone so that she could contact her mother. She telephoned her mother to explain her situation and asked for her to visit. Her mother commenced an in-depth conversation on what had happened and Lindsey found herself discussing her experience in detail in front of the other mothers in the ward.

On discussion with other mothers in the ward they told me in graphic terms about Lindsey's experience, describing in detail issues relating to her pregnancy, labour and shock at being a new mother. The indignity of being placed in this situation was overwhelming for Lindsey. The whole process of ensuring that you maintain your dignity during pregnancy and childbirth focuses upon the respect that a mother has for herself and her situation. By placing mothers, in this case Lindsey, in a position where their private life is under scrutiny, in what is a sensitive situation, a person's ability to ensure their own privacy and maintain their self-respect is decreased. While this example could be considered extreme, it can be applied to similar situations, for example where healthcare professionals discuss cases behind curtains or in a public place while the mother or patient is present. Now carry out Reflective activity 8.4, based on Lindsey's story.

Reflective activity 8.4

➤ Reflect upon Lindsey's predicament and consider how a practitioner could have helped her maintain her self-respect and dignity in this situation.
➤ Consider your own practice environment and reflect upon any similar situations that may have occurred and how they can be prevented.

CONCLUSION

Privacy and dignity are interrelated concepts. Without privacy a mother has no protective mechanism to maintain her dignity. The repetitive nature of examinations during pregnancy and birth desensitises mothers to their invasive nature. This helps mothers determine what is necessary for monitoring the health of their baby so they are considered as part of the normal childbearing process. By achieving this status, a mother does not perceive her dignity to be compromised. In situations where mothers are participating in a normal birth, then it is important for the midwife to act as advocate for the mother to ensure that her privacy and dignity needs continue to be met while the mother engages in self-introversion. However, where a mother finds herself in a situation of compromise, such as when admitted to an antenatal ward or requiring an operative delivery, it is important for healthcare professionals to ensure that mothers are treated with respect. Where mothers feel they are not respected and their privacy is not promoted, then they perceive their dignity to be compromised after their baby is born. Healthcare professionals have a role to play in ensuring that mothers maintain their dignity during pregnancy and childbirth, to ensure they have a positive birthing experience.

REFERENCES

Applegate M, Morse J (1994) Personal privacy and interactional patterns in a nursing home. *Journal of Ageing Studies* 8(4): 413–34.
Aveyard H (2002) The requirement for informed consent prior to nursing care procedures. *Journal of Advanced Nursing* 37(3): 243–9.

Berg J, Appelbaum P, Lidz C, Parker L (2001) *Informed Consent: legal theory and clinical practice* (2e). New York: Oxford University Press Inc.

Bloustein E (2003) *Individual and Group Privacy.* London: Transaction Publishers.

Burden B (2007) *Privacy in Maternity Care Environments.* Unpublished PhD thesis. Buckingham: Open University.

Fried C (1970) *An Anatomy of Values.* Cambridge, MA: Harvard University Press.

Goffman E (1959) *The Presentation of Self in Everyday Life.* London: Penguin Books.

Goffman E (1961) *Asylums: essays on the social situation of mental patients and other inmates.* New York: Doubleday.

Goffman E (1963) *Behavior in Public Places.* New York: The Free Press.

Goffman E (1967) *Interaction Ritual: essays on face-to-face behavior.* New York: Pantheon Books.

Halmos P (1953) *Solitude and Privacy: a study of social isolation, its causes and therapy.* New York: Philosophical Library Inc.

Lawler J (1991) *Behind the Screens: nursing somology and the problem of the body.* London: Churchill Livingstone.

McHale J, Gallagher A (2003) *Nursing and Human Rights.* London: Butterworth Heinemann.

Rachels J (1975) Why privacy is important. *Philosophy and Public Affairs* **4**: 323–33.

Rosen J (2001) *The Unwanted Gaze: the destruction of privacy in America.* New York: Vintage.

Rossler B (2005) *The Value of Privacy.* Cambridge: Polity Press.

Royal College of Nursing (2005) *Informed Consent in Health and Social Care Research: RCN guidance for nurses.* London: Royal College of Nursing.

Rykwert J (2001) Privacy in antiquity. *Social Research* **68**(1): 29–40.

Schneider C (1977) *Shame, Exposure and Privacy.* London: WW Norton and Company.

Simmel A (1971) Privacy is not an isolated freedom. In: Pennock, JR, Chapman JW (eds) *Privacy.* New York: Atherton.

Westin A (1970) *Privacy and Freedom.* London: The Bodley Head.

CHAPTER 9

Dignity and older people

Wilfred McSherry and Helen Coleman

INTRODUCTION

Statistics tell us that currently within the United Kingdom (UK) and globally, there are more people aged 80 years and over than those aged 16 years and below (Office for National Statistics, 2010). We don't have to be mathematicians to predict that at some point in the future this will have a significant impact on all sections of our society but especially with regard to those working within the health and social care sectors.

Ageing is non-discriminatory, it comes to all people because it is a natural and inevitable process as one moves along the life span continuum from birth to death. However, in contemporary society, ageing seems to be feared and discussions on the subject avoided. Until the advent of an 'elixir of life' or the development of genetic engineering that switches off or halts the ageing process, everyone is destined to grow old – unless they die prematurely. Therefore, the fact that we are all destined to live longer, fuller and healthier lives should be a cause for celebration, and the contribution that older people make to the fabric, culture and social structure of society remembered and welcomed. For some older people, retirement or social ageing is positive, enjoyable and life enhancing. It is an opportunity to spend time with family and friends, participating in recreational activities, engaging in new pursuits and experiences. However, for others ageing will mean a decline in physical and cognitive functioning as a result of illness, disease or trauma. This may result in increased morbidity, a loss of independence and social isolation. The onset of illness or disease may result in periods of hospitalisation. Depending on the nature and severity of an illness or disease, this may necessitate long-term health and social care. The quality of this care has the potential to preserve the older person's dignity and identity or rob them of a fundamental aspect of their humanity and human rights.

Health and social care professionals are in a unique and privileged position to safeguard and preserve the dignity of older people. Therefore, this chapter will first explore why dignity is important for older people and why older people might be vulnerable to a loss of dignity, drawing on research findings and reports about older people's dignity. The chapter will explain what is important for older people's dignity, by providing illustrated examples of where dignified care for older people may not have been achieved in various settings.

LEARNING OUTCOMES

By the end of this chapter you will be able to:

➤ understand what is meant by the phrase 'dignity in care' when caring for older people
➤ demonstrate an awareness of how care and services may be organised to preserve the dignity of older people
➤ be aware of the strategies that can safeguard the dignity of older people
➤ transfer the knowledge and skills gained throughout this chapter into the delivery of health and social care.

DEMOGRAPHICS OF AGEING

The World Health Organization (2000) estimates that by 2025, there will be 1.2 billion people in the world over the age of 60 years. In developing countries the over-60s will account for 70% of the populations. Interestingly, the fastest-growing age group is the over-80s.

These statistics suggest that globally the number of older people is due to increase. The fact that more people are living longer in the developed and developing world should not really be viewed negatively, but should be a cause for celebration. There have been tremendous improvements in health, education and welfare, eradicating diseases and illness. Changes in welfare standards such as sanitation and housing, and measures taken to remove poverty and social inequality have all contributed to an increased life expectancy.

It is easy to look at statistics and figures and think that these do not really matter because they are not directly relevant. The following may help to illustrate how these global trends in relation to older people directly impact upon healthcare.

➤ We undertook a review of the patients who were in hospital on one day. Over 68% of all the people in hospital were over the age of 65 years, with a large proportion being over the age of 80 years.

This finding illustrates that the global predictions with regard to an increasing older population are occurring within the UK. They also indicate why there is a need to look at dignity and older people, because older people are the largest consumers of health and social care and one of the largest groups within society.

ATTITUDES TOWARD AGEING AND OLDER PEOPLE

Within some sections of society there seems to be a general lack of tolerance, sensitivity and disregard towards the needs of older people. Older people are often portrayed as a burden and demanding; healthcare is not immune to these negativities. There are many prejudices and myths that require dispelling, with regard to caring for older people (see Box 9.1).

BOX 9.1 *Reflection: dispelling myths!*

Caring for older people, especially within the acute hospital environment, suggests images of hard graft and dirty work! Not too long ago one of the authors of this chapter was dissuaded by a senior manager from applying for a nursing post within older people services. Suffice it to say that the person concerned did not listen and spent many satisfying and rewarding years caring for older people. In fact, this person learned more about care, caring, dignity and respect than they had at any other time in their nursing career. This anecdote illustrates that it is not all doom and gloom and detrimental to one's nursing career, as implied by the senior manager; on the contrary, nursing older people is professionally fulfilling and enabling.

The above reflection emphasises the need for us all to challenge our attitudes towards ageing. The so-called age or generation gap still exists, despite many drives in society and health and social care to eradicate age discrimination and stereotyping in the drive for equality (Department of Health [DH], 2001). The fact that there is a chapter in this book dedicated to dignity and the older person is itself a form of discrimination. It highlights that the needs and perceptions of older people are different from those of other groups within society. However, this form of discrimination is positive because it focuses attention on how older people may perceive dignity and respect and how intergenerational differences may be overcome so that their dignity and respect can be preserved, enabling older people to feel valued and integrated within society.

There are numerous incidents highlighted in the media where older people are subjected to all forms of abuse, whether emotional, physical, financial, sexual or social. Furthermore, some older people become fearful of crime, meaning they may withdraw from wider society. Evidence suggests that some older people, for example those suffering from dementia, can be treated with a general disregard and a lack of respect within our communities and within diverse healthcare settings (Alzheimer's Society, 2009). Older people can often be left feeling useless and unwanted in a society that seems to value youthfulness and beauty over wisdom, experience and knowledge. There needs to be a realisation that older people make a significant contribution to society. How many of us have relied upon grandparents to provide child care? And are we aware of the vast amount of voluntary work undertaken by older people?

Now carry out Reflective activity 9.1.

Reflective activity 9.1

Before proceeding you might want to make a note or recall some of the words, phrases or terms used to describe older people

---

Your reflections may have seen you producing a list of terms, some of which may view older people in a very negative light – terms such as 'wrinklies', 'old dear', 'old boy', 'old girl', 'pet', 'love', 'dear'. Older people are often seen as being slow, forgetful, out of touch, technophobes, unable to make decisions. While some of these stereotypical images and terms may not be intentional, they often leave older people feeling patronised, disempowered and degraded, losing self-respect and value as a person.

A sense of proportion

It would be very wrong to think that all older people are treated with a general lack of dignity and respect within society. On the contrary, for example within healthcare, many older people using healthcare services report a high level of satisfaction with the treatment and care that they receive. Garratt, for the Acute Co-ordination Centre for the NHS Patient Survey Programme (Garratt, 2009; p.2), reported that:

> Nearly 8 in 10 patients (79%) rated the care they received in hospital as 'excellent' (43%) or 'very good' (35%) with those rating their overall care as 'excellent' increasing from 42% in 2007 to 43% in 2008 (reproduced with permission from the Picker Institute Europe).

Therefore, the vast majority of adults and older people are satisfied with the hospital care received. The challenge for all working in health and social care is to improve services for the small proportions of patients who are dissatisfied with the care provided, so that everyone is satisfied.

Dignity and older Europeans

The European Commission (2004) funded a project called Dignity and Older Europeans. This is an influential study that explored older Europeans' understanding of the concept of dignity. The project brought together academics, clinicians and user groups. Please look at the following web link for further information and access to the reports and resources that were produced: http://medic.cardiff.ac.uk/archive_subsites/_/_/medic/subsites/dignity/index.html

The findings from this study provide an in-depth account of what older people from across Europe feel about dignity, detailing how healthcare professionals can preserve the older person's dignity. Within the educational material produced it is evident that using inappropriate terms of endearment is something that many older people find intolerable, unacceptable and offensive:

➤ when meeting an older person for the first time, always call them by their family/surname, not their first name, until they have given you permission to do so. Never use inappropriate terms of endearment
➤ when caring for older people in whatever setting, always knock on the door or seek permission prior to entering their house, room or personal space.

RECENT POLICY AND PUBLICITY

Within the UK there have been a number of drives to enhance the care of older people. There are clear steps being taken across health and social care (full health economy) to raise the quality and standards of care delivered. There is a notable emphasis placed on the concepts of dignity and respect. Lord Darzi's review states:

> Quality of care includes quality of *caring*. This means how personal care is – the compassion, dignity and respect with which patients are treated. It can only be improved by analysing and understanding patient satisfaction with their own experiences (DH, 2008, p.47).

Yet, despite a great deal of investment and publicity with campaigns (DH, 2006a; Royal College of Nursing [RCN], 2008) and dignity champion programmes (DH, 2009b) seeking to raise the standards of care for all, especially older people, there are a growing number of publications emerging that highlight that older people are still being subjected to and are vulnerable to undignified care. This is despite all the drives to combat the negativities and discrepancies in care provided to older people, especially within acute care (DH, 2001).

Rayner, president of the Patients Association, writes in the foreword of the report:

> For far too long now, the Patients Association has been receiving calls on our Helpline from people wanting to talk about the dreadful, neglectful, demeaning, painful and sometimes downright cruel treatment their elderly relatives had experienced at the hands of NHS nurses (Rayner, 2009, p.3, reproduced with permission from the Patients Association).

The content of this foreword is extremely sad and concerning because it indicates that some older people are still not receiving a quality and level of care that respects their humanity, despite all the policy and guidelines attempting to reverse these negative cultural trends.

This quotation also reinforces why there is an urgent need to focus upon the dignity of older people within society and healthcare specifically.

THE MEANING OF DIGNITY FOR OLDER PEOPLE

Fenton and Mitchell (2002) provide a useful definition of dignity that underlines the fundamental principles of dignity and older people. It describes clearly what older people consider dignity to be (*see* Reflective activity 9.2).

Reflective activity 9.2

Please revisit the following definition that was referred to in Chapter 2, identifying the main dimensions of dignity, reflecting on how these may relate to older people.

Dignity is a state of physical, emotional and spiritual comfort, with each individual valued for his or her uniqueness and his or her individuality celebrated. Dignity is promoted when individuals are enabled to do the best within their capabilities, exercise control, make choices and feel involved in the decision-making that underpins their care (Fenton and Mitchell, 2002, p.2, reproduced with permission from the RCN).

Your reflections may have revealed that older people want to be:
➤ treated in an individual and holistic manner, with equal attention paid to the physical, psychological, social and spiritual aspects of their lives
➤ accepted as unique individuals and have this individuality celebrated
➤ involved to the best of their ability in decisions and choices
➤ in control and exercise control of their own lives.

Crucially, this definition implies that dignity is fundamental to the older person's identify, self-worth and ultimately their individuality and humanity. Implicit in the word dignity is the word respect. Fenton and Mitchell's (2002) definition implies that respect concerns seeing the older person as an individual with a past, present and a future. It is all too easy to focus upon the person as a condition rather than the individual.

A theoretical model of dignity

Nordenfelt and Edgar (2005) present a theoretical model of dignity created within the Dignity and Older Europeans project. By analysing older people's responses, descriptions and experience of dignity, they were able to develop a theoretical model (Figure 9.1). This model suggests that older people described or felt that there are four types of '*dignity*'. The dashed lines indicate that all types of dignity are interrelated and share equal importance. They build on Fenton and Mitchell's (2002) definition by presenting a model that may assist healthcare professionals to understand the relevance and importance attached to dignity by older people.

Now carry out Reflective activity 9.3.

Reflective activity 9.3

Study the four types of dignity and ask yourself: what do these mean? Can you think of any examples that may illustrate these meanings within everyday life and practice?

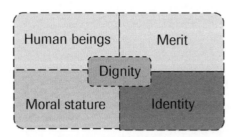

Figure 9.1 A theoretical model of dignity (Nordenfelt and Edgar, 2005).

Chapter 2 explored meanings of dignity, including Nordenfelt and Edgar's (2005) theory. Here, the four types of dignity are defined and there is application to older people.

➤ *Menschenwürde*: this word is translated from German as 'humanness'. Therefore, this type of dignity refers to the dignity inherent within every human being. This type affirms that dignity is something universal. This may indicate that dignity is now enshrined within the Human Rights Act (Great Britain, 1998) and legislation. Therefore, if we deny older people the right to express individuality and their humanity, whether intentionally or unintentionally, then we may be violating their primary right to dignity.

➤ *Dignity as merit*, either formal or informal, is dignity conferred upon someone as a result of either merit or rank. Some people may inherit titles. However, in this classification, dignity is usually earned or conferred by others because of deeds or actions. As an example of people who may be conferred a level of merit, think of a good ward manager who inspires through their leadership. Such people are conferred a level of merit from all with whom they work.

➤ *The dignity of moral stature* refers to one's own moral identity and stature and how a person may lose this if they fail to act in accordance with their guiding principles and values. Think of the recent UK scandal about 'MPs' expenses' and how the lack of moral principles displayed by some MPs shattered public trust and confidence.

➤ *The dignity of personal identity* concerns the identity of the person. A person can be robbed or violated by physical assault or humiliation. The notions of integrity and physical identity, autonomy and inclusion are all important aspects of the person's identity. This type of dignity has the most profound impact upon health and social care. If one studies this definition, it is easy to see how a healthcare professional's actions, attitudes and behaviour can either preserve a patient's identity or destroy it. This can be illustrated in the following example taken from the Healthcare Commission (2009, p.6):

> The care of patients was unacceptable. For example, patients and relatives told us that when patients rang the call bell because they were in pain or needed to go to the toilet, it was often not answered . . . Some relatives claimed that patients were left, sometimes for hours, in wet or soiled sheets . . . (Healthcare Commission, 2009, p.6, © Care Quality Commission).

It is clear that such practices had a demeaning and distressing impact upon the individual's sense of identity. These behaviours and practices robbed the individual and their families of dignity and humanity.

Now carry out Reflective activity 9.4.

Reflective activity 9.4

Spend a few minutes reading through the extract from the report. Ask yourself how would you expect to be treated?

WHAT OLDER PEOPLE WANT

The previous section highlighted some very serious failings in the care of older people. By reflecting on the implications of such reports and by assessing our own perceptions, attitudes and practices towards dignity in care, the culture within healthcare may be changed. The danger is that such reports are so pain-ful and distressing to read that we avoid engaging with them. Yet, explicit within such reports are the foundations and recommendations for a sustained change in practice. They also tell us something about older people's expectations and standards with regard to dignity and respect.

Now carry out Reflective activity 9.5.

Reflective activity 9.5

Look at Box 9.2, which contains the DH (2006c) ten-point dignity challenge (also discussed in relation to health policy in Chapter 4). Take each clause in turn and ask yourself what this may mean for you personally and for the older people for whom you care.

BOX 9.2 *The Department of Health ten-point dignity challenge*

High-quality care services that respect people's dignity should:
1.   have a zero tolerance of all forms of abuse
2.   support people with the same respect you would want for yourself or a member of your family
3.   treat each person as an individual by offering a personalised service
4.   enable people to maintain the maximum possible level of independence, choice and control
5.   listen and support people to express their needs and wants
6.   respect people's right to privacy
7.   ensure people feel able to complain without fear of retribution
8.   engage with family members and carers as care partners
9.   assist people to maintain confidence and a positive self-esteem
10. act to alleviate people's loneliness and isolation.

(Department of Health, 2006c, Crown copyright; reproduced with permission from the Controller of HMSO and the Queen's Printer for Scotland)

The origin of the DH's Dignity in Care campaign was discussed in Chapter 4. This section demonstrates how the DH (2006a,b,c) dignity challenge was intro-duced to raise awareness of the importance of preserving the dignity of older people. This also coincided with the recruitment of regional dignity champi-ons who were asked to register with the DH in order to challenge some of the practices that were detrimental to older people. A full summary of the impact of dignity champions was published (DH, 2009a). A similar campaign was launched by the RCN (2008). It is sometimes easy to be cynical and think that such campaigns have little impact. However, it must be emphasised that both these campaigns have had a significant impact with regard to raising awareness of dignity in care by challenging practice, breaking down barriers and, importantly, changing cultures.

Different organisations have responded in diverse ways to implementing the dignity challenge within their organisational structures and processes. Some of the 'good practice stories' and 'bright ideas projects' initiated to promote and preserve the dignity of older people are outlined on the DH Dignity in Care website: www.dignityincare.org.uk.

Each point in the ten-point challenge relates to a fundamental aspect of dignity. For a more in-depth explanation and discussion on how each point applies to older people and healthcare, please look at the following material developed by the Health and Social Care Advisory Service (HASCAS) (2010) *Dignity Through Action (Older People) Resource Package*, which can be downloaded from: www.hascas.org/hascas_publications_downloads.shtml.

The dignity challenge alerts us to what is important for older people in preserving dignity. It focuses attention on areas that healthcare professionals must consider when caring for older people.

PRESERVING THE DIGNITY OF OLDER PEOPLE

Previous sections have outlined what older people understand by the concept of dignity. This section explores strategies, practices, behaviours and attitudes that will preserve the dignity of older people. The RCN's (2008, p.6) definition of dignity (Box 9.3) highlights a number of key factors and strategies that are central to the dignity of older people. It reveals that 'people, processes and places', as outlined in Chapter 2, must be considered when preserving the dignity of older people

---

Box 9.3 *Royal College of Nursing definition of dignity*

Dignity is concerned with how people feel, think and behave in relation to the worth or value of themselves and others. To treat someone with dignity is to treat them as being of worth, in a way that is respectful of them as valued individuals.

In care situations, dignity may be promoted or diminished by: the physical environment; organisational culture; the attitudes and behaviour of the nursing team and others; and the way in which care activities are carried out.

When dignity is present people feel in control, valued, confident, comfortable and able to make decisions for themselves. When dignity is absent people feel devalued, lacking control and comfort. They may lack confidence and be unable to make decisions for themselves. They may feel humiliated, embarrassed or ashamed.

Dignity applies equally to those who have capacity and to those who lack it. Everyone has equal worth as human beings and must be treated as if they are able to feel, think and behave in relation to their own worth or value.

The nursing team should, therefore, treat all people in all settings and of any health status with dignity, and dignified care should continue after death.

(RCN, 2008, p.6, used with kind permission from the Royal College of Nursing)

Now carry out Reflective activity 9.6.

Reflective activity 9.6

Read the case study in Box 9.4, which is an extract taken from a case presented in the Patients' Association report (2009). While reading through this, ask yourself the following questions:

➤ what steps could have been taken to preserve Ann's dignity?
➤ which of the four types of dignity are violated?
➤ how did people, processes and places influence this situation?

BOX 9.4 *Ann McNeill by her husband Richard McNeill*

My wife Ann McNeill died on 15 January 2008. Ann was 71 when she had to undergo a succession of major operations in the months preceding her death. She was a patient at both Barnet Hospital and Edgware Community Hospital, moving between the two. Ann had spent decades working as a nurse, she trained with Claire Rayner, and she put a lot of pride in the role of nurses as caring professionals.

Whilst I struggle to remember exact dates and details, during her time there were things that happened to my wife that I will remember forever. I feel that poor nursing care over a long period of time contributed to her death. Ann couldn't relate the attitude and actions of some of the nurses with how she had been trained to look after people.

In October 2007, following surgery at Barnet Hospital she was transferred to Edgware Community General Hospital in North London. It was supposed to be an intermediate step whilst she recovered. I was appalled at how my wife was treated by some of the staff. Her legs were raw and covered in bandages both to protect her wounds, and the fragile skin surrounding them as she had developed blisters and lesions from deep vein thrombosis and other problems. The dressings were supposed to be changed regularly, every few days, but the nurses at Edgware didn't bother. One night two nurses were hoisting her into bed and one handled her very roughly, knocking her legs. She gasped in pain and the nurse said 'Oh, we've got a drama queen here'. That description didn't match my wife in the slightest.

Later that night, the other nurse who had been more considerate and careful came and checked on Ann. There was blood on the bed sheets and her bandages from where she had been knocked. The other nurse said to the nurse who had shown such little care to Ann, 'you did this, now you clear it up'.

(Patients Association, 2009, p.31, used with kind permission from the Patients Association)

This case study illustrates how healthcare professionals' attitudes are fundamental to communicating empathy and an essential component of care and caring. The qualities that practitioners display in their interaction with older people can make a person feel respected, valued and important. However, the nurses in this situation showed no respect for Ann as an individual. Their actions, attitudes and words destroyed Ann's dignity, violating her humanity and sense of identity. Furthermore, the processes and places that were supposed to care for Ann failed in every respect.

Again there is a need for balance and proportion as it must be emphasised that the majority of nurses and healthcare professionals do a brilliant job in circumstances that are often difficult and challenging. But as indicated, these tragic cases must be reviewed so that lessons can be learnt and remedial action taken to prevent any reoccurrence.

FUNDAMENTAL ASPECTS OF DIGNITY FOR OLDER PEOPLE

Matiti et al (2007) outline several fundamental aspects of dignity. All these must be present if older people are to feel valued, respected and equal partners in society and care. These are all essential to preserving the identity and self-worth of older people. They are especially important to the delivery of world-class health and social care, irrespective of the context in which care is delivered:

➤ need for information
➤ communication
➤ how older people are addressed – courtesy

➤ choice and decision making
➤ respect
➤ treated with decency
➤ participation in care delivery
➤ autonomy and independence
➤ confidentiality
➤ privacy.

An additional one that we have added is: attitude.

Many of these are self-explanatory. These fundamentals are central to the delivery and implementation of the theoretical model of dignity outlined earlier. Similarly, if these are not incorporated in the caring relationship and organisational culture then older people will be left feeling vulnerable, isolated and potentially violated. Many organisations are now seeking to capture older people's experiences of care. Magee *et al* (2008) undertook a review of the different tools available to measure the level of dignity provided to older people. Some of the key areas outlined in this report are similar to those offered by Matiti *et al* (2007).

SAFEGUARDING THE DIGNITY OF OLDER PEOPLE

Figure 9.2 outlines the primary domains of dignity that are considered central to the dignity of older people (Magee *et al*, 2008). These domains are also evident in a number of other publications:

➤ hospital ward exit surveys
➤ DH (2009b) *Dignity Maps*
➤ DH (2003) *Essence of Care Patient-focused Benchmarks for Clinical Governance*
➤ Social Care Institute For Excellence (2006) *SCIE Guide 15: Dignity in Care*
➤ Magee *et al* (2008) *Measuring Dignity in Care for Older People*
➤ Healthcare Commission (2009) *Investigation into Mid Staffordshire NHS Foundation Trust*
➤ The Patients Association (2009) *Patients . . . Not Numbers, People . . . Not Statistics.*

Many organisations are now assessing these domains to determine the overall quality and standard of care provided. These areas have also been recognised by older people as being essential to preserving dignity (The Patients Association, 2009; Alzheimer's Society, 2009).

Our organisation has developed a 'Care with Dignity Indicator Tool' as one measure that can be used to capture older people's experience and satisfaction with the quality of care received. The different domains are described below. It

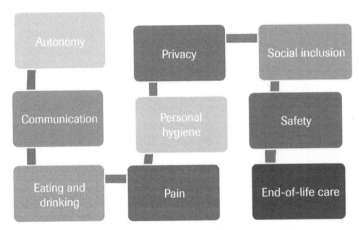

Figure 9.2 Domains of dignity (Magee *et al*, 2008).

must be emphasised that these domains are not in any order of priority since they are all essential to older people whether delivering care in a residential setting or hospital. Some of these domains are also relevant and appropriate in everyday interaction with older people.

➤ *Autonomy*: means involving the older person in decisions about their life, future and care or treatment.

➤ *Communication*: listening to and facilitating positive communication with the older person. Being non-patronising and courteous at all times.

➤ *Eating and drinking*: older people must be given control about the food they eat by offering choice. Appropriate, timely and sensitive assistance should be given with eating and drinking if this is required. Nutritional support is essential to maintain and aid recovery and the general well-being of the person.

➤ *Privacy*: the older person's privacy must be maintained and preserved at all times, especially when carrying out personal care or when using wash or toilet facilities. Consideration must be given to the location of care – whether or not this is the older person's own home. Personal space is important and older people like to feel secure and safe. Curtains must be drawn, doors closed and personal space respected. Consent should be obtained prior to carrying out any care or examinations and older people tell us that permission should be gained for students to be in attendance or for them to carry out essential care. Knocking on doors and seeking consent to enter, whether a cubicle or the person's own home, is funda-mental. All caring environments should comply with national directives regarding single-sex accommodation.

➤ *Personal hygiene*: a loss of independence and autonomy can have a very profound impact on older people's sense of worth and identity. Providing timely assistance and involving the older person in personal care empowers and removes the loss of control that can be experienced. It is imperative that older people are given a choice in decisions made about their own personal hygiene. There is a need to ensure all facilities are clean and suitable.

➤ *Pain*: there must be timely and appropriate intervention for pain or discomfort. It must be remembered that older people or their carers may know more about the treatment and management of their condition than the person providing care. This knowledge and expertise must be acknowledged and respected. The older person could be responsible for their own pain relief, should this be desired. There must be avoidance of practices that may cause or contribute to the older person experiencing pain or discomfort.

➤ *Social inclusion*: older people should be able to practise and maintain their own personal, religious and spiritual beliefs. Nurses should value the older person, ensuring that there is no age discrimination. Contact and access should be maintained with family, friends and community, if requested.

➤ *Safety*: nurses must undertake a thorough individualised assessment of each older person, identifying potential environmental or personal risks; these may include assessments for falls, use of bed rails, mobility, pressure area care, nutrition support, and necessary documentation completed. Where required, refer people to the protection of vulnerable adults team in suspected cases of elder abuse or neglect. Nursing staff must comply with all infection and prevention control measures.

➤ *End-of-life care*: death is an inevitable part of life and growing old. Older people indicate that there needs to be openness and willingness on the part of healthcare professionals to discuss and support older people with decisions that they may have made with regard to their own death. There is a danger of adopting a paternalistic attitude when dealing with matters of death and dying, to protect the older person from additional suffering. This practice must be avoided and older people must be consulted, informed and involved in all decisions made. Consideration must be given to advance directives and 'living wills'. Nurses must be culturally sensitive to religious or spiritual needs and have awareness of how these may impact upon attitudes to death and care of the person following death. Provision must be made to discuss personal wishes and preferences about end-of-life care.

CONCLUSION

This chapter has explored dignity and older people. It has highlighted what older people across Europe consider dignity to be and how dignity can be preserved within everyday interactions. It is evident that the interpersonal skills and qualities displayed and the attitudes adopted are critical when dealing with older people, whether in a caring context or in general encounters. Dealing with older people requires sensitivity and communication that is non-patronising. It must be remembered that older people are equal members of society, who have made and are still making a significant contribution to its welfare and structure. Older people must always be treated with courtesy and respect. There is a fundamental need for all of society to confront ageism, prejudice and discrimination wherever these are encountered, so that negative attitudes can be eradicated and growing old is celebrated and not feared.

REFERENCES

Alzheimer's Society (2009) *Counting the Cost Caring for People with Dementia on Hospital Wards.* London: Alzheimer's Society. http://alzheimers.org.uk/site/scripts/download_info.php?fileID=787 (accessed 11 October 2010).

Cardiff University (2004) *Dignity and Older Europeans: Final Report.* Cardiff: Cardiff University. www.cardiff.ac.uk/medic/subsites/dignity/index.html (accessed 11 October 2010).

Department of Health (2001) *National Service Framework for Older People.* London: Department of Health.

Department of Health (2003) *Essence of Care Patient-focused Benchmarks for Clinical Governance.* London: Department of Health.

Department of Health (2006a) *'Dignity in Care' Public Survey, October 2006. Report of the survey.* London: Department of Health. www.dh.gov.uk/prod_consum_dh/groups/dh_digitalassets/@dh/@en/documents/digitalasset/dh_4139558.pdf (accessed 11 October 2010).

Department of Health (2006b) *Dignity in Care. A Report on People's Views, October 2006. What you had to say. . .* London: Department of Health. www.dh.gov.uk/prod_consum_dh/groups/dh_digitalassets/@dh/@en/documents/digitalasset/dh_4139559.pdf (accessed 11 October 2010).

Department of Health (2006c) *Dignity Challenge: high quality care services that respect people's dignity.* London: Department of Health. www.dh.gov.uk/prod_consum_dh/groups/dh_digitalassets/documents/digitalasset/dh_085105.pdf (accessed 11 October 2010).

Department of Health (2008) *High Quality Care For All – NHS Next Stage Review Final report.* Gateway reference 10106. London: Department of Health.

Department of Health (2009a) *Final Report on the Department of Health's Dignity Campaign.* www.dhcarenetworks.org.uk/_library/Opinion_Leader_Final_Report_to_DH.doc.pdf (accessed 11 October 2010).

Department of Health (2009b) *Dignity Maps.* London: Department of Health. www.dhcarenetworks.org.uk/dignityincare/Topics/championresources/Dignity_Map/ (accessed 11 October 2010).

European Commission (2004) *Educating for Dignity. Dignity and older Europeans. A multidisciplinary workbook.* http://medic.cardiff.ac.uk/archive_subsites/_/_/medic/subsites/dignity/resources/Educating_for_Dignity.pdf (accessed 11 October 2010).

Fenton E, Mitchell T (2002) Growing old with dignity: a concept analysis. *Nursing Older People* **14**(4): 19–21.

Garratt E (2009) *The Key Findings Report From the 2008 Inpatient Survey. Acute Co-ordination Centre for The NHS Patient Survey Programme 2008.* Oxford: Picker Institute Europe. www.nhssurveys.org/Filestore//documents/Key_Findings_report_for_the_2008_Inpatient_Survey.pdf (accessed 11 October 2010).

Healthcare Commission (2009) *Investigation into Mid Staffordshire Foundation Trust.* London: Commission for Healthcare Audit and Inspection.

Human Rights Act (1998) www.opsi.gov.uk/acts/acts1998/ukpga 19980042 en 1 (accessed 11 October 2010).

Magee H, Parsons S, Askham J (2008) *Measuring Dignity in Care for Older People.* London: Picker Institute Europe for Help the Aged.

Matiti M, Cotrel-Gibbons E, Teasdale K (2007) Promoting patient dignity in healthcare settings. *Nursing Standard* **21**(45): 46–52.

Nordenfelt L, Edgar A (2005) The four notions of dignity. *Quality in Ageing* **6**(1): 17–21.

Office for National Statistics (2008) *Ageing: fastest increase in the 'oldest old'.* National Statistics. www.statistics.gov.uk/cci/nugget.asp?id=949 (accessed 11 October 2010).

Patients Association (2009) *Patients . . . Not Numbers, People . . . Not Statistics.* London: Patients Association.

Rayner C (2009) Foreword. In: *Patients . . . Not Numbers, People . . . Not Statistics.* London: Patients Association.

Royal College of Nursing (2008) *Defending Dignity – Challenges and Opportunities for Nursing.* London: Royal College of Nursing.

Social Care Institute for Excellence (2006) *SCIE Guide 15: Dignity in Care.* London: Social Care Institute for Excellence. www.scie.org.uk/publications/guides/guide15/index.asp (accessed 11 October 2010).

World Health Organization (2000) *Social Development and Ageing: Crisis or Opportunity?* Geneva: World Health Organization. www.who.int/ageing/publications/development/alc_social_development.pdf (accessed 11 October 2010).

CHAPTER 10

Dignity at the end of life

Davina Porock

INTRODUCTION

Dignity is one of the first things people mention when asked about the care they would like at the end of life. However, understanding what people really mean by dignity is not easy because most people have a great deal of difficulty in saying what they mean by it. In fact, mostly we know how it feels when we have lost our dignity rather than how it feels when we have dignity. Not only that, but most people do not like thinking and talking about their own death and unfortunately health professionals also find it difficult to talk to their patients about planning for end-of-life care (Hopkinson *et al*, 2003). As a result, facilitating high-quality end-of-life care that promotes dignity is some-times very difficult to achieve.

The purpose of this chapter is to explore why dignity is so important at the end of life and how we, as health professionals, can facilitate respect for dignity with the dying person and their family. The chapter is divided into two main sections: the meaning of dignity at the end of life, and facilitating dignified dying. The chapter will focus mainly on dying and death in older age groups because that is predominantly when death occurs in our society. There are texts available on the specialist area of care of dying children and young people, for example Pfund and Fowler-Kerry (2010).

LEARNING OUTCOMES

By the end of this chapter you will be able to:
➤ describe the context of dying and death in the modern United Kingdom and consider the implications of current trends
➤ identify social and historical themes that influence our understanding of a good death and dignity at the end of life
➤ reflect on dignity, suffering and comfort as interrelated concepts that have particular meaning and resonance in care at the end of life
➤ identify practical but meaningful actions to promote dignity at the end of life.

THE MEANING OF DIGNITY AT THE END OF LIFE

There is one assured fact for any living being and that is the reality that we will die. No matter how long science can increase the length of human life with improvements in health and technology, we will still all die. We spend our lives mostly *not* thinking of this fact, and yet the threat of death is very much integrated into the way we organise our lives and respond to risk – from what we eat, to wearing a seat belt or washing our hands (Douglas, 2004). Every health professional will come in contact with dying and death even if they do not specialise in palliative care. Most people who are dying, whether it is from cancer or non-malignant disease, will be cared for by health professionals who are not palliative care specialists (Shipman *et al*, 2007). Although admissions to hospital are more frequent as patients approach death, it is unlikely that specialist palliative care teams will direct the care or even be consulted as part of the care. The last year of life is most commonly spent in the community, being cared for by family and friends with the support of district nurses, the general practitioner and community health and social services (Shipman *et al*, 2007; Gomes and Higginson, 2008).

In this section we will look first at when and where death occurs in the United Kingdom (UK), how it has changed over the past decades, and what it will look like in the future if current trends continue, as this will set the context for understanding dignity and the barriers to care provision at the end of life. Then, we will explore the research about people's preferences for end-of-life care and their concerns around dignity. The differences between what is happening and what people want, and how that affects the sense of dignity that people experience in end-of-life care, will be discussed.

DEATH: PAST, PRESENT AND FUTURE

Looking at death statistics in the UK reveals some interesting information. Table 10.1 shows the distribution of deaths over age groups in 2005 (Department of Health [DH], 2005). What can be seen from this table is that in the UK, as in all western developed countries, death is most common in older people. Over 80% of deaths occur in people over the age of 65 years, and two-thirds of all deaths occur in people over 75 years. Furthermore, two-thirds of acute hospital beds are occupied by people over 65 years of age (DH, 2005), with one-quarter of all hospital patients being people in their last year of life (Higginson *et al*, 1998). From this it can be seen that those at greatest risk of dying are old or very old and they are often in contact with acute health services in addition to community health and social services.

Currently in the UK, almost 80% of all deaths each year occur in either a hospital or a nursing home, with hospitals accounting for close to 60%. Only 19% of deaths occur at home and less than 5% of deaths occur in hospices

Table 10.1 Summary of death statistics (Office for National Statistics, 2009)

Age group (years)	Total deaths (%)
≤14	0.9
15–44	3.5
45–64	13.1
65–74	16.2
75–84	30.5
≥85	35.8

(National End of Life Care Programme, 2010). Patients with cancer and who are younger (less than 45 years old) account for the majority of the home and hospice deaths, which means that although most people die of something other than cancer and when they are old, the likelihood of a home death for these individuals is very low (Gomes and Higginson, 2008). Gomes and Higginson's (2008) comprehensive analysis of mortality statistics over the past 30 years shows that the proportion of home deaths has steadily decreased from 31.1% in 1974 to 18.1% in 2003. If this trend continues, then by 2030 only one in ten deaths will occur at home, which, coupled with an increasing death rate after 2012 due to the baby boomers reaching very old age, will result in a need for expanding inpatient facilities by more than 20%. However, most agree that hospital, with its focus on interventional medicine, is not the best place to be for high-quality end-of-life care, so this expansion of services for the dying is needed in hospices and care homes. If reducing hospital inpatient deaths could be achieved, then a great deal more support will be needed in the community to help families care for the dying. Gomes and Higginson calculate that if support from community health and social services for care of the dying was doubled, then the proportion of deaths at home could be one in three in 2012 instead of the current value of less than one in five.

There are many complex reasons for the changes over the last few decades in where people die. For example, there is an increasing number of people living alone, which means there is no one else at home to provide care (Grundy et al, 2004). General practitioners make fewer home visits than they did 30 years ago and this has resulted in more hospitalisations (Gomes, 2006, cited in Gomes and Higginson, 2008). For older people, too, the availability of informal (family) caregivers may be limited, and their concern for the burden caregiving places on family members may also be a reason for older people dying in hospital (Patrick et al, 2001; Vig et al, 2002). As a result of changes in society, the conventional ideal of a good death is difficult to achieve. What is important to know is what people want when it comes to care at the end of life. Sutton and Coast (2006) reviewed the literature in relation to older people's preferences at the end of life and found three main areas of focus in the research: treatment decisions; the good death; and place of care/death. The idea of what is a good death is particularly important in getting to the heart of understanding what people think respecting dignity at the end of life really means in practice.

PREFERENCES FOR END-OF-LIFE CARE

The idea of a good death is a widespread concept but it varies culturally and has its roots in social history (Seale, 1998; Walters, 2004). Our current 'western' view of a good death has evolved from influences in the recent past. From a health perspective, there has been a transition from acute conditions to chronic conditions as the predominant problem, a transition that has diminished some of the reality of death by changing illness from being life threatening to life limiting. From a health service perspective, care has been institutionalised away from the home and into acute hospitals as care has become more professionalised and technology based. Furthermore, the advances in technology in healthcare have emphasised the importance of restorative and 'heroic' interventions to the exclusion of other goals of care. These changes have not only resulted in people becoming distanced from the experience of caring for a dying relative or friend, but have also resulted in death being seen as failure and something preventable or at least able to be postponed (Christakis, 1999; Timmermans, 2005).

Similarly the euthanasia debate, including the use of so-called 'physician-assisted suicide', influences people's ideas about options at the end of life. On one side it is suggested that to take control of the timing of death before one's quality of life is too greatly impaired represents a good death, allowing one to die with dignity. On the other side, the management of suffering at the end of life through expert palliative care is offered as a way to maintain dignity and remove the need to end one's life (Materstvedt et al, 2003). Needless to say, these are essentially contested concepts and thus neither side will win the argument or convince the other side to alter their views, since they are based on values and not facts (Gallie, 1955–1956). The scare tactics of some activists that old people will be euthanised unwillingly and the current limited access to specialist palliative care make both these arguments a source of concern rather than a solution. Another 'western' trend, connected with the self-determination element of the euthanasia debate and which has influenced the social perception of a good death, has developed out of the rise of individualism in the pursuit of happiness and success. This is reflected in bioethics as we see that autonomy is given more importance over the other main bioethics principles of non-maleficence (do no harm), beneficence (do good) and justice (Beauchamp and Childress, 2008; Tsai, 2008).

Out of these influences, what appears to be important in terms of dignity is how we define personhood. Being a person is being someone who is rational, self-aware, and capable of valuing their own life, entitled to freedom and therefore having the right to make choices for themselves (Locke, 1964; Tsai, 2008). This western view of human personhood and the right to be treated with dignity can be supplemented by an 'eastern' view of personhood. Tsai (2008) explains that there are two layers of personhood in Confucian philosophy. In addition to the autonomous self, personhood also relies on one's relationships and support of others, particularly family and community. This is an interesting addition to understanding personhood, which is not absent from the way ordinary western people think but has certainly not been included explicitly in formal philosophical and ethical definitions.

These social and historical influences are reflected in older people's views on preferences for end-of-life care. Sutton and Coast's (2006) review identified the main preferences of older adults, which are summarised in Box 10.1.

BOX 10.1 *Summary of preferences at the end of life*

➤ To have family and friends present during the dying process and at the end
➤ To be pain free and have symptoms managed effectively
➤ To be treated as a whole person, including psychospiritual support
➤ To be prepared for death
➤ To maintain independence and control over activities and care
➤ To be able to access well-coordinated care services
➤ To be cared for and to die in the place of choice

These points illustrate an integration of the elements of personhood as already presented. Clearly people are connected with their families and friends, and maintaining relationships is very important. Being treated as a whole person, and having symptoms attended to in order to maintain a sense of self and control over one's body is also necessary for personhood. Being prepared for death and maintaining independence are both related to control and can be interpreted as the continuation of adult life where the person had autonomy and conducted their affairs independently. The final two items can be viewed together, since the ability to be cared for and to die in the place of choice is reliant on access to services that meet the needs of the patient and family.

These are the important features that, if present or managed will facilitate the best death possible. They are also the same factors that promote dignity for the individual. Definitions of dignity related to healthcare incorporate a few agreed concepts. Dignity is an innate or intrinsic part of being human and is related to self-esteem and social roles (Sandman, 2002; Badcott, 2003). Furthermore, dignity is manifested through our personal behaviour (Jacelon, 2003) and in the way we recognise the dignity in others (Pleschberger, 2007).

The central idea of the behavioural component is that an action 'shows respect' either to oneself or to others. If dignity is known through human behaviour then it must be learned, and that suggests also that there may be cultural differences in how dignity is expressed. Nordenfelt's (2004) typology of dignity (*see* previous discussions in Chapters 2, 3 and 9) is of use to us here in that two of the four types of dignity he defines are particularly important in the care of the dying: the dignity of *Menschenwürde* (the German term for dignity attributed simply because we are human) and the dignity of personal identity.

As Wainwright and Gallagher (2008) ably argue, nurses have unparalleled opportunity to demonstrate respect for life, not just in saving life but in protecting patients' vulnerability to the embarrassment and humiliation that can so readily accompany healthcare interventions. The dignity of personal identity carries with it considerable risk of loss since it relates to self-respect and concepts like integrity, autonomy and inclusion. When patients are unconscious, cognitively impaired or indeed so close to death that they are unresponsive, then these virtues associated with dignity have disappeared. As nurses, though, the dignity of *Menschenwürde* means that we will treat these people with all due respect despite their having lost elements of personal identity and personhood as formally defined.

Dying is a very problematic concept in relation to dignity because everything that points to the attributes of personhood and therefore to commanding respect for personal dignity is at risk. In all other areas of healthcare, restoration of personhood and dignity is a foreseeable and achievable goal as the aim of treatment and invasive procedures is recovery. During these periods of vulnerability, dignity can be palliated by the actions and communications of health professionals. For example, providing privacy, being respectful in communication and giving patients as much choice as possible help people retain their dignity and personhood despite their vulnerabilities. In healthcare in general, any loss of personhood and dignity can be seen as transitory. But with dying, the real and present threat of non-existence, of non-personhood, makes the risk to dignity greater than at any other time in life. The fear of an undignified dying is magnified by the grief not only of losing autonomy and freedom during the dying process, but of losing self entirely. Thus the need to be treated with respect is even more important at the end of life.

FACILITATING DIGNIFIED DYING

The statistical picture painted above, alongside the areas of preference for a good death, suggests that we are not doing very well at facilitating end-of-life care in the way that patients say they want it. Since the early 2000s, the Department of Health has had an increasing policy focus on end-of-life care in the UK which aims to promote patient choice, support end-of-life care in the community and ensure that not just cancer patients get a 'Rolls Royce' service (Clark *et al*, 2005). But the reality of caring for the dying comes down to the individuals who attend to that person and family. No policy, however well thought through and implemented, can substitute for excellent, compassionate care by well-educated professional nurses who provide a person-centred, evidence-based approach to their work.

This section of the chapter is divided into two parts. First we will explore the nature of suffering, which is the antithesis to dignity, and how dignified dying may provide a better alternative for approaching the care of the dying. Then we will examine the interventions designed to facilitate dignified dying, before concluding the chapter.

Dignity and suffering

Understanding what dignity is at the end of life, from the dying person's perspective, is a fundamental step toward facilitating dignified dying. Several studies have shown that the descriptors of personhood and dignity as described above hold true for the dying person. Self-image, self-determination and a sense of personal identity remain important (Chochinov *et al*, 2002; Ternestedt *et al*, 2002; Enes Duartes, 2003; Pleschberger, 2007). The centrality of social relationships is also confirmed as essential to dignity at the end of life (Street, 2001; Ternestedt *et al*, 2002; Enes Duartes, 2003; Pleschberger, 2007). However, the impact of the body's deterioration is a feature that is particular to dignity in the dying person. Street (2001) suggests that dignity is embodied as it is found to be so related to the loss of bodily function and process of decay associated with dying. Similarly, in the work of Franklin *et al* (2006), the themes revealed that the greatest threats to dignity were the 'unrecognizable body' and 'fragility and dependency', both starkly revealed by the process of dying. The connection between the dying body and loss of dignity clearly directs us to provide comfort through managing the physical as well as psychological, social and spiritual needs, in order to maintain dignity and prevent or minimise suffering.

Suffering and dignity are integrated concepts, particularly at the end of life or in life-threatening situations. Not only does suffering cause loss of dignity but it is also the case that a loss of dignity causes suffering. The fear of dying often relates to the desire not to suffer and this fear of suffering is at the core of the problems associated with the end of life. The fear of suffering itself causes suffering. Suffering is a complex, multidimensional and subjective concept that varies in intensity, severity and bearability (Ruijs *et al*, 2009). Despite its persistent presence with health-related problems, suffering has not been well described from the patient's point of view.

Ruijs *et al* (2009) attempted to conceptualise and measure unbearable suffering by developing a questionnaire based on the elements of suffering identified from research in health professionals' views of suffering. The 69 items fall into five domains: medical signs and symptoms (37 items); loss of function (seven items); personal aspects (17 items); social and environmental aspects (six items); and nature and prognosis of disease (two items). Participants were asked to rate not only the severity of each item but also the degree of unbear-able-ness. The fifth domain on the nature and prognosis of disease asks patients to rate two interesting statements, one on the 'fear of future suffering' and the second on the 'fear of not any longer having the strength to bear the suffering' (p.4). The analysis showed strong relationships between presence and bear-ability, supporting the idea that relieving symptoms or concerns in one domain may result in an increase in the availability of capacity to bear suffering within that domain or perhaps in other domains.

Similarly, Chochinov and colleagues considered the relationship between suffering and dignity, developing from that the dignity model as an empirically testable approach to intervening rather than measuring suffering (Chochinov *et al*, 2002, 2008). The components of the model are: illness-related concerns – including level of independence and symptom distress; dignity-conserving repertoire – including dignity-conserving perspectives and practices; and the social dignity inventory – including privacy boundaries, social support, care tenor (attitude and approach of staff), burden to others, and aftermath con-cerns (concerns about what will happen after death).

Kolcaba's work on the theory of comfort in nursing also provides some insight (Kolcaba, 2009). She suggests that there are three levels of comfort out-comes: to relieve discomfort, to ease discomfort or to transcend discomfort. These goals work well with the concept of suffering at the end of life in that it may be possible to relieve completely some forms of suffering and to ease to some degree other forms of suffering. However, sometimes it is necessary to assist patients and families in transcending, rising above, the suffering and sup-porting them to find some level of comfort in very discomforting situations. In Kolcaba's theory, discomfort can be experienced in three domains: physi-cal, psychospiritual and environmental. These are not dissimilar domains to those of Ruijs *et al*'s (2009) work on suffering or Chochinov *et al*'s (2002) work on dignity, and confirm the hypothesis that suffering and comfort, and there-fore dignity, are all multidimensional, whole-person experiences. Furthermore, these three theoretical views highlight that the relationship between suffering and dignity can be balanced by comfort. Taking these three related concepts together, one can see how comfort measures counteract the effects of suffering and promote dignity.

Interventions for dignified dying

The term 'dignified dying' has only appeared in the nursing literature in the past five years. It is an important component of a good death, since dignity figures highly in the construction of a good death for most people. The good death poses some problems in that there is a tendency to have a rigid, idealised view of what is a good death, and if those components are not there, then the circumstances of the death can be construed as a failure of care (Walters, 2004). For example, many nurses both in the community and in hospital value a home death over and above all other considerations, so much so that they believe they have failed if the patient is moved to hospital; thus a good death could not be achieved even if the family is relieved and the patient's pain is better managed in hospital (Smith and Porock, 2010). The professionals' view of what constitutes a good death can sometimes be in conflict with what patients and families want or need and families can feel under pressure to comply with what professionals consider to be a good death (Walters, 2004).

The dying scene is idealised in a good death scenario, in a similar way that the birth plan for the delivery of a baby can be idealised. When things do not go quite to plan with the delivery, there can be great disappointment, guilt and grief. With dignified dying, the aim is simply to ensure the patients' and families' dignity throughout the process, whatever that may entail, wherever it may occur. For the dying person and family, the intention may be to die at home but because of unfamiliarity with the dying process, and with the success of medical treatment, this sometimes does not happen. For example, over the last year or so of the patient's life when a crisis has occurred, such as an infection or uncontrolled pain, the patient has gone to hospital, been treated, and gone home again. The family is not to know that this time it is the terminal event. So they go to hospital with the patient fully expecting sufficient recovery to go home, albeit aware that the patient will die at home. When the infection or metabolic crisis cannot be reversed, the patient then enters the active phase of dying but is not in the place of choice. The idealised death scene has to be abandoned and the patient and family begin to face uncharted and unprepared-for waters. Thus, dignified dying provides a way of thinking about facilitating the best death possible for both the patient and family without the constraints of the idealised good death.

As we have seen, dignity is a multidimensional, subjective concept; therefore, multidimensional and dynamic interventions are needed as solutions when dignity is threatened by suffering at the end of life. Physical suffering is probably the area of palliative care specialty that is best developed and most widely recognised. The assessment and management of pain in particular are critical to dignity-preserving care. Psychological, social, spiritual and existential suffering is less well understood and not amenable to intervention or management – at least not in the same way that physical symptoms are. For example, there is no dose, route or frequency of administration for a social intervention. Chochinov (2006) notes that many of the interventions for dignity that have been noted would be categorised as 'niceties' of care or 'touchy-feely', but emphasises the centrality of these actions and interactions as of the highest priority if we are to maintain and support dignity at the end of life. Fundamental to providing dignity-preserving care is finding out who the patient is, what is important to them and what they value. This is the assessment process for dignity. From that, creative and individual care can be designed. The simple act of recognising the suffering as experienced by the patient, validating that experience as real, is in itself a dignity-preserving intervention. As Chochinov (2006) states, '. . . patients are looking for affirmation regarding their sense of worth in spite of their dyspnoea, incontinence and disfigurement' (p.94).

Suffering cannot be palliated in the same way as pain at the end of life. Rather than masking with analgesia or sedation, as is acceptable and effective with physical pain, the issues underlying psychological, social and spiritual and existential suffering should be explored and, as far as possible, resolved. Rousseau (2000) suggests the following dignity-preserving activities in addition to controlling symptoms and providing supportive presence: use life review to recognise purpose, value and meaning in life and in dying; explore guilt, remorse, forgiveness and reconciliation; and facilitate religious expression and focus on meditative practices that promote healing rather than cure. These interventions require great skill and courage, particularly in a healthcare system where these activities are not valued or built into the workload. However, health professionals caring for the dying must not shy away from allowing the patient time to express their concerns, or from supporting family members wherever possible in this process, as well as facilitating access to those who can support more in-depth exploration.

Kissane (2001) uses the term 'demoralising syndrome' to describe the impact of suffering on dignity. His suggestions for care are very similar to Rousseau's and Chochinov's but he adds the importance of balancing support for grief with the promotion of hope and suggests that continuity of care is essential to providing this kind of support. Hopelessness is highly correlated with suicidal ideation and desire for death, more so than depression (Chochinov et al, 1998), and fundamentally undermines the sense that life has any value or worth (Chochinov, 2006). It might seem difficult, if not impossible, to find hope at the end of life. However, the key is in reframing what is hoped for. Hope is a way of coping, a way of enduring suffering. Patients may hope for no more suffering, or for living each day, or for a peaceful death and they may hope for their family's future (Duggleby, 2000; Duggleby and Wright, 2004).

Dignity therapy is a specific technique developed and tested by Chochinov and colleagues (2005), which focuses on finding meaning. Patients are asked to relate the elements of their personal history that they most want to be remembered or to focus on things that they feel must be said. The sessions are recorded and then transcribed and presented back to the patient who can then distribute them to family members. The impact of this simple act is profound as it provides comfort to relatives and generates a tangible legacy for the patient. Measuring the impact has shown improvements in depressive symptoms and desire for death.

Fear of the dying process is part of psychological suffering and it can be experienced by family as well as patients. As with the fear of any new experience, education and support are of vital importance. Teaching patients and families about the dying process may seem a daunting prospect but is essential for dignified dying. Many hospices and palliative care services provide descriptions of the final hours and days of life so that fear of the unknown can be reduced. Many services have these descriptions on line and they are well-accessed sites. Teaching about the dying process has been recognised as part of family care and has been confirmed, along with privacy for the family and encouraging involvement in care, in several countries as a positive intervention for dignified dying (Wilson *et al*, 2006; Coenen *et al*, 2007).

Privacy is often connected with dignity but listed as if they were separate concepts. Privacy is a part of dignity and it is important to consider this element in more detail. The home death is appealing in part because of its ability to keep the dying process private. Dying in a public place is not part of the idealised death. In their critical look at end-of-life care at home, Exley and Allen (2007) describe the institutionalisation and medicalisation of the home where the sick room takes on the appearance, and sometimes the routine, of the hospital. Although this is probably not what people have in mind with a home death, it does afford one feature not always present in hospital and that is privacy from other patients and relatives. Porock *et al* (2009) provide an explicit description of the lack of privacy for dying people in general hospitals in the UK. An extract from this work is presented in Box 10.2. The field note extract relates to a situation where an older patient's two daughters arrived on the ward and a nurse asked the doctor to speak to them about their mother's condition. There followed a conversation in the ward with the daughters sitting at a table, a cleaner nearby, and several doctors and a nurse standing by the daughters. The doctor explained to the patient's daughters that most older people with dementia die of pneumonia rather than their dementia. He then asked them how they wished their mother to be treated, pointing out that there were very limited choices. As you read in Box 10.2, not only was there a lack of privacy but the staff apparently displayed a lack of empathy for the patient's daughters.

Providing privacy is more than just pulling a curtain around the bed. The impact of watching another patient dying on those sharing a bay is raised in Porock *et al*'s work, but more research is needed to really understand the implications and be able to act effectively on patients' behalf. Dilemmas between the idealised good death being facilitated by offering a single room and the desire not to hide away the dying was another feature of providing end-of-life care in such a public arena. Street and Love (2005) attend to the issue of privacy

BOX 10.2 *Field note extract from 'Dying in public: the nature of dying in a public hospital'*

Daughters' eyes begin to well up. One states clearly that they do not want any heroics if their mother has a heart attack, and that this has already been decided. She wants to know what the options are. Doctor suggests that it may be kindest to allow the mother to die in peace with no pain rather than continue with active treatment (antibiotics). Daughters both agree but they want her fed to the end and kept pain free. Doctor states that he will note their wishes. This seems a very private conversation to have in the middle of a busy ward with trolleys and cleaners all around. The daughters are left welling up and go to see their mum. No assistance is offered by staff for chairs or cup of tea or anything remotely empathic. Both daughters are clearly fighting back the tears on seeing their mum in bed. The ward round continues in this bay with this family left exposed in the rawness of their newly realised embarkation on a journey toward the loss of their mother. It is surreal and yet ordinary.

(Porock *et al*, 2009, p.16, reprinted by permission of the publisher Taylor & Francis Group, www.informaworld.com)

BOX 10.3 *Characteristics of dignified dying, adapted from Wilson et al (2006), p.38*

➤ Verbalises relief of pain
➤ Expresses control of symptoms
➤ Participates in decisions for care and treatment
➤ Verbalises physical comfort
➤ Verbalises spiritual contentment
➤ Reviews life experiences
➤ Resolves personal and family concerns
➤ Feelings of sorrow, grief and detachment processed through mourning
➤ Expresses feelings of loss
➤ Consciously dealing with emotions relating to impending death
➤ Shares feelings of loss with significant others
➤ Expresses spiritual concerns
➤ Expresses expectations about the impending end of life
➤ Expresses acceptance of dying
➤ Verbalises any lack of control in treatment decisions
➤ Verbalises any lack of respect from healthcare providers

and caution us to consider privacy not just in terms of environment but also in terms of psychosocial and moral dimensions. Providing privacy as a means of preserving dignity is an essential intervention in care of the dying.

With all interventions, it is important to evaluate and determine their effectiveness. The concept of dignified dying is being developed and tested as a nursing diagnosis. Wilson *et al* (2006) suggest 16 characteristics that would indicate that the patient's dignity is maintained. These are listed in Box 10.3.

These are helpful indicators of dignified dying but they do rely on the patient being sufficiently cognitively intact and assertive, particularly with professional caregivers, and that might not be the case. It also assumes that acceptance is a necessary part of dignified dying when clearly there are many examples of patients who at best may be feeling resigned to the fact of their impending death but not really prepared to accept it (Walters, 2004). These feelings are also legitimate and need to be accepted as part of the human experience at the end of life. Dignified dying cannot be any more uniform than the idealised 'good death', as that would inhibit the individual's own expression of dignity.

What is similar about all dignity-preserving interventions is the need not only for presence and time but also for the courage to spend time with a person who is dying, an activity that can seriously challenge our own sense of stability and ability to cope with our own mortality. Thus an important intervention for dignity-preserving care is for professional and family caregivers to be cared for and supported themselves.

CONCLUSION

This chapter has reviewed death in our society in terms of where and when people die, and has explored the preferences for end-of-life care, particularly in older adults, in order to provide a context for understanding dignity at the end of life and how to facilitate dignified dying. Facilitating dignified dying through dignity-preserving strategies is an achievable goal. It takes the courage to talk to people about their deaths and is contingent on the recognition and open awareness of death. Providing end-of-life care that preserves dignity is not an easy area of care but it is a privilege and one that can be immensely rewarding and life affirming. NB: Chapter 11 (Community care and dignity) includes exploration of a community-based case study of end-of-life care.

REFERENCES

Badcott D (2003) The basis and relevance of emotional dignity. *Medicine Health Care and Philosophy* **6**: 123–31.

Beauchamp TL, Childress JF (2008) *Principles of Biomedical Ethics* (6e). London: Oxford University Press.

Chochinov HM (2006) Dying, dignity and new horizons in palliative end-of-life care. *CA: A Cancer Journal for Clinicians* 5: 84–103.

Chochinov HM, Wilson KG, Enns M *et al* (1998) Depression, hopelessness and suicidal ideation in the terminally ill. *Psychosomatics* 39: 366–70.

Chochinov HM, Hack T, Hassard T *et al* (2002) Dignity in the terminally ill: a cross-sectional cohort study. *Lancet* 360: 2026–30.

Chochinov HM, Hack T, Hassard T *et al* (2005) Dignity therapy: a novel psychotherapeutic intervention for patients nearing death. *Journal of Clinical Oncology* 23: 5520–5.

Chochinov HM, Hassard T, McClement S *et al* (2008) The patient dignity inventory: a novel way of measuring dignity-related distress in palliative care. *Journal of Pain and Symptom Management* 36(6): 559–71.

Christakis N (1999) *Death Foretold: prophecy and prognosis in medical care.* Chicago, IL: University of Chicago Press.

Clark D, Small N, Wright M *et al* (2005) *A Bit of Heaven for the Few? An oral history of the modern hospice movement in the United Kingdom.* Lancaster: Observatory Publications.

Coenen A, Doorenbos A, Wilson SA (2007) Nursing interventions to promote dignified dying in four countries. *Oncology Nursing Forum* 34(6): 1151–6.

Department of Health (2005) *The National Service Framework for Long-term Conditions.* London: HMSO.

Douglas K (2004) Death defying. *New Scientist* 28 August: 40–3.

Duggleby W (2000) Enduring suffering: a grounded theory analysis of the pain experience of elderly hospice patients with cancer. *Oncology Nursing Forum* 27: 825–30.

Duggleby W, Wright K (2004) Elderly palliative care patients' descriptions of hope-fostering strategies. *International Journal of Palliative Nursing* 10: 352–9.

Enes Duartes SP (2003) An exploration of dignity in palliative care. *Palliative Medicine* 17: 263–9.

Exley C, Allen D (2007) A critical examination of home care: end of life care as an illustrative case. *Social Science and Medicine* 65(11): 2317–27.

Franklin L-L, Ternestedt B-M, Nordenfelt L (2006) Views on dignity of elderly nursing home residents. *Nursing Ethics* 13(2): 130–46.

Gallie WB (1955–1956) Essentially contested concepts. *Proceedings of the Aristotelian Society, New Series* 56: 167–98.

Gomes B, Higginson IJ (2008) Where people die (1974–2030): past trends, future projections and implications for care. *Palliative Medicine* 22: 33–41.

Grundy E, Mayer D, Young H *et al* (2004) Living arrangements and place of death of older people with cancer in England and Wales: a record linkage study. *British Journal of Cancer* 91(5): 907–12.

Higginson IJ, Astin P, Dolan S (1998) Where do cancer patients die? Ten year trends in the place of death of cancer patients in England. *Palliative Medicine* 12: 353–63.

Hopkinson J, Hallet C, Luker K (2003) Caring for dying people in hospital. *Journal of Advanced Nursing* 44(5): 525–33.

Jacelon CS (2003) The dignity of elders in an acute care setting. *Qualitative Health Research* 13(4): 543–56.

Kissane DW (2001) Demoralization: its impact on informed consent and medical care. *Medical Journal of Australia* 175: 537–39.

Kolcaba C (2009) Comfort. In: Peterson SJ, Bredow TS (eds) *Middle Range Theories.*

Application to nursing research (2e). Philadelphia: Lippincott Williams and Wilkins, pp.254–70.

Locke J (1964) *An Essay Concerning Human Understanding Book 2*. London: Oxford University Press.

Materstvedt LJ, Clark D, Ellershaw J *et al* (2003) Euthanasia and physician-assisted suicide: a view from an EAPC Ethics Task Force. *Palliative Medicine* **17**: 97–101.

National End of Life Care Programme (2010) *Variations in Place of Death in England. Inequalities or appropriate consequences of age, gender and cause of death?* London: NHS.

Nordenfelt L (2004) The varieties of dignity. *Health Care Analysis* **12**(20): 69–89.

Office for National Statistics (2009) www.statistics.gov.uk/downloads/theme_health/dr2009/dr-09.pdf (accessed 26 October 2010).

Patrick DL, Engelberg RA, Curtis JR (2001) Evaluating the quality of dying and death. *Journal of Pain and Symptom Management* **22**(3): 717–26.

Pfund R, Fowler-Kerry S (2010) *Perspectives on Palliative Care for Children and Young People: a global discourse*. Oxford: Radcliffe Publishing.

Pleschberger S (2007) Dignity and the challenge of dying in nursing homes: the residents' view. *Age and Ageing* **36**: 197–202.

Porock D, Pollock K, Jurgens F (2009) Dying in public: the nature of dying in an acute hospital setting. *Journal of Housing for the Elderly* **23**(1): 10–28.

Rousseau P (2000) Spirituality and the dying patient. *Journal of Clinical Oncology* **18**: 2000–2002.

Ruijs KDM, Onwuteaka-Philipsen BD, van der Wal G *et al* (2009) Unbearability of suffering at the end of life: the development of a new measuring device, the SOS-V. *Biomed Central Palliative Care* **8**(16). www.biomedcentral.com/1472-684X/8/16 (accessed 12 October 2010).

Sandman L (2002) What's the use of human dignity within palliative care? *Nursing Philosophy* **3**: 177–81.

Seale C (1998) *Constructing Death: the Sociology of Dying and Bereavement*. Cambridge: Cambridge University Press.

Shipman C, Higginson IJ, White P *et al* (2007) *Scoping Exercise on Generalist Services for Adults at the End of Life: research, knowledge, policy and future research needs. Report 3: the consultation report for the National Co-ordinating Centre for NHS Service Delivery and Organisation R&D (NCCSDO)*. London: King's College London.

Smith R, Porock D (2010) Caring for people dying at home: a research study into the needs of community nurses. *International Journal of Palliative Nursing* **15**(12): 601–8.

Street A (2001) Constructions of dignity in end-of-life care. *Journal of Palliative Care* **17**(2): 93–101.

Street AF, Love A (2005) Dimensions of privacy in palliative care: views of health professionals. *Social Science and Medicine* **60**: 1795–1804.

Sutton E, Coast J (2006) Older people's preferences at the end of life: a review of the literature. In: Woodthorpe K (ed) *Layers of Dying and Death: papers presented at the 4th Global Conference of Dying and Death. Wed 12th–Friday 14th July 2006. Mansfield College, Oxford*. Oxford: Inter-Disciplinary Press.

Ternestedt B-M, Andershed B, Eriksson M *et al* (2002) A good death: development of a nursing model of care. *Journal of Hospice and Palliative Nursing* **3**: 153–60.

Timmermans S (2005) Death brokering: constructing culturally appropriate deaths. *Sociology of Health and Illness* **27**: 993–1013.

Tsai DF-C (2008) Personhood and autonomy in multicultural health care settings. *American Medical Association Journal of Ethics* **10**(3): 171–6.

Vig EK, Davenort NA, Pearlman RA (2002) Good deaths, bad deaths and preferences for the end of life: a qualitative study of geriatric outpatients. *Journal of the American Geriatrics Society* **50**(9): 1541–8.

Wainwright P, Gallagher A (2008) On different types of dignity in nursing care: a critique of Nordenfelt. *Nursing Philosophy* **9**: 46–54.

Walters G (2004) Is there such a thing as a good death? *Palliative Medicine* **18**(5): 404–408.

Wilson SA, Coenen A, Doorenbos A (2006) Dignified dying as a phenomenon in the United States. *Journal of Hospice and Palliative Nursing* **8**(1): 34–41.

CHAPTER 11

Community care and dignity

Candice Pellett

INTRODUCTION

People live their lives primarily in their own homes and communities, where their health and well-being are influenced by the events in which they find themselves involved. Primary care is diverse and can be complicated, with a vast and increasing range of care, treatments and support being delivered in the community setting. This chapter will explore issues relating to dignity in care for patients in the community in the United Kingdom (UK). Care delivery by the district nursing team in patients' own homes, residential homes and clinics will be focused on, though the principles discussed apply to other healthcare professionals working in the community, and indeed will be relevant in other countries too.

Community staff often work with patients and their families over a long period of time, so it is imperative to build trusting relationships to promote, where possible, independence, choice and empowerment along their health-care journey. Lack of respect for people's dignity can take many forms and may be experienced differently from person to person. Dignity should permeate care delivery and includes people having choices about how their care is delivered and having their religious and cultural needs considered.

This chapter includes case studies that focus on the dignity of patients at the end of their lives, patients requiring wound care, and adults with long-term conditions, as these are all situations commonly encountered in community care. The case studies are based on the author's practice experience; all patients' names and identifying features have been altered to maintain anonymity.

LEARNING OUTCOMES

By the end of the chapter you will be able to:

➤ discuss the context of dignity in community care, with reference to current UK health policy and the district nursing team
➤ identify key principles relating to dignity within patients' own homes and residential settings

➤ explain how the district nursing team can promote dignity for patients in the community, with specific reference to patients with chronic wounds, patients undergoing palliative care and patients with long-term conditions.

DIGNITY IN COMMUNITY CARE: THE CONTEXT

Dignity is important to every individual, irrespective of the situation and the healthcare setting in which they find themselves. Increasingly, care takes place in the community rather than in hospital; indeed, in the UK, 90% of people accessing healthcare do so in primary and community settings (Darzi, 2009). *Our Health, Our Care, Our Say* (Department of Health [DH], 2006) asserted that healthcare is shifting from hospital to primary care across the health spectrum, from complex disease management to end-of-life care, giving patients and carers preference where possible to be treated closer to home. The DH (2006) discussed the importance of supporting and caring for people at home, particularly those aged over 65 years and those with long-term conditions. This was further supported by *High Quality Care for All* (DH, 2008a), which sets out the vision for a modern, responsive, high-quality service delivered to people nearer to home and aimed at preventing unnecessary hospital admissions. Furthermore, services should focus on the importance of patients' experiences in terms of quality of care and caring, which includes 'compassion, dignity and respect with which patients are treated' (DH, 2008a, p.47). These principles should be applied across all settings within the community, including general practitioners' (GPs') surgeries, health clinics, community hospitals and within patients' own homes.

In the UK, community care is usually led by district nurses (DNs) for people who require nursing in their own homes. DNs hold a post-registration specialist practitioner qualification and are responsible for the delivery of patient and carer-centred care. DN team members may include registered nurses and healthcare support workers who have a wide range of skills. DNs are usually attached to GPs and cover a defined geographical area. They provide care to patients aged 16 years and over who are registered with the practice and who are usually confined to their home or live in a residential setting. The DN service provides care 365 days per year, and in many parts of the UK there is 24 hour support. Visits are often on a regular basis and over a long period of time; therefore, DNs are in a position to accurately assess the needs of the patient and their family. With health policy aiming to provide care closer to home, the DN service is rapidly taking on ever-increasing roles as more complex care is delivered in the community, whether managing long-term conditions, preventing unnecessary emergency admissions or delivering end-of-life care. The team is well placed to liaise across the boundaries of primary and acute services, working with all professionals involved in patients' care pathways to maximise and coordinate care to deliver a high-quality service. Maintaining patient dignity is central to good community nursing practice, particularly as DNs often care for patients at a vulnerable time in their lives.

The fundamental role and responsibility of the DN service are to offer full holistic assessment of patients in addition to recognising their carers' needs, and to provide skilled nursing care to meet assessed needs. The service endeavours to empower patients and their carers by working in partnership and where possible, promoting independence. The skills offered by the DN team include assessment, planning, implementing and evaluating the needs of the patients and their carers/families within their own homes. This may include assessment and treatment of incontinence and assessment and prescribing of equipment to facilitate care in patients' homes, thus enabling individuals to maximise their quality of life within the limits of their illness or disease, or to enable a full recovery. DNs use personalised care planning with patients, rather than setting patients' goals for them, thus actively involving patients in deciding, agreeing and owning how their health will be managed, promoting choice and enhancing dignity. This philosophy is supported by the Government's principle of shared decision making of 'no decision about me without me' (p.13) which involves patients working in partnership with clinicians in choosing their care and treatments that will improve their health outcomes (DH, 2010).

DIGNITY IN PEOPLE'S OWN HOMES

District nursing teams undertake the majority of care in patients' own homes; therefore, they are 'guests' in the patients' environment. Nurses and other healthcare professionals are there by the patient's invitation and consent and often have information and knowledge about the patient, their family and their lifestyle. Therefore, confidentiality of information is paramount, including that relating to the patient's health, values, beliefs, home environment, finances and relationships. This information must be treated with respect for the patient's and their family's right to privacy, as otherwise dignity will be compromised. Some communities, especially in village settings, are very close-knit and it can sometimes be difficult to maintain confidentiality when the nurse works and lives in the same environment. Relatives, friends or neighbours of the patient may ask for information without the patient's knowledge or consent and may become quite affronted when the community team is unable to answer their questions. However, information about patients is private and nurses have a duty of confidentiality to respect and protect their patient (Nursing and Midwifery Council [NMC], 2008), as do other healthcare professionals.

The majority of patients on a DN caseload are older people who may be frail and vulnerable, and it is important that they are treated as individuals, valuing them as people who, although they may require support, still have much to give to their families and the wider community. The dignity of older people can easily become compromised as they find themselves in vulnerable situations, often with less control (*see* Chapter 9 for a detailed exploration of dignity and older people). The Royal College of Nursing (2008) suggests that when dignity is present, people feel in control, valued, confident and comfortable and able to make decisions for themselves; however, when dignity is absent, people feel devalued, lacking control and comfort. Being unable to manage and control activities of daily living may have a devastating impact on a person's self-respect and dignity.

When a person requires nursing in their home on a regular basis, they and their family may feel that they lack privacy in many areas of their lives. Dignified care starts when the DN knocks on the door and greets the patient. Asking a person how they would like to be addressed is essential, as a person's name is very personal to them and in some cultures to use a first name as a form of address is considered very disrespectful. Dignity is about respecting the person, which is more than ensuring their physical dignity. It is about maintaining a sense of self-worth, being listened to and being able to make choices about their lives.

Some people require 24-hour care in either their own home or a residential home, and everything they do is open to observation by another person. Conversations, telephone calls, expressions and feelings are on show to others. Personal and intimate care should be sensitively provided to ensure that the dignity of the person remains intact throughout. Attention to preserving privacy and modesty while giving personal care is paramount, as a person's dignity could easily be encroached upon by carelessly exposing their body during intimate care such as undertaking hygiene needs or delivering bowel care. When a person requires help with washing and bathing at home, it is important to ensure that the room door is closed and the window curtains are drawn if the room is overlooked. Staff should also ensure that only the area being washed is uncovered and that the person is warm at all times, which is sometimes difficult to achieve if the bedroom is cold. Often members of the family are present in the house and the person's privacy and dignity should be protected at all times. Consent must be gained from the patient before any discussion about their care takes place when others are present.

DIGNITY IN RESIDENTIAL CARE HOMES

Often people do not want to leave the comfort and privacy of their own homes to live in shared accommodation with strangers. When nursing people living in residential care, it is important to minimise intrusion on their privacy, as they are often in a shared room and they may only be separated from their neighbour by a curtain around the bed. It must be recognised that their room in the residential setting is now their home, so even the most basic step of knocking on the door before entering is important. Bedside curtains may give the illusion of privacy but they do not provide protection from the activities that are occurring behind them. Using a clip or peg to secure the curtain will prevent gaps and remind staff not to enter without warning. The curtains are not smell-proof or sound-proof and it can be very embarrassing when the person is having an enema administered, using the commode or having a bed bath. Respecting a person's privacy and personal space is imperative. Many people are embarrassed if they are moved using a hoist, especially if they wish to use the toilet or commode, and it is important that their clothes are adjusted to ensure that they are not exposed to other residents. An engaged sign on the door will ensure that visitors do not go in and cause embarrassment to the person who is washing or having their wound dressings changed.

To preserve a person's self-respect, it is important to keep their individuality. We must never assume what the patient wants but must respect their individuality at all times. On one occasion, I visited an older person in a residential home to undertake wound dressings and found her crying and withdrawn. After sitting with her, it transpired that it had been her birthday the day before and during tea a carer had placed a large 'top hat' on her head complete with material candles. She would never have agreed to this if she had been asked and felt like she had been treated as a child. The person has since died but her daughter still remembers with sadness how upset her mother had been because she had not been treated as an individual and had felt patronised. It is so important that everyone caring for older people sees beyond a group of residents living in a home and respects them as individuals. All residents are people with life experiences and staff can connect with who they were in the past by using appropriate language and involving them in decision making wherever possible. Dignity must be enforced, not eroded, and at the heart of everything we do, and carers should be seen as expert partners in care rather than controllers of care.

The next sections explore case studies of community patients undergoing wound care, end-of-life care, and care when living with long-term conditions. These case studies illustrate the practical steps that can be taken to promote dignity in community care.

DIGNITY DURING WOUND CARE

Dignity for people undertaking treatments is a basic human right but it is something that could be overlooked in busy clinics. Many leg ulcer clinics are run by DNs in GP surgeries or health clinics. Thousands of people in the UK are affected by leg ulceration, primarily as a consequence of chronic venous insufficiency, with estimated annual costs of care of £200 million (Posnett and Franks, 2007). Essential to patient dignity is promotion of quality of life for individuals, particularly if they have a chronic wound like a leg ulcer, which can often have far-ranging effects on all activities of living. Restrictions in carrying out paid employment, the inability to cope with household activities and loss of mobility can result in loss of control and anxiety and will impact negatively on the patients' quality of life. Various studies have reported the negative impact of leg ulcers on a patient's life (Charles, 1995; Walshe, 1995; Douglas, 2001; Persoon *et al*, 2004).

Reflective activity 11.1 presents questions to help you to consider how a chronic wound affects dignity.

Reflective activity 11.1 The impact of a chronic wound on dignity

If you had a chronic open wound on your lower leg, what impact would this have on your dignity? For example, consider the impact on dignity of:

➤ probable malodour and a constantly oozing wound
➤ associated chronic pain
➤ restricted mobility
➤ having leg bandages in place 24 hours a day.

As you might have considered, malodour from wounds can cause embarrassment for patients and can affect all areas of their lives, causing social isolation and loss of self-esteem. This can be exacerbated when toe-to-knee compression bandaging has to remain in place for up to a week, which may prevent patients from having a shower or bath. Leakage from the ulcer may prevent the person leaving their home between clinic appointments, and cause them to suffer loss of dignity in their outward appearance. A majority of patients experience problems with body image when coping with bandaging. One of the most significant problems that occurs is the visible physical change in the shape and size of the leg, and for some people this necessitates a complete change of preferred style of dress – trousers with wide legs or long skirts are examples of clothing that people with lower leg ulceration adopt whatever their former personal preference. People with oedema to the leg find activities requiring the limb to bend particularly difficult, and swollen and bandaged feet can make shopping for shoes time consuming, costly and depressing. This can have a profound effect on a person's occupation and lifestyle, with feelings of loss of dignity, isolation, anxiety and depression.

The case study in Box 11.1 illustrates the impact of a chronic wound on a patient's dignity and how a DN addressed this situation. As you will read, a crucial factor was listening to Jean's concerns and involving her in planning a solution. Webster and Bryan (2009) found that people value being included in decisions about their care, which allows them to maintain independence and feel more in control about their situation. Although their research was based in a hospital setting, the findings are applicable to the community environment, with the belief that communication is the intervening factor in maintaining control, independence and dignity.

BOX 11.1 *Case study: wound care*

Jean attended an afternoon leg ulcer clinic run by DNs after an absence of some time. She had been referred to the clinic by the practice nurse six months previously, with a venous leg ulcer due to an accidental injury to the lower leg. Walking was a problem due to the increased oedema exacerbated by the failure to wear compression bandaging. Although Jean had been advised on many occasions to maintain good skin care, her skin condition was dry, particularly on her toes and feet. From the documentation it was clear that, gradually, failure to attend the clinics became more frequent despite the DN phoning her and inviting her to attend.

When Jean arrived at the clinic it soon became apparent that she was extremely apprehensive and close to tears, and conversation was difficult. While the nurse was washing Jean's leg she confided that her mother had suffered from leg ulceration due to diabetes which had eventually resulted in amputation of one of her legs. Jean had vivid memories of the discomfort and pain that her mother had experienced and the total loss of dignity and despair she had felt. Jean's situation had brought back all the negative memories of her mother's condition, which had culminated in her not attending the clinics or wearing her bandages. Jean's life was very demanding; combining family commitments and a working day meant she was finding it very difficult to take time off to attend the clinics and she worried that she may lose her job.

After discussions with Jean, the DN suggested that she could attend the evening clinic to have her ulcer redressed by the practice nurse. This enabled Jean to carry on as normal with her employment and maintain control over her day rather than feeling that she was being controlled by her ulcer. Jean's wound healed within ten weeks of attending regular clinic appointments.

DIGNITY IN END-OF-LIFE-CARE

Most deaths occur following long-term illness; according to the DH:

> Around half a million people die in England each year, of which two thirds are aged over 75. The large majority of deaths at the start of the 21st century follow a period of chronic illness such as heart disease, cancer, stroke, chronic respiratory disease, neurological disease or dementia (DH, 2009a, p.123).

Recently, the End of Life Strategy (DH, 2008b), which promotes high-quality care for all adults at the end of life, has stated that most people will spend the majority of the last year of their lives in the community. Therefore, although death itself occurs in hospital for many people (*see* Chapter 10), caring for patients who are dying is a large part of the DN community caseload.

A loss of dignity at the end of life is feared by many people (*see* Chapter 10) and some people feel that lack of support to be able to die in their own home undermines their dignity (Help the Aged, 2007). People must receive excellent care at the end of their lives to give them and their loved ones confidence that they can stay at home if that is their choice. Macleod (2003) suggests that loss of dignity may cause hopelessness, depression and a longing for a quick death. Many people feel that a 'good death' means they have adequate pain relief, privacy, dignity and some control over how and where they die. They may initially receive the bad news of diagnosis in the acute setting, but many aspects of this news and subsequent care are delivered by the primary healthcare team. *Transforming Community Services* (DH, 2009b) suggests the use of an established systematic framework to optimise care delivery. There are best-practice models that aim for dignity as they identify and address people's preferences and needs at the end of life, for example:

➤ *The End of Life Care Transformational Guide* (DH, 2009b)
➤ The Gold Standards Framework (www.goldstandardsframework.nhs.uk)
➤ Liverpool Care Pathway (www.liv.ac.uk/mcpcil/liverpool-care-pathway/)
➤ *Preferred Priorities for Care* (www.endoflifecareforadults.nhs.uk/assets/downloads/ppc.pdf).

The DN service is committed to facilitating patient choice during end-of-life care provision, to allow all patients to die at their preferred place of care with privacy and dignity and with their symptoms controlled. Care includes daily monitoring of a patient's condition, administration of prescribed drugs and assessment of additional support, for example, referral to the Marie Curie service (a UK-based charity delivering home care for people with cancer), and using evidence-based practice in line with national and local policies, guidelines, pathways and protocols. Bereavement visits are also offered to families.

Being involved at the end of someone's life is a privilege. There is only one opportunity to get it right and ensure that the person has a dignified death and their family are well supported. Box 11.2 details a case study as an example of care given to a patient on the DN caseload. As you read the case study of Alan, consider what the community team did to preserve his dignity. A discussion on Alan's care then follows.

BOX 11.2 *Case study: end-of-life care*

Alan was a 73-year-old retired builder who was diagnosed with colorectal carcinoma with lung metastases. He was known to the DNs as they had undertaken flushing of his Hickman line 2 years previously when he was undergoing chemotherapy. As his disease progressed he had been attending a city hospital once weekly for abdominal paracentesis but was finding the sheer effort of travelling to, and waiting for, his treatment more exhausting as his health deteriorated. Alan was placed on the Gold Standard Framework supportive care register. His care plan and needs were discussed at the monthly primary healthcare meetings. Alan's GP and DN were approached by the hospital to discuss the possibility of undertaking ascites drainage at home. Following insertion of a permanent drainage system under local anaesthetic, Alan returned home under the care of the primary healthcare team. Close communication between the DNs, GPs and Macmillan nurse* allowed flexible and timely care to be delivered to Alan when it was appropriate for him.

  For the last three months of Alan's life, the nurses visited at least three times a week to assess for re-accumulation of ascites and to observe for abdominal distension and pain. Alan was averaging between 4 and 5 litres drainage per week and was well aware when the drainage needed to be undertaken as he would experience a 'dull, continuous' ache across his abdomen; otherwise he had very little discomfort. He would phone the DN team if extra visits were required to drain the ascitic fluid, thus giving him control of the situation. Alan gradually became more jaundiced and was diagnosed with pruritus. Over time Alan became hypotensive and had increased peripheral oedema. He was eventually placed on the Liverpool Care Pathway and all non-essential medication was stopped. Alan's symptoms were well controlled on a regular prescription administered via a syringe driver. Nursing support was increased to several visits a day. Alan died peacefully within the comfort of his own home in the presence of his family.

*Macmillan nurses are funded by Macmillan Cancer Support, a UK cancer charity.

Discussion

Alan had lived an active, independent life and had found that his advancing illness meant loss of independence and increasing dependence on his wife and health professionals. He initially found this situation very hard to cope with as he felt his freedom of choice and autonomy had diminished. Decision making is the key to our autonomy and determines our lifestyle. Freedom of choice and autonomy are essential components to experiencing dignity. Alan wanted to maintain as much control and choice over his illness and pending death as was possible. Making decisions about our lives, like what to eat and drink, what we wear and whom we choose to live with, is, for most people, something we take for granted and see as a fundamental human right. Nuland (1993) stated that 'The greatest dignity to be found in death is the dignity in the life that preceded it'; therefore, dignity is fundamental in the maintenance of well-being in people who are approaching the end of life.

Over many months, Alan had formed a relationship with the community nursing team as they had been visiting to flush his Hickman line between chemotherapy. A personalised care plan was written that was centred on Alan's needs and concerns and this was shared, with Alan's consent, with every professional involved in his care. As Alan's health eventually deteriorated, his religious and spiritual needs were included in his plan of care. Promoting autonomy of Alan's wishes and values was central to his care delivery and treatment, and respecting his religious needs was essential to maintain his dignity. It is equally important that families and carers feel emotionally supported during end-of-life care delivery. They need confidence to believe that symptoms can be controlled and the dignity of the patient maintained with support from the professionals to help them cope with an acute time of difficulty in their lives.

DIGNITY AND LONG-TERM CONDITIONS

Long-term conditions are described as conditions that currently cannot be cured but can be controlled by medication and other therapies (DH, 2008c). There are approximately 17.5 million people in the UK with a recorded long-term condition and numbers are rising (DH, 2009c). People with a long-term condition want to remain healthy and live independently for as long as possible. Putting people at the heart of their care allows them to make choices about their lives, what is important to them and how they like their care delivered. This can be applied by using a personalised care planning approach to fit in with people's needs, and improvement to the provision of information about long-term conditions to help people manage their own conditions (DH, 2009a). The NHS *Next Stage Review* (DH, 2008d) also suggests that care planning will help to ensure that people with more complex and long-term care needs receive the best, most appropriately tailored package of care to meet their individual needs and requirements. Multidisciplinary team working of nurses, intermediate care and rehabilitation services can support people with long-term conditions to achieve the optimum level of independence for their long-term future.

Box 11.3 provides an example of a man (Tom) living with a long-term condition. As you read the case study, consider the impact of a long-term condition on Tom's dignity, how concurrent social and psychological factors further affect his dignity, and the role of the community team in promoting his dignity. A discussion of Tom's care then follows.

BOX 11.3 *Case study: living with a long-term condition*

Tom lived with his mother who died when he was 56 years of age. He was diagnosed with type 2 diabetes 20 years previously and, due to this condition, was registered blind. Tom has a mild learning disability which means he needs supervision with all his activities of living, including the drawing up and administration of his daily insulin. With DN visits and regular daily visits by carers, Tom managed to remain at home for the next two years. Tom then developed ulcers on both feet, and despite being admitted into a nursing home for care, his skin deteriorated rapidly and a few months later resulted in him having both legs amputated below the knee.

Tom was eventually transferred back to the nursing home but he felt lonely and isolated and he was anxious to return to his own home environment. After several months of rehabilitation, Tom was offered a ground floor apartment in a warden-controlled complex, which he accepted. Tom is totally dependent on others to help him and continues to have daily visits from the DNs to give him his insulin and assess his general health. Agency carers visit every morning to apply Tom's artificial legs, support him with his hygiene needs and prepare his breakfast. Transport collects him every morning to take him to a day centre where he is cared for in a social environment and provided with a hot meal. Carers then visit Tom at his apartment at tea time to prepare his supper, and then again in the early evening to help him prepare for bed. The DNs work closely with the diabetes specialist nurse and GP to monitor Tom's diabetes.

Discussion

As you read, chronic illness and failing health have had an immense impact on Tom's life. He did not want to move out of his home into the nursing home and into unfamiliar surroundings. Being blind made him disorientated and anxious in his new environment. Since Tom has moved into his new flat, he is highly dependent on others for all his needs, and his dignity can very easily be seriously compromised. The timing of visits between carers is crucial for Tom's care planning. If the care agency staff arrive late in the morning Tom gets very upset as he feels 'trapped in his bed' and worries that he won't be ready to go on the transport to the day centre. He says that he cannot make decisions on a day-to-day basis as he is totally dependent on rotas and visits of carers. Tom's feelings of anxiety, helplessness and uncertainty often accompany the reality of total reliance on others. People generally want as much control as possible over their lives. When one is so dependent on others for care, control is easily lost and social isolation and depression are a reality for many people with long-term health conditions. Asking Tom what clothes he would like to wear and what he would like to eat promotes ownership and control that otherwise could easily be compromised. Maintaining privacy and respect are essential aspects of delivering personal care, and matters of personal appearance and hygiene are paramount in preserving dignity.

Tom is confined to bed until the carer attaches his artificial legs, when he can then transfer safely to use the commode. Dignity can be difficult for people who need to use a commode or bedpan (British Geriatrics Society, 2006), and loss of autonomy may result in loss of respect and dignity. In order to maintain dignity, it is suggested by Sturdy (2007, p.9) that healthcare professionals need to 'protect those who are exposed to the alien and often frightening environment of care services'. The DNs who visit Tom are aware that he often needs reassurance and encouragement to boost his confidence with his package of care. Good support is about understanding the needs of the patient, and this can be achieved by working in partnership with them and really listening to their concerns rather than making assumptions about what they want. Communicating effectively with Tom meant that the DN was able to assess his needs and listen to his worries. Finding out details on Tom's daily lifestyle, including what Tom can do for himself and what he cannot manage, built up an overall picture of Tom's life.

Living independently relies on the ability of individuals to carry out a range of personal activities, which can be difficult if there are specific medical conditions. Degeling *et al* (2006) argued that care models must acknowledge the rights and responsibilities of people with long-term conditions to be informed, consulted and included in decision making with their providers of care to determine what they can expect from others and what others can expect from them. Achieving a successful care plan depends on effective communication between all agencies; therefore, the DN liaises regularly with the care agency manager to ensure that Tom's visits are timely. This means that his dignity is not compromised by late visits and stops Tom worrying that he will not be ready for transport every morning, which gives him confidence and reassurance about the coordination of his care plan.

CONCLUSION

As discussed in Chapter 2, dignity can be difficult to define but people know when they have not been treated with respect and dignity. Nurses have a key role in robust care planning for patients in the community environment, whether in a GP surgery, clinic, residential home or the person's own home. Personalising services and listening to what patients really want put them on an equal footing with the professional and allow them control over their lives. All people have histories and lives behind them and hopefully a future too. Shorter futures for older people or people who are near the end of their lives make the time more significant. Working in partnership improves the quality of the patient pathway through joint and effective care planning. Close working with the multidisciplinary team to deliver the care plan helps people maintain optimum functioning, health, well-being, dignity and quality of life. The DH (2009c, p.4) identified that personalised care planning recognises:

> an individual's full range of needs, taking into account their health, personal, family, social, economic, educational, mental health, ethnic and cultural background and circumstances.

People from varying backgrounds may find themselves requiring care in the community setting; therefore, it is imperative that their specific needs are acknowledged. These include the person's ethnic and cultural needs as well as spiritual needs, which are particularly important when delivering end-of-life care. Putting people at the heart of their care allows them to make choices about their lives and express what is important to them. The maintenance of patients' dignity within the community setting is essential to enable the person to feel empowered at a vulnerable time and retain a feeling of control about their care. We all have a duty to deliver dignified care. If dignity is absent then it is very hard to imagine how what is delivered can ever be considered as 'care'.

REFERENCES

British Geriatrics Society (2006) *Dignity Behind Closed Doors.* www.bgs.org.uk/campaigns/dignity.htm (accessed 12 October 2010).

Charles H (1995) The impact of leg ulcers on patients' quality of life. *Professional Nurse* 10: 571–3.

Darzi A (2009) *Foreword: Transforming Community Services Clinical Guides: ambition, action, achievement.* London: Department of Health, pp.4–5. www.dh.gov.uk/prod_consum_dh/groups/dh_digitalassets/documents/digitalasset/dh_102200.pdf (accessed 12 October 2010).

Degeling P, Close H, Degeling D (2006) *Re-thinking Long Term Conditions. A report on the development and implementation of co-produced, year-based integrated care pathways to improve service provision to people with long term conditions.* Durham: The Centre for Clinical Management Development, Durham University.

Department of Health (2006) *Our Health, Our Care, Our Say: a new direction for community services.* London: Department of Health.

Department of Health (2008a) *High Quality Care for All: NHS next stage review final report*. London: Department of Health.

Department of Health (2008b) *End of Life Strategy: promoting high quality care for all adults at the end of life*. London: Department of Health.

Department of Health (2008c) *Raising the Profile of Long Term Conditions: a compendium of information*. London: Department of Health.

Department of Health (2008d) *NHS Next Stage Review: a vision for primary and community care*. London: Department of Health.

Department of Health (2009a) *Transforming Community Services and World Class Commissioning: resource pack for commissioners of community services*. London: Department of Health.

Department of Health (2009b) *Transforming Community Services: transformational guides*. www.dh.gov.uk/tcs (accessed 12 October 2010).

Department of Health (2009c) *Supporting People with Long Term Conditions: commissioning personalised care planning*. London: Department of Health.

Department of Health (2010) *Equity and Excellence: Liberating the NHS*. London: The Stationery Office.

Douglas V (2001) Living with a chronic leg ulcer: an insight into patients' experiences and feelings. *Journal of Wound Care* 9: 355–60.

Help The Aged (2007) *The Challenge of Dignity in Care – Upholding the Rights of the Individual*. London: Help the Aged.

Macleod R (2003) Setting the context: what do we mean by psycho-social care in palliative care? In: Lloyd-Williams M (ed) *Psychosocial Issues in Palliative Care* (2e). Oxford: Oxford University Press, pp.1–21.

Nuland SB (1993) *How We Die*. London: Chatto and Windus.

Nursing and Midwifery Council (2008) *Confidentiality*. London: Nursing and Midwifery Council. www.nmc-uk.org/Nurses-and-midwives/Advice-by-topic/A/Advice/Confidentiality/ (accessed 12 October 2010).

Persoon A, Heinen M, Van Der Vleuten C et al (2004) Leg ulcers: a review of their impact on daily life. *Journal of Clinical Nursing* 13: 341–54.

Posnett J, Franks P (2007) The costs of skin breakdown and ulceration in the UK. In: Smith and Nephew Foundation. *Skin Breakdown – The Silent Epidemic*. UK: SNFoundation.

Royal College of Nursing (2008) *Defending Dignity – Challenges and Opportunities for Nursing*. London: Royal College of Nursing.

Sturdy D (2007) Indignity in care: are you responsible? *Nursing Older People* 19(9): 9.

Walshe C (1995) Living with a venous leg ulcer: a descriptive study of patients' experiences. *Journal of Advanced Nursing* 22: 1092–100.

Webster C, Bryan K (2009) Older people's views on dignity and how it can be promoted in a hospital environment. *Journal of Clinical Nursing* 18: 1784–92.

CHAPTER 12

Dignity in acute and critical care

Lesley Baillie

INTRODUCTION

Patients are admitted for acute and critical care due to a wide range of health problems, including planned surgery, emergencies such as trauma, or acute problems associated with long-term health conditions. These admissions are often accompanied by anxiety, fear, loss of control and dependency. Patients in acute and critical care settings are also particularly vulnerable to diminished dignity due to the health conditions that led to their hospital admission, the associated procedures and care activities, and the nature of the care environment. Even someone who is usually fit and well and is admitted for planned surgery can be vulnerable to diminished dignity due to loss of control and temporary dependence. Patients who are admitted as emergencies face additional uncertainties and even less control over their situation. A relative in Douglas-Dunbar and Gardiner's (2007) study highlighted that going into hospital 'is one of the most vulnerable times of your life' (p.29).

Thus although staff working in these areas are often under immense pressure, they still need to deliver care with dignity. This chapter focuses on the dignity of adults undergoing acute and critical care and highlights the care activities, treatments, procedures and processes in these settings that may undermine dignity. The chapter will specifically consider how dignity can be promoted in accident and emergency (A&E) departments, intensive therapy units (ITUs), and during perioperative care.

LEARNING OUTCOMES

By the end of the chapter you will be able to:
➤ analyse the challenges to dignity in acute and critical care settings, including the vulnerability of patients and care environment issues
➤ explain how dignity can be promoted for patients undergoing acute and critical care in accident and emergency departments, intensive therapy units, and during perioperative care.

CHALLENGES TO DIGNITY IN ACUTE AND CRITICAL CARE SETTINGS

Changes in health and social care provision have led to the inpatient population being increasingly frail and with complex needs (Bridges *et al*, 2010) and thus many people who are admitted for acute and critical care are already vulnerable. Two-thirds of hospital beds in the UK are occupied by people aged over 65 years (Department of Health [DH], 2001) and one study found that 18% of patients attending A&E departments were older people (Downing and Wilson, 2005), many of whom may have complex and multiple needs, including cognitive impairment. The population of people with learning disabilities is increasing and living into older age, and they are very likely to need emergency care due to a high risk of acute health problems (Brown, 2005). Mencap's (2007) report detailed several acute hospital admissions of people with learning disabilities and highlighted many affronts to their dignity (*see* Chapter 14 for a detailed exploration of dignity for people with learning disabilities).

Patients admitted to acute hospitals follow a pathway through departments and wards, encountering numerous different staff and procedures along the way. Individual staff members therefore rarely see the patient's whole acute care experience, but in Box 12.1 I have related my mother's journey through acute and critical care. As you read this, reflect on the factors that might have affected her dignity, in relation to her health condition, the procedures she experienced, and the care environment factors.

Box 12.1 illustrates how a usually independent woman in control of her own life and health developed an acute illness leading to her emergency admission and rapidly increasing helplessness. On the orthopaedic ward she could do very little independently as she could not move, eat or carry out personal care without help. Many patients find it undignified to have to be assisted with personal care, and at one point my mother said to me: 'I have lost all my dignity now – there's none left'. Unusually for the UK, and because of her infection, she had the privacy of being in a side room; many other patients in acute care settings are cared for in multi-bed areas with privacy provided by curtains. In theatre and ITU, my mother was totally dependent on the healthcare team and technology to support her bodily functions. She was physically examined by various doctors, requiring bodily exposure, and she had necessary but invasive procedures including urinary catheterisation and intravenous cannulation. Box 12.1 highlights the vulnerability of patients admitted to acute and critical care. You will be able to relate this to many other patients who follow similar paths through acute and critical care services.

As well as caring for an increasingly vulnerable population of patients, staff in critical care settings deal with a rapid throughput of patients which includes transfer and admission at short notice and little time in which to build relationships. In my doctoral research based on a surgical ward (Baillie, 2007), several patients commented on the staff's excessive workload and most perceived

BOX 12.1 *An acute admission to hospital*

My mother was 72 years old, lived in her own house with her older
husband and was usually independent. One Sunday evening, she
was taken to the A&E department by ambulance on a stretcher after
a home visit by her general practitioner. My mother had developed
a severely swollen and painful knee and her doctor suspected an
abscess. In A&E she was transferred onto a trolley. Her vital signs
were recorded and oxygen administered as her oxygen saturation was
low. She was examined by an orthopaedic doctor, blood samples
were taken, she had an intravenous cannula inserted, intravenous
fluids were started and she had an X-ray of her leg. She was admitted
into a side room (due to her suspected infection) on an orthopaedic
ward. Her leg remained painful and she had difficulty in moving.
She was unable to pass urine and so a urethral catheter was inserted.
The following day she was prepared for theatre and her abscess was
drained under general anaesthetic. Over the next few days, despite
intravenous antibiotics, her condition deteriorated. Following blood
cultures, she was diagnosed with septicaemia. She became increasingly
breathless and she could eat only very small amounts, which were
given to her on a spoon. She had a bedbath each day and used a
bedpan to empty her bowels. She was examined by the orthopaedic
and medical teams regularly. On her 7th day of admission she
returned to theatre for a further drainage of abscess, after which she
developed respiratory failure in recovery. She remained in recovery for
several hours while an ITU bed was made available so she could be
ventilated. On the 4th day in ITU her active treatment was stopped as
she was now in multi-organ failure. Her sedation was increased and
she died, with us, her family, by her bedside.

(source: Lesley Baillie)

a resulting adverse effect on their dignity, mainly because staff could appear
brusque or off-hand. For example, one patient in this study commented that
due to workload, staff did not introduce themselves, as 'They haven't time to
keep stopping to talk to people' (p.147). Another patient, who had had major
surgery, expressed that the hospital's busy routine and associated paperwork
took priority over what he termed the 'care aspect', which he associated with
dignity:

Because it's a busy hospital – you've got such a busy routine that's perpetually changing – there's so much emphasis on them doing their work and they will do that and the patient just happens to be there. Their work goes before the patient . . . they're so busy doing what they're doing, filling in their forms, doing every-thing in the way they have to do it. The care aspect – it's quite difficult to know whether the care aspect is really really there (Baillie, 2007, p.148).

Another patient considered that the high workload led to a lack of individual-ity, illustrating her view by explaining that when she arrived at theatre she had to wait outside on a stretcher for a long time as the anaesthetist was double booked:

It just makes you aware that you are patient number nine hundred and fifty-nine and you don't matter. You're in a meat market. And you're on a conveyor belt (Baillie, 2007, p.147).

Nursing staff, too, recognised the impact that busyness had on dignity; one senior nurse said:

I suppose if staff appear very busy then that can impact upon dignity . . . that's almost unavoidable as well. If people are busy then they are busy and we both know how difficult it is when you've got a bay with six beds in and you've got somebody dying in that bay and you've got somebody else who's getting better and going home and you're trying to deal with different people going through different experiences (Baillie, 2007, p.148).

Nevertheless, I observed some staff who were working under immense pres-sure on the ward and yet still promoted patients' dignity. Staff who work in acute and critical care settings need skills to rapidly build rapport with patients and relatives despite the busy workload. As Bridges *et al* (2010) highlighted, for older people undergoing acute care, relationships with staff have a crucial impact on their care experience. Furthermore, Douglas-Dunbar and Gardiner (2007) asserted the importance of hospital staff developing a therapeutic rela-tionship with the carer as well as the person with dementia.

Acute and critical care settings generally use a lot of technical equipment, which may impact on caring (Randle, 2001; Picker Institute, 2008). In Douglas-Dunbar and Gardiner's (2007) study of relatives of people with dementia admitted to hos-pital, one carer expressed that while the technology used may be life saving, 'the treatment of the person as an individual has somehow been lost' (p.29).

However, in Alliex and Irurita's (2004) study, nurses described making addi-tional efforts to meet patients' humanistic needs in the presence of technology, which they referred to as 'maximising', and which consisted of:

➤ *maintaining presence*: offering help, popping in, giving time. For example, A&E staff can pop in to cubicles and check whether patients need anything
➤ *minimising the impact of technology*: staff can use social interaction, including humour if appropriate, and understate the technology used rather than focusing on it
➤ *individualising interactions*: considering patients' likes, doing little things (for example, making a telephone call for a patient), portraying a caring demeanour and kindness.

In essence, technology should not pose a barrier to dignified care, as long as staff continue to focus on the patient as a human being rather than on the technology alone. In my own experience as a relative (Box 12.1), most ITU staff did convey compassion alongside efficient use of technology in my mother's care.

Overall, patient frailty and vulnerability, invasive treatments and care, rapid patient throughput and technology are all challenges to dignity in acute and critical care. Nevertheless, there is much that staff in these settings can do to promote the dignity of patients. Earlier chapters of this book considered in detail how the care environment (Chapter 5) and staff behaviour (Chapter 6) can promote dignity in care. These principles can all be applied to acute and critical care settings. The next sections of this chapter consider some specific aspects of how healthcare professionals can promote dignity in A&E departments, during perioperative care and in ITU settings.

PROMOTING DIGNITY IN ACCIDENT AND EMERGENCY DEPARTMENTS

The Healthcare Commission (HCC) (2008) reported that during 2007/2008, there were 19.1 million attendances at A&E departments and urgent care centres in England and most patients were positive about their experiences. However, the HCC (2008) expressed concern that the needs of patients with complex or particular individual needs (such as vulnerable adults, people with disabilities) were not always met and patients were not always treated with dignity and respect. The HCC (2008) pointed out that when patients have negative experiences in A&E, particularly if they feel they have not been treated with dignity, they will feel upset and anxious about using services in the future. Reflective activity 12.1 includes some reflective questions about dignity in A&E.

Byrne (1997) found that A&E nurses viewed their role as one that was predominantly concerned with providing urgent physical care. While they acknowledged that many people attending A&E would be anxious, one nurse expressed that when A&E is busy 'the "patient as a person" thing gets forgotten' (p.97). However, just treating patients' physical conditions, without treating them as human beings, can lead to a negative experience of the A&E department. Look at your answers to the reflective questions: did you feel you were treated as a

> **Reflective activity 12.1** Reflecting on A&E experiences
>
> You will almost certainly have attended A&E at some stage as a patient or relative. Reflect on the following:
> ➤ how did you feel when you first arrived in A&E?
> ➤ what were your *first* impressions of the staff you met and the A&E environment? How did these affect the rest of your A&E visit?
> ➤ how did the A&E environment affect your dignity?
> ➤ how did the way staff behaved towards you affect your dignity?

human being in A&E? An A&E visit is a significant event for many people, as it occurs suddenly, is often accompanied by pain, fear, stress and anxiety, and patients have had no opportunity to prepare physically, socially or psychologically (Baillie, 2005). Ford *et al* (2008) pointed out that emergency care settings are often the 'front doors' through which many patients start their healthcare journeys, so it is very important that dignity begins there. At the 2007 Royal College of Nursing (RCN) Emergency Care Association annual conference, the Patients Association gave examples of staff behaviour that diminished dignity in emergency departments (Ford *et al*, 2008). As a result, the two organisations jointly developed a set of nine 'dignity principles' that patients accessing emergency care should expect (*see* Box 12.2). Adhering to the principles in Box 12.2 should help to ensure that patients feel comfortable, in control and valued, which is important for patients to feel that their dignity is promoted (Baillie, 2009). Here we will consider patients' A&E experiences in more detail and include further details about promoting dignity in this environment.

In the UK, there is currently a four-hour target for A&E departments: patients should have been assessed, treated and either discharged or admitted within four hours. The Healthcare Commission (2008) reported that 97.9% of patients in A&E departments and urgent care centres were dealt with within four hours. While a speedy journey through A&E is generally in patients' best interests, staff have a tight time frame during which they must help patients feel that they have been treated as individuals and cared for as human beings. Therefore, A&E staff need to be able to develop a rapport with patients rapidly, and furthermore:

> Nurses should aim to be kind and courteous and even in the hectic pace of an A&E department it should be possible to accompany physical care with pleasantries and friendliness which helps people feel that they matter (reprinted from Baillie, 2005, p.13, with permission from Elsevier).

BOX 12.2 *The nine emergency care dignity principles: what patients can expect*

1. The reception staff will be welcoming, courteous and helpful.
2. You will be given a rough estimate of how long you should expect to wait before being seen by a healthcare professional.
3. All healthcare professionals dealing directly with you will formally introduce themselves and their role.
4. All staff will ask you how you would like to be addressed, either formally, by using your title and surname, or more informally, by using your first or other preferred name.
5. You will be looked after in a clean and safe environment. All staff will wash or cleanse their hands regularly and before each patient contact.
6. You will be asked for your informed consent before any procedure is initiated.
7. You will be kept up to date with information about your treatment plan. Any information obtained will be recorded and remain strictly confidential. We may, however, need to share some information with other health and social care professionals. Please feel free to ask about this in more detail.
8. You will be treated with respect and dignity at all times.
9. Staff will do their best to respect and address any religious or cultural needs if you make them aware.

(RCN, 2008; used with kind permission from the Royal College of Nursing)

This statement is applicable to all staff dealing with A&E patients, such as radiographers and medical staff, as well as nurses. When meeting patients for the first time in an acute care situation, staff should adopt a non-judgmental approach, avoid stereotyping and portray an appropriate level of understanding and compassion for the person's situation (Bowman and Thompson, 1998). In A&E, this must be portrayed during an initial brief encounter where there is, correctly, a focus on identifying urgent needs.

Patients attend A&E departments for all sorts of reasons. Initially they are triaged and from there they are referred to the appropriate area of the department, which might be the minor injuries area, major area or resuscitation area. In the minor injuries area, staff should be courteous, keep patients informed and protect privacy during treatment. Patients treated in the minor injuries area may be upset due to the cause of injury (for example, dog bite, assault), anxious and in some discomfort. They may be concerned about the effect on their body image (for example, with facial injuries) or on their employment (for example, a self-employed carpenter with a hand injury). The approach of staff has a strong influence on the dignity of patients in these situations.

In the major area of A&E, the patient care pathway usually involves initial assessment and undressing for examination, followed by further investigations and treatment. Staff can do much to promote dignity through introducing themselves to patients and their relatives, addressing patients politely and by the name they prefer, explaining what will happen, keeping patients and their relatives informed, and ensuring that they have call bells, which gives some control. Relatives or friends who are accompanying patients should remain with them as much as possible, as long as this is the patient's wish. Douglas-Dunbar and Gardiner (2007) highlighted how vulnerable older carers can feel when their relative with dementia is admitted to hospital; they reported feeling ignored and not kept informed. While most patients will need to undress so that they can be properly examined and no important problem is missed, staff should approach this sensitively. They should explain why it is necessary to undress, and gain consent to proceed, leave underwear on unless there is a reason to remove it (for example, soiling), provide a gown to wear and linen to cover the patient, and put clothing carefully into a labelled bag. Staff should ensure that the patient knows where their belongings are and that they are safe, and put any soiled clothing into a separate bag. If it is not necessary to keep the patient nil by mouth, then staff should offer a drink. They should explain to patients who must remain nil by mouth (for example, swallowing problem, likelihood of emergency surgery) why they cannot have a drink, and offer mouthwashes for comfort.

Privacy should always be given during examinations and this is of paramount concern for intimate examinations (for example, vaginal or rectal). The RCN (2006) *Guidelines for Vaginal and Pelvic Examinations* advise the use of a warm private room with a lock on the door, that couches and trolleys should face away from the door, and that there should be toilets and bathrooms near the examination rooms. For women having miscarriages in the emergency department, Bryant (2008) suggested that all equipment needed should be available so staff do not have to leave the room during procedures, and that hygiene packs should be available containing pants, pads, wipes and disposal bags. Prior to examinations, staff should explicitly ask for consent to examine, and recheck consent during the procedure as necessary. A chaperone will be required during intimate examinations; chaperones should introduce themselves and stay where the patient can see them. If the examination is uncomfortable or distressing, the chaperone should offer a hand to hold and express concern and reassurance. Certain procedures need a team of staff; for example, a patient with a suspected cervical spine injury will need four staff to log-roll while the patient is examined, which will include checking for sensation down to the base of the spine. Dignity can be promoted by introductions, explanations and minimising exposure. Some A&E patients will be embarrassed by their appearance; they may have been incontinent, or not have bathed today or put on clean clothes. For some patients, having to have an intimate examination, use a bedpan or give a urine sample will be the first time they have experienced this in their lives. Therefore, staff dealing with A&E patients should be sensitive, reassuring and aware of cultural and religious needs too.

Patients treated in the resuscitation area of an emergency department are those who are most acutely unwell or unstable, for example, those with cardiac chest pain or major trauma. The priority is to assess them rapidly, and carry out urgent investigations and treatments. The team may have to quickly remove clothing, possibly by cutting, in order to examine and treat the patient. Staff should approach these urgent activities in a way that promotes dignity; it is still possible to give explanations and gain consent, keep patients' bodies covered most of the time and address patients' concerns. Resuscitation attempts can appear very undignified indeed, as cardiac compressions, airway management and defibrillation are all rapidly delivered. It is very important that, following the initial urgent activity, any dignity loss is quickly restored. When relatives are brought in to see patients following an unsuccessful resuscitation attempt, the patient's appearance may remain with them forever. It is paramount to spend some time tidying up the patient and the near environment, removing used equipment, washing away any blood, closing eyes and putting in dentures, wiping away blood, vomit, etc. from the face, putting a clean gown on the

---

BOX 12.3 *A relative's experience*

When we were taken to his bed we were not prepared for the horrific sight of seeing him, eyes wide open with a resuscitation tube down his throat. This image has traumatised not only us but also my sister and brother in law for the rest of our lives! When my daughter asked if the tube could be removed the nurse informed us that it had to stay for legal reasons. We should have been warned beforehand so that we could have made an informed choice of whether to see him or not. This haunting image of a proud man who looked as if he had starved to death will stay with us forever!

(Patients Association, 2009, pp.34–5, reprinted with permission from The Patients Association)

patient, spigoting any tubes attached, covering the patient with a blanket and putting a clean pillow under the patient's head. Airway equipment inserted during the resuscitation attempt may have to be left in for post mortem, as per hospital guidelines. It is important to explain to relatives, and significant others who wish to see the patient, exactly what to expect prior to visiting, thus enabling them to make an informed choice. Box 12.3 includes a relative's account which illustrates the consequences of a lack of preparation. A&E staff should aim to portray to relatives that the patient who has died suddenly has been treated with dignity and care, with recognition for the important human being that they are. Relatives should be treated with dignity; nursing and medical staff should display kindness and compassion and provide information in a non-hurried manner and give time for questions.

PROMOTING THE DIGNITY OF PATIENTS DURING PERIOPERATIVE CARE

Perioperative care has many potential effects on dignity; we will consider pre-operative care, dignity in the operating theatre, and immediate postoperative care.

Preoperative care

There are a number of ways in which preparation for theatre can impact on dignity; for example, Goldberg et al (2009) highlighted that marking surgical sites on patients' bodies, particularly in more intimate areas, can undermine dignity. Matiti and Sharman (1999) identified how traditional practice in preoperative care can threaten dignity as patients may be asked to remove their clothes, jewellery, cosmetics and dentures, all of which can be part of their identity. However, jewellery only really needs to be removed if it will interfere with the operation site, and jewellery that may come into contact with diathermy equipment can be covered with tape. Matiti and Sharman (1999) highlighted patients' discomfort about removing their dentures, for example: 'I was very, very embarrassed, as I cannot take my dentures out, even in front of my family'. However, securely fitted dentures do not actually need removing prior to surgery. Dentures that do need removal can be taken out in the anaesthetic room, put into a labelled pot and replaced as soon as the patient wakes up in recovery. Patients can be encouraged to wear disposable underwear to theatre. Hair removal can diminish dignity, especially hair on the head. Shaving can be avoided as much as possible; if skin is prepared with appropriate solution, procedures can often be carried out with no or minimal hair shaving.

Operation gowns have been found to threaten dignity as they can expose patients (Walsh and Kowanko, 2002; Woogara, 2005; Baillie, 2009). Therefore, ward staff should not ask patients to change into gowns earlier than necessary and patients who walk to theatre in gowns must have dressing gowns to wear. On arrival in theatre, patients enter the anaesthetic room. Here, staff should greet the patient and introduce themselves and explain what is going to happen. They should ask the patient how they would like to be addressed and record this so that the recovery room staff can use the patient's preferred name when waking them. While preparing to administer the anaesthetic, staff should be pleasant and conversational and not talk over the patient. The aim is for the patient to feel cared about and safe in the hands of the operating department staff.

Care during theatre

Marshall (1994) highlighted that anaesthetised patients entrust the theatre team with maintaining their dignity and safety. However, Chapter 8, Box 8.1 provides an example of a mother who, following caesarean section, was left exposed and ignored. She described her shame and embarrassment at being left exposed like 'a slab of meat'. Operating department staff should attend to privacy of the patient by avoiding any unnecessary exposure and not having extra observers present unless the patient gave permission. Some patients will be awake or sedated during the procedure (rather than unconscious) as they have local or epidural anaesthesia. Communication with these patients is absolutely crucial: politeness and courtesy, explanations and keeping patients informed along with a kind and caring approach.

Patients are often acutely aware that intimate areas of their bodies will be exposed and invaded in theatre. For example, a patient expressed embarrassment about having bladder surgery, saying:

> I mean in my case, I had an operation on the bladder so obviously the thought of what they were going to do to me was a feeling of – oh – how awful, you know (Baillie, 2007, p.166).

Her embarrassment led to her opting for a general anaesthetic, as undergoing surgery while she was awake during epidural anaesthesia would have been too 'humiliating' to contemplate.

Many other patients will have such procedures carried out while they are awake and operating staff should be sensitive and discreet and attend to privacy. Theatre staff should also ensure that they clean the patient thoroughly when surgery is completed, before transfer to recovery, so that they are not covered by dried blood or other body fluids and solutions.

Immediate postoperative care

Immediately postoperatively, in the recovery room and following transfer to the ward or unit, patients are in a very vulnerable situation. There is potential for them to be in pain or to vomit, though this should generally be controlled with medication. They are unable to move or do anything for themselves. In addition, they may be cared for in a multi-patient area with only curtains for privacy. Staff should ensure that patients' comfort, safety and dignity are promoted. They should ensure dentures are replaced (if applicable) and that, despite the many bodily attachments (drains, catheter, infusions) that may be present, patients' bodily privacy is maintained. Staff should address the patient by their preferred name while awakening them, give explanations and gently find out the cause of any apparent distress.

PROMOTING THE DIGNITY OF PATIENTS IN INTENSIVE THERAPY UNITS

Patients admitted to ITU are critically ill and totally dependent on the staff caring for them. While some patients are unconscious, others will be awake as they are being weaned from mechanical ventilation but they will be physically too weak to self-care. Holland et al (1997) interviewed patients about their recollections of their ITU stay; they stated that it was easier to cope with the stress of ITU if nurses treated them with respect and dignity. Several other studies have investigated perspectives of dignity for ITU patients. In the study of Plakas et al (2009), based in Greece, relatives of ITU patients considered that dignity related to cleanliness of the patient's body and respectful care of the patient, including relief of pain and suffering. Pokorny (1989) interviewed patients who had been in ITU for at least 24 hours following cardiovascular bypass surgery about their perceptions of their dignity while they were in ITU. The patients identified privacy, control, independence, competence and caring as attributes of dignity. Arguably, ITU patients and their relatives should be able to count on staff to be competent and caring, but control and independence could be more elusive. However, staff could consider how these attributes might apply, for example, by including and involving patients' relatives. Finding out from relatives about the patient, their likes and dislikes and how they like to be addressed can help staff to approach the patient as an individual. Engström and Söderberg (2004) found that partners of critically ill spouses felt secure when they were kept informed. They also considered it important that staff showed respect for the critically ill person and acted as if they were conscious and could hear everything. One patient's partner said that the nurses were good 'acting as if my husband was conscious' but that one of the doctors 'was the only one who didn't' (p.302). She said that he had stood smiling, making a long speech, which she thought was 'terrible'.

Challenges to the privacy of patients in ITU relate to both the care environment and the nature of patients' conditions. In ITU, patients are likely to be cared for in bays with screens used for privacy, and they have multiple attachments to their bodies, for treatment and monitoring purposes. Thus, Turnock and Kelleher (2001) asserted that it is common practice in ITU for patients to be nursed naked (though covered with linen), for the convenience of clinical procedures such as patient observation or integrity of invasive equipment. They further suggested that minimising exposure of genitalia can be problematic due to the invasive equipment attached and that the clinical team require great skills to prevent patient exposure. Other factors highlighted were reduced patient consciousness, and the need to perform many tasks rapidly to avoid compromising a physiologically unstable patient. Turnock and Kelleher (2001) found that most exposure occurred during clinical procedures, in particular, technical procedures and repositioning. Some staff demonstrated a lack of awareness for unconscious patients' dignity by saying, of the impact of bodily exposure on patients and their relatives: 'If the patients can't be asked, they can't get stressed by it'. However, one nurse acknowledged the impact on relatives and another nurse recognised that failing to cover patients up could lead to dehumanisation. Turnock and Kelleher (2001) identified that exposure could be reduced by staff being more vigilant about clothing and screening patients, thoroughly preparing the bed area and removing unnecessary equipment, encouraging staff to ask permission before entering bed curtains, and assessing patients' privacy and dignity needs by involving relatives. Thus, although it may be more challenging to promote privacy in ITU, it is still possible, with care and thoughtfulness.

A certain number of patients in ITU, like my mother (*see* Box 12.1), will deteriorate and die. Chapter 10 explores dignity at the end of life in detail, and much of this discussion is relevant in ITU as well. However, in ITU, dying has added complexity; the major focus is on reviving and saving so once the care focus changes to de-escalation of treatment and allowing the dying process, some staff may view the situation as failure. Nevertheless, critical care nurses have expressed that facilitating dying with dignity is important in end-of-life-care (Kirchhoff *et al*, 2000; Beckstrand *et al*, 2006; Plakas *et al*, 2009). Beckstrand *et al* (2006) suggested that facilitators to providing a good death include encouraging family members to stay with the patient, providing facilities for the family, soothing music, quiet places for prayer and meditation and family gatherings. However, not all ITUs will have ideal facilities for relatives, and privacy for the patient and family can be difficult as many patients will be in a screened bay, outside which the busy unit's work continues. ITU staff can, nevertheless, do much to promote dignity through their communication with patients and their relatives and attending to comfort and fundamental care.

CONCLUSION

In acute and critical care settings, patients are particularly vulnerable to a loss of dignity due to their health status and the treatments needed. The care environment can be depersonalising and unwelcoming to patients and their relatives. Staff working in these settings are often under considerable pressure and are dealing with groups of acutely unwell patients, in sometimes less than ideal environments. However, as dignity is very important to acute and critical care patients, staff must attend to privacy, ensure treatments and care are performed competently and confidently to a high standard, and that they communicate with patients and their relatives in a way that helps them to feel comfortable, in control and valued. The care environment plays an important role in supporting staff to promote dignity and should have the facilities to enable privacy and high-quality care. Acutely unwell patients who feel that their dignity is preserved by staff caring for them can concentrate on their recovery and feel confident in those they are dependent on.

ACKNOWLEDGEMENTS

I would like to thank Jessica Baillie, Lorraine Ilott, Sue Maddex and Ibraheim Almakari for their comments and suggestions during the preparation of this chapter.

REFERENCES

Alliex S, Irurita VF (2004) Caring in a technological environment: how is this possible? *Contemporary Nurse* 17(1–2): 32–43.

Baillie L (2005) An exploration of nurse-patient relationships in Accident and Emergency. *Accident and Emergency Nursing* 13(1): 9–14.

Baillie L (2007) *Patient Dignity in an Acute Hospital Setting* Unpublished thesis. London: South Bank University.

Baillie L (2009) Patient dignity in an acute hospital setting: a case study. *International Journal of Nursing Studies* 46: 22–36.

Beckstrand RL, Callister LC, Kirchhoff KT (2006) Providing a 'good death': critical care nurses' suggestions for improving end-of-life care. *American Journal of Critical Care* 15(1): 38–45.

Bowman GS, Thompson DR (1998) Therapeutic nursing in acute care. In: McMahon R, Pearson A (eds) *Nursing as Therapy* (2e). Cheltenham: Stanley Thornes.

Bridges J, Flatley M, Meyer J (2010) Older people's and relatives' experiences in acute care settings: systematic review and synthesis of qualitative studies. *International Journal of Nursing Studies* 47: 89–107.

Brown M (2005) Emergency care for people with learning disabilities: what all nurses and midwives need to know. *Accident and Emergency Nursing* 13: 224–31.

Bryant H (2008) Maintaining patient dignity and offering support after miscarriage. *Emergency Nurse* 15(9): 26–9.

Byrne G (1997) Understanding nurses' communication with patients in accident and emergency departments using a symbolic interactionist perspective. *Journal of Advanced Nursing* 26(1): 93–100.

Department of Health (2001) *The National Service Framework for Older People.* London: Department of Health.

Douglas-Dunbar M, Gardiner P (2007) Support for carers of people with dementia during hospital admissions. *Nursing Older People* **16**(5): 810–18.

Downing A, Wilson R (2005) Older people's use of Accident and Emergency services. *Age and Ageing* **34**: 24–30.

Engström Ä, Söderberg S (2004) The experiences of partners of critically ill persons in an intensive care unit. *Intensive and Critical Care Nursing* **20**: 299–308.

Ford P, Hayward M, Baillie L *et al* (2008) Sticking to our principles. *Emergency Nurse* **16**(4): 4–5.

Goldberg AE, Harnish JL, Stegienko S, Urbach DR (2009) Attitudes of patients and care providers toward a surgical site marking policy. *Surgical Innovation* **16**: 249–57.

Healthcare Commission (2008) *Not Just a Matter of Time: a review of urgent and emergency care services in England.* London: Healthcare Commission.

Holland C, Cason CL, Prater LR (1997) Patients' recollections of critical care. *Dimensions of Critical Care Nursing* **16**(3): 132–41.

Kirchhoff KT, Spuhler V, Walker L *et al* (2000) Intensive care nurses' experiences with end-of-life care. *American Journal of Critical Care* **9**(1): 36–42.

Marshall C (1994) The concept of advocacy. *British Journal of Theatre Nursing* **4**(2): 11–13.

Matiti MR, Sharman J (1999) Dignity: a study of preoperative patients. *Nursing Standard* **14**(13): 32–5.

Mencap (2007) *Death by Indifference.* London: Mencap.

Patients Association (2009) *Patients . . . Not Numbers, People . . . Not Statistics.* London: Patients Association.

Picker Institute (2008) *The Challenge of Assessing Dignity in Care.* London: Help the Aged.

Plakas S, Cant B, Taket A (2009) The experiences of critically ill patients in Greece: a social constructionist grounded theory study. *Intensive and Critical Care Nursing* **25**: 10–20.

Pokorny ME (1989) *The Effect of Nursing Care on Human Dignity in the Critically Ill Adult.* Unpublished PhD thesis. University of Virginia.

Randle J (2001) Past caring? The influence of technology. *Nurse Education Today* **1**: 157–65.

Royal College of Nursing (2006) *Guidelines for Vaginal and Pelvic Examinations.* London: Royal College of Nursing.

Royal College of Nursing (2008) *Dignity A&E poster.* London: Royal College of Nursing.

Turnock C, Kelleher M (2001) Maintaining patient dignity in intensive care settings. *Intensive and Critical Care Nursing* **17**(3): 144–54.

Walsh K, Kowanko I (2002) Nurses' and patients' perceptions of dignity. *International Journal of Nursing Practice* **8**(3): 143–51.

Woogara J (2005) Patients' privacy of the person and human rights. *Nursing Ethics* **12**(3): 273–87.

CHAPTER 13

Dignity in mental health: listening to the flying saint

Gemma Stacey and Theodore Stickley

INTRODUCTION

Research exploring the views of people who use mental health services has found people often feel stripped of dignity in the mental health system, even though the maintenance of dignity is recognised as crucial to recovery from mental health problems. This chapter explores the key areas identified within recent policy and research, which require substantial attention if practitioners are to maintain the dignity of people who use mental health services. We aim to expose the constraints of the current mental health system that contribute to the lack of dignified care reported by service users and carers. The dilemmas which face mental health practitioners will be critically discussed in light of the impact of mental health law and professional ethics surrounding this issue.

We hope that this chapter will enable you to understand the importance of promoting dignified care by relating theoretical concepts and discussions of dignity to practical examples. You will be encouraged to critically reflect upon the influence of public and practitioners' attitudes towards people who use mental health services in all healthcare settings. This will enable you to consider ways in which you can contribute to providing dignified care, and in doing so challenge the stigma and discrimination towards people who use mental health services, which is prevalent not only amongst wider society, but also within healthcare itself.

LEARNING OUTCOMES

By the end of this chapter you will be able to:
➤ discuss the position of dignity in mental healthcare and its relationship with the concept of recovery
➤ critically consider the underlying issues that present barriers to maintaining dignity within mental healthcare
➤ explore the significance of values when promoting dignified mental healthcare

➤ identify the issues within specific mental healthcare settings where provision of dignified care is most at risk

➤ apply these discussions to practice-based scenarios to consider how to promote dignity in practice.

A BRIEF HISTORY OF MENTAL HEALTHCARE

Before we begin to consider dignity in mental healthcare, it is important to give a brief historical background of the development of mental health services in the United Kingdom (UK). This will allow you to see the origins of current approaches to working with people who have been diagnosed with mental health problems and consider how these historical influences impact on the way people are viewed and treated in society today.

Treatment in mental health has had a chequered history. In fact, while medical care might have its origins in ancient Greece, mental healthcare only dates back to the Enlightenment era (the 'Age of Reason'). It was during this period that in Europe, social care became formalised and institutional solutions were offered to people who were considered 'mad'. These people were often referred to as 'lunatics'. Madhouses and lunatic asylums therefore came into existence. Before this development, those considered mad were often left to fend for themselves, and were cared for by families and communities or religious institutions. Around the 1790s, humane methods of treatment were being developed in institutions and this became known as 'moral treatment of the mentally ill'. In the Victorian period, large institutions were built, many of which exist to this day, although virtually all of the people who lived within these settings have long since been discharged into the community.

What became established during this fairly recent era, however, was the recognition that 'madness' or 'lunacy' was in fact a medical condition. This apparent progression in thinking coincided with the rise of the medical profession and it was at this point in history that 'madness' became medicalised. As such, mental illnesses had symptoms; these symptoms could be interpreted by a medical practitioner as symptoms of a recognisable illness. Thus, the illness could be diagnosed and a treatment could be prescribed. While on the one hand this significant development was seen as scientific progress, on the other hand people's social, psychological and emotional experiences came to be regarded as 'illness'. Therefore, people often received treatment inappropriately. Sometimes these treatments were later considered barbaric. For example, people were admitted to asylums for reasons we would now consider extraordinary, such as being pregnant outside wedlock, for having religious experiences, for being homosexual. Treatments included mechanical restraints, straitjackets, muzzles and so on. In the last century, insulin shock therapy was introduced, as well as electroconvulsive therapy, which is still used today.

Thousands of people had parts of their brains removed through a procedure called 'lobotomy'. At the time, these treatments were not generally considered barbaric; rather, they were implemented because they were based upon the best evidence of the day.

In the middle of the last century, more efficient drugs were developed which, some would argue, have effectively restrained people through chemicals rather than through chains and locks. Furthermore, although hospital wards were unlocked from the 1960s onwards, they have quite recently become locked once again in the UK under the era of New Labour (van der Merwe *et al*, 2009). Drug treatments have improved enormously, enabling people to lead seemingly normal lives, although the side-effects of psychotropic medication are themselves devastating for some people.

The effect of both the confinement of the mentally ill and subsequent seemingly punishing treatments was that people with a mental illness diagnosis became deeply stigmatised in society. The asylums became feared and threatening institutions. People who were treated in them became social pariahs. While we may like to think we live in more enlightened times, research evidence suggests that this social stigma is as strong today as it ever was. For a more detailed account of the history of mental health services and its relationship with nursing, please see Nolan (1999).

Complex mental health laws have been developed that enforce treatment for some people diagnosed as mentally ill who are considered to be a danger to themselves or to the public. The implementation of the Mental Health Act (1983), amended by the Mental Health Act 2007, falls upon mental healthcare workers and is fraught with complexity. It is hard to argue against mental health law that seeks to protect individuals and society from harm. However, the issues are not straightforward. Often, people are sectioned under mental health law and detained in hospital because there are no other alternatives. Issues of dignity in mental healthcare therefore may relate to legal issues such as human rights. Later in this chapter we offer two scenarios that illustrate the complexities in maintaining dignity in mental healthcare.

THE POSITION OF DIGNITY IN MENTAL HEALTHCARE

The following section of this chapter identifies the current mental health policy, which supports the need for improvements in the provision of dignified care as part of the recovery and social inclusion agenda. It explores the research evidence which has contributed to this political recognition by considering the issues of service user and carer experiences of using mental health services, public and professional attitudes towards this client group and the impact of stigma and discrimination on maintaining dignity.

The concept of recovery in mental healthcare

Contemporary mental health policy has identified recovery as a priority and it is currently positioned at the heart of its agenda. When related to mental health, the term 'recovery' has a slightly different meaning. It does not necessarily refer to a cure or restoration to the person's previous state of health. This is due to the recognition that people can and do live meaningful and fulfilling lives despite their mental health problems. The recovery movement was originally initiated by people who used mental health services, as many began to reject the labels and limitations that were placed upon them by mental health services and society. People began to tell their story of surviving the mental healthcare system and regaining a sense of self following many years of being exposed to dehumanising practices and undignified care. An excellent anthology illustrating such stories can be found in Barker *et al* (1999). The UK government began to incorporate concepts associated with recovery into policy in 1999 with the *National Service Framework* (NSF) *for Mental Health* (Department of Health [DH], 1999). This document identified that health and social care professionals should contribute to challenging the stigma and discrimination directed towards people with mental health problems and promote their social inclusion. To see examples of how this might be achieved through mental health promotion strategies, you should now complete Reflective activity 13.1.

Reflective activity 13.1 Investigate some mental health promotion strategies

Look up some examples of mental health promotion strategies that are using the media in a positive way by accessing the following:

➤ Shift: www.shift.org.uk/
➤ Time to Change: www.time-to-change.org.uk/
➤ BBC Headroom: www.bbc.co.uk/headroom/

This *National Service Framework for Mental Health* placed mental health promotion as a high priority for service providers which is certainly justified, as recent research exploring public attitudes towards people who use mental health services in England has found that negative attitudes have increased (Rethink, 2006; DH, 2008). The association between mental health problems and violence has worsened, and in a recent study, only 65% of respondents believed that people with mental health problems should be entitled to the same job opportunities as anyone else (TNS for Shift, CSIP, 2007). These findings are supported elsewhere. For example, in a study carried out by a mental health charity, 84% of people who use mental health services reported problems in gaining employment, accessing healthcare, and establishing relationships (Mind, 2004), and 49% have been harassed or physically attacked (Read and Barker, 1996).

With regard to dignity, the effects that stigma and subsequent discrimination may have on the individual cannot be emphasised enough. People who are diagnosed with a mental health problem often report experiencing a downward spiral of loss, social disadvantage and isolation. These experiences are regularly attributed to the media portrayal of people who use mental health services; however, some service users feel that it is also a consequence of the way people are treated in health services (Campbell, 1999). Tackling the stigma and subsequent discrimination attached to mental health problems must be a key role for the mental health worker if they are to promote recovery, and providing dignified care is an essential aspect of this. While there have been a number of high-profile campaigns in recent years (*see* Reflective activity 13.1), these are no substitute for the necessary grass-roots day-to-day work of tackling stigma and discrimination that workers and carers need to do among the people they come in contact with. If this is hard to imagine, you might like to consider how racial prejudice has been confronted in our society. While we are not asserting that this has been eliminated, it is much better than it was, say, 50 years ago. But this change has only come about by people standing up for what they believe in and fighting and arguing for social justice (Sayce, 2000). If this example is hard to relate to, you might also like to think about rights for women over the last 100 years or the rights of people described as lesbian or gay. We have a long way to go before we can say that people with mental health problems enjoy these same rights and protection in law. This is one reason why we discussed the law earlier, because it could be argued that the mental health law reinforces negative stereotypes because it emphasises danger and risk.

The *National Service Framework for Mental Health* (DH, 1999) also recognised that contemporary community mental health services should be organised in a way that would enable people who experience mental health problems to be cared for during periods of crisis in the least restrictive environment. This hoped to reduce the 'revolving door' scenario where people's lives were continuously disrupted, sometimes beyond repair, by frequent hospital admissions. This has resulted in the development of a model of community mental health services that can respond quickly to crisis and provide intensive treatment in the person's home environment in order to prevent or facilitate shorter admission to hospital. It is hoped that by enabling people to maintain their roles and relationships, the downward spiral of loss, which has previously been observed, can be challenged.

A number of other policy documents have continued to emphasise the importance of undoing the legacy of the large institutions and the stigma inherited from them (for example, *Modernising Mental Health Services*: DH, 1998; *The NHS Plan*: DH, 2000a). These documents include instructions for creating safe, sound, supportive services that should meet the needs of those who use them, and ways of involving and including people with mental health problems as equal citizens in society. The directives that have arisen from these documents are summarised in the first policy document directly advocating the recovery approach in mental healthcare, *The Journey to Recovery* (DH 2001a), which aims to inform all service providers of the significant shifts required in order to modernise mental healthcare.

The role of values

The directives outlined in the *National Service Framework for Mental Health* were supported by the publication of *The Ten Essential Shared Capabilities* (National Institute for Mental Health in England, 2004), which was developed in consultation with service users, carers and practitioners to provide a training and development framework for the mental healthcare workforce. It was acknowledged that previous frameworks did not go far enough in emphasising the influence of the values of practitioners in relation to the care they deliver or the importance of working in collaboration with service users and carers to focus on their strengths and challenge inequalities. This document makes specific reference to dignity in relation to respecting the diversity of people who use mental health services and promoting their right to make informed choices and for staff to take therapeutic risks. Some have referred to this as a 'dignity of risk' (Parsons, 2008). It recognised that a shift is required in the attitudes and values of practitioners if they are to genuinely facilitate recovery and give choice and control back to people who use mental health services.

The Chief Nursing Officer's review of mental health nursing (DH, 2006) also provides some valuable recommendations for mental health practice across the professions. This document is named *From Values to Action* and reiterates the principles of the essential shared capabilities. It identifies that dignity should be upheld by respecting the values of people who use mental health services through creating forums for shared decision making. The review recognises that this will sometimes involve advocating for vulnerable individuals who may not have a voice or may feel unable to assert their perspective. It also adds that the physical health of people who use mental health services has been severely neglected. It is proposed that their right to receive healthcare provision is often hindered by lack of recognition by mental health professionals and lack of access due to dismissive and stigmatising attitudes among general healthcare professionals.

Underpinning each of these policy documents and their successful implementation is the significance of the values and attitudes that the practitioner holds towards those with whom they are working. These initiatives are supported by the Values Based Practice agenda, which recognises that the decisions we make and the way we care for people are influenced not only by evidence, but also by what we believe is morally and ethically right (Woodbridge and Fullford, 2005). It is here where we can see how the issue of dignity is central to our actions. In order to explore the values you bring to your practice, you should now complete Reflective activity 13.2.

Reflective activity 13.2 Writing a professional philosophy statement

A professional philosophy is a personal statement that describes your own values, beliefs and theories about how nurses and midwives should practise and care for people who use health services. There is not necessarily a 'right' or 'wrong' way to write your statement. However, there are certain issues that you should probably consider when making the connections between what you believe about practice, how you practise and how you evaluate your practice.

Most simply, you can start by asking yourself:

➤ What are health services for?
➤ What do you think people who use health services should expect from care?
➤ What are your values, attitudes and beliefs about people who use health services?
➤ So, what approaches do you use that reflect this position (perhaps with a couple of examples)?

Now that you have written your professional philosophy statement, use a highlighter to identify which parts are influenced by your values.

How do you think this relates to providing dignified care?

DIGNITY IN SPECIFIC MENTAL HEALTH SETTINGS

The Dignity in Care campaign in England was launched in 2006 (*see* Chapter 4) and aims to eliminate tolerance of services that do not respect dignity (DH, 2009). This campaign has now been extended from older adults' services to include mental health services. The campaign has highlighted the key areas where maintaining dignity is at risk, one of which includes tackling stigma. Additionally, the campaign also prioritises older people's mental health and acute inpatient care. The campaign utilises dignity champions who are volunteers and work to increase the profile of dignity in practice areas. You can find out more about the Dignity in Care campaign by completing Reflective activity 13.3. This will give you the opportunity to see some examples of where dignity has been addressed in mental healthcare, for example, advocating working in partnership with people who use mental health services to achieve their goals to improve quality of life.

Reflective activity 13.3 Find out more about Dignity in Care within mental health

➤ Follow the link provided: www.dhcarenetworks.org.uk/dignityincare/ index.cfm
➤ Read about some of the 'ideas from practice'
➤ What are your thoughts about these initiatives?

Older adults' mental healthcare

Chapter 9 discusses dignity in the context of older adults; however, a significant area of concern regarding the provision of dignified care arises from research exploring older people's experiences of using mental health services. Some older people might be considered the most vulnerable in society. This vulnerability might be multiplied if the person has experienced years of mental health problems, subsequent treatments and the social consequences. Furthermore, many thousands of people also become mentally unwell through dementia and Alzheimer's disease. When physical frailty is accompanied with mental frailty, the individual's dignity is at greatest risk.

The *National Service Framework for Older People* (DH, 2001b) emphasises the need for person-centred care. If care that is delivered to older people with mental health problems is truly person centred, then their dignity would be protected. However, there are multiple factors that jeopardise people's dignity in practice. As a principle, one key way to preserve the dignity of older people is to ensure that the views and wishes of service users or their carers are elicited and acted upon in meaningful ways. We would assert that this is the first key to ensuring dignity among this client group. A great deal more importance needs to be placed upon the needs of older people, especially those with mental health problems. This will become a considerably growing issue as the retired population increases. As with all areas of mental health, workers need to campaign for the needs of our clients and ensure that they receive the same rights and privileges as others in our society.

Stories are all too frequently told of abuse of older people in institutional care (Penhale, 2008). Significant improvements may only take place when individual workers demand the kind of quality of care at grass-roots level that is called for at policy level (DH, 2001b). Another area of concern is when older people with mental health needs are admitted to acute general health wards for physical conditions. Often, their mental health needs are not understood or catered for, perhaps because of the lack of understanding of mental health needs among general nurses. Obviously, this calls for greater education for inpatient staff and increased practice development in physical healthcare wards.

Inpatient mental healthcare

Our final area to consider, when thinking about the importance of dignity within mental healthcare, is the issues that arise for people who are admitted to inpatient units during periods of crisis. The Sainsbury Centre for Mental Health (SCMH) has identified from its research that the top priority for mental health service users is the improvement of conditions on inpatient units (SCMH, 2004). The research evidence suggests that people feel they are treated with far less dignity in these settings than in physical healthcare settings (SCMH, 1998, 2002, 2004), which is clearly a cause for concern. To illustrate the seriousness of these concerns, consider the following: in 2009, the NHS was criticised for the four unnecessary deaths a day among those in psychiatric inpatient care (Campbell, 2009). The National Patient Safety Agency (NPSA) reports that 1282 people in England died in what it calls 'patient safety incidents in mental health settings' in the period 2007–2008 (this is helpfully collated by Campbell, 2009). The figures include people who committed suicide, and those who died through violent incidents, medication safety errors and accidents, although it is unclear how many deaths were in each category.

Acute inpatient mental health services in the UK have been considered dysfunctional, failing (Dodds and Bowles, 2001), and denying individuals their human rights (SCMH, 2002). Staff morale is low and recruitment, retention and sickness are problematic. These problems are recognised by the DH (2002) and there are moves to improve care.

The mental health charity Mind (2004) has reported similar findings: only one in five of the respondents to their survey on acute wards felt that they were treated by staff with respect and dignity. Almost the same proportion (17%) stated that they were never treated by staff with respect and dignity. In its 13th biennial report 2007–2009, the Mental Health Act Commission (2009) has authoritatively addressed dignity in mental healthcare. It gives many examples of how this can be compromised, including absence of appropriate bedding and dirty linen. Restraint procedures are a common complaint in mental healthcare. The report gives an example of how undignified restraint can become, as people reported being restrained for lengthy periods in full view of others on the ward. It was identified that the absence of a seclusion room means that people may be restrained in the main ward area until they are considered calm enough to be released. It is recognised that this is clearly upsetting not only for the restrained person but also for those witnessing the restraint. There are examples in the literature that call for a positive focus on promoting dignity in physical restraint (Moylan, 2009).

Not all is bad, and blame should not rest with the nurses who work at grass-roots level with resource problems and low morale. The problems on acute wards are systemic. Answers to problems will only be found by looking at the bigger picture, incorporating philosophy, research, theory, practice and, most importantly, what service users say. However, for mental health workers to maintain the dignity of the individual on acute wards is exceptionally difficult.

There has been much research into service users' views of inpatient care, and familiar themes emerge:

➤ overuse of medication
➤ lack of therapy – counselling
➤ lack of therapeutic activities
➤ not socially inclusive
➤ poor environment
➤ poor resources
➤ frightening atmosphere (especially for women)
➤ lack of goals of the service
➤ inadequate evidence base for treatments
➤ lack of information
➤ lack of involvement and choice
➤ not person-centred care, little regard for background and culture
➤ African-Caribbean people overrepresented and more likely to be sectioned
➤ disconnection from community workers when inpatient
➤ staffing problems: low morale, lack of support, overuse of agency staff, inadequate training
➤ boredom (SCMH, 2002).

Very recently, there has also been an emphasis upon the negative effects of mixed-sex wards. The dangers posed to women, highlighted in the NPSA report (2006), showed that over 100 women were raped, sexually assaulted or sexually harassed in NHS mental health units over a two-year period monitored in this research. Almost three years after these findings have been made public, the issue of keeping vulnerable women safe while detained under section is still a long way from being resolved.

Specific recommendations have been made by the government in relation to mixed-sex accommodation on wards. In *Modernising Mental Health Services* (DH, 1998), the government outlined a strategy that aimed to ensure that people who were admitted to wards were protected from physical, psychological or sexual harm, as a means of providing dignified care. This document drew attention to the ward environment and attempted to enforce the eradication of any mixed-sex accommodation. However, a further operational policy was later published named *Safety, Privacy and Dignity in Mental Health Units*, which lowered expectations to single-sex sleeping accommodation and washing facilities (DH, 2000b). This is despite the recognition that a number of people admitted to these practice areas may have a history of being abused and may not feel safe mixing with the opposite sex. Furthermore, during periods of crisis some people's distress may lead to violent or abusive behaviour and therefore place people who are vulnerable at risk. This document also identifies the importance of assessment, in order to judge if a person is vulnerable to being abused or may abuse others. Additionally, the significance of fully investigating accusations of abuse is emphasised.

THINKING ABOUT DIGNITY IN MENTAL HEALTHCARE

In summary, the policy documents, research evidence and discussion outlined here identify several areas where dignity is central to providing recovery-orientated care. These include:
- challenging stigma and discrimination
- promoting social inclusion
- respecting diversity
- advocating for the individual's right to make choices and take risks
- facilitating shared decision making
- challenging disempowering practices
- promoting awareness of physical health issues
- providing safe care environments
- thinking about people holistically, not just medically.

In this chapter we have only introduced some of the complex ways to think about dignity in mental healthcare. The truth is, we could write a whole book on the subject. We want to emphasise that issues of dignity in mental healthcare are complex. With this in mind, we have included some complex scenarios for you to consider. Having said they are complex, they are based upon the authors' experiences in mental health settings and unfortunately are quite typical of situations that may arise in mental health work. Take a look at the scenarios in Reflective activities 13.4 and 13.5. Each scenario is followed by some critical questions. Please take time to think about these questions and have a go at answering them. By doing so, you will be addressing some of the complex questions workers need to grapple with when thinking about dignity in mental healthcare. Pseudonyms have been used in these exercises.

CONCLUSION

The material presented in this chapter is only a brief introduction to some of the issues that illustrate how dignity threads through all aspects of recovery-

Reflective activity 13.4 Maintaining dignified care in complex situations

Case study: Bernie

Bernie is a 24-year-old West Indian man living on his own in a small flat in a poor inner-city area. His neighbours have complained to the police that he has been playing loud music through the night. Bernie is a very big gentleman, and some of his (white) neighbours are frightened of him. Bernie is known to smoke cannabis. When the police arrived to investigate the situation, Bernie was shouting out of his window that he was the true king of Jamaica and was able to walk on water. When they discovered he had previous contact with social services, and a history of violent offences, the police arranged for a Mental Health Act assessment. When the doctors and the approved mental health practitioner (AMHP) arrived to assess him, Bernie refused to open his door. In preparation for the assessment, the AMHP had obtained a warrant to enter Bernie's premises by force if required. The riot police were called to break down the door and an ambulance was called to transport Bernie to hospital if required. A small group of Bernie's neighbours gathered around his flat to watch the proceedings. As the police broke down the door to Bernie's flat, they entered using CS gas and restrained him by force before leading him to the ambulance in handcuffs.

Critical questions
➤ How was Bernie's dignity compromised?
➤ How might some of this have been avoided?
➤ What might be the social consequences for Bernie following this incident?
➤ Imagine the effect of this incident on Bernie: how might he respond and how might he feel in the future about this incident?
➤ How would you feel if you were Bernie?
➤ Imagine the role of the nurses on the ward when Bernie is admitted: what problems might they face both immediately and in the days to follow?
➤ How might this incident affect Bernie's future?
➤ What might be some of the social influences related to this story?
➤ What might be some of the psychological influences related to this story?

Reflective activity 13.5 Maintaining dignified care in complex situations

Case Study: Imogen

Imogen is 17 years old. Her parents are both successful, well-educated professional people. She is an only child, and her parents have been told that she is predicted to achieve four grade As in her A-level exams. They are hoping she will be successful in gaining a place at Oxford University. Under the strain of her studies and the pressure she has felt from her parents, Imogen has been admitted to an assessment ward, having experienced what had been described as a 'mental breakdown'. Imogen prefers to dance around the ward naked claiming that she is Saint Catherine de Vigni, and she prefers to fly rather than walk. Her parents are clearly embarrassed by her behaviour as it started at home and she had previously paraded around the village wearing nothing more than a silk scarf.

Critical questions
➤ How was Imogen's dignity compromised?
➤ How might these incidents have been avoided?
➤ What might be the social consequences for Imogen following these incidents?
➤ Imagine the effect of these incidents on Imogen: how might she respond and how might she feel in the future about these incidents?
➤ How would you feel if you were Imogen?
➤ Imagine the role of the nurses on the ward with Imogen. What problems might they face both immediately and in the days to follow?
➤ How might these incidents affect Imogen's future?
➤ What might be some of the social influences related to this story?
➤ What might be some of the psychological influences related to this story?

orientated mental healthcare. As you can see, the issues are complex and there are many barriers to making dignified mental healthcare a reality in practice. However, if the fundamental values that inform our work are underpinned by a belief in the person's rights to equality and inclusion, dignified care will follow despite these barriers. Small shifts in the way we communicate choice to people who use mental health services and challenge disempowering practices will, and do, make a significant difference to individuals and families.

The European Parliament (2006), in its Green Paper entitled *Improving the Mental Health of the Population: a Strategy for the European Union,* calls for all people with mental health problems to be treated with dignity and humanity and for them to have their human rights upheld by healthcare professionals. Excellent examples of dignified approaches to mental healthcare are reported in the literature, which remind us that barriers are challenges that can be overcome; however, there is still much more to be done in order to say that we have succeeded in providing wholly dignified mental healthcare.

REFERENCES

Barker P, Campbell P, Davidson B (1999) *From the Ashes of Experience: reflections on madness, survival and growth*. London: Whurr.

Campbell D (2009) Four psychiatric patients dying each day in NHS care. *Observer* 12 April.

Campbell P (1999) The service user/survivor movement. In: Newnes C, Holmes G, Dunn C (eds) *This is Madness: a critical look at psychiatry and the future of mental health services*. Ross-on-Wye: PCCS Books, pp.195–210.

Department of Health (1998) *Modernising Mental Health Services*. London: Department of Health.

Department of Health (1999) *The National Service Framework for Mental Health*. London: Department of Health.

Department of Health (2000a) *The NHS Plan*. London: Department of Health.

Department of Health (2000b) *Safety, Privacy and Dignity in Mental Health Units: guidance on mixed sex accommodation for mental health services*. London: Department of Health.

Department of Health (2001a) *The Journey to Recovery*. London: Department of Health.

Department of Health (2001b) *The National Service Framework for Older People*. London: Department of Health.

Department of Health (2002) *Mental Health Policy Implementation Guide: adult inpatient care provision*. London: Department of Health.

Department of Health (2006) *From Values to Actions: the Chief Nursing Officer's review of mental health nursing*. London: Department of Health.

Department of Health (2008) *Attitudes to Mental Illness Research Report*. London: Department of Health.

Department of Health (2009) *Dignity in Care*. London: Department of Health. www.dhcarenetworks.org.uk/dignityincare/index.cfm (accessed 13 October 2010).

Dodds P, Bowles N (2001) Dismantling formal observation and refocusing nursing activity in acute in-patient psychiatry. *Journal of Psychiatric and Mental Health Nursing* 8: 173–88.

European Parliament (2006) *Improving the Mental Health of the Population: a Strategy for the European Union*. www.europarl.europa.eu/oeil/file.jsp?id=5319462 (accessed 13 October 2010).

Mental Health Act Commission (2009) *Coercion and Consent: monitoring the Mental Health Act*. London: Mental Health Act Commission.

Mind (2004) *Ward Watch: Mind's campaign to improve hospital conditions for mental health patients*. London: Mind.

Moylan LB (2009) Physical restraint in acute care psychiatry. *Journal of Psychosocial Nursing and Mental Health Services* 47(3): 41–7.

National Institute for Mental Health in England (2004) *The Ten Essential Shared Capabilities: a framework for the whole of the mental health workforce.* London: National Institute for Mental Health in England.

National Patient Safety Agency (2006) *With Safety in Mind: mental health services and patient safety.* London: National Patient Safety Agency.

Nolan P (1999) *A History of Mental Health Nursing.* Cheltenham: Nelson Thornes Ltd.

Parsons C (2008) The dignity of risk. *Australian Nursing Journal* **15**(9): 28.

Penhale B (2008) Elder abuse in the United Kingdom. *Journal of Elder Abuse and Neglect* **20**(2): 151–68.

Read J, Barker S (1996) *Not Just Sticks and Stones: a survey of the stigma, taboos and discrimination experienced by people with mental health problems.* London: Mind.

Rethink (2006) *Stigma Shout: service user and carer experiences of stigma and discrimination.* London: Rethink.

Sainsbury Centre for Mental Health (1998) *Acute Problems: a survey of the quality of care in acute psychiatric wards.* London: Sainsbury Centre for Mental Health.

Sainsbury Centre for Mental Health (2002) *An Executive Briefing on Adult Acute Inpatient Care for People with Mental Health Problems.* London: Sainsbury Centre for Mental Health.

Sainsbury Centre for Mental Health (2004) *Acute Care: a national survey of adult psychiatric wards in England.* London: Sainsbury Centre for Mental Health.

Sayce L (2000) *From Psychiatric Patient to Citizen: overcoming discrimination and social exclusion.* London: Macmillan Press.

TNS for Shift, CSIP (2007) *Attitudes to Mental Illness in England.* London: TNS.

van der Merwe M, Bowers L, Jones J *et al* (2009) Locked doors in acute inpatient psychiatry: a literature review. *Journal of Psychiatric and Mental Health Nursing* **16**(3): 293–9.

Woodbridge K, Fullford B (2005) *Whose Values? A workbook for values-based practice in mental health care.* London: Sainsbury Centre for Mental Health.

CHAPTER 14

Dignity and people with learning disabilities

Bob Hallawell

INTRODUCTION

This chapter will explore specific aspects of dignity related to the concept of learning disability and the particular context of the promotion of dignity within services designed to meet the needs of people with learning disabilities.

Learning disability is defined for the purposes of this chapter as a significant impairment of intellectual functioning with significant limitations in adaptive behaviour as expressed in conceptual, social, and practical adaptive skills, which are evident during the developmental period (prior to the age of 18 years) (Department of Health [DH], 2001). Learning disability is not to be confused with learning difficulty, as more broadly defined in education. Other terms that may be used globally to represent learning disability include 'intellectual disability' and 'mental retardation'.

People with learning disabilities have experienced a contravention of their dignity through a number of historical and social manifestations, and such breaches of dignity continue to this day. The origins and nature of such breaches will be explored here, together with contemporary ideas that seek to enable people with learning disabilities to lead dignified and rewarding lives. The discussion will be founded on the notion of dignity as an individual feeling of worthiness and respect (NHS Modernisation Agency, 2003) or, as the Royal College of Nursing stated:

> Dignity is concerned with how people feel, think and behave in relation to the worth or value of themselves and others. To treat someone with dignity is to treat them as being of worth, in a way that is respectful of them as valued individuals (RCN, 2008, p.6, reproduced with permission from the Royal College of Nursing).

LEARNING OUTCOMES

After reading this chapter you will be able to:

➤ explain how historical and social influences created devalued identities for people with learning disabilities, and a consequent lack of dignity in their lives
➤ appreciate how social policy may both hinder and promote dignity in the lives of people with learning disabilities
➤ identify contemporary thinking about the promotion of dignity within health and social care settings for people with learning disabilities
➤ identify how individuals and services may promote dignity through their thinking and actions.

SOCIAL INFLUENCES AND SOCIETAL IMPRESSIONS

Social policy for people with learning disabilities in the latter part of the 19th century and the early decades of the 20th century was partly driven by segregationist principles that underpinned the eugenics movement of the time. These segregationist principles were themselves based on three beliefs: first, that intelligence and ability were inherited; secondly, that people with a learning disability bred at a faster rate than the rest of society; and thirdly, that there were strong links between 'feeble-mindedness' and major social problems (Emerson, 2005). 'It was as a social grouping and as a social problem that individuals with a learning disability were perceived, treated and ultimately constructed' (McClimens, 2005, p.43). Within such a socially constructed identity, people with learning disabilities were not afforded rights to choice, decision making or involvement in the nature of service delivery. Thus, social policy based on eugenic principles served to stigmatise specific groups of individuals and denied them their basic human rights (Richardson, 2005).

Now carry out Reflective activity 14.1.

Reflective activity 14.1

➤ How important is inclusion, choice and the right to make decisions to you?
➤ In the absence of such factors, is it possible to feel worthy and respected?

Economic imperatives also drove the legislation for, classification of and segregation of madness (and other deviance) in the 19th century. Classifications of disability can be linked back to the 'deserving' and 'undeserving' poor criteria established in the Poor Law Reforms of 1834. Thus, industrialisation and a dominant capitalist ideology resulted in the social exclusion of people with physical or mental impairments in the 18th and 19th centuries (Richardson, 2005). A political response to this exclusion and marginalisation was to institutionalise provision for the disabled, first in workhouses and later in specialised institutions. Within these closed, segregated and often authoritarian environments, disabled people 'were socialised into a view of themselves as sick, helpless, inferior and in need of help and care to survive' (Goble, 2004, p.41).

Chapter 2's exploration of dignity introduced 'place, people and process' as factors affecting dignity. Table 14.1 presents how the socialisation process engendered by institutionalisation was characterised by a lack of dignity expressed in place, people and process. After reading the table carry out Reflective activity 14.2.

Table 14.1 Institutions and a lack of dignity (RCN, 2010)

Place	*People*	*Process*
• Little or no privacy in the environment	• The promotion of personal identity was largely absent, e.g. shared clothing, shared toiletries, shared living space	• Rigid, prescribed regimes, e.g. drinks at set times; fixed bedtimes; fixed bathing times
• Barren, impoverished environments	• People had very little in terms of personal possessions	• Lack of choice
• Institutions/hospitals were often situated at a distance from the person's home, family and friends	• The language of the institution was often stigmatising and undignified, staff to patient and patient to patient	• Families had to apply in writing to obtain permission to take their relative out of the grounds of the institution
• Restricted or no access to the outside world		
• All resources, activities, experiences were supplied within the institution by the institution		

> **Reflective activity 14.2**
>
> ➤ Do the characteristics of the institution (*see* Table 14.1) sound familiar to you today?
> ➤ Can you think of other examples from your own experiences of large institutions within society, for example, schools or hospitals?

A lack of dignity within institutional settings has also been reflected in the personal accounts of those who lived within the institutions. For example, Atkinson and Williams's (1990) book of narratives from people with learning disabilities has provided vivid examples. Peter Stevens (p.191) related the constraints and authoritarianism of hospital life: 'You have to be told what to do in hospital'; 'You rely on the food being dished up and I don't like it'. When he was young, he said: 'we always had to go to bed early' and he further said of the charge nurses and nurses: 'I have the strange feeling that they think they are the ones that know better'. Ronnie Gaukrodger (p.198) explained how they were not allowed to talk at the table and that on one occasion, while sitting with others around the table, he started talking, with the result that a nurse: 'just came and pulled me in the pantry, and walloped me on the back of me earhole'. He went on to say that she 'threw a basin at me and split me head open'. The nurse then told him: 'you don't say anything to the doctor'. Ronnie described feeling 'very frightened. I couldn't say anything'.

Now carry out Reflective activity 14.3.

Reflective activity 14.3

➤ Is it likely that such provision and the resultant self-perception will promote worthiness and respect?
➤ How much do social environments determine your feelings of dignity and respect? Can you identify any experiences that were either positive or negative in nature?

IDENTITY, NORMALISATION AND PERSONALISATION

People with learning disabilities who experienced the effects of institutional living have, through such accounts, enabled us to better understand both their personal and social identities. Personal identity may be formed through experience – a sense of belonging, of being loved and valued; being treated as an adult; and being able to value one's self (Atkinson and Williams, 1990). Such characteristics sit well with the idea of dignity as individual feelings of worthiness and respect. However, personal identity is not developed without interaction with a social world that further enables the establishment of a social identity. Social identity may be defined as:

> . . . the ways in which collectivities and individuals are distinguished in their relations with other collectivities or individuals; the establishment, signification and organisation of relationships of similarity and difference between collectivities and individuals . . . (Jenkins, 1998, p.6, reproduced with permission from Cambridge University Press).

The manner in which identities, roles and labels are negotiated and constructed will determine who is considered disabled (Goodley, 2004). Historically, people with learning disabilities have been represented within society under a number of identities. These include the subhuman, the holy innocent, the sick, the eternal child, the vagabond, the ineducable, the defective, the idiot, the mentally subnormal and the mentally handicapped (Gates, 1997; Grant *et al*, 2005).

Both personal and social identities develop as a result of the socialisation processes experienced by the individual, and individuals may inherit included or excluded identities (Borland and Ramcharan, 1997). The adoption of certain social roles, the achievement of a valued status and the acquisition of useful skills or accomplishments all contribute to the individual's social identity (Atkinson and Williams, 1990). People with learning disabilities may at times have struggled to establish valued personal and social identities in the face of stigmatisation by both society and powerful and articulate individuals. Powerful individuals may set the tone for dialogue about less powerful individuals. For example, identities such as 'able-bodied' and 'normal' are constructed by those who wield power as a result of status and authority conferred by legitimated knowledge (Thomas, 2004). However, Ward (2000), referring to earlier work by Lukes (1974), argued that one should refrain from solely focusing on the behaviour of specific decision makers but also consider how systems may both define and work against people's interests. This form of power '. . . is not only the capacity to impose (if necessary in the face of opposition) but [. . .] also the capacity to set the terms of debate' (Ward, 2000, p.50).

Calhoun (1994) argued that where such dominant discourses repress, delegitimate or devalue a particular identity, a fundamental response may be to claim value for those labelled by a given category (for example, learning disabilities). Inclusion in society is central to the development of self-concept and identity, and if subject to exclusionary experiences then: 'it is likely that the person will be socialised into an excluded self-concept and identity' (Borland and Ramcharan, 1997, p.88). Gates (1997) further notes how social incompetence may result from the segregation and devalued lifestyles to be found within the learning disability hospitals that provided care during the 20th century. People with learning disabilities may continue to be seen as people who have to be cared for, and thus they are disregarded and excluded and seen as 'the other' (Walmsley, 2000). Mackenzie (2005) argues that 'learning disabilities has come to be understood as a socially constructed condition to which the most helpful response is social inclusion' (p.47). Thus, inclusive identities, with other groups and individuals, are dependent upon inclusionary socialisation processes.

Now carry out Reflective activity 14.4.

Reflective activity 14.4

➤ Can you think of situations through which your involvement gave you a sense of being included?
➤ What strategies did you adopt in order to become included?
➤ How dependent were you on others to include you?
➤ Did you alter any aspects of your personal identity in order to take on a new social identity?

The advent of normalisation philosophy, participatory research and the self-advocacy movement in the late 20th century and the early 21st century were crucial in enabling people with learning disabilities to be heard and to enable them to adopt valued social roles (Atkinson, 2005). Normalisation theory originally developed partly as a reaction to institutional care and proposed that people with learning disabilities should be enabled to live ordinary lives, such as those experienced by other members of society. The theory was based on three central tenets: first, that people with learning disabilities should experience the normal rhythms of life such as those based on work, play and a varied day; secondly, that there should be a separation of life functions, in contrast to institutional life where often all functions would be carried out in one ward; and thirdly, that service provision should be based on culturally valued analogues, that is, services should be based on culturally valued ways of meeting the needs of people who use services (Cocks, 2001). Later conceptualisations of normalisation (Wolfensberger and Thomas, 1983) acknowledged social identity in emphasising how people with learning disabilities were portrayed and perceived by the public. These conceptualisations articulated the need to develop valued social roles for this group of people (Means and Smith, 1998, p.72), while Williams and Tyne (1988) noted the need to develop 'value based services' in order to militate against negative social values and the concomitant negative life experiences of people with disabilities.

The 1960s also saw an extension of the notion of rights to more 'marginal' groups within society, including people with disabilities (Emerson, 2005). Professional ideologies were also influenced in the 1960s and 1970s by the United Nations's (1948) declarations on human rights and the rights of mentally retarded persons (Office of the United Nations High Commissioner for Human Rights, 1971). These developments built upon the influence of parental pressure groups, the disability rights movement, and social research during the middle decades of the 20th century. Such developments had led to the awareness that people with learning disabilities may grow and develop with the removal of adverse social circumstances, such as institutionalisation and social exclusion (Richardson, 2005). Walker (1997) argued that services delivered within a user-centred framework would '. . . be organised to respect the users' right to self-determination, normalisation and dignity . . .' (p.216). Dawson (1997) also noted that active participation in services was occurring because people with learning disabilities were seen to be of equal worth to non-learning disabled people and were valued as expert consultants because of their direct experience of services. Thus, the personal and social identities of people with learning disabilities had undergone a transformation leading to a new sense of worth and value and a new sense of dignity based upon respect for the individual and their unique expertise.

DIGNITY, HEALTH AND SOCIAL CARE

The physical environment, service cultures, the attitudes and behaviours of the care team, and the manner in which care is delivered may individually or together determine whether dignity is diminished or promoted (RCN, 2010). The notion of dignity applies equally to those who may lack intellectual capacity as it does to individuals who are held to be mentally competent. This requires that care staff treat people of any health status in any setting with dignity. Now carry out Reflective activity 14.5.

Reflective activity 14.5

➤ Think about your previous experiences of healthcare.
➤ What aspects of that care led you feel that you were treated with dignity?

People with learning disabilities (RCN, 2010) identified the following characteristics:
➤ an understanding of their health needs
➤ being treated with respect.
➤ people taking the time to get to know them
➤ having choices and making decisions
➤ feeling safe.

The presence or absence of dignified care may lead to a range of feelings and outcomes for people. The earlier discussions in this chapter noted how people with learning disabilities felt devalued, controlled and excluded by the conditions under which care was provided at the time. The provision of the right social circumstances, environments and approaches to care, and the resultant promotion of dignity can lead to alternative outcomes and feelings (*see* Table 14.2).

Table 14.2 Outcomes and feelings associated with the presence or absence of dignity (RCN, 2010)

Dignity present	Dignity absent
In control	Lack of control
Valued	Devalued
Confident	Lacking confidence
Comfortable	Uncomfortable
Able to make decisions	Unable to make decisions
	Humiliation
	Embarrassment
	Shame

Although it is important to treat all individuals with dignity, there are some particular measures or strategies that may need to be put into place to promote the dignity of people with learning disabilities. There are some particularly damning reports of the experiences of people with learning disabilities when they access mainstream healthcare facilities (Disability Rights Commission, 2006; Mencap, 2007; Michael, 2008). The commonly reported difficulties include:
➤ discrimination against individuals
➤ healthcare professionals who do not understand the law about capacity and consent to treatment
➤ healthcare professionals do not always see the lives of people with a learning disability as worth saving
➤ assumptions made about individuals by professionals, with no assessment to substantiate them
➤ lack of communication between professionals, the individual and their carers
➤ difficulty for people with learning disabilities in accessing services
➤ staff who lack knowledge and skills in working with people with learning disabilities
➤ abuse of individuals and neglect by services, sometimes leading to unnecessary deaths (Mencap, 2007; RCN, 2010).

People with learning disabilities may also find healthcare particularly difficult for a number of reasons. It is likely that they will find it difficult to explain what they are experiencing in terms of pain or discomfort, and they may also struggle to make a rapid adjustment to changing routines and environments that may be part of healthcare services. Healthcare staff may not fully understand their cognitive, health and personal needs and the individuals may have themselves experienced poor healthcare in the past (Hebron, 2009).

Read through Michael's scenario in Reflective activity 14.6 and then consider the questions that follow.

Reflective activity 14.6 Scenario – Michael goes to the hospital

Michael is a 22-year-old man with Down's syndrome, who lives at home with his family. He has moderate learning disabilities and is capable of managing some of his daily life independently, for example eating and personal hygiene. He has some speech but others often find it difficult to understand what he is saying. Staff at the day resource that he attends have been working with him to help him use a sign language known as Makaton. It is known that Michael likes to organise his life around specific routines and activities and he has particular possessions that he likes to keep around him at all times.

Michael has been admitted to hospital by his consultant for cardiac surgery.

➤ What information would be needed to support Michael's care? Where might such information come from?
➤ How would you establish what Michael's support needs are?
➤ How might you communicate with Michael?
➤ How might you give information to Michael about the routines and practices within the hospital?
➤ Might Michael's need to have his possessions with him pose any problems? Would there be any strategies that might help with this situation?

Resource
You may find the following resource helpful in answering the questions: *Working Together: easy steps to improving how people with a learning disability are supported when in hospital:* www.library.nhs.uk/learningdisabilities/ViewResource.aspx?resID=305541

Michael's situation might raise some questions that are difficult to answer, but there are some very practical steps suggested by both people with learning disabilities and learning disabilities professionals that may be taken in order to provide dignified care to Michael and other people with learning disabilities. For example:

➤ all nurses and support staff should have training about people with learning disabilities

➤ healthcare staff should be familiar with any policies and procedures for
the safeguarding of vulnerable adults and children

➤ people with learning disabilities should have regular health checks and
each have a health action plan that can be used as information for others.
They might also have something called a health passport or health profile
that provides information on health needs, choices, likes and dislikes,
reactions to medication or pain and required levels of support

➤ community teams for people with learning disabilities should give other
nurses information and support

➤ it should be established whether there is a learning disability liaison nurse
or health facilitator for the hospital

➤ nurses should understand their responsibilities with respect to capacity
and consent. They should thus appreciate the key principles of the Mental
Capacity Act

➤ people with learning disabilities should be given information and help
about how to stay well, such as eating healthily or exercising. This information should be provided in understandable formats as required, for
example, pictures and symbols

➤ the person with the learning disability, and not only the carers or other
staff, should be spoken to about their needs. They should be addressed in
the manner preferred by the person

➤ people with learning disabilities should be included at all stages of the
care planning process. They may need to know what to expect, what might
happen and how they may feel

➤ people with learning disabilities may require more intensive preparation.
A preadmission visit might therefore be arranged to identify potential
risks, to establish levels of dependency and to define the necessary levels
of support. Balancing the need to manage risks against the person's independence is crucial to providing a safe and dignified experience

➤ nurses should seek to establish what the person can do for themselves –
not assume a lack of capability. They should also be asked what support
they do need and in what form that support might be best provided

➤ more time should be allowed for consultations/assessments – double
appointments may be necessary. Also, more time should be allowed for
self-care

➤ private, accessible and clean environments should be provided, with
understandable signs and/or information.

➤ communication should use simple, everyday language and concrete terms
rather than abstract ideas. Consider the use of photographs, pictures and
symbols to assist communication

➤ new events or procedures and the reason for the change should be explained. This may require pictorial or symbolic forms of communication in addition to verbal language
➤ information about the staff and their roles should be provided
➤ if giving medication, people with learning disabilities should be told:
  – what it is for
  – why it should be taken
  – how it will help
  – about the side-effects
  – the information in a format that is easy to understand
  – how to take the medication
➤ feedback should be provided to the person on procedures and progress and their particular response to the treatment
➤ particular discharge arrangements that may need to be made to support the person in their home should be thought about
➤ a learning disabilities champion should be established within the service area, who can be a source of information and advice to the staff team (Hebron, 2009; RCN, 2010).

Dignified care for people with learning disabilities need not be an extremely complex episode if some of these practical steps are taken before, during and after access to healthcare services and professionals.

CONCLUSION

People with learning disabilities may experience a lack of dignity fostered by historical and social impressions of their worth and value to society. A devalued personal and social identity may in turn lead to dehumanising practices and service provision that may result in undignified lifestyles and, in the worst instances, abuse, neglect and unnecessary deaths. Changes in thinking, policy and practice have led to the emergence of new, valued social roles for people with learning disabilities that foster choice, respect, rights and dignity. An awareness of this, aligned with some specific policy imperatives and new models of care within health and social systems, may lead to the enhancement of dignified practice by health and social care professionals. This, in turn, may result in people with learning disabilities having a new-found sense of personal worth. People with learning disabilities are not a homogenous group, and, as such, dignity can be promoted through the recognition of each person as an individual with a unique personality, history and range of abilities (RCN, 2010).

REFERENCES

Atkinson D (2005) Narratives and people with learning disabilities. In: Grant G, Goward P, Richardson M, Ramcharan P (eds) *Learning Disability – A Life Cycle Approach to Valuing People.* Maidenhead: Open University Press, pp.7–27.

Atkinson D, Williams F (eds) (1990) *Know Me As I Am: an anthology of prose, poetry and art by people with learning difficulties.* London: Hodder and Stoughton.

Borland J, Ramcharan P (1997) Empowerment in informal settings – the themes. In: Ramcharan P, Roberts G, Grant G, Borland J (eds) *Empowerment in Everyday Life – Learning Disability.* London: Jessica Kingsley Publishers, pp.88–97.

Calhoun C (ed) (1994) *Social Theory and the Politics of Identity.* Oxford: Blackwell.

Cocks E (2001) Normalisation and social role valorisation: guidance for human service development. *Hong Kong Journal of Psychiatry* **11**(1): 12–16.

Dawson P (1997) Service planning and people with learning disabilities. *British Journal of Nursing* **6**(2): 70.

Department of Health (2001) *Valuing People: a new strategy for learning disability for the 21st century.* London: The Stationery Office.

Disability Rights Commission (2006) *Equal Treatment: closing the gap – a formal investigation into physical health inequalities experienced by people with learning disabilities and/or mental health problems.* London: Disability Rights Commission.

Emerson E (2005) Models of service delivery. In: Grant G, Goward P, Richardson M, Ramcharan P (eds) *Learning Disability – A Life Cycle Approach to Valuing People.* Maidenhead: Open University Press, pp.108–27.

Gates B (1997) The nature of learning disability. In: Gates B, Beacock C (eds) *Dimensions of Learning Disability.* London: Baillière Tindall, pp.3–25.

Goble C (2004) Dependency, independence and normality. In: Swain J, French S, Barnes C, Thomas C (eds) *Disabling Barriers – Enabling Environments.* London: Sage Publications, pp.41–6.

Goodley D (2004) Who is disabled? Exploring the scope of the social model of disability. In: Swain J, French S, Barnes C, Thomas C (eds) *Disabling Barriers – Enabling Environment.* London: Sage Publications, pp.118–24.

Grant G, Goward P, Richardson M, Ramcharan, P (eds) (2005) *Learning Disability – A life Cycle Approach to Valuing People.* Maidenhead: Open University Press.

Hebron C (2009) Working together to ensure equal healthcare for all. *Learning Disability Practice* **12**(6): 27–30.

Jenkins R (ed) (1998) *Questions of Competence – Culture, Classification and Intellectual Disability.* Cambridge: University Press.

Lukes S (1974) *Power: a radical view.* London: Macmillan.

MacKenzie F (2005) The roots of biomedical diagnosis. In: Grant G, Goward P, Richardson M, Ramcharan P (eds) *Learning Disability – A Life Cycle Approach to Valuing People.* Maidenhead: Open University Press, pp.47–65.

McClimens A (2005) From vagabonds to Victorian values. In: Grant G, Goward P, Richardson M, Ramcharan P (eds) *Learning Disability – A Life Cycle Approach to Valuing People.* Maidenhead: Open University Press, pp.28–46.

Means R, Smith R (1998) *Community Care – Policy and Practice.* Basingstoke: Macmillan Press Ltd.

Mencap (2007) *Death by Indifference: following up the Treat me Right! Report.* London: Mencap.

Michael J (2008) *Healthcare For All: report of the independent inquiry into access to health-care for people with learning disabilities.* London: Aldridge Press.

NHS Modernisation Agency (2003) *The Essence of Care – patient focused benchmarks for clinical governance.* London: NHS Modernisation Agency. www.dh.gov.uk/dr_consum_dh/groups/dh_digitalassets/@dh/@en/documents/digitalasset/dh_4127915.pdf (accessed 13 October 2010).

Office of the United Nations High Commissioner for Human Rights (1971) *Declaration on the Rights of Mentally Retarded Persons.* www2.ohchr.org/english/law/res2856.htm (accessed 13 October 2010).

Richardson M (2005) Critiques of segregation and eugenics. In: Grant G, Goward P, Richardson M, Ramcharan P (eds) *Learning Disability – A Life Cycle Approach to Valuing People.* Maidenhead: Open University Press, pp.66–89.

Royal College of Nursing (2008) *Dignity: at the heart of everything we do.* London: Royal College of Nursing. www.rcn.org.uk/newsevents/campaigns/dignity (accessed 17 August 2010).

Royal College of Nursing (2010) *Dignity in Healthcare for People with Learning Disabilities – RCN guidance.* London: Royal College of Nursing.

Thomas C (2004) Disability and impairment. In: Swain J, French S, Barnes C, Thomas C (eds) *Disabling Barriers – Enabling Environments.* London: Sage Publications, pp.21–7.

United Nations (1948) *The Universal Declaration of Human Rights.* www.un.org/en/documents/udhr/ (accessed 13 October 2010).

Walker A (1997) Community care policy: from consensus to conflict. In: Bornat J, Johnson J, Pereira C, Pilgrim D, Williams F (eds) *Community Care: a reader.* London: Macmillan Press Ltd, pp.196–220.

Walmsley J (2000) Caring: a place in the world?' In: Johnson K, Traustadottir R (eds) *Women with Intellectual Disabilities: finding a place in the world.* London: Jessica Kingsley, pp.191–212.

Ward D (2000) Totem not token – groupwork as a vehicle for user participation. In: Kemshall H, Littlechild R (eds) *User Involvement and Participation in Social Care.* London: Jessica Kingsley, pp.45–64.

Williams P, Tyne A (1998) Exploring values as the basis for service development. In: Towell D (ed) *An Ordinary Life in Practice: developing comprehensive community-based services for people with learning difficulties.* London: King's Fund Publishing, pp.23–31.

Wolfensberger W, Thomas S (1983) *PASSING: Program Analysis of Service Systems Implementing Normalisation Goals.* Toronto: National Institute on Mental Retardation.

SECTION 3
Developing dignity in healthcare

CHAPTER 15

Education to promote dignity in healthcare

Liz Cotrel-Gibbons and Milika Ruth Matiti

INTRODUCTION

The public's desire for healthcare that promotes the dignity of clients has become an overt demand – it is therefore vital that healthcare professionals are formally educated about what dignity means and how it can be promoted. This chapter will focus on the approaches to education that can be employed to promote dignity in care and is aimed at both students and educators in healthcare. There is specific reference to pre-registration nurse education but the content is also applicable to other students receiving their initial education in healthcare.

In the first section of the chapter the rationale for 'values education' in nursing and healthcare and the position of dignity within 'values education' will be presented. Challenges to dignity education will be identified. The educational theories of deep learning, andragogy, constructivism and transformative learning, and their relevance for dignity education, are discussed. This will provide a solid theoretical foundation for the section on the implementation of educational strategies.

The second section uses the six questions posed by Kipling in 1902 (1989) as a framework: What? Why? When? How? Where? Who? An example of a programme for dignity education is outlined and specific examples of how to implement this programme are given. Some of the content is based on our personal experiences. Reflective exercises are included to enable readers to experience and evaluate some of the strategies.

LEARNING OUTCOMES

By the end of the chapter you will be able to:

➤ identify the rationale for 'values education'
➤ be aware of the challenges to 'values education'
➤ discuss the relevance of deep learning, andragogy, constructivism and transformative learning to dignity education

➤ discuss the implementation of values/dignity education
➤ experience and evaluate learning exercises.

A CASE FOR DIGNITY IN THE CURRICULUM

As stated in previous chapters of this book, dignity is a value; it is more than an attitude, knowledge or a skill. A value is a belief that guides behaviour and provides criteria for making choices (Vezeau, 2006). Dignity does not stand alone – other relevant values in healthcare include integrity, empathy, compassion, caring and respect. However, dignity has been claimed to be a core value of nursing practice. In Norway, Fagermoen (1997) investigated values embedded in nursing practice by asking 767 qualified nurses: 'What is most meaningful in your work as a nurse?'. The findings indicated that dignity was a core value for nurses when caring for patients. Fagermoen (1997) found that the other values the nurses identified, such as integrity, either arose from the value of dignity or were aimed at preserving dignity, for example privacy.

The values of integrity (Teeri *et al*, 2008), empathy (Fahrenwald *et al*, 2005; Manthey, 2008), compassion (Fahrenwald *et al*, 2005; Kalb and O'Connor-Von, 2007; Cornwell and Goodrich, 2009), caring (Fahrenwald *et al*, 2005) and respect (Kalb and O'Connor-Von, 2007; Manthey, 2008; Teeri *et al*, 2008; Cornwell and Goodrich, 2009) are all bound together; if one is missing from healthcare practice, the ability to promote dignity is compromised. It therefore follows that these values need to be incorporated in the curriculum.

Raya (1990) argues that universities have a responsibility to teach values, not just knowledge, because values direct the use of knowledge and encourage respect for truth and for the worth and rights of other people. Hoover's study (2002) demonstrated that values education enhanced students' knowledge and intent to practise in a caring way. Improvement in the care experiences of patients and their families is the main aim of values education. The ways in which values are incorporated in the education of healthcare professionals indicate how the promotion of dignity may be learned.

The need for explicit dignity education for nurses is recommended by many authors including Johnston *et al* (2004) in Australia, Jacelon *et al* (2004) in the United States of America, and Matiti (2002), Tschudin (2004) and Woogara (2005) in the United Kingdom (UK). The necessity for dignity to be explicit in educational programmes is supported by the American Association of Colleges of Nursing (1998), which identified five core professional nursing values – altruism, autonomy, human dignity, integrity and social justice. In the UK, the Nursing and Midwifery Council (NMC; 2007) published the 'Essential Skills Clusters', with one section on 'care, compassion and communication', which specifically encompasses dignity.

However, there are some challenges to values education that need to be kept in mind by healthcare educators. The first challenge is that dignity is, as has been discussed in earlier chapters, difficult to define and subjective. As a consequence, lecturers might have different perceptions of dignity, which can pose problems when considering how to incorporate dignity into educational programmes. A second challenge is the current lack of literature and evidence on the implementation of values education in pre-registration curricula. A third is the limited amount of time available due to a packed curriculum (Warburton, 2003). Vezeau (2006) identifies that values education is difficult as it raises potentially uncomfortable questions and may challenge self-image. Despite all these challenges, it is our contention that healthcare education should aim to develop knowledge, skills and appropriate attitudes among students in relation to the concept of dignity. The next section identifies and discusses the educational theories that can be utilised when teaching about dignity.

EDUCATIONAL APPROACHES AND THEORIES

When reviewing the literature on how the concept of dignity is transmitted to others, there are three main approaches:

➤ *ethical*: moral judgements on how people ought to be treated
➤ *political*: legal rights as in the Human Rights Act (1998)
➤ *spiritual*: as a dimension of the person's self-concept.

While all three are underpinned by values and have merit, the majority of nursing literature focuses on the ethical approach. This chapter draws on all three approaches but focuses on application to practice.

There are a number of educational theories but four will be outlined and their relevance to dignity education discussed: deep learning, andragogy, constructivism and transformative learning.

Deep learning

Dignity is both a multifaceted and a personal concept. Each person has a personal concept of dignity which shapes their attitudes and actions. Healthcare professionals interact with clients and, in addition to enacting their own concept of dignified behaviour, have to develop an understanding of each client's dignity and then provide conditions to promote the dignity of that client. In order to achieve this level of practice, healthcare professionals must develop an understanding of what dignity means both to themselves and to others, such as clients. This can lead to a dilemma, as values are embedded in a person's self-concept and are difficult to change. Any challenge to a person's values causes a need for them to review core aspects of themselves, which may lead to dissonance between who they are and who they feel/think they should be. A specific example is the debate about what constitutes a dignified death. On the one hand, there is the argument for the sanctity of life and promotion of dignity through palliative care, while on the other there is the right to self-determination including choosing when and how to die.

In educational terms, developing this understanding requires deep as opposed to surface learning (Clare, 2007). Beattie *et al* (1997) define deep learning as 'learning with understanding'. The distinction between deep and surface learning was first made in 1976 by Marton and Saljo. Surface learning is identified as being extrinsically motivated, passive and requiring reproduction of knowledge, while deep learning is an 'intrinsically motivated process of personalised meaning construction'. Clare (2007) used deep learning strategies with her social work students by encouraging them to use a reflective journal and facilitating dialogue between the student and the content, other students and the teacher. She found that her students developed critical thinking about practice and themselves as practitioners, which she attributed to employing deep learning strategies. The students felt that they had 'a stronger foundation for entering the professional practice arena' (p.443).

It is, however, acknowledged that learning about dignity may also have extrinsic motivators such as health and social policy and practice guides, for example Dignity in Care (Department of Health, 2006). These motivators need to be examined, analysed and critiqued before being included in the students' personalised meaning constructions. Merely presenting policies leads to surface learning, what Beattie *et al* (1997) would identify as rote learning, with limited ability to instigate professional practice.

According to Entwistle (2000), the intention of deep learning is to extract meaning; this requires the student to be actively involved in their learning. Pask (1988) identified two strands to deep learning: first the holist strategy, which involves looking for patterns and principles; and secondly the serialist strategy, which uses evidence and logic. Both of these strategies are relevant when enabling students to develop an understanding and application of a complex and difficult-to-define concept such as dignity. The holist strategy encourages reflection on students' personal concepts and practice experiences; the serialist strategy uses research and planning processes to support students in making changes to their own practice.

Key concepts that are relevant to deep learning are:
➤ internal motivation of the student
➤ active learning – engagement with the topic (Warburton, 2003)
➤ provision of opportunities to develop enhanced personal meaning (Entwistle, 2000; Warburton, 2003)
➤ relevance of teaching – from the student's perspective (Warburton, 2003).
➤ self-assessment to guide the learning process (Sandberg and Barnard, 1997).

These concepts can be applied to dignity education in the following ways. Internal motivation can be stimulated by encouraging students to analyse their own personal concept of dignity and to consider what makes them feel respected. In the authors' experiences, the student's inbuilt desire to care for others is a strong motivator for promoting dignity for patients. The learning activities that are incorporated into an educational programme need to enable students to critically analyse and reflect on their personal attitudes, knowledge and skills, as well as on the literature and policies. This provides students with the opportunity to develop their personal concept of dignity and their role in promoting dignity for patients. Focusing on their role ensures that the learning has professional relevance for students. In addition, the opportunity to develop an aspect of practice through action planning, and then evaluate the effectiveness of how this has led to service improvement, incorporates all five of the key concepts.

Andragogy

In the education of healthcare professionals, the philosophy of andragogy needs to run alongside the principle of deep learning. The students are adults, and therefore an andragogical approach needs to underpin all teaching strategies; this is a fundamental way of treating students with respect and so maintaining their dignity. In turn, being valued themselves will reinforce the importance of promoting the dignity of others. The elements of andragogy that are particularly relevant for values education are:

➤ the adult's accumulation of life experiences, which can act as a resource for learning, for example, their personal experience of dignity or of dignity promotion in practice

➤ the adult's readiness to learn is related to what they need to know or do in their life; for example, how will learning about dignity help to develop their practice? (Jarvis, 1987; Quinn and Hughes, 2007).

In addition, Quinn and Hughes (2007) and Henschke and Cooper (2009) suggest that an adult is predominantly internally motivated, for example, by job satisfaction, as opposed to relying on approval from others. However, this may not always be the case in professional education when learning is assessed by the same people who are facilitating the adult's learning; gaining these facilitators' formal approval becomes paramount in order to pass the course (Entwistle, 2000; Warburton, 2003). An example that relates to dignity is the healthcare student placing a higher priority on working quickly rather than on respecting the patient's need for compassionate communication. The role of assessment in values education therefore needs to be considered carefully if it is to promote and not restrict learning.

Two further learning theories that have relevance to values education are:
➤ constructivist learning
➤ transformative learning.

Both of these theories are from the cognitive school of learning and focus on internal mental processes, not just demonstrated behaviours (Mezirow, 2000).

Constructivism

Constructivist learning is based on the work of Piaget who rejected the idea of the teacher pouring knowledge into the empty student vessel (Weinberg and Weinberg, 1983). Constructivism assumes that learners build their knowledge by identifying meanings from their own experiences. This requires active learners with the ability to use past and present experiences, thus linking to both deep learning and andragogy. In relation to dignity education, constructive learning can be facilitated by asking the students trigger questions about their own experiences or actions and then asking the students to consider how this affects their professional practice.

Transformative learning

Transformative learning is based on Mezirow's work (Williams, 2001). This takes account of the ideas of constructivism, moving on to use the meanings that the learner identifies to transform their view of others or self and to guide future action. This is vital in practice-based professions. Strategies to promote transformative learning may set out to challenge existing 'frames of reference', as in Rush's (2008) study. Rush examined the impact of employing mental health service users to teach nursing on the nursing students' attitudes about the potential capabilities of these mental health service users. The students' previous experiences of mental health service users had been as providers of their care rather than as recipients of their knowledge. In relation to promoting dignity, working with clients to formulate a dignity charter would enable students to work in partnership with clients. This challenges the usual relationship of caregiver and recipient and enables students to work in new ways. Providing opportunities for students to experience the world from the clients' perspectives, reflecting on how that makes them feel and then identifying actions that they could undertake to promote dignity, would also be transformative.

In order to evaluate the teaching strategies, Reflective activity 15.1 will help you to understand the relevance of these educational theories.

An example would be:

> My experience relates to riding a horse. I am not a confident rider. I don't believe that I can influence the horse if he doesn't want to listen. I would increase my enjoyment in riding if I felt that I could have more control through working with the

---

Reflective activity 15.1 Educational theories

➤ Describe an occasion when you felt that you had a good learning experience. It may have been during your professional education, at school/college or be related to a hobby.

➤ What was it that made it a good experience? It may have been because you enjoyed the learning activity, or because you learned something or because you felt supported by the teacher or fellow learners.

➤ Did this experience use any of the four educational theories discussed in this chapter?

---

horse. I discussed this with my instructor who knew that I was ready to learn and motivated to improve my riding [key concepts of *deep learning* and *andragogy*]. My instructor knew that I had knowledge of anatomy and movement. She built on this knowledge and related this to my riding technique and the movement of the horse, thereby using my previous life experiences [key concepts of *deep learning, andragogy* and *constructivism*]. I was given practical exercises to undertake, so engaged in active learning – both cognitive and psychomotor. Undertaking these exercises enabled me to assess my own progress [key concept of *deep learning*] and to discuss this with my instructor. I was able to identify new meanings from my discussion and experiences, which then led to a transformed view of myself in relation to the meaning of control and risk. This in turn influenced my willingness to extend my riding skills [*transformative learning*].

The theories of andragogy, constructivism and transformative learning all support deep learning, which is crucial if students are to develop their abilities to promote dignity. Sandberg and Barnard (1997) acknowledge that deep learning is difficult and that students require teachers to create learning environments that enable them to actively construct knowledge. Entwistle (2000) suggests that teachers who are student focused and learning orientated, as opposed to teacher focused and content orientated, place a greater emphasis on encouraging students to develop deep levels of understanding. It is with this in mind that the implementation of educational strategies will be discussed in relation to dignity.

IMPLEMENTATION OF EDUCATIONAL STRATEGIES TO PROMOTE DIGNITY IN CARE

In this section the five Ws and one H of Rudyard Kipling (1989) will be used to guide the discussion.

➤ What?
➤ Why?
➤ When?
➤ How?
➤ Where?
➤ Who?

This is a simple framework that ensures that the elements of curriculum planning are considered: content (*what*), rationale for content and method (*why*), logical sequencing (*when*), learning and teaching methods (*how*), learning environment (*where*) and appropriate expertise and skills of the facilitator (*who*). The *why* will be included with each of the other questions in turn.

What needs to be learned?

Education for dignity needs to be included in a wider programme of values education (see Box 15.1 for suggested topics), which includes:
➤ ethics
➤ spirituality
➤ professionalism
➤ attitude formation
➤ communication skills
➤ law and policy relevant to dignity and human rights.

Dignity needs to be considered from three perspectives: personal dignity, patient dignity and the dignity of professional colleagues.

It is acknowledged that the time that can be allocated to specific education about dignity will be limited and that dignity also needs to be incorporated in all sessions that involve interaction with others. However, relying on incorporation alone can lead to the devaluing of dignity as a topic with it being hidden amongst other content – perpetuating the issue of 'dignity being a taken for granted concept'. Therefore specific content that needs to be learned about dignity should be identified.

There needs to be an increase in the complexity of this content to enable the student to develop their cognition and application to practice in relation to dignity. Initially students need to consider their own concept of dignity, explore how it relates to other people's concepts and then move on to reflecting on their own actions. The next stage is to apply their skills and knowledge through working with service users who have a variety of needs and then identifying individual needs within the competing demands of practice. Finally students should develop an understanding of how they can influence colleagues and the organisational culture.

BOX 15.1 *Suggested topics for inclusion in a values education programme*

➤ Altruism – beneficence, non-maleficence
➤ Attitude formation
➤ Autonomy – self-care – choice
➤ Change process
➤ Compassion
➤ Confidentiality
➤ Communication
➤ Consent
➤ Culture – diversity
➤ Dignity
➤ Disability
➤ Discrimination, harassment and exploitation
➤ Diversity
➤ Embarrassment, humiliation, shame
➤ Equality
➤ Ethics – value, worth, personhood
➤ Gender
➤ Mental capacity
➤ Professional code – integrity/accountability
➤ Role modelling
➤ Safeguarding and/or public protection
➤ Sexuality
➤ Social justice
➤ Spirituality
➤ Stigma

Considering the when

In the UK, most pre-registration healthcare education programmes are three years long. Table 15.1 suggests how content about dignity can be sequenced across a three-year nursing programme; this sequence could be applied to other healthcare programmes. For trainee assistant practitioners and healthcare support workers, the timescale is shorter but the sequence of content in Box 15.2 is still applicable; the year 3 content could be reduced to take account of the different roles of these students. Dignity should be introduced early in the curriculum as this allows concepts to be developed and reflected upon as students grow in their professional role.

Table 15.1 Sample programme for dignity education

Year (when)	Content (what)	Method (how)	Rationale (why)
Year one			
Session 1	Explore dignity as a concept and relate it to practice	Reflective exercise as a trigger (*see* Reflective activity 15.2)	Exploration of personal concept
	What does the term 'dignity' mean to you?	Concept analysis – individual and then shared with other group members	Identification, sharing and comparing of elements that make up the concept
	What do the terms 'privacy', 'individuality', 'respect' mean to you?	Concept analysis – individual and then shared with other group members	Identification, sharing and comparing of meanings
	How do people show you respect? When are the times that you get privacy? What qualities and characteristics make you an individual?	Trigger questions; discussion	Identifies personal values
	What happens to dignity when someone is in need of nursing care?	Trigger question; discussion	Makes links to patients/clients
	What actions can nurses take to maintain the person's dignity?	Trigger question; discussion	Links maintenance of dignity to professional role
	Person's view	Poem – *Crabbit Old Woman*	Appreciation of expert (patient's) view
Session 2	Policies; literature on empathy, compassion and caring – suggested articles given to the student	Directed reading and reflection	Opportunity for active engagement and for the student to formulate own ideas before sharing with fellow students
		Post on computer forum and comment constructively on peers' contributions	Group reflection may facilitate the presentation of alternative solutions and different interpretations of experiences but may suppress personal learning by leading to conformity (Jarvis, 1985, p.107). This is avoided by sharing after individual reflection. Places dignity in context with related values
Session 3	Appropriate attitude in relation to dignity	Trigger questions on verbal and non-verbal interactions, e.g. Do you say 'please' and 'thank you' to clients? Do you walk into a room/bed space before getting permission?	Students to relate these questions to themselves and decide on whether or not they are respectful

Year (when)	Content (what)	Method (how)	Rationale (why)
	Factors that influence the maintenance of patient dignity, e.g. gender, age, sexuality, disability, mental capacity	Reflection – identify groups of clients and an individual that the student has found easier to show respect to and less easy to show respect to	Consider factors that affect personal capacity to demonstrate respect. Compare personal factors to literature
		Discussion of literature on staff attitudes and equality and diversity	Consider the impact of experiences on self and how it shapes personal professional practice
	Promotion of choice	Trigger questions – list the choices that you have every week. Consider the choices that different client groups have in a week. How do they compare?	Consider the impact of experiences on self and how it shapes personal professional practice
	Promotion of privacy	Discussion on intrusion into own life and into clients' lives	
Year two			
Session 4	How dignity of clients can be maintained in student's own field of practice	User involvement – sharing their experience of dignity in healthcare and constructing a charter for dignity with the students	Gain client perspective
	Explore factors that could influence the maintenance of patient dignity and staff dignity in own field	Users to take the lead in formulating dignity charter, which students implement on placement	Experience the concept of partnership working and view the client as a colleague/ leader not a passive recipient
Session 5	Explore the concept of humanness and personhood	Experiential exercise, i.e. role play or simulation – sensory deprivation, disabled, homeless, confined to bed; or client/ family's narratives	First-hand experience of client situation. Not all students may wish to take part; or reflection on client/ family account
		Followed by reflective discussion on personhood. Bring in scenarios from other fields	Apply dignity to other fields
	Review charter from session 4	Discussion	Reflect on the experience of using the charter. Highlights barriers to and positive aspects of working for a client group

Table 15.1 continued

Year (when)	Content (what)	Method (how)	Rationale (why)
Year three			
Session 6	The emotionally vulnerable person	Trigger DVD followed by discussion and care planning	Taking time to 'see' what is happening for the patient during a time when there are clinical priorities that may be the staff's focus. Identifying actions that students can take to promote dignity
Session 7	The nurse's role in facilitating a culture that promotes dignity	Discussion on facilitating organisational culture. Reflective exercise (*see* Reflective activity 15.3). SWOB (strengths, weaknesses, opportunities, barriers) analysis of own ability to influence practice. Action planning – identify actions that the student will take to promote dignity – mini project on placement	To empower the students to influence the promotion of dignity in practice
	Dealing with challenging situations	Role play of challenging situations	To practise (through role play) relevant skills in a safe environment
Session 8	The nurse's role in facilitating a culture that promotes dignity	Feedback on the progress the student has made with his/her personal action plan	To review the impact the student has had on influencing promotion of dignity in practice – improving the service to patients
	Review and evaluate own practice		To enable the student to make the cognitive transition to qualified nurse

A detailed programme for dignity education in the university setting is outlined in Table 15.1. The programme would need to be linked to other educational sessions relating to values.

Selecting the how

A number of learning strategies can be considered when selecting the *how*. As previously discussed, strategies should adhere to the principles of deep learning, andragogy and constructive learning and some will aim to develop transformative learning. Examples of learning strategies include:

BOX 15.2 *Example of sequencing education about dignity in a three-year nursing programme*

First year: exploration of dignity as a concept and its relationship to practice
Two teacher contact sessions and one directed study
➤ Session 1: to take place before the first placement
➤ Session 2: directed study
➤ Session 3: to take place after placement experience

Second year: application of the concept to all fields of nursing
➤ Session 4: to take place in first half of year 2
➤ Session 5: to take place in second half of year 2

Third year: promoting dignity through influencing others
➤ Session 6: to take place in first half of year 3
➤ Session 7: to take place in first half of year 3
➤ Session 8: to take place in second half of year 3

➤ concept exploration (Fahrenwald *et al*, 2005; Vezeau, 2006; Vacek, 2009)
➤ use of triggers for discussion, for example, written scenarios, DVD, poetry, vignettes (Elfrink and Lutz, 1991; Gallagher, 2004; Shaw and Degazon, 2008)
➤ discussion/public dialogue/performance (Entwistle, 2000; Yorks and Sharoff, 2001; Warburton, 2003; Clare, 2007)
➤ narratives (Paterson and Crawford, 1994; Heliker, 2007; Cornwell and Goodrich, 2009; Trueland, 2009)
➤ reflection on practice including use of journals (Paterson and Crawford, 1994; Yorks and Sharoff, 2001; Lockyer *et al*, 2004; Chirema, 2006; Clare, 2007)
➤ role play (Shaw and Degazon, 2008; Cornwell and Goodrich, 2009)
➤ simulation (Elfrink and Lutz, 1991; Fahrenwald *et al*, 2005)
➤ role modelling and mentoring (Elfrink and Lutz, 1991; Paterson and Crawford, 1994; Stern, 2000; Weis and Schank, 2002; Illingworth, 2006; Peters, 2006; Vezeau, 2006; Armstrong, 2008; Cornwell and Goodrich, 2009)
➤ user involvement (Stuhlmiller, 2003; Clare, 2007; Morris and Faulk, 2007; Rush, 2008; Davison and Williams, 2009)
➤ action planning (Matiti *et al*, 2007).

Where should learning take place?

Some of the learning will occur in the formal education setting; other learning will occur in practice when the student is either trying out prior learning or being exposed to further new experiences. By far the majority of learning will need to take place in the student's own psychological space, if enduring and transformative learning is to occur.

Learning can occur in a range of physical environments: classroom, simulation, in a laboratory, or in practice. An environmental culture that promotes learning is pivotal to promoting dignity and it is the role of the teaching institution and individual teacher to promote a positive learning environment that enables deep learning to take place. This encompasses enthusiasm and empathy of the teacher (Entwistle, 2000), a caring and safe learning environment (MacNeil and Evans, 2005) and ensuring relevance of content and variation of teaching styles (Warburton, 2003) to take account of students' preferred learning styles, thus encouraging engagement with the topic. Entwistle (2000) cites Marton and Booth's (1997) idea of 'meetings of awareness': the teachers use their empathic awareness of what students already know and how they learn to develop their teaching strategies. Role modelling of nursing values by faculty staff forms a bridge between the environment and teaching strategies (Paterson and Crawford, 1994; Chou *et al*, 2003); for example, the teacher's willingness to accept a student's challenge to her opinion can lead to empowerment of the student – this willingness is an attribute of the teacher that will influence the culture of the environment and the strategies that will be used to teach.

Who is involved in promoting learning about dignity?

First and foremost, students themselves need to be receptive, active and reflective. Practitioners and service users have a large influence on students' learning too. Teaching staff have less opportunity in terms of time with students to facilitate learning; therefore, sessions need to be carefully planned to maximise their impact.

One learning strategy that illustrates how the questions of *'what, how, where, who* and *when'* form a useful framework is that of role modelling:

➤ *what* - according to the NMC (2007), student nurses should act as role models in promoting a professional image and in developing trusting relationships; therefore students are expected not only to become competent practitioners but to influence others

➤ *how* – can a person learn to be a role model? The evidence from the literature is that one learns to be a role model from another role model (Illingworth, 2006); this is particularly relevant to professionalism and values

➤ *where* – professionalism and values can be learned both in practice and in the academic setting

➤ *who* – in the practice setting, role modelling is learned from practitioners and the mentor has a key role (Armstrong, 2008); in the academic setting it is the responsibility of the educators (Paterson and Crawford, 1994) and other faculty staff. Peters (2006) discusses the value of educators in supporting students in clinical practice, thus bridging both settings

➤ *when* – role modelling of professionalism and values such as respect needs to be a continuous process; it cannot be switched on and off for a session if it is to be perceived as a genuine value of the role modeller.

Two Reflective activites (15.2 and 15.3) are included for you to consider – these form part of the sample programme in Table 15.1 (*see* sessions 1 and 7). These exercises will enable you to experience elements of the programme and evaluate their usefulness.

Reflective activity 15.2

You are attending an outpatients appointment for an examination and investigations due to recent rectal bleeding.

➤ What concerns do you have about the visit to the outpatients department?
➤ Does the thought of this appointment make you feel uncomfortable? If so, in what way?

You meet one of your neighbours in the waiting room – you know that, in the past, this neighbour has discussed other people's lives with other neighbours.

➤ What could the outpatient department staff do to prevent you feeling uncomfortable?

Reflective activity 15.3

➤ Identify one occasion when you maintained or promoted a person's dignity.
➤ Describe what you did.
➤ How do you know that this maintained/promoted this person's dignity?
➤ Why were you successful in maintaining/promoting this person's dignity?
➤ What can you take forward from this occasion to maintain/promote the dignity of others?

ASSESSMENT

Assessment has been suggested as a way of stimulating learning (Morris and Faulk, 2007). In a small qualitative study, ten students evaluated a range of assessments, including a community assessment, which involved assessing, planning, implementing and evaluating care outcomes from a holistic base and an individualised care planning assignment, and reported personal development in the value of human dignity (Morris and Faulk, 2007). Entwistle (2000) supports the use of assignments as a way of enabling students to demonstrate their understanding in an observable way. He also sees these 'performances of understanding' as an opportunity to develop the student's ability to think at a higher level. However, as previously discussed, formal assessment can impede deep learning and lead to what Entwistle (2000) terms 'an apathetic approach to study and surface learning'. To avoid this, the assessments need to be designed to reward personal understanding rather than reproducing knowledge. Formative rather than summative assessment will allow more freedom for the student to develop, as it reduces the fear of failing.

CONCLUSION

This chapter has emphasised the responsibility of universities to provide values education, incorporating dignity and respect. Other relevant values are integrity, empathy and compassion. It was argued that the ethical approach to teaching dignity should be most influential; however, the importance of both spirituality and politics was acknowledged. Application to practice is fundamental, as dignity education aims to improve the care experiences of service users. Due to the complexity and enduring nature of concepts that are part of a person's self-image, changes are difficult to effect. Therefore, education must provide opportunities for deep learning and facilitate learners in constructing their own meanings from their educational experiences in the university and practice environments. Only then can students transform their personal constructs and their professional practice. Educators must ensure that the environment is conducive to learning.

To be effective, theoretical educational approaches need to be translated into practical application. Kipling's five Ws and one H provide a useful framework for planning an educational programme. There are many learning strategies available; the final choice of strategy – *how* – for a session depends on the *what*, *when*, *where* and *who*. Role modelling was used as a bridge between concepts and application of theory. Assessment of learning is important to enable students to internalise their concept of dignity and transform their practice, thereby influencing others as a role model, as well as by explicit activities such as acting formally as an advocate. Summative assessment may impede internalisation and lead to surface learning; therefore, formative assessment may be more effective.

The chapter included a sample programme with suggestions for dignity education. As in any educational programme, the learning strategies used should be tailored to the learning styles of the students and the resources available. To conclude, deep learning and improving practice are fundamental in education for dignity in care.

ACKNOWLEDGEMENT

The authors would like to thank Mr R Brittle, lecturer, for his input to the questions in the sample programme for dignity education.

REFERENCES

American Association of Colleges of Nursing (1998) *The Baccalaureate: education for professional nursing practice.* Washington: American Association of Colleges of Nursing.

Armstrong N (2008) Role modelling in the clinical workplace. *British Journal of Midwifery* 16(9): 569–603.

Beattie V, Collins B, McInnes B (1997) Deep and surface learning: a simple or simplistic dichotomy? *Accounting Education* 6(1): 1–12.

Chirema KD (2006) The use of reflective journals in the promotion of reflection and learning in post-registration nursing students. *Nurse Education Today* 27: 192–202.

Chou S-M, Tang F-I, Teng Y-C *et al* (2003) Faculty's perceptions of humanistic teaching in nursing baccalaureate programs. *Journal of Nursing Research* 11(1): 57–63.

Clare B (2007) Promoting deep learning: a teaching, learning and assessment endeavour. *Social Work Education* 26(5): 433–46.

Cornwell J, Goodrich J (2009) Exploring how to enable compassionate care in hospital to improve patient experience. *Nursing Times* 105(15): 14–16.

Davison N, Williams K (2009) Compassion in nursing 2: factors that influence compassionate care in clinical practice. *Nursing Times* 105(37): 18–19.

Department of Health (2006) *Dignity in Care Public Survey October 2006. Report of the survey. Gateway number: 7213.* London: Department of Health.

Elfrink V, Lutz EM (1991) American Association of Colleges of Nursing essential values: national study of faculty perceptions, practices and plans. *Journal of Professional Nursing* 7(4): 239–45.

Entwistle N (2000) *Promoting Deep Learning Through Teaching and Assessment: conceptual frameworks and educational contexts.* Paper presented at the Teaching Learning Research Programme Conference, Leicester. www.tlrp.org/acadpub/Entwistle2000.pdf (accessed 13 October 2010)

Fagermoen MS (1997) Professional identity: values embedded in meaningful nursing practice. *Journal of Advanced Nursing* 25(3): 434–41.

Fahrenwald NL, Bassett SD, Tschetter L *et al* (2005) Teaching core nursing values. *Journal of Professional Nursing* 21(1): 46–51.

Gallagher A (2004) Dignity and respect for dignity – two key health professional values: implications for practice. *Nursing Ethics* 11(6): 587–99.

Heliker D (2007) Story sharing: restoring the reciprocity of caring in long-term care. *Journal of Psychosocial Nursing* **45**(7): 20–23.

Henschke JA, Cooper MK (2009) *International Research Foundation for Andragogy and the Implications for the Practice of Education with Adults.* www.umsl.edu/continuinged/education/mwr2p06/pdfs/B/Henschke_Cooper_International_research_foundation.pdf

Hoover J (2002) The personal and professional impact of undertaking an educational module on human caring. *Journal of Advanced Nursing* **37**(1): 79–86.

Human Rights Act. C.42. (1998) London: Her Majesty's Stationery Office.

Illingworth P (2006) Exploring mental health students' perceptions of role models. *British Journal of Nursing* **18**(13): 812–15.

Jacelon CS, Connelly TW, Brown R *et al* (2004) A concept analysis of dignity for older adults. *Journal of Advanced Nursing* **48**(1): 76–83.

Jarvis P (1985) *The Sociology of Adult and Continuing Education.* London: Croom Helm.

Jarvis P (1987) *Adult Learning in the Social Context.* London: Croom Helm.

Johnston MJ, Dacosta C, Turale S (2004) Registered and enrolled nurses' experiences of ethical issues in nursing practice. *Australian Journal of Advanced Nursing* **22**(1): 24–30.

Kalb KA, O'Connor-Von S (2007) Ethics education in advanced practice nursing: respect for human dignity. *Nursing Education Perspectives* **28**(4): 196–202.

Kipling R (1989) *Just So Stories for Little Children.* Harmondsworth: Penguin.

Lockyer J, Gondocz T, Thivierge RL (2004) Knowledge translation: the role and place of practice reflection. *Journal of Continuing Education in the Health Professions* **24**(1): 50–6.

MacNeil MS, Evans M (2005) The pedagogy of caring in nursing education. *International Journal of Human Caring* **9**(4): 45–51.

Manthey M (2008) Social justice and nursing: the key is respect. *Creative Nursing* **14**(2): 62–5.

Marton F, Saljo R (1976) On qualitative differences in learning. 1. Outcome and process. *British Journal of Educational Psychology* **46**(1): 4–11.

Matiti M (2002) *Patient Dignity in Nursing: a phenomenological study.* Unpublished PhD thesis. Huddersfield University.

Matiti M, Cotrel-Gibbons E, Teasdale K (2007) Promoting patient dignity in healthcare settings. *Nursing Standard* **21**(45): 46–52.

Mezirow J (2000) *Learning as Transformation.* San Francisco: Jossey Bass.

Morris AH, Faulk D (2007) Perspective transformation: enhancing the development of professionalism in RN-to BSN students. *Journal of Nurse Education* **46**(10): 445–51.

Nursing and Midwifery Council (2007) *Essential Skills Clusters for Pre-registration Nursing Programmes.* London: Nursing and Midwifery Council.

Pask G (1988) Learning strategies, teaching strategies and conceptual or learning style. In: Schmeck RR (ed) *Learning Strategies and Learning Styles.* New York: Plenum Press, pp.83–100.

Paterson B, Crawford M (1994) Caring in nursing education: an analysis. *Journal of Advanced Nursing* **19**(1): 164–73.

Peters MA (2006) Compassion: an investigation into the experience of nursing faculty. *International Journal for Human Caring* **10**(3): 38–46.

Quinn FM, Hughes SJ (2007) *Principles and Practice of Nurse Education* (5e). London: Croom Helm.

Raya A (1990) Can knowledge be promoted and values be ignored? Implications for nursing education. *Journal of Advanced Nursing* **15**(5): 504–509.

Rush B (2008) Mental health service user involvement in nurse education: a catalyst for transformative learning. *Journal of Mental Health* **17**(5): 531–42.

Sandberg J, Barnard Y (1997) Deep learning is difficult. *Instructional Science* **25**: 15–36.

Shaw HK, Degazon C (2008) Integrating the core professional values of nursing: a profession, not just a career. *Journal of Cultural Diversity* **15**(1): 44–50.

Social Care Institute for Excellence (2006) *Dignity in Care*. London: Social Care Institute for Excellence.

Stern DT (2000) The development of professional character in medical students. *Hastings Center Report* **30**(4): S26–9.

Stuhlmiller CM (2003) Breaking down the stigma of mental illness through an adventure camp: a collaborative education initiative. *Australian e-journal for the Advancement of Mental Health* **2**(2): 1–9.

Teeri S, Valimaki M, Katajisto J et al (2008) Maintenance of patients' integrity in long-term institutional care. *Nursing Ethics* **15**(4): 523–35.

Trueland J (2009) Compassion through human connection. *Nursing Standard* **23**(48): 19–21.

Tschudin V (2004) Editorial. *Nursing Ethics* **11**(6): 539–40.

Vacek JE (2009) Using a conceptual approach with concept mapping to promote critical thinking. *Journal of Nurse Education* **48**(1): 45–8.

Vezeau TM (2006) Teaching professional values in a BSN Program. *International Journal of Nursing Education Scholarship* **3**(1): 1–15.

Warburton K (2003) Deep learning and education for sustainability. *International Journal of Sustainability in Higher Education* **4**(1): 44–56.

Weinberg D, Weinberg GM (1983) Learning by design: constructing experiential learning programs. Proceedings of the Second Annual Information Systems Education Conference, 21–23 March, 1983, Chicago, USA.

Weis D, Schank MJ (2002) Professional values: key to professional development. *Journal of Professional Nursing* **18**(5): 271–5.

Williams B (2001) Developing critical reflection for professional practice through problem based learning. *Journal of Advanced Nursing* **34**(1): 27–34.

Woogara J (2005) Patients' rights to privacy and dignity in the NHS. *Nursing Standard* **19**(18): 33–7.

Yorks L, Sharoff L (2001) An extended epistemology for fostering transformative learning in holistic nursing education and practice. *Holistic Nursing Practice* **16**(1): 21–9.

CHAPTER 16

Enabling dignity in care through practice development

Kate Sanders and Jonathan Webster

Awakening, whilst all around sleep,
icy cold encapsulates my world,
I persevere, I reach, I grow, I look upwards.
Light comes from my strength,
strength comes from my inner light.
I reach, I look upwards, I grow,
whilst all around awakens.

(Jonathan Webster)

INTRODUCTION

Defining dignity is complex; similarly, helping practitioners to develop practice (the ultimate aim being to improve the person's experience of care) in
the context of complex work-based cultures and ever-changing services can be
challenging. This chapter will consider how practice development can enable
practitioners to improve dignity in care through creative, transformational ways
of learning supported by skilled facilitation.

The first part of this chapter provides a brief history of practice development
to set it into the context of the United Kingdom (UK) healthcare modernisation
agenda. Practice development will then be defined and the key characteristics
identified. Two pictures from practice describe how practice development can
facilitate the development of people, practice and workplace cultures towards
enabling the delivery of person-centred, evidence-based care. This chapter will
also acknowledge some of the challenges within complex healthcare contexts
and will identify core components that will help sustain and enable ongoing
practice development.

LEARNING OUTCOMES

By the end of this chapter you will be able to:

➤ describe how practice development has emerged in the context of health-care modernisation
➤ identify the key concepts and methods of practice development
➤ recognise how practice development methods can be used to develop both practice and practitioners, to improve dignity in patient care
➤ understand some of the challenges of developing practice in complex workplace cultures.

PRACTICE DEVELOPMENT: A BRIEF HISTORY

Achieving and sustaining improvements in care is challenging, particularly when there is a constant drive to achieve economic efficiency and cost savings at all levels across organisations. It is therefore essential in our view that the workplace is receptive and open to ways of working that have improving quality at their core, but where staff feel empowered and enabled to think critically and work in new ways, the ultimate goal being to improve the quality of care for patients and for those people who support them.

Practice development has become a commonly used phrase to describe the variety of ways in which healthcare professionals develop their knowledge and skills to improve patient care (Titchen and Higgs, 2001; Garbett and McCormack, 2002; McCormack and Garbett, 2003; Manley and McCormack, 2004; McCormack et al, 2006) and that encompasses both nursing (Manley, 1997; McCormack et al, 1999) and the broader multiprofessional team (Walsh, 2000).

In order to understand the significance of practice development, it is useful to look at its emergence alongside other patient and healthcare developments.

In a recent review of the practice development literature, Shaw (2009) traces the development of practice development as a concept in the UK over the last three decades. She identifies the late 1970s as the starting point, with the move for nursing to become more patient centred through the introduction of the nursing process. This was followed by an increased emphasis on achieving quality healthcare through efficiency and productivity, which characterised the general management ideology of the 1980s (Griffiths, 1983), alongside which came further developments in nursing, including primary nursing (Pearson, 1983), nursing development units (NDUs) and, subsequently, practice development units (PDUs). Shaw (2009, p.24) suggests that the PDUs provided 'stepping stones toward the emergence of practice development as a concept', with the focus being on delivering patient-centred care that was of high quality and achieved through effective multidisciplinary working and a commitment to the development of nursing practice.

The 1990s saw an increased emphasis on the need for healthcare to be based on research evidence, which brought the concept of evidence-based practice to the fore (Shaw, 2009). However, the implementation of evidence into practice, for example via guidelines, is a complicated process (Royle and Blythe, 1998; Rycroft-Malone *et al*, 2002) and the assumption that once research and/ or evidence is made available, it will be accessed by practitioners, appraised and then applied into practice is naïve (*Effective Healthcare Bulletin*, 1999) and often proves to be ineffective (Rycroft-Malone *et al*, 2002). Such findings suggest that alternative approaches to developing practice that take into account the complexities of healthcare practice contexts are needed.

The new British government in 1997 and their strong healthcare modernisation agenda could be seen as one of the most significant factors to support the emergence of practice development in the UK over recent years (McSherry and Warr, 2006). This agenda, supported by the introduction of new frameworks of accountability such as clinical governance, a variety of new roles, for example, practice development nurse, clinical practice facilitator, and new organisations such as NHS Quality Improvement Scotland and NHS Institute for Innovation to champion improvement in all four countries of the UK, has continued to be a major influence into the new millennium, with 'quality of care' as 'a central principle' being positioned alongside 'access, volume and cost of healthcare' (Royal College of Nursing, 2009).

Over the past ten years, there have been significant advances in the development of frameworks to guide practice development activities, and an increased understanding about the key underlying principles and methodological perspectives (McCormack *et al*, 2004; Manley *et al*, 2008). This work has been further strengthened by growing international collaboration, particularly between practitioners in the UK, Australia, New Zealand and Holland.

PRACTICE DEVELOPMENT: AN OVERVIEW

The term 'practice development' has frequently been used 'loosely' and interchangeably with others such as 'research into practice' (Mallett *et al*, 1997), and also to describe a broad range of educational (McKenna, 1995), continual professional development (Aggergaard *et al*, 2005; Walsgrove and Fulbrook, 2005), research (Rolfe, 1996) and audit (National Health Service Executive, 1996) activity. However, while in the past there has been a lack of clarity, a stronger and clearer understanding of practice development is emerging.

It can be argued that while practice development is directly concerned with the world of practice, if practice developers are to be effective, there is a need for them to be aware of and understand the assumptions that underpin the way that they work, and to use approaches that are systematic, rigorous and informed by their specific intended purposes (Manley and McCormack, 2004).

DEFINING PRACTICE DEVELOPMENT

The Department of Health (1993, 2003) has defined development (as in practice development) as a systematic process for change; however, Tolson et al (2006) argue that such a simplistic definition gives a false impression of the complexity of developing practice. A variety of more detailed definitions of practice development have been offered, and a summary of a selection (those based upon literature and/or contextually based evidence rather than opinion alone) is shown in Table 16.1.

These definitions help us to identify the key concepts of practice development, as they suggest both the purpose of practice development as well as the means by which this purpose is achieved. In summary, these definitions suggest that the purpose of practice development is improvement in healthcare, towards the achievement of effective and good-quality patient-centred care. The means by which this purpose is achieved have become increasingly refined but essentially include facilitation, the development of knowledge and skills, the use of processes that are systematic and rigorous and the transformation of contexts and cultures of care. It is argued that these activities need to be directly targeted at practice to have an impact on how practitioners work with patients, as opposed to just focusing on personal and/or professional development, which may or may not directly impact on practice (Manley and McCormack, 2004). Shaw (2009, p.63) argues that it is 'the emphasis practice development places on patients, their needs and their care that makes it distinct and arguably more effective in transforming practitioners and their practice.'

Practice development has, on occasions, been presented as a 'linear' or 'simple' educational process; however, there is increasing recognition that it is much more 'complex' and 'multifaceted' (Dewing and Wright, 2003). This complexity is articulated in an 'emancipatory' methodology of practice development (Manley and McCormack, 2004), which uses the concepts of critical social theory and emphasises the development of individual practitioners and the cultures and contexts within which they work to achieve sustainable changes in practice. This methodology is further refined in a recent revision of the McCormack and Garbett (2000) definition of practice development, proposed by Manley et al (2008) following critical dialogue with members of the International Practice Development Colloquium (a cooperative inquiry of practice developers, practitioner researchers and educators). It proposes that:

> Practice development is a continuous process of developing person-centred cultures. It is enabled by facilitators who authentically engage with individuals and teams to blend personal qualities and creative imagination with practice skills and practice wisdom. The learning that occurs brings about transformations of individual and team practices. This is sustained by embedding both processes and outcomes in corporate strategy (Manley et al, 2008, p.9, reproduced with permission from Wiley-Blackwell).

Table 16.1 Definitions of practice development

Author(s)	Definition of practice development	Informed by
Kitson (1994, p.5)	Practice development: • is a 'system' for introducing 'new activities or practices' • involves 'change agents' who 'work with staff' • is based on research, experience or 'trying out new ideas' • should be 'systematic' and 'carefully evaluated'	This definition emerged from nursing research and development activity supported by the National Institute for Nursing in Oxford
Mallett et al (1997, p.38)	Practice development is: • a 'continuous process' • linked to but different from professional development • concerned with using 'knowledge, skills and values' (professional development) to 'provide good-quality patient-focused care'	Mallett et al (1997) conducted a pilot study to explore the nature of professional development and practice development roles using questionnaires with nurses who were part of a professional and practice development nurses' forum
Unsworth (2000, p.323)	Practice development: • requires practitioners with multiple skills • introduces 'new ways of working' • is concerned with improving care or services • is concerned with sustaining or developing services • introduces changes that respond to client needs • results in effective services	These critical attributes of practice development were identified through the process of concept analysis, which was informed by dictionary definitions and literature
Garbett and McCormack (2002, p.88)	Practice development: • is a 'continuous process of improvement' • focuses on increasing 'effectiveness in patient-centred care' • focuses on achieving changes that reflect the perspective of service users • transforms cultures and contexts of care • is enabled by facilitation • uses 'systematic' and 'rigorous' processes	This definition emerged from a concept analysis, which was informed by literature analysis, telephone interviews and focus groups

This latest definition proposes that the purpose of practice development is the development of person-centred cultures, and places greater emphasis on the role of facilitation and the use of creativity (which has grown from the theoretical and methodological work of McCormack and Titchen [2006]) as the means for achieving transformations. This definition also highlights the importance of ensuring that practice development is not only embedded in practice but forms part of a strategic, corporate focus that will enable ongoing and active support for individuals and teams at a 'high level' within an organisation.

How is practice development approached?

Much of the success of practice development can be attributed to the way it is approached, and the connection between this and its outcomes for practice (Shaw, 2009).

A review of the evidence around practice development published in 2006 recommended that all practice development work should have evidence of a 'participatory, inclusive and collaborative methodology being used' (McCormack *et al*, 2006, p.11). In addition, 18 methods were identified that practice development projects should be able to demonstrate using. These methods have been themed by Shaw (2009, p.88; *see* Box 16.1), who suggests that an effective practice development project would emphasise each of six areas of significance.

Practice development or service improvement?

We have already acknowledged that the need to continuously improve the quality of care provided in the NHS is at the core of the UK government's programme for health service modernisation. It could be argued, however, that it is service improvement not practice development that has been embraced as a means of achieving these reforms. So what is the difference between practice development and service improvement?

Henderson and McKillop (2008) and Shaw (2009) have taken a closer look at the two concepts and acknowledge the similarities. They identify that both are concerned with improving patient care and use systematic and rigorous processes of change that are enabled by facilitators. Additionally, they both support the involvement of service users and other stakeholders; joint working across all healthcare services and settings; patient-centred care; and learning in and from practice. However, Henderson and McKillop (2008, p.339) believe that although there are many similarities between ideas and approaches, there are significant differences in the methods and the tools that are used. To summarise, service improvement largely focuses on 'systems and processes', while practice development concentrates on 'people and their practices.'

BOX 16.1 *Eighteen essential processes or methods for practice development identified by McCormack et al (2006) and themed by Shaw (2009) into six areas of significance*

1. Person-centred care
➤ Agreed ethical processes – 1
➤ Stakeholder analysis and agreed ways of engaging stakeholders – 2
➤ Person-centredness – 3

2. Collaboration and partnership
➤ Agreed ethical processes – 1
➤ Stakeholder analysis and agreed ways of engaging stakeholders – 2
➤ Person centredness – 3
➤ Values clarification – 4
➤ Developing a shared vision – 5
➤ Collaboration and participation – 7
➤ Developing shared ownership – 8

3. Enabling facilitation and support
➤ Methods to facilitate critical reflection – 10
➤ High challenge and high support – 11
➤ Facilitation of transitions – 15

4. Commitment to active learning and development
➤ Reflective learning – 9
➤ Methods to facilitate critical reflection – 10
➤ High challenge and high support – 11
➤ Feedback – 12
➤ Knowledge use – 13
➤ Giving space for ideas to flourish – 16
➤ Dissemination of learning – 17

5. Transforming workplace culture
➤ Workplace culture analysis – 6
➤ Rewarding success – 18

6. Evaluation
➤ Process and outcome evaluation – 14
➤ Dissemination of learning – 17

While there is a growing body of evidence to demonstrate the valuable contribution of service improvement to healthcare service development (Henderson and McKillop, 2008), Shaw (2009, p.301) argues that the use of practice development methodology 'could strengthen service development activity and increase participation in and sustainability of healthcare service improvement initiatives'.

PRACTICE DEVELOPMENT AND DIGNITY: 'PICTURES OF PRACTICE'

Picture one

This programme of practice development has been published (Webster *et al*, 2009) and presented at several conferences (Partners in Practice – University College London Hospitals NHS Foundation Trust 2008; International Practice Development Conference, Koningshof, The Netherlands 2008; Royal College of Nursing – Nursing Older People Conference, Manchester 2009).

Background

The profile and importance of dignity as a core component of essential care and a fundamental human right have attracted much attention. Different authors have identified the challenges of defining what is meant by 'dignity' (Fenton and Mitchell, 2002; Webster and Byrne, 2004; RCN, 2008); how patients (people) experience dignified or undignified care (Calnan *et al*, 2003; Woolhead *et al*, 2004; Age Concern, 2006) and the impact on person-centred outcomes and therapeutic relationships. In addition, sustaining and embedding dignity in how both individuals and teams work with older people remain challenging (Webster, 2007a).

Within the NHS trust in which this programme of practice development ran, I (Jonathan Webster), as consultant nurse for older people, had been asked to take a trust-wide lead in raising the profile of the importance of dignity in care at a time when there had been much publicity concerning the role of the 'dignity nurse' (Womack, 2006). This didn't mean that care within the trust was not dignified but rather that there was a need to make explicit the importance of dignity and to raise the profile of the importance of dignity and respect as part of all activities that involved patients.

I recognised how easy it was to espouse the importance and value of dignity in care (who wouldn't say that dignity is important?); however, more important, in my view, was the need to help staff embed change in clinical practice, to promote critical reflection leading to better understanding and insight, the core goal being to improve the patient's (person's) experience of care. While teaching, training and awareness raising play an important part in technical learning, I recognised that this was only a small part of the approach needed to enable change to occur (when it is needed) in highly complex and challenging work-based cultures and settings. As a nurse working with older people, practice development has played an important part in how I have worked with both individuals and teams (Webster, 2007b) in a number of different posts and organisations; the ultimate aim is to help individuals transform the way in which they work with patients and provide care, through skilled facilitation and work-based support.

Synopsis of the programme of practice development

The programme of practice development (reported in full by Webster *et al*, 2009) that ran for six months brought eight nurses and eight older people together to explore the meaning and understanding of dignity in care, using a variety of creative approaches such as collage and dance. Supporting each of the facilitated sessions was a reflective learning group for the nurse participants.

At the end of the programme, the nurses described how they had led changes in their clinical settings aimed at improving and raising the profile of dignity in care. These included improving methods of communication across the multiprofessional team; introducing preoperative visits to assess and meet patients; and the introduction of music to the clinical setting as part of the hospitals arts programme. Additionally, participants (both nurses and older people) described how the programme had not only raised their awareness but had enabled them to learn and share in an open, supportive environment. One older person stated:

> The discussions allowed me to open up and share experiences which have not been expressed before. I was comfortable but glad to get rid of the pain. The relief was immense.

Eloise (one of the nurse participants) described her experience of taking part and completing the programme (*see* Box 16.2).

Reflections/critique on learning

Throughout the programme of practice development the '18 essential processes or methods for practice development', as identified by McCormack *et al* (2006) and themed by Shaw (2009) earlier in the chapter, were evident at different times and stages of the journey.

This programme of practice development was not without its challenges. The real world of clinical care can be a highly challenging setting in which to work with practitioners, not only because of the day-to-day pressures of delivering services but also because of the broader influences asserted by both the work-based and organisational culture, which can be either enabling or disen-

BOX 16.2 *Vignette 1: Eloise*

This type of learning was very new to all of us. As nurses we were all used to the conventional teaching in a classroom where the teacher (the main focus) told you what you need to know, while in the approach taken with us as part of the programme we were teachers to each other, reflecting out loud or through the creative arts on good and bad practice. This allowed each of us to reflect on our own and with other group members' experiences. I wanted to immediately go straight back to the ward and share with my colleagues the type of 'care' patients are exposed to that compromises dignity, and to find out how our patients felt and from there how to change practice. This type of learning was very real; we saw group members' facial expressions of hurt, the pain in their eyes, when they had to share what had happened, and it reaffirmed (if there was any doubt) what a privilege it is, that people allow us as nurses, into their personal space at some of the hardest times in their lives. What became clear hearing people's stories was that what makes people feel respected is ensuring that care is given in a safe place, to be nursed by caring staff who will deliver individual patient centred care in a respectful, sensitive manner.

At the start of the programme we (the nurses and older people) were sitting at opposite sides of the room but by the end of the sessions we were working together and focused on making a difference to improve experiences of dignity. What was highlighted from the sessions was that everyone had their own meaning of dignity, but we all share the same idea that it is a fundamental human right and should be implicit as part of providing care. We each made our own objectives and plans of changing practice to bring back to our wards.

Within my own ward, a colleague and I set up a noticeboard where we could put up our names to highlight our roles to patients, families and staff as dignity champions, and also put up-to-date information on dignity in care and a suggestion box with comment cards to be filled in by patients during their stay so that they could tell us about their experiences of dignity in care on the ward. We recognised from listening to older people who took part in the programme that the environment in which care is delivered is important; rooms are now checked regularly to ensure curtains are fitted perfectly around the beds. Also we encouraged patients to wear their own night and day clothes and explained to patients and families the importance of upholding the rest period. On our wards the rooms are mostly single, so lack of privacy may not always be an issue but isolation and loneliness is a problem (this is something I had never thought about); plans are under way for a day room to be opened on the ward to enable patients to mix (if they wish) and to be able to eat away from the bedside too.

It is crucial in my area of practice (cardiothoracic surgery) to understand the complexities of caring for older people, as thoracic and cardiac surgery is invasive, and is being carried out increasingly on older people. It is essential for them to be supported and fully informed from admission to aftercare, as it will encourage faster recovery and enhance the experience of care. The next step for me is to translate my understanding of the importance of dignity in care into the clinical setting in which I work to help raise awareness in staff of the importance of dignified care. Even though this was a pilot programme of practice development, it would be so beneficial for all areas and teams to reflect and learn in a similar way, as the approach taken has transformed both my understanding and how I work as a nurse, which in turn has transformed care and raised the profile of the importance of dignity within the team in which I work.

Included with the permission of Eloise Horgan, Staff Nurse, University College London Hospitals NHS Foundation Trust.

abling to developing practice and new ways of working when there are competing pressures.

Through the sharing of stories based on reflection on action, nurse participants described how they were using the knowledge gained from the programme and their learning/collaboration with older people to influence how they worked with older people in their clinical settings on a day-to-day basis, with a clear focus on developing a greater person-centred approach to care. Conversely, through reflection, participants also described how they were increasingly reflecting in action when working with older people, and making sense of situations that they were facing.

Through facilitation (as part of the programme for nurses and older people) and group reflective learning for nurse participants, there was also evidence of group members increasingly challenging each other and their assumptions, beliefs and current ways of working. Such 'high challenge' required 'high support' to enable learning and better insight into their practice and the development of a shared understanding and, in turn, a shared vision. In the early stages of the programme, the majority of 'challenge' was provided by the older people as they shared stories and reflections of care; however, as the programme developed, nurse participants increasingly challenged each other and themselves, leading to a transition in both their understanding and how they practised.

Nurse participants described the importance of disseminating learning/knowledge and the need to help their colleagues to find both space and time to critically reflect on their own practice and to develop new ideas. Leadership and support in practice played a key role in enabling participants to 'grow', to carry the dignity agenda forward in their clinical setting and to 'own' developments. The ward sisters/charge nurses shaped this agenda and I observed that where developing practice and care was central to how the team worked and the work-based culture, the themes from the programme were more readily embraced by the team as a whole and applied to day-to-day practice with older people. More broadly, this also highlighted that the 'unseen' power of culture and the place of tradition and ritual should not be underestimated when helping practitioners to explore and critically question their practice. It appeared that for those nurse participants who were working in less 'receptive' work-based cultures, their need for support was greater as they tried to influence colleagues, peers and more senior staff.

Picture two

> The person with dementia is an individual with feelings – treat them with respect and dignity (Alzheimer's Disease International, 2009).

The purpose of this practice development initiative was to improve dignity in care for patients with dementia on an acute orthopaedic ward. It arose from concerns of senior nursing staff who had observed some of their nursing team delivering care that disregarded the older person involved, as they were focusing on achieving a task rather than the needs, desires or wants of the patient, causing distress for the patients and their families. Through discussions with the staff involved, and more general conversations with the clinical teams, it became apparent that development directly targeted at practice was needed to enhance staff awareness and understanding of the concept of dignity from the perspective of patients with dementia.

There were three key elements to this practice development initiative:
- ➤ three workshop days held in the hospital education centre facilitated by a clinical specialist in dementia care
- ➤ the development of a designated bay allocated for trauma patients with dementia called the 'forget me not' bay
- ➤ the creation of a working group of 'forget me not champions' to facilitate the exchange of ideas and implementation of actions to improve the hospital experience for this group of patients.

The world of practice – enhancing understanding of dementia and maintaining dignity

Following discussions with the senior nursing team, a workshop programme was developed and delivered by an external facilitator with expertise in dementia care and practice development. The workshop activities were targeted at practice, reflecting on and working with real clinical situations surrounding person-centred dementia care. The workshop was run on three occasions to enable day, night and therapy staff to attend. The involvement of as many staff as possible was seen to be essential, so that, collectively, they could explore and challenge current practice and develop a shared understanding of how care should be delivered and experienced.

Enhancing the environment

Practical and environmental measures can be taken to help support patients with dementia in the acute setting (Archibald, 2002). To achieve this, a six-bedded bay was designated for female patients with dementia. Using charitable funds, the room was decorated and furnished to provide a homely atmosphere with a sense of calm and with noise from the clinical unit reduced. Personal care plans have been introduced to enable staff to learn more about the patient and to enable them to communicate their likes, dislikes, needs and wants. Relatives are encouraged to provide information for the care plans and to bring in personal and familiar belongings for the patient. The introduction of open visiting has also enabled relatives to have greater involvement in care.

Stimulating and sustaining change

Staff were invited to form a working group to support the ongoing development of practice relating to dignity in care for patients with dementia. Twelve members of the multidisciplinary team now meet regularly to discuss issues, exchange ideas and reflect on how they can lead and facilitate new ways of working to continuously improve care. The demands of the unit are such that nursing time is precious, and so these meetings are short, but remain vital to ensure ongoing critique and to maintain motivation and enthusiasm.

Evaluating the impact

At a variety of stages through the process, staff and relatives were asked for their views and perspectives on how the workshops and environmental changes had impacted on the way in which care was delivered and experienced. This included the use of group reflection, written reflections and questionnaires. The following examples illustrate the ways in which staff believed that their knowledge and understanding of dementia had improved and how, as a result, the care they are giving has become more dignified, with greater emphasis on taking time and listening to the patients' needs and wants (also *see* Box 16.3).

I am now able to approach patients with an altogether new awareness of how they may perceive the environment around them.

I will no longer think of the job that has to be done. I will now look at the patient and wonder what they would like. I will listen more.

I enjoy working in the "forget me not bay". The focus of care is different. I can really relate to the patients and concentrate on what they need and what is going on.

When a patient is upset, angry and aggressive, I now try and see it from their point of view, be on their side and try and help them sort out the problem, or leave them alone if that's what they want. I used to ignore these emotions and carry on regardless, as I wanted to get the care delivery done. Now I wait until the patient is ready and in a state of well-being.

Relatives also reported positive experiences of care by the patients.

I feel you understand what my mother needs. I like the friendly atmosphere. It feels welcoming in here. I like the lights, pictures and music.

Thank you for letting me be involved in the care of my Mum. I like to be included and I always feel welcome. I like to help, and I know how busy you all are. This room has a special feel, and am pleased you make meal times and feeding an important issue.

Reflection on processes
The purpose of practice development as identified earlier in the chapter is continuous development towards the delivery of care that is person centred, and this picture from practice has demonstrated how this can be achieved for older people with dementia.

Within the context of therapeutic working with older people, Pritchard (2002, p.28) describes practice development as: '. . . helping practitioners within their real world context . . . to find creative and positive ways forward through the demanding, often confusing and draining day-to-day trials and tribulations of practice'. This view highlights the 'helping' and 'facilitative' approach needed by practice developers to work creatively with practitioners to help them to critically explore, and in doing so develop their practice at times when there may be immense pressure, or delivery of the 'quality' agenda may be difficult to achieve (Pugh *et al*, 2005).

Similarly, recognising that practice development's key aim is to 'improve' the person's experience of care, Hamer (2002, p.66) states: 'If practice devel-

BOX 16.3 *Vignette 2: Nikki*

Patient care is now delivered in a calm, quiet and relaxed atmosphere. Patients' personal needs are assessed and delivered in a timely and patient-focused manner according to what the individual wants. Ward routine is not adhered to in the bay and personal care is given as and when the patient needs. This is supported by personal care plans, which contain details of the patient's personal life stories, likes and dislikes.

The culture has shifted hugely. We are slowly becoming well known in the trust for delivering optimal and dignified care for this group of patients. The team are proud of the 'forget me not bay', and this sense of pride is reinforced by the positive feedback that we are constantly receiving from relatives and members of the multidisciplinary team. It is now a common conversation within the team to discuss individual patients and how we can meet their personal needs, however difficult this may be. The approach now is not how to get the job done but how can we make this as pleasurable as possible for the patient – going with the patient's flow and mood rather than a list of tasks. We enjoy their company and the bay has its own atmosphere and feeling.

At the beginning the staff strongly opposed the idea. New things were often met with suspicion and it was felt that the work load would be greatly increased as this group of patients had a poor status within the ward, as they were generally considered to be difficult and demanding to care for. From my perspective, there was an obvious lack of knowledge and understanding about dementia amongst staff. The workshop days were therefore really important in enabling change. The learning opportunities helped staff to develop an insight into the illness and to discover the ways in which they could meet the needs of patients and ensure that their experience of care was dignified and stress free. This involved exploring how to enter the patients' perspective and not to impose our reality. The 'forget me not champions' provided visible leadership and also helped to motivate the team.

With hindsight, I should have involved higher management more throughout the development to enable the initiative to have become trust-wide.

Included with the permission of Nikki Haak, Ward Manager, Royal Surrey County Hospital NHS Foundation Trust.

opment is a patient centred rather than a professional centred activity, as we believe it must be, then the extent to which we are able to gain insight into the perspective of service users, their perceptions, needs, wants and expectations, must be key to our success in this field'.

It is evident that skilled facilitation and transformational leadership have been fundamental to enabling this nursing team to critically explore their current ways of working, develop a deeper understanding of the patients' perspectives and consequently effect changes in the ways in which care is delivered and experienced. The culture of care within the 'forget me not bay' is now one that is centred on the needs and wants of the patients.

While it was senior staff who initially recognised the need for change, the processes used in this development enabled the multidisciplinary team to work collaboratively to achieve a shared understanding of how care should be delivered and experienced and to take ownership of the necessary changes to practice and the environment. Active involvement of relatives continues to enhance the person-centred approaches to care. The 'forget me not champions' and meetings provide ongoing critique and commitment to care and provide the time and space for new ideas to flourish.

While this project focused on enhancing dignity in care for patients with dementia, it would be interesting to explore how the methods used have impacted on dignity in care for patients on the ward who do not have dementia, as practice development is an approach that enables practitioners to work in person-centred ways regardless of the focus of care (Manley et al, 2008). Additionally, the need for active support from senior management and organisational strategy is recognised to enable the spreading, sharing and sustaining of good practice.

CONCLUSION

In healthcare today, traditional methods of integrating research and practice have been problematic, probably as a result of failing to recognise the complexity of the practice setting (Page and Hamer, 2002) and the competing pressures faced by practitioners and managers to deliver 'quality services' within strict financial constraints at times of immense change. Balanced against this is the need to recognise the requirement for sustained and systematic approaches to changing cultures of practice, in which we move beyond traditional notions of respecting and acknowledging individuality, and individualised care, to being person centred. Practice development has much to offer in meeting these competing demands.

At the start of this chapter, we identified that defining what is meant by 'dignity' is complex; similarly, helping practitioners to develop and change practice can be 'challenging' when the work-based culture is not supportive or open to enabling transformation in practice to occur. Embedding dignity and respect in the way in which practitioners work with patients and their supporters is core to delivering quality-focused services. However, we know that this can be problematic, as illustrated in a number of high-profile publications underpinned by harrowing stories when dignity has been diminished. Balanced against such harrowing stories and examples of undignified practice is the need to recognise in equal measure examples of practice where dignity and respect are core to how teams work and fundamental to how patients experience care.

We would argue that simplistic approaches to understanding complex phenomena such as 'dignity', 'clinical practice' and 'culture' will invariably lead to limited (if any) successful, sustainable improved outcomes for patients. In our view, both understanding and being able to work with complex work-based cultures are key to enabling the development of effective, person-centred practice. However, this doesn't happen haphazardly, it requires leadership, skilled facilitation and an approach to practice development that enables transformational change to occur and be sustained.

ACKNOWLEDGEMENTS

Eloise Horgan, Staff Nurse, University College London Hospitals NHS Foundation Trust; Nikki Haak, Ward Manager, Royal Surrey County Hospital NHS Foundation Trust; Theresa Shaw, Chief Executive, Foundation of Nursing Studies.

REFERENCES

Age Concern (2006) *Hungry to be Heard. The scandal of malnourished older people in hospital.* London: Age Concern.

Aggergaard Larsen J, Maundrill R, Morgan J *et al* (2005) Practice development facilitation: an integrated strategic and clinical approach. *Practice Development in Healthcare* 4(3): 142–9.

Alzheimer's Disease International (2009) *Living With and Caring For a Person with Dementia.* www.alz.co.uk/carers/caring.html#dignity (accessed 14 October 2010).

Archibald C (2002) *People with Dementia in Acute Hospital Settings.* Stirling: Dementia Services Development Centre, University of Stirling.

Calnan M, Woolhead G, Dieppe P (2003) Courtesy entitles. *Health Service Journal* 113(5843): 30–1.

Department of Health (1993) *Report of the Taskforce on the Strategy for Research in Nursing, Midwifery and Health Visiting (The Webb Report).* London: HMSO.

Department of Health (2003) *Report of the Taskforce on the Strategy for Research in Nursing, Midwifery and Health Visiting.* London: HMSO.

Dewing J, Wright J (2003) A practice development project for nurses working with older people. *Practice Development in Health Care* 2(1): 13–28.

Effective Healthcare Bulletin (1999) Getting evidence into practice. *Effective Healthcare Bulletin* 5(1): 1–16.

Fenton E, Mitchell T (2002) Growing old with dignity: a concept analysis. *Nursing Older People* **14**(4): 19–21.

Garbett R, McCormack B (2002) A concept analysis of practice development. *Nursing Times Research* **7**(2): 87–100.

Griffiths R (1983) *NHS Management Inquiry Report.* London: Department of Health and Social Security.

Hamer S (2002) Innovation in practice. *Practice Development in Health Care* **1**(2): 66.

Henderson L, McKillop S (2008) Using practice development approaches in the development of a managed clinical network. In: Manley K, McCormack B, Wilson V (eds) *International Practice Development in Nursing and Healthcare.* Oxford: Blackwell Publishing, pp.319–48.

Kitson A (1994) *Clinical Nursing Practice Development and Research Activity in the Oxford Region.* Oxford: Centre for Practice Development and Research, National Institute for Nursing.

Mallett J, Cathmoir D, Hughes P *et al* (1997) Forging new roles: professional and practice development. *Nursing Times* **93**(18): 38–9.

Manley K (1997) A conceptual framework for advanced practice: an action research project operationalising an advanced practitioner/consultant nurse role. *Journal of Clinical Nursing* **6**(3): 179–90.

Manley K, McCormack B (2004) Practice development: purpose, methodology, facilitation and evaluation. In: McCormack B, Manley K, Garbett R (eds) *Practice Development in Nursing.* Oxford: Blackwell Publishing, pp.33–50.

Manley K, McCormack B, Wilson V (2008) Introduction. In: Manley K, McCormack B, Wilson V (eds) *International Practice Development in Nursing and Healthcare.* Oxford: Blackwell Publishing, pp.1–16.

McCormack B, Garbett R (2000) *A Concept Analysis of Practice Development.* London: Royal College of Nursing.

McCormack B, Garbett R (2003) The meaning of practice development: evidence from the field. *Collegian* **10**(3): 13–16.

McCormack B, Titchen A (2006) Critical creativity: melding, exploding and blending. *Education Action Research* **14**(2): 239–66.

McCormack B, Manley K, Kitson A *et al* (1999) Towards practice development – a vision in reality or reality without vision. *Journal of Nursing Management* **7**(5): 255–64.

McCormack B, Manley K, Garbett R (2004) A clearer vision of practice development? In: McCormack B, Manley K, Garbett R (eds) *Practice Development in Nursing.* Oxford: Blackwell Publishing, pp.315–29.

McCormack B, Dewar B, Wright J *et al* (2006) *A Realist Synthesis of Evidence Relating to Practice Development: Final Report to the NHS Education for Scotland and NHS Quality Improvement Scotland.* Edinburgh: NHS Quality Improvement Scotland.

McKenna H (1995) Nursing skill mix substitutions and quality of care: an exploration of assumptions from the research literature. *Journal of Advanced Nursing* **21**(3): 452–59.

McSherry R, Warr J (2006) Practice development: confirming the existence of a knowledge base. *Practice Development in Healthcare* **5**(2): 55–79.

National Health Service Executive (1996) *Clinical Guidelines: using clinical guidelines to improve patient care within the NHS.* London: HMSO.

Page S, Hamer S (2002) Practice development – time to realize the potential. *Practice Development in Healthcare* **1**(1): 2–17.

Pearson A (1983) *The Clinical Nursing Unit.* London: Heinemann.

Pritchard E (2002) Practice development, trials and triumphs. *Nursing Older People* **14**(5): 28.

Pugh E, Locky M, McSherry R *et al* (2005) Innovation in practice: creating order out of chaos. Towards excellence in practice. *Practice Development in Health Care* **3**(3): 138–41.

Rolfe G (1996) *Closing the Theory–Practice Gap: a new paradigm for nursing.* Oxford: Butterworth-Heinemann.

Royal College of Nursing (2008) *Defending Dignity – Challenges and Opportunities for Nursing.* London: Royal College of Nursing.

Royal College of Nursing (2009) *Breaking Down Barriers, Driving up Standards. The role of the ward sister and charge nurse.* London: Royal College of Nursing.

Royle J, Blythe J (1998) Promoting research utilisation in nursing: the role of the individual, organisation and environment. *Evidence-based Nursing* **1**: 71–2.

Rycroft-Malone J, Harvey G, Kitson A *et al* (2002) Getting evidence into practice: ingredients for change. *Nursing Standard* **16**(37): 38–43.

Shaw T (2009) *A Qualitative Descriptive Exploration of the Experiences of Healthcare Practitioners Involved in Practice Development.* Unpublished NursD thesis. University of Nottingham.

Titchen A, Higgs J (2001) A dynamic framework for the enhancement of health professional practice in an uncertain world: the practice–knowledge interface. In: Higgs J, Titchen A (eds) *Practice Knowledge and Expertise in the Health Professions.* Oxford: Butterworth Heinemann, pp.215–25.

Tolson D, Schofield I, Booth J *et al* (2006) Constructing a new approach to developing evidence based practice with nurses and older people. *Worldviews on Evidence Based Nursing* **3**(2): 62–72.

Unsworth J (2000) Practice development: a concept analysis. *Journal of Nursing Management* **8**(6): 317–22.

Walsgrove H, Fulbrook P (2005) Advancing the clinical perspective: a practice development project to develop the nurse practitioner role in an acute hospital trust. *Journal of Clinical Nursing* **14**(4): 444–55.

Walsh M (2000) Chaos, complexity and nursing. *Nursing Standard* **14**(32): 39–42.

Webster J (2007a) We all need to challenge practices that do not value a person's right to dignity. *Nursing Times* **103**(15): 10.

Webster J (2007b) *Person-centred Assessment with Older People. An Action Research Study to Explore Registered Nurses' Understanding of Person-centred Assessment within a Framework of Emancipatory Practice Development.* Unpublished PhD thesis. University of Portsmouth.

Webster J, Byrne S (2004) Strategies to enhance privacy and dignity in care for older people. *Nursing Times* **100**(8): 38–40.

Webster J, Coats E, Noble G (2009) Enabling dignity in care through practice development with older people. *Practice Development in Healthcare* **8**(1): 5–17.

Womack S (2006) *Dignity Nurse in Every Hospital.* www.telegraph.co.uk/news/uknews/1516209/Dignity-nurse-in-every-hospital.html

Woolhead G, Calnan M, Dieppe P *et al* (2004) Dignity in old age: what do older people in the United Kingdom think? *Age and Ageing* **33**: 165–70.

CHAPTER 17

Dignity in care: the way forward

Lesley Baillie and Milika Ruth Matiti

INTRODUCTION

This book has explored the concept of dignity from various perspectives, the factors influencing dignity for people in different care settings, and how dignity can be promoted. The two previous chapters of this section explored ways of educating about dignity and developing practice, with illustrative examples. In this final chapter, we will highlight key messages about dignity in care from this book and some of the challenges in the promotion of dignity in care, linking back to previous chapters. We will then focus on the implications for management and education. Finally, we will review research conducted about dignity in healthcare and consider further research needed to continue to develop the body of knowledge about dignity in care. The emphasis in this final chapter is on the way forward, for promoting dignity in care across the healthcare sector.

LEARNING OUTCOMES

By the end of this chapter you will be able to:

➤ explain the key messages relating to dignity in the care of people across diverse settings
➤ analyse challenges facing healthcare professionals striving to promote dignity in care
➤ discuss implications for healthcare management and education in relation to dignity in care
➤ consider further research needed to support dignity in care in the future.

DIGNITY IN THE CARE OF PEOPLE ACROSS DIVERSE SETTINGS: KEY MESSAGES

We have established the importance of dignity in healthcare for patients and clients, whether they are in hospital or community, acutely ill or living with a long-term condition, and whether they are at the beginning or end of their lives. A commitment to the concept of human dignity (*see* Chapter 2) is an important starting point for healthcare as it follows that all health service users should be treated as valued human beings by the healthcare system as a whole, and by the staff who work within healthcare organisations.

While we acknowledge the inherent dignity of each person, there are other meanings of dignity identified in the literature (*see* Chapter 2), which can be diminished within a healthcare context: for example, 'social dignity' (Jacobson, 2007, 2009) and the dignity of personal identity (Nordenfelt, 2003). A person's sense of dignity may alter during the course of a day, being affected by their circumstances and surroundings and their interactions with other people. Human beings, when ill or during life-stage processes such as giving birth (*see* Chapter 8) or dying (*see* Chapter 10), may experience changes in themselves that can threaten their dignity. The healthcare setting (*see* Chapter 5), other people's behaviour (*see* Chapter 6), and treatments, investigations and care activities further influence patients' dignity. For example, the dignity of people with mental health problems (*see* Chapter 13) or learning disabilities (*see* Chapter 14) has been diminished by society's attitudes, the care environment and the way in which these individuals have been treated by staff responsible for their care. Many reports have uncovered breaches of dignity of patients in acute hospital settings, due to a combination of healthcare systems, ward culture, individual staff behaviour, poor staffing levels and lack of resources. Reports from the United Kingdom (UK) such as the Patients Association's (2009) *Patients . . . Not Numbers, People . . . Not Statistics* indicate that there is much to be done before all patients, particularly those who are most vulnerable, can feel confident that their dignity will be protected and promoted in healthcare.

In Section 2, the chapters focused on dignity in different care settings and for varied patient or client groups, exploring specific factors that may increase vulnerability to diminished dignity and how staff can promote dignity. This section also considered contextual factors, including in some instances (*see* Chapter 13, mental healthcare) the historical factors. Dignity is complex: there is no one 'solution' or one way of working that will necessarily protect each individual patient's dignity in every setting and at every moment of the day. All these are challenges that healthcare professionals face in practice.

CHALLENGES FACING HEALTHCARE PROFESSIONALS WHO STRIVE TO PROMOTE DIGNITY IN CARE

Healthcare workers should not assume that promoting the dignity of patients or clients is 'easy' all of the time. There are challenges involved in the process. We argue that healthcare organisations and healthcare professionals should recognise the challenges, and indeed barriers, to promoting dignity in today's healthcare settings. Only then can we address these issues, through our healthcare practice, management of staff and organisations, and education. Here we identify key challenges for the promotion of dignified care, with examples from this book's chapters.

Challenge 1: attitudes and behaviour of staff

Staff attitudes and behaviour have a major influence on patient and client dignity (*see* Chapter 6). While we could assume that those who choose to work within healthcare professions will believe in the dignity of human beings and act accordingly in the care of patients and clients, we know that we cannot take this for granted as UK reports suggest otherwise (*see* Healthcare Commission, 2007, 2009; Patients Association, 2009). The issue is not confined to the UK; Jacobson's (2009) research details violations of dignity in Canadian healthcare settings and almost all relate to staff behaviour: rudeness, indifference, condescension, disregard, dependence, intrusion, objectification, restriction, labelling, contempt, revulsion, deprivation and abjection.

Other chapters detailed how the attitudes of healthcare professionals can affect the dignity of patients in specific patient groups or in particular settings; some examples follow. Paula Reed in Chapter 7 points out that staff may overlook the dignity of children and babies and that adults are used to having control over this age group within society. Staff may not always listen to young children as they try to express their needs, and instead communicate with parents, rather than the whole family. In Chapter 9, Wilfred McSherry and Helen Coleman suggest that negative attitudes towards older people and ageing in society as a whole may spill into healthcare too and lead to behaviour that undermines older people's dignity. In Chapter 13, Gemma Stacey and Theodore Stickley highlight that clients in acute mental health settings may not feel that they are treated with dignity, and while some factors are related to the care environment, procedures conducted by staff in mental health settings, such as restraint, may undermine dignity.

The challenge is therefore that each individual healthcare worker must recognise the inherent importance of dignity for each human being no matter what their situation or health condition, and ensure that dignity is central to their treatment and care. Staff should therefore constantly examine their attitudes and behaviour towards other people through self-reflection, which is an essential prerequisite to promoting dignity.

Challenge 2: vulnerability of patients and clients

Many of this book's chapters identified that patients' specific health conditions may affect their dignity, and thus healthcare staff have the challenge of promoting the dignity of people who may not be feeling dignified due to their situation; some examples drawn from this book's chapters follow. In Chapter 11, Candice Pellett explores the vulnerabilities of patients cared for in the community, many of whom may have long-term debilitating conditions that affect their everyday life. Gemma Stacey and Theodore Stickley in Chapter 13 highlight that older people may have experienced years of mental health problems alongside associated social consequences, and older people with Alzheimer's disease can be both physically and mentally frail. In Chapter 12, Lesley Baillie highlights the particular vulnerability of patients in acute and critical care settings, as they often experience anxiety, fear, loss of control and dependency, and undergo procedures that are invasive, exposing and embarrassing. Patients could be unconscious, and undergo surgery or resuscitation; in such situations patients have no control over their bodies and are dependent on staff to promote their dignity. Furthermore, an individual's dignity may be affected by life stage; Paula Reed (Chapter 7) identifies particular dignity issues of different age groups. Young children and babies cannot always clearly identify their needs, and adolescents are undergoing considerable physical and emotional changes.

Challenge 3: the care environment

In the Royal College of Nursing's (RCN; 2008) nursing workforce survey, many respondents gave examples of how resource shortages (staff, space and equipment) affected delivery of dignified care. These factors may lead to staff feeling that their own dignity is diminished by their employing organisation, affecting their ability to promote patients' dignity. In Chapter 4, Alistair Hewison examines how healthcare staff are confronted by apparently conflicting priorities; they have time-driven targets to meet, which in turn impact on the patient care experience. Ann Gallagher's exploration of how the care environment affects patients' dignity (*see* Chapter 5) highlights aspects such as privacy and organisational culture. Kate Sanders and Jonathan Webster, in Chapter 16, discuss how practice developments in dignity are influenced by environmental culture. Other chapters provide specific examples of how the care environment can impinge on staff who are striving to promote dignity; here are some examples. In Chapter 7, Paula Reed discusses how lack of privacy affects children's dignity in hospital, as wards may have mixed age groups and the imposed mealtimes and other routines remove independence and control from children. In Chapter 12, Lesley Baillie details how the high workload of acute hospitals impacts on patients' dignity. She highlights that staff–patient relationships are affected by healthcare systems in acute care that lead to frequent transfers of patients. In Chapter 13, Gemma Stacey and Theodore Stickley explain how mental healthcare systems and care environments have encroached on the dignity of people with mental health problems.

These challenges all have implications for healthcare management and education.

THE IMPLICATIONS FOR HEALTHCARE MANAGEMENT

Managerial issues might relate to resources, systems and processes (for example, excessive patient transfers) and care environment concerns, as well as managing individual staff behaviour. The promotion of dignity in healthcare needs commitment from politicians and healthcare management authorities as well as individual healthcare organisations, such as hospitals, community services or care homes. It is evident in the literature that healthcare settings lack resources on a worldwide basis. There should be continuous lobbying of governments so that more resources are allocated to healthcare services because, without enough resources, it is difficult to promote dignity in healthcare, even for highly committed healthcare workers. However, healthcare workers should maximise the use of limited resources, which can be achieved better with improved knowledge, skills and appropriate attitudes and behaviour. In the UK, the Darzi report emphasised that organisations should 'organise care around the individual, meeting their needs not just clinically, but also in terms of dignity and respect' (DH, 2008, p.21). There are many managerial strategies in place already to facilitate dignity in care for patients and clients.

From a human resource dimension, wards need an adequate and stable workforce, with dignity-promoting leadership and a whole-ward culture and commitment to patient dignity. Healthcare organisations need to consider how they can recruit and select staff with appropriate attitudes and insights that will promote patient or client dignity. Staff recruited to work in healthcare must have insight into the reasons why patients may be vulnerable to their dignity being diminished, and display compassion for those whom they care for. They should want to do their best for patients, understand how to behave towards patients in a way that will promote dignity, and have a willingness to challenge dignity compromises. Therefore, we suggest that interviewers should explore understandings of dignity with applicants and set out an absolute expectation that all staff will behave towards patients in a way that promotes dignity. Box 17.1 suggests interview questions to use and the types of responses an interviewer would look for. Some organisations include service users in interview panels so that they can consider whether the interviewee is the type of person who they would like to care for them.

Once staff are employed, organisations should have strategies for supporting staff to promote the dignity of patients and clients. Managers should consider what type of policies and regulations they have in place to specifically address the dignity of patients and clients. For example, in the UK, the Department of Health's (DH) ten-point challenge for healthcare organisations (*see* Chapter 4) sets out expectations (DH, 2006a). There are NHS trusts that require all staff to sign a pledge that they will behave in accordance with the DH dignity challenge, thus setting a clear expectation that their staff will promote dignity in care. As discussed in previous chapters (*see* Chapters 1 and 3), registered healthcare professionals are required to behave according to their professional bodies' codes of conduct and ethics too, and can be called to account for their behaviour. Strong leadership for dignity is very important within healthcare

---

BOX 17.1 *Key questions to explore at interview*

➤ Why do you want to work for this organisation/study this course? *Look for: an interest in people and a desire to care for/help people who are undergoing healthcare.*

➤ We expect all healthcare staff to behave towards patients in a way that promotes their dignity. Please give some examples of how you could promote dignity for patients. *Look for: communicating respectfully (for example, introducing yourself and addressing the person by their preferred name), treating people as individuals and as important and valued human beings, providing privacy, explaining and informing patients, being kind and compassionate.*

➤ Why might people (*individualise question to relevant client group, for example, children, older people, people with mental health problems or learning disabilities*) be vulnerable to a loss of dignity when undergoing healthcare? *Depending on the client group and setting, look for: loss of independence and control, fear and uncertainty, being undressed and undergoing procedures, lack of privacy.*

➤ What do you think could cause a lack of dignity for patients? *Look for: lack of privacy, staff behaving as though the patient does not matter by ignoring, talking down, being rude, disrespectful or unkind; lack of attention to fundamental human needs, such as hygiene, comfort and food.*

➤ What would you do if you thought a patient was being treated with a lack of dignity? *Look for actions to promote dignity, such as kindness and providing comfort and privacy, challenging the colleague, reporting to a senior colleague.*

---

organisations (*see* Chapter 5), and an ethos of dignity in care needs to pervade the whole organisation.

Organisations should create a culture that encourages feedback from staff and patients and have procedures to monitor dignity on an ongoing basis. There should also be clear and accessible procedures for reporting and dealing with dignity compromises. In England there are mandatory inspections for health-care organisations (the Care Quality Commission, Patient Environment Action Team), which include criteria for dignity, respect and privacy. These inspections ensure that dignity and privacy are seen as important in organisations, as their ratings are published and no organisation would want to score badly on these aspects. However, the more qualitative aspects of a patient's healthcare experience are not easily measured in such quantitative terms (Picker Institute

2008), so organisations need to consider how they can gain more meaningful feedback from their local populations. The UK government recommends that trusts, clinical teams, professionals and commissioners develop their own quality indicators, tailored to local needs, specific conditions and specialties (Sizmur *et al*, 2009). Organisations should therefore work closely with their local service user groups to gain feedback and evaluate improvements made. Many organisations have their own systems for monitoring dignity, such as dignity audits and matrons' rounds. For example, in the RCN survey, a manager reported:

> We have a stop-and-look programme in which matrons walk the wards with staff of different grades and challenge them to look into patient bays and think whether, if their family members were there, they would be happy or confident about their care. This has made nurses really look at their practice and how their patients are treated (RCN, 2008, p.39, reproduced with permission from the Royal College of Nursing).

Some organisations use electronic patient experience trackers to measure patient and staff satisfaction at the point of delivery. These devices can be used to evaluate dignity and privacy issues, as well as any other aspect of patient experience, and they can instantly capture the patient's experience on a 24-hour basis, enabling timely feedback on any developments implemented to enhance care. Dewar *et al* (2010) described using 'emotional touch-points' to elicit patients' and relatives' views of their care from an emotional perspective. Patients and families are asked about key points in the patient's journey and they select emotional words (provided on cards) to portray how they felt at that point. Dewar *et al* (2010) argue that this method leads to a more balanced and meaningful representation of patients' care experiences. The findings were then used to improve compassionate care within an action research project.

In terms of care environments, as Ann Gallagher discussed in Chapter 5, there are fundamental aspects of the physical environment that are necessary to promote patients' dignity or at least to make it easier for staff to do so. Some factors relate to privacy, for example, single-sex accommodation, bed curtains that fit properly, bed spaces of adequate size and sufficient toilets and bathrooms. In England recently, the Design Council worked with the DH on a project called 'Design for Patient Dignity' which aimed to tackle environmental challenges to dignity (particularly privacy) from a design perspective (see www. designcouncil.org.uk). Other essential factors are environmental cleanliness and easy access to appropriate food for patients.

Healthcare organisations should have systems that treat patients as valued individuals. However, in the UK, bed shortages in some hospitals have led to the constant moving of patients between wards, and to patients being in mixed-sex accommodation (now being eliminated, *see* Chapter 4's discussion). Bed management systems should ensure single-sex environments and minimal transfers, and that patients with similar conditions are cared for together, thus promoting social support and mutual understanding (Baillie, 2009). For many patients, their relationships with staff and sometimes with other patients (Baillie, 2009; Bridges and Nugus, 2010) are important for their self-esteem and for feeling that they are cared for as individuals. Frequent moving of patients between wards disrupts relationships with both staff and other patients.

The dignity of healthcare workers is also important. The UK has a 'Dignity at Work' policy (*see* www.dignityatwork.org). The underlying assumption is that it is difficult to expect healthcare workers to think about patients' dignity if their own dignity is at stake. Watson (1996) claims that only if nurses treat themselves or are treated with dignity will they treat their patients or clients with respect, care, gentleness and dignity. In the RCN (2008) survey, nurses confirmed her view; for example, one hospital staff nurse said:

> My last shift only stopped for lunch at 4pm and I did not have time to have a drink with it. I did not have time to drink a hot drink from 10am to 6pm. I think nurses need to be treated with dignity if we are to deliver the same (RCN, 2008, p.31, reproduced with permission from the Royal College of Nursing).

In Chapter 5, Ann Gallagher considers how organisational culture influences dignity. Staff who appear uncaring could be suffering from burnout or may be exhausted and demoralised. Staff are human beings too, whose dignity can be threatened by circumstances and how others behave towards them, for example, inadequate resources to carry out their job, excessive workload and unsupportive colleagues and senior staff.

In England, under the auspices of the DH Dignity in Care campaign (DH, 2006a), many staff have signed up as dignity champions (*see* Chapter 4). In some organisations, there are dignity champions throughout the organisation. While any staff member can ensure that their own individual practice with patients promotes dignity, a group of dignity champions, recognised and supported by their organisation and with opportunities to share good dignity practices through forums, can make a much larger and more sustained impact on dignity within an organisation. Local dignity champions can work with their teams and patient groups to identify dignity issues and tackle these and develop dignity-promoting practice. In Chapter 16, Kate Sanders and Jonathan Webster explain how practice can be developed, including detailed examples of how a planned approach can lead to real differences being achieved. Crow *et al* (2010) established a 'dignity forum' in a hospital, in response to individuals feeling isolated in their efforts to enhance dignity.

IMPLICATIONS FOR EDUCATION OF HEALTHCARE WORKERS

Recruitment and selection, as discussed earlier (*see* Box 17.1), also apply to recruitment of healthcare students, so that educators can ensure that students recruited hold the fundamental values necessary to underpin care with dignity. We must then consider how healthcare education can further develop appropriate attitudes and from what base point. Dignity education should start in pre-registration programmes, as students are the future workforce of healthcare organisations. Patient dignity should be explicit and integral in pre-registration and postregistration healthcare courses, so that students can explore and understand the subject. Thus, curriculum teams must plan effective education to enable healthcare students to learn about dignity and apply their learning in practice. We suggest that curricula for healthcare students should be evaluated to see what, how, where and when dignity is being taught. In Chapter 15, Liz Cotrel-Gibbons and Milika Ruth Matiti detail approaches to education about dignity that can help to develop knowledge, skills and appropriate attitudes among healthcare students.

Healthcare settings need to have staff who understand the meaning of dignity, are vigilant about, and sensitive to, how the dignity of patients could be undermined, are committed to promoting dignity in care, and act as role models for dignified care in practice. Therefore, all staff with patient contact (including non-clinical staff such as receptionists) need education about patient dignity, as recognised by a number of writers (Lothian and Philp, 2001; Woogara, 2004a). As Alistair Hewison points out in Chapter 4, there are many sources of information available to practitioners to inform them about how to care for patients with dignity. The challenge is more about staff accessing and then applying this information in their practice. Healthcare workers need to acquire sound knowledge to underpin dignified care delivery and develop healthcare skills related to dignity in care. Staff also need to develop appropriate attitudes and values, as it is through attitudes that staff portray that the patient is valued (Bayer *et al*, 2005). Some staff may lack the specific knowledge to underpin behaviour that promotes dignity; for example, they may lack the knowledge and skills to care for people with specific needs, such as those with learning disabilities or a mental health problem. They could lack skills in fundamental care, for example, supporting patients with nutritional intake, pain management or end-of-life care. A lack of knowledge and skills may lead to inappropriate and unhelpful attitudes, avoidance of patients, or omissions in care. Therefore, staff must have further education about dignity, to ensure that they acquire the knowledge, skills and attitudes that underpin behaviour that promotes dignity in care. Education can also affirm the organisation's commitment to patient dignity and help staff to understand how to recognise and deal with any dignity compromises encountered.

Education should include service user involvement, as listening to and exploring patients' real experiences of dignity in care is meaningful and has a high impact. Patients' real experiences can be explored through digital story-telling and extracts from reports (for example, Patients Association, 2009 – *see* Chapter 9 as an example). Teaching methods should be active, with participants rehearsing interactions that promote dignity, and practising how they can provide privacy, in simulated care situations. Active learning promotes deep learning (*see* Chapter 15), which can be applied more readily in practice (Biggs, 1999). The teaching methods used need to trigger awareness of students' practice: how their own actions affect the dignity of patients and how their behaviour can influence their colleagues' behaviour. With every care activity or procedure healthcare students learn, the teaching of care with dignity should be integral, with facilitators asking, how might this procedure affect dignity and how can you protect dignity? Clinical staff education should give special consideration to promoting patients' dignity during intimate and invasive care and examinations. Healthcare students and employees need to develop awareness of their ethical and professional responsibilities to promote dignity (*see* Chapter 3), learn to take individual responsibility for patients' dignity and develop an understanding of how the impact of their own actions and omissions in care could affect the dignity of patients. They also need to learn to recognise and report factors that affect dignity, such as the care environment and resource issues, and consider how to address dignity compromises. Staff must therefore be educated about managing ethical dilemmas; the use of critical incidents and reflective practice can help staff to learn from their experiences.

As promoting dignity is a collective responsibility of all healthcare workers, all those involved in the patient or client journey in healthcare should have the opportunity of learning together through interprofessional education. Barr and Goosey (2002, p.2) cited a revised definition of interprofessional education for the Centre for the Advancement of Inter-professional Education (1997) as: 'when two or more professions learn, from and about each other to improve collaboration and quality of care'. Collaboration between different professions is important if quality care is to be achieved; therefore, students and staff from different professions need to learn together. It was evident from Matiti's (2002) study that some indignities to patients result from healthcare workers not understanding or appreciating other professionals' roles.

RESEARCH THAT WILL SUPPORT DIGNITY IN CARE IN THE FUTURE

Considering how important dignity is to patients and clients in every society, there is comparatively little research carried out worldwide. However, if a concept is important in clinical practice, then even limited study of the concept is useful (Chinn and Kramer, 1995). Studies have mainly focused on the meaning of dignity and factors affecting dignity in healthcare settings, while research about how dignity issues can be tackled, and the barriers to dignified care, are less apparent. Most studies have been conducted in the last decade, perhaps due to a greater awareness of the importance of patient experience and human rights as a whole, particularly in the UK. These studies are all important, in that they have made a contribution to the body of knowledge about patient dignity and they have raised awareness of the indignities that patients and clients face while receiving healthcare. Research has focused predominantly on hospital patients and adults. Few studies have considered community patients, children, women using maternity services, or people with mental health problems or learning disabilities.

Table 17.1 summarises designs and methods used to study dignity. Most studies have been qualitative, which is unsurprising, as qualitative research is more suited to studying human experiences, such as dignity.

Table 17.1 Research designs and methods used to study dignity

Design and methods	Researchers
Questionnaire survey	Matiti and Sharman, 1999; Rylance, 1999; Whitehead and Wheeler, 2008
Internet/online survey, including free-text answers	Gamlin, 1998; DH, 2006b; RCN, 2008
Rating scales	Hack *et al*, 2004
Phenomenology – interviews	Pokorny, 1989; Matiti, 2002; Walsh and Kowanko, 2002; Enes, 2003; Widäng and Fridlund, 2003; Öhlén, 2004; Widäng *et al*, 2008; Webster and Bryan, 2009
Ethnography – interviews and observation	Reed *et al*, 2003; Woogara, 2004a,b; Reed, 2007
Grounded theory – interviews/observation	Jacelon, 2003; Jacobson, 2009
Case study – observation, interviews, documentary analysis	Baillie, 2007; Baillie and Gallagher, 2010
Discourse analysis – interviews and documentary analysis	Street, 2001
Qualitative – interviews	Chochinov, 2002; Matthews and Callister, 2004; Bridges and Nugus, 2010; Slettebo *et al*, 2009
Quasi-experimental pilot study – observation, attitude measurement scales, interviews	Seedhouse and Gallagher, 2002
Focus groups	Stabell and Nåden, 2006; Bayer *et al*, 2005; Stratton and Tadd, 2005; Ariño-Blasco *et al*, 2005
Observation	Randers and Mattiasson, 2004; Lundqvist and Nilstun, 2007
Action research	Turnock and Kelleher, 2001; Crow *et al*, 2010

Most studies included patients and/or nurses as participants; only a few studies included interviews with relatives or carers (Seedhouse and Gallagher, 2002; Street, 2001; Jacelon, 2002, 2003; Enes, 2003; Bridges and Nugus, 2010). However, relatives of patients are often highly distressed by indignity (*see* Patients Association, 2009), and therefore exploring their views is very relevant. Many of the most vulnerable patients (for example, unconscious, dying, advanced dementia) are the most difficult to include in research due to access and consent issues, and they have therefore been excluded from studies. Including relatives of vulnerable patient groups in future research could be most insightful. Interviews with healthcare professionals other than nurses is noticeably absent, even though promoting dignity is an interprofessional activity.

Although a number of studies about dignity have been published, as discussed above, there is a need for further research in different settings and from different perspectives. We suggest that there should be research about how patients in different healthcare settings and in different countries perceive their dignity. Dignity is a cultural concept and it should be understood within the different contexts/organisational cultures. Intercultural research about the concept of patient dignity might provide a global operational definition. Furthermore, the healthcare setting's culture is continually changing and evolving due to developments such as technology. It is logical, therefore, to assume that perceptions of dignity will also change, necessitating updating of the concept. Practical ways of promoting dignity that are based on evidence should continue to be identified. More research on influencing factors such as the environment, attitude of patients and behaviours of different staff in different professions is also needed. Research to investigate gender influences on the dignity of patients or clients would provide useful insights. Action research studies, which would enable study of how practice might be changed, incorporating study of dignity-promoting organisational cultures, would make a valuable contribution too.

Although this book is primarily concerned with patient or client dignity, it is worth mentioning that research about the dignity of healthcare staff is very difficult to find. As discussed earlier, the dignity of healthcare workers needs to be upheld too, so that they in turn can effectively promote patient or client dignity. Researchers could explore the interrelationship between staff and patient dignity. It is also evident from the literature that there is a paucity of tools to evaluate dignity in practice.

CONCLUSION

Dignity in healthcare needs commitment at all levels, from government, healthcare organisations, teams and individual staff. Dignity must be tackled from an environmental and resource perspective but we also need healthcare staff who feel confident that they can make a difference to dignity in care and that their team, their organisation and managers will support them. While research studies about dignity have grown in number over the last decade, we have identified a number of gaps and suggested further areas for research. Findings from empirical studies should inform healthcare practice and policy and also inform healthcare curricula and influence how dignity in care should be taught. Healthcare workers must have the support of their organisations so that they can promote patients' dignity, and they should feel confident that their own dignity will be preserved at work.

All healthcare patients are vulnerable to their dignity being threatened; conversely, patients who feel that their dignity is promoted will have a better healthcare experience. Patients may have illnesses that cannot be cured and they may face an uncertain future and prognosis. They should always be able to be confident that they will be treated with dignity.

REFERENCES

Ariño-Blasco S, Tadd W, Boix-Ferrer JA (2005) Dignity and older people: the voice of professionals. *Quality in Ageing* 6(1): 30–5.

Baillie L (2007) *A Case Study of Patient Dignity in an Acute Hospital Setting.* Unpublished thesis. London South Bank University.

Baillie L (2009) Patient dignity in an acute hospital setting: a case study. *International Journal of Nursing Studies* 46: 22–36.

Baillie L, Gallagher A (2010) Evaluation of the Royal College of Nursing's 'Dignity at the heart of everything we do' campaign: exploring challenges and enablers. *Journal of Research in Nursing* 15(1): 15–28.

Barr H, Goosey D (2002) *Inter-Professional Education: selected case studies.* Commissioned by the Department of Health from the UK Centre for the Advancement of Inter-professional Education (CAIPE). www.dh.gov.uk/en/Publicationsandstatistics/Publications/PublicationsPolicyAndGuidance/DH_4139354

Bayer T, Tadd W, Krajcik S (2005) Dignity: the voice of older people. *Quality in Ageing* 6(1): 22–7.

Biggs JB (1999) *Teaching for Quality Learning at University.* Buckingham: Open University Press.

Bridges J, Nugus P (2010) Dignity and significance in urgent care. *Journal of Research in Nursing* 15(1): 43–53.

Centre for the Advancement of Inter-professional Education (1997) *Inter-Professional Education – A Definition.* London: Centre for the Advancement of Inter-professional Education.

Chinn PL, Kramer MK (1995) *Theory and Nursing – A Systematic Approach* (4e). London: Mosby.

Chochinov HM, Hack T, McClement S, Kristjanson L, Harlos M (2002) Dignity in the terminally ill: a developing empirical model. *Social Science and Medicine* 54(3): 433–43.

Crow J, Smith L, Keenan I (2010) Sustainability in an action research project: 5 years of a dignity and respect action group in a hospital setting. *Journal of Research in Nursing* **15**(1): 55–68.

Department of Health (2006a) *Dignity in Care*. Gateway reference 7388. London: Department of Health.

Department of Health (2006b) *Dignity in Care Public Survey October 2006 – Report of the Survey*. Gateway reference 7213. London: Department of Health.

Department of Health (2008) *High Quality Care For All – NHS Next Stage Review final report*. Gateway reference 10106. London: Department of Health.

Dewar B, Mackay R, Smith S, Pullin S, Tocher R (2010) Use of emotional touchpoints as a method of tapping into the experience of receiving compassionate care in a hospital setting. *Journal of Research in Nursing* **15**(1): 29–41.

Enes SPD (2003) An exploration of dignity in palliative care. *Palliative Medicine* **17**(3): 263–9.

Gamlin R (1998) An exploration of the meaning of dignity in palliative care. *European Journal of Palliative Care* **5**(6): 187–90.

Hack TF, Chockinov HM, Hassard T *et al* (2004) Defining dignity in terminally ill cancer patients: a factor-analytic approach. *Psycho-oncology* **13**: 700–708.

Healthcare Commission (2007) *Caring for Dignity: a national report on dignity in care for older people while in hospital*. London: Commission for Healthcare Audit and Inspection.

Healthcare Commission (2009) *Investigation into Mid Staffordshire Foundation Trust*. London: Commission for Healthcare Audit and Inspection.

Jacelon CS (2002) Attitudes and behaviours of hospital staff towards elders in an acute care setting. *Applied Nursing Research* **15**(4): 227–34.

Jacelon CS (2003) The dignity of elders in an acute care hospital. *Qualitative Health Research* **13**(4): 543–56.

Jacobson N (2007) Dignity and health: a review. *Social Science and Medicine* **64**(2): 292–302.

Jacobson N (2009) Dignity violation in healthcare. *Qualitative Health Research* **19**(11): 1536–47.

Lothian K, Philp I (2001) Maintaining the dignity and autonomy of older people in the healthcare setting. *BMJ* **322**(7287): 668–70.

Lundqvist A, Nilstun T (2007) Human dignity in paediatrics: the effects of healthcare. *Nursing Ethics* **14**(2): 216–28.

Matiti MR (2002) *Patient Dignity in Nursing: a phenomenological study*. Unpublished thesis. University of Huddersfield School of Education and Professional Development.

Matiti M, Sharman J (1999) Dignity: a study of pre-operative patients. *Nursing Standard* **14**(13–15): 32–5.

Matthews R, Callister LC (2004) Childbearing women's perceptions of nursing care that promotes dignity. *Journal of Obstetrics, Gynaecologic and Neonatal Nursing* **33**(4): 498–507.

Nordenfelt L (2003) Dignity of the elderly: an introduction. *Medicine, Healthcare and Philosophy* **6**(2): 99–101.

Öhlén J (2004) Violation of dignity in care-related situations. *Research and Theory for Nursing Practice* **18**(4): 371–85.

Patients Association (2009) *Patients . . . Not Numbers, People . . . Not Statistics*. London: Patients Association.

Picker Institute (2008) *The Challenge of Assessing Dignity in Care.* London: Help the Aged.

Pokorny ME (1989) *The Effect of Nursing Care on Human Dignity in the Critically Ill Adult.* Unpublished PhD thesis. University of Virginia.

Randers I, Mattiasson A (2004) Autonomy and integrity: upholding older adult patients' dignity. *Journal of Advanced Nursing* **45**(1): 63–71.

Reed P (2007) *Dignity and the Child in Hospital.* Unpublished PhD thesis. University of Surrey.

Reed P, Smith P, Fletcher M, Bradding A (2003) Promoting the dignity of the child in hospital. *Nursing Ethics* **10**(1): 67–76.

Royal College of Nursing (2008) *Defending Dignity: challenges and opportunities for nurses.* London: Royal College of Nursing.

Rylance G (1999) Privacy, dignity and confidentiality: interview study with structured questionnaire. *BMJ* **318**(7179): 301.

Seedhouse D, Gallagher A (2002) Undignifying institutions. *Journal of Medical Ethics* **28**: 368–72.

Sizmur S, Redding D (2009) *Core Domains for Measuring Inpatients' Experience of Care.* Oxford: Picker Institute Europe.

Slettebo A, Caspari S, Lohne V *et al* (2009) Dignity in the life of people with head injuries. *Journal of Advanced Nursing* **65**(11): 2426–33.

Stabell A, Nåden D (2006) Patients' dignity in a rehabilitation ward: ethical challenges for nursing staff. *Nursing Ethics* **13**(3): 236–48.

Stratton D, Tadd W (2005) Dignity and older people: the voice of society. *Quality in Ageing* **6**(1): 37–45.

Street A (2001) Constructions of dignity in end-of-life care. *Journal of Palliative Care* **17**(2): 93–101.

Turnock C, Kelleher M (2001) Maintaining patient dignity in intensive care settings. *Intensive and Critical Care Nursing* **17**(3): 144–54.

Walsh K, Kowanko I (2002) Nurses' and patients' perceptions of dignity. *International Journal of Nursing Practice* **8**(3): 143–51.

Watson J (1996) Watson's theory of transpersonal caring. In: Walker PH, Newman B (eds) *Blue Print for Use of Nursing Models – Education, Research, Practice and Administration.* New York: National League for Nursing Press, pp.141–84.

Webster C, Bryan K (2009) Older people's views of dignity and how it can be promoted in a hospital environment. *Journal of Clinical Nursing* **18**(12): 1784–92.

Whitehead J, Wheeler H (2008) Patients' experience of privacy and dignity. Part 2: an empirical study. *British Journal of Nursing* **17**(7): 457–64.

Widäng I, Fridlund B (2003) Self-respect, dignity and confidence: conceptions of integrity among male patients. *Journal of Advanced Nursing* **42**(1): 47–56.

Widäng I, Fridlund B, Martenssen J (2008) Women patients' conceptions of integrity within healthcare: a phenomenographic study. *Journal of Advanced Nursing* **61**(5): 540–8.

Woogara J (2004a) Patient' rights to privacy and dignity in the NHS. *Nursing Standard* **19**(18): 33–7.

Woogara J (2004b) *Patient Privacy: an ethnographic study of privacy in NHS patient settings.* Unpublished PhD thesis. University of Surrey.

Index

abuse 19, 72, 111, 178, 181, 193
accident and emergency (A&E)
    departments 56, 57, 157, 158,
    160–5
accountability 222
acknowledgement of value 31, 34, 35
action planning 212
action research 249, 250
active learning 204, 207, 226, 248
acute and critical care 156–69
  A&E departments 160–5
  challenges facing health professionals
    242
  challenges to dignity 157–60
  end-of-life care 127
  intensive therapy unit 167–8
  learning outcomes 156
  overview xv, 156, 168–9
  patients' and healthcare professionals'
    views 4
  perioperative care 165–7
adolescence 84, 88, 90
adult learning 205–6
advance directives 123
Age Concern 44, 73
ageing 110, 111–13, 241
aggressive care 85
Allen, D 136
Alliex, S 159
Allingham, Henry 25, 27
altruism 202
Alzheimer's disease 178, 241
American Association of Colleges of
    Nursing 202
American Nurses Association (ANA) 28
Amsterdam Declaration (1994) 3
anaesthetic room 166

analgesia 135
andragogy 205–6, 207, 212
Applegate, M 69, 102
approved mental health practitioners
    (AMHPs) 182
Arman, M 63
arts 13, 48, 228
assessment 216
asylums 172, 173
Atkinson, D 189
attitudes of staff 69–72
attributes of dignity 16–20
audit 222
auditory privacy 57, 69
Aung Sang Suu Kyi 25, 27
autonomy
    children 89, 92
    community care 151, 153
    concept of dignity 12, 16, 17
    education 202
    end-of-life care 129, 130, 131
    older people 122

babies 83, 85, 88–9, 241, 242
Baillie, L 12, 15, 72, 83
Balen, R 83
Barker, P 174
Barnard, Y 207
Barr, H 248
Bayer, T 62
BBC Headroom 174
Beach, M 4
Beattie, V 204
Beauchamp, TL 12
Beckstrand, RL 168
bedbaths 72–3
bed-management systems 246

bedpans 153, 164
'behavioural dignity' 14, 16
beneficence 129
bereavement visits 149
Beyleveld, D 26, 27, 28
bioethics 129
birth *see* childbirth
Blake, William 29
bodily privacy 66–9, 87, 97, 157, 167–8
body image 147
Booth, F 204
Boseley, S 37
Bostrom, N 24
breastfeeding 96, 99
Bridges, J 159
Bristol Inquiry 58
British Geriatrics Society 43
Brownsword, R 26, 27, 28
Bryan, K 148
Bryant, H 163
Burke, Edmund 29
Burns, Robert 29
Byrne, G 160

caesarean section 166
Calhoun, C 190
Campbell, Thomas 29
Campinha-Bacote, J x
cancer patients 17, 91, 128, 149–51
Cann, P 48
capitalism 188
care environments 52–60
    acute and critical care 168–9
    challenges facing health professionals
        242
    challenges in implementing dignity
        policy 44–5
    children 85–6, 92
    dignity and the care environment 52–6
    dignity and the physical environment
        56–7
    implications for healthcare
        management 245
    learning outcomes 52
    other aspects of the organisation 57–9
    overview xiii, 52
    practical application 59–60

    practice development 232, 233
    staff behaviour and attitudes 64
career satisfaction 5
care homes 41, 128, 145–6
care planning 144, 151, 153, 154, 234
Care Quality Commission 48, 244
Care with Dignity Indicator Tool 121
Carnevale, F 85
Carter, B 84
Casals, Pabo 25
Centre for the Advancement of Inter-
        professional Education 248
cervical smears 97
chaperones 68, 163
child abuse 19
childbirth
    being overheard while in labour 104–7
    implications for future practice 240
    indignity of ward-based treatment
        103–4
    pregnancy and childbirth 95–6
    solitude and withdrawal 99–103
children 81–92
    challenges facing health professionals
        241, 242
    dignity and the child 82–3
    end-of-life care 126
    environment 85–6
    family-centred care 83–5
    learning outcomes 82
    overview xiv, 81–2, 92
    power and the child 83
    privacy 86–90
    staff–patient relationships 90–1
Chinn, PL 16
Chochinov, HM 4, 14, 133, 134, 135
Clare, B 204
cleanliness 53, 64, 245
Clegg, A 4
clinical gaze 87
clinical governance 222
clothing 19, 67–8, 72, 88, 163, 165–6
Coast, J 128, 130
codes of ethics 5, 27, 72
cognitive impairment 157
cognitive school of learning 205
collage 228

comfort 133
commodes 153
communication
    children 83, 88–9, 90, 91, 92
    end-of-life care 131
    learning disabilities 193, 195, 196
    older people 122
    staff behaviour and attitudes 63,
        69–72
community care 142–54
    context 143–4
    dignity and long-term conditions
        151–3
    dignity during wound care 146–8
    dignity in end-of-life care 148–51
    dignity in people's own homes
        144–5
    dignity in residential care homes
        145–6
    end-of-life care 127
    learning outcomes 142–3
    mental healthcare 175
    overview xv, 142, 153–4
    patients' and healthcare professionals'
        views 4
    perceptions of dignity 20
    vulnerability of patients 241
compassion 202
Comus 29
concept analyses of dignity 13–14
concept exploration 213
confidentiality 5, 14, 68–9, 74, 87, 92,
    144
consent
    acute and critical care 163
    community care 144, 145
    learning disabilities 193
    maternity care 98, 100
    older people 122
    research to support future dignity in
        care 250
    staff behaviour and attitudes 64
constructive feedback 58
constructivism 206, 207, 212
continence 45, 69
continuing professional development
    222

control
    children 83
    community care 145, 149, 151, 153
    end-of-life care 130
    intensive therapy unit 167
    maternity care 99, 102, 104
    perceptual adjustment level 16
Convention of the Rights of the Child
    (1989) 82
Cooper, MK 205
Cornwell, J 71
Coyne, I 84
creative arts 13, 48, 228
critical care *see* acute and critical care
critical incidents 248
Crow, J 246
cultural sensitivity 4, 19, 154, 164, 250
cystic fibrosis 88

Daily Mail 41
dance 228
Darbyshire, P 89
Darzi review 37, 113, 243
Dawson, P 192
death and dying
    community care 149
    death past, present and future 127–9
    facilitating dignified dying 131–8
    intensive therapy unit 168
    learning disabilities 193
    mental healthcare 179
    overview xiv–xv
    patients' and healthcare professionals'
        views 4
    professional practice 26, 27, 31
    staff behaviour and attitudes 69
deep learning 203–5, 206, 207, 212, 216,
    248
Defending Dignity report 55
Degeling, P 153
dehumanisation 168
dementia
    acute and critical care 159, 163
    care environments 56, 57
    end-of-life care 136
    mental healthcare 178–9
    older people 111, 123

dementia – *contd*
  policy issues 48
  practice development 231–2, 234, 235
  research to support future dignity in
    care 250
  staff behaviour and attitudes 70
demoralising syndrome 135
dentures 165, 167
Department of Health (DH)
  children 91
  community care 143, 148–9, 154
  end-of-life care 131
  implications for healthcare
    management 243, 245, 246
  mental healthcare 179
  older people 117, 118, 121
  policy issues 37, 41–4, 47
  practice development 223
  staff behaviour and attitudes 73
depersonalisation 98
depression 135
Design Council 245
Design for Patient Dignity 245
Dewar, B 245
DH *see* Department of Health
diabetes 152
Diario de Barcelona 25
dignified dying 131–8, 149, 204
dignity
  concept of dignity 9–21
    attributes of dignity 16–18
    concept analyses of dignity 13–14
    definitions of dignity 11–16
    factors influencing perceptions of
      dignity 18–20
    learning outcomes 9
    overview 9, 21
    research findings on the meaning of
      dignity 14–16
    theories of dignity 11–13
  patients' and healthcare professionals'
    views 3–6
  the way forward 239–51
    challenges facing professionals
      240–2
    implications for education of
      healthcare workers 247–8

    implications for healthcare
      management 242–6
    key messages 239–40
    learning outcomes 239
    overview 239, 250–1
    research to support future dignity in
      care 248–50
'Dignity and Older Europeans' project
  14, 112–13, 115
dignity as merit 12, 13, 33, 115–16
Dignity at Work policy 246
dignity audits 245
dignity challenge 42, 117, 118, 243
dignity champions 43, 47–8, 113, 177,
  246
Dignity in Care campaign
  deep learning 204
  implications for healthcare
    management 246
  mental healthcare 177, 178
  older people 117, 118
  overview x, xiii
  policy issues 41–3, 44, 47
  quality fundamental care 73
'dignity-in-relation' 13, 16
Dignity Maps 121
dignity nurses 227
dignity of moral stature 12, 115, 116
dignity of personal identity 12, 28, 115,
  116, 131, 240
dignity of risk 176
'dignity-of-self' 13
dignity therapy 135
*Dignity Through Action (Older People)
  Resource Package* 117
disability 12, 82, 89 *see also* learning
  disabilities
discourse analysis 249
discrimination 111, 174, 175, 181, 193
district nurses (DNs) 143–4, 145, 149,
  150, 152, 153
domains of dignity 121–2
Douglas-Dunbar, M 156, 159, 163
Down's syndrome 194
dress *see* clothing

eating assistance 72, 73, 122

Edgar, A 12, 115
education 201–17
  assessment 216
  a case for dignity in the curriculum
      202–3
  educational approaches and theories
      203–7
    andragogy 205–6
    constructivism 206
    deep learning 203–5
  implementation of educational
      strategies 207–15
    considering the when 209–12
    selecting the how 212–13
    what needs to be learned? 208–9
    where should learning take place?
        214
    who is involved? 214–15
  implications for education of
      healthcare workers 247–8
  learning outcomes 201–2
  overview xvi, 216–17
Edvardsson, D 67
Einstein, Albert 53
elderly people *see* older people
electroconvulsive therapy 172
electronic patient experience trackers 245
emergency care dignity principles 161,
    162
'emotional touch-points' 245
empathy 35, 119, 136, 202, 214
end-of-life care 126–38
  community care 148–51
  death past, present and future 127–9
  facilitating dignified dying 131–8
  implications for education of
      healthcare workers 247
  intensive therapy unit 168
  learning outcomes 126
  meaning of dignity at the end of life
      127
  overview xiv–xv, 126, 138
  patients' and healthcare professionals'
      views 4
  preferences for end-of-life care 129–31
  safeguarding the dignity of older
      people 123

End of Life Care Transformational Guide
    149
End of Life Strategy 149
Enes, SPD 14
engagement 31, 32, 34, 35
Engström, A 4, 167
Entwistle, N 204, 207, 214, 216
environment of care *see* care
    environments
epidural anaesthesia 166
Eriksson, K 62
Essence of Care 59, 72
*Essence of Care Patient-focused Benchmarks
    for Clinical Governance* 121
essential shared capabilities 176
'Essential Skills Clusters' 202
ethics 5, 27, 40, 72, 177, 243
ethnic needs 154
ethnography 82, 249
eugenics 187
European Commission 112
European Parliament 183
European Region of the World
    Confederation for Physical Therapy
    5
euthanasia 129
Every Child Matters 83
evidence-based practice (EBP) 222
Exley, C 136

Fagermoen, MS 5, 202
family-centred care 83–5, 92
feedback 58, 244, 245
Fenton, E 13, 114, 115
Fielding, Henry 29
Firth-Cozens, J 74
focus groups 249
Ford, P 161
'forget me not champions' 231, 233–5
formative assessment 216
forms of address 19, 64, 71–2, 113, 145
Foucault, M 87
Fowler-Kerry, S 126
'frames of reference' 206
Francis, Robert x, 54, 55
Franklin, L-L 132
freedom of choice 151

Fridlund, B 62
From Values to Action 176
fundamental care 72, 247

Gallagher, A 12, 31, 131
Garbett, R 223, 224
Gardiner, P 156, 159, 163
Garratt, E 112
Gates, B 190
Gaukrodger, Ronnie 189
gender 250
general anaesthetic 166
General Medical Council (GMC) 5
General Pharmaceutical Council 5
generation gap 111
Goffman, E 100, 103
Goldberg, AE 165
Goldsmith, Oliver 29
Gold Standards Framework 149, 150
Gomes, B 128
'good death'
    community care 149
    end-of-life care 128, 129, 133, 134, 138
    intensive therapy unit 168
Goodrich, J 71
Goossey, D 248
grounded theory 249
The Guardian 25

Haddock, J 13
hair removal 165
Haiti earthquake 25
Halldorsdottir, S 63
Ham, C 40
Hamer, S 233
handling aids 46, 47, 146
harassment 180
Headroom 174
Health Advisory Service (HAS) 74
Health and Social Care Advisory Service
    (HASCAS) 117
Healthcare Commission (HCC)
    A&E departments 160, 161
    older people 116, 121
    policy issues 40
    staff behaviour and attitudes 64, 73,
        74

healthcare professionals
    challenges facing health professionals
        240–2
    dignity of healthcare professionals 250
    implications for education of
        healthcare workers 247–8
    implications for healthcare
        management 242–6
    views on importance of dignity 3–6
health policy *see* policy issues
hearing impairments 69
Help the Aged 19, 43, 71
Henderson, L 225
Henschke, JA 205
Hickman line 91, 151
Higginson, IJ 128
High Quality Care for All 143
hoists 46, 47, 146
holist strategy 204
Holland, C 4, 167
home deaths 127, 128, 134, 136, 149
home visits 128, 144–5
Hoover, J 202
hope 16, 135
hospices 14, 127, 128, 136
hospital clothing 67–8, 88, 165–6
hospitals
    acute and critical care 156, 157, 159
    attributes of dignity 18
    care environments 53
    children 83, 86, 88, 89, 90
    end-of-life care 127, 128, 136, 137, 149
    maternity care 103–4
    patients' and healthcare professionals'
        views 4
    'perceptual adjustment level' 14, 15
    policy issues 37, 40, 41
    staff behaviour and attitudes 64, 71
Hughes, SJ 205
human dignity 12, 13, 30, 202, 239
human rights 3, 27, 115, 179, 191, 249
Human Rights Act (1998) 3, 115
Hungry to Be Heard report 73
hygiene 72, 73, 122–3, 153

ICN *see* International Council of Nursing
ideal-self 19

identity
  children 86
  dignity of personal identity 12, 28,
      115, 116, 131, 240
  learning disabilities 189–92
  older people 109, 114, 116, 120
  professional practice 27, 28, 31, 35
  staff behaviour and attitudes 67
  theories of dignity 12
*Improving the Mental Health of the
    Population: a Strategy for the European
    Union* 183
incontinence 69, 73, 144, 164
independence 16, 92, 167
Independent on Sunday 25
individuality 146
industrialisation 188
information giving 68–9
informed consent 98
inhibitions, loss of 96–8
inpatient mental healthcare 179–81
inspections 244
institutional culture 73–5
institutionalisation 188, 191
insulin shock therapy 172
integrity 202
intensive therapy unit (ITU) 4, 160,
    167–8
International Council of Nursing (ICN)
    5, 27–8
International Practice Development
    Colloquium 223
interpersonal dignity 16
interviews 249
intimate examinations
  A&E departments 163, 164
  children 87
  community care 145
  implications for education of
      healthcare workers 248
  maternity care 96, 97, 104, 107
  staff behaviour and attitudes 69
Irurita, VF 159
Ishiguro, Kazuo 26, 27
ITU *see* intensive therapy unit

Jacelon, CS 13, 202

Jacobs, MK 16
Jacobson, N 12, 13, 71, 241
jewellery 165
Johnston, MJ 202
Johnstone, MJ 5
The Journey to Recovery 175
justice 129, 202

Kant, Immanuel 11–12
Kelleher, M 167–8
Kelly, B 5
Kennedy, John F 25
Kingdon, JW 40
Kipling, Rudyard 201, 207
Kirk, Ron 53
Kissane, DW 135
Kitson, A 224
Kolcaba, C 133
Kolnai, A 32, 33, 34, 35
Kowanko, I 62, 70, 74
Kronkite, Walter 25

labour *see* childbirth
Lawler, J 87, 100
leadership 57, 58
learning disabilities 186–96
  acute and critical care 157
  children 90
  community care 152
  dignity, health and social care 192–6
  identity, normalisation and
      personalisation 189–92
  implications for future practice 240,
      247
  learning outcomes 187
  overview xv–xvi, 186, 196
  social influences and societal
      impressions 187–9
learning environment 214
learning styles 214
leg ulceration 146–7, 148
Levi, Primo 27
Lewis, Ivan 41
Lewis, P 86
life expectancy 110
Lindsay, Reed 25
Liverpool Care Pathway 149, 150

living wills 123
lobotomy 173
long-term conditions 151–3, 241
loss of inhibitions 96–8
Love, A 136
lunatic asylums 172, 173

Mackenzie, F 190
Macleod, R 149
Macmillan Cancer Support 150
Magee, H 121
Mairis, ED 13
Makaton 194
Mallett, J 224
Mandela, Nelson 25
Mantel, Hilary 25
Marcel, Gabriel 9
Marie Curie service 149
Marley, J 14
Marshall, C 166
Marton, F 204, 214
maternity care 95–107
    being overheard while in labour 104–7
    indignity of ward-based treatment
        103–4
    learning outcomes 95
    loss of inhibitions 96–8
    overview xiv, 95, 107
    patients' and healthcare professionals'
        views 4
    pregnancy and childbirth 95–6
    solitude and withdrawal 99–103
Matiti, M 14, 71, 120, 121, 165, 202, 248
Maxwell, S 48
McCormack, B 223, 224, 225, 226, 228
McKillop, S 225
meaning of dignity 14–16, 21, 114–16,
    127
Measuring Dignity in Care for Older People
    121
media 26, 39, 47
'meetings of awareness' 214
Menschenwürde 12, 28, 33, 115, 131
mental capacity 193, 195
Mental Health Act 173, 182
Mental Health Act Commission 53, 179
mental healthcare 171–84

brief history 172–3
care environments 53
challenges facing health professionals
    241, 242
children 90
dignity in specific mental health
    settings 177–81
implications for future practice 240,
    247
learning outcomes 171–2
overview xv, 171, 181–4
position of dignity 173–7
thinking about dignity in mental
    healthcare 181
transformative learning 206
mentoring 212, 215
merit, dignity as 12, 13, 33, 115–16
Mezirow, J 206
mid-Staffordshire hospitals x, 53, 121
midwives 5, 98, 100, 102, 105 *see also*
    maternity care
Milton, John 29
Mind 179
minifisms 87
miscarriages 163
Mitchell, T 13, 114, 115
mixed-sex accommodation 17, 44, 45,
    64, 180, 246
Modernising Mental Health Services 175,
    180
Molzahn, A 5
morality 33, 40, 177
moral worth 32, 35
Morse, J 69, 102
mortality statistics 127–9

Nåden, D 62
narratives 212
National Dignity Tour 43
National Health Service (NHS) 37, 41–3,
    45, 151, 243
National Patient Safety Agency (NPSA)
    179
National Service Framework for Children
    84
National Service Framework for Mental
    Health 174, 175, 176

National Service Framework for Older
People 178
near misses 59
Next Stage Review 37, 151
NHS *see* National Health Service
NHS Institute for Innovation 222
NHS Patient Survey Programme 112
The NHS Plan 175
NHS Quality Improvement Scotland 222
NMC *see* Nursing and Midwifery Council
Nolan, P 173
non-maleficence 129
Nordenfelt, L 12–14, 28, 33, 34, 115, 131
normalisation theory 191
Nuland, SB 151
nursing
  acute and critical care 159
  end-of-life care 131
  importance of dignity in healthcare 3,
    4, 5
  practice development 221
  professional practice 27, 28–30, 32, 35
Nursing and Midwifery Council (NMC)
    27–8, 30, 44, 45, 202, 214
nursing development units (NDUs) 221
nursing homes 46, 127
nutrition 43, 72, 73, 247

Obama, Barack 25
observation 249
Occupational Therapy Association of
    South Africa 5
older people 109–24
  acute and critical care 157, 159
  attitudes toward ageing and older
    people 111–13
  community care 144–5
  concept of dignity 12, 13
  demographics of ageing 110
  end-of-life care 126, 130
  fundamental aspects of dignity 120–1
  importance of dignity in healthcare 4
  learning outcomes 110
  meaning of dignity for older people
    114–16
  mental healthcare 178–9
  overview x, xiv, 109–10, 123–4

policy issues 40–3, 45
preserving the dignity of older people
    118–20
professional practice 26, 31
recent policy and publicity 113–14
safeguarding the dignity of older
    people 121–3
staff behaviour and attitudes 62, 64,
    71, 73, 241
what older people want 116–18
organisational culture 73–5, 83, 242,
    244, 246, 250
Our Health, Our Care, Our Say 143

pain management
  end-of-life care 134, 135, 149
  implications for education of
    healthcare workers 247
  intensive therapy unit 167
  maternity care 99, 100, 102, 104–6
  older people 123
palliative care 14, 127, 129, 136
Panorama 37
'parenting in public' 89
Parkinson, Sir Michael 43
Pask, G 204
Patient Environment Action Team 244
patients
  the dignity of a practice 35
  privacy of patients' bodies 66–8
  privacy of personal space 64–6
  staff behaviour that diminishes dignity
    63–4
  views on importance of dignity in
    healthcare 3–6
  vulnerability 241–2
Patients Association
  A&E departments 161
  care environments 53–4
  implications for future practice 240,
    248
  older people 113, 119, 121
  policy issues 37
  staff behaviour and attitudes 63, 73
*Patients...Not Numbers, People...Not
    Statistics* 53, 63, 121, 240
perceptions of dignity 18–20, 21

'perceptual adjustment level' 14
perioperative care 165–7
Perry, B 5
personal appearance 153
personal hygiene 72, 73, 122–3, 153
personal identity *see* identity
personalised care planning 144, 151, 154, 234
personal space 64–6
person-centred care 178, 226
personhood 129–30, 132
Peters, MA 215
Pfund, R 126
phenomenology 249
physical environment 55, 56–7, 59 *see also* care environments
Piaget, Jean 206
Pinker, Steven 24
place, people and process 20, 21, 59, 188
Plakas, S 167
plateaux of disinvolvement 103
Pokorny, ME 167
policy issues 37–48
    challenges in implementing dignity policy 44–7
    Dignity in Care campaign 41–3
    getting dignity on the policy agenda 40–1
    implementing policy 44
    learning outcomes 38
    overview xiii, 37–8
    the policy process in healthcare 38–40
    progress 47–8
Poor Law Reforms 187
Porock, D 136
postoperative care 166–7
power and the child 83
practice development 220–36
    brief history 221–2
    defining practice development 223–7
    the dignity of a practice 32–4
    enhancing the environment 232
    evaluating the impact 232–3
    implications for healthcare management 246
    learning outcomes 221
    overview xvi, 220, 222, 235–6

pictures of practice 227–32
    reflection on processes 233–5
    stimulating and sustaining change 232
practice development units (PDUs) 221
Preferred Priorities for Care 149
pregnancy xiv, 95, 97–9 *see also* maternity care
preoperative care 165–6
pre-registration healthcare education 201, 203, 209, 247
preservation of value 31, 34, 35
primary care 143
Pritchard, E 233
privacy
    acute and critical care 157, 163, 167
    care environments 57, 59, 242
    children 86–90, 92
    community care 144, 145, 146, 149, 153
    concept of dignity 14, 16, 17, 19
    end-of-life care 131, 136, 138
    implications for future practice 242, 245
    importance of dignity in healthcare 5
    maternity care 95–100, 102, 104–7
    older people 122
    policy issues 44, 45, 48
    privacy of information 68–9
    privacy of patients' bodies 66–8
    privacy of personal space 64–6
    staff behaviour and attitudes 63, 64–9, 70, 74
privacy and dignity fund 45
Privacy and Dignity report 17
professionalism 214, 215
professional philosophy statement 177
professional practice 24–35
    dignity as the basis for nursing 28–30
    dignity in common language 25–7
    the dignity of a practice 32–4
    learning outcomes 24
    overview xiii, 24, 34–5
    philosophical basis for dignity 28
    professional expectations 27–8
    worth, dignity and respect 30–2
Proverbs from Hell 29

psychotropic medication 173
Public Interest Disclosure Act (1998) 74

quality fundamental care 72–3
quality of life 129, 147, 154
questionnaires 249
Quinn, FM 205

Rachels, J 100
rape 180
rating scales 249
Raya, A 202
Rayner, C 113
Ray, SL 74
Raz, Joseph 31, 34
RCN *see* Royal College of Nursing
reception area 53
reciprocity 15, 16
recovery 174
recruitment of staff 244, 247
Reed, P 14, 89
reflective activities
  acute and critical care 161
  care environments 60
  children 91
  community care 20, 147
  definitions of dignity 10, 17
  education 207, 215
  learning disabilities 187, 188, 189,
    191, 192, 194
  maternity care 98, 99, 104, 107
  meaning of dignity 10
  mental healthcare 174, 177, 178,
    182–3
  older people 112, 114, 115, 116, 117,
    119
  perceptions of dignity 18
  policy issues 45
  staff behaviour and attitudes 64, 71,
    73, 74
reflective journals 204, 212
reflective practice 248
regression 103
Rehnsfeldt, A 63
religious beliefs 68, 151, 164
The Remains of the Day 26
reporting staff behaviour 74, 75

research
  meaning of dignity 14–16
  practice development 222
  supporting future dignity in care
    248–50
respect
  community care 153
  concept of dignity 15, 16, 17, 18–19
  education 202
  end-of-life care 131
  importance of dignity in healthcare 4,
    5
  maternity care 102
  older people 114
  policy issues 45
  professional practice 28, 31, 34, 35
restraint procedures 179, 182
resuscitation 164–5
rights
  children 82
  concept of dignity 17
  importance of dignity in healthcare 3,
    5
  learning disabilities 191
  mental healthcare 175, 179
  older people 109, 115
  professional practice 27
  research to support future dignity in
    care 249
  right to health 13
Robb, Barbara x
role modelling 57, 58, 212, 214, 215
role play 212
rote learning 204
Rousseau, P 135
Royal College of Nursing (RCN)
  A&E departments 161, 163
  care environments 55, 57, 58, 59
  community care 145
  definitions of dignity 118–19
  implications for future practice 242,
    245, 246
  learning disabilities 186
  older people 117, 118–19
  policy issues 43, 44, 47
  staff behaviour and attitudes 62, 74
Ruijs, KDM 132, 133

Rush, B 206

safety 47, 123
Safety, Privacy and Dignity in Mental Health Units 180
Sainsbury Centre for Mental Health (SCMH) 179
Saljo, R 204
same-sex accommodation *see* single-sex accommodation
Sandberg, J 207
Scarry, E ix
sectioning 173
sedation 135
Seedhouse, D 9
self 15
self-advocacy 191
self-concept 19
self-esteem 13, 15, 19, 130, 147, 246
self-image 19, 132
self-introversion 99–103
self-respect 13, 14, 16, 145
self-worth 14, 15, 114, 120, 145
sexual assault 180
sexuality 87
Shakespeare, William 29
shared decision making 144
Sharman, J 165
shaving 165
Shaw, T 221, 223, 225, 226, 227, 228
Sherman, J 71
Shift 174
Shotton, L 9
Siblin, Eric 25
sign language 194
Sigsworth, J 48
single-sex accommodation 45, 55, 122, 181, 245, 246
Smith, P x
social care 192–6
Social Care Institute for Excellence (SCIE) 9, 44, 121
social dignity 12, 13, 240
social identity 189, 190, 191
socialisation 19, 190
social justice 202
Söderberg, S 4, 167

solitude 99
Southampton University Hospitals NHS Trust 57
spinal anaesthesia 101
spiritual needs 151
staff behaviour and attitudes 62–76
    acute and critical care 157–8, 159, 161
    behaviour that diminishes dignity 63–4
    children 90–1
    communication and attitudes 69–72
    implications for future practice 241, 242, 250
    learning outcomes 63
    older people 119–20
    organisational culture 73–5
    overview xiii–xiv, 62–3, 75–6
    providing privacy 64–9
    quality fundamental care 72–3
stagist model of policy 39, 40
status 13, 33, 34
Stevens, Peter 189
Stockwell, F 90
'stop-and-look' programme 58
Street, AF 136
strokes 4
Sturdy, D 153
suffering 132–3
suicide 135, 179
summative assessment 216
surface learning 204
surgery 166
surveys 249
Sutton, E 128, 130

teaching styles 214
team working 57
technology 159, 160
The Ten Essential Shared Capabilities 176
theories of dignity 11–13
'3Ps' model (people, place and process) 20, 21, 188
Time to Change 174
Titchen, A 225
toilets 46, 47, 146, 153, 245
Tolson, D 223
torture 19

transformative learning 206–7, 212
Transforming Community Services 149
Tschudin, V 202
Turnock, C 167–8
Tyne, A 191

United Nations (UN) 82, 191
United Nations General Assembly
    Declaration (1948) 3
United Nations International Bill of
    Rights 3
Unsworth, J 224

vaginal examinations 96, 97, 163
value based services 191
values 176–7, 202, 203
Values Based Practice 176
values education 201–17
    assessment 216
    a case for dignity in the curriculum
        202–3
    educational approaches and theories
        203–7
    implementation of educational
        strategies 207–15
    implications for education of
        healthcare workers 247–8
    learning outcomes 201–2
    overview xvi, 216–17
violence 174, 179, 181

Wainwright, P 12, 131
waiting times 55
Walker, A 192
Walsh, K 62, 70, 74
Ward, D 190
washing assistance 72–3, 145
Watson, J 246
Webster, C 148
Webster, Jonathan 220
whistle-blowing policies 74, 75
WHO *see* World Health Organization
Widäng, I 62, 70
Williams, F 189
Williams, P 191
Wilson, D 67
Wilson, SA 137, 138
withdrawal 99
Woogara, J 71, 202
Woolhead, G 73
workhouses 188
working practices 45–7
Working Together resource 194
World Health Organization (WHO) 3,
    5, 110
worth 17, 30, 31, 33–5, 135
wound care 146–8
Wynne, A 26

Yonge, O 5